Eugenio Garosi

Projecting a New Empire

Studies in the History and Culture of the Middle East

Edited by
Stefan Heidemann, Gottfried Hagen, Andreas Kaplony,
Rudi Matthee, and Kristina L. Richardson

Volume 42

Eugenio Garosi

Projecting a New Empire

Formats, Social Meaning, and Mediality of Imperial Arabic in the Umayyad and Early Abbasid Periods

DE GRUYTER

ISBN 978-3-11-154386-4
e-ISBN (PDF) 978-3-11-074082-0
e-ISBN (EPUB) 978-3-11-074097-4
ISSN 2198-0853

Library of Congress Control Number: 2021947926

Bibliographic information published by the Deutsche Nationalbibliothek
The Deutsche Nationalbibliothek lists this publication in the Deutsche Nationalbibliografie; detailed bibliographic data are available on the Internet at http://dnb.dnb.de.
 Typesetting: Integra Software Services Pvt.
This volume is text- and page-identical with the hardback published in 2022.

www.degruyter.com

Acknowledgements

The present book is a revised version of my homonymous dissertation, completed in 2019 at the Department of Ancient Civilizations of the University of Basel and the Institute for the Near and Middle Eastern Studies of the Ludwig Maximilian University Munich in the framework of a *Cotutelle de Thèse*. It could not have been written without the generosity of several institutions and foundations. Most of my doctoral research was carried out under the auspices of the SNSF project *Change and Continuities from a Christian to a Muslim Society – Egyptian Society and Economy in the 6th to 8th Centuries*. Concomitantly, I benefitted from an "Excellent Junior Researcher" Completion Grant by the Research Fund of the University of Basel as well as the Dissertation Award of the Faculty of Cultural Studies of the Ludwig Maximilian University. Finally, the revision of the book's manuscript was finalized during my fellowships at the Israel Institute for Advanced Studies (Jerusalem) and at the RomanIslam Center for Comparative Empire and Transcultural Studies (University of Hamburg).

It is with great pleasure that I acknowledge the contributions by mentors, colleagues, and friends, which, great and small, were integral to my efforts. Pride of place goes to my main advisors Andreas Kaplony and Sabine Huebner, who guided and encouraged me in very different, yet perfectly complementary ways. With my best interest at heart, they always gave my – at times chaotic – personality a direction and purpose. For their generous counsel, I am furthermore indebted to my other advisors Ronny Vollandt and Matthias Müller. I owe special thanks to the colleagues and student assistants of the research teams *Change and Continuities*, *The Arabic Papyrology Database*, and *Cultural Brokerage in Pre-Modern Islam* for the long hours spent conversing on late antique documents and society, both within and outside the university's halls. To Andreas Kaplony and the research group of the *APD*, in particular, I extend my gratitude for the far too under-appreciated work they put in every day pushing the boundaries of the discipline of Arabic Papyrology.

It was my good fortune that several scholars took the time to answer my naïve questions, read drafts of my works, and make unpublished and rare material available to me. These include Jelle Bruning, Lajos Berkes, Hubert Kaufhold, Isabelle Marthot-Santaniello, Michael Shenkar, Daniel Potthast, Stefanie Schmidt, Matthias Stern, Dieter Weber, and Luke Yarbrough. I had the pleasure to present my research at several international conferences where many specialists critiqued and made useful comments on my preliminary results. In the process of turning my dissertation into a book I could count on the keen eye of Victoria G. D. Landau. For their useful feedback, I would further like to thank the anonymous reviewers of De Gruyter. I also want to express my gratitude to the Staatliche

https://doi.org/10.1515/9783110740820-202

Münzsammlung in Munich and the Vienna Papyrussammlung for allowing me to work on their collections. I have spent a significant portion of the last five years in the reading rooms of the libraries at the Universities of Basel and Munich, the Bavarian State Library, and the Israel National Library, whose staffs kindly and patiently facilitated my search for rare material.

My thankfulness for the academic assistance I received is matched only by the obligation I feel towards the people closest to me for their loving support. My gratitude for Lucia's sacrifices, loving care, and inspiration far exceeds what I can put into words. Finally, what little I have achieved I owe most of all to my parents, Monica Lippi and Luciano Garosi, who supported me emotionally and financially every step of the way. They were the first to open my eyes to the wonders of the ancient world and to plant in me the seeds of curiosity for all things distant and unknown. I could never hope to repay such a debt; dedicating this work to them is a symbolic token of my gratitude.

The Eye of the Beholders — 163

Conclusion — 166

III Shaping Official Umayyad Arabic

Introduction: *Reichsarabisch* or Early Islamic Official Arabic? — 171

If the Mountain Will Come: Arabic Letters — 174
Formulary — **176**
Long Prescript — **178**
Short Prescript — **181**
Parallel Parameters of Scribal Politesse: Long-Prescript Letters to and from Christians — **183**
Translating Structure into Visuals — **185**
Striving for Proficiency — **187**

If the Mountain Will Not Come: Official Inscriptions — 192
Formulary — **195**
Disposition of Text — **198**

Umayyad Official Documentary Standard as Early Islamic Documentary Standard — 199
Hegemonic and Minority Scribal Traditions in Imperial Arabic — **200**
Plurality within the Same Standard: Private Letters on Papyrus and Related Materials — **202**
Multiple Parallel Formal Standards: Private Epigraphy — **207**

Conclusion — 212

IV A Culture of Ambivalence

Negotiating "Arab Style" — 217
Greek Arab-Style Letters — **219**
Arab-Style Coptic Letters — **225**
The "Arabic" Letters from Sogdia — **228**
Arab-Style Middle Persian letters — **232**

Trading Rank Identifiers — 233
Arab-Style Epistolography: *mise en page* — 236

Shifting Boundaries between Scribal Cultures in the Umayyad Empire — 239

Parallel Scribal Traditions: Numismatics — 242
The Pahlavi Precursors — 242
Early Islamic Latin Coinage and the Arab-Style Bible — 245

Parallel Scribal Traditions: Independent Arab-Style Scribal Practices — 254
Arab-Style Greek Legal Documents — 254
The Arab Style on the Eastern Frontier — 255

Conclusion — 259

V An Empire of Words

Regional Idiolects in the Use of Administrative Loanwords in Documentary Arabic — 263

The Loanwords in Imperial Arabic (640–800) — 266
Loanwords only Attested in Documents from Egypt (640/641–800) — 268
a) Fiscal Administration — 268
b) Institutions and Officials — 271
c) Infrastructure — 273
d) Coinage — 274
e) Metrology — 274
f) Military — 281
Loanwords Attested in Documents from Egypt and other Regions (640/641–800) — 283
a) Fiscal Administration — 283
b) Institutions and Officials — 290
c) Infrastructure — 295
d) Coinage — 297
e) Metrology — 303
f) Military — 307
Loanwords Attested only Outside Egypt (640/641–800) — 307
a) Fiscal Administration — 307

b) Institutions and Officials — 308
c) Metrology — 308

Regional Diversity in the Use of Administrative Loanwords in Early Islamic Documentary Arabic — 310

Terminology and Regional Settings: The Role of Umayyad Syria and the Looming Shadow of Abbasid Iraq — 314

Conclusion — 322

Summary and Conclusions — 324
The "Elephant in the Dark" — 324
Brief Outline of Research Outputs — 324
Re-orienting Egypt — 328
An Implosion of Late Antiquity — 330
Imperial Arabic as a Mirror of Early Islamic Society — 331
Concluding Note — 334

Appendices

Appendix 1: Formal and Layout Structure of Early Islamic Arabic Official Letters — 337

Appendix 2: Formal and Layout Structure of Early Islamic Official Inscriptions — 339

Appendix 3: Comparative Table of Early Islamic Arab-style Letters — 345

Bibliography — 353

Indices

General Index — 415

Index Locorum I: Papyri — 427

Index Locorum II: Inscriptions — 441

List of Illustrations

Map 1 Places of Discovery of Early Islamic Arabic Documents (Egypt and Syria-Palestine) —— **XIX**

Map 2 Places of Discovery of Early Islamic Arabic Documents (Iran) —— **XX**

Map 3 Places of Discovery of Early Islamic Arabic Documents (Central Asia) —— **XXI**

Fig. 1 Bilingual protocol of ʿAbd al-ʿAzīz b. Marwān (P.Vind.inv. G 39763 r)
© Österreichische Nationalbibliothek, Vienna —— **62**

Fig. 2 Arab-Byzantine *fals (ABAZ* type)
© Dumbarton Oaks, Byzantine Collection, Washington, DC —— **65**

Fig. 3 Bilingual tax demand of Qurra b. Sharīk (P.Heid.inv. Arab. 13 r)
© Institut für Papyrologie, Universität Heidelberg —— **69**

Fig. 4 Arab-Byzantine *fals* ("Umayyad imperial image coinage" type) from Ḥimṣ
© Staatliche Münzsammlung, Munich —— **81**

Fig. 5 Bēk family tree —— **108**

Fig. 6 Arab-Sasanian drachm of ʿAbd al-Raḥmān b. Ziyād, dated to 673/674
© Staatliche Münzsammlung, Munich —— **140**

Fig. 7 Reformed *dīnār* dated to 710/711
© Staatliche Münzsammlung, Munich —— **143**

Fig. 8 Reformed *dirham* dated to 711/712
© Staatliche Münzsammlung, Munich —— **144**

Fig. 9 Gold *solidus* ("three standing imperial figures" type)
SICA I 607 —— **151**

Fig. 10 Gold solidus of caliph ʿAbd al-Malik ("standing caliph" type), dated to 696/697
© Ashmolean Museum, University of Oxford —— **152**

Fig. 11a *Fals* of caliph ʿAbd al-Malik ("standing caliph" type) from Aleppo
© Staatliche Münzsammlung, Munich —— **153**

Fig. 11b "Muḥammad" *fals* ("standing caliph" type) from Jerusalem
© Dumbarton Oaks, Byzantine Collection, Washington, DC —— **154**

Fig. 12 Arab-Sasanian silver drachm ("standing caliph" type) dated to 694/695
Gyselen 2000, pl. 15 no. 7 —— **155**

Fig. 13 Arab-Sasanian silver drachm ("sacrum and spear" type)
Treadwell 1999, 268 —— **155**

Fig. 14 Arab-Sasanian silver drachm (*orans* type) of Bishr b. Marwān dated to 692/693
Treadwell 2005, 261 A1 —— **158**

Fig. 15 Arab-Sasanian *fals*, drawing ("standing caliph" type)
Gyselen 2000, 146 —— **159**

Fig. 16 Arabic letter of Qurra b. Sharīk to the pagarch of Ihnās dated to 709 (P.Vind.inv. A. P. 378 r)
© Österreichische Nationalbibliothek, Vienna —— **186**

Fig. 17 Arabic scribal exercise on a marble tile from Khirbat al-Mafjar
Baramki 1953: pl. xi —— **190**

Fig. 18 Epigraphic Latin *solidus* from Spain dated to 712/713
© Staatliche Münzsammlung, Munich —— **246**

Fig. 19 Arab-Byzantine *semissis* (TIB type)
© Staatliche Münzsammlung, Munich —— **247**

Fig. 20 Bilingual *dīnār* from Africa
© Staatliche Münzsammlung, Munich —— **251**

https://doi.org/10.1515/9783110740820-204

Note on Conventions

Transliteration

Transliterations from Arabic follow the guidelines of the *International Journal of Middle East Studies*.

Transliterations from Ancient South Arabian Languages follow the guidelines of P. Stein, *Lehrbuch der sabäischen Sprache I: Grammatik*, Wiesbaden: Harrassowitz, 2013, 38–40.

Transliterations from Ancient North Arabian Languages follow the system used by A. al-Jallad, *An Outline of the Grammar of the Safaitic Inscriptions*, Leiden/Boston: Brill, 2015.

Transliterations from Hebrew, Aramaic, Greek and Coptic follows the guidelines of P. H. Alexander, J. F. Kutsko, J. D. Ernest, Sh. Decker-Lucke and D. L. Petersen, eds., *The SBL Handbook of Style*, 2nd edition, Atlanta: SBL Press, 2014, 25–30.

Transliterations from Middle Iranian languages follow the guidelines of W. B. Henning, "Mitteliranisch", in: K. Hoffmann, W. B. Henning, H. W. Bailey, G. Morgenstierne and W. Lentz, *Iranistik* (Handbuch der Orientalistik 4, 1), Leiden: Brill, 1958, 20–126, at 120–126.

In order to increase the text's legibility, the names of Arab dynasties within the main body and footnotes have been written without diacritics (e.g., Abbasid instead of ʿAbbāsid). In the case of references to the Qurʾān/Qurʾānic, I have opted to exclude diacritics (Qur'an or Qur'anic).

Toponyms

I have used the current English nomenclature for well-known cities and place names. When specifying the provenance of documentary sources, I have used the standard Arabic name (e.g., Madīnāt al-Fayyūm, instead of Arsinoē). For the sake of convention, I use Nessana instead of Naṣṭān. In cases of multiple possible spellings, I have opted for the version of the name used in the *Arabic Papyrology Database* for papyri, and in the *Thesaurus d'Épigraphie Islamique* for inscriptions (e.g., al-Ushmūnayn instead of al-Ashmūnayn). For sources of unknown origin, I have indicated the geographical area (e.g., Egypt) to which they belong.

https://doi.org/10.1515/9783110740820-205

Editorial Conventions

For quotations from text editions the following system of abbreviations and brackets has been used:

r	recto
v	verso
ov	obverse
rv	reverse
fd	field
mg	margin
()	Round brackets enclose solutions of abbreviations
[]	Square brackets enclose text lost in a lacuna supplied by the editor
⟦ ⟧	Double square brackets enclose erasures
< >	Angular brackets enclose text omitted in error by the writer
{ }	Curly brackets enclose text included in error by the writer
\ /	Diagonal strokes enclose interlinear text

References and Abbreviations

Citations from modern secondary literature follow the format of author-date. Abbreviations of editions and literary sources are discussed in a dedicated section in the bibliography (*Abbreviations of Quoted Editions*). Unless otherwise specified, the translations are my own. Abbreviations of titles of books of the Old and New Testament follow the guidelines of P. H. Alexander, J. F. Kutsko, J. D. Ernest, Sh. Decker-Lucke and D. L. Petersen, eds., *The SBL Handbook of Style*, 2nd edition, Atlanta: SBL Press, 2014, 73–75. As has become commonplace, references to the Qur'an are abbreviated as Q Sura number: verse number (e.g., Q 1:1).

Languages and Scripts:

arab.	Arabic
aram.	Aramaic
CPA	Christian Palestinian Aramaic
JBA	Jewish Babylonian Aramaic
JPA	Jewish Palestinian Aramaic
bac.	Bactrian
copt.	Coptic
ENA	Epigraphic North Arabian
ESA	Epigraphic South Arabian
dem.	Demotic
eth.	Ge'ez

gr.	Greek
lat.	Latin
MP	Middle Persian
syr.	Syriac

Dates and Calendars

Unless otherwise specified, dates are given according to the Common Era system (CE). Other chronological systems referenced in the text are:

Islamic (*hijrī*) Era (AH)	Day 1, year 1 = July 16, 622 CE
Era of Bosra (EB)	Day 1, year 1 = Mar. 22, 105 or 106 BCE
Yazdgerd Era (AY)	Day 1, year 1 = June 16, 632 CE
Post-Yazdgerd Era (PYE)	Day 1, year 1 = June 16, 652 CE
Bactrian Era (BE)	Day 1, year 1 = Oct. 2, 223 CE

Where relevant to the argument, I have used double dates, indicating the non-Common Era year followed by the Common Era year in round brackets, e.g., 77 AH (696/697).

Varia

Further terminological choices and concepts are explained in the dedicated section of the introduction (*The Definitional Trap*).

Maps

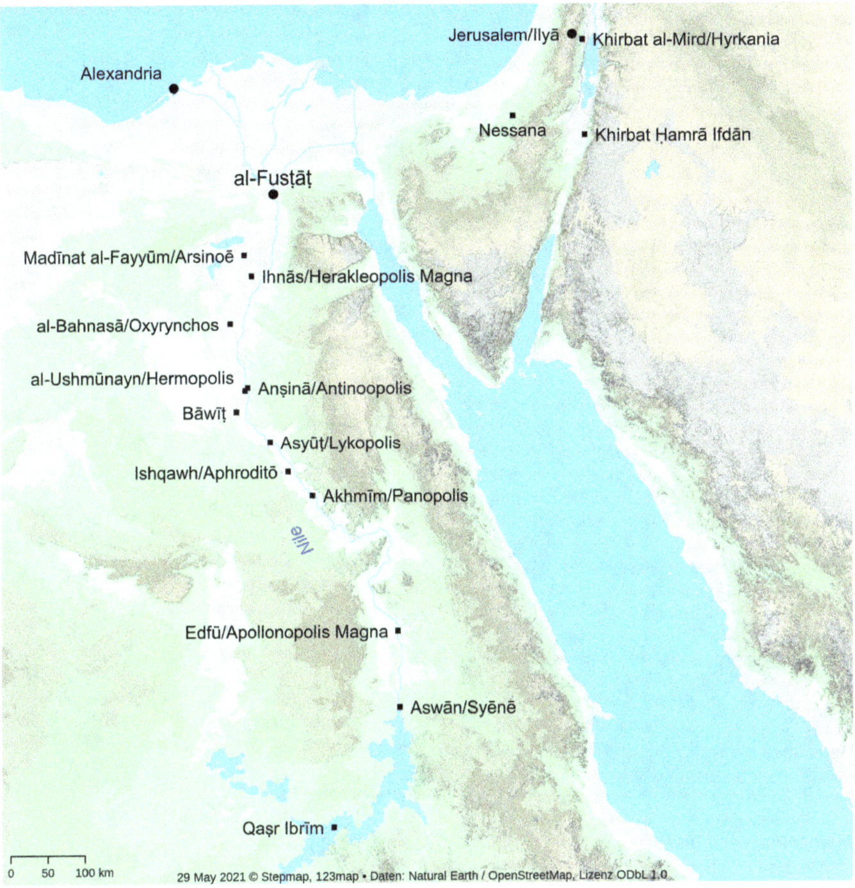

Map 1: Places of Discovery of Early Islamic Arabic Documents (Egypt and Syria-Palestine).

https://doi.org/10.1515/9783110740820-206

Map 2: Places of Discovery of Early Islamic Arabic Documents (Iran).

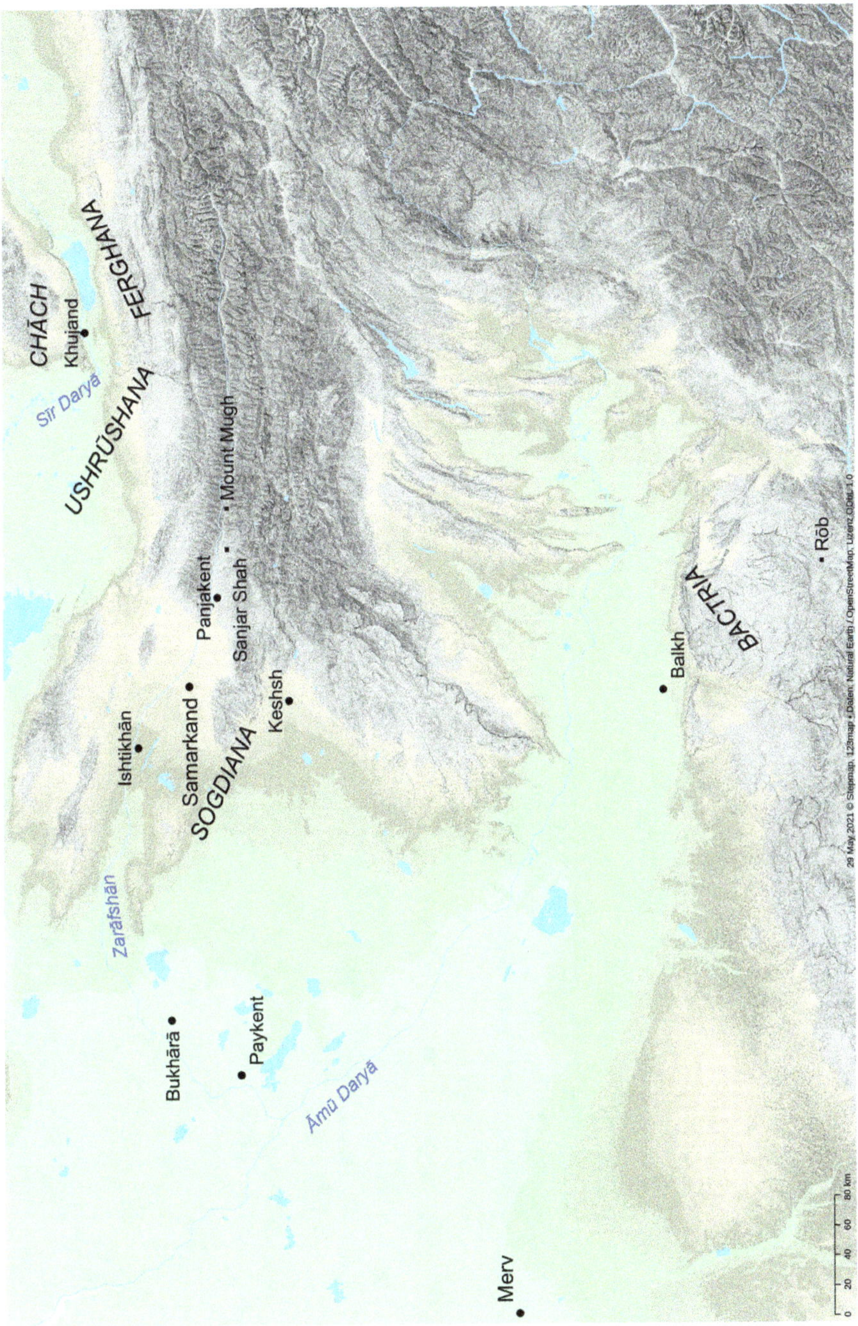

Map 3: Places of Discovery of Early Islamic Arabic Documents (Central Asia).

Introduction

(...) it is detestable that a man should become accustomed to speaking in something else than Arabic. Because the Arabic language is one of the symbols of Islam and Its people. Languages are among the prominent symbols by which communities are told apart.

Ibn Taymiyya, *Iqtiḍāʾ al-ṣirāṭ al-mustaqīm.*

Becoming Empire

One of the restrictions allegedly imposed on Christians from Syria – and by analogy all other protected minorities – by the caliph ʿUmar I (*rg.* 634–644), in exchange for protection and security, explicitly forbade them from engraving Arabic inscriptions on their signet seals. In this narrative, the public use of the Arabic *script* (not so much the practice of Arabic *per se*)[1] is presented as a symbol of high social standing and a monopolistic prerogative of the Muslim overlords. To be sure, the different transmitted versions of the so-called "Pact of ʿUmar" are in all probability historicizing inventions of the 9th century.[2] In fact, the pact's stipulations very possibly reflect a stage in the development of Christian-Muslim relations in which ideological emphasis on distinctive "cultural stuff" (language, customs, dress etc.) functioned as a means to articulate and organize difference in a culturally mixed environment, in which social divides were becoming increasingly blurred.

Questions of historical veracity aside, the anecdote lays out a story of the formation of the Muslim Empire that runs parallel to the accounts of the seemingly unstoppable advances of the Muslim armies[3] in the Byzantine Levant, Egypt, and North Africa, in Visigothic Spain and in Sasanian Iraq and Iran. The prohibition of Christians carrying Arabic signet rings presents a culturally defensive – if military hegemonic – minority of Arab-Muslim conquerors confronted by a multitude of cultures and peoples, striving to articulate its privileged status around a set of distinctive and monopolizable cultural markers. It also alludes to the role played by Arabic writing as a – even visually – distinctive public symbol in the transformation of a small minority, descended from merchants and nomads from Western Arabia, into a self-conscious ruling elite of the largest political entity of their time.

On the eve of the Arab conquest of the Middle East, Arabic vernaculars were widely spoken in pre-Islamic north-west Arabia, Syria-Palestine, and in the borderlands along the Syrian Desert and Southern Iraq. In most territories of the

---

1 A strikingly similar injunction (though seemingly addressed to Muslims) can be found in a *ḥadīth* with an Iraqi *isnād*; see e.g. Wensinck 1936–1988, VI, 535. I thank Luke Yarbrough for the reference.

2 For comprehensive bibliographical references on versions of and studies on the Pact of ʿUmar, see Levy-Rubin 2009, 362–364.

3 For non-Muslim and/or non-Arab components of the Early Islamic conquest armies, see al-Qāḍī 2016 and Hoyland 2015a, 56–61; for non-Arab retainer forces in the early Islamic Empire, see Gordon 2001, 151–156. Here and in the rest of the book I will refer to "Muslim" and "Arab" conquest armies for the sake of conciseness.

https://doi.org/10.1515/9783110740820-001

rising Islamic Empire stretching from the Atlantic to the Hindu Kush, however, Arabic was a superstratum language introduced by the new rulers.

The question that served as the point of departure for the present study was the *quality* of the relationship between Early Islamic imperial governance and practices of Arabic literacy. More specifically: how did language tie in with the broader policies of the Early Islamic Empire to create and organize "difference"? How did different groups experience communicative acts by the Arab imperial elite? What was the nature of Arabic interaction with substrate scribal traditions? Was there a correlation between regional varieties of Arabic and the social geography of the Early Islamic Empire? And, finally, what social connotations were attached to practices of Arabic and how did these practices influence the subsequent development of Arabic as a written language?

I will approach these lines of investigation through the lens of official documents, coins, and inscriptions, which represent the earliest, most distinctive, and pervasive demonstration(s) of imperial presence in the 7th- and 8th-century material record. The dissertation addresses strategies of communication, legitimization and assertion of authority, from the perspective of a cluster of intertwined linguistic and social dynamics underscored by: 1) the functional interplay of Arabic and other languages used in the Early Islamic chanceries, 2) the development of Arabic from a minority language into a lingua franca for medium- and long-term exchange across the Mediterranean basin and beyond, 3) the "mediality" of practices of public Arabic writing, meaning those features that operated beyond and independently of a semantic comprehension, 4) the formulaic and graphic distinctiveness of Early Islamic Arabic documentary standards compared to previous and neighbouring scribal traditions, and 5) the regional influences that shaped local styles of imperial representation.

Semantics of Empire

These few opening considerations immediately betray the underlying assumption of the present work that the peculiarities of Early Islamic official practices in Arabic writing originated in the socio-cultural framework of imperial policies. Using modern notions of empire as an analytic category for empire-like antique, medieval and early modern polities can be controversial. Part of the problem is strictly terminological. The Latin *imperium* from which the word "imperial" ultimately derives, connotes "command", "authority", "supremacy" and came to be associated with a territorial entity only in the Middle Ages,[4] while the modern theory of "empire" is essentially a concept from the 18th and later centuries.[5] While this is certainly true, the use of the notion of empire to describe antique phenomena is no more anomalous than that of other terms that were unknown to coeval societies such as "ideology" (< 19th century), or were used in markedly different meanings such as "hegemony" or "republic".

A stronger objection pertains to the evocative overtones inherent in empires. In its contemporary acceptation, "empire" is almost synonymous with imperialism, and western European imperialism in particular, and thus carries the pejorative connotation of the oppressive rule of one people over another. The implicit risk is that of projecting complex antique phenomena onto a not simply anachronistic, but also prejudiced and ultimately inadequate framework. It could be added that historical polities that defined themselves or that are commonly labelled "empires" showed a wide array of political systems and ideological outputs that would be difficult to bring together under one definition.[6]

These difficulties call for a working definition of empire.[7] In other words, what are the common characteristics of empires? What are the distinctive prerogatives of imperial rule? The definition of empire used in this study does not

4 On the development of the concept of *imperium* in the Middle Ages, see Folz 1953.

5 The etymologically closest Arabic equivalent to "empire", *imāra* (lit. "the prerogative of command"), is one of the central attributes claimed by the earliest leaders of the Muslim community, the *umarā' al-mu'minīn* "Commanders of the Believers" (sing. *amīr al-mu'minīn*), but is not used with the hegemonic connotation of the modern understanding of empire.

6 A synthetic survey of the political systems from which empires originate is given by Eisenstadt 1969, 10–12.

7 From time to time, scholars have proposed the use the more neutral term "hegemony" to describe empire-like authority relations between pre-modern polities. I prefer to employ the term "empire", as "hegemony" indicates the supremacy within a group of formally equal political actors (Münkler 2005, esp. 67–77) whereas "empire" entails a hierarchical relation between dominant and subordinate political actors. "Empire" further more concretely implies a territorial dimension.

https://doi.org/10.1515/9783110740820-002

claim to have definitive validity or to be universally applicable to all empire-like entities.[8] Furthermore, I do not wish to imply that the scions of conquerors who forged the Early Islamic Caliphate set out with a program and notions of Imperialism (founders of empires rarely do) nor that the Early Islamic Empire possessed a heavily bureaucratic structure comparable to that of 18th- and 19th-century empires.[9]

Empires are composite multicultural and multi-ethnic polities bound by a central power. An empire is held together by a dominant ruling class occupying the highest echelons of the administration and exerting political and military control over groups ethnically and culturally distinct from itself. Characteristic of imperial rule is the distinctiveness and autonomy of the imperial metropole, which manifests itself in the centre's ability to develop and maintain specific criteria of recruitment and organization. The imperial context provides a new locus of identity for the ruling elite, which manifests itself in the development and public display of monopolizable cultural and social identifiers and parameters of social behaviour. This fortifies the pan-imperial ruling class's internal sense of belonging and loyalty towards the central metropole.

In the initial stages, membership of the imperial elite tends to overlap with belonging to the ethnic group of the hegemonic segment of the polity. With time, however, the imperial elite becomes increasingly separated from ethnicity. The imperial elite's status identifiers not only demarcate the distinctiveness of the ruling class *vis à vis* the subjugated segments of the imperial polity, but increasingly *vis à vis* the imperial elite's own culture of origin as well.[10] Through the adoption of the imperial elite's identifiers (language, religion, lifestyle etc.) individuals born into subordinated segments of the polity can claim factual or symbolic membership among its ranks. The rise of cultural brokers[11] catalyzes the assimilation of non-dominant cultures in the imperial *Leitkultur*.

---

8 The concept of an imperial system applied in this study was greatly influenced by the definitions of empires crafted by Eisenstadt 1969, esp. 12–29, Doyle 1986, 12, Tilly 1997, 3–4, Hardt/Negri 2001, Kennedy 2004, 3n1, Barkey 2008, esp. 9–27, Münkler 2005, 16–20, and Cline/Graham 2011, 1–9.

9 The notion of empire gains momentum in the study of the first two centuries of Islamic rule. It is lamentable, however, that its use is rarely accompanied by a precise working definition of the peculiarities of imperial rule. This lack of theoretical consideration is best exemplified in the interchangeable use of the concepts of "empire" and "state" in many recent studies. See e.g. Legendre 2013; Sijpestein 2013; Foss 2009; Hoyland 2006; Fowden 1993.

10 A reflection of the self-awareness of the Umayyad imperial family can be seen in the marital policy of the Umayyad clan that became increasingly endogamous. Robinson 2016.

11 On cultural brokerage, see Burt 2005, and Szaz 2001, esp. 294–310 with reference to further literature. Jezewski 1995, 18 defines cultural brokers as possessing 12 distinctive attributes: (1) intervening

Regardless of the strength of the metropolitan centre, the ability of the imperial elite to maintain political and military control over the periphery and to access economic resources, manpower, and information depends on cooperation with peripheral groups. Vertical interactions between the ruling group and the common population are thus usually mediated by intermediate governing bodies. This role is mostly discharged by local elites with a local power base and relatively loosely integrated in the imperial administration. "Horizontal" interactions between subordinated segments of the polity rarely take place. On the contrary, the centre holds a close to monopolistic position as the interlocutor with subordinated segments of the polity.

Thus, in this study, I understand empire to be a complex network of indirect authority relations between the trans-regional imperial elite and the differentiated populations of the periphery, through the mediation of intermediate governing bodies. These mediators are caught in a system of conflicting loyalties alternating between their local network and powerbase and the central polity. If left unchecked, these centrifuge impulses can cripple imperial control of the periphery and potentially even threaten the unity of the imperial polity. Although authority remains the prerogative of the centre, the ruling group negotiates over degrees of autonomy in exchange for agency, loyalty, and compliance. Authority relations between imperial and local elites, structurally unbalanced in favour of the centre as they are, are therefore constantly brokered. Empires survive as long as they are able to organize and rule over difference.[12]

in conflict situations when tensions exist in interactions; (2) standing guard at critical junctures in the context of interactions; (3) possessing role ambiguity in the context of brokering and functioning in asymmetric relationships; (4) functioning marginally in one or more systems while brokering between systems; (5) encouraging potential for changing systems; (6) dealing with others positively and cultivating varied social relationships; (7) mediating between traditions; (8) innovating when traditions are inflexible; (9) facilitating communication by translating interests and messages between groups; (10) bridging value systems; (11) functioning as a go-between; and (12) bringing people together through networking. The figure of the cultural broker is therefore to be distinguished from that of the interpreter (someone who facilitates communication between users of two different languages through competence in both of them) and from that of the transculturate (someone who moves from one culture to live in another). For seminal case studies, see Wolf 1956 and Geertz 1960. For some reflections on the application of the concept of cultural brokerage to Early Islamic society, see Reinfandt 2020a.

12 On general considerations on the process of the disintegration of empires, see Tilly 1997 and Motyl 2001. On the dissolution of the early Islamic Empire in particular, see Kennedy 2004.

Empires and Arab History

Arabian potentates were involved in imperial policies centuries before the rise of Islam. The first Muslim invaders originated in a culturally permeable borderland situated at the margins of overlapping spheres of influence wrestled over by the Himyarite Kingdom and later the Axumite vice-kingdom, the Byzantine Empire, and the Sasanian Empire.[13] Arab Himyarite, Byzantine, and Sasanian vassals such as the Ḥujrids, Ghassānids, and Lakhmids relied on imperial subsidies and exploited their military capital to broker autonomy and social prestige. From the scant information that transpires from their inscriptions, Arab vassal kings took great pride in their bonds with imperial formations. In its epitaph in Namāra, the "king of all Arabs" Imru' al-Qays (332)[14] boasts of his exploits in Central Arabia on behalf of the Byzantines (*l-rwm*). Ghassānid phylarchs likewise ostentatiously proclaimed their ties with Byzantium by converting to Christianity, patronising Christian architecture, writing in Greek, and adopting Roman titles of rank such as *flaouios, paneuphēmos, patrikios, endoxotatos, phylarchos*.[15]

The Islamic conquests that turned the Middle Eastern and Mediterranean world on its head in a period of under 30 years, exponentially increased the conquerors' symbolic capital but also called for carefully balanced policies of difference and incorporation. The lands the Arabs appropriated were home to ancient cultural traditions, signified by the visible landmarks left by previous civilizations. On one hand, the rich representative repository of Late Antiquity commanded admiration and notions of greatness worthy of emulation. On the other, it held a dangerous potential for cultural assimilation and the dissolution of distinctive Arab-Muslim cultural traits. The polyglot not-yet Arabized nor Islamized self-aware local elites were furthermore a powerful reminder of the Arab-Muslims' minority status. The decision attributed to the second caliph ʿUmar I (*rg.* 634–644) to prevent Arab fighting men from owning land, and to encourage them to settle in walled-off garrison-cities rather than spreading over the countryside, for instance, is indicative

13 Marsham 2009b, 481–483; Sizgorich 2004, 16–22 with references to further literature.
14 The traditional reading of the date on the Namāra epitaph (Kaslūl 7th 223) has been revised by Robin to "Kaslūl 3rd 227" EB thereby giving the year 332 instead of 328 for the death of Imru' al-Qays. Robin 2016, 376–377; on the interpretation of the fourth cipher on the inscription as the Nabatean numeral for 5 see *ibid.*, 375. The identification of Imru' al-Qays with the homonymous Lakhmid king is possible, but hypothetical.
15 A synoptic survey of Ghassānid inscriptions is given by Gatier 2015. See also the seal of one "Gabala *patrikios*" possibly owned by the Ghassānid Jabala b. Ayhām († 640/641), in Shahid 2001.

https://doi.org/10.1515/9783110740820-003

of the lengths to which the Early Muslim rulers went to contain the risk of cultural assimilation.[16]

The challenge was more than symbolic. Byzantine counteroffensives in Egypt and North Africa resulted in the successful – if short-lived – re-conquest of the provincial capitals of Alexandria (645) and Carthage (698). The Mardaite mercenaries dispatched by Constantine IV (*rg.* 668–685) to the Lebanese coast even managed to carve out an independent territory from which they attacked the heartland of the Umayyad caliphate in Syria for years.[17] Furthermore, Constantinople took advantage of periods of struggle within the Caliphate to impose favourable peace conditions on the Muslims in 658,[18] 677/678,[19] and repeatedly between 685 and 687.[20] Likewise, the spectre of the house of Sāsān loomed menacingly in the Far East where the last members of the royal family had found asylum at the Tang court, beseeching support in claiming back their ancestral lands. One of Pērōz III's sons, Narseh (ironically allegedly a maternal uncle to Yazīd III), led an abortive attempt to invade Iran in 677 with Chinese help[21] and a brother of his, Khusraw, reportedly accompanied a Turkic army in an effort to drive the Arabs out of Transoxiana (729).[22]

These struggles were compounded by friction stemming from within the Caliphate. Local uprisings by disparate social matrices punctuated Early Islamic history. The implementation of centralizing fiscal reforms was the main trigger of the Coptic agrarian revolts from the late 7th to the 9th century,[23] while eschatological expectations are said to have played in the background of an early Jewish uprising in Iraq in the 640s[24] and a mix of cultural resentment and longing for past glory seems to have animated the revolt of Sunbādh, a descendant of Sasanian aristocracy, in 755.[25] Foreign powers could also and did take advantage of social tensions among the Empire's population. The leader of the Turgesh Suluk, for instance, triggered a rebellion in Sogdiana that crippled Arab presence in

---

16 Sijpesteijn 2013, 115–116; Morony 2005, 236–264.

17 Howard-Johnson 2010, 4–9 and Lilie 1976, 83–96 and 99–112. For enigmatic imitations of Byzantine *folles* from late 7th-century Syria with Pahlavi inscriptions, possibly struck by the Mardaites, see Schindel/Hahn 2010a.

18 For the conditions and setting of the treaty, see Kaplony 1996, 37–46.

19 *Ibid.*, 77–97.

20 *Ibid.*, 99–136.

21 Rezakhani 2017, 183–184 with further literature.

22 Christensen 1936, 502–503.

23 Mikhail 2014, 118–127; Frantz-Murphy 2001, 26–29; Morimoto 1981, 145–172.

24 Morony 2005, 327.

25 Crone 2012, 32–40.

Transoxiana (720),[26] and the ranks of the above-mentioned Mardaites were inflated by prisoners of war freed from Muslim captivity. But local rebels were also an attractive ally for recalcitrant Arab tribes and Islamic sectarian movements at odds with imperial rule. In 658, for instance, Kurds from Fars flocked to the Khārigite ranks.[27] A few decades later, the pro ʿAlid agitator al-Mukhtār employed slaves in the service of the Kufans in his army in the period 686–687[28] and the rebellious Arab general ʿAbd al-Raḥmān b. Muḥammad b. al-Ashʿath was in league with the population of Sistān and with the ruler of Zābulistān (*rutbīl*) against al-Hajjāj b. Yūsuf in 699.[29]

The most fundamental test to the Empire's resilience, however, came with the clash of elites and concepts of legitimacy within the Arab-Muslim community. Growing discontent with the allegedly nepotistic and worldly-minded policies of the third caliph ʿUthmān resulted in the latter's assassination. The civil war that eventually ensued (arab. *fitna*, literally "temptation") marked the rise to power of the Umayyad dynasty (656–660). A generation later, a second civil uprising triggered by Muslim Meccan aristocracy following the death of Muʿāwiya I (*rg.* 661–680) in turn pushed the Umayyads to the brink of annihilation (680–692). This was the catalyst for the extensive administrative reforms started by the Marwanids at the beginning of the 8th century. The Umayyads held power for another 60 years before eventually succumbing to their distant cousins, the Abbasids (Banū Hāshim), in yet another civil war (746–750). The political unity of the Muslim Empire, although deprived of its westernmost extremity, survived and even flourished for another 80 years after the collapse of its first great dynasty, before slowly dissolving into the Abbasid commonwealth.

---

26 Karev 2015, 221; Hoyland 2015a, 184–185; Beckwith 2009, 133–134.

27 Morony 2005, 265.

28 Hoyland 2015a, 167; Morony 2005, 211.

29 Hoyland 2015a, 152–153; Morony 2005, 272.

Views on Early Islamic History

The broadest avenue for the study of the formative phase of the Early Islamic Empire is offered by the rich medieval Islamic historical memory collected in chronicles, religious and juridical treatises, and collections of the Prophet's sayings (arab. *aḥādīth*, sing. *ḥadīth*), but also biographical lexica and court poetry. Historiographical and legal oeuvres, in particular, contain echoes of debates on the nature of temporal authority and legitimacy.[30] Chronicles further expound the grand narrative of how the mosaic of peoples and cultures in the Middle East and North Africa was moulded, seemingly effortlessly, into an integrated polity by the administrative and monetary reforms of ʿAbd al-Malik b. Marwān and al-Ḥajjāj b. Yūsuf, and by the steady advance of the Islamic religion and the Arabic language across the lands of the Empire.

The question of representativeness of these oeuvres that have informed traditional notions of how Islam began has been the subject of critical studies since the late 19th century. These include studies by Julius Wellhausen, Ignaz Goldziher, Leone Caetani, and Henri Lammens.[31] The most immediate cause for caution is the time gap that separates the redaction of this composite literary corpus and the events referenced in it. The overriding mass of information filtered through medieval Islamic historiographical works has its roots in fluid oral traditions reaching as far back as the formative period of Islam in the early 7th century. But this was not committed to writing until the 9th, 10th, and later centuries. The work of collecting and redacting these materials typically occurred at the hands of an urban intellectual elite of mostly Mesopotamian and Iranian origin.[32] Furthermore, most of the authors were active at the Abbasid court where they absorbed its cultural premises and, particularly, its anti-Umayyad predisposition. Finally, by the 9th century, definitive concepts of Islam had formed, which exercised a retroactive homogenizing effect on notions of Islam's earliest days.

In their 1977 book *Hagarism: The Making of the Islamic World,* Patricia Crone and Michael Cook were among the first to champion the systematic use of coeval 7th- and 8th-century Greek and Syriac (and mainly Christian) narrative sources to write a history of the formation of Islam to counterbalance the partialities of later Muslim accounts. Crone and Cook finally postulated a systematic reassessment of basic aspects of Early Islamic civilization, gravitating towards the view of a radical rupture between an embryonic phase of Islam in the 7th and 8th centuries

30 Most notably Donner 1998, 98–125.

31 For a synoptic assessment on this early scholarship, see *ibid.*, 9–20.

32 Brockopp 2017, esp. 98–133.

https://doi.org/10.1515/9783110740820-004

and its maturity in the 9th and following centuries.[33] Several studies followed this path, based on analogous methodological assumptions. Some postulated that the figure of Muḥammad[34] or even the Muslim conquests were never historical but were instead later inventions.[35] Others claimed that Islam originated as a Judeo-Christian movement[36] and that its formative environment should be situated in the Fertile Crescent[37] rather than in the Arabian Peninsula. Still others suggested that the Qur'an was a product of the late 8th and later centuries[38] and was composed in a hybrid mix of Syriac/Aramaic and Arabic.[39] Such radical rethinking of the origins of Islam have since come to be regarded by most as provocative intellectual exercises at best, providing ultimately "wrong answers" despite "asking the right questions".

The methodological points raised by *Hagarism*, however, became the book's most enduring legacy. Recent contributions to Early Islamic history have adopted a stance of "healthy scepticism" towards traditional Muslim accounts and have assimilated the need for more scrupulous methodological premises and for corroboration by integrating more secure evidence.[40] Moreover, extra-Muslim accounts have since become an unalienable component of academic discourse on the making of Islamic civilization.[41] The perspective of the vanquished on the Islamic Empire cannot of course reasonably be expected to be less biased and prejudiced than that of the conquerors. The main advantage of dealing with these extra-Muslim sources is rather chronological, as about two dozen such accounts were first written during the 7th and 8th centuries. It goes without saying that extra-Muslim literary works have transmission and redaction problems of their own.[42] The nature of this body of evidence is moreover highly heterogeneous,

33 Donner 1998, 20–25. For a synopsis of the positions of "revisionist" scholars in Qur'anic studies and of their different approaches, see in particular Reynolds 2008, 8–17.
34 Popp 2010; Luxemberg 2000; Nevo/Koren 2003.
35 Nevo/Koren 2003.
36 E.g., Popp 2010; Nevo/Koren 2003; Crone/Cook 1977.
37 E.g., Hawting 1999; Sharon 1988; Wansbrough 1978; Crone/Cook 1977.
38 Most notably, Wansbrough 1977 and *id.* 1978.
39 Luxemberg 2000.
40 E.g., Brockopp 2017; Mikhail 2014; Borrut 2011; Robinson 2000; Donner 1998.
41 Compilations of extra-Muslim narrative writings on the beginnings of Islam in Syriac are to be found in Brock 1982, Palmer 1993, and Penn 2015. More comprehensive are Hoyland 1997a and Thomas/Roggema 2009 in that they include also Greek, Latin, Coptic, and Armenian, and even Persian and Chinese sources. For Egypt in particular see Mikhail 2014. For sources in Sanskrit, see Chattopadhyaya 1998.
42 A poignant case is the destiny of the work of John of Nikiou, whose world history composed around the year 700 survives in an early 17th-century Ethiopian version based on an Arabic translation of the original.

ranging from homiletic literature to accounts by pilgrims and wayfarers and apocalyptic literature. Cross-checking between Muslim and non-Muslim literary accounts, however, can certainly provide a framework for distinguishing actual historical information from polemical, aprioristical or idealizing projections.[43] The authors in question were mostly Christian ecclesiastics working in monastic contexts, often residing in but also traveling to the Middle East and operating outside the milieu of imperial rule. Cases like that of John of Damascus († 754), who possibly held an office in the Umayyad administration, as had his father before him,[44] are highly exceptional. To sum up, whether the information they provide is historically accurate or not, neither Muslim (on account of their date of composition) or extra-Muslim (on account of their social environment) literary works are representative of the scribal culture defined by imperial officials of the Early Islamic period. For this reason, this study focuses mainly on communicative acts *by* the Early Islamic Empire preserved in their original form rather than on works *on* the Early Islamic Empire.

43 For the use of non-Muslim literary sources on the development of Islam and the Islamic empire and its problematic aspects, see in particular Hoyland 1997a, 545–597.

44 For the Manṣūr family's ties with the Umayyad administration, see Griffith 2016. On a critical assessment of John of Damascus' belonging in the same family, see Anthony 2015.

A Review of the Documentary Evidence and Coping with its Limitations

Hagarism was methodologically ground-breaking in that it advocated the use of documentary and archaeological evidence as a corrective measure for the literary accounts. These sources are contemporaneous with the events they narrate and are not distorted either by temporal or geographical distance. Content and structure of documentary sources can be shaped by ideological calculations; these reflect, however, the issuers' agenda at the time and place of the document's production rather than being interpretative retrospections of geographically and/or chronologically distant contexts. Arabic official documents of various types survive in numbers sufficient to provide a fairly varied picture of the rhetorical, linguistic, and visual means employed by the early "Commanders of the Believers" to define and display their power *vis à vis* different audiences.

The surviving corpus of documentary texts ranges from papyrus, parchment, and paper documents to epigraphic and numismatic items, each possessing a different kind of relevance to the subject of this inquiry. For purposes of comparison, this study examines sources in Greek, Middle Persian, Coptic, Syriac, Sogdian, and Latin as long as they are the product of the social milieu of the Early Islamic pan-imperial elite. Architectural and iconographic motifs are only discussed if closely bound to public forms of Arabic writing.

A further body of textual evidence that has increasingly attracted scholarly attention in the last decades are early Arabic fragments of the Qur'an[45] preserved in *geniza*-like deposits.[46] Unfortunately, none of the earliest copies is provided with a colophon. Increasingly refined palaeographical models and radiocarbon dating, however, suggest that at least part of the Qur'anic corpus had taken on

45 For an up-to-date list of all known non-Qur'anic pre-900 Arabic manuscripts not including Christian works, see Brockopp 2017, 199–209. The earliest dated specimen, a portion of the *History of David* attributed to Wahb b. Munabbih housed in the Heidelberg papyrus collection is dated to 844. Cf. Déroche 1987–1989 including a Christian Arabic fragment of the Gospel of John dated 859/860.

46 The bulk of early Arabic manuscripts stems from the repositories of the Umayyad Mosque in Damascus (housed in the Museum for Turkish & Islamic Art in Istanbul), the Great Mosque of Kairouan (Tunisia), and the Great Mosque of Ṣanʿāʾ (Yemen). For an overview of Qur'anic fragments datable between the 7th and 10th century, see the *Manuscripta Coranica* database in the framework of the *Corpus Coranicum* project https://corpuscoranicum.de/handschriften/uebersicht (accessed Apr. 28, 2021).

https://doi.org/10.1515/9783110740820-005

a recognizable form by the 7th century.[47] Stylistic features of fragments from (arguably) the late Umayyad period even hint at a degree of official regulation in manuscript production.[48] The relationship between early Qur'an manuscripts and contemporary documentary evidence has been the subject of a number of recent studies;[49] here I have limited my discussion to the use of Qur'anic formulae in Early Islamic Arabic documents (Chapters III–IV).

Papyrus, Parchment and Paper Documents

Since the editing of the first Arabic papyri almost 200 years ago by the French scholar Antoine-Isaac Silvestre de Sacy (1825), papyri and related sources have become almost universally accepted as the main window into aspects of personal and administrative daily life that have been largely overlooked by literary accounts. The favourable climatic conditions have made Egypt the source of the overwhelming majority of preserved texts from the 7th and 8th centuries.

The thousands of papyri in Arabic, Coptic, and Greek unearthed in the region, dated or datable to the Early Islamic period, illustrate the coeval bureaucratic machinery with a degree of detail that is unimaginable for other provinces.[50] The

---

47 Déroche 1992 remains the most authoritative and extensive paleographic model for early Islamic Arabic manuscripts. See also Déroche 2014, 11–106, *id.* 2009, and *id.* 2002; George 2010, 31–93; Blair 2006, 101–140. On the challenges of dating early Qur'an copies, see Grohmann 1958, 221–222. Radiocarbon examinations have indicated that some of the early Qur'anic fragments may date as far back as the mid-7th century. Analysis of later specimens, however, has brought to light discrepancies between colophon dates and radiocarbon dating, with the result that C_{14} results should be taken with a grain of salt. See Déroche 2014, 11–13. It should also be added that C_{14} analysis can date only the material support, and not when a work was actually committed to writing.

48 Déroche 2014, esp. 107–134. On the process of collection and redaction of the Qur'anic corpus under official sponsorship, see in particular Sinai 2014 and Kaplony 2018, 312–343.

49 In particular Kaplony 2018, 312–343 and the contributions to the volume *Qur'ān Quotations Preserved on Papyrus Documents, 7th-10th Centuries* (2019) referenced in the bibliography. For a recent assessment on overlaps and discontinuities between early Islamic documentary texts and Qur'anic manuscripts with regard to orthographical and paleographical features, see, in particular Sijpesteijn 2020b with further references.

50 The large number of fiscal documents in different languages illustrates the limited administrative novelties implemented ad hoc by the Arabs in a climate of overall resilience of administrative practices and personnel. See Sijpesteijn 2007a, *ead.* 2007b, and *ead.* 2013, 49–114; Legendre 2013, 78–154 and *ead.* 2016, Foss 2009; and Bruning 2018a. More extensive interventions in the administrative structure are first discernible in 8th-century papyri, when Arab or Arabicized personnel are increasingly active at an administrative middle layer. These changes coincide with the first attestations of Muslim presence in the Egyptian countryside. See Sijpesteijn 2013, esp.

most immediate sign of continuity with late antique practices that papyri have to offer is represented by their use of pre-Islamic administrative languages. Multilingual archives and dossiers[51] illustrate the functional interplay in the Early Islamic chanceries of Arabic, Greek, and Coptic in Egypt (7th–8th century),[52] of Arabic and Greek in Palestine (7th century),[53] and of Arabic and Sogdian and Bactrian in Central Asia (8th century).[54]

But papyrus documents also offer insights into the gradual process of cultural assimilation by the local population signalled by the adoption of Arabic names, Arabic language, and sometimes – but not necessarily – of the Islamic religion.[55] The circumstances of the discovery of documents as well as internal references also elucidate the way these texts were kept, utilized and disposed of.[56] Papyri in Arabic and Coptic likewise show the slow transition from Byzantine and hybrid judicial practices to an Islamic judicial system in the 9th and 10th centuries.[57] In tandem with documents in Greek and Coptic, Arabic papyri furthermore reveal aspects of Egypt's agrarian economy and even prices and wages of the labour force.[58] By the late 8th century, Muslim traders involved in transregional mercantile networks spreading over the Early Islamic Empire also made their appearance in Arabic papyri.[59] Finally, papyri also illuminate aspects of social behaviour in private contexts.[60]

199–216; Legendre 2013, 158–213; Bruning 2018a. Cf. Robinson 2000, 90–97 for similar developments in 8th-century Northern Mesopotamia. On the differing pace of the process of Arabization of the administration in Egypt and Syria-Palestine, see Kaplony 2016.

51 For the concepts of "archive" (a collection of documents made in antiquity) and "dossier" (a group of documents brought together today), see Vandorpe 2009, esp. 218–219.

52 See in particular Richter 2010 and *id.* 2013. Cf. Kaplony 2016, 392–394 (7th–8th century) and 396–399 (8th century). See also *infra* pp. 54–77.

53 See in particular Stroumsa 2008 and *ead.* 2014, 185–213. Cf. Kaplony 2016, 294–296. See also *infra* pp. 77–87.

54 Khan 2007, 19. See also *infra* pp. 101–108.

55 For Egypt, see Frantz-Murphy 1991, 15–17, Fournet 2009b, Legendre 2013, 138–142, and Reinfandt 2020a; for Afghanistan, see Khan 2007, 16.

56 Sijpesteijn 2007c and *ead.* 2012a; cf. Bravmann 2012.

57 *I.a.*, Tillier 2013 and Richter 2001 and 2009.

58 Ashtor 1969; Shatzmiller/Pamuk 2014, 198–208 (mainly based on later Genizah sources); Morelli 2019. For a comparison with microeconomic aspects elucidated by the pre-conquest Nessana papyri, see Trombley 2014, 184–212.

59 Rāġib 1991. Cf. also *P.HindsNubia* (Qaṣr Ibrīm; 758) in which the governor Musā b. Kaʿb negotiates the release and safety of merchants with Arabic names. The letter is part of a dossier comprising four other missives in Coptic. A monographic study of the entire dossier is being prepared by Joost Hagen.

60 E.g., Younes 2013.

In recent years, interdisciplinary research projects have followed integrated approaches to papyrology, encouraging cooperation between the neighbouring fields of Arabic, Greek, and Coptic studies.[61] Increasing digitization has greatly improved the accessibility of the ever-growing corpus of published papyri and substantially reduced the linguistic and graphic recalcitrance of this body of evidence.[62] For all their advantages, the study of papyri has critical limits. In sharp contrast to Egypt, only a few hundred 7th- and 8th-century Greek, Arabic, and Christian leather Aramaic (CPA) papyri survived in Syria-Palestine at the sites of Nessana,[63] Khirbat al-Mird,[64] and Khirbat Ḥamrā Ifdān.[65] Some 250 documents on paper and leather in Arabic (35),[66] Bactrian (ca. 150),[67] and Sogdian (ca. 72)[68] from Early Islamic Central Asia can be added to this corpus. A number of Early Islamic documents in Middle Persian[69] and Arabic[70] on paper and textiles has surfaced in Iran.[71] But even within Egypt, the representativeness of papyri suffers from an imbalance. Besides these limitations, the bulk of the evidence stems from rural areas, with comparatively few testimonies coming from urban centres and

61 Most notably, *The formation of Islam – The view from below* (Leiden, 2009–2014); *Imperium and Officium* (Vienna, 2009–2015); *The Early Islamic Empire at Work – the view from the regions towards the center* (Hamburg, 2014–2019); *Embedding Conquest – Naturalising Muslim Rule in the Early Islamic Empire (600–1000)* (Leiden, 2016–2021); *Change and Continuities from a Christian to a Muslim Society – Egyptian Society and Economy in the 6th to 8th centuries* (Basel, 2016–2018).
62 In particular, the *Arabic Papyrology Database* (*APD*), http://www.naher-osten.lmu.de/apd (accessed Apr. 30, 2021) providing full-text and metadata on published Arabic papyri; the *Arabic Papyrology School* (*APS*), http://www.naher-osten.lmu.de/aps (accessed Apr. 28, 2021), a didactic tool for deciphering Arabic papyri; *Papyri.info*, http://papyri.info/ (accessed Apr. 30, 2021) providing full-text and metadata on published documentary papyri, mainly in Greek and Latin but with substantial contributions in Coptic, Arabic, Demotic, Aramaic, and Hebrew; *Trismegistos*, https://www.trismegistos.org/ (accessed Apr. 28, 2021) providing metadata of papyri and related sources in all languages; and the *Bruxelles Coptic Database*, https://dev.ulb.ac.be/philo/bad/copte/baseuk.php?page=accueiluk.php (accessed Apr. 28, 2021) providing metadata on published Coptic documentary texts.
63 *P.Ness.* and *P.HoylandDhimma*.
64 *P.Mird*.
65 Friedman/Vorderstrasse/Mairs/Adams 2017.
66 *P.Khurasan*, *P.Kratchkovski*, and *P.HaimPaper*.
67 *BD* I–III.
68 Mugh.
69 Berk.
70 *P.KhanBerkley*.
71 The Arabic (*P.KhanBerkeley*) and Middle Persian (Berk.) documents from early Islamic Iran housed at Berkeley most probably belong to two different phases of the same archive. The scant Arabic material is in all probability to be dated to the 9th century and is therefore not examined in this study. See Khan 2003.

scarce documentation existing on the Delta region. Besides, domains such as literature, intellectual history and jurisprudence are comparatively underrepresented in the 7th- and 8th-century papyri, while others such as religious conversion have left mostly indirect traces.

Epigraphy

Epigraphy, the writing on stone for the purpose of perpetuating and displaying the relationship between persons and certain places, objects, and edifices, is the only pre-Islamic form of Arabic writing for which physical evidence survives.[72] The main epigraphic categories attested in the Early Islamic period are private epitaphs and, first and foremost, building and restoration inscriptions. The latter were produced mainly under the aegis of Early Islamic rulers and officials to celebrate their patronage of public buildings or luxury objects. Inscriptions of this kind – when intact – are always dated and designed for public display with a wider reception than official chancery documents.[73] They are of paramount importance not only for reconstructing the development of an Arab-Muslim imperial culture but also for the analysis of Early Islamic dispositional practices of public texts.

From a geographical viewpoint, Arabic inscriptions are comparatively more widely spread across the lands of the Early Islamic Empire than papyri. Conversely, official inscriptions are incommensurably fewer than papyrological and related sources.[74] In addition, despite being attested in the area between North Africa and the Caucasus, official inscriptions are themselves geographically unevenly distributed and mostly concentrated in core regions of the Early Islamic Empire, in particular in Greater Syria and the Ḥijāz. Early Islamic official epigraphy has furthermore little of the linguistic plurality of papyri, as all public epigraphic texts connected with the Early Islamic ruling elite are redacted in Arabic – with the unique exception of a Greek inscription commemorating the restoration of a bathhouse in Hammat Gader under the auspices of the local Muslim governor.[75]

72 There is a gap of roughly one hundred years between the latest pre-Islamic inscription in Ḥarrān (548) and the earliest known Islamic Arabic graffito in Muthallath (643).

73 Cf. Biermann 1998, 14–15.

74 For a survey with commentary of Early Islamic Arabic inscriptions, see *infra* pp. 192–194 and Appendix II.

75 Di Segni 1997, 237–240.

Parallel to inscriptions proper, there is a numerically more consistent and ever-growing corpus of Arabic graffiti.[76] As a genre, Arabic graffiti are embedded in an epigraphic scribal tradition that had its roots in the Arabian Peninsula centuries before the rise of Islam. Arabic graffiti may be considered to be direct epigones of the tens of thousands of graffiti in Old North and South Arabian languages.[77] In fact, the appearance of Early Islamic Arabic graffiti predates that of the earliest Arabic monumental inscriptions by a generation. Graffiti moreover betray a very different framework of scribal conventions and formulae compared to official inscriptions and chancery documents. Both in terms of geographical distribution and semantic domains, graffiti differ markedly from more elaborate epigraphical testimonies. Early Islamic graffiti are mostly tokens of private piety in the form of invocations, prayers, and benedictions (or maledictions), which offer a precious window into the development of Early Islamic spirituality and even into the formation of the Qur'anic text.[78]

By contrast, the ruling elite rarely, if at all, resorted to graffiti for public communications, although prominent figures of the Muslim community have occasionally left traces on this medium.[79] Owing to their informal character and the circumstances of their production,[80] Arabic graffiti dated or datable to the 7th and 8th centuries are primarily diffused in regions in which native Arabic speakers made up a large proportion of the local population; mainly in Syria-Palestine and north-west Arabia. Conversely, very few examples of this genre are found in other regions of the Early Islamic Empire. Overall, graffiti provide an excellent source of information on the internal spiritual development of the contemporary Arab-Muslim milieu and are particularly valuable as a medium for inquiring into Arabic scribal traditions developing outside the formal framework defined by imperial officials (see Chapter III). However, they offer comparatively little

76 The *Thesaurus d'Épigraphie Islamique* (*EPI*) (http://www.epigraphie-islamique.org/epi/login.html; accessed Apr. 23, 2021) database provides data on about 500 graffiti dated or datable before 800. For more accurate quantitative esteems on the ever-growing corpus of early Islamic Arabic graffiti, see Imbert 2013a, 101–102 and *ibid.*n4.

77 Cf. *infra* Ch. III, *If the Mountain won't come* (Formulary).

78 See in particular Imbert 2000 and *id.* 2013a.

79 See in particular *id.* 2015.

80 On graffiti as a form of leisure in nomadic societies, see MacDonald 2009a, IV, 180. Besides their informal, accidental, and personal nature graffiti distinguish themselves from inscriptions proper both by their graphic features – often characterized by the heterogeneity of the characters – and by technical peculiarities – graffiti being (literally) "scratched" on the stone's surface rather than engraved. Cf. McLean 2002, 207–208. Graffiti are moreover materially produced by their author, whereas inscriptions are usually commissioned by their putative author. A perfect separation of the labels "graffito" and "inscription", however, is admittedly difficult at times.

information on the relation of the early Muslim community to culturally different milieus.

Numismatics and Sphragistics

Coins are the single most numerically plentiful, evenly distributed, and chronologically continuous textual source on the Early Islamic period. Two of the greatest advantages of using numismatic evidence as a historical source are the resilience of metal as a writing material and the fact that coins are usually dated.

Coins are indicators of the monetization of ancient economies and the locations of coin hoards are a crucial element in mapping mercantile networks. Arabic epigraphy and numismatics have also been treated in tandem with other types of material evidence in order to trace the development of institutions in the Early Islamic Empire on a transregional scale. They are the main windows on the centralizing reforms undertaken during the reign of the caliphs Muʿāwiya I and particularly ʿAbd al-Malik b. Marwān.[81]

Seventh and 8th-century Islamic coinage moreover offers the widest – if relatively superficial – picture, not visible in other sources, of the relationship of the Early Islamic elite with a number of cultural milieus. For instance, Arab-Byzantine coinage from North Africa and Spain constitutes the only direct evidence of the resilience of Latin as an administrative language in the Muslim administration. As textual media, Islamic coins encompass condensed forms of imperial ideology and styles of legitimization that may at times comprise more than a hundred words. Numismatic evidence is crucial to a reconstruction of styles of representation in the Early Islamic Empire and particularly to an understanding of the evolution of the role of the Islamic religion in Early Islamic public promulgations.[82]

Of singular interest, furthermore, is the interplay and blending of the textual component with iconographical motifs derived from previous imperial traditions that characterizes Islamic coins issued in the first three generations of Arab rule (see Chapter II).[83] What is more, coinage provides virtually unique original evi-

---

81 *I.a.* Donner 2012; Hoyland 2006; Johns 2003. See also *infra* Ch. II, *From Image to Word*.
82 *I.a.* Treadwell 2015 and *id.* 2017; Bacharach 2010; Bacharach/Anwar 2012; Heidemann 2010a.
83 Comprehensive editions of pre-reform coinage are *ASCC*, *BMC* I–II, *DOC*, and *SICA* I. For a synoptic overview of the typologies of pre-reform Islamic coinage, see Album 2011, 21–39.

dence for concepts of legitimacy and propaganda strategies crafted by defeated claimants to the leadership within the Muslim community (see Chapter III).[84]

In addition to coins *stricto sensu*, thousands of Early Islamic seals, stamps and standard measures on metal, glass, and clay survive. These testimonies share similar structure and sets of formulae with coins.[85] In particular, Arabic numismatic and sigillographic sources operate within a set of fixed operative clauses that mirror different layers of the administrative chain of command.[86] In contrast, the coverage of information provided by coinage and related sources is severely limited by the small writing surface and by the serial nature of coin production. Numismatics is in addition the least synoptic of the main categories of Early Islamic material sources and the one which suffers most from a structural lack of digital tools.[87]

84 Most notably, Geiser 2010 and Foss 2002 on Khārijite coinage; Foss 2013 on Zubayrid coinage; Treadwell 2012 on ʿAlid and (revolutionary) Abbasid coinage. See also Wurtzel 1978.

85 Extensive collections of Islamic measures and stamps are *BM*, *EIGS*, and *UAT*.

86 Balog 1977. Cf. also Stefan Heidemann's unpublished paper held at the conference *The Measure of Integration – Economic Structures and Resources of the Early Islamic Empire* (Hamburg; Febr. 16–17, 2018). I thank Stefan Heidemann for sending me a transcript of his paper.

87 To date, no database for Islamic coins comparable to the *EPI* and *APD* exists. Collections around the world have in recent years increasingly put effort into digitizing their holdings of Islamic coins on dedicated websites of varying quality. The oldest and most extensive website of this kind to date is hosted by the American Numismatic Society http://numismatics.org/search/department/Islamic (accessed Apr. 21, 2021). The largest digital corpus of Islamic coins is collected on the website *Zeno.ru* https://www.zeno.ru/ (accessed Apr. 27, 2021) which to date includes close to 155 000 commented images of oriental coins, about 41% (65641) of which stem from the Islamic world. A welcome addition is the Kenom Virtuelles Münzkabinett https://www.kenom.de/ (accessed Apr. 5, 2021) which – despite the small *corpus* (to date about 200 items of pre-800 early Islamic coins) – allows for textual searches in Arabic.

Previous Studies

A number of works have integrated, to varying degrees of detail, documentary sources on the study of the development of concepts of royalty and legitimacy in the Early Caliphate into their research, complementary to data filtered through the literary tradition. Most of these studies are neither exclusively nor mainly concerned with the role of the Arabic language in this process and use documentary texts as ancillary evidence to integrate or correct the historical narrative of literary accounts, rather than treating them as a field of study themselves.[88]

Discussion of official uses of the Arabic script in public contexts, in particular, has been traditionally confined to a few contributions from the fields of Arabic epigraphy and numismatics, mostly those by Oleg Grabar (*i.a.* 1987 and 2006b), Holly Edwards (1991), Richard Ettinghausen (1974), and Erica Dodd (1969). The sole systematic study on the practice of Arabic public writing is an extensive study by Irene Biermann (1998) on the Fatimid public text. Biermann's opening section, in particular, contains a survey on the use of inscriptions from Late Antiquity to the rise of the Fatimids, including considerations on aspects of public writing in the Umayyad and Abbbasid Empire.[89] While building on Biermann's treatment of the subject matter, the present work differs substantially from it in thematic focus, evidentiary base, and approach. Unlike Biermann, who essentially uses previous forms of public writing in order to outline a background for her main inquiry into Fatimid sources, I delve into practices of public writing during the first 150 years of the Islamic era. In contrast to Biermann, who focuses on inscriptions, coins, and – to a lesser extent – on textiles, excluding papyrological and sigillographic evidence,[90] the present study also tackles materials "not used officially in communal gathering spaces".[91]

Most importantly, Biermann's analysis operates on two main communicative levels: the material surface and the ideological content of public texts.[92] My work

88 *I.a.* Marsham 2018 and *id.* 2009a; Crone 2004; al-Azmeh 2001 [1997]; Crone/Hinds 1986. Al-Qāḍī 2012 merits special mention, basing her research on the "semi-documentary" corpus of state letters attributed to the Umayyad secretary ʿAbd al-Ḥamīd († 750).

89 Biermann 1998, 28–59.

90 *Ibid.*, 14–15.

91 *Ibid.*, 14.

92 Biermann 1998 identifies three main functions of public writing: a) territorial function (using a group-specific alphabet to mark boundaries), 31–48, b) aesthetic function (the use of certain materials and styles of writing to reference the process of production and the patrons), 48–56, and c) referential function (intertextuality through semantic reference to scriptures and other socially well-established corpora of writings), 56–59.

https://doi.org/10.1515/9783110740820-006

expands on this model by providing a deeper examination of the internal structural features of official texts, in particular formulae and layouts as well as less eye-catching instruments of symbolic meaning such as technical terms and the set of references they imply.

Interest in the *Sitz im Leben* of Arabic official documents in the cultural framework of the Early Islamic Empire is still in its infancy. The link between 7th- and 8th-century practices of Arabic and imperial policies is explicitly addressed in articles by Andreas Kaplony (2008; 2016; 2018; 2019) and Lucian Reinfandt (2015) for papyrological sources, and by Stefan Heidemann (2010; forthcoming) for numismatics. My work expands on these efforts by taking a more integrated approach to the Early Islamic scribal culture that accounts for epigraphic, papyrological, and numismatic evidence, discussing as well communicative acts which do not rely on semantic comprehension.

Approach and Methodology: Form over Substance

The present study's approach to the cumulative body of Early Islamic Arabic writing emphasizes the view from the centre. Specifically, it focuses on authority relations, spreading vertically from the imperial metropole as reflected in documentary sources produced for the most part in the imperial periphery. The array of original textual promulgations that constitutes the starting point of my discussion comprises 758 Arabic documents on papyrus and related materials, a selected corpus of 869 Arabic inscriptions and graffiti,[93] around 550 coin types and subtypes,[94] and a selected body of 1684 glass, metal and clay seals, stamps and standard measures[95] dated or datable before the year 800.

Papyri are both the most detailed of the sources considered in the present work and the most challenging to integrate in this line of inquiry. In the style of a statement by Richard Bulliet,[96] one can affirm that Arabic documentary papyrology has always privileged the view from the periphery or from below. This is largely dictated by the geographical provenance and dominant functional domains and contents of the overwhelming majority of Early Islamic documentary papyri. The natural wealth of the land preserved Egypt's role as a crucial economic and strategic asset well into the Early Islamic period. The region was, however, neither the seat of power nor the spiritual centre of the Early Islamic world and cannot be used to outline a representative picture of other regions in the Empire. Furthermore, the study of papyrological evidence is characterized by significant methodological constraints. Occasionally, single documents such as the famous letter by the Muslim governor Musā b. Kaʿab detailing the peace treaty (*baqṭ*) with the ruler of Nubia (*P.HindsNubia* (Qaṣr Ibrīm; 758)) will illustrate macro-historic events. More often, however, it is only by abstraction and through contextualization in large corpora that documentary papyri allow one to address issues of a broader social, economic, cultural, and political nature. This implies that the availability of numerically rich bodies of evidence is a necessary condition to tackle questions of wider historical significance, and that the potential for contextualizing evidence from Egypt in a wider trans-regional framework

93 The collection of epigraphic material has been made with the help of the *EPI* database.
94 Based on Album 2011, more particularly 549 types and subtypes (324 for the pre-reform coinage; 180 for Umayyad reformed coinage and revolutionary Abbasid coinage; 45 for early Abbasid coinage).
95 The collection of sigillographic sources has been done without the help of digital tools.
96 Bulliet 1994, 5, "The story of Islam has always privileged the view from the centre".

https://doi.org/10.1515/9783110740820-007

depends on the availability of a fairly commensurate number of documents from other regions.

In this regard, Egypt's status as a province within a larger imperial formation can be exploited. Papyri, like all other kinds of textual evidence examined in my discussion, belong to the environment of written communication in which interlocutors do not share a common spatial and temporal context, language exists visually, and style, register, and social etiquette (as opposed to content) are determined by carefully considered social factors.[97] As is the case with all other types of documentary evidence, papyri do not exist as independent, individual creations; rather, they operate within a closely defined set of formal, formulaic, graphic, aesthetic, and even terminological conventions, which offer a larger, broader context for their study. Arabic scribal conventions, in particular, originated in the cultural superstratum imported by the Arabs into Egypt (see Chapter I and III). In this respect, Egypt is no different from the other regions of the coeval Islamic Empire from which Arabic papyri and related sources have emerged. Scrutinizing official promulgations issued in hugely diverse geographical backgrounds for aspects of consistency in layout, formulae, arrangement, and technical terminology provides a measure of the reach of the central administration (see Chapters I–III). Conversely, variations in secondary formulaic and terminological features of imperial documents can be used to examine if, how, and to what extent aspects of the imperial canon were adapted to the peculiarities of a given regional context (Chapters IV–V) and/or how substratal cultural elements were echoed in the local version of official documents.

Although a comparatively understudied field, research on formal typologies of Arabic documents has made great leaps in recent years. Most treatments of this topic pertain to Arabic epistolography[98] and Arabic legal documents[99] with the notable addition of Adolf Grohmann's comprehensive study of Islamic protocols.[100] Eva Grob's (2010) ground-breaking monograph on private Arabic letters on papyrus is to date the most comprehensive treatment of the formal taxonomy of Arabic papyrus documents and systematizes previous research on the subject. Following this path, a comprehensive digital tool for formal typologies of Arabic documents on papyrus, parchment, and paper has been developed at the Ludwig

97 Barton 2007 esp., 86–100. My considerations apply to pre-modern societies.
98 Jahn 1937, esp. 157–173; Khan 1990 and *id.* 1992, 63–66; Diem 2004 and *id.* 2008; Sijpesteijn 2013, 222–229; Reinfandt 2015, esp. 282–286; Kaplony 2018.
99 Frantz-Murphy 1981–1989 and *ead.* 2001; Khan 1994 and *id.* 2008.
100 Grohmann 1923–1924, IX–CII.

Maximilian University (Munich).[101] These endeavors have greatly improved our understanding of the operational logic (the "algorithm", in Grob's terminology) of the documents, of the interrelation between formal and functional types, and have facilitated the process of cataloguing, dating and editing unpublished documents. At the same time, they provide the groundwork for expanding the possibilities for a more integrated approach to Arabic papyrology.

Like much of our knowledge of Early Islamic documentary practices, formalistic and typological studies on Early Islamic papyrus documents and related sources are largely dependent on papyri from Egypt. Unlike a content-based analysis, however, a comparison of documents from different regions based on their formal skeleton is neither dependent on the sheer quantitative mass of texts at our disposal nor bound by their thematic constraints. Granted that a document's functional type can overlap with a certain formal typology,[102] the formulae, layout, and script of official Arabic writings on papyrus are independent of their specific circumstantial content. An approach based on form thus provides the much-needed basis for a comparison of the proportionally overrepresented papyrological documentation from Egypt and the proportionally underrepresented evidence on papyrus and related materials from other regions, particularly Greater Syria and Central Asia. This in turn allows, as I shall argue, for an assessment of the degree of integration of the Early Islamic imperial system with particular reference to official scribal practices.

Islamic numismatics and epigraphy provide direct insights into the Early Islamic imperial metropole, in terms of both geographical provenance and functional typology. Conversely, formal features of Early Islamic epigraphic and numismatic texts – with the notable exception of palaeography[103] – have received a less systematic treatment than those of papyri and related sources.[104] I discuss papyrological evidence in tandem with epigraphic and numismatic sources in order to obtain a more complete panoramic view of the analysed phenomena, and to avoid geographical and chronological gaps in the documentation. At the same

101 Schematics of the formal types of Arabic documents can be viewed through the function "Types" of the *APD* (https://www.apd.gwi.uni-muenchen.de/apd/typology.jsp; accessed Apr. 30, 2021). I thank the research group *A Digital Typology of Arabic Documents* (*APT*) for keeping me updated on their progress and discussions, and for making internal data available to me.

102 Cf. Kaplony 2018, who distinguishes five functional types of Arabic documents on papyrus: 1) letter, 2) register, 3) agreement, 4) semi-literary document, 5) literary document.

103 *I.a.* Robin 2006; Blair 2006, 77–100; Gruendler 1993; Grohmann 1967–1971, II.

104 Partial outlines of the formal structure of Early Islamic inscriptions can be found in Gaube 1982, 213–215 and Ritter 2016a, 64–72 and 75–80. For some reflections on graffiti, see in particular Hoyland 1997b.

time, this study incorporates formalistic approaches developed by papyrologists into the discussion of Early Islamic imperial numismatics and epigraphy for a better understanding of the cultural trends that inform their formal templates.

A further advantage of dealing with original sources is that they not only survive in their unaltered, unredacted meaning and phrasing but are also preserved with their original materials, layouts, and script (see Chapters II–III). Even more than a document's formulaic features, the "mediatic" dimension of Early Islamic official promulgations entails communicative statements that are not only not content-related but also independent of a text's semantic comprehension. Inscriptions placed in contexts that made readability an issue – like those in the Dome of the Rock[105] or the small legends on Islamic coins – were, for instance, hardly meant to engage their public in intensive reading. In the mainly aural environment[106] in which Early Islamic imperial textual promulgations operated, the visual surface of public texts further constituted a key component of how textual communicative acts were experienced. I have devoted particular attention to "impressionistic" aspects of official writing, channelling the charismatic dimension and visual distinctiveness of the written word and conveyed through stylistic, graphic, visual, referential, and material qualities of documents (see Chapter II).

From the parallel discussions of communicative acts that presupposed a semantic comprehension of a text's content and those that did not, one infers furthermore which rhetorical strategies different target-audiences were exposed to – or rather, were expected to be exposed to by the issuers of the documents. The main divides were of course determined by literacy (who could read?) and language mastery (who could read which language?). Throughout the 8th century, Arabic supplemented the use of the administrative languages of the Byzantine and Sasanian Empires and of the potentates of Central Asia. Greek, Latin, and Middle Persian remained dominant at first among the middle cadres of the imperial administration, while regional vernaculars like Coptic and Bactrian were used at the bottom level of the imperial bureaucracy.[107] Nonetheless, in the first half of the 8th century, local languages were also used for communication between Arab-Muslim high-ranking officials and non-Arab/non-Arabicized lower ranking officials. Documents operating at this juncture between cultural and linguistic milieus present hybrid formal characteristics and constitute a unique source of

---

105 Dodd/Khairallah 1981, 24–25.

106 There is to date no analysis of literacy levels (and literacy in which language?) in the early Islamic Empire. Documentary sources, however, indicate that relatively ample segments of the population (literate or not) were exposed to writing. For thoughts on this topic based on documents from Egypt, see Sijpesteijn 2013, 217–219 and Grob 2010, 87–89.

107 See *infra* Ch. I, *The Rise and Dissolution of "Imperial Arabic"*.

information on the way parameters of social behaviour were negotiated when the conditions of language accessibility shifted (see Chapter IV).

It goes without saying that an analysis based on these selective parameters is not a comprehensive attempt to reconstruct the complex set of interactions between the Early Islamic imperial elite and its subordinate groups "as it really was", but rather how it was expressed and reflected in the contemporary promulgations of the Early Islamic Empire.

The Definitional Trap: A Note on Terminology and Anachronism

In an unpublished paper delivered at the workshop *Towards a Typology of Arabic Documents* (Vienna 16–19 August 2016), Fred Donner opened his talk by stating that one of the greatest challenges faced by anyone studying the development of the Early Islamic state is definitional. Indeed – and in no small part owing to Donner's own contribution to the field – scholarly attention has increasingly been devoted in recent years to elements of anachronism, ambiguity, and inaccuracy in established terminology pertaining to various aspects of the academic discourse on Early Islamic civilization. Part of the difficulty lies in the sedimentation of concepts and the projection of later times on the Early Islamic polity, both in literary sources and in modern historiographical writing.

Documentary sources from the 7th and 8th centuries do not refer to different aspects of Islamic civilization in terms commonly used today. The first adherents to the religious movement that came to be known as Islam that we encounter in papyri and inscriptions, for instance, for the most part refer to themselves as "Believers" (*mu'minūn*) rather than "Muslims"[108] (*muslimūn*).[109] Building on passages from the Qur'an and from the Constitution of Medina, Donner argues that the early community of "Believers" included Christians and Jews, and viewed itself as a pan-Abrahamic pietistic movement, which only later took the shape of the confessionally distinctive religion known as Islam.[110]

Arab individuals, and particularly those involved in the military, are also addressed in 7th- and 8th-century Greek and Syriac sources as *moagaritai*/*mhaggrayē*, a rendering of the Arabic *muhājirūn* "emigrants/settlers"[111] found in Early Muslim poetry and *ḥadith*.[112] Both terms used as collective designations of the conquerors, *muhājirūn* and *mu'minūn* differed in that the former did not

108 For recent assessments of the meaning of the verb *aslama* (*li*-) and the substantive *islām* as used in the Qur'an, see Kister 2018, Cole 2019, and Lindstedt 2019, 184–186.
109 Donner 2002–2003 and *id.* 2010, 56–89.
110 *Ibid.*; for an expansion on Donner's theses based on pre-Abbasid epigraphic evidence, see Lindstedt 2019. Cf. however, Cole 2019, with conclusions partially incompatible with Donner's.
111 On the semantic connotation of the root *h-j-r* in early Islamic times, see Crone 1994. *Mhaggrayē* and *moagaritai* could – though less likely – also be derivatives of Hagar, the biblical progenitrix of the Arabs. Cf. e.g. the Syriac colophon to MS BM add. 14,666 fol. 56 reading "this writing of the New (Testament) was completed in the year 993 of the Greeks corresponding to (the year) 63 of *mhaggrayē*, the sons of Ishmael, the son of Hagar and Abraham".
112 Hoyland 1997a, 547 and *ibid.*n13.

https://doi.org/10.1515/9783110740820-008

encompass nomadic tribes who refused to settle down and grant military support to the Early Islamic conquests, nor converts.[113] In a recent monograph, Peter Webb likewise argues that 7th- and 8th-century groups, commonly referred to today as "Arabs", resorted to other collective terms for themselves and that the "Arab" ethnonym is a retrospective construct from the 9th and later centuries.[114] The term "Islam" itself is not attested before the year 691, when it appears on a private tombstone from Aswān (*CG* IX 3201); it occurs in official texts only from the following century on, and even then only sporadically.[115]

In Enzensberger's words, anachronisms are "no avoidable error but rather a basic condition of human existence".[116] A degree of anachronism both of a conceptual and a terminological nature is inherent in studies concerning times in the distant past. Implementing a terminology completely compatible with 7th- and 8th-century definitions and concepts is beyond the scope of this work. Key notions are consciously addressed in this study in terms that do not reflect coeval descriptions. This choice is an attempt to avoid unfamiliar periphrases in the belief that even anachronistic terminology – if properly contextualized – can be productive on account of its associative potential for the modern reader.[117] Some of the more recurrent instances of potentially ambiguous terminological choices in this essay will be briefly explained.

For the purpose of this study and without addressing the thorny issue of the existence (or lack thereof) of an "Arab" identity in the Early Islamic period, the use of the term "Arab" is strictly applied to the practice of Arabic and refers to the group encompassing 7th- and 8th-century *native* Arabic speakers and writers. I refer to the religion professed by the overwhelming majority of Arabic practitioners in their writings as "Islam" and to its adherents as "Muslims", although both terms become common only from the 9th century onwards. This preference is motivated not only by the wish to avoid less familiar terms *à la* Donner, such as "Believers", but also by the need to prevent the dangerous assumption that a

---

113 Lindstedt 2015.

114 Webb 2016, esp. 1–60, summarizing the main debates on the subject. For a recent discussion of pre-Islamic material evidence in particular, see al-Jallad 2020a.

115 The first attestation of the term *islām* in an official inscription is *RCEA* I 18* (Damascus; 705/706), which is, however, only known through literary reports. The word's first appearance in an official papyrus letter is *P.MuslimState* 8 (Fayyūm; 730–743), 8, 10, and 17. *Islām* is otherwise used in another graffito (Imbert 2013, 113) and in an official letter on papyrus (*P.HindsNubia*) before the turn of the 9th century. On the date of *CG IX* 3201 cf., however, *infra* p. 208n215.

116 *Die Elixiere der Wissenschaft. Seitenblicke in Poesie und Prosa*, Frankfurt 2002, 231 quoted in Landwehr 2013, 5; the English translation is my own.

117 For a useful discussion on anachronisms in historical writing and on their descriptive potential, see Landwehr 2013.

faith's content should conform to its public display. Following the papyrologist's mantra, absence of evidence is not evidence of absence. The lack of distinctive Muslim markers in public promulgations from the first 60 years of "Muslim" dominion should not automatically rule out their existence.[118] I do not wish to imply, however, that the credo professed by 7th- and 8th-century "Muslims" was identical to Islam as defined in the 9th and later centuries.

In order to refer to the Early Islamic imperial polity and its rulers I use the terms "Caliphate" and "caliph" interchangeably with Early Islamic Empire and *amīr al-muʾminīn*, despite the former (*khilāfa*/*khalīfat allāh*) being rarely used by contemporaries.[119] Dates according to the Muslim era are abbreviated as A(*nno*) H(*egirae*) although the eponymous event of the *hijra* is never mentioned in the documentary sources using the Islamic calendar.[120] The label "Islamic" implies *stricto sensu* explicit references to the Muslim creed. I use the term in a purely chronological sense, however, when referring to concepts such as Early Islamic Empire, Islamic coinage, and Islamic conquest(s).

A second major source of terminological ambiguity stems from the confluence of the different disciplines and areas of expertise involved in the study of the rise of Islam. Each field of study has developed its own conceptual categories and technical terminology to suit or reflect its stage of development, the sources it uses, and how it approaches them. Publications dedicated to the first centuries of Islamic rule are punctuated by a set of partially overlapping terminological choices. For example, Islamicists usually refer to the historical period between Muḥammad's predication and the appearance of the landmarks of classical Islamic culture as Early Islamic time. Byzantinists, on the other hand, might prefer the label Early Byzantine, and ancient historians in turn the more inclusive umbrella terms of Late Antiquity or Early Middle Ages. The same label can also be used to convey different periods. For an historian of Roman Egypt, for instance, Late Antiquity would commonly denote the time span stretching from the reign

118 Brockopp 2015.
119 Marsham 2018, 7 *contra* Crone/Hinds 1986, 4–23 and Nadler 1990, 34–51. Cf. also *infra* p. 153.
120 The only early Islamic document mentioning the *hijra* is a controversial inscription of unknown location on Cyprus and no longer extant, quoted by the Arab traveller al-Harawī (*RCEA* I 5*) and dated to the year "29 according to the *hijra* (*li-l-hijra*)". Donner 1998, 86 and *ibid.* n88 disputes the inscription's authenticity; in his extensive review of Donner's work, Elad (2002, 284–287) argues that the inscription should be considered authentic but admits that the phrase *li-l-hijra* may have been added by al-Harawī. For a recent discussion on the origins of the Islamic era, see Tillier/Vanthieghem 2019.

of Diocletian to the Islamic conquest, while for an Islamic historian the term may encompass the entire Umayyad period and beyond.[121]

As with all constructs, the stringency of such labels is not dependent on the inherent qualities of the phenomena or the concepts to which they are applied, but on the extrinsic set of relationships they unveil for the scholar. Depending on the context, partially overlapping terminologies have been used in this study. They are not meant to be interchangeable but to open different and parallel webs of references. Returning to our example, the use of the labels "Late Antiquity" and "late antique" is intended to emphasize the connection a phenomenon has with the pre-Islamic world, whereas "Early Islam" and "Early Islamic" are meant to underline a relation with or a formative influence on later Islamic culture. What these designations do not imply, however, is a strict chronological succession between a late antique and an Early Islamic period, nor are they used with the intent of setting a date at which Late Antiquity came to a close.

---

121 For an overview on the evolution of the concepts of Late Antiquity and End of Antiquity, see Johnson 2012, XII–XVIII with further references.

Timeframe

No historical event marks the exact moment at which Arabic ceased to be an immediate marker of inclusion in the ruling elite of the Islamic Empire (although it certainly remained one among several others). An estimated date can be assigned to the point when Arabic supplanted Greek and Middle Persian irreversibly in the public sphere in ca. the year 800.[122] At about this time, Arabic lost its immediate association with Islam and came to supplement Greek as the language of choice for Melkite authors from Syria-Palestine such as Theodore Abū Qurra († after 820).[123] Most importantly, starting with the late 8th/early 9th century, characteristic 7th- and 8th–century formal components of Arabic documentary sources on papyrus and related materials disappear and are replaced by formulaic novelties originating in Iranian scribal traditions (see Chapters III and V).[124] In parallel, from the 9th century onwards, the number of Arabic documents increases exponentially, signalling the adoption of the Arabic language (together with other cultural markers) by people from a different ethnic background than that of the Arab conquerors and their descendants (see Chapter I).[125] Concomitantly, the early 9th century saw the maturation of classical Muslim scholarship and historiography. This development opened for the Islamic culture the first period of systematic elaboration and reflection on itself and its origins. Through this process, a class of scholars, mostly of Iraqi and Iranian background, laid claim to a key role in preserving, defining, and interpreting the collective Muslim memory and Islam itself.[126]

Ninth- and 10th-century biographical information further suggests that the first community of Muslim scholars was formed beyond the circles of Umayyad imperial bureaucracy.[127] This is corroborated by the different scribal practices evident in early Islamic papyri and the prestige of literary corpora referenced by later grammarians (pre-Islamic poetry, the Qur'an, and *ḥadīth* literature).[128]

On the basis of these considerations, the time span surveyed in this study extends from the first attestation of Islamic Arabic documentary writing (640/641)

122 See *infra* Ch. I, *The Rise and Dissolution of "Imperial Arabic"*.
123 Throughout the 8th and early 9th century, language choice in Melkite circles appears to have been largely dictated by the targeted readership. See Griffith 1997, esp. 25–30, *id.* 2012, and Mavroudi 2015, esp. 316–318.
124 See especially Khan 2008, 888–889 and 896–897.
125 Webb 2016, 244. For Egypt in particular, see Grob 2010, 8–11 with references to further literature.
126 Brockopp 2017.
127 *Ibid.*, 50–58.
128 *Ibid.*, 65–83, Potthast 2019, and Kaplony 2019, 314–317.

https://doi.org/10.1515/9783110740820-009

until the beginning of the 9th century. As is often the case when setting definite chronological boundaries, there is an element of arbitrariness in the aforementioned criteria. In particular, it will not escape the reader's attention that the specified chronological boundaries do not coincide with any major political development or dynastic shift within the Muslim Empire. With a preponderant focus on textual sources, the trajectory of this study follows instead the development of the first Arabic imperial scribal culture from its formative phase in pre-Islamic times, through the Medinan Caliphate until its reformulation in the early Abbasid age. On account of this premise, the present work focuses primarily on concepts of authority and legitimacy as theorized and displayed by the Umayyad dynasty.

Organization of this Study

The subjects of this book are organized into five chapters, each dedicated to a different facet of Early Islamic scribal culture.

Chapter I begins by analyzing the social reach of Arabic in the Early Islamic administration and society, based on a quantitative and typological evaluation of the documentary evidence. I argue that pre-800 Arabic scribal practices reveal close ties to the ambit of official administration (Imperial Arabic). I then proceed to compare the process of Arabization of official and private writing in Egypt, Palestine, Iran, and Central Asia from the 7th to the 8th century.

In *Chapter II*, I discuss extra-textual properties of official Arabic promulgations. In particular, I focus on the use of Arabic writing in the Umayyad visual culture to redefine the referential dimension of established symbols of authority. I then discuss the development of Arabic into an emblem of the Islamic Empire on reformed Islamic coinage.

Chapter III examines the origins of distinctive formulaic features of early Islamic documentary sources. In particular, the discussion concerns a comparison of official Arabic writings with more informal ones (graffiti and private correspondence) on a formal level. The assessment of distinctive formal features of official documents sheds light on the process of selection that shaped Arabic scribal culture.

Chapter IV examines the social behaviour of Arab-Muslim imperial officials *vis à vis* local elites, as reflected in their non-Arabic correspondence. The chapter traces a shift in social etiquette in the official correspondence of Arab-Muslim officials, signalled by the adaptation of distinctive formal features of Arabic epistolography into Greek, Coptic, Sogdian, and Latin, with particular attention to religious formulae. This chapter includes some remarks on the progressive adoption of the Arabic language and Arabic script by the non-Arab population of the Muslim Empire, including a discussion of the emergence of cultural mediators in the documentary record.

In *Chapter V*, I provide a list of lexical borrowings reflected in 7th- and 8th-century Arabic documents. Through a comparison of regional differences in the use of technical loanwords across documents from Egypt, Syria, and Central Asia, I provide a tripartite model of overlapping layers of technical language: imperial, super-regional, and regional. On the basis of this model, I formulate a pattern of "directional" hierarchical influxes between metropolitan and peripheral regions of the early Islamic Empire.

https://doi.org/10.1515/9783110740820-010

I Towards an Ecology of Documentary Arabic

(. . .) they who lately disdained the tongue of Rome now coveted its eloquence. Hence, too, a liking sprang up for our style of dress, and the "toga" became fashionable. Step by step they were led to things which dispose to vice, the lounge, the bath, the elegant banquet. All this in their ignorance, they called civilization, when it was but a part of their servitude.

Tacitus, *Agricola*; trans. Bryant.

Introduction

The first monument on which a language that can be recognized as Arabic appears is a fourth-century epitaph in Nabatean characters.[1] Subsequent direct testimony of Arabic in the centuries leading up to the rise of Islam rests entirely on a few graffiti and commemorative inscriptions, comprising just a handful of words and proper names. These are the cultural products of an area that extends between the central Arabian Peninsula, the edges of Byzantine Syria-Palestine, and Sasanian Southern Mesopotamia.

The extent of this body of material shares little more than a common geographic origin with diverse uses of writing which Islamic-age reports ascribe to pre-Islamic Arabs.[2] Particularly interesting here is the contrast between the scant pre-Islamic Arabic epigraphic testimonies and the supposedly coeval poetic flowering of the 5th–7th centuries preserved through the redaction, compilation, and – frequently – interpolation at the hands of Islamic-age literates of the 9th and later centuries.[3] In fact, as is made clear by internal references, pre-Islamic Arabic poems were mainly circulated orally and were only rarely committed to writing in the form of *aide-mémoires*.[4] It is difficult to imagine how pre-Islamic poetry would have fared any better than the few coeval relics of Arabic without the historical momentum of the Arab conquests and their profound consequences for the dissemination of the Arabic language among the peoples of both Arab and non-Arab descent.

Wherever a slim superstrate of Arab settlers came into extended contact with indigenous populations, linguistic penetration followed relatively rapidly, even occurring before or without any ethnic mingling. In the entire area under direct control of the Early Islamic Empire, local literatures experienced a progressive contraction either reaching a complete stasis or surviving as vernacular or liturgical literacies. Even if the process of Arabicization proved reversible in the Westernmost and the Easternmost extremities of the Early Muslim territory, namely in Spain and the Iranian World, the literary *koine* of Classical Arabic continued to

---

1 *RCEA* I 1 (Namāra; 332) with improved readings by Bellamy 1985; on the dating of the inscription in particular, see Robin 2016, 376–377. On the language displayed in the 1st century inscription from Qaryat al-Faw, see *infra* p. 43.

2 For pre-Islamic uses of Arabic writing, see Serjeant 1983, Schoeler 1992, 1–6; *id.* 1997, 424–426; and *id.* 2009, 1–16.

3 For an introductory overview of pre-Islamic poetry, see Caskel 1930; el-Tayib 1983; and Jones 1992–1996.

4 Pre-Islamic graffiti occasionally preserve samples of poetic metre. See Bellamy 1990 with corrections by Knauf 2010, 233–234 and al-Jallad 2015c. For a recent reassessment on the inscription of ʿAyn ʿAbada, see Kropp 2017.

https://doi.org/10.1515/9783110740820-011

provide a powerful symbol of unity for the Islamicate Commonwealth well after the political fragmentation of the Abbasid Caliphate.

The rise of Arabic from a localized to a transregional idiom accords well with the often-quoted maxim of the Spanish grammarian Antonio de Nebrija († 1522) that "language was always a companion of the empire" (*siempre la lengua fue compañera del imperio*). The Islamic tradition indeed explicitly acknowledges close ties between the implementation of Islamic state structures and the dissemination of Arabic in the lands conquered by the nascent Islamic Empire. Medieval Arab historical narratives on the banishment of languages other than Arabic from the Islamic chanceries and coinage ordered by the caliph ʿAbd al-Malik (*rg.* 685–705) are imbued with a sense of self-assertion towards the Byzantines[5] as well as the non-Arabicized aristocracies within the Empire.[6] At the other end of the spectrum, testimonies of subordinated minorities residing within the Islamicate World stigmatized knowledge of Arabic as a conduit to identity-loss and assimilation into the politically dominant Arab culture. Writing in 9th-century Cordoba, the theologian Paulus Alvarus, for instance, laments the eagerness of the Iberian Christian elites to assimilate themselves into Arab customs and their zeal to learn Arabic.[7] In a similar vein, the likely Fatimid-age *Apocalypse* by the Pseudo-Samuel of Qalamūn presents the Egyptians' neglect of their native Coptic in favor of the "language of the *hijra*" as an eschatological omen.[8]

Each shaped by its own ideological notions, Muslim tales of ʿAbd al-Malik's reforms and accounts like Alvarus' and ps. Samuel's equally linger on the teleological and "eventual" character of Arabization. Where it survives, documentary evidence can be mobilized to complement the literary narratives and provide a substantiated measure of the impact of Arabic on the conquered societies. Through a repartition of the available material into functional and institutional domains (both in absolute and relative terms), the opening chapter sets out to outline the ecology[9] of *written* Arabic from the mid-7th to the closing of the 8th

5 Cf. for instance the episode of ʿAbd al-Malik's confrontation with Justinian II about Greek and Arabic formulae on papyrus rolls and coinage in Balādhurī, 240 (trans. Hitti, 383–384). For the Byzantine perspective on the events, see Theophanes, 365, 10f. 14–18 (trans. Mango, 509–510). For the political background, see Kaplony 1996, 151–156.

6 Cf. for instance the story of the rivalry between the *mawlā* Ṣāliḥ b. ʿAbd al-Raḥmān and the Persian secretary of al-Hajjāj, Zādān Farrūkh b. Yabrā. See *i.a.* Balādhurī, 300–301 (trans. Hitti, 455–456) and Ibn al-Nadīm, 242 (trans. Dodge, II, 381–582).

7 Alvarus, § 35, see also Wasserstein 1998.

8 Ziadeh 1915–1917.

9 For the concept of language ecology, see Haugen (esp. 1972). For more recent assessments on the *status questionis*, see Barton 2007 and Ludwig 2016. For an introduction to the ecology of languages of power in particular, see Versteegh 2018.

century. Throughout the following pages I will refrain from attempting a precise quantification of the spread of Arabic or even Arabic literacy during the Early Islamic period.[10] Such an endeavor lacks both an adequate evidentiary basis and solid methodological premises. Rather, the chapter ventures an assessment of the environment in which Arabic emerged in the Early Islamic Empire. This line of inquiry is ultimately related to the question of determining *which* Arabic, that is, which different forms of Arabic are reflected by documentary evidence. The outline of the "reach" of documentary Arabic[11] in administration and society will serve as the basis for further formal and visual analyses of the Early Islamic documentary culture in Chapters 2 and 3.

10 For provisional estimates of Arabic literacy in Egypt, see Sijpesteijn 2013, 217–219 and Grob 2010, 87, and further references in both. For a more general overview of literacy in Islam, see Eickelman 1978.

11 For the label "documentary Arabic", see Grob 2010, 157–158; cf. the discussion on "Official Umayyad Arabic" in Ch. III.

A Sudden Language: Pre-Islamic Arabic Writing and the Epigraphical Habit

Old Arabic is the umbrella term usually used to refer to the first attested stage of the language which later evolved into the Arabic on display in Early Islamic documents.[12] References of widely differing reliability to an "Arabic idiom" (*hē Arabōn phonē*/*arabicus sermo*) are found in Greek and Latin classical authors. Sparse items of vocabulary and linguistic features interpretable as Arabic further punctuate epigraphical evidence and literary accounts in different languages dating as far back as the 9th century BCE.[13] Material remains and indirect testimonies alike indicate that Arabic vernaculars were relatively widely spoken languages across Northern Arabia, Syria-Palestine, and Southern Iraq.[14] Practices of Arabic literacy proper, however, appear to be a comparatively late phenomenon and are first attested in the historical record in the late 5th- and early 6th-century Near East.

Old Arabic was furthermore not associated with a distinctive script until the late 5th/early 6th century and overall remained an almost exclusively spoken language for most of the pre-Islamic period. It is assumed that (Old) Arabic was the native language of populations who embedded themselves in the more developed writerly systems of the neighbouring societies for entertainment or commemorative purposes – be it Greek and Nabatean Aramaic in Syria-Palestine, Safaitic and Dadanitic in North Arabia, Epigraphic South Arabian (ESA) in Yemen and neighbouring regions, among others.[15]

The only direct evidence for the use and, subsequently, the diffusion of Arabic in pre-Islamic time is epigraphical. While constituting a distinct language, epigraphical Old Arabic is admittedly difficult to differentiate from the Old North Arabian idioms practiced in Northwest Arabia and the surrounding areas until the 5th century.[16] The task is aggravated by the fact that the epigraphical testimonies typically display very simple formulaic structures, often shared across a variety of neighbouring languages. Unsurprisingly, the assessment of discrimina-

12 For the label "Old Arabic", see in particular MacDonald 2008.

13 Hoyland 2004, 183–187.

14 Fiema *et al.* 2015, 429–430.

15 For an outline of the language situation in the Arabian Peninsula, see MacDonald 2009a III and Knauf 2010.

16 MacDonald 2008, 465–466.

https://doi.org/10.1515/9783110740820-012

tive features of the (Old) Arabic language in written artefacts crossing a variety of scripts and languages has proven a thorny issue among Semitists.[17]

The use of the definitive article *ʾl* has been traditionally considered as the principal signpost of (Old) Arabic. This position, however, has weakened considerably in recent years[18] as the use of the determinative *ʾl* has been proven in several North Arabian languages.[19] To complicate matters, several potentially discriminative morphological features remain hidden behind the consonantal writing systems employed by potential Old Arabic testimonies. Greek transliteration of Arabic speech on epigraphs and papyri are the main source for reconstructing the pronunciation and several aspects of the flection of pre-Islamic Arabic.[20] It is also not unusual for texts to contain a mixture of (Old) Arabic and other idioms.

These difficulties reverberate in the recent critical interest in determining the number of legitimate Old Arabic testimonies pre-dating the Islamic conquests. In 2008, MacDonald published a list comprising 13 inscriptions containing Old Arabic in five different scripts plus a few others showing "mixed" linguistic features.[21] The language on display on the oldest item of the list, an inscription in Old South Arabian script located in Qaryat al-Faw (dated paleographically to the 1st century BCE), has since been reclassified as a transitional form between Old North Arabic and Old South Arabic.[22] The language of the 4th-century graffito of Jabal Ramm, long considered the oldest testimony of Arabic *script*, has recently been reclassified as Nabatean Aramaic, while Christian Palestinian Aramaic rather than Arabic is now considered to be on display in the bilingual so-called "*Saōla* mosaic" in St George's Church on Mount Nebo (completed by 530).[23] Conversely, the language of a Greek inscription discovered in pre-Islamic Arabic northern Jordan displays distinctive features of Old Arabic.[24]

A more unequivocal marker of Arabic is the use of a form of what is presently referred to as the Arabic script. There is scholarly consensus that the Arabic verbal

---

17 E.g., MacDonald 2000; 2008; and 2009a and al-Jallad 2014 and 2018a. For a synoptic assessment on the *status questionis* on the innovative features of (Old)Arabic, see Huehnergard 2017 and al-Jallad 2018a with references to further literature.

18 MacDonald 2008, *s.v.* "Safeao-Arabic inscriptions".

19 Al-Jallad 2014, 449–450 and 457–459.

20 For the pronunciation of pre-Islamic Arabic, see Fiema *et al.* 2015, 431–432; Kaplony 2015, and al-Jallad 2017a. For flection in Qur'anic Arabic in particular, see van Putten/Stokes 2018.

21 The identification of Arabic features in MacDonald 2008 is largely based on the use of the determinative article *ʾl* discussed above in the main text.

22 Al-Jallad 2014.

23 Hoyland 2010.

24 Al-Jallad 2015b.

root *k-t-b* (originally meaning "sewing together") only acquired the semantic aspect of "writing" as a loan from the homonymous Aramaic root.[25] The history of the term is evocative of the historical beginnings of Arabic writing more generally. What is presently known as the Arabic script as well as several features of Arabic orthography developed from Nabatean Aramaic.[26] In particular, Arabic characters *proprio sensu* as they feature in late 5th and mid-6th century epigraphic evidence appear to have evolved from a progressive cursivization of the Nabatean script through continuous practice on perishable materials.[27] This process is on display quite early as the script used in Nabatean papyri from the 1st and 2nd century is notably more cursive than that used in coeval lapidary inscriptions.[28] This development was possibly catalyzed by the increased use of Arabic in chancery environments at the hands of the phylarchs serving in the Roman armies and their counterparts on the Sasanian side – most conspicuously the Ghassānid and the Lakhmid confederations.[29] Unfortunately, no such document has been found to confirm this supposition.

The transition from a recognizably "Nabatean" to a recognizably "Arabic"[30] script is, nonetheless, partially illustrated by the ever-expanding corpus of so-called Nabateo-Arabic[31] graffiti dated to the 4th and 5th centuries and exhibiting – both graphically and linguistically – mixed features of Arabic and Nabatean Aramaic.[32] In such transitional inscriptions Aramaic tends to be restricted to the formulaic parts of the text such as invocations (e.g., the Aramaic *dkyr* N.N. "(may) N.N. (be) remembered"), dating formulae, and filiation (Aramaic *br* instead of Arabic *bn* or *ʾbn*).[33] Similar language dynamics can be seen to be at play in the Graeco-Arabic inscription from the Wādī Salma (ca. 140 km north-east of Amman) in which the author writes his name, patronym, papponym, and propapponym in

25 On the etymology and use of *kataba* and its derivatives, see *infra* Ch. V, *The Loanwords in Imperial Arabic*, s.v. "*kitāb*".

26 For the relation of Arabic and Aramaic orthography, see Diem 1979–1983 and Sijpesteijn 2020b, 446–455 with further references.

27 Gruendler 1993 and Nehmé 2010.

28 Starcky 1954, 11. For an extensive discussion of the development of the Nabatean script, see Yardeni 2001, 221–263.

29 *I.a.* Hoyland 2009a, 391–392, Toral-Niehoff 2014, 114–116, and Nehmé 2017b, 78.

30 Nehmé 2010, 48–54.

31 For the different terminologies used to label 4th- and 5th-century inscriptions in a script presenting both Nabatean and Arabic features, see Nehmé 2017b, 74–75 and further references there. See also Robin 2014, 311.

32 Nehmé 2017a estimates the corpus of Nabateo-Arabic inscriptions to ca. 120 specimens.

33 The use of a logogram derived from a fossilized Aramaic *bar* is evidenced in early Islamic Arabic papyri, see Sijpesteijn 2020b, 445–450.

Greek but switches to Arabic in the main body of the inscription.[34] This suggests that the language of the engravers was an (Old) Arabic vernacular whereas distinctively Aramaic formulae constituted a link to previous epigraphic practices and were possibly even used as fossilized ideograms.[35]

Since the late 5th and early 6th century, recognizably Nabatean script forms blend with recognizably Arabic ones so gradually[36] that one should refrain from speaking of distinct Nabatean and Arabic scripts and rather interpret Nabatean and Arabic characters as two stages of the same script.[37] In 2014, the Franco-Saudite expedition to Najrān discovered about 30 texts in al-Ḥīma which combined language features of Arabic and Nabatean Aramaic and whose script resembled very closely that of the slightly later pre-Islamic Arabic inscriptions from Syria. Several of the graffiti from al-Ḥīma are marked with crosses and possibly represent tokens of devotion by the local Christian community.[38] One of the graffiti, *Ḥimā-al-Musammāt PalAr* 1, is dated 513[39] CE and another, *Ḥimā-Sud PalAr* 1, dated to 470,[40] making this the earliest unequivocally dated text in "Arabic" characters.[41] The earliest inscriptions in Epigraphic Old Arabic from al-Ḥīma thus pre-date their pendants in Syria by about one generation. These latter comprise the trilingual Greek/Syriac/Arabic inscription of Zebed (512)[42] and a graffito in Jabal Usays (532/533).[43] A further Arabic Christian pious text originates from North Arabia in the region of al-Jawf, and is dated 548/549.[44] Finally, a monumental dedicatory inscription in Arabic is known through literary reports by Yāqūt

34 Al-Jallad/al-Manaser 2015, 54. For Arab anthroponyms in Greek graffiti, see al-Jallad 2020b, 111–123.

35 For the use of fossilized Aramaic expressions in Old Arabic graffiti, see MacDonald 2010, 20n41, Fiema *et al.* 2015, 398–399, and Nehmé 2017b, 93.

36 Hoyland in Ghabban 2008, 233–234; Hoyland 2009a, 391–392 and *id.* 2010, 35.

37 MacDonald 2008; *id.* 2009a, III, 58; and *id.* 2009b, 217–229.

38 Robin 2014, 1052–1054.

39 On the dating of *Ḥimā-Sud PalAr* 2, see previous footnote and Robin 2016. The language of the inscription is classified by Robin 2016, 306 as "pre-Islamic Arabic" ("vorislamisches Arabisch").

40 *Ḥimā-Sud PalAr* 1 bears the date *burak* (February–March) of the year 364 which Robin interprets as referring to the era of the Roman province of *Arabia* or era of Bosra. See Robin 2016, 317–318. For the months employed in *Ḥimā-Sud PalAr* 1 and *Ḥimā-al-Musammāt PalAr* 1 see *ibid.*, 318–329.

41 While the script of *Ḥimā-Sud PalAr* 1 closely resembles the one used in 6th-century Arabic inscriptions, the language is still Nabatean. See Robin 2016, 303.

42 Robin 2016, 306n17 rightly points out that the date of the Zebed inscription is not given in the Arabic version but only in the Syriac and Greek one.

43 The date of the Jabal Usays graffito has been recently re-read by Robin 2016, 378 as 427 EB instead of 423 [427+105 or 106 = 532/533 CE].

44 Nehmé 2017a, 124–131.

(† 1229) and al-Bakrī († 1094) on the construction of a monastery in al-Ḥīra[45] sponsored by Hind, daughter of the Kindite king al-Ḥārith b. ʿAmr b. Ḥujr and wife to the Lakhmid al-Mundhir III (*rg.* 504–554). The already mentioned inscription of the phylarch Sharaḥīl b. Ẓālim in Ḥarrān[46] (568) – likely affiliated to the Ghassān confederation –[47] closes the series of (dated) epigraphs in Arabic script and languages that fall within pre-Islamic times.

Compared to the limited number of pre-Islamic inscriptions in Arabic script, their geographical distribution is staggering. Throughout the 5th and particularly the 6th century, Arabic script was in use, albeit sporadically, in far-flung regions. The northern-, southern-, and easternmost extremities of this area are delineated respectively by the trilingual inscription of Zebed in the region of Aleppo, the inscriptions from al-Ḥīma near Najrān at the gates of the Himyarite kingdom in Yemen, and the dedicatory inscription from al-Ḥīra.

The common denominator of all material evidence for the pre-Islamic use of Arabic script is that all belong in a Christian milieu and are concentrated in territories under the sphere of influence of Arab "client-kingdoms". Robert Hoyland (2009a; 2009b; 2018b) has argued that together with the rise of a provincial Arab elite, the activity of Christian missionaries among Arabic-speaking communities was instrumental to the emergence of Arabic as a written language.[48] The link between the diffusion of Arabic script and Christian missionary activities is substantiated by the use of the Era of Bosra (EB) – the standard chronographic system of the Roman province of Arabia – in the already mentioned Christian Nabateo-Arabic graffiti of al-Ḥīma and al-Jawf.[49] As the period of maximum diffusion of Old Arabic texts coincides with the apogee of Arab potentates in the service of the Late Antique imperial powers, their disappearance overlaps with the collapse of the three main Arab client-kingdoms of the Late Antique Near East: the Lakhmids, the Ḥujrids, and the Ghassānids. The inscription of Ḥarrān is followed by a silence of the epigraphical record of about 80 years, when Arabic papyri surfaced in Egypt in a world already bearing the marks of the Islamic conquests.

---

45 For the linguistic constellation of Late Antique al-Ḥīra, see Toral-Niehoff 2014, 113–124.

46 For the pre-Islamic inscription of Ḥarrān, see Robin 2006, 332–336 with further references.

47 In order to counteract the increasingly daring incursions of the Lakhmid al-Mundhir, Justinian united all the phylarchies in the Byzantine Levant under the command of the Ghassānid al-Ḥārith in 528/529. See Fisher 2011 and Edwell *et al.* 2015.

48 See in particular Hoyland 2009b. Cf. Robin 2014, 1050–1054 who argues that the political activity of the Christian Ḥujrid dynasty in Central Arabia was instrumental to the diffusion of Arabic script throughout the Peninsula.

49 Robin 2016.

The Rise and Dissolution of "Imperial Arabic" (From Reichssprache to Lingua Franca)

Arranging the cumulative corpus of Arabic written artefacts from the 7th and 8th centuries according to functional and institutional domains is key in reaching an assessment of the nature, extent, and social connotation of Arabic writing in the Early Islamic Empire. As these will be addressed in greater depth in the following sections, a brief overview of the size and nature of the sources at our disposal will suffice here.

Among all sorts of preserved evidence for Early Islamic written Arabic, documents on papyrus and related materials cover the largest range of genres and represent the best conduit to the "quality" and social reach of Early Islamic practices of Arabic literacy. At present, the body of edited Arabic documents dated or datable before 800 comprises ca. 760 papyrus, parchment, and paper documents, as well as ostraca, about a fifth of which is bi- or trilingual. The relative share of texts connected with the Muslim administration in the form of official letters (ca. 210), protocols (ca. 280), official accounts and quittances (ca. 60) constitutes about 70% of the total evidence. At the other end of the spectrum, private and business letters (ca. 160), legal agreements and receipts (ca. 25), and private accounts and lists (ca. 15) amount to about 25% of the total, with another approximately 5% claimed by literary texts.[50] Roughly another 400 Arabic and – to a lesser extent – bilingual Arabic/Greek documents dated

50 Estimates on published Arabic texts on papyrus and related materials are based on the data provided by the *APD* (data extracted on Nov. 3, 2018); cf. the figures on Early Islamic Arabic documents given by Kaplony 2019, 314–315. Included in my estimates are 116 bilingual Greek/Arabic protocols, 39 bilingual Greek/Arabic demand notes, nine bilingual Greek/Arabic official receipts, a bilingual Arabic/Coptic demand note, a bilingual Arabic/Coptic official receipt, a bilingual Arabic/Coptic magical prescription, a trilingual official declaration, and a trilingual writing exercise. Not included in the computation are 16 Arabic one-line administrative remarks and addresses that can be read on Greek letters, all issued by the Arab governor Qurra b. Sharīk (see *infra A Language of Distinction*). For the scope of the present work, Arabic documents exhibiting Greek numerals and Greek or Coptic dockets but not otherwise containing Greek and/or Coptic text have not been counted as bilingual. For a prolegomenon to a typology of multilingual Early Islamic documents on papyrus and related materials, see Lucian Reinfandt's and Sven Tost's paper presented at the *28th International Congress of Papyrology* (Barcelona; Aug. 1–6, 2016) and Reinfandt 2020a, 143–146. Cf. Reinfandt/Tost 2017. For the relation between absolute numbers of Arabic documents and number of archives, see *infra*nn56 and 85.

Note: For the notion of "Imperial" Arabic, see Kaplony 2019, 314–317 as well as Kaplony's paper presented at the *33. Deutscher Orientalistentag* (Jena; Sept. 21, 2017)

https://doi.org/10.1515/9783110740820-013

or paleographically datable to the 7th and 8th centuries have at present been catalogued in collections worldwide.[51]

Only in Egypt are preserved documents on papyrus and related supports diachronically continuous within a geographically coherent context. Throughout the time span surveyed in the present study, Arabic texts from Egypt are furthermore not only numerically the most plentiful but are also enriched with ample contextual evidence in other languages. The roughly 600 Arabic documentary texts on papyrus excavated in Egypt are counterbalanced by about 1800 (mostly private) Coptic[52] documents for the mid-7th until the end of the 8th century, as well as about 1100 in Greek.[53] Based on onomastic and formulaic data, no Arabic text among this collective body of evidence is of obvious Christian authorship and only two or three are of Jewish[54] ascendancy. Taking into account papyrological and related testimonies from outside Egypt, only two other pre-800 letters are explicitly marked as Christian.[55]

Using Egypt as a proxy, the quantitative and typological figures on Early Islamic practices of Arabic literacy strongly suggest that the use of Arabic mostly clustered within the domain of imperial administration throughout the 7th and most of the 8th century. At the other end of the spectrum, the comparatively low share of Arabic documents of a private and business-related nature – and of explicitly non-Muslim authorship – indicates that the social reach of Arabic into the private sphere was generally limited outside the Arab-Muslim minority community. These considerations are corroborated by a repartition of the Arabic texts into official and private domains within multiligual archives, a topic which

---

51 I thank the staff members of the *APD* project (Munich) for making the internal data available to me on which my estimates on unpublished Early Islamic Arabic documentary texts are based.
52 I thank Eline Scheerlinck for correcting my estimates on Coptic documents (p. c. Oct. 12, 2018).
53 Estimates on Greek and Coptic documentary texts are based on data provided by the *papyri.info* (data extracted on Aug. 15, 2018) and *Trismegistos* databases (data extracted on Aug. 15, 2018). For the purpose of this work, multilingual documents have resulted in one entry for each of the featured languages. Coptic documents containing Greek invocations and/or recapitulations have been counted as monolingual.
54 P.Vind.inv. A. P. 849 (VIII), currently being prepared for publication by Petra Sijpesteijn, and *P.HanafiTwoPaperDocuments* 3 (Egypt; 761/762). Abū Yazīd and his son-in-law Yahūdā, to whom *P.Jahn* 10 (Fayyūm; late VIII) is addressed, are certainly Jewish as well. Whether the sender also belonged to a Jewish milieu, however, remains unclear. For references to Jews in early Islamic documentary sources, see Sijpesteijn 2020a, 428–429.
55 *P.Mird* 45 and 46 (both from Khirbat al-Mird; VIII). For the emergence of a Christian Arabic documentary tradition, see *infra* Ch. III, *Umayyad Official Documentary Standard as Early Islamic Documentary Standard* (Hegemonic and Minority Scribal Traditions in Imperial Arabic).

I shall return to later.[56] Evidence of a numismatic and epigraphic nature is similarly characterized by a preponderance of officially sponsored items in regions in which Arabic vernaculars were not already widespread in pre-Islamic times.

Contrary to the trends identified by papyrological evidence, in epigraphy the number of Early Islamic Arabic private graffiti greatly outweighs that of commissioned official inscriptions. Precise quantitative estimates are made difficult by the brevity and poor execution of texts of the former category which in turn hinders an accurate palaeographical dating. The *Thesaurus d'Épigraphie Islamique* contains entries for over 500 Early Islamic Arabic graffiti either dated or (more often) datable to the Early Islamic period; further 200 specimens are collected in the *Arabic Inscriptions from the Ḥarra* database. From a geographical viewpoint, Early Islamic Arabic graffiti essentially overlap with the distribution of pre-Islamic Arabic inscriptions and mostly cluster along a virtual line connecting Damascus' hinterland to the North to the area of Najrān to the South passing through the caravan routes of the Syrian Desert and Western Arabia.[57] Easy-to-produce, Early Islamic Arabic graffiti can, however, also bear witness to the occasional movement of people over long distances within the Islamic Empire and beyond. Obvious examples thereof are the graffiti left by Arab troops campaigning in the Aegean in Kos and Knidos[58] and the enigmatic Abbasid plaster inscriptions

56 For the 7th and 8th centuries the database *Trismegistos* contains entries for only two archives featuring documents in Arabic. These figures can be refined: Among archives listed in *Trismegistos* the ones of the pagarchs of Heracleopolis (TM 572), of Papas (TM 170), of Georgios and Sergios (TM 92), and of Rāshid b. Khālid (TM 467) do in fact contain single documents and/or seals in Arabic or bilingual. Archives comprising Arabic texts not included in the list of *Trismegistos* are the monolingual archive of ʿAbd Allāh b. Asʿad and the bi- and trilingual archives of Mēnas s. of Senouthios and of the monasteries of Apa Apollo in Bāwiṭ, of Apa Jeremias in Saqqāra, of The Holy Rock of Apa Thomas in Wādī Sarga, and of Apa Apollo in Balāʾizah. *Trismegistos* further does not contain data on archives from the eastern provinces of the Empire, most notably the bilingual so-called Pahlavi Archive, the bilingual Chāl Tarkhān archive, the quadrilingual Mount Mugh archive, and the bilingual Bēk family archive. In addition, most of contemporary dossiers with documents in Arabic stem from official environments. For an overview of Early Islamic archives and dossier containing Arabic documents, see Sijpesteijn 2010 and *infra* in this section.

57 Extensive collections of Early Islamic Arabic graffiti are to be found in Hamidullah 1939, Miles 1948, Grohmann 1962, al-Muaikel 1994, al-Rāshid 1993, al-Kilābī 1995, *ead.* 2009, Ghabban 2011, and Imbert 2015 (Arabian Peninsula); Ory 1967 (Lebanon), Nevo/Heftman/Cohen 1993, and Nevo 1994 (Palestine); Baramki 1964, Imbert 1996, al-Jbour 2006, al-Salameen 2010 (Jordan); al-Ushsh 1963 (Syria). Several other graffiti from Palestine and Jordan are collected in the volumes of the *Corpus Inscriptionum Arabicarum Palestinae* (*CIAP*).

58 Imbert 2013b. For a brief overview of Arabic graffiti in the Eastern Mediterranean, see A. Pralong in the annexure to Rāġib 2013.

in an Armenian church in Zvartʿnocʿ.[59] The second most plentiful source for Early Islamic private epigraphy is represented by tombstones, of which 23 items dated before 800 survive. The bulk of this group of texts stems from a single find in the so-called "Fatimid" cemetery in Aswān.[60] Single dated specimens have also been found in Iraq,[61] Arabia,[62] and North Africa.[63] Another 32 funerary inscriptions distributed across the Levant[64] and the Arabian Peninsula have been assigned to the 8th century on paleographical grounds. A sub-branch of early Islamic Arabic epigraphy is a corpus of several dozen small inscriptions on mobile objects such as lamps, cans, vases, and textiles, mostly found in Palestine and Jordan, with single finds from Iraq, Egypt, North Africa, and even Central Asia.[65] These include two fragments of *ṭirāz*s produced in officially sanctioned factories in North Africa during the reign of Marwān II (*rg.* 744–750).[66]

More numerous and evenly widespread among Early Islamic commissioned inscriptions proper are the items connected with official patronage in the form of the foundation, restauration, or decorative inscriptions that punctuate the few surviving Early Islamic building complexes. Over 40 monumental inscriptions commemorating Umayyad and early Abbasid architectonic endowments are preserved from Greater Syria (28) and the Holy Cities of the Ḥijāz and their surroundings (13).[67] A few early Abbasid inscriptions found at the margins of the Empire in North Africa,[68] Yemen,[69] and the Caucasus[70] contribute to a more equal distribution of the evidence. The texts of another dozen lost Umayyad as well as Abbasid official inscriptions from Fusṭāṭ, Mecca, Medina, Acre, Sidon, Iran, and Tlemcen are transmitted in travel reports by medieval authors. On the basis of formal affin-

59 See the latest edition by Hoyland in Greenwood 2004, 88–89.

60 Mostly collected by el-Hawary/Rached 1932 (= *RCEA* I 55–63). For the reconstruction of the provenance of several Aswān tombstones scattered across different collections, see Schmidt (in press).

61 Al-Ṣandūq 1955, 214, no. 1 (Ḥafnat al-Abyaḍ; 683/684).

62 Al-Faqīh 1992 (*non vidi*), 341 (Masʿūda; 773/774).

63 Tütüncü 2013, 399 (Biskra; 743/744).

64 Most 8th-century Arabic epitaphs from Syria are represented by the steles found in the cemetery annexed to the Mibrak *madrasa* in Bosra, orientatively assigned to the Umayyad period. For the archaeological context, see Ory 1970.

65 The *EPI* contains 25 entries for Arabic inscriptions on mobile objects dated or datable before 800.

66 Day 1952 and Grohmann 1972, 74 and *ibid.*n4.

67 For a commented list of Early Islamic inscriptions, see *infra* pp. 192–194 with a typological survey in Appendix 2, I.

68 *IM* p. 28–29 (Monastir; 797/798) and Abdeljaouad 2001 (*non vidi*), 43, no. 2 (Monastir; related to 797/798).

69 Mittwoch 1935 p. 235–236 (Ṣanʿāʾ; 753/754).

70 Gadjev/Shikhsaidov 2002 p. 4 (Derbent; 792/793).

ities with known examples of Arabic monumental epigraphy, these reports are generally accepted as reliable. Finally, twelve milestones located along travel arteries in Greater Syria, the pilgrimage route connecting Kūfa to Mecca commonly known as Darb Zubayda, and in the Caucasus have also been discovered.[71]

Coinage best underscores the interregional character of Early Islamic official Arabic written artefacts. The several tens of thousands of Early Islamic coins containing bi- and trilingual or entirely Arabic legends minted before 800 CE amount to more than 550 types and subtypes, about 320 of which belong to pre-reform coinage.[72] Arabic legends appear as short validating marks on Arab-Sasanian silver coinage with increasing regularity after 651,[73] while in the Levant similar validating countermarks are attested on Arab-Byzantine anonymous copper coinage in the 660s.[74] During the years of the Second Civil War (680–692) and those immediately preceding and following it, longer Arabic formulae of Islamic coloring appear on the coinage of all opposing sides.[75] Over their main phases of production, Arab-Sasanian coins bear over 70 mint marks, most of which are identifiable with official minting centers throughout the entire former Sasanian Empire. Bilingual (Greek/Arabic) marks, mint names, and short formulae appear on Umayyad Imperial Image copper coinage issued at 12 imperial mints stretching between Ḥimṣ and Jerusalem from the 670s to the 690s (Fig. 4).[76] During the early years of ʿAbd al-Malik's reign, the first gold and copper coinage bearing solely Arabic legends surfaced in Syria and was minted at 14 mints from Northern Mesopotamia to Palestine.[77] Finally, in 697, non-figural all epigraphic coinage in all three metals (gold, silver, copper) was introduced in Damascus, and the following year in the Eastern provinces. All-epigraphic Arabic copper coins were produced in Egypt shortly afterwards.[78] Transition from pre-reform to all-epigraphic coinage appears to have progressed rather swiftly in the Levant and slightly slower in Iraqi and Iranian mints. In the outermost Eastern territories, however, the process was much more gradual. In the Arab provinces encircling the fringes of Iran, such as

71 See *infra* pp. 194 and 196–197.
72 Estimates on Islamic coins are based on Album 2011.
73 Heidemann 2010a, 162–163.
74 Schulze/Goodwin 2005, 47–49.
75 *I.a.* Album /Goodwin 2002, 19–26, Heidemann 2010, 166–169, and Bacharach 2010, 8–15. Cf. *infra* Ch. II, *From Image to Word* (Becoming Word).
76 For the so-called "Umayyad Imperial Image coinage", see Album/Goodwin 2002, 81–91; Foss 2008, 42–55 ("bilingual coinage"); and Heidemann 2010a, 156–161.
77 For the so-called "standing caliph" coinage, see Album/Goodwin 2002, 91–98; Foss 2008, 66–74; Heidemann 2010a, 171–172; and *id.* 2010.
78 For the chronology of the introduction of all-epigraphic Arabic coinage in Egypt, see *infra* p. 66 and references there.

Sistān, Ṭabaristān, Khwārazm, and Sogdia, in particular, figural coinage of Sasanian ascendancy was still issued parallel to Abbasid an-iconic coinage into the 9th century and continued to circulate for centuries thereafter.[79] At the Western end of the Empire, in Ifriqiyya and the Maghreb, Arabic legends appear on Arab-Byzantine coppers minted during the governorate of Ibn al-Nuʿmān (in office 699/700).[80] The new governor Mūsā b. Nuṣayr, however, reintroduced Latin coinage, with bilingual Arabic/Latin coinage appearing in Spain and North Africa only from 715/6 onwards.[81] Related to numismatic evidence are seals, stamps, and standard measures with Arabic inscriptions and validating marks. The rich findings of glass stamps and standard weights excavated in Egypt constitute the bulk of Early Islamic sigillographic evidence, but metal and clay specimens have been found virtually everywhere throughout the Empire, from Spain to Central Asia.

Fast-forwarding another 150 years beyond the surveyed time span, the absolute numbers of Arabic documents and their relative typological distribution reflect a progressive shift in the social reach of Arabic. Conservative estimates[82] on the number of Arabic documents dated or datable between 800 and 950, at present, amount to more than 5400 known documents worldwide.[83] Of these, fewer than 1300 have been edited while descriptions of roughly another 750 have been published in collection catalogues.[84] A prudent reorganization into functional typologies can only be based on the latter two categories of documents. In comparison with the figures for the preceding century and a half, the relative share of 9th- and 10th-century documents belonging within the domain of the Islamic administration (mainly protocols, tax receipts, official lists and surveys etc.) drops to 20 to 30% of the total. Conversely, documents related to private and business matters rise to 60 to 70% and display a much wider typological range (mainly private and business letters but increasingly also contracts of sale and marriage, private notes and accounts etc.). These developments correspond to a proliferation of Arabic private archives.[85]

---

79 For the coinage of Early Abbasid Tabaristān, see in particular Malek 2004; for Sistān, see in particular Sears 1999 and Album/Goodwin 2002, 43–45; for Sogdiana, see in particular Treadwell 2007.
80 Jonson 2015, 227–230. Cf. *ibid.*, 233–238.
81 For Early Islamic Iberian and North African coinage, see in particular Bates 1992, *id.* 1995, and Jonson 2015.
82 Not included are documents dated by their editors or cataloguers based on the paleography to the 10th century.
83 See *supra*nn50–51.
84 Cf. Grob 2010, 8–9 and Kaplony 2018.
85 Regrettably, there is no systematic survey of Arabic archives from the 9th and 10th centuries. Examples of Arabic private and business archives from this time frame include the papers of several traders from the Banū ʿAbd al-Muʾmin based in the Fayyūm (*P.Marchands* I–III; V/I and *P.Van-*

Zooming in on Egypt, Greek texts of documentary nature virtually disappear[86] while the number of Coptic texts drops less drastically to about 500. For the same time span, the number of edited Arabic graffiti rises to over 1500, that of epitaphs and funerary inscriptions – again heavily influenced by findings from the Fatimid cemetery of Aswān – to over 4600, and small inscriptions on portable objects reach over 500 items. It goes without saying that at this time, Arabic is still the language of the administration and of official public statements but now permeates the private sphere much more thoroughly than in the previous century and a half while also functioning as a transcultural language of communication and learning.[87]

The increasing Arabization corresponds with a weakening of the association of Arabic language and script with Islamic religion throughout the 9th century. Several 9th- and 10th-century papyri from Egypt betray a recognizably Christian authorship.[88] At the same time, Christian Arabic devotional inscriptions and graffiti, such as those discovered in the Basilica of the Holy Cross in Resafa,[89] enter the record. The progressive transformation of Arabic into a transcultural language of communication and learning is signaled by the first Christian Arabic literary compositions by authors like Theodore Abū Qurra († after 820). This coincides with the earliest manuscript evidence for Christian-Arabic translations of the Holy Scriptures, such as the fragment of the Gospel of John (859), and the Pauline epistles fragment (867) housed at St Catherine's monastery in Sinai.[90] Around this time, the emergence of forms of allography such as the Graeco-Arabic psalm fragment from the Umayyad Mosque in Damascus,[91] and a recently published

---

thieghemAbuHurayra), of an unnamed merchant of horses (*P.Vente* 16–23 and *P.Vanthieghem-Maquignon*), of one Abū ʿAbd Allāh (*P.Berl.Arab.* II 38–43), and of an anonymous merchant from Edfū (*P.David-WeilEdfou* A–B and *P.RagibEdfou* 1). For some general considerations on archival culture in the Islamicate Middle Ages and the question of preservation of archives in Islam, see Rāġib 1984, Tillier 2009, el-Leithy 2011, van Berkel 2014, Liebrenz 2020, and Rustow 2020.

86 For 9th-century Greek documentary texts, see Berkes 2019. The latest Greek document edited to date is, to the best of my knowledge, *SPP* III_2 577 (Fayyūm; 825), reedited by Berkes 2019. For Greek epigraphy under Arab rule, see di Segni 2009. For Greek education in the Early Islamic period, see Mavroudi 2015.

87 For the role of Islamic learning for the diffusion of Arabic, see in particular Versteegh 2015.

88 *CPR* XVI 14 (Egypt; IX/X) and 34; *P.AnawatiPapyrusChretien* (Fuṣṭāṭ; IX); *P.Heid.Arab.* II 34 (Egypt; X); *P.Vind.Arab.* III 20 (al-Lakhūn; X).

89 Khoury 1986, 179 and 180 (both IX).

90 Déroche 1987–1989, 346, no. 4. For the translation of the Bible into Arabic in general, see Vollandt 2015; for the earliest Christian manuscripts in Arabic, see in particular *ibid.*, 27–28.

91 Violet 1901, 384–403, 425–441, 475–488. The text has been re-edited by Blau 2002, 68–71 and al-Jallad 2020b, 79–91 (Arabic text only). See also Corriente 2007, 303–320; Mavroudi 2008, 321–329; Vollandt 2015, 55–58; and al-Jallad 2020b, esp. 35–56.

9th-century Latin and Latino-Arabic double-letter mentioning Jerusalem[92] further reveals the increasing interference of Arabic in its neighbouring languages.

Compared to the progressive dissemination of practices of written Arabic across social and confessional domains in the 9th and 10th centuries, we might characterize Arabic documentary evidence from the time before 800 as belonging to an "imperial" phase: As local languages retained their role as idioms of choice for short- and medium-term written communication, the majority of the Empire's population experienced Arabic mainly through the media and standards determined by imperial officials.[93] Within these broad outlines, the way Arabic interacted with substrate languages in different regional contexts varied to a considerable extent.

A Language of Difference: Arabic in Egypt 641–ca. 680

Distant from the major Late Antique theatres of war, Egypt had experienced a comparatively peaceful history during the six centuries of Roman rule, only interrupted by the Palmyrene annexation of 270 and a decennial Sasanian occupation (619–629) in the 7th century. In 639, however, an Arab host moved into Egypt from Palestine and brought the provincial capital of Alexandria to its knees in 641 – though the exact logistics of the Arab invasion are partially unclear.[94] The Arabs introduced some novelties into the administrative geography of the province by merging the four Roman eparchies into a single province under the authority of a governor appointed by Medina and, soon enough, Damascus. The operational base of the first conquering army next to the Roman stronghold of Babylon was in due course turned into a permanent fortified settlement (*miṣr*) known as al-Fusṭāṭ (< gr. *to fossaton*) and the provincial capital was moved there.[95]

Overall, however, the Arabs left Byzantine Egypt's administrative and institutional skeleton nearly intact. As during the Persian occupation 20 years before,[96] the local administrative bureaucracy proved to be able to function smoothly under

---

92 P.BL 3124 (origin unknown; VIII?). See Internullo 2016 and Internullo/D'Ottone Rambach 2018, 53–72.

93 For the role of imperial officials in shaping early Islamic Arabic scribal practices and language, see Grob 2010, 157–158, and Kaplony 2016 and *id.* 2019.

94 For a recent assessment of the Arab conquest of Egypt, see Booth 2013. For the conquest of Upper Egypt in particular, see now Bruning 2018a, 89–97 and Schmidt 2020, 207–210.

95 For the foundation and the development of Early Islamic al-Fusṭāṭ, see Bruning 2018a.

96 For Pahlavi documentary evidence dating to the Persian occupation of Egypt, see Weber 2013a. For the Coptic documentation, see MacCoull 1987.

the new masters despite its connection with Byzantium having been severed. At the time of the conquest, Greek was the dominant language of the administration and culture, whereas the majority of the population – especially outside the Hellenized urban centers – spoke Coptic as a native language. As Arab-Muslims quickly took over the leading administrative posts, the garrisoning Arab forces stationed in the region introduced an Arabic element to the linguistic constellation of the provincial administration, effectively turning the region into a *populus trilinguis*.[97]

Alone among the discoveries of Early Islamic Arabic documentary texts, papyrus findings from Egypt cover the entire spectrum of the bureaucratic apparatus from the top layer of the imperial administration to items of private and legal exchange between individuals and even include literary compositions.[98] The repartition of Arabic text materials is quite uneven from a chronological viewpoint. Particularly small is the number of writs that can be definitely dated to the Medinan and Sufyanid period. Specifically, the total number of the hitherto published Arabic documents from Egypt dated to before 685 amounts to a staggeringly low seven exemplars, with a handful of others awaiting publication. By comparison, the total number of documents dated to the following 40 years attests to about 200 mono- and bilingual Arabic texts. The scant evidence for Arabic writing from the first decades of Muslim rule over Egypt is furthermore restricted to a small roster of documentary types. The bulk of the earliest surviving testimonies is represented by economic documents. These include four individual records of written obligations (*dhikr ḥaqq*)[99] and a receipt[100] concerning monetary debt and three possibly official registers of debt acknowledgements.[101] A handful of similar exemplars of the latter can be found among unpublished

97 On the question of Arab settlements in pre-Islamic Egypt, see Sijpesteijn 2013, 34 and *ibid*.n 115 with further literature. The references to Arabs and Arab-like terms in pre-Islamic papyri are discussed by De Jong 2017.

98 For literary texts on papyrus, the reference text is still Abbot 1957–1972.

99 *P.BruningSunna* (664/665), P.Utah inv. 520 (Fusṭāṭ; 676/677), now edited by Tillier/Vanthieghem 2019, 177–179), and probably *P.RagibAn22* (Egypt; 642/643) with emendations by Tillier/Vanthieghem 2019, 155–156.

100 *Chrest. Khoury* 48 (Qahqahwe; related to 641) with emendations by Tillier/Vanthieghem 2019, 168–172.

101 P.Cambr. UL inv. Michael. 893 (Fusṭāṭ; 667/668), now edited by Tillier/Vanthieghem 2019, 176–177, *P.RagibJurisdiction* 1 (662/663) and 2 (676/677) to which the fragments P.Vind.inv. A. P. 11153 (49/670), 11012 (674), 11074 (676/677), 11076 (676/677), 11086 (668 or 677), 11078 (undated) as well as P.Paris BNF inv. 7075(9) probably belong; see Tillier/Vanthieghem 2019, 148–149; cf. also the list of documents provided by Bruning 2015, 354n7. I do not agree, however, with Bruning's repartition of the documents which, under the vague label "legal documents", groups texts of administrative pertinence together with agreements between private parties. See further the list of documents.

material assigned to the 7th century together with private deeds of acquittal (*barā'*).[102]

Even thinner is the evidence for the use of Arabic in matters of official bureaucracy. Presently, only one published pre-680 Arabic papyrus of this period can *positively* be placed within the domain of the imperial administration with a few others awaiting publication.[103] This is a bilingual Greek/Arabic receipt (*SB* VI 9576) issued by the commander ʿAbd Allāh b. Jābir[104] to the heads of the provincial district (pagarchy) of Heracleopolis Magna/Ihnās, Theodorakios and Christophoros for the delivery of 65 sheep destined for Arab soldiers dated 643/644. An arguably pre-680[105] fragment of an Arabic receipt for wheat may or may not also be related to requisitions for the Muslim army.[106] The document is headed by a protocol penned in the "perpendicular writing" (*Schraffenschrift*)[107] characteristic of the Byzantine period.[108] Two further unpublished Arabic fiscal documents dated to the 660s pertaining to allowances (*rizq*) for the Muslim army and other taxes have been described by Y. Rāġib.[109] Further discussion of these specimens will have to await their publication. Finally, two bilingual tax receipts dated

102 E.g., P.Vind.inv. A. P. 11086 and 11163 currently prepared for publication by Fred Donner.
103 See in particular the unpublished bilingual document discussed *infra*n146.
104 Legendre 2013, 77n8 identifies the ʿAbd Allāh b. Jābir of *SB* VI 9576 as ʿAbd Allāh b. Jābir al-Ḥajrī.
105 *P.GrohmannPapyrusProtokoll* 1. The editor assigned a date before 674 to the text. This is based on the fact that the text at issue is headed by a Byzantine style protocol, which the editor at the time believed to have disappeared from Islamic administrative practice by 674. The question of when Byzantine style protocols were supplanted by bilingual ones and whether the process was an immediate and homogeneous one is, however, open to debate. Based on the current state of research, the 690s seem to be a more reliable *terminus post quem*. On this question, see *infra* p. 83.
106 The editor interpreted *P.GrohmannPapyrusProtokoll* 1 (of which only the first line is preserved) as an official receipt connected with the collection of the wheat tax (*ḍarībat al-ṭaʿām*). I am, however, personally unaware of any other official receipts displaying the same opening clause *hādhā mā aʿṭā* + *fulān* "this is what N.N. has delivered". In addition, individual tax receipts in Arabic are first attested in the mid-8th century. Bilingual Arabic/Greek exemplars are first attested in the first quarter of the 700s; see *infra* p. 83 and references there.
107 For the stylization of perpendicular writings on Byzantine protocols, see Turner 1978, 21–22.
108 For the evolution and characteristics of the Byzantine papyrus protocol, see Diethart/Feissel/Gascou 1994.
109 Rāġib 2013, 706, no. 10 (660) and *ibid*., 707, no. 13 (quoted without inventory numbers) (*non vidi*). These two are, together with *P.RagibJuridiction* 1 and *P.BruningSunna* (664/665), the "quatre actes" dated between 660 and 665 and referred to by Rāġib 1991, 16. The document first confirmed by Rāġib 1996b, 14 Fig. 3 as concerning the capitation tax and then in *id*. 2013, 707, no. 14 as pertaining to the land-tax (= *P.BruningSunna*), is now accepted as being a private written obligation.

by their editor to 677[110] and 694[111] respectively have recently been convincingly re-dated to the early 8th century through new readings of the Arabic absolute dates.[112] The translation of a further Arabic papyrus letter allegedly dated to 660 was published by Silvestre de Sacy (1827). The location of the original is presently unknown. The missive is addressed to Usāma b. Zayd by ʿAbd Allāh b. ʿAmr b. al-Ashʿath b. Nuʿmān and Mahdī b. Nuʿmān[113] and consists of a wish for the good health of the addressee.

More insights on the language use in the high and middle layers of the provincial administration of Early Islamic Egypt throughout the 640s to the 680s are outlined by the documentation in Greek and Coptic. Most of the evidence for the early decades of Arab rule in Egypt stems from the official archive of the then pagarch of the Heracleopolite, Apakyros, and the latter's already referenced sons Theodorakios and Christophoros dated from 639 to 647. Arab military officials, including ʿAmr b. al-ʿĀṣ, the first Muslim governor, appear in the archive throughout the 640s and 650s as the issuing authority in eight Greek documents addressed to Christian pagarchs and village officials[114]. These texts mostly consist of demand notes or receipts for the delivery of allowances for the Arab armies stationed in the province. Of the archive's 18 Greek texts only the already mentioned *SB* VI 9576 includes an Arabic translation.[115] This can be explained by the nature of the document: contrary to most other items in the dossier, *SB* VI 9576 is a receipt – as opposed to a demand – issued by Arab authorities and therefore conceived so as to allow a check by Arab officials.[116]

Contextual evidence in Greek and Coptic confirms the impression of marginality of Arabic in the post-conquest administrative machinery. Roughly contemporaneous with the archive of the pagarchs of the Heracleopolite is the administrative correspondence of Senuthios *anystes*, a middle-level administrator in the

110 *P.StoetzerSteuerquittungen* 2 (Ihnās).
111 *P.StoetzerSteuerquittung* (al-Ushmūnayn).
112 Barański 2019. Cf. *BL* XII p. 222, no. 13771 and 269, no. 1198.
113 For the possible identity of the sender, see Becker 1906, 2 who argues for a later dating of the letter.
114 The relevant texts are collected and discussed by Grohmann 1957 and, more recently by Trombley 2015, 19–38. See, however, Morelli's *caveats* in Morelli 2013, 164–168. For the single texts, see in particular *ibid.*n7.
115 For the relation between the Greek and Arabic text of *SB* VI 9576, see in particular Kaplony 2016, 392–394.
116 *SB* VIII 9755, a Greek receipt issued by several Arab *magaritai* to the head of a district (*skelos*) of the Heracleopolite, explicitly states that the *magaritai* are addressing the recipient through an intermediary, the addressee's financial secretary (*chartoularios*). This might explain why the document is penned only in Greek contrary to *SB* VI 9576.

Hermopolite.[117] The over 30 published Greek[118] and few Coptic Senouthios papyri are part of a much larger ensemble of other unedited Greek and Coptic[119] documents. Unlike documents preserved in the coeval Heracleopolite, the Senouthios papyri published so far offer a window into the middle-level provincial administration, coping with requests from the high echelons of the Arab administration. While Arab military officials are referenced in the archive's documents, they appear to deal directly only with Senouthios' superior, the pagarch Athanasios. Accordingly, items of official communication in *Arabic* are completely absent from the archive.

The bilingual (Greek/Coptic)[120] archive of Flavius Papas, pagarch of Edfū (ca. 660s–680s), provides a glimpse into the administrative language use of the generation following the Sufyanid takeover in Syria. Papas' documents touch upon different facets of the local fiscal and legal[121] administration but also contain texts pertaining to the internal administration of the pagarch's own estates.[122] Written communication between Papas and his entourage is carried out both in Greek and Coptic, without a clear sociolinguistic pattern.[123] Instructions from above are transmitted to the pagarch through a chain of command mediated by the duke of the Thebaid and his lieutenant (*topotērētēs*) residing in relatively distant Antinoe.[124] This top-down communication is usually penned in Greek alone. Whether instructions were issued to the duke from al-Fusṭāṭ in Arabic or (more likely) in Arabic and Greek is lost to us. A number of "Byzantine"-type protocols in the archive of Papas further bears witness to continuity with pre-Islamic bureaucratic practice.[125]

117 Morelli 2010a, 1–12.

118 *CPR* XXX. Add the letter edited by Berkes/Claytor 2017 and Berkes 2020.

119 For Coptic documents in the Senouthios' archive, see Krall/Wessely 1902, 346–347; Till 1958, x and *ibid.*n3; and Morelli 2010a, 5–6. Cf. *id.* 2013, 169–170.

120 The Greek documents in the archive of Fl. Papas have been edited in *P.Apoll.* Part of the Coptic documents belonging to the same archive has been published by MacCoull 1988. A much larger cache of mainly Coptic documents from the same archive found stored in a jar are in the process of publication. For a current update, see Boud'hors 2020.

121 For the judiciary aspects evidenced by the documents of the archive of Papas, see in particular Tillier 2013, 21–22.

122 For the archive of Papas, see in particular Foss 2009.

123 Boud'hors 2020, 68–70.

124 On the evolution of the office of the duke of the Thebaid in the Early Islamic period, see Legendre 2016.

125 *P.Apoll.* 105a carrying an account of wine, *P.Apoll.* 97 on the back and *P.Apoll.* 105b, written on the back of a fiscal register, *P.Apoll.* 82 (both dated before 693). For the dating, see Gascou/Worp 1982, 84 and 88. Of Byzantine type are also possibly *P.Apoll.* 105c and d. See Gascou/Worp 1982, 85 and *ibid.*n13.

Epigraphic and numismatic evidence from Sufyanid Egypt equally registers an almost complete lack of Arabic in the official domain. The earliest coinage issued in the province under Arab authority consists of crude imitations[126] of Constans' II copper *dodecanummia*, depicting a standing emperor holding a cross scepter and a globe *cruciger* on the obverse and a cross enclosed by the Greek numeral *IB* (=12) surmounting the abbreviated mint name *ΑΛΕΞ* (=Alexandria) – or a variant thereof – on the reverse.[127] The crude quality of the local coinage is particularly surprising in view of the fact that Alexandria was – together with Carthage in the West – the only Byzantine mint still active by the time of the conquest. In particular, the awkwardness and often inaccuracy of the inscriptions together with the low quality of the images have cast doubts as to whether those coins could have been the product of an official "Byzantine" mint. It has been argued therefore that the *ΑΛΕΞ*-coppers may have been the fruit of semi-official production.[128] The mint name *ΑΛΕΞ* should then be understood as a vestigial feature and a symbolic link to Byzantine administrative practice.[129]

The first monetary issues showing clear marks of the Arab dominion belong to a series exhibiting similar features to the above-mentioned but bearing the mint name *MACP* in Greek characters and showing an astral symbol beside the standing figure on the obverse.[130] The puzzling mint name has since been convincingly interpreted as a rendering of the Arabic *Miṣr*, the eponym of Egypt and an alternative term to indicate the provincial capital Fusṭāṭ.[131] Thus, the *MACP* coins suggest that the Egyptian mint was relocated from Alexandria to al-Fusṭāṭ at some point, although it is also possible that the older mint continued to function alongside the newly opened one. A particularly controverted Egyptian type is one presenting a cross between two crowned figures (inspired by *folles* of Heraclius dated 629) on the obverse and showing an unprecedented reverse with a cross enclosed by an *A* and a *Ω* instead of the usual *I* and *B*.[132] This type appears both with an abbreviated mint name *ΠΑΝ* and without mint indications. The

---

126 On the problematics inherent in the use of the term "imitations" to describe the earliest Arab coinage from Egypt, see Domaszewitz/Bates 2002, 95–96.

127 Awad 1972.

128 Domaszewitz/Bates 2002, 96–97. Cf. Treadwell 1999, 226.

129 For pre-reform Egyptian bronze coinage, see Domaszewitz/Bates 2002, 95–103 with extensive corrections by Metlich/Schindel 2004; Foss 2008, 99–105; and Goodwin 2015.

130 Foss 2008, 102; Metlich/Schindel 2004, 13; the type corresponds to Awad 1972, type IV(a).

131 Domaszewicz/Bates 2002, 97; cf. Foss 2008, 102. The interpretation of Greek *masr* as a transliteration of Arabic *Miṣr* casts some doubts about the original vocalization of the term in Arabic; see Awad/Bacharach 1981, 51–52. For the etymology of *miṣr*, see *infra* p. 267.

132 Foss 2008, 104; Metlich/Schindel 2004, 12; Album/Goodwin 2002, 108.

ΠAN inscription has traditionally been interpreted as Pan(opolis)[133] and even as a corruption for *POM* (= Rome).[134] More recent contributions have suggested the reading *P(olis) AN(tinoeōn)* (= Antinoe) instead, based on the distribution of the findings – abundant in Antinoe while very rare outside – and on papyrological parallels.[135] On account of the prominent Christian symbolism and of technical peculiarities (almost all of the known specimens are cast not struck), it has been hypothesized that these coins constituted an emergency issue, or were possibly not even meant as coins at all but rather as devotional tokens.[136] As for the epigraphical evidence, the only surviving record of Arabic dated to the first 40 years of Muslim rule in Egypt is the tombstone of the commander ʿAbd al-Raḥmān b. Khayr al-Ḥajrī[137] dated 652, whose provenance is still a matter of debate.[138]

To summarize, what little evidence survives for practices of Arabic literacy in pre-Marwanid Egypt reflects the functional needs of an insular Arab-Muslim community. All items of private Arabic correspondence from pre-680 Egypt accordingly reflect short-term exchange between all-Arab – and presumably native Arabic – parties. In the few documented instances in which Arabic finds its way into administrative documents, Arab officials are always among the intended readership. Furthermore, the continuous use of Byzantine protocols and Greek mint marks by the Arab authorities signals continuity with pre-conquest administrative practices. Unpublished evidence appears to confirm these broad outlines. Outside the boundaries of the insular Arab cultural milieu, Arabic seems to have had at first little to no impact on either private or administrative practices of literacy. Top-down communication with Hellenized intermediate governing bodies in the local bureaucracy is always dealt with in Greek and internal communication at middle and lower administrative echelons is carried out exclusively in Greek and Coptic.[139]

---

133 First suggested by Kubitschek 1897, 194–5. Cf. for instance Wroth 1908, 228–229 and Phillips 1962, 237.

134 Domaszewitz/Bates 2002, 103, who consider *ΠAN* coins to be western imports. This interpretation has, however, been convincingly refuted by Metlich/Schindel 2004, 12.

135 Suggested by Castrizio 2010, 28–32 (see in particular 31 and *ibid.*n16).

136 Foss 2008, 104. Cf. Castrizio 2010, 31–32. Noeske 2000, I, 173 speculated that *ΠAN* coins could have been issued by Benjamin, the miaphysite patriarch expelled from Alexandria by Heraclius. For the figure of Benjamin and the sources related to him, see Mikhail 2014, 94–100.

137 *CG* I 1 (= *RCEA* I 6 = l-Hawary 1930).

138 The origin of the funerary stela of ʿAbd al-Raḥmān b. Khayr is somewhat debated. El-Hawary 1930, 332–333 argued in favor of Gizeh as the probable provenance of the stela based on prosopographical data. Schmidt (in press) defends a possible origin from Aswān.

139 Cf. Richter 2010.

A Language of Distinction: Arabic in Egypt ca. 680–800

The 680s represent a turning point for the use of Arabic in Egypt, not just in terms of sheer quantity of documents but also of documentary typologies. In 684, at the peak of the second civil war, a congregation of Kalb tribes appointed the already aging Marwān b. al-Ḥakam as caliph in an attempt to fill the power vacuum left by the death of Yazīd I. Marwān in turn appointed both his elder sons as heirs apparent. It fell to the second born, ʿAbd al-ʿAzīz[140] to recover Egypt from the Zubayrids and to be subsequently installed as governor over the province (in office 685–705). When shortly thereafter Marwān died, his firstborn ʿAbd al-Malik succeeded him on the throne. It is likely within the broader framework of ʿAbd al-Malik's far-reaching administrative reforms that the language constellation of Egypt began to mutate during the 680s–690s.

Leading the way is a new typology of bilingual papyrus protocols featuring Muslim slogans in Arabic and Greek issued in the name of the new governor (Fig. 1).[141]

Considering the low number of preserved specimens, the distribution of bilingual protocols dated to the governorate of ʿAbd al-ʿAzīz is telling. Exemplars have been found in the Fayyūm,[142] the Thebaid,[143] the Hermopolite,[144] and the Antaiopolite,[145] which indicates a widespread administrative practice.

Starting from the last quarter of the 7th century, Arabic appears in the communication between the governor's office and the provincial aristocracy. While the demand notes issued by Arab high-ranking officials of the 640s and 650s are without exception monolingual in Greek, by the following generation orders for the delivery of labor force and *naturalia* from the governor's office are bilingual Arabic/Greek. An unpublished document from the governorship of Maslama b. al-Mukhallad (in office 667–682) indicates that this practice was already introduced in the late Sufyanid period.[146] A more sizable dossier of six such bilingual demand notes survives from ʿAbd al-ʿAzīz b. Marwān's time. These documents are

140 For ʿAbd al-ʿAzīz, see the recent monograph by Mabra 2017, who makes an argument for its title figure pursuing a policy of semi-independence from Damascus. For some counter arguments from documentary evidence, see Marie Legendre's unpublished paper held at the conference *The Reach of Empire – The Early Islamic Empire at Work* (Hamburg; Oct. 11–13, 2018).

141 Grohmann 1923–1924, II, XXVII–XLVIII.

142 *CPR* III 8.

143 *P.BellTwoLetters* 1 and *CPR* III 9 (both from al-Uqṣur).

144 *P.Gascou* 27a and *CPR* III 4 (both al-Ushmūnayn).

145 *CPR* III 2 and 10 (both from Ishqawh).

146 P.Wash.Libr. of Congress inv. Ar. 1+ 40 (Ṭuṭūn; 670/671 or 679/680). The document is being prepared for edition by Lev Weitz and Naïm Vanthieghem. On the text, see Weitz's presentation

Fig. 1: *Bilingual protocol of ʿAbd al-ʿAzīz b. Marwān (P.Vind.inv. G 39763 r).*
© Österreichische Nationalbibliothek, Vienna.

framed as letters and addressed to the inhabitants of villages and cities in three different pagarchies.[147] This again hints at a generalized administrative practice. Furthermore, both the Arabic and the Greek version of these demand notes operate within a standardized set of formulae and operative clauses underscoring an organized secretarial system. Arabic and Greek versions of these documents are both similarly structured.

(1) They open with a monotheistic invocation
(Arabic) *bi-sm allāh al-raḥmān al-raḥīm* "In the name God, the Merciful, the Compassionate"
(Greek) *en onomati tou theou* "In the name of God"

(2) This is followed by an internal address.

at the *8th ISAP Conference* (Online; Mar. 16, 2021). For references to inscriptions allegedly commissioned by Maslama, see *infra*n164 in this chapter.

147 *P.DelatterEntagion* (694), *P.KarabacekBemerkungenMerx* (= *P.MerxDocuments* p. 55) (697/698), and *P.DiemFruheUrkunden* 1 (undated/685–705) are addressed to the villages in al-Fayyūm; *P.Gascou* 27b to those of al-Ushmūn; and *P.DiemFruheUrkunden* 2 and P. Vind.inv. G 43234 to those of Ihnās. (undated/685–705). The community addressed in a further specimen, P.CtYBR inv. 71 (693?), is unknown.

(3) The main body of the document detailing the deliveries is introduced by the operative clause
(Arabic) *fa-aʿṭū* "and deliver . . ."
(Greek) *pareschete* "deliver . . ."

(4) Next follows the date according to
(Arabic) the Muslim calendar and *hijrī* year
(Greek) the Egyptian calendar and indiction year in Greek.

Only the Arabic version reports the name of the scribe above the date.[148] At the bottom of the papyrus sheet, summaries of the deliveries due were added, folded over, and sealed.[149] The seal could be broken for control purposes should the need have arisen. Interestingly, sealed administrative summaries are penned in Greek only. The picture of language use that emerges from the early Marwanid bilingual demand notes is therefore one in which Greek retains functional primacy (as underscored by the summaries) despite visual representational primacy being claimed by the Arabic text placed on top.

Meanwhile, Arab appointees at the level of the pagarchy appear for the first time in the papyrological record. The earliest and best documented of such instances is the figure of Flavius[150] Atias son of Goedos (arab. ʿAṭīya b. Juʿayd), who served as pagarch of the Fayyūm before being appointed as *dux* of the Arcadia and Thebais around 695.[151] The entirely Greek and Coptic papyrus dossier[152] related to Atias indicates that the appointment of Arabs as pagarchs did not immediately lead to a wider dissemination of Arabic among the middle layers of Egyptian administration. In fact, the language choice in the chancery of the

---

148 See, however, the mention of the Greek scribe in *P.BeckerPapyrusstudien* (Anṣinā; 713/714) issued by the chancery of Qurra b. Sharīk. Unlike in bilingual gubernatorial requisition and tax orders, the names of the Greek scribes are mentioned in the bilingual requisition orders from Nessana as well as in several bilingual receipts from 7th- and early 8th-century Egypt. See the list of references in Sijpesteijn 2020b, 439n15. Sijpesteijn *op. cit.* 466 suggests that the lack of scribal signature in the Greek part of bilingual documents might indicate that both the Arabic and the Greek part were penned by the same scribe. For an alternative explanation for the lack of scribal signatures in the Greek version of bilingual fiscal documents, see Kaplony 2016, 388–389.
149 For sealing practices in the Early Islamic administration, see Sijpesteijn 2012b and *ead.* 2018.
150 For the use of the Roman honorific "Flavius" by Arab officials, see Gonis/Morelli 2000, 194 and Papaconstantinou 2009, 453–454. See also *infra* Ch. IV, *Negotiating "Arab Style"* (Trading Rank Identifiers).
151 On Flavius Atias and his dossier, see Sijpesteijn/Worp 1983, 189–197; Cromwell 2013; Legendre 2016, 11–15; and Delattre/Vanthieghem 2016, 122–125.
152 *CPR* IV 3–6, *P.Gascou* 28, and *SB Kopt.* IV 1783 and 1785 (all in Coptic) and *CPR* VIII 72(?)–84, *P.Ross.Georg.* III 23, *SB* III 7240 and XXIV 16219 (all in Greek).

pagarch and the duke evidences notable differences with documentary practices of the gubernatorial chancery in al-Fusṭāṭ.

Noticeable is the apparent functional overlap between the Greek and Coptic demand notes for the requisition of manpower,[153] and allowances for wheat[154] and other goods[155] issued in Atias' chancery and the already mentioned coeval bilingual injunctions dispatched to communities under Atias' jurisdiction directly from the governor's office.[156] Legendre (2016) interprets the functional overlapping between the governor's and the duke's offices in the late 7th century as an indicator of the parallel administrative structures that ultimately led to the suppression of the by then superfluous office of the duke.[157] As far as language choices go, the documents in Atias' dossier may suggest an alternative interpretation: that bilingual requisition orders were dispatched by the governor to the duke's office from whence they were forwarded to the addressed communities in Greek or Coptic. This conclusion is in fact suggested by the reference to previous written orders (*epistalmata*) by the governor in Atias' demand notes.[158] An example of this bureaucratic *iter* is in all probability the "doublets" *P.Gascou* 27 and 28, an Arabic/Greek and a Coptic demand note issued by the governor and by the duke Atias respectively. The two demand notes are addressed to the same community (Ushmūn), in the same year (695), and concern an identical delivery (two sailors with their allowances for a period of 2 months). It is therefore plausible that *P.Gascou* 28 is nothing but the Coptic translation (prepared in the duke's office) of the original bilingual order *P.Gascou* 27, issued by the governor.

From the beginning of ʿAbd al-ʿAzīz's governorate also stems the first monolingual Arabic letter concerning administrative instructions proper.[159] The document is torn on the upper, right and left margins, and neither the sender's nor the recipient's name survive. The format, graphic peculiarities, and most of all the technical jargon of the fragment are very reminiscent of those seen in the Arabic gubernatorial letters[160] in the following generation. Based on these similarities, Werner Diem interpreted the document as a missive by the governor probably addressed to a pagarch. As Arab pagarchs are first – and even then

153 *CPR* VIII 74 (698) addressed to the village of Dikaiou in the Fayyūm.

154 *CPR* VIII 74 and *CPR* VIII 75 (698) addressed to the village of Aninou in the Fayyūm.

155 *P.Gascou* 28 (695) addressed to the inhabitants of Hermopolis.

156 Legendre 2016, esp. 14.

157 For the instalments of Arab-Muslim administrative personnel and the implementation of new offices in Lower Egypt and Alexandria in particular, see Bruning 2018a, 22–57.

158 *CPR* VIII 74, 4 and 75, 4 (both from the Fayyūm; 698).

159 *P.DiemGouverneur* (= *P.Ryl.Arab.* I XV 59) (al-Ushmūnayn; 684–685).

160 For a detailed discussion of the formal and layout features of Early Islamic official documents on papyrus, see *infra* 176–187 with references to previous literature.

sporadically – attested only from the 690s onwards,[161] the addressee is likely to have been a member of the rural Hellenized aristocracy who had not yet mastered Arabic – provided that Diem's interpretation is correct. The letter might have been accompanied by a Greek copy or a translation could have been prepared *in loco* by Arabic scribes in the pagarchial chancery.

The development of new styles of Arabic public writing in Marwanid Egypt is indicated in both the documentary and literary record. An echo of the Marwanid monumental projects from coeval Greater Syria is felt in the notice regarding the installation of an Arabic inscription on the bridge of al-Fūsṭāṭ.[162] Like several of the known Marwanid public inscriptions, the text at issue is no longer extant and is only known through a literary report by al-Maqrīzī († 1442). Compared to coeval examples, the formulary of the text, however, suggests that al-Maqrīzī's transmission is true to the original.[163, 164]

Fig. 2: ABAZ, fals, *no mint (Fusṭāṭ?), no date (685–705?), 6,55 g.*
© Dumbarton Oaks, Byzantine Collection, Washington, DC.

In the numismatic realm, a series of Arab-Byzantine copper coins from Egypt display a crowned royal bust holding a palm frond which has no exact counterpart in Byzantine coinage. The coins at issue distinguish themselves by the calcu-

161 The first Arab pagarch of whom evidence survives is Flavius Atias son of Goedos; see *supra* pp. 63–64.
162 *RCEA* I 8* (688).
163 Hoyland 1997a, 694n27.
164 According to literary reports, inscriptions in the name the Umayyad governors Maslama b. Mukhallad (in office 667–682) and on Qurra b. Sharīk (in office 709–715) commemorated renovation works in the mosque of ʿAmr b. al-ʿĀṣ in Fusṭāṭ. Of the first inscription, only mentions are known while the text of the second survives only in a 17th-century French translation from a seemingly lost Arabic chronicle. See *MCIA* I 546* (711 or 712) and commentary on pages 4–9.

lated absence of Christian religious symbolism and by the legend *ABAZ* placed in the lower reverse margin (Fig. 2). N. Schindel has ingeniously suggested that the inscription be interpreted not as a corrupted form of the usual mint name *ΑΛΕΞ* (=Alexandria) but rather as an abbreviated name of the acting governor, *AB(dal) AZ(iz)*.[165] It is unclear when exactly Egyptian Arab-Byzantine copper coinage was finally replaced by undated all-epigraphic emissions. If a report by the 10th-century administrator and chronicler al-Jahshiyārī († 942) is to be believed, the secretary al-Ḍaḥḥāk b. ʿAbd al-Raḥmān was sent to Egypt upon the death of ʿAbd al-ʿAzīz (705). He found the local treasury to consist "mainly of coppers made in the land of Rūm", likely meaning Arab-Byzantine coinage. This would suggest that all-epigraphic copper coinage was introduced to Egypt only after 705.[166]

The evidence for Arabic writing expands exponentially both in terms of sheer quantity of documents and of their typology roster in the archives from the 8th century. This coincides with the tightening of direct central control in the provincial administrative structure, most notably the disappearance of the relay office of the *dux*.

The single richest 8th-century coherent group of Arabic texts is found amid the roughly 400 documents in Greek, Coptic, and Arabic that comprise the archive of Basileios, an early 8th-century (705–721) administrator (*dioikētēs*)[167] of Aphrodito/Ishqawh (44 km south of al-Asyūṭ). Basileios' archive distinguishes itself by the high percentage of incoming correspondence issued directly from the gubernatorial chancery in al-Fusṭāṭ. This includes 41 lengthy Arabic letters addressed to Basileios by the governor Qurra b. Sharīk (in office 709–715). Nothing indicates that the putative addressee of Qurra's Arabic missives possessed any mastery of Arabic at this time. In fact, the complete absence of Arabic documents produced in Basileios' office points strongly in the opposite direction. Lists and accounts pertaining to the management of Basileios' chancery are prevalently redacted in Greek with a few additional examples in Coptic.[168] Coptic guarantee declarations addressed to the governor through the intermediary of the pagarch are instead redacted in Coptic with additional recapitulations in Greek.[169] A number of private documents are also authored in Coptic with seemingly no connection with the rest of the archive.[170] More to the point, the correspondence between

165 Metlich/Schindel 2004; Foss 2008, 99–105; Goodwin 2015; and Mabra 2017, 113–118.
166 Foss 2008, 103–104. Cf., however, the glass weights produced during ʿAbd al-ʿAzīz's governorship, which are based on the standard of the reformed *dīnār* (4,25 g); see Morton 1986 (n. 2).
167 The official titulature of Basileios is discussed *in extenso* by Marthot-Santaniello 2013.
168 Richter 2010, 203.
169 *Ibid.*, 204–207.
170 *Ibid.*, 207–208.

Qurra and Basileios embraces 74 further *Greek* letters which are concerned with analogous topics (e.g., delivery of tax money, specialized workers, fugitives etc.) as their Arabic *pendants*. It is generally assumed that a Greek translation was provided for every Arabic letter despite the fact that no such match can be identified beyond doubt.[171] Alternatively, translations of the Arabic letters coming from al-Fusṭāṭ in Greek and/or Coptic may have been prepared in the pagarchial chancery itself, as the presence of Arabic scribes is mentioned in the Basileios archive.[172] Based on similarities in content and phraseology with extant Greek Qurra letters, E. Scheerlinck has recently made a convincing case for interpreting *P.Ryl.Copt.* 277 as one such a Coptic translation from a Greek or Arabic original prepared in Basileios' office.[173]

A handful of bilingual (Greek/Arabic) orders for the delivery of manpower and raw materials for the Arab fleet[174] also belongs to Qurra's dossier in the Aphrodito archive and is structured in the same vein as those issued by the chancery of Abd alʿ Azīz and displaying the same operative clause *fa-aʿṭū* "and deliver . . . "/ *pareschete* "deliver . . .".[175] In addition, the archive includes a series of bilingual demand notes, detailing amounts for the gold[176] and wheat[177] taxes, addressed by the governor to hamlets under Basileios' jurisdiction. Though – even visually – similarly structured as the orders for delivery in manpower and kind, tax demands in Basileios' archive exhibit a different set of operative clauses and thus form, formally speaking, a separate (sub-)typology of documents (Fig. 3).

---

171 Bell 1910, XLIIn2 suggested a number of pairs between Greek and Arabic missives from Qurra to Basileios. The difference in wording between the hypothetical Greek and Arabic double letters (*P.Lond.* IV 1349 and *P.Heid.Arab.* I 1, *P.Lond.* IV 1359 or 1345 and *P.BeckerPAF* 3, and *P.Lond.* IV 1389 and *P.BeckerPAF* 3 frag. 4) is, however, very noticeable.

172 *P.Lond.* IV 1434, 229 and 1447, 140 and 190.

173 See Scheerlinck's talks at the conference *The Reach of Empire* (Hamburg; Oct. 11–13, 2018) and at the *29th International Congress of Papyrology* (Lecce; July 28–Aug. 3, 2019).

174 *P.Heid.Arab.* I 22; *P.BeckerPAF* 8 (= *P.Heid.Arab.* I 7); *P.Mudun* 32 (= *P.BeckerPAF* 9 = *P.Heid. Arab.* I 8), all to Ishqaw/Aphroditō, 709–710 and *P.BeckerPapyrusstudien* sent to Anṣinā/Antinoopolis in 714.

175 Cf. however, *P.BeckerPAF* 10 (= *P.Heid.* I 9) (709), 2 in which the operative clause reads *fa-arsilū* "and send . . .".

176 *P.Heid.Arab.* I b; *P.Heid.Arab.* I d; *P.Heid.Arab.* I f; *P.Heid.Arab.* I h; *P.Heid.Arab.* I i; *Chrest. Khoury* I 94 (= *P.Heid.Arab.* I 6); *P.Cair.Arab.* 161 (= *P.BeckerNPAF* 14); *P.Cair.Arab.* 162 (= *P.BeckerNPAF* 15); *P.Cair.Arab.* 163 (= *P.BeckerNPAF* 16), all sent to Ishqaw/Aphroditō, 709–710.

177 *P.Heid.Arab.* I a; *P.Heid.Arab.* I c; *P.Heid.Arab.* I g; *P.Heid.Arab.* I k; *P.Heid.Arab.* I l; *P.Mudun* 11 (= *Chrest.Khoury* I 93 = *P.Heid.Arab.* I 5); *P.Cair.Arab.* 160 (= *P.BeckerNPAF* 13), all sent to Ishqawh between 709–710.

In particular:

(1) They open with the same invocation as the requisition orders
(Arabic) *bi-sm allāh al-raḥmān al-raḥīm* "In the name God, the Merciful, the Compassionate"
(Greek) *en onomati tou theou* "In the name of God"

(2) Likewise followed by an internal address.

(3) The main body of the document detailing the deliveries, however, is introduced by the operative clause
(Arabic) ***inna-hu aṣāba-kum*** "that it has befallen you . . .".[178]
(Greek) ***elachen hymin*** "it has been allotted to you . . ."

(4) The dating formulae are otherwise the same
(Arabic) the Muslim calendar and *hijrī* year
(Greek) the Egyptian calendar and indiction year in Greek.

Like the demand notes of the previous generation, bilingual requisition orders from the Basileios archive continue to exhibit Greek administrative summaries at the bottom of the papyrus sheet. Bilingual tax demands in gold, or in gold and in kind, issued by Qurra are additionally headed by a Greek title indicating the addressed community and the amount due. The presence of titles and recapitulations in Greek offers just a glimpse of an administrative machinery still effectively operating in Greek behind an Arabic façade.[179]

The panoramic of the language dynamics laid out by the documents of the archive of Basileios notoriously lacks commensurate contextual evidence from other regions of Egypt. There is no indication, however, that Aphrodito enjoyed any privileged or special status within the Egyptian administrative machinery. In fact, a recent study by I. Marthot-Santaniello on the toponyms mentioned in the Basileios archive (2013) has established that the taxable area under the *dioikētēs'* jurisdiction was comparatively small, comprising little more than a couple dozen square kilometers and measuring close to 2,5 kilometers in diameter. One Arabic letter by Qurra in the Vienna collection is in fact addressed to the pagarch of Heracleopolis/Ihnās[180] and another one from Heidelberg to the pagarch of Hermopolis/al-Ushmūnayn,[181] suggesting that the use of Arabic for official missives between al-Fusṭāṭ and the pagarchial offices was by then standard administrative procedure. Furthermore, the remains of the Arabic portion of a supposedly bilingual demand note issued in Qurra's name with a

178 For the different operative clauses used in the Greek version of tax demands and requisition orders produced in Qurra's chancery, see Bell 1945, 535.

179 Kaplony 2016, 397–399.

180 *P.GrohmannQorraBrief* (709).

181 *P.Heid.Arab.* I 10 (710).

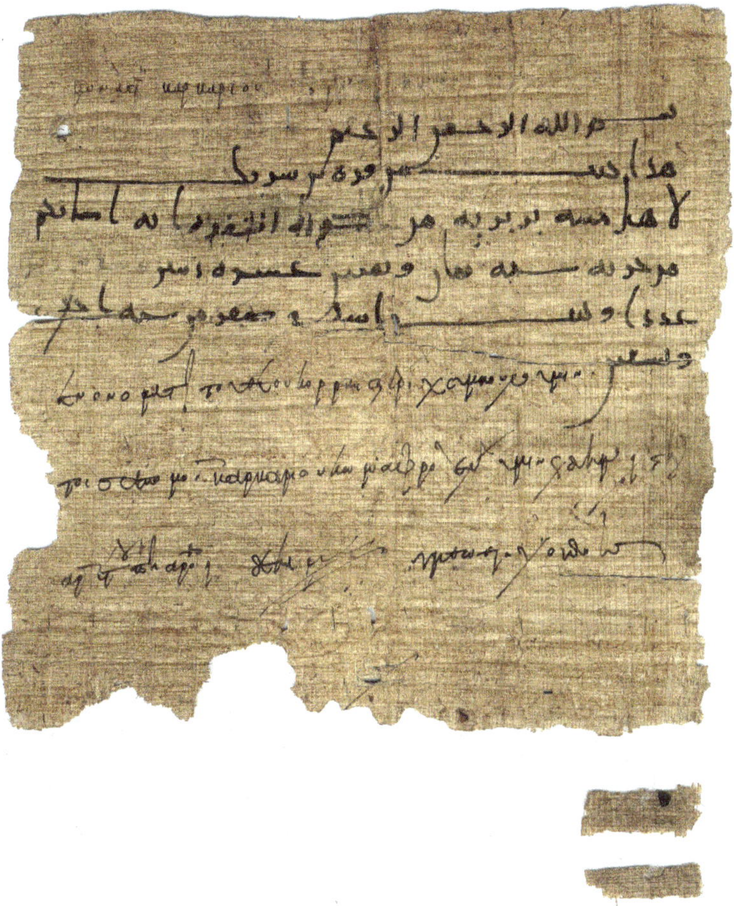

Fig. 3: *Bilingual tax demand of Qurra b. Sharīk (P.Heid.inv. Arab. 13 r).*
© Institut für Papyrologie, Universität Heidelberg.

Coptic endorsement on the *verso* have been recovered at the site of the Apa Thomas monastery in the Wādī Sarga near Edfū.[182] Yet another Arabic[183] and two Greek[184] fragments of demand notes by Qurra have been excavated in the Apa Apollo monastery in Balā'iza – though not all of them were originally sent there.[185] One can thus pru-

182 Text edited in Crum/Bell 1922, 9n2.
183 *P.DonnerFaagments* 1.
184 *P.Bal.* 181 and 182.
185 Only *P.Bal.* 182 mentions the Apa Apollo monastery. *P.DonnerFragments* 1 is addressed to "the head of the district of Ishqawh" and probably belonged in the Basileios archive. The address of *P.Bal.* 181 is lost.

dently conclude that the administrative culture on display in the Aphrodito papyri was not substantially divergent from coeval administrative practices in the rest of the Egyptian countryside.

One blind spot in the archive of Basileios and in the overall documentary record of Early Islamic Egypt is language use in bottom-up administrative communication between sub-provincial administrators and the highest echelons of the provincial administration. The few documents operating at this specific administrative layer are all between Arabs. One such example is a letter found in the monastery of Apa Apollo at Dayr al-Balāʾiza addressed by the pagarch of the Hermopolite Khālid b. Yazīd (in office in the early 720s) to the financial director al-Qāsim b.ʿUbayd Allāh (in office 734–742) possibly requesting the issuing of a safe-conduct for one of the inhabitants of the monastery.[186] Another example is the *incipit* of a letter addressed by the pagarch of the Fayyūm Maymūn b. Kaʿb to the governor Yazīd b. Ḥātim (in office 762–769).[187] Whether Hellenized intermediate governing bodies of the 7th and early 8th centuries would have communicated with al-Fusṭāṭ in Greek, Arabic or both remains unknown.

Starting with the second quarter of the 8th century, Muslim landowners are attested in the Egyptian countryside.[188] This change in landholding patterns is accompanied by the appearance in coeval documents of distinctively Muslim legal practices outside the garrison cities.[189] The increased presence of Arab lower-ranking officials in the Egyptian countryside further emerges from new typologies of Arabic documents related to fiscal checks. In the Heracleopolite and the Hermopolite as well as in Aphrodito, bilingual tax receipts issued to both village communities and individual taxpayers appear throughout the 700s and 710s.[190] The inclusion of an Arabic translation on fiscal quittances was no doubt designed

186 *P.DonnerFragments* 3 see also Sijpesteijn 2012a, 707–709.
187 *P.Christ.Musl.* 23.
188 Sijpesteijn 2009 and *ead.* 2013, esp. 105–110.
189 For the terminological innovations introduced in Coptic documents through a process of borrowing from Arabic juridical terminology, see Richter 2001 and *id.* 2009, 424–425. For the progressive development of Islamic judicial structures in Egypt over the 8th and later centuries, see Tillier 2013a and *id.* 2015; a very useful synoptic overview of the development of legal practice in Egypt from the Medinan to the end of the Marwanid period is provided by Bruning 2018a, 124–151. For Khurāsān, see Khan 2007, 28–30.
190 *P.StoetzerSteuerquittungen* 2 (Ihnās; 707?) and *P.BaranskiArabisation* = *SPP* VIII 1198 (Ihnās; 709?), both issued by ʿAbd al-Raḥmān b. Abī ʿAwf, *P.Christ.Musl.* 1 (= *P.Cair.Arab.* 286 = *P.BeckerPAF* 16 = *SPP* VIII 1345) (Ishqawh; 706) issued by ʿUmar b. Ḥabīb, *P.Christ.Musl.* 2 (Ishqawh?; VII/VIII), issuer unknown, *P.StoetzerSteuerquittung* (al-Ushmūnayn; 709?) issued by Sufyān b. Ghunaym and *P.Grenf* II 105 and 106 (both from Ihnās; 719) issued by Zubayr b. Ziyād. On the dating of *P.Stoetzer-Steuerquittungen* 2 and *P.StoetzerSteuerquittung*, see *supra*n112. On Zubayr b. Ziyād, see *infra*n192.

to enable controls at the hands of Arab officials. By contrast, coeval individual tax demands continue to be penned exclusively in Greek and Coptic until the mid-8th century. This is well-illustrated by a small ensemble of documents which appears to be the private archive of one Mēnas son of Senouthios, head of the village of Leukogion in the Heracleopolite. Mēnas is the addressee of three tax receipts, *SB* XVIII 13268 (722) and 13269 (719) and *P.Grenf* II 106 (= *SPP* III 259) (719), and one tax demand, *SB* XX 14234 (716).[191] The senders of *SB* XVIII 13268 and 13269 (both in Greek) are anonymous. Arab officials[192] are explicitly stated as the issuing authority of both the tax demand *SB* XX 14234, written in Greek, and the tax receipt *P.Grenf.* II 106, which conversely is bilingual Arabic/Greek.

Fiscal checks operated by Arab officials are also behind the issuing of Arabic safe-conducts serving as long term travel permits[193] at the hands of Arab "agents" (arab. *ʿummāl*, sing. *ʿāmil*) of pagarchs appearing in the documentation since the 710s.[194] The majority of Early Islamic Arabic safe-conducts whose finding context is known were issued to residents in the Apa Jeremias monastery at Saqqāra[195] but exemplars issued to villagers of Lower Egypt are also attested.[196] When preserved, the names of the addressees are invariably Greek or Coptic, which most probably indicates indigenous villagers who had not yet mastered Arabic. It is to be expected that such safe-conducts would have to be shown at administrative checkpoints and verified by Arab fiscal agents.[197] In addition, the use of the Arabic script imbued the visual appearance of the document with the added value of conveying an aura of officiality (Chapter II).

In contrast, for one-way top-down administrative communication with the native population, the use of Arabic remained marginal at first. Within the trilin-

191 On the dating of *SB* XX 14234, see Gonis 2001, 225–226.
192 Muḥammad b. Abī al-Qāsim (*Maamed ouios Aboul Kasem*) in *SB* XX 14234 and Zubayr b. Ziyād (*Zubeeir ouios Ziada*) in *P.Grenf.* II 106.
193 For a synoptic overview of the different typologies of travel permits in early Islamic Egypt, see Delattre 2018, 543, for documents in Arabic in particular, see *ibid.*, 533–536.
194 The oldest preserved exemplar of Arabic safe-conducts is *P.VanthieghemSaufConduit* (Egypt; 717). For this typology of documents, see Sijpesteijn 2012a, 708–709 and *ead.* 2013, 241–244 (n41) and 311–312; Vanthieghem 2014a, 266–271; Rāġib 1997, 143–168. For similar coeval documents in Coptic and Greek, see Boud'hors 2007, 115–129.
195 *P.RagibSauf-conduits* 1 (VIII); *P.PiletteSauf-Conduit* (729); and *P.RagibSauf-conduits* 5–8 (all dated between 750–751). On the discovery of Arabic papyri at the Apā Jeremias monastery, see De Sacy 1825 and Pilette/Vanthieghem 2016, 234n8. For the documents related to the monastery, see most recently Lajos Berkes' and Naïm Vanthieghem's paper held at the *29th International Congress of Papyrology* (Lecce; July 28–Aug. 3, 2019).
196 *P.RagibSauf-conduits* 3 (Armant; 733/734).
197 Delattre 2018.

gual ensemble of ca. 540[198] papyri[199] and ostraca[200] dating from the late Byzantine to the early Arab period excavated at the monastery of Apā Apollo in Bāwiṭ, documents pertaining to fiscal accounting and internal management are penned both in Coptic and in Greek. Except for the reuse of bilingual protocols as writing material,[201] the only Arabic document connected to the monastery is an incoming bilingual Arabic-Coptic tax demand for the capitation of one of the monks dated 753.[202] Otherwise, incoming demand notes issued to monks in the monastery by Arab pagarchs are only attested in Coptic.[203]

In another large trilingual repository of late 7th- to late 8th-century documents found in the Apa Apollo monastery in Balāʾiza, Arabic documents similarly claim but a fraction of the over 300 texts excavated at the site, which are mostly Coptic and Greek.[204] The Arabic papyri[205] are all fragmentary to different extents and all but one[206] pertain to official business. Furthermore, none of the Arabic papyri shows direct connections with the monastery and all have been reused as writing material for Coptic texts. Most likely, the Arabic Balāʾiza texts came to the monastery incidentally as second-hand papyrus rather than having been addressed to local residents.[207]

In coeval official dossiers from Middle Egypt, Arabic documents for top-down communication with local communities likewise have a primarily representative function. The fiscal documents issued by the chancery of the pagarch of Heracleopolis/Ihnās (in office 718–723) and Hermopolis/al-Ushmūnayn (in office 710–716 or 725–731) Rāshid b. Khālid are in Greek and Coptic.[208] The impression of the pagarch's personal seal with Arabic inscriptions is preserved on two tax demands,[209] establishing Arabic

198 Estimates on Coptic documents from Bāwiṭ are based on the data provided by the *Brussels Coptic Database* (*BCD*) https://dev.ulb.ac.be/philo/bad/copte/baseuk.php?page=accueiluk.php (data extracted on Dec. 12, 2018).

199 In particular *P.Bawit Clackson*, *P.Brux.Bawit*, *P.Clackson*, and *P.Mon.Apollo*. For a list of Bāwiṭ-related documents scattered across non-dedicated volumes or smaller contributions, see Delattre 2007, 117–124.

200 In particular *O.Bawit* and *O.Bawit IFAO*. See also previous footnote.

201 *P.Bawit Clackson* 76 as well as *P.Brux.Bawit* 9, 17, 19, and 44.

202 *P.Clackson* 45. On the taxes levied in the Bāwiṭ monastery, see Delattre 2015, summarizing previous research on the topic.

203 *P.Mon.Apollo* 28–30 and *P.Vat.Aphrod.* 135 (VIII).

204 *P.Bal.*

205 *P.DonnerFragments* 1 and 3. For unpublished Arabic texts from Balāʾiza, see Sijpesteijn 2012a.

206 Bodleian MSCopt d 23, being prepared for publication by Petra Sijpesteijn.

207 Sijpesteijn 2012a, esp. 710–713.

208 On the career of Rāshid b. Khālid, see now Gonis 2022.

209 *Nilus* IV 1 (= *PERF* 577) and *PERF* 578. See also Garel 2018.

as the language of the validating authority, while not being the functional language of the actual demand.

The most detailed information on the use of Arabic in the Egyptian chanceries of the mid-8th century has been recovered from the Fayyūm. The trilingual dossier related to the pagarch of Ihnās (in office 728–730) and the Fayyūm (in office ca. 730–743[210]), Nājid b. Muslim, still evidences a similar language choice to that of previous generations. Top-down communication between the pagarchal office and the villagers under Nājid's jurisdiction continues to be kept in Greek or Coptic as attested by a series of Greek tax demands[211] as well as by a Coptic letter to the "headmen of the village of Arsinoe".[212] As in the case of Rāshid b. Khālid's dossier, the only attestation of Arabic in this domain is in the bilingual Greek/Arabic personal seal attached to a fiscal document in Greek.[213] Arabic is also the language on a seal[214] of another 7th/8th-century pagarch of the Fayyūm, Ibrahīm b. Yaḥyā[215] of whom two Greek tax demands[216] survive. At other end of the spectrum, however, the appointment of Arab-Muslims to the mid-tiers of the provincial administration manifests itself in an increasing use of Arabic in both horizontal and top-down communication between offices. This is the background to *P.DiemAmtlicheSchreiben* 1,[217] an Arabic letter in which the mid-8th-century pagarch of the Heracleopolite, ʿAbd al-Malik b. Yazīd, instructs a (arguably Arab)[218] subordinate with regard to issues brought to the pagarch's attention by Nājid b. Muslim in a (lost) previous letter.

The archive of ʿAbd Allāh b. Asʿad, head of a sub-division (*ḥayyīz*) of the Fayyūm pagarchy during Nājid's tenure,[219] in particular, consists of his Arabic correspondence with the pagarch as well as with other Arab lower ranking officials. The most interesting element of novelty in ʿAbd Allāh's archive is a letter

210 On the end of Nājid's term as pagarch of the Fayyūm, see Berkes/Vanthieghem 2020, 157 and *ibid.*n11 quoting the unedited P.Louvre inv. 6420.

211 *CPR* XXII 8–9, and (Ihnās; 729–730) and 10 (Egypt; 727–743); *SB* I 5130 (Fayyūm; 730–743), XVI 12857 (Ihnās; 727–730); and *SPP* VIII 1184 (Ihnās; 728).

212 See the re-edition of *KSB* II 912 (Fayyūm; 743) in Berkes/Vanthieghem 2020, 158–159.

213 *CPR* XXII 9. For sealing practices in Early Islamic Egypt in general, see Sijpesteijn 2012b and *ead.* 2018.

214 The name on Ibrahīm b. Yaḥyā's seal (= *PERF* 572) was originally read by Karabacek and subsequently by Grohmann 1957, 39 as Abū Haym b. Yaḥyā.

215 For Ibrahīm b. Yaḥyā, see Morelli's commentary to *CPR* XXII 13.

216 *CPR* XXII 13 and *SB* VIII 9760 (vii/viii) with extensive corrections by Gonis and Morelli; See Morelli's commentary to *CPR* XXII 13 and Gonis' commentary to *P.Clackson* 46.

217 See now the re-edition by Berkes/Vanthieghem 2020, 154–157 (*P.BerkesCareers*).

218 The salutation and valediction formulae used in *P.BerkesCareers* (= *P.DiemAmtlicheSchreiben* 1) are those typically reserved for Muslim addressees. On this subject, see *infra* pp. 73–74.

219 On ʿAbd Allāh b. Asʿad, see Sijpesteijn 2013, 136–151. Cf. also *P.Heid.* XI 500–501.

addressed by one arguably Christian village tax official (arab. *simmāk* < gr. *symmachos*),[220] Georgios, requesting a loan. In another papyrus from the same archive, ʿAbd Allāh references one – arguably Arabic – scribe (*kātib*) by the name Abūla (< copt. Apollō).[221] These documents represent early examples of Arabic being used for transcultural bottom-up official communication at village level. It also indicates that for a village authority in the 8th- century Fayyūm to address an Arab Muslim in the latter's native language had become a question of either necessity or simply personal prestige.

Like in the Heracleopolite, however, in the Fayyūm as well the use of Greek and Coptic for top-down communication between the pagarchal chancery and the local population remained substantially unchallenged into the late 8th century. Still in the dossier of the pagarch of the Fayyūm Yaḥyā b. Hilāl (in office 744–760?)[222] all outgoing and incoming correspondence at the level of the pagarchy, as well as the internal business of the pagarch's office, was dealt with in Greek or Coptic. The use of Arabic is instead limited to correspondence between Arab-Muslim officials or to receipts addressed to Muslims.[223] Furthermore, the relatively high number of writing exercises in Greek,[224] Coptic,[225] and bilingual (Greek/Coptic)[226] in Yaḥyā's dossier implicates that the practice of a proper Greek and Coptic documentary hand was still held to be a priority as late as the second half of the 8th century.[227] This is further reinforced by the documents left by Yaḥyā's successors in office, Maymūn b. Kaʿb, Abd Allāh b. Qays, and Khālid b. Yazīd,[228] all known through Arabic as well as Greek and Coptic documents. In all dossiers, the Arabic items[229] are reports by/orders to Arab lower ranking agents

220 See Sijpesteijn's commentary to *P.MuslimState* 14, l. 5.
221 *P.MuslimState* 34, 5.
222 Garel/Vanthieghem 2022. Cf. Gonis 2004, 189–193.
223 *P.Christ.Musl.* 6 (ca. 740), 7 (743/744), 8–10 (= *P.Jahn* 3–4) (744/745), and 11–14 (743–749).
224 *MPER* XV 106 v; *MPER* XV 106a r; *SB* XVIII 13247 (all from the Fayyūm; undated); *CPR* XXII 18v (Fayyūm; 761); *SPP* VIII 1333 (Fayyūm; 751/752?).
225 *MPER* XV 106 av (Fayyūm; 744–760?).
226 *MPER* XV 106r (Fayyūm; 744–760?).
227 Bucking 2007, 240 argues that the clerical personnel in Yaḥyā b. Hilāl's chancery was mainly made up by Coptophones who practiced Greek as a second language, as suggested by the several scribal mistakes in their Greek writing exercises.
228 The exact chronology of the office of the pagarch of the Fayyūm in the 760s–770s is somewhat opaque, see now Garel/Vanthieghem 2022 and Gonis 2004, 192–195.
229 *P.Berl.Arab.* II 23 addressed to ʿAbd Allāh b. Qays and *P.RagibLettres* 2a–b containing a letter addressed to Khālid b. Yazīd on the *recto* and the *incipit* of a letter by Khālid on the *verso*. For the Coptic docket on *P.Berl.Arab.* II 23 v, see Gonis 2004, 193. See also *P.Christ.Musl.* 19–21 (ca. 762–763), three epistolary exercises in the name of Maymūn b. Kaʿb and *P.Christ.Musl.* 23 (772–778), a model for a tax receipt issued in the name of Khālid b. Yazīd.

concerning issues of tax collection. Both ʿAbd Allāh's[230] and Khālid's[231] dossier further comprise Greek scribal exercises implying that formal training in Greek minuscule was still required for outgoing administrative correspondence.

Throughout the later 8th century, the formal typologies of documents written in Greek progressively narrow down as Greek's role in the administration is functionally absorbed by Arabic and, to a lesser extent, by Coptic. A contraction of the administrative use of Greek is first discernible in the top layers of the provincial administration. The last dated specimens of bilingual protocols reach back to the reign of Yazīd (II) b. ʿAbd al-Malik (*rg.* 720–724 CE). Likewise, after the governorate of Qurra, gubernatorial letters are only attested in Arabic.[232] The use of Greek and Coptic for fiscal administration proved more resilient. Transitional trends, however, are evidenced in papyrological documentation throughout the 8th century. Monolingual Arabic tax demands addressed to individual villagers appear in the documentary record in the 720s and 730s in the Hermopolite.[233] The latest known dated example of a tax order issued in Greek comes from the Fayyūm and is dated 752.[234] However, coeval tax demands were also issued in Arabic and Coptic.[235] Although tax registers in Arabic had already appeared in the 730s,[236] the use of Greek for accounting carried on the longest and only died out in the early decades of the 9th century.[237] An enduring heritage of the Greek administrative tradition lived on in continuing use of Greek numerals in Arabic documents for centuries after the disappearance of Greek as a language of bureaucracy.[238] Documentary uses of Coptic on the other hand extend well beyond the timeframe surveyed in the present study. By the mid-9th century, however, Coptic – though sporadically attested into the early 11th century – had given way to Arabic even among Christians in the ambit of private law, as well as for matters of personal accounting.[239] Late Coptic legal documents further betray a process of assimilation into the

230 *SPP* X 169 (Fayyūm).
231 *CPR* XXII 18 and 20 (Fayyūm).
232 See *P.AbbottUbaydAllah* and *P.HindsNubia*.
233 P.Gen.inv. 713 (722); *P.Cair.Arab.* 180 (al-Ushmūnayn; 731–732).
234 *SPP* III 260 (Fayyūm); on the dating of the document, see Gonis 2004, 191–192.
235 *P.Clackson* 45 (Bāwiṭ; 753).
236 E.g., *P.Mil.Vogl.* I 8 a-b (Egypt; 731–734).
237 See *supra*n86.
238 Cf. the anecdote reported by Theophanes according to which Arab authorities dismissed all Greek-writing administrative personnel from Egyptian chanceries in the year 758/759 but were forced to reinstate them shortly thereafter due to the Arab functionaries' inability to write numbers.
239 Richter 2009, 417–418.

Arabic superstrata writerly culture in the form of Arabic addenda, technical loanwords, and loan translations of Arabic formulae.[240]

The progressive embedding of substrate writing cultures into the Arabic scribal tradition is illustrated by the shifting boundaries between the Arabic and the Greek and Coptic scribal practices in the later 8th century, as has been recognized by L. Reinfandt and S. Tost. Characteristic of the first bilingual texts appearing in 7th- and early 8th-century Egypt and Palestine is a functional "supplementarity": the Arabic text is a translation or rendition of a functionally equivalent one in Greek or Coptic. This typology of documents is best represented by the bilingual demand notes and the bilingual protocols of the early Marwanid period. Discrepancies in formal structure, handwriting as well as writing instruments[241] further reveal that in these types of texts, the Arabic and Greek/Coptic versions were the work of scribes who underwent distinct scribal training.[242] Whenever mentioned, scribes of the Greek parts of bilingual documents are distinguished from those of the Arabic and – judging by the fact that they all carry Greek personal names – apparently stem from a different cultural background. Conversely, all the names of the scribes responsible for the Arabic parts are Arab.[243]

The turn of the 8th century is marked by the appearance of documentary types in which Arabic is used to *complement* rather than supplement the main text penned in Greek or Coptic and vice versa. Arabic and non-Arabic parts of the text are usually both functionally and positionally distinct and addressed to different readers. This is the case, for instance, with administrative dockets attached to the letters of Qurra to Basileios.[244] Other similar language uses are represented by seals containing Arabic inscriptions and mottos attached to documents written

240 Richter 2008a, 161–165 and *id.* 2009, 419–421. For Arabic loanwords in Coptic, see in particular *ibid.*, 422–426 and *id.* 2004, 107–112.

241 See in particular the different thickness of the *kalamos* used by early Islamic Greek and Arabic scribes. Sijpesteijn 2020b, 439 and 444–445.

242 *I.a.* Richter 2010, 211–213; Sijpesteijn 2013, 231; Reinfandt 2015, 282–283; and Kaplony 2016, 392–399.

243 *I.a.* Rāghib 1996a, 21–26, Richter 2010, 213–214, and Sijpesteijn 2020b, 439 and *ibid.*n15. The mention of one Basīl as the scribe of *P.Qurra* 2 has probably been misread by the editor (cf. Richter *loc. cit.*n96). I propose to read the name as "Muslim" and to identify him with the homonymous scribe of *P.Cair.Arab.* 153 (= *P.BeckerNPAF* 6) and *P.Heid.Arab.* I 11 and probably the same individual as the Muslim b. Lubnān credited as the scribe of several letters copied by the copists al-Ṣalt (b. Masʿūd?) (*P.BeckerPAF* 1, *P.CairArab.* 154 and 155, and *P.Sorb.* 2346) and Saʿīd (*P.Heid. Arab.* I 10). Cf. in particular the scribal signature in *P.Qurra* 2 with Muslim's autographed one on *P.Cair.Arab.* 153.

244 Richter 2010, 199.

in Greek or Coptic.[245] Over the course of the 8th century, multilingual documents appear in which Arabic and Greek/Coptic text-parts are *integrated* in the same document and addressed to (arguably) the same person. An example of this typology is an unpublished fragment of a bilingual legal document housed at the Austrian National Library in which an Arabic witness signature is followed by a Greek notarial subscription.[246] In documents of this type, the Arabic and Greek/Coptic text/text portions are at times even penned by the same writer. A handful of bi- and multilingual scribal exercises that punctuate the papyrological record of the 8th century falls into this category.[247] This typology of multilingual and multigraphic documents bears witness to the rise of experts bridging separate clerical systems and languages, and heralds the assimilation of the local elite into the hegemonic Arabic scribal culture.[248]

A Language of Exchange: Arabic in Syria-Palestine (7th–8th Centuries)

The material evidence for Arabic writing from other regions of the Early Islamic Empire does not allow for a scrutiny of the language dynamics in the Early Islamic administration to a degree even remotely comparable with that of Egypt. In the winter of 1935–1936, an exceptional drought forced the American Colt archaeological expedition to relocate to the site Nessana in the Negev. During the excavations, about 200 papyri were discovered in *geniza*-like repositories[249] in the two churches of Theotokos[250] and of St Sergius.[251] Part of the findings consisted of literary material including several items in Greek,[252] a Latin fragment of

245 Sijpesteijn 2012a.
246 P.Vind.inv. A. P. 8711 (Fayyūm, VIII).
247 P.Vind.inv, G 39752 (= *PERF* 594). Berkes/Younes 2012; Reinfandt 2020a.
248 Reinfandt/Tost 2017 and Reinfandt 2020a. For the emergence of bilingual Coptic/Arabic scribes, see Reinfandt 2020a, 146–150. For trilingual scribes, see Berkes/Younes 2012. As a similar instance may be considered the *Ničeh p-tĕrkouman* (< arab. Najīḥ *at-tarjumān* “the translator”) signing a quittance in Coptic in *P.Ryl.Copt.* 214 (Hermopolite; VIII). See also *infra* pp. 239–241.
249 Unlike in archives proper, the storage of texts in *genīzōt* lacks an arrangement aimed at facilitating the retrieval of documents in view of potential further use. On this subject, see Rustow 2020, 2.
250 Colt 1962, plate 57, room 3.
251 Colt 1962, plates 53 and 54, room 8.
252 *P.Ness.* 3–13.

the Aeneid,[253] a Latin/Greek glossary,[254] a fragment of a Syriac religious poem,[255] and a handful of CPA – possibly liturgical – texts,[256] all datable to between the 6th and the 8th century. In addition, the excavations yielded close to 190 texts of a documentary nature. About 40 of the documents found in the church of St Sergius are dated or datable to the Early Islamic period and include texts in Greek (30), Arabic (2) as well as bilingual Arabic/Greek (10) dated between 674 and 689 CE. Arabic toponyms and proper names encountered throughout pre-conquest Greek papyri and Greek[257] and Nabatean[258] graffiti and inscriptions from Nessana underscore the familiarity of the local population with an Arabic spoken vernacular.[259] Neither papyrological nor epigraphic texts dated before the Islamic conquest, however, are redacted in Arabic script or language. Furthermore, cultural affinities between the conquerors and the Arab population of Syria ought not to be exaggerated. Later Muslim literary accounts suggest that the Arab population of Greater Syria was perceived by the new conquerors as possessing a liminal cultural profile.[260]

The documents from Nessana provide insights into the lower levels of the provincial administration of the *jund Filasṭīn* in the Sufyanid and early Marwanid period. By then, Nessana belonged to a subdivision (*iqlīm*/*klima*)[261] of Elousa, in turn subordinated to the district (*kūra*/*chōra*)[262] capital of Gaza. The town appears to have been under the jurisdiction of an administrator (*dioikētēs*), called Georgios, drawn from the ranks of the local Hellenized landowning class.[263] Georgios received written orders concerning the management of revenues as well as other

253 *P.Ness*. 2.
254 *P.Ness*. 1.
255 Kraemer 1958, 9. Eline Scheerlinck kindly informed me that she was unable to locate the Syriac fragment referred to by Kraemer during her research stay at the Morgan Library (p.c. Aug. 1, 2019). For conjecturally Syriac influences on the religious environment of Nessana, see Stroumsa 2008, 230–237.
256 No CPA papyri from Nessana are mentioned by Kraemer 1958. For these texts, see in particular the conference panel dedicated to the Nessana papyri at the *29th International Congress of Papyrology* (Lecce; Aug. 1, 2019).
257 Kirk/Welles 1962.
258 Rosenthal 1962.
259 Stroumsa 2008, 196–197 and *ead*. 2015, 147–148.
260 Stroumsa 2008, 124–125.
261 On the term *iqlīm*, see *infra* Ch. V, *The Loanwords in Imperial Arabic*, *s.v.* "*iqlīm*".
262 On the term *kūra*, see *ibid*. *s.v.* "*kūra*".
263 The Georgios *dioikētēs* (or Georgios of Nessana) addressed in *P.Ness*. 70 (685?), 73 (683), and 74 (ca. 685) is possibly to be identified with the abbot of St Sergius, Georgios son of Patrikios, to which the tax receipts on behalf of other residents, *P.Ness*. 55 (682) and 59 (684), are addressed and who is commemorated by a marble column together with his wife Anastasia (*P.Ness*. I inscr. 77).

ad hoc tasks from the provincial governor (*symboulos*).[264] Similar missives could, however, be addressed to the resident population without explicitly mentioning Georgios as intermediary.[265] In terms of language use, all letters addressed by the governor to Georgios directly are in Greek. Greek is also the language in which lists and accounts pertaining to the internal management of the town's administration are kept in the Nessana dossier.[266]

The process of tax collection proper appears to have been in the hands of local Hellenized village officials, featuring as the issuing authority of tax quittances.[267] In parallel, however, Arab personnel are portrayed as involved in similar capacities. The *recto*, of a single papyrus sheet contains two Arabic letters by an otherwise unknown Bayyān b. Qays, probably a senior Arab official; the *verso* of the papyrus sheet is inscribed with a Greek register of tax payments (*P.Ness.* 76). In the upper letter on *recto*, the sender reproaches two Arab Muslim addressees along with a further Muslim official for the unlawful appropriation of goods belonging to the villagers of Nessana. The lower missive addresses frictions between Muslim officials pertaining to the jurisdiction over unnamed villages. From the content of the texts, as well as its reuse for a tax register, one can infer that the misconduct deplored in the first missive was connected to fiscal tasks. At the very least, the letters by Bayyān b. Qays attest to the presence of Muslim officials operating at a village level and communicating with their superiors in Arabic roughly 50 to 70 years before analogous items appeared in Egypt.[268]

The Nessana dossier includes a group of seven bilingual Arabic/Greek orders for the requisition of wheat and oil destined for the allowances of Muslim troops dated between 674 and 689. One of the requisition orders found in Nessana (*P.Ness.* 64) is addressed to the villagers of Sykomazon, another town in the *iqlīm* of Elousa, and was likely sent to Nessana by oversight.[269] This suggests a systematic use of Arabic in the communication with all towns located in the jurisdiction of Gaza.

In his discussion of the demand notes from Nessana, Kraemer points to several minor differences between the bilingual demands from Nessana and their counterparts issued by the chancery of Qurra b. Sharīk, while remarking

---

See Kraemer 1958, 8 and Sijpesteijn 2010, 111. For the identification of the *dioikētēs* Georgios with Georgios of Nessana, see Kraemer 1958, 8.

264 *P.Ness.* 68, 71, and 72. *P.Ness.* 70 and 74 are addressed to the *dioikētēs* Georgios by a homonym whose office is never specified but who apparently occupied a higher hierarchical position.

265 *P.Ness.* 73.

266 *P.Ness.* 69, 76–77, and 92–93.

267 *P.Ness.* 55 and 58–59.

268 Kaplony 2016, 399–401.

269 Bell 1945, 536.

on their overall formal affinity.[270] Upon closer examination, several of the minor discrepancies between the Nessana and Aphrodito bilingual demand notes can be contextualised. These discrepancies are first and foremost definitional and depend on the vagueness of the term *entagion* under which Kraemer surmises both orders for the delivery of material, food, and manpower (attested both in Nessana and Aphrodito) and tax demands in money (attested only in Aphrodito). From a formal point of view, however, Arabic monetary tax demands and requisition orders for goods and labor form two distinct documentary sub-typologies, each displaying different operative clauses. This is apparent not just between Egypt and Syria but also within the Qurra dossier itself – as shown above.[271] In fact, when only the demands for deliveries in kind from the Qurra dossier are concerned – the same as those issued under ʿAbd al-ʿAzīz – the requisitioning phrase is always introduced by the same clause *fa-aʿṭū* "and deliver . . ." (Arabic)/ *pareschete* "deliver . . ." (Greek), which is also on display in the Nessana bilingual demand notes. It is further worth mentioning that the differences concerning the notation of dates between the Nessana and Aphrodito *bilinguae* pointed out by Kraemer (with Islamic year, indiction year, and Roman months in Nessana; with indiction year only in Aphrodito) only concern the *Greek* portion of the texts. The Arabic one, by contrast, bears an almost total resemblance to Marwanid examples from Egypt.[272] In other words, while the Greek portion of bilingual fiscal documents from Nessana and Egypt indicates the existence of – if only slightly – different *Greek* clerical practices in Syria and Egypt, the Arabic one indicates a common transregional administrative culture and jargon.

The formal affinities of the bilingual demand notes from Nessana and their Egyptian counterparts transcend the formulary. In particular, the formatting of these texts, with the Arabic version placed above the Greek, is virtually the same as in their counterparts from Marwanid Egypt. Slight differences in administrative practices, however, can also be evidenced. A factor distinguishing the bilingual demand notes found in Nessana from those excavated in Egypt is first and foremost that the former operate at a lower administrative level, namely that of the *iqlīm*, and not of the *kūra* like the demand notes of ʿAbd al-ʿAzīz and Qurra. Most importantly, in terms of language use, administrative recapitulations at the bottom of the sheet in Nessana are noted in both Greek *and* Arabic. The Nessana requisition orders further display signs of the linguistic penetration of Arabic into Greek. Unlike in Egyptian Greek documents, in the Nessana papyri the filia-

270 Kraemer 1958, 175–177.
271 See *supra* pp. 62–63 and 67–68.
272 Cf. Diem 1984b, 114–115.

tion (*nasab*) of Arab individuals is transliterated (as opposed to translated) into Greek characters,[273] as are names of Muslim months.[274] All this concurs to convey the impression of a deeper dissemination of Arabic in the local administrative machinery compared to early Marwanid Egypt.[275] The fact that bilingual demand notes are attested in Nessana a generation before their first counterparts in Egypt points to Sufyanid Syria as the probable origin of the administrative practices taking root in Marwanid Egypt.

Fig. 4: *Anonymous,* fals, *Ḥimṣ, no date, 6,86 g.*
© Staatliche Münzsammlung, Munich.

A comparandum is provided by the bronze coinage minted in the 660s–670s in Greater Syria (so-called "Umayyad Imperial Image coinage")[276] which displays Greek/Arabic legends with validating remarks (e.g., *ṭayyib*/*kalon* "good") and mint names both in Greek and Arabic (Fig. 4). This is notably different from Egyptian coinage in which Arabic appears only 30 to 40 years later, and from coeval bilingual Arabic/Middle Persian Arab Sasanian coinage, on which Arabic and Pahlavi legends build two functionally and graphically independent components of the coin.[277] Furthermore, while administrative information proper (date,

---

273 Cf. however, the Greek transliteration of the name ʿAbd Allāh b. Abū Hāshim (or ʿĀṣim) in the inscription from Hammat Gader, in which the filiation is translated and correctly declined (= *ouiou*). See Hasson 1982, 100.
274 Kaplony 2016, 395–396.
275 Cf. *ibid.*, 399–401.
276 For the definition "Umayyad Imperial Image coinage", see Album/Goodwin 2002, 74–75 and Goodwin 2012, 186. For an overview of the different terminologies used by scholars to refer to the different phases of Islamic transitional coinage, see Oddy/Schulze 2012, 187–193.
277 In Arab-Sasanian coinage before the second civil war (680–692), Arabic is used for validating marks as well as for short religious invocations placed on the outer margins of the coins. Conversely, Middle Persian in Pahlavi script is used for the obverse field legends – including

issuing authority, and mint) is only detailed in Middle Persian on pre-Marwanid Arab-Sasanian coinage, it appears on coeval Levantine copper coinage in both Greek *and* Arabic. The picture that emerges is that of a functional (rather than complementary) bilingualism in local provincial coinage 20 years before the implementation of the Arabic and all-epigraphic coinage at the hands of ʿAbd al-Malik.[278]

The epigraphical record from early Islamic Greater Syria also anticipates the development of forms of Arabic public writing in other regions by decades. Some light is shed on the dawning of Arabic monumental epigraphy in Medinan Syria by the so-called "Jerusalem 32" inscription, excavated in a small mosque at the foot of the Ḥaram al-Sharīf.[279] The official nature of the inscription is suggested by both its content and the high profile of the individuals mentioned in it. Despite the loss of much of the body of the main text, "Jerusalem 32" appears to commemorate the fall of Jerusalem and the implementation of the restrictions on "protected peoples" (*ahl al-dhimma*)[280] and is "witnessed" by the governor of Syria and later caliph Muʿāwiya and by the Companion of Muḥammad, ʿAbd al-Raḥmān b. ʿAwf al-Zuhrī as well as by the conqueror of Syria, Abū ʿUbayda b. al-Jarraḥ.[281] If the date on the inscription is to be believed, "Jerusalem 32" anticipates the first Sufyanid official epigraphies from the Arabian Peninsula by more than 20 years, and the Marwanid monumental inscriptions by 40. Unfortunately, the original context of the inscription – later reused as building material for the little mosque in which it was found – is lost, so that the dispositional practices connected with it are unknown. Use of Arabic in public epigraphy was not immediately monopolistic. As much is suggested by a Greek inscription which commemorates the restoration of the bathhouse in Hamat Gader[282] (ca. 190 km north of Jerusalem), patronized by the otherwise unknown governor (*symboulos*)[283]

Sasanian royal mottos like *GDH APZWT* "may kingship increase", the name of the issuing authority, and the reverse legends comprising mint name and date. Cf. the separation between administrative information (in Arabic) and propagandistic affirmations (in Sogdian) on the bilingual coin issued by Yazīd b. Ghūrak (776/777); see Naymark/Treadwell 2011. I thank Michael Shenkar for the reference.

278 Cf. Kaplony 2016, 400 and Legendre 2016, 17.

279 The so-called "Jerusalem 32" (mentioned in *CIAP* I, p. xiii and Rāġib 2013, 705, no. 6) inscription was found already in 1968 and has subsequently been in the editing process for 50 years.

280 For the early Islamic concept of *dhimma*, see Hoyland 2015b.

281 The text of "Jerusalem 32" has been edited and commented by Sharon 2018.

282 Di Segni 1997, 237–240 (54). For the transcription of Arabic names in the inscription in particular, see Blau 1982.

283 For the possible interpretations of the title *symboulos* in the inscription of Hammat Gader, see Hasson 1982, 100–101.

ʿAbd Allāh b. Abī Hāshim (or ʿĀṣim) (*fl.* 662), and mentions the caliph Muʿāwiya I using his full Arabic titulature.[284]

Returning to documents on papyrus, a comparatively high degree of Arabization of administrative practices in Syria-Palestine is suggested by what appears to be the remains of a bilingual Arabic/Greek protocol on *P.Ness.* 60.[285] The document is dated to 674, which would indicate that the provincial administration in Palestine had switched from a Byzantine protocol to a newer bilingual type 20 years before it was introduced in Egypt.[286] The nature of the supposed protocol, however, remains somewhat doubtful,[287] especially since the use of Byzantine protocols in Nessana is attested until 689.[288] Furthermore, whereas the "protocol" from Nessana is penned with a thin *kalamos* in dark brown ink, Egyptian examples are usually executed with brushes and, occasionally, using red ink.[289]

Contrary to coeval Egypt, in 7th-century Nessana Arabic was used for private financial documents involving both (arguably) Arabic and Greek contracting parties.[290] *P.Ness.* 56 is a bilingual Arabic/Greek deed of release in which one al-Aswad b. ʿAdī acknowledges the settlement of a considerable debt of fifty *solidi* contracted by a certain Apa[291] Kyros. As the document informs us, 30 of the 50 *solidi* were paid by Apa Kyros to al-Aswad in full; the remaining 20 were remitted by al-Aswad – though the exact nature of the transaction remains unclear.[292]

---

284 On the Greek transcriptions of Arabic terms in the inscription of Hamat Gader, see Hasson 1982, 99–101.

285 *P.GrohmannPapyrusProtokoll* 2 (= *P.Ness.* 60a).

286 The earliest specimen of a bilingual protocol from Egypt, *P.Gascou* 27a, is dated to 695.

287 Delattre/Vanthiegem 2016, 116 and Sijpesteijn 2020b, 466–467n111.

288 *P.Ness.* 76.

289 For the preparation of red tint in Islamic times, see Schopen 2006, 125–138. On the subject of ink manufacture in the Arabic writing tradition, see also the recent dissertation by Claudia Colini. I thank Tea Ghigo for the reference.

290 Cf. however the unpublished P.Vind.inv. A. P. 8711 (VIII), containing the remains of Arabic witnessing clauses followed by a notarial subscription in Greek by one Theodoros son of Apion (*supra* p. 77).

291 For the use of the title *abba* in papyri, see Derda/Wipszycka 1994. Cf. Papaconstantinou 2001, 241–245.

292 The editor of *P.Ness.* 56 interpreted the document as a release from a labor contract. Following this interpretation, the son of Apa Kyrin would have compensated 20 *solidi* of his father's original debt of 50 *solidi* through a period of work in al-Aswad's service. The sum of 20 *solidi*, however, seems much too high for this scenario. For comparison, the price of a slave boy is registered in *P.Ness.* 89 (Nessana; early VII) as 6 *nomismata*, and that of a camel oscillates between 4 1/3 and 15. See Trombley 2014. Cecilia Palombo ingeniously suggested to me that the document might concern an endowment rather than a personal debt as possibly hinted at by the use of the verb *ṣadaqa* (p.c. Mar. 23, 2018). Upon an examination of a digital picture of the document,

Though similarly structured, the Greek and the damaged Arabic versions differ considerably in wording. The Greek version is dated by day, month, and year after the Roman calendar, indiction year, and the provincial era; the Arabic version, after the Muslim era, by year only. Both versions of the agreement further include their own sets of witnesses. In the Arabic text, the signatures are not autographs, as is customary in legal papyri from this period.[293] The Greek version shows only one witness clause by one Sergios son of Georgios and a scribal signature by one Georgios son of Victor. Both scribe and witness of the Greek version are church clerks known from other documents in the Nessana dossier.[294] Though evidence is admittedly limited, the Nessana dossier underscores scribes' practical mastery of Arabic extending beyond merely administrative purposes and involving exchanges between Arabic- and Greek-writing population groups.

For southern Palestine, additional context for the comparatively swift Arabicization of local clerical practices is provided by pre-conquest documentary evidence. In particular the anthroponyms and toponyms as well as phonological peculiarities and formulaic phrases attested in the Greek from 6th- and early 7th-century Nessana and Petra (*P.Petra* I–V) indicate fluency in Arabic among the local Hellenograph population.[295] The fact that written Arabic had gained visibility and wider use in the region under the auspices of the Christian phylarchs of Late Antiquity, might also have provided the groundwork for its more capillary employment after the Arab conquest.[296]

however, I was unable to confirm F. Day's reading of the verb. I propose to read the verb as *haddā* instead. I thank Robert Hoyland for sharing with me a preliminary re-edition of *P.Ness.* 56.

293 Cf. Sijpesteijn 2020b, 440–441n20. Khan argues that for the first century and a half of Islamic rule, witnesses' autographs were registered in a separate document rather than on the legal deed they referred to. See Khan 1994, 200–201 and *id.* 2003, 234. *P.RagibJuridiction* 1 (Egypt; 662/663) and 2 (Egypt; 676/677) may possibly represent examples of such compilation of witness statements.

294 Kraemer 1958, 6–8; Montevecchi 1988, 261n96.

295 For the Arabic vernacular of pre-conquest Nessana, see Stroumsa 2008, 191–193 and *ead.* 2014. Cf. also the entries in Kaplony 2015. For Petra, see al-Ghul 2006, al-Jallad/Daniel/al-Ghul 2013, and al-Jallad 2018b. For traces of an Arabophone substrate in phonological features of the Greek papyri from Petra, cf. also Vierros 2018. For a more general overview, see also al-Jallad 2017a discussing papyrological material in tandem with (Old) Arabic items in epigraphic evidence from the region.

296 Hoyland 2018b, 335–336 in particular, challenges the notion that the adoption of written Arabic by Christians of the Syro-Arabian region was a consequence of religious conversion and the influence of the Umayyad administration. Rather he argues in favor of a continuity of use of written Arabic by Christians across the pre-Islamic and Early Islamic period. Hoyland's main piece of evidence, the Christian Arabic inscription from Kilwa, however, can possibly be dated to the Early Islamic period. On this inscription, see *infra* p. 308 and references there.

The latest documents in the Nessana dossier are dated or datable to the 690s, after which the town was seemingly abandoned. An outline of the subsequent permeation of Arabic in the administration and society of Syria-Palestine is provided by the trilingual group of documents unearthed at the site of Khirbat al-Mird (ca. 20 km east of Jerusalem). About 100 Arabic specimens – together with a handful of Greek and Christian Palestinian Aramaic ones – were discovered in the ruins of the former Herodian fortress of Hyrkania, converted in 493 into the Byzantine monastery *Kastellion*, known in Syriac as *Mardā* (>arab. *Mird*).[297] Unfortunately, most of the Arabic documents are in a poor state of preservation. The specimens bearing an absolute date or that can be dated on onomastic grounds go back to the early to mid-8th century, while a handful of undated texts can be assigned to the late 8th and even early 9th century based on paleographical and formulaic features.

Though a precise typological repartition of the Mird papyri is sometimes hindered by the fragmentary status of the documents, it is clear that the relative share of items between private and business correspondence is higher than in both coeval Egyptian papyri and the older group of documents from Nessana. In particular, the number of items of private (45), business-related (9), and legal (2) correspondence surpasses that of documents of administrative pertinence (ca. 24 official letters, 12 protocols, and 4 official lists). Of interest are also a few Arabic literary fragments[298] that possibly constitute the earliest dated literary pieces preserved on papyrus with a narrative structure.[299] These findings bear witness to the comparative variety of uses of Arabic literacy in mid-8th-century Syria-Palestine and herald the rise of Arabic as a language of scholarship and entertainment. By contrast, Greek and Christian Palestinian Aramaic (CPA) texts found at the site are almost exclusively items of liturgical literature.[300] A CPA papyrus represents the only non-Arabic documentary text in Mird and likely dates to the 7th century. From the content of the missive, as well as from the many figures of Christian religious speech and symbols, one may infer that the letter, addressed by one Gabriel (*gbryl*) to the abbot of the nearby Sabas monastery, belonged in a monastic context.[301]

297 For the discoveries of papyrological material at Khirbat al-Mird, see Wright/Milik 1961; Bardtke 1962, 51–53; and Grohmann 1963, XII–XIII.

298 *P.Mird* 71–73 (VIII).

299 On the shortcomings of the dating of several literary papyri from Egypt based on ascriptive criteria and prosopographical data, see Brockopp 2017, 104–113.

300 Milik 1953.

301 *Ibid.*, 533–537 with emendations by Wright/Milik 1961, 25–26.

Contrary to coeval Egypt, Arabic is furthermore employed in 8th-century Mird for both top-down and bottom-up, as well as horizontal official and private correspondence alike. Several Mird official letters portray local Arab (or Arabized?) village officials being instructed by their superiors on adjudicating local disputes[302] and reporting back to them.[303]

The onomasticon of the Mird documents equally reveals the prominent Arab component of the town. Of the 135 to 139 individuals' names attested in the Mird documentary papyri, all are Arabic and only three are explicitly Christian.[304] Only in very few instances does the onomasticon enable a distinction to be made between Arab immigrants,[305] an Arabicized local population, or an Arab local population. This is aggravated by the fact that very little is known of the nature of the settlement in Early Islamic times. Only a few names suggest a process of religious conversion. An individual whose first name is lost in a lacuna acting as witness in *P.Mird* 8 (728–737), son of Jurayj (the Arab diminutive version of Georgios), possibly hints at a first generation convert, though this is by no means a straightforward conclusion. With the addressee of *P.Mird* 48, a seemingly private letter, a certain Umm Sulaymān bt. Marqōs, one may possibly face a similar scenario. Three other individuals, referred to as *mawālī* (clients) in a fragmentary list of names, are potentially first generation converts as well.[306] In contrast, the mention of an individual as "father Yusūf" in *P.Mird* 50, a fragmentary letter concerning the land tax that can be dated to the early 9th century based on formulary and paleographical features, identifies him as a Christian.

An Arabic letter by one Anbā Magnillē, "the preacher" (*al-khāṭib*) to one Ḥabbān b. Yūsuf and the latter's answer on the *verso* of the same missive (*P.Mird* 45, 46) are of particular cultural interest with regard to the social reach of (written) Arabic in the region.[307] Both letters stand out for their use of the invocation *bi-sm al-āb wa-l-ibn wa-l-rūḥ al-quds bi-jawhar wāḥid* "in the name of the Father the Son and the Holy Ghost, in one essence" used as an opening invocation instead of the confessionally neutral – but culturally Muslim connoted – *basmala*. The two letters at issue constitute the first recorded use of Arabic in a recognizably

302 *P.Mird* 18 (viii), 19 (viii), 20? (754/755 or 756/757), 25 (viii), 29? (vii), 30? (viii), and 31 (viii).
303 *P.Mird* 23 (mid-viii) and 24 (viii).
304 Majilleh (< gr. Magnillos) in *P.Mird* 46v 1 (= *P.Mird* 45 r), 1; Faṭrīq (< gr. Patrikios) in *P.Mird* 19, 9; and Jurayj ("the little George") in *P.Mird* 8, 5.
305 Grohmann 1963, 39, 64, and 77 discusses *en passant* the few clan names and *nisbas* attested in the Arabic papyri from Khirbat al-Mird.
306 The *mawlā* of Madhḥij, the *mawlā* of al-Asad, and the *mawlā* of Ibn Kināna, in *P.Mird* 33, 4, 6, and 15 respectively.
307 *P.Mird* 45 and 46 (Khirbat al-Mird; viii).

inter-Christian milieu. By comparison, the earliest attestations of distinctively intra-Christian epistolography in Islamic Egypt date from the 9th and 10th centuries.[308] That one of the correspondents of *P.Mird* 45 and 46 has an Arab name and patronym, and can only be identified as a Christian by his use of a Trinitarian invocation, further alerts us to the permeability of onomastic and linguistic boundaries in the Arabophone Christian milieu in Syria-Palestine.

Though the evidence is circumstantial, in Khirbat al-Mird, close to the provincial capital of Jerusalem, the practice of Greek and CPA appears to have been confined to the liturgical ambit. By the mid-8th century, written Arabic appears to have entered private everyday short-term communication irrespective of confessional boundaries. Corroborating the impression of a comparatively swift spread of written Arabic among the – at least partially – already Arabophone Syrian Christians is a number of Arabic-inscribed lamps produced at several arguably Christian workshops in the Decapolis.[309] In turn, papyrological and archaeological evidence is substantiated by the comparatively early production of Arabic liturgic texts and Scripture by Melkite Christians in the monasteries of Palestine and the Sinai Peninsula, with dated specimens reaching as far back as the last quarter of the 8th century.[310]

A Language of Leisure: Arabic in the Arabian Peninsula (ca. 640–660)

Compared to the relative richness and typological variety of evidence for Early Islamic use of Arabic in Egypt and Palestine, information on the Arabian Peninsula, the core of the Medinan Caliphate, is restricted to a relatively limited semantic and typological spectrum. The scant archaeological information dated or datable to the 6th and 7th century further provides little context.

308 The first paleographically dated distinctively Arabic letter between Christians from Egypt is *P.AnawatiPapyrusChrétien* (Fusṭāṭ; IX).
309 Clermont-Ganneau 1900a; *id.* 1900b; Day 1942; Bagatti 1947, 141; *id.* 1963–1964, 267–269; Kennedy 1963, 89–90; Avigad 1976, 193, no. 53; Rosenthal/Sivan 1978, 133, no. 542–544; Tzaferis 1983, pl. XIV, no. 4; ʿAmr/Khairy 1986; ʿAmr 1986, 165–168; *id.* 1988; Walmsley *et al.* 1993, 228, no. 3; Hadad/Khamis 1998, 66–72. Cf. also the several Arabic graffiti and ink inscriptions occurring together with Greek letters and staurograms on amphorae from the recently discovered late 7th-/early 8th-century Maʿagan Mikhael B shipwreck (ca. 90 km north-west of Jerusalem). See Creisher/Goren/Artzy/Cvikel 2019, 111–112; I thank Uriel Simonsohn for the reference.
310 See *i.a.* Vollandt 2015, 27–28.

As already mentioned, distinct from other regions of the Empire, Arabic was a widespread vernacular in the north-west of the Arabian Peninsula prior to the rise of Islam. Together with comparatively few dedicatory and funerary inscriptions, the overwhelming majority of the North Arabian pre-Islamic written record consists of rock graffiti characterized by their informal and habitual nature and often containing little more than personal names.[311] Only rarely can these epigraphical testimonies be associated with the environment of written communication proper and only in a few instances are Arabian graffiti written for obvious practical purposes (e.g., the demarcation of property). Rather, graffiti prospered on the Arabian routes as a pastime and relief from boredom.[312] Invariably, pre-Islamic North Arabian epigraphic traditions became extinct in the material record before the rise of Islam. The tens of thousands of graffiti and inscriptions in the several ancient North Arabian scripts (Epigraphic North Arabic = ENA) dominate the epigraphical record of the region between the 6th century BCE and the 4th century CE, although there is a significant presence of inscriptions and graffiti in Achaemenid Official Aramaic,[313] as well as in several post-Achaemenid forms of Aramaic and – to a lesser extent – Greek. Based on the absence of references to Christianity (or Christians) in ENA graffiti, it is assumed that the ENA epigraphic tradition died out before the 4th century CE.[314] Nabatean inscriptions and graffiti survive into the 6th century, but no item is dated or datable to Islamic times. Similarly, dated ESA texts at the southern edge of the Peninsula disappear after the 6th century.[315]

The first sign of disruption of pre-Islamic literacy practices introduced to the Arabian Peninsula by the Islamic conquests is the "lifting the ban" on written Arabic. As early as 644 one Zuhayr, client of a certain Bint Shayba, engraved his name and affiliation in recognizably Arabic characters and Arabic language in the area of Madāʾin Ṣāliḥ (ca. 20 km north of al-ʿUlā) in the northern Ḥijāz.[316]

311 Updated checklists and preliminary editions of the known epigraphical testimonies from ancient North Arabia can be accessed on the website of the Online Corpus of the Inscriptions of Ancient North Arabia (*OCIANA*) http://krc.orient.ox.ac.uk/ociana/ (accessed Jan. 29, 2021). Useful introductory remarks to Ancient North Arabian graffitology can be found in al-Jallad 2015a, 2–25.
312 MacDonald 2009a, I, 84–85 and *id.* 2010, 15–16.
313 On the definition of Achaemenidian Official Aramaic and its discriminative linguistic and orthographic characteristics within the broader family of Imperial Aramaic (*Reichsaramäich*), see Gzella 2015, 157–165.
314 Hoyland 2009a, 391; al-Jallad 2015a, 17–18.
315 The latest dated inscription in Epigraphic South Arabic is *CIH* 541 dated 548. Radiocarbon dating analysis of private and legal documents on wooden sticks has also failed to individuate items datable to later than the 6th century. See Drewes *et al.* 2013 and Stein/Jocham/Marx 2016.
316 Ghabban 2008.

A second (undated) graffito by the same author was found nearby and is in all probability coeval.[317] Unlike their pre-Islamic counterparts, these epigraphies are devoid of Aramaic formulaic components and inaugurate a series of hundreds more, punctuating the caravan routes of the Arabian Peninsula and the Syrian Desert over the 7th and 8th centuries.

Functionally, Early Islamic Arabic graffiti follow essentially in the steps of their pre-Islamic counterparts. The continuity with the pre-Islamic epigraphical habit is also evidenced by structural features of several texts dated to the Early Islamic period. The formulaic structure of graffiti in Old North Arabic languages, *anā fulān* "I am N.N.", corresponds to *w-ʾn* N.N. in ENA graffiti.[318] At the same time, graffiti from the Islamic era also exhibit a number of innovative features mixed with more ancient scribal conventions. From the viewpoint of content, the most distinguishable characteristic of Early Islamic Arabic graffiti are pietistic invocations of both monotheistic and distinctively Islamic flair.[319] Some specimens even include quotations from the Qur'an.[320] When dated, Early Islamic Arabic graffiti further invariably display the newly implemented Islamic counting after the *hijra*. In addition to *hijrī* dates, however, several early Islamic Arabic graffiti use the vestigial Arabian dating system after several eponymous events. The already mentioned graffito of Zuhayr, for instance, exhibits a double dating clause: "at the time ʿUmar died, in the year 24". Similarly, a graffito left by one al-Rayyān b. ʿAbd Allāh in Ḥumā al-Numūr (ca. 30 km north-west of Ṭāʾif) is dated to "the year the Masjid al-Ḥarām was built (i.e.) in the year 78 (697/698)".[321] Similar double dating clauses are by contrast never encountered in coeval official inscriptions and other types of documentary sources. Furthermore, whereas dating clauses in papyrological and numismatic sources always use the term *sana* to indicate the year, in graffiti the use of the term *ʿām* is attested as well.[322] This is again never the case in documentary papyri, coins and official inscriptions.[323]

---

317 *Ibid.*, 214–215.

318 Al-Jallad 2015a, 95; King 1990 I, 4. A.5.

319 Ory 1990 and Imbert 2011.

320 Imbert 2000 and *id.* 2013a.

321 Published by Nāṣir b. Alī al-Hārithī in 2007 (*non vidi*). The image of the *graffito* with transcription and English translation is accessible on the *Islamic Awareness* website (https://www.islamic-awareness.org/history/islam/inscriptions/haram1.html; accessed Apr. 22, 2021).

322 See the graffito mentioned in the previous note.

323 Though inherently confined to the realm of private literacy practices, a number of Arabic graffiti directly address leading figures of the Early Islamic community including mentions of and possibly even autographs by various caliphs and members of the royal family from the Medinan to the Abbasid period. From a formal point of view, these testimonies belong in the broader cultural framework of coeval Arabic graffiti. For instance, a possibly autograph graffito by ʿAbd

A neater caesura with the pre-Islamic Arabian epigraphical habit is marked by the appearance of commissioned Arabic inscriptions conceived for public display and charged with imperial prestige. Two inscriptions dated to the reign of Muʿāwiya I demarcate dams of caliphal estates near Ṭāʾif[324] (ca. 780 km west of Riyadh) and Medina.[325] Almost contemporary and functionally identical, the two inscriptions nonetheless differ substantially in terms of formal structure:

Hoyland 2006: 413 (Medina: 661–680)

Invocation	(1) *bi-sm allāh al-raḥmān al-raḥīm* "In the name of God, the Merciful, the Compassionate"
Endophoric reference	(2) *hādhā al-sadd li-ʿabd allāh* (3) *muʿāwiya amīr al-muʾminīn* "this is the dam of the Servant of God Muʿāwiya, the commander of the believers"
Blessing	(4) *allāhumma bārik la-hu fī-hi* (5) *rabb al-samāwāt wa-l-arḍ* "Oh God, bless him for it, Lord of Heavens and the Earth"
Executive clause	(6) *banā-hu abū raddām mawlā* (7) *ʿabd allāh b. ʿabbās* "Has built it Abū Raddām, client of ʿAbd Allāh b. ʿAbbās"
Doxology	*bi-ḥaw*(8)*l allāh wa-quwwati-hi* "with God's help and His might"
Operative clause 2	(9) *wa-qāma ʿalay-hi kathīr b. a*(10)*l-ṣalt wa-abū mūsā* "and oversaw it Kathīr b. al-Ṣalt and Abū Mūsā"

AI Z 68 (Ṭāʾif; 677/678)

Endophoric reference	(1) *hādhā al-sadd li-ʿabd allāh muʿāwiya* (2) *amīr al-muʾminīn* "this is the dam of the Servant of God Muʿāwiya, the commander of the believers"

al-Malik b. Marwān adopts a subjective style rather than the "monumental" third person and follows the already mentioned *anā* + N.N. structure. For this body of material, see Imbert 2015.

324 *AI* Z 68 (= Miles 1948).

325 Hoyland 2006, 413. On the political dimension of Umayyad estates, see now Munt 2018 who interprets Umayyad concerns for acquiring or appropriating landed property in the hinterland of Medina as a means to contrast rival elite families – particularly the Zubayrids and the Alids – propertied in the same region.

Executive clause	*banā-hu ʿabd allāh b. Ṣakhr* "Has built it ʿAbd Allāh b. Ṣakhr"
Doxology	(3) *bi-idhn allāh* "With God's permission"
Date	*li-sanat thamān wa-khamsīn* "in the year fifty-eight"
Blessing	*a*(4)*llāhumma iġfir li-ʿabd allāh muʿāwiya a*(5)*mīr al-muʾminīn wa-thabbit-hu wa-unṣur-hu wa-mattʿ a*(6)*mīr al-muʾminīn bi-hi* "Oh God, forgive the Servant of God Muʿāwiya, the commander of the believers, fortify him, make him victorious, and grant the Commander of the believers enjoyment of it"
Scribal note	*kataba ʿamrū b. ḥabbāb* "ʿAmr b. Ḥabbāb wrote (it)"

The two inscriptions reveal evident formulaic affinities but also significant divergences from a structural point of view. In the first place, the inscriptions present a different number of lines. Furthermore, while for the inscription from Medina – albeit somewhat crudely executed – a purposefully cut and placed stone was used,[326] the one from Ṭāʾif is engraved on a loose rock which was even reused for a private graffito.[327] Both epigraphies contain an endophoric reference framed as *hādhā al-sadd li-ʿabd allāh muʿ(ā)wiya amīr al-muʾminīn* "this is the dam of the Servant of God Muʿāwiya, the commander of the believers". However, while the endophoric reference opens the inscription from Ṭāʾif, in that from Medina it is preceded by the invocation *bi-sm allāh al-raḥmān al-raḥīm*. In the inscription from Medina, the endophoric reference is followed by a benediction on the Caliph, by the executive clause *banā-hu* "has built it" followed by the name of the constructor, a short doxology, and a second executive phrase specifying the supervisor of the works. On the contrary, in the inscription from Ṭāʾif the blessing on the caliph and the second executive clause are missing, while the doxology is slightly different from the one used in the inscription from Medina. Rather, the specimen from Ṭāʾif displays a date after the doxology and the "signature" of the engraver, which are lacking in the Medina counterpart. The similarities between the phraseology of Muʿāwiya's inscription in Medina and that in Ṭāʾif implicates a process of standardization of official formulae. At the same time, the structural

326 A color image of Muʿāwiya's inscription near Medina is provided by al-Zalaʿī 2010, 487.
327 *AI* Z 69 (VII).

differences between the two epigraphies is testimony to the fluidity of official formularies in the Sufyanid period.

As in the papyrological and numismatic record, the rise to power of the Marwanid dynasty is marked by a new dimension in the use of public epigraphy in Arabic to promulgate imperial ideology across the lands of the Empire. Marwanid monumental Arabic inscriptions have been found at the 8th-century Umayyad residences of Qaṣr al-Ḥayr al-Gharbī[328] (ca. 94 km south-east of Homs), Khirbat al-Minya[329] (ca. 130 km north of Jerusalem), Qaṣr al-Ḥayr al-Sharqī[330] (ca. 120 km north-east of Palmyra), and Qaṣr Burquʿ[331] (ca. 245 km north-east of Amman). Umayyad patronage is connected with other coeval infrastructural projects by the inscriptions found in Baysān/Scythopolis,[332] al-Muwaqqar[333] (ca. 25 km south-east of Amman), and Bouar[334] (ca. 32 km north of Beirut). To these, a series of eight milestones originally installed along routes built or renovated during ʿAbd al-Malik's reign along the routes connecting Damascus and Tiberias,[335] Jerusalem and Ludd/Jaffa,[336] and Jerusalem and Damascus[337] can be added. Of arguably more "intimate" nature but still to some extent conceived for larger audiences are the Arabic fresco inscriptions that adorned the interior of the reception hall in the Umayyad reservoir in Quṣayr ʿAmra.[338] Inscriptional programs linked to Marwanid endowment of cultic architecture are attested

328 *RCEA* I 27 (727).
329 Ritter 2016a p. 65 (743–744?).
330 *RCEA* I 28 (729).
331 *RCEA* I 12 (700/701).
332 *CIAP* II p. 207, no. 1 (737/738?).
333 Hamilton 1946, 70–72 (722/723).
334 *RCEA* I 25. For a possible integration of the inscription and a dating in the reign of al-Walīd II (*rg.* 743–744), see Sauvaget 1944, 96–102.
335 *CIAP* III p. 220, no. 1 (Fīq; 704), *CIAP* III p. 221, no. 2 (Fīq; 704). The beginning of works on the route between Damascus and Tiberias is attested by a further inscription *AI* p. 368 (692) commemorating the levelling of the mountain pass of Fīq.
336 *CIAP* I p. 4 no. 1 (= *RCEA* I 17) (Abū Ghūsh; 685–705), *RCEA* I 15 (Bāb al-Wādī; 685–705), and Silverman 2007 p. 605 (ʿAyn Ḥamad; 685–705).
337 *CIAP* III p. 104, no. 1 (= *RCEA* I 16) (Dayr al-Qalt; 685–705) and *CIAP* III p. 104–105 no. 2 (= *RCEA* I 14) (Dayr al-Qalt; 685–705).
338 See now Imbert 2016, 332 (south wall above west window), 337 (south wall, at eye-level), 340 (south wall, central niche), 341–342 (south wall above east window). The pictorial decoration of Quṣayr ʿAmra also comprises bilingual Arabic/Greek labels flanking the figures of the so-called "six kings" fresco on the west wall, Imbert 2016, 344–346 (= *RCEA* I 23) and Greek labels flanking personification of History, Poetry, and Inquiry in the east aisle of the south wall and of Grace(?) and Victory over a royal scene depicted the south wall of the west aisle, see Fowden 2004, 87–88 and 192–194 respectively.

for the Dome of the Rock,[339] with the two inscriptions on copper plaques over the eastern[340] and northern[341] entrances, as well as the epigraphical frieze on the outer[342] and inner[343] side of the octagon and for the al-ʿUmarī Mosque in Bosra.[344] Whereas in Greater Syria several Umayyad building projects and inscriptional cycles have survived to the present day with little alteration, officially sponsored Umayyad architecture on the Arabian Peninsula has been unrecognizably tampered with over the centuries and is only known through later literary reports. Inscriptions commemorating Umayyad restorations of the Prophet's Mosque in Medina in 706/707[345] and 749/750[346] are known through accounts by Ibn Rustah (*fl.* x). Al-Azraqī († 837) further reports on two inscribed crescent-shaped ornaments sent by al-Walid II to be kept in the Kaʿba.[347] The text of the running mosaic inscription from the Umayyad Mosque of Damascus is described in reports by al-Masʿūdī and al-Balādhurī.[348] Al-Maqrīzī is further the source for the already mentioned inscription on the bridge of al-Fuṣṭāṭ.[349] Finally, al-Jahshiyārī († 942) provides the text for a mosaic inscription of the Umayyad residence in Acre[350] and of two specular inscriptions originally allocated on the entrance to the ports of Sidon and Acre.[351]

We will turn to the stylistic dimension of the formal and aesthetic features of the Early Islamic official written artefacts *in extenso* in the following two chapters. Here it will suffice to remark that the relative numerical plenty of Marwanid official Arabic inscriptions corresponds to a much closer standardization of formulaic, layout, and aesthetic features of Marwanid (and later Abbasid) official

339 The question of the date of the *completion* of the Dome of the Rock was at the center of some debate in the 1990s and early 2000s. See Blair 1992, who suggests that the traditional date for the construction of the Dome of the Rock (692) refers to the beginning of the works. This interpretation has been addressed and rejected by Johns 2003, 424–426.
340 *RCEA* I 10 (691/692).
341 *RCEA* I 11 (691/692).
342 *RCEA* I 9.
343 *RCEA* I 10.
344 Suvaget 1947 p. 52, no. 2 (745/746). See also the re-edition by Ory 2005 no. 2.
345 Sauvaget 1947 p. 66*.
346 Sauvaget 1947 p. 58 E* (= *RCEA* I 46* with corrections in *RCEA* XIV p. 275) (749/750).
347 *RCEA* I 26*; the date of the inscriptions is reported by al-Azraqī as 101 (719/720) which must be a mistake; cf. Grabar 1959, 50 and *ibid.*n98.
348 The literary descriptions of the inscriptional program of the Umayyad mosque of Damascus are collected by Flood 2001, 252–253 (= *RCEA* I 18a–b*) (705–706).
349 *RCEA* I 8*.
350 *CIAP* I p. 30–31, no. 1*(= *RCEA* I 32*) (ca. 742/743).
351 *CIAP* I p. 31, no. 2* (= *RCEA* I 37*) (750).

inscriptions as compared to the Medinan and Sufyanid period.[352] The formulary and set of operative clauses characterizing Marwanid period inscriptions further find close parallels in coeval numismatic and sigillographic evidence, as well as on Arabic papyrus protocols.[353]

To summarize, an overview of Early Islamic Arabic epigraphy in the Arabian Peninsula evidences the existence of two parallel formal registers. Substratal centuries-old pre-Islamic epigraphical habits and scribal convention live on in informal practices of Arabic literacy. Concomitantly, more representational uses of Arabic public epigraphy betray an endeavor towards an imperial canon culminating in the formal *koine* of Marwanid and later official epigraphy.

The Former Sasanian Domains (7th–8th Centuries)

The ravages of time have been especially unforgiving towards Early Islamic administrative documentation from the core lands of the former Sasanian Empire in Iraq and Iran. The initial spread of Arabic in the region is almost exclusively traceable through the appearance of Arab-Sasanian coinage produced in former Sasanian mints. The Sasanian-style coinage minted by the invading Arabs dovetails nicely with the route of the retreating Yazdgerd III. These early monetary issues are almost indistinguishable from regular ones minted in the territories still under the aegis of the last *Shāhān-shāh* apart from the odd combinations of mintmarks and dates and a few stylistic *minutiae*.[354]

Within the limited range of text information they provide, Arab-Sasanian coins nonetheless offer valuable information on the implementation of novel administrative practices. From 651 onwards, dates on Arab-Sasanian silver coinage according to the Yazdgerd Era are progressively supplanted by *hijrī* dates, and Arabic legends appear as validating marks on the coins' outer margin.[355] In notable contrast with the so-called copper "Umayyad Imperial Image coinage" from Greater Syria, Arab-Sasanian monetary emissions are not functionally bilingual. Arabic and Pahlavi legends are not translations of each other but rather two visually and semantically independent components of the coins (Chapter II). More specifically, administrative information proper is kept only in Middle Persian, whereas Arabic is only used for validating marks on the outer margin – usually

352 Gaube 1982, 213–214; Blair 1998, 29–42; and Ritter 2016a 64–68.

353 For issuing clauses in Early Islamic sigillography, see in particular Balog 1976, 4–9. For numismatics, see in particular Balog 1977, 63. For protocols, see Grohmann 1923–1924, XXVII–C.

354 Nikitin/Roth 1995.

355 Heidemann 2010a, 163.

left blank on standard Sasanian coins.[356] This repartition establishes Arabic as the language of the validating authority operating at the highest echelons of the provincial administration. Pahlavi administrative legends on Arab-Sasanian coinage, however, indicate the resilience of Sasanian administrative practices functioning almost unaltered at a provincial level.

Insights into daily administrative routines at a localized level are faced with insurmountable geographic constraints with one notable exception. A cache of around 300 (mostly unedited) post-Sasanian documents on parchment, leather, and linen is housed at the Berkeley collection, at the Freie Universität in Berlin, as well as in minor deposits scattered across various private collections. Several of the toponyms mentioned in the so-called "Pahlavi Archive" can be identified with historical and modern localities situated in the area surrounding the city of Qom[357] (140 km south-west of Tehran), whence the documents probably originated.[358] Qom and its hinterland were reportedly subdued by the Arabs after brief resistance in the aftermath of the decisive Sasanian defeat at Nihānwand (642), likely at the hands of the commander Abū Mūsā al-Ashʿarī († 662?) or by one of his lieutenants – though several details on the modalities and chronology of the conquest remain unclear.[359]

Thematically, the documents of the Pahlavi Archive are overwhelmingly concerned with economic and fiscal issues related to the internal administration of a number of rural estates.[360] Several of the documents bear dates. Internal and prosopographical data indicate that the dating system used in several of the documents from Qom is according to the post-Yazdgerd era (PYE).[361] The hitherto edited or otherwise discussed texts extend over roughly a century, from the mid-7th to the mid-8th century.

The MP documents profile a conglomerate of settlements of different dimensions organized in a single administrative unity (*ostān*) headed by an omnipresent, yet never referred to by name, *ostāndār*.[362] Single settlements are placed under the leadership of members of the local Zoroastrian aristocracy. One of the most prominent of these, Yazdānpādār, can be confidently identified with the

356 Gaube 1973, 9–55.
357 See in particular Weber 2010, 37–45.
358 See in particular Gignoux 2004.
359 The narratives concerning the Arab conquest of Qom are examined in detail by Drechsler 1999, 69–74.
360 Azarpay *et al.* 2003; Gignoux 1991, 1996, 2001, 2004, 2008, 2009, and 2010; Weber 2008b, 2011, and 2012.
361 On the question of the dating of the Middle Persian documents in the Berkeley collection, see in particular Weber 2008b; cf. Azarpay *et al.* 2003.
362 Weber 2010, 57–60.

local leading Zoroastrian magnate Yazdānfādhār, known from the late 10th-century Arabic *History of Qom* by Ḥassan al-Qommī († 988/989).[363] According to the *History*, Yazdānfādhār co-opted Arab tribes in protecting Qom's countryside against local bandits in exchange for land in 702. After the death of Yazdānfādhār in 733, however, social tensions between the new settlers and the native Persian population reportedly escalated in the murder of the local Zoroastrian nobility and the confiscation of their estates, thus prompting more extensive Arab settlement in the area.[364]

Arab presence in the region is in fact sporadically referenced in the MP documents, most notably in the form of the mention of several Muslim fiscal authorities and institutions. The involvement of Arab officials in the local fiscal administration is evidenced by the reference to an *'myl* < arab. *amīr*.[365] A measurer of land subjected to the *kharāj* (*frashn-hargarīg*) is mentioned in Berk. 27 (693/694),[366] while the institution of a poll-tax (*gazīdag*) is referenced in Berk. 67 (667/668).[367] Little context is given in the Pahlavi Archive for the agency of these officials, who did not exercise nominal civil authority in the region, as this appeared to have lain with the *ostāndār*. By analogy, it is tempting to see the *amīr*s mentioned in the Pahlavi Archive as serving in similar functions as the amirs placed by the central Arab authority at the side of Christian dukes and pagarchs in the 640s and 650s in Egypt.[368]

It is clear that the entourage of Arab officials comprised local "liaison officials". Berk. 244, for instance, mentions one Māhgušnasp serving as a scribe (*dibīr*)[369] of one *amīr* Abdīn.[370] Other references to an Arab presence in the region include the mention of the office for the "surveillance of the mosque" (*peshānīg*

363 Weber 2008b.

364 For a detailed account, see Drechsler 1999, 78–102.

365 The MP lemma *'myl* occurring in the Pahlavi Archive was originally interpreted by the editor as a rendering of the Arabic term *'āmil* (lit. "agent"), a denomination for tax collectors in Early Islamic documents from Egypt and Central Asia. This reading has now been reinterpreted as a rendering of the Arabic *amīr*; see Weber 2014, 181 and *ibid*.n14. I thank Dieter Weber for the reference.

366 First published by Gignoux 2001, no. 2 with emendations by Weber in Azarpay *et al.*, 27; reedited by Weber 2013b, 172–174.

367 Weber 2013b, esp. 174–175 and *id.* 2008b, 218. To the best of the author's knowledge, the only other reference to *gazīd(ag)* in MP can be found in a Medieval poem edited by de Blois (2000). I thank Thomas Benfey for the reference.

368 For the role of Early Islamic *amirs*, see Morelli 2010b and Legendre 2016, 7–9.

369 For possible Arabic cognates of the term *dibīr*, see Frye 1977, 239.

370 I thank Dieter Weber for discussing Berk. 244 with me (p.c. Nov. 16, 2018). The reading of the names should be considered tentative until its publication.

ī mazgītan) in Berk. 187, a letter addressed to the *ostāndār*.[371] Assuming that the issuing official was an Arab, it appears that as elsewhere in the Empire at this stage, the members of the Arab-Muslim elite used the local idiom to communicate with the local land aristocracy. The complete absence of 7th- and 8th-century documents in Arabic in the Pahlavi Archive is in fact not completely unexpected, as the thematic focus of the archive revolves around the internal management of local rural communities where Arab presence at this historical juncture would have been minimal. The lack of demand notes concerning taxes, however, is noticeable. A few MP documents from Berkeley furthermore stem from the immediate entourage of the *ostāndār*.[372] At this layer of the local administration as well, however, neither the content nor the onomasticon of the documents so-far published betrays the presence of Arab or Arabic practicing personnel.

Public use of Arabic in the region is in fact attested at a higher administrative layer through numismatics. Bilingual Arabic/MP Arab-Sasanian silver coinage of the Khusraw type had been issued by Umayyad governors in the neighbouring districts of Rayy, Hamdān, Jayy, and possibly in Qom itself[373] since the 660s. That the local population was exposed to other forms of Arabic writing is further indirectly evinced from some of the later documents from the Pahlavi Archive. Three documents exhibiting a particularly cursive late ductus (B2)[374] distinguish themselves by the occurrence of the opening invocation *pad nām ī yazd* "In the name of god".[375] The use of religious invocations in the heading is unattested in pre-Islamic Pahlavi documents as well as in the earlier dated or datable texts from Qom. Rather, the invocation indicates a transposition of the Arabic *basmala*.[376] Unfortunately, in all three examples only the lower section of the letter – where address and greeting formulae are repeated – [377] is preserved so that it is unclear whether the missives contained other adaptations of Arabic formulae (Chapter IV).

A group of five undated fragmentary Arabic papers housed in the Berkeley collection[378] appears to share the same provenance as the MP documents.[379] The

371 Weber 2008b, 219 and *id.* 2014, 181.
372 Most notably Weber 2011.
373 Gyselen 1983, 236–238 argues in favor of interpreting the Pahlavi mintmark *GW* on Arab-Sasanian drachms of the Khusraw type as Qom.
374 For the different ductus attested in the Pahlavi Archive, see Weber 2008b, 215–216.
375 Weber 2008b, 216 and *id.* 2014, 180. On the formula *pad nām ī yazd*, see *infra* Ch. IV, *Negotiating "Arab Style"* (Arab-style Middle Persian Letters).
376 The transposition of group-specific Arabic formularies into substrate languages (including MP) is extensively discussed in Ch. IV.
377 Weber 1992, 234–236 and *id.* 2008a, 804–809 (part C).
378 *P.KhanBerkeley* 1–5.
379 Azarpay *et al.* 2003, 17 and Khan 2003.

mention of the *kharāj* tax in one of the Arabic items[380] hints at official correspondence while the other fragments appear to be tokens of private written exchange. The use of paper,[381] together with formulaic and terminological choices, as well as the cursive features of the documents suggest that the Arabic materials should be dated no earlier than the 9th century.[382] Notably, none of the published MP documents can be dated as late.

To summarize, the evidence from the Pahlavi and Arabic documents from Qom does not allow for the reconstruction of a linear progression of the Arabization of the local communities. It is tempting to interpret the abrupt shift from MP to Arabic in the Berkeley archive as the long-term consequence of the appropriation of Qom's countryside by Arab tribesmen described in al-Qommī's *History*.

Some contextual evidence for the Pahlavi Archive can be found in the hundreds of MP ostraca that have surfaced at several sites in Iran and Khurāsān[383] – most of which were unearthed by Herzfeld in 1926 in Warāmīn (near Rayy).[384] The overwhelming majority of these texts is undated and can be roughtly assigned to the late Sasanian period based on linguistic and palaeographic features.[385] One exception to this rule is *CII, O.* 197 from the town of Qaṣr-ī Abū Naṣr (near Shiraz), which seemingly bears the date 83 PYE (= 714/715 CE). This indicates that it cannot be *ipso facto* excluded that further undated MP ostraca may have been penned during the early Islamic period as well.

Of particular interest in this regard is the bilingual dossier found in a palatial complex at Chāl Tarkhān-ʿEshqābād (ca. 20 km south-east of Rayy), close to the larger finspot of the late Sasanian ostraca in Warāmīn. The site appears to have been a late Sasanian foundation but stylistic details of the stucco decoration indicate contined use into the Umayyad and possibly Early Abbasid period.[386] As much is also suggested by Umayyad and Abbasid coinage struck in Rayy found at the site and minted as late as 822/823.[387] A dating into the late

380 *P.KhanBerkeley* 5.

381 In the 9th-century cache of documents found in the *Dār al-ʿAmma* in Sāmarrā' both papyrus (*P.HerzfeldSamarra* 1 and 2) and paper (*P.HerzfeldSamarra* 3, 4, 5, and 6) are used. For these documents, see Reinfandt 2012. With the help of Peter Arnold Mumm, Desmond Durkin-Meisterernst, and Michael Shenkar, I was able to determine that the unedited backside of *P.HerzfeldSamarra 6* is written in Sogdian and not in Arabic as previously presumed by Herzfeld and all subsequent scholars.

382 Khan 2003, 34.

383 Mostly published in *CII* (*O.* 1–199); see also Nikitin 1992 and Weber 2003.

384 *CII, O.* 1–190.

385 On the problem of dating MP ostraca, see in particular Weber 2003, 277.

386 The stuccos from Chāl Tarkhān-ʿEshqābād are published by Thompson 1976.

387 Some of the coins found in Chāl Tarkhān-ʿEshqābād were discussed by Miles 1938.

Sasanian and Early Islamic period is corroborated by a cache of MP (ca. 25)[388] and Arabic (ca. 6)[389] ostraca excavated in the complexes.[390] Based on the late ductus, Frye and Weber tentatively assigned the MP pieces to the 7th/8th century.[391] As for the Arabic ones, the images published by Thompson suggest a dating no earlier than the 9th century.[392] As for the content, there are hints of functional overlap between the Pahlavi and Arabic ostraca, both of which contain receipts for deliveries of bread[393] as well as other texts pertaining to the internal administration of the estate.[394] The uncertain palaeographic dating of the documents, combined with the lack of prosopographical links,[395] however, makes it difficult to divine the exact functional and chronological interplay of the Arabic and Pahlavi ostraca.

Ṭabaristān

For the sake of completeness, mention should be made of a cache of documents yielded by Early Abbasid Ṭabaristān between the Caucasus Mountains to the south and the Caspian shores to the North. The richness of the deposits of

---

388 CT-75, CT-85/1, CT-85/2 r/v, CT-94, CT-97, CT-101 (?), CT-102, CT-110, CT-133/1, CT-133/2, CT-133/3, CT-133/4, CT-134, CT-135/2, CT-135/4 (?), CT-135/5 r/v, CT-139 (?), CT-140/1, and Thompson 1976, pl. XXXII, Fig. 2 (no inv. no.). Cf. the slightly different numbers given by Weber 2003, 276–277. Another 4 MP ostraca not listed by either Thompson or Weber could be located at the Oriental Institute in Chicago (CT-205/1, CT-205/3a, CT-205/3b, and CT-205/4). I thank Helen McDonald for this information (email of May 20, 2021) and for sending pictures of the ostraca to Thomas Benfey and myself.

389 CT-92/1, CT-123, CT-195, and Thompson 1976, pl. XXXII, Fig. 1 (no inv. no.). CT-162/2 is possibly bilingual. CT-40 r/v, which was identified as Sogdian by Chr. Reck and W. Sundermann *apud* Weber 2003, 276, seems to me to be Arabic as well.

390 The MP ostraca are edited by Weber 2003. Images of the MP and Arabic ostraca from Chāl Tarkhān-ʿEshqābād are published by Thompson 1976, pls. XXVI–XXVI.

391 Thompson 1976, XII.

392 Cf. the dating suggested by Heidemann *apud* Weber 2003, 276. The dating to the 4th/5th c. AH suggested by Heidemann for CT-123 (= Arab. 02 in Weber 2003) seems to be too late to me.

393 See Weber 2003, 278–279 (in Pahlavi) and Thompson 1976, pl. XXXV (Fig. 1) (in Arabic): *bi-sm allāh al-raḥmān al-raḥīm*| *ʿalā yaday muḥammad*| *ithnā ʿashar akhbāzan* (sic?)| *wa-qabaḍtu*(?) *ʿalā yaday aḥmad* (. . .) "In the name of God, the Merciful the Compassionate| at the hands of Muḥammad 12 pieces of bread| and I received at the hands of Aḥmad (. . .)".

394 See for instance Thompson 1976, pl. XXXVI (Fig. 1), which appears to be a scribal exercise of numerals between 13 and 19.

395 All individuals mentioned in the (edited) Pahlavi ostraca from Chāl Tarkhān bear Iranian names. Judging from Thompson's (1976) plates, it seems to me that all names mentioned in the Arabic ostraca are likewise Arab.

silver and the agricultural lowlands made Ṭabaristān a worthy prize for foreign would-be conquerors, were it not for the infamous unevenness of its terrain and the ruthlessness of its rulers often immortalized by medieval Muslim accounts. Arab attempts to invade the country were repelled in 670 and 712 by the Dābūyid dynasty. It was not until half a century later that the armies of the future caliph al-Mahdī (*rg.* 775–785) found their way into the region in an attempt to recover the treasure of Abū Muslim, reportedly smuggled into Ṭabaristān by the fleeing rebel Sunbadh.[396]

The years leading to the annexation of Ṭabaristān by the Abbasid caliphate are documented in a dossier of about 30 MP documents housed in a private collection.[397] Several texts are dated according to the post-Yazdgerd era and cover a time span dated between 738 and 759. Thus, the latest specimens in the dossier are contemporaneous with the Abbasid invasion of the region (759), culminating in the overthrow of the Dābūyids and the submission – at least *de iure* – of Ṭabaristān in 761.[398]

The documents seemingly belonged to a private archive located in the unidentified village of Haspīn-raz (possibly to be identified with modern Rūdbār)[399] in the Daylam region. Most texts are court records of civil cases debated in the presence of local dignitaries as well as leases, loans, and compensation agreements. In fact, macro-historical events are never referenced in the Ṭabaristān archive. Structural, onomastic, and formulaic features of the documents furthermore reveal no signs of influence from the Arabic legal and/or scribal tradition.[400] In particular, studies in the juridical technical terminology and the formal structure of the legal documents from Ṭabaristān reveal close conformity with Sasanian legal practice and juridical jargon as known through later Zoroastrian literature.[401]

---

396 For Sunbadh's uprising, see Crone 2012, 32–40.

397 Gignoux 2012 (Tab. 1–8, 10, 12, 14, 21, 22, 26, and 28), *id.* 2014 (Tab. 11, 13, 15–20, 23, and 27); and *id.* 2016 (Tab. 24 and 25). Tab. 1–8, and 10 have been thoroughly reedited by Weber 2016a with useful commentaries by Macuch 2016; Tab. 12 and 26 by Weber 2016b; Tab. 13–15, 17, 18, and 23 by Weber 2017 with useful commentaries by Macuch 2017.

398 For the history of Ṭabaristān in the early Abbasid period, see Haug (forthcoming).

399 On the tentative reading of Haspīn-raz, see Weber 2016a, 124; on the possible location of this site, see *id.* 2017, 131–132.

400 For examples of Arabic scribal influences on Early Islamic documents produced outside the Early Islamic Empire, see Ch. IV and especially *Parallel Scribal Traditions* (The Arab Style on the Eastern Frontier).

401 Macuch 2016; *ead.* 2017; Weber 2016; and *id.* 2017.

A Language of Pledge: Arabic in Central Asia (8th century)

Much like Ṭabaristān, the natural defenses and the hostile terrain combined with the geographical remoteness ensured the resilience of the Central Asiatic principalities to military conquest at the hands of the Arabs. In the regions to the south of the Hindukush in particular, conquering efforts were repeatedly frustrated by the counterattacks of the *rutbīl*s of Zabulistān. The latest and most thorough Umayyad attempt to set foot in the region famously backfired as the proverbial "peacock army" lead by Ibn al-Ash'ath formed a coalition with the *rutbīl* and rose in rebellion against al-Ḥajjāj b. Yūsuf. An echo of the Arab losses in the region even found its way into the coinage of the local rulers, at times boasting their success against the invading Arab armies.[402]

Overall, the Arabs had better luck to the North with the Sogdian cities located along the course of the river Zarafshān and the Bactrian settlements around the oasis of Balkh. Even there, however, caliphal expansion was faced with severe setbacks and the establishment of an Arab presence in the region had to be negotiated rather than gained through sheer martial superiority. Despite the successful incursions of the Medinan and Sufyanid age, the Arabs had yet to establish a firm footing in the region when the Second Civil War broke out and resulted in their gains largely being reversed. Most of the area finally fell to the armies of Qutayba b. Muslim († 715/716) only to be swamped again by Turgesh incursions in the 720s. Although the Arabs were ultimately successful in driving the Turgesh out, the caliphal hold over the lands to the north of the Hindukush, except for a few crucial strongholds, was tenuous and the region remained a borderland for which the Muslims, the Chinese, the Turgesh as well as local principalities contended.

Unlike southern Afghanistan, our knowledge of Early Islamic Sogdia and Bactria is blessed with comparatively rich findings of coeval documentary materials.

Sogdia

In 1932, local shepherds found a paper document in an enigmatic script amidst the ruins of the fortress of Mount Mugh in the Zarafshān valley in modern-day Tajikistan. Upon competent examination, the script of the document was determined to be Sogdian. The discovery triggered more systematic excavations by Soviet archaeologists in 1933, which resulted in the emergence of hundreds of objects including a quadrilingual archive of documents on paper, leather, and

402 See *i.a.* Sims-Williams 2008, 123–125.

textiles. In addition to the already mentioned Sogdian text, other 75 Sogdian documents, an Arabic letter on parchment, several Chinese texts on textiles, and one letter in Turkish runic script could be identified.[403] The texts belonged to the archive of the ruler of Panjakent and self-styled king of Sogdia Dēwāshtīch, who took refuge in the Mugh fortress in 722 after his involvement in a local uprising. He was subsequently besieged and eventually captured by the troops of the Arab governor Saʿīd b. ʿAmr Ḥarashī (in office 722–723) to be pubblicaly executed shortly thereafter.[404]

The Sogdian documents from the Mugh archive are mostly intelligence reports produced in the later years of Dēwāshtīch's rule, as well as legal documents belonging to Sogdian aristocrats. In the archive, three letters stand out for detailing incoming and outgoing correspondence of Arab governors of Khurāsān. *P.Kratchkovski*, the only Arabic item of the archive, is a letter addressed by Dēwāshtīch to the *amīr* of Khurāsān al-Jarrāḥ b. ʿAbd Allāh (in office 717–719), petitioning for the custody of the sons of the former ruler of Samarkand for safekeeping. Two other items are in Sogdian. The first is a fragmentary letter by the *amīr* Saʿīd b. ʿAbd al-ʿAzīz (in office 720–721) to a "chief scribe of Samarkand" whose name is lost in a lacuna.[405] The second is a letter by the *amīr* ʿAbd al-Raḥmān b. Ṣubḥ to Dēwāshtīch himself. The capacity of the sender is somewhat opaque: possibly ʿAbd al-Raḥmān was acting as an intermediary between Dēwāshtīch and the governor of Khurāsān as the mention of a letter by the latter would suggest.[406]

A second smaller dossier of Early Islamic documents has been excavated in nearby Sanjar-Shah. Seven Arabic paper fragments were unearthed there in a fortified structure and could be combined to form three fragmentary letters.[407] As the site was abandoned in the 770s–780s,[408] the letters should be dated between 721 (when the first Arab presence in the region is recorded) and that time. Though the documents are too fragmentary to enable a precise assessment of their nature, the mention of a military commander (*amīr*), the purely Arab onomasticon, the

403 For the discovery, the archaeological context, and the edition of the Mugh documents, see Yakubovich 2002, 232–234; Semenov 2002; and Livshits 2015, 15–16.

404 For Dēwāshtīch's role in the anti-Arab Sogdian revolts, see Yakubovich 2002, 244–249 and Grenet/de la Vaissière 2002. On the function of public executions in the affirmation of Umayyad legitimacy, see Marsham 2011 and Anthony 2014.

405 The text was partially edited by Livshits 1962, 221 without being assigned an edition number. An image of the document is provided by Livshits 2015, 204–205.

406 The interpretation of several key passages in the letter remains open to interpretation, see Yakubovich 2002, 235–244.

407 *P.HaimPaper* 1–3. *P.HaimPaper* 2 and *P.HaimPaper* 3 may theoretically be two fragments of the same letter.

408 Haim/Shenkar/Kurbanov 2016, 142 and 157.

general tone of camaraderie[409] in the missives, and the place they were found coincide to suggest that we are dealing with the correspondence of Arab forces stationed in the region.

In its limited extent, documentary evidence provides a comparatively variegated outline of the language dynamics involved in written communication in early 8th-century Central Asia. These largely conform to those in coeval Egypt. Arab authorities *in loco* notably rely on local vernaculars to carry out top-down written communication with the local aristocracy, while the Arab military elite uses Arabic in insider communication. Whether the missives of the *amīr*s of the Khurāsān or those of middle-ranking officers like ʿAbd al-Raḥmān b. Ṣubḥ to Dēwāshtīch and his like were also accompanied by an Arabic copy like those of Qurra to Basileios is not known. Then again, Dēwāshtīch was a formally independent ruler and not directly subordinate to Arab authorities like Basileios.

Dēwāshtīch's Arabic petition to al-Jarrāḥ is an unparalleled example of bottom-up communication involving the uppermost layers of the Arab imperial administration. The document shows a scribal addendum (l. 11, *ilā \sulaymān b. abī al-sarī/*) and was possibly a draft as its finding in Dēwāshtīch's refuge would suggest. As I shall discuss later in greater detail (Chapters II, III, and IV), the letter's formulary and *mise en page* show an effort to reproduce the typical layout and formulaic structure of Arabic official epistolography known from similar documents from Egypt and Syria. From other reports in the Mugh archive one infers that Dēwāshtīch employed Arabs in his service[410] – though no scribe is mentioned – but the letter could also have been penned by a Sogdian bilingual scribe as some formal anomalies in the text could indicate.[411] For the purpose of the present chapter, it is the decision to use Arabic that holds relevance. Dēwāshtīch's resolve to issue a letter in Arabic entailed a symbolic *captatio benevolentiae* towards the addressee as well as a form of scribal politesse but is also indicative of social prestige being associated with Arabic. A few generations later, both Arabic and bilingual Sogdian/Arabic legends likewise occasionally appear in the coinage of Sogdian tributaries of the Arabs, such as the *ikhshīd*s of Ishtikhān and the *dehqān*s of Keshsh.[412] Once more, one can but speculate

409 The use of *kunya*s to identify sender and addressee in *P.HaimPaper* 1, in particular, suggests a discourse between equals. See Haim/Shenkar/Kurbanov 2016, 159 and *ibid.*n75.

410 See, for instance, the mention of a letter carrier by the name of *mrwʾn* (= arab. Marwān) in Mugh A 14, 31. See also Lurje 2008, 42 (12).

411 See Huseini (in press). Cf. *infra* Ch. IV, *Negotiating "Arab Style"* (The "Arabic" Letters from Sogdia) and Appendix 3.

412 Smirnova 1963, ns. 797 and 798; *ead.* 1981, ns. 1660–1681 and Naymark/Treadwell 2011. On the ruling dynasties of Central Asian principalities in the 8th and 9th centuries, see Karev 2015, 336–344.

whether this was also standard practice for bottom-up communication between non-Arabized local elites and the Arab imperial establishment in other regions of the Early Islamic Empire.

Language choice in everyday writing is, by comparison, poorly documented. A glimpse into the wider language dynamics in the region is offered by several Sogdian economic texts, vessel labels as well as school exercises on potsherds excavated in Panjakent – most of which remains unpublished.[413] One fragmentary account, in particular, is headed by the *basmala*[414] in Arabic script.[415] This suggests that Arabic (or rather Arabic formulaic phrases) had made inroads in local scribal practices by the late 8th-century.[416] The fragmentary report in question is directed at some high authority addressed as "the lord [*khūv*?][417]" (*ʾt βyw* [*xwβw*]), which might explain the use of an Arabic header.[418] A further ostracon found in the citadel of Panjakent and datable to the first quarter of the 8th century is fully Arabic. The document is a fragmentary list of names, which according to the editors, was possibly connected to the distribution of booty among soldiers.[419] Of interest is particulary one individual mentioned in the text by the name of (…) al-Raḥmān son of *al-Dibīr*, the MP word (*dbyr*) for "scribe". This possibly hints at the early stages of the Arabicization of Iranian clerks – a point that I will return to in Ch. IV and V).

Bactria

Among the over 180 Bactrian and Arabic documents found in Northern Afghanistan and currently housed at the Khalili Collection in London,[420] about 40 belong to a common private archive of one Qārwāl b. Mīr b. Bēk (II) b. Kamir-far b. Bēk (I)

413 Livshits/Raspopova 2015. I thank Michael Shenkar for the reference.
414 For the use of the *basmala* in early Islamicate Central Asia, see *infra* pp. 228–229 and 255–258.
415 Livshits/Raspopova 2015, 335–336, no. 6 (Fig. 7).
416 Archaeological and numismatic evidence indicates that the city of Panjakent was largely abandoned in the the 770s.
417 For the title *khūv*, see de la Vaissière 2007, 28–29.
418 The same formula is used in Sogdian letters addressed to Dēwāshtīch in the Mugh archive. Cf. also the formula "to the Lord of Lords" allegedly used in letters addressed to the *afshīn* of Ushrūsana Khaydar b. Kāwūs (commonly known simply as al-Afshīn). See Ṭabarī, II, 1310–1311 (trans. Bosworth, XXXIII, 189 and *ibid*.n542) and de la Vaissière 2007, 135.
419 Belenitsky/Isakov 1969.
420 The documents emerged on the antiquities market in the early 1990s after being smuggled into Pakistan during the Soviet occupation of Afghanistan. There is, however. no precise record of their discovery. For the background of the collection, see Sims-Williams 1999, 246–247, *id*. 2000, 7, Khan 2007, 15–19, and Rezakhani 2010, 193–194, and De Blois/Sims-Williams 2018, 7.

and his family (Fig. 5). Based on the toponyms mentioned, it can be established that the archive's owners were based in the area of Rōb (modern Ru'i), southeast of Balkh.[421] The time span covered by the documents stretches from the early 8th century up to the reign of al-Mahdī (*rg.* 775–785), spanning over six generations. It is unclear whether the parchments from the Bēk family archive are related to the other Bactrian and Pahlavi documents in the Khalili Collection – some of which are coeval.

The repartition of items in the archive according to functional domains unveils a double administrative system. Matters pertaining to tax collection, in particular, were safely in the hands of the Arab authorities. In matters of private law, however, a local ruler based in Rōb known as the *sēr* acted as guarantor. Closely reflecting this binary constellation, the documents that can be directly connected with the family of Bēk are bilingual, comprising 33 items in Arabic[422] and six to seven in Bactrian.[423] It is unclear whether a Pahlavi letter (P.Khalili inv. 129) which entered the Khalili Collection with the Bactrian documents is connected to the archive.[424] The use of Bactrian and Arabic does not follow a strict chronological pattern. If the earliest Bactrian documents in fact pre-date the appearance of the Arabic ones by as much as 50 years, the latest ones are contemporaneous with the Arabic parchments in the archive.[425] The functional repartition of the

421 According to *BD* I W (747) and Y (771), Qārwāl's father Mīr b. Bēk himself resided in a town called Asp. Tax receipts addressed to members of the Bēk family are issued by financial administrators acting under the authority of local *amīr*s whose jurisdiction extended over several towns in the region including Rōb, Samangān, Madr, and Rizm. On the location of these sites and other toponyms mentioned in the Bēk family archive, see Khan 2007, 17–22 and De Blois/Sims-Williams 2018, 11–13.

422 *P.Khurasan* 1–32. The picture of a further unedited Arabic document related to the Bēk family archive is reproduced by Khan 2008, fig. 7.2. The text is a letter between one Maysara (?) and one Sām (probably the same person acting as a witness in *P.Khurasan* 29, 10) both styled *mawlā* of Ghālib (probably the same person whose clients are mentioned in *P.Khurasan* 29, 10 and 30, 13).

423 *BD* I T (700), U (712), V (729), W (747), X (749), and Y (771). It is unclear whether the Meyam son of Bēk to which the Bactrian letter *BD* II je is addressed is connected with the Bēk family. The paleographical features of the latter (possibly late V) would point towards a distant ancestor of the owners of the archive. See De Blois/Sims-Williams 2018, 39. For the era used in the Bactrian documents of the Bēk family archive (starting point 223 CE), see De Blois 2006 and De Blois/Sims-Williams 2018.

424 The document was edited by Weber in De Blois/Sims-Williams 2018, 99–108 and can be assigned to the second half of the 6th century based on paleography.

425 The latest Arabic document in the Bēk family archive is the emancipation of a slave dated to 777 (*P.Khurasan* 30).

archive's texts partially overlaps with their linguistic subdivision. In particular, all the tax quittances issued to the archive owners by tax collectors operating in the name of local Arab officials styled as *amīr*s are redacted in Arabic. Further, one of the Arabic documents[426] is an official land survey. At the other end of the spectrum, all the documents in the archive penned in Bactrian are of an economic or legal nature. Several of both fiscal "agents" and local *amīr*s have Iranian patronyms indicating converted (or simply Arabized) local rural elites.[427] The patronym of the *amīr* Abū Ghālib b. al-Iṣbahbadh (< MP *spāhbed*, a high-ranking Sasanian military official) in particular seems to point at a local aristocratic family.[428]

The use of Bactrian and Arabic in the archive, however, defies a clear-cut repartition into functional domains. Specifically, a functional overlap can be seen in settlements concerning legal and economic activities. Agreements pertaining to the buying and selling, as well as the legal status of landed property are mostly detailed by Bactrian documents, three of which are roughly contemporaneous with the Arabic material.[429] Remarkably, however, a further deed of acknowledgement (*P.Khurasan* 25 (762)) in which one Maskan renounces his claim to the price of a sale against Mīr b. Bēk (II) under the guarantee that the *sēr* will assume Mīr's debt, is redacted in Arabic.[430] As we learn from the document, the transaction involved a third Arab (or Arabicized) party by the name Ibrāhīm. In fact, the list of witnesses in *P.Khurasan* 25 includes both Iranian and (mostly) Arabic names.[431] The deed is also validated by the *bulla* of a certain Naṣr b. al-Qāsim, probably a local official, who also subscribes the deed as a witness (l. 7). A further portion of the Arabic parchments likewise deals with half-legal, half-economic private deeds of settlement. Three Arabic documents pertain to the dowry of Mīr b. Bēk (II)'s daughter Ḥamra.[432] The other four are related to the manumission or eman-

---

426 *P.Khurasan* 24 (Rōb; 771).

427 Khan 2007, 19. For a synoptic overview of the fiscal authorities involved in the documents from the Bēk family archive, see *ibid.*, 22–24.

428 Khan 2007, 19.

429 *BD* I W (747), contract of purchase of land by Mīr and his brother Wahran; BD I X (749), in which Bāb and Kamird-far agree to settle a quarrel with their brothers Mīr and Wahran and to share with them equally their movable properties and estates; and *BD* I Y in which the *sēr* serves as guarantor of an acknowledgement that Mīr b. Bēk (II) has dissociated himself from his brother Bāb and that his properties and land are therefore not liable for his brother's debts.

430 For more background on *P.Khurasan* 25, see Khan 2007, 49–50.

431 Muḥammad client of Ṣayfī and Khālid son of Slkyān acting as the witnesses in *P.Khursan* 25 (ll. 9–10), are possibly first generation converts.

432 In *P.Khurasan* 26–27 one Khīb b. Nashbūb, betrothed to Mīr b. Bek's daughter Ḥamra, and his legatees acknowledge receiving instalments of a dowry of 500 *dirhams*; *P.Khurasan* 28 concerns a series of witnesses who attest that Ḥamra has received her dowry, presumably after Khīb's death.

cipation of slaves from the Bēk family's household.[433] Interestingly, these Arabic legal deeds are invariably also issued by or involve one or more parties bearing Arab names, while Mīr or his familiars are always on the receiving end of the exchange. The documents relative to Ḥamra's dowry, as well as those dealing with the emancipation of slaves, even display technical legal jargon known from coeval Iraqi Muslim jurisprudence and appear to be embedded in Islamic legal categories and juridical language.[434]

The resulting picture of the language interplay within the archive is one that transcends a situation of purely functional bilingualism and is rather interwoven with matters of social etiquette. Arabic is not merely the language of the administration and official business but also the socially accepted language of choice for private exchange between the native Bactrians and Arabs (or Arabicized locals). Business and legal documents not involving Arab parties, on the other hand, are instead dealt with in the archive owners' native Bactrian. A useful *comparandum* is provided by the onomastic pattern of the fourth and fifth generations of the Bēk family which are contemporaneous with the Arabic documents in the archive (Fig. 5). All known members of the Bēk family including the four sons of Bēk (II) (*fl.* 712/713) still have Iranian names.[435] The emergence of Arabic documents in the archive coincides with a shift in onomastic patterns. Bēk (II)'s sons Mīr and Kamird-far (II) give their legitimate children both Bactrian[436] and Arabic[437] names whereas only Wahran's progeny bears an exclusively Bactrian onomasticon.[438] Furthermore, all legitimized children and grandchildren of Kamird-far (II), by his union with the emancipated (and probably converted) slave Zerān, carry Arabic names.

Finally, the social behaviour of Mīr's brother Kamird-far (II) is indicative of a double social etiquette. In *P.Khurasan* 29 (755), which sanctions the emancipation of the *umm walad* Zerān and her children, Kamird-far notably appears with

433 *P.Khurasan* 29–32.
434 The legal context of the Arabic documents in the Bēk family archive is discussed in detail in Khan 2007, 59–64.
435 Sims-Williams 2010, 38–39 (41), 75 (200), 88 (253), and 103 (320).
436 *Ibid.*, 46–47 (79) and 88 (253).
437 The name Ḥamra (bt. Mīr) is of uncertain reading and may be a dialectal variant (or variant orthography?) of the standard al-Ḥamrāʾ "the red one". See Khan's commentary to *P.Khurasan* 26 l. 6 with further literature. The name Khamir (b. Kamird-far (II)) is a Bactrian rendering of the Arabic title *amīr* "commander". See Lurje 2008 and Sims-Williams 2010, 147 (514).
438 The identification of the progeny of Wahran son of Bēk (II) is dubious, see Khan 2007, 21–22.

the Arab name Saʿīd[439] "fortunate" – a partial translation of his Bactrian name (*Kamird-far* "Kamird's fortune").[440]

The discriminating factor for the language choice in the private documents of the Bēk family archive seems not to have been of a merely functional but additionally of a social nature. Notably, parties with Arab names are never mentioned in the latest Bactrian economic and private documents from the archive; Arab (or Arabized) parties are instead a constant of the coeval Arabic documents. Together with the Bēk family's onomastic pattern, this strongly suggests that Arabic was by then recognized as a language of social prestige and its use was considered a matter of scribal etiquette whenever Arabic-practicing parties were involved.

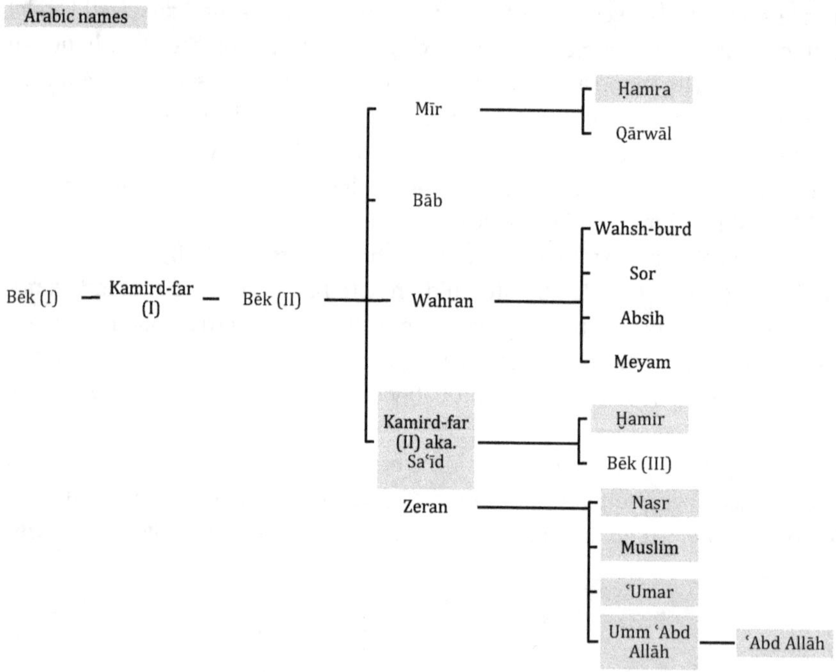

Fig. 5: *Bēk family tree (adapted from Khan 2007: 22 and De Blois / Sims-Williams 2018: 37).*

439 For the identification of Kamird-far (II) with the Saʿīd of *P.Khurasan* 29, see Sims-Williams 2010, 64 (152) and De Blois/Sims-Williams 2018, 37–38.

440 The use of double names is attested in legal documents from 9th-century Egypt. See Khaled Younes' unpublished paper held at the *25th Congress of Papyrology* (2010).

Concluding Remarks

Language is possibly the one component of "cultural stuff" (Barth 1969) which is most easily mobilized in order to create and maintain social boundaries. It is against this background that the rise of Arabic from the *Reichsprache* of a powerful few to a transcultural *lingua franca* of the Islamic Commonwealth of the 9th and later centuries plays out.

A quantitative examination of evidence for Early Islamic practices of literacy alone firmly dismisses the notion of a swift spread of Arabic among the conquered societies. The language of the Arab *ferus victor* did ultimately win the day not only in the administration but also as a language of science, literature and, eventually, of private exchange for the majority of the population within the Islamicate world. As far as the documentary evidence is concerned, however, the emergence of Arabic as a language of religion, learning, and trade was largely still a thing of the future. Both quantitatively and typologically, it was not the Arabic of science and knowledge, *belles lettres*, and trade, nor even the Arabic of Islamic teaching or of the epigraphic pastime that left the deepest mark on the Early Islamic material record. It is rather the Arabic (and the documentary formats) of the Umayyad and early Abbasid administration and imperial rule that enjoyed the widest geographical dissemination, sheer quantitative primacy, as well as the most social visibility.

While close ideological ties between the practice of written Arabic and the halls of power transcend and antedate the administrative reforms commanded by ʿAbd al-Malik, the homogenizing effect of the Marwanid public epigraphy, coinage, as well as papyrus protocols and official writs, doubtlessly informed much of the way subordinated segments of the imperial polity experienced Arabic, or rather *imperial* Arabic. Direct evidence and especially official writs, protocols, tax demands, as well as coins and official inscriptions comes from Egypt, Syria-Palestine, the Arabian Peninsula, and Central Asia. The common formal framework of documents produced in such disparate regions adumbrates the agency of imperial officials and provided a powerful marker of inclusion to those that co-participated in the transregional official Arabic writerly culture. That the material record from Sufyanid Greater Syria anticipates documentary types attested in Egypt and elsewhere only generations later, suggests that Marwanid imperial documentary practices resulted from the export of an Arabic administrative culture which first developed in the political core of the Umayyad Empire in Sufyanid Greater Syria.[441] The appearance of monumental inscriptions

441 For the conjecturally Syrian component of Early Islamic Arabic administrative jargon, see *infra* Ch. V, *Terminology and Regional Settings*.

https://doi.org/10.1515/9783110740820-014

in Greater Syria a generation before their earliest counterparts from the Arabian Peninsula, and the central role of the Damascus mint for the reform of imperial coinage further corroborates this view.

The social reach of Arabic and its interplay with neighbouring vernaculars and previous languages of power progressed of its own accord in the different regions of the Umayyad and Early Abbasid Empire. If Arabic had gained a firm footing in the bureaucratic machinery and was beginning to spread among the local rural elites in both Egypt and Central Asia in the late 8th century, it was still delegating most administrative matters to Middle Persian in coeval rural North-western Iran. There were, however, shared traits. Up to the mid-8th century in Egypt and Sogdia, to the late 7th century in Syria-Palestine, and to the early 9th century in the Qom hinterland, exchange within the top layers of the imperial administration took place in Arabic, as did representational public statements. Incoming bottom-up communication by subordinate segments of society, as well as top-down pragmatic administrative communication, could instead be carried out in the regional vernaculars. Furthermore, in all surveyed regions, the appointment of Arab-Muslim officials at a local level preceded and vehicled recognizable cases of Arabization.

The assimilation of subordinated groups into the Arabic – not automatically Islamic – imperial writerly culture was born out of this system of language hierarchy, based on the restrictive access to the dominant language and the specific formats associated with it. Lying behind the adoption of Arabic by Egyptian Coptic lower tax officials and scribes, Sogdian princes, and Bactrian landowners is a common recognition of the practice of Arabic as a social statement.

In regions like Syria-Palestine and the Ḥijāz in which Arabic vernaculars were already widely practiced before the rise of Islam, the most immediate consequence of the emergence of the Early Islamic Empire was overcoming the "reluctance" to write in Arabic. In these areas, Arabic substrate written artefacts and pre-Islamic formal conventions lived on beneath the surface of a homogeneous transregional Early Islamic imperial documentary standard in informal practices of literacy such as graffiti. While these practices of Arabic literacy thrived under Islamic rule, they remained confined to the Arab (mostly Muslim) cultural milieu and spread as a consequence of its expansion rather than being its primary cause.

II Imperial Arabic: Between Text and Visual Text

Que la luna del persa y los inciertos
oros de los crepúsculos desiertos
vuelvan. Hoy es ayer. Eres los otros
cuyo rostro es el polvo. Eres los muertos.

Jorges Luis Borges, "Rubaiyat", *Elogio de la sombra*

Introduction

The previous chapter surveyed the spread of Arabic as the chief representational and, increasingly, administrative means of written expression in the Early Islamic imperial polity. This happened at the expense of rival local languages. It also suggested a broad-scale characterization of documentary uses of Arabic in an "imperial" phase (7th–8th centuries) followed by a period of slow transformation into a *lingua franca* (9th and later centuries).

The initial horizontal dissemination of Arabic documentary evidence from the Maghreb to Central Asia is best explained against the background of the deep ties between Arabic and Arab imperial rule. The imperial setting also shaped the social profile of Early Islamic Arabic documents: featuring mainly in the top layers of administration, Arabic spread the fastest in highly visible written corpora such as monumental inscriptions and coinage, but also official writs and papyrus protocols. Arabic's vertical spread across the layers of Early Islamic multicultural and multilingual society was asymmetrical and more gradual by comparison, taking as long as two centuries to catch up.

The difference in pace at which an officially sponsored and a private/informal Arabic documentary culture evolved in most of the Islamic Empire indicates a gulf between the proportionally high degree of exhibition of official practices of Early Islamic Arabic writing and their proportionally limited social reach among many strata of the population. This disproportion in (comparatively high) visibility and (comparatively low) potential readership had important implications for the modes that guided the experience of Early Islamic official public promulgations and how those who issued them intended these promulgations to operate.

It is plausible that the practice and experience of spoken Arabic shared the social connotations of its written counterpart among the newly formed Early Islamic imperial elite, and among those wishing to join it. Indications of the performative nature of Arabic documents or even reading certificates for public audiences (*samāʿ*) are occasionally found in later documentary and manuscript material.[1] Such internal indications, unfortunately, are only rarely found in Early Islamic documents.[2] As the social implications of Early Islamic spoken Arabic remain almost entirely beyond the reach of any inquiry, scrutiny of the modalities

1 See for instance Hirschler 2012, 33–37.

2 In *P.Lond.* IV 1343 (Ishqawh; 709) Qurra b. Sharīk instructs Basileios to have the people under the latter's jurisdiction make copies of the governor's letter and put them on display in the churches of the district.

https://doi.org/10.1515/9783110740820-015

in which Early Islamic Arabic was experienced is constrained to written forms and their inherent peculiarities.

Written communication lacks the relative spontaneity and immediacy of language choices in oral settings and is instead born out of careful consideration. Moreover, in written communication, language – through the representation by written characters – exists visually. The actual physical presence of written language means that a statement does not require human intermediaries but only human viewers and readers. In societies in which audio recording had yet to be invented, the potential for perpetuity (*scripta manent*) further separated written messages from the ephemeral character of spoken utterances (*verba volant*). Furthermore, in written communication, meaning finds expression not only through the text proper and its register but also through the mediation of supports and form as well as position in space.

The present chapter expands on the previous assessment of the social environment of Early Islamic documentary sources to examine questions of their placement and extra-textual properties. By taking into closer consideration their most superficial level of experience and conception, the following pages will analyze the referential component of Arabic promulgations as a means to articulate difference in a culturally mixed environment.

Images of the Word

New powers in a culturally alien environment have a way of marking their presence through visually perceptible and culturally denotative statements. The most obvious imprint left by Early Islamic rulers on their conquered lands was the establishment of permanent military garrisons and, soon enough, administrative centers both at the site of or in close proximity to pre-Islamic urban centers (e.g., Fusṭāṭ near the Roman fort of Babylon, Kūfa near the Lakhmid capital of al-Ḥīra, and Baṣra near Vaheshtābādh Ardashīr). Umayyad residences and estates scattered across Palestine, Lebanon, Syria, and Jordan,[3] commonly referred to as "desert castles",[4] similarly signaled the growing presence of the ruling elite in the imperial metropolitan territory. Specifically, some Umayyad age facilities were located on the site of previous Ghassānid structures, which possibly indicates the Umayyads' intent to exploit Ghassānid networks and tribal strategies for the control of the Syrian steppe.[5] By the end of the 7th century, the erection of monuments to the new faith at the sites of Christian and Jewish shrines embodied the search for a separate identity *vis-à-vis* the non-Muslim subjects of the Empire. The Dome of the Rock and al-Aqṣā Mosque on the Temple Mount and the Umayyad Mosque of Damascus at the site of John the Baptist's Cathedral serve as primary examples, but less prominent instances are also evident in archaeological records.[6] A further facet of this process of appropriation was the frequent re-use of Christian architectonic *spolia* in imperial complexes.[7] The latter had the

---

3 For an explanation of the location of Umayyad "desert castles" as a mirror of the regional base and patronage strategy of various members of the Marwanid family, see Bacharach 1996.
4 Despite its use by scholars since the 19th century, the term "desert castles" is a shorthand and partially misleading cumulative definition for a group of about 20 edifices with a wide array of functional purposes. For a synoptic account, see Gaube 1979; for a more detailed one, see Cresswell 1989, esp. 91–216.
5 Gaube 1979; MacAdam 1986; Shahid 1989; *id.* 1992; Key-Fowden 2004; Tohme 2009. For Late Antique-Umayyad continuity in residential complexes in the former Sasanian East, see Morony 2004, 282–284.
6 King 1983 and Hoyland 1997a, 564. For a more comprehensive survey and a recent assessment of forms of contiguity between churches and mosques, see Guidetti 2013 and *id.* 2017, 30–70. Cf. also Q 18: 21 "Build over them a building; their Lord knoweth best concerning them. Those who won their point said: We verily shall build a place of worship over them" (trans. Pickthall).
7 For a detailed overview of the Early Islamic use of Christian *spolia*, see Guidetti 2017, 97–131, Flood 2001, 200–203, and Meinecke 2020, 113–114. For the use of South Arabian *spolia* in the Great Mosque of Ṣanʿāʾ in particular, see Costa 1994, II, esp. 11–16.

Note: For the term "image of the word" to refer to Arabic public writing, see Dodd 1969 and Dodd/Kheirallah 1981.

https://doi.org/10.1515/9783110740820-016

effect of incorporating the familiar visual vocabulary of the past and rival imperial traditions, while at the same time proclaiming the supremacy of the new Arab imperial rule.

In terms of less grand statements, few instruments are more readily accessible in delineating boundaries and territory in multilingual environments than group-specific alphabets and scripts.[8] Formal consistency (Chapter III), geographical outreach, sheer quantity, and cultural distinctiveness (Chapter I) granted the use of Arabic for public writing pride of place among the preferred means of expression by the Early Islamic imperial elite outside Islam's homeland on the Arabian Peninsula.

Rewriting Public Space: Written Arabic and Territoriality

Among the anti-Christian measures allegedly undertaken by the governor of Egypt, ʿAbd al-ʿAzīz b. Marwān, described in the *History of the Patriarchs*, one reads of the governor's resolve to place inscriptions echoing the *Sūrat al-Ikhlās* on the front doors of churches across Egypt.[9] Within the corpus of Early Islamic Arabic writings, the number of items designed to intrude in public spaces and establish difference among mixed audiences is comparatively low. Nonetheless, some of the most prominent examples of public employment of the Arabic script can be connected with the symbolic appropriation of urban and extra urban landscapes.[10]

Both the Umayyads and the Abbasids revived the Roman custom of erecting milestones along crucial road arteries. The geographic distribution of extant Early Islamic items of this kind indicates that this expression of imperial presence primarily involved landscapes of symbolic significance. In particular, Umayyad age milestones are concentrated on the road network connecting the imperial capital

---

8 For the socio-cultural implications of languages and scripts in ancient or pre-industrial multilingual societies in general, see Ferguson 1971, 234–253; Scribner/Cole 1981; and Goody (ed) 2005. For classical antiquity, Bodel 2001, 25–30; Adams 2003, 271; Mullen/James (eds) 2012; Graham 2013; the contributions in Keegan/Sears/Laurence (eds) 2013; Bolle 2019; and Leatherbury 2019. For the European Middle Ages, see e.g. Stock 1983, Adamska 2013, 354–356, and Snijders 2015. For the Late Antique and Early Islamic world in particular, see Biermann 1989 and *ead.* 1998, esp. 36–48.

9 "Moreover he [ʿAbd al-ʿAzīz] wrote certain inscriptions and placed them on the doors of the churches at Miṣr and in the Delta saying in them: 'Muḥammad is the great Apostle of God, and Jesus also is an Apostle of God. But verily God is not begotten and does not beget'" *HP* I, XVI, 25 (transl. Evetts, 279).

10 Grabar 1987, 43–64; Biermann 1998, 28–48; and Blair 1998, 41. Cf. Ettinghausen 1974 and Eck/Gronke/von Hesberg 2007, 227–233.

of Damascus with Palestine and with the holy city of Jerusalem at its center.[11] *Amyāl* (sing. *mīl* “mile”, “milestone”)[12] erected by the future Marwān I between ʿArafa and Mecca during his first governorship of Medina (in office 661–668) are referenced in the literary sources.[13] Early Abbasid milestones, on the other hand, were erected along the Darb Zubayda highway, the pilgrimage route connecting lower Iraq with the Holy Cities of the Ḥijāz.[14]

Other symbolic uses of Arabic epigraphy included the placement of inscriptions over city gateways such as in the case of the Egyptian gate of Ayla (present-day Aqaba).[15] Similar inscriptions were reportedly placed at the entrance to the harbors of Sidon and Acre.[16] An Arabic inscription likewise marked the entrance to the Early Abbasid citadel of Monastir (ca. 120 km south-east of Tunis)[17] and a mosaic inscription was allegedly placed on the exterior of a gubernatorial estate in Acre.[18] Within urban perimeters, Early Islamic Arabic inscriptions could be used to intrude upon public spaces that were not group-specific, such as the double Umayyad Arabic mosaic inscription placed at the entrance to the market in Baysān/Scythopolis.[19] More often, however, Arabic epigraphic programs complemented architecture in delineating Muslim sectarian places. Inscriptions in Arabic characters, for instance, adorned the doorways of the Dome of the Rock[20] in Jerusalem and of al-ʿUmayrī Mosque[21] in Bosra.[22] Within Muslim compounds set in prevalently Christian environments such as the Dome of the Rock and the Umayyad Mosque in Damascus, interior inscriptions comprising lengthy Qur’anic paraphrases[23] probably had a more prominent role in enforcing the perception of Muslim sectarian space than analogous inscriptions from the coeval Arabian Peninsula.

---

11 See *supra* p. 92.
12 On the etymology of *mīl*, see infra Ch. V, *The Loanwords of Imperial Arabic s.v.* “*mīl*”.
13 For a discussion of the nature of the so-called milestones of Marwān I and the sources related to them, see Elad 1999, 41–44.
14 See *supra* p. 51. For a synopsis of Early Abbasid building activities along the Darb Zubayda route, see Creswell 1989, 280–284.
15 Whitcomb 1989.
16 *CIAP* I p. 31, no. 2* (= *RCEA* I 37*) (before 750).
17 Abdeljaouad 2001 p. 43, no. 2 (related to 797/798) (*non vidi*).
18 See *infra* p. 172.
19 *CIAP* II p. 207 no. 1 (738?); for the context of the inscription, see in particular Khamis 2001.
20 See *supra* p. 93 and nn340 and 341.
21 See *infra* p. 172.
22 On access to Early Islamic sectarian spaces, see *infra* p. 106 and references there.
23 A quote of Q 2:256 is only attested to in the version of the Umayyad foundation inscription of the Mosque of Damascus related by al-Kutubī († 1363). For further Qur’anic paraphrases inscribed on bands on the *qibla* wall, see Flood 2001, 247–251.

Furthermore, the original placement of several Early Islamic Arabic inscriptions on door lintels of Umayyad estates underscores the use of the written word as a means to organize internal space and demarcate boundaries, both within a single edifice and in building complexes.[24] One might expect the potential audiences of these latter inscriptions to have embraced mainly Arab Muslims but it is probable that these facilities were used for the official reception of mixed spectatorship as well.[25] Finally, the direction of the writing in the mosaic inscriptions inside the Dome of the Rock – at least theoretically – [26] served as a means to direct the beholder's movement within the building.[27]

Perhaps less impressive, but by far the most consistent official use of Arabic throughout the territory of the Early Islamic Empire is to be found on coinage. Coins are the only surviving original sources of written Arabic whose production and circulation extended to the political borders of the Empire and beyond. Writing in group-specific scripts and languages, in particular, already characterized the coinage of all political actors of the pre-Islamic Middle East. The appearance of the Arabic script in addition to and, eventually, in substitution for other languages of power signaled that the ultimate authoritative instance in the lands in which the coins circulated now rested with the Arab-Muslim imperial elite.[28]

On a more focused geographical scale, Arabic official documents on papyrus and similar materials could be put to use for the same effect. I have argued that Arabic official letters and protocols in particular responded to more than strictly functional needs for Arabic in the local administration (Chapter I). While the *dioikētēs* Basileios and his like most probably had no textual access to Qurra's Arabic missives they – as Reinfandt puts it – "well understood the implicit message of the Arabic letter, its script and language choice being the symbolic expression of rule".[29] Notions of sovereignty and territoriality conveyed by Arabic writing not only accompanied those who actively practiced it, but extended more generally to the institutions in whose name those writings were issued. Arabic documents dispatched by high-ranking Muslim officials to peripheral regions

---

24 Umayyad official inscriptions placed on door lintels are *RCEA* I 12 (Qaṣr Burquʿ; 700/701); 27 (Qaṣr al-Ḥayr al-Gharbī; 727); and Ritter 2016a p. 65–66 (Khirbat al-Minya; 743–744?). A lintel inscription is also Ory 2005 no. 1 (Bosra 720/721) from al-ʿUmayrī Mosque.

25 Shalem 2006. Cf. also *infra* pp. 105–106.

26 On the question of visibility of the Dome of the Rock's mosaics on the inner and outer octagon, see *infra*n41 in this chapter.

27 See Milwright 2016, 49–79.

28 Heidemann 2010a, 159 and *ibid.*n31 and *id.* 2010b, 25.

29 Reinfandt 2015, 282.

such as Aphrodito[30] or Nessana served, *inter alia*, as a proxy for the Arab central government.[31]

In a multilingual framework in which knowledge of Arabic distinguished only an insular and politically hegemonic segment of Early Islamic society, official Arabic writing on inscriptions and coins as well as on papyrus protocols and official missives did not indicate a community united by one shared language, but rather one bound together by the same imperial rule.

Readership and Spectatorship of the Imperial Arabic Public Text

A significant portion of Early Islamic Arabic documentary evidence belongs to the inner-Arab/Arabic-reading milieu. This is the case with regard to Arabic missives featuring both Arabic writers and recipients, and Arabic inscriptions that adorn the interior of Early Islamic structures. As we have seen, however, the *Sitz im Leben* of a substantial part of officially sponsored Arabic documentary evidence from the 7th and 8th centuries rested – potentially at least – among culturally mixed audiences. Some documents were specifically addressed to non-Arab and – arguably – non-Arabic "readers". These documents include Qurra's Arabic letters to Basileios and the Marwanid bilingual papyrus protocols and orders for delivery. Other forms of officially sponsored Arabic public writing such as the Umayyad and early Abbasid milestones, the inscribed copper plates placed above the entrances to the Dome of the Rock in Jerusalem, and Arabic inscriptions on coinage were presumably exposed to a prevalently non-Arab and non-Arabic literate readership.

Even the interior Arabic inscriptions that punctuate Early Islamic residences and estates hint at mixed audiences. This much is suggested, for instance, by the Greek[32] and bilingual Greek-Arabic labels on the mosaic decoration of the Umayyad residence in Quṣayr ʿAmra.[33] It is further worth pointing out that access to Muslim cultic facilities need not have been exclusive. On one hand, literary and documentary materials suggest that clear religious boundaries between the conquerors' community and other monotheistic creeds were only gradually formu-

30 Cf. *supra* pp. 68–70 with references there.
31 Cf. the reference to practices of public display of official documents quoted *supra*n2.
32 See *i.a.* Fowden 2004, 87–88 and 191–196 and Vibert-Guige/Bisheh 2007, pls. 130a; 140 d–e; and141 d–e.
33 See *infra* p. 134.

lated throughout the Early Islamic period.[34] On the other, Muslim tradition itself holds that more rigid restrictions on Christian and Jewish access to mosques were first implemented during the reign of ʿUmar II (717–720).[35] Finally, Muslim anecdotal evidence suggests that adherents of competing faiths – and particularly Christians – formed part of the intended spectatorship of Early Islamic monumental enterprises.[36] What is more, literary information makes clear that imperial residential complexes and cultic facilities alike could function as majestic arenas for the reception of foreign diplomatic embassies.[37]

Early Islamic Arabic writing culture differed from calligraphic developments characterizing the artistic writing of the later Islamic world, at the expense of the actual transmission of text.[38] Although not devoid of enriching aesthetic features, practices of officially sponsored Early Islamic Arabic writing were in fact such that most viewers would have understood them as forms of writing regardless of their knowledge of the Arabic language and/or script.[39] Recognition of written

---

34 For a critical view of confessional identities during the Early Islamic period, see Donner 2002–2003 and *id.* 2010. On accounts of Early Islamic Muslim prayer held in churches, see Bashear 1991 and Elad 1995, 138–141. Corroborative documentary evidence is possibly provided by *P.Ness.* 72–73, which documents Muslim visits to St. Catherine's Monastery in the Sinai.

35 Pedersen 1991, *s.v.* "Masdjid". On Islamic traditions preventing non-Muslims from entering mosques, see Yarbrough 2012, esp. 26–47 and Melchert 2013. I thank Luke Yarbrough for the references.

36 See for instance Muqaddasī, 159 "(. . .) Talking to my father's brother one day, I said: 'O my uncle, surely it was not fitting for al-Walīd to expend the resources of the Muslims on the mosque at Damascus. Had he expended as much in building roads, or the water tanks, or in repairing the fortresses, it would have been more proper and more to his credit.' Said he: 'You simply do not understand, my dear son. Al-Walīd was absolutely right, for he accomplished a worthy work. He saw that Syria was a country settled by Christians, and he noted in that place all their churches so handsome with their enchanting decorations, renowned far and wide, such as the Church of the Holy Sepulchre and the churches of Ludd (Lydda) and al-Ruhā (Edessa). So he undertook for the Muslims the building of a mosque that would divert their attention from the churches, and make it one of the wonders of the world' (. . .)" (trans. Collins, 146).

37 *I.a.* Canard 1964; Grabar 1987, 159–162; and Shalem 2006.

38 Grabar 1992 defines aesthetic writing *stricto sensu* (i.e., characterized by an intent to generate pleasure through the visual component of writing with primacy over or regardless of the actual transmission of a text) as "terpnopoietic". On the development of Arabic calligraphy, see in particular George 2010.

39 I have presented a group of students at the University of Basel who had no previous knowledge of either Arabic, Greek, or Middle Persian with several examples of Early Islamic official documents on papyrus and coins in all three languages (date Apr. 17, 2016). All were able to tell texts apart from figural depictions and to distinguish between Arabic and Greek, and two out of four could distinguish between Arabic and Pahlavi script. I thank Audric Wannaz, Dario Giacometti, Florence Anliker, and Marie Besso for indulging me in this small experiment; see also

language of course did not equal understanding. In order to be informative, a written artifact should address a literate public familiar with the language being written, be placed so as to be easily visible and be written in easily decipherable and legible characters. Projecting these parameters onto the cumulative corpus of Early Islamic Arabic writing reveals obvious grey areas. Although no precise quantitative estimates can be drawn, contextual evidence – and particularly the resilience of local languages in the private ambit – suggests that Arabic literacy remained a minority phenomenon for centuries after the Islamic conquests, even among populations already literate in a local language (Chapter I). Even in regions such as Palestine, in which Arabic vernaculars were spoken in pre-Islamic times, Arabic nonetheless lacked a writing tradition *proprio sensu* and the local educated population continued to use Greek for their own record-keeping and everyday businesses.[40]

"Condensed" writing on small surfaces such as coins and seals, for instance, challenged the eye of even skilled Arabic readers. It is also worth mentioning that before the introduction of electrical illumination, natural lighting was a key factor in the legibility of inscriptions. In the absence of other means of artificial lighting, various parts of complex inscriptional programs might have been legible only at specific times of the day.[41] Abbreviations in Arabic inscriptions on coins and on papyrus protocols further complicated the encoding of textual meaning for uninitiated readers.[42] Circumstantial factors also aggravated textual understanding among people possessing less than proficient Arabic literacy. The graphic ambiguity of the (mostly unpunctuated and unvocalized)[43] Arabic script, well known to its own practitioners,[44] in itself constituted an obstacle to deciphering Early Islamic documents.

---

*infra*n93. For approaching writing through visual forms in pre-schooled adults, see Kurvers/van Hout/Vallen 2009, 882–883.

40 Cf. for instance the dossier of the abbot George of Nessana. See *supra* pp. 79–80.

41 For the question of legibility of the inscriptions in the Dome of the Rock, see Grabar 1959, 53 and Edwards 1991, 65. Cf. however, Milwright 2016, 61–65 and figs. 2.20 and 2.21 for a recent assessment on the Umayyad ceiling and lighting in the Dome of the Rock.

42 As indicative examples, see *CPR* III 35 (Ishqawh; 706/707), l. 4 (<*a*>*llāh*), l. 8 (*rasū(l)* and *arsa(l)a-hu*), and l. 12 (*a*(*mara*)); *CPR* III 37 (= *P.BeckerLateinisches* 6) (Fayyūm; 706/707),l. 7,(*amīr al-mū'*)*minīn*; *CPR* III 325 (= *P.KarabacekPapyrusprotokolle* p. 42) (al-Ushmūnayn; VIII), l. 7, *li-yuẓhira-hu* (*'alā al-dīn*) *kulli-hi*; and *P.DelattreSymbole* (Egypt 799–803) l. 6, *arsala-hu bi-l-hudā* (*wa-dīn*) *al-ḥaqq* and l. 8, *amīr al-mu'minīn* (*akrama-hu*) *allāh*.

43 For the use of diacritical dots in Early Islamic documentary texts, see Kaplony 2008.

44 See for instance the often-quoted remark by al-Birunī († 1050) that "The Arabic script has one decisive disadvantage: the similarity of the letters' shapes and the need to differentiate them with diacritical marks and vowel marks. If these are omitted the sense becomes unclear and if,

In addition, the ideologically charged Early Islamic formulaic parts of inscriptions, coinage, papyrus protocols, and epistolary prescripts resorted to an array of Qur'anic paraphrases and quotes[45] with three main referents. The first was the highly standardized framework of official documentary formulae and the institutions it represented (Chapter III). The second was the general Muslim audience who could recognize itself on the shared basis of a common faith running through a fairly consistent *Vulgata* of Qur'anic passages.[46] Finally, particular groups within the Early Muslim community itself linked their sectarian orientation with specific mottos such as the Khārijite *lā ḥukma illā li-llāh* "judgment belongs to God alone". While all these referential dimensions were possibly widely meaningful within the insular Arab-Muslim community,[47] they were most probably lost on outsiders. This further hindered access by non-Muslims to official texts through contextual information and forms of collective literacy.[48]

Accordingly, the composite audience of Early Islamic Arabic public writing possessed widely differing patterns of access to inscriptional declarations. Literate insiders would have been able to access the textual meaning of Early Islamic Arabic public promulgations. In turn, they would have served as a proxy for illiterate members of the Arab-Muslim community. Access to textual meaning through intermediaries would of course have been viable also for outsiders, especially those sharing similar cultural traits with the Arab-Muslim hegemonic minority. Yet it was likely that broad strata of the population of the Empire lacked social, cultural, and linguistic connections to the still relatively confined Arab-Muslim community.

Semantic access is not the sole or the most immediate means by which information and meaning are encoded or decoded in written texts. Support, size, script, layout, disposition, color, and more can enhance the aesthetic or even

furthermore, the text is not compared and corrected by collation – and this is common practice among contemporaries – it is as if the text has never existed and it is of no consequence whether one is acquainted with its content or not" (trans. Hirschler 2012, 93).

45 For Qur'anic quotes and paraphrases on Early Islamic coinage, see Treadwell 2012b. For papyri, see Almbladh 2010 and Potthast 2019. For inscriptions, see Dodd/Kheirallah 1981. For graffiti, see Imbert 2000 and *id.* 2013a.

46 A hint of broader resonance of the Qur'anic phraseology used on official coinage, inscriptions, and papyrus documents is its recurrence on the earliest examples of Arabic amulets such as *P.Bad.* V 143 (Fayyūm; VII/VIII) and 152 (Fayyūm; VIII) or on tombstones like the already mentioned one of ʿAbbāsa bt. Jurayj. Cf., however, *infra* p. 202 and references there. On Qur'anic quotations on papyrus amulets, see now Bsees 2019.

47 Cf. Brockopp 2017, 65–70.

48 On contextual information use in pre-readers, see Blair/Savage 2006, 993 and further references there. For the Islamic world in particular, cf. Ettinghausen 1974, 306 and *ibid.*n57.

iconic quality of a text and guide its interpretation and frame of reference. The centrality of the extra-textual dimension in channeling the experience of the written word is all the more central in social contexts in which access to literacy is limited.[49] It was through the lens of the latter features that those on the outside of the imaginary boundary traced by the language and script of Arabic public writing experienced Early Islamic imperial promulgations.

Arabic as an Element of Visual Discourse

From the late 7th century onwards, Early Islamic inscriptional programs connected with caliphal patronage underlined an aesthetic *koinē*. Monumental building projects in Marwanid Greater Syria and the Arabian Peninsula show the makings of a trans-regional framework of epigraphic ornament realized in gold lettering on a blue background. Leading the way are the mosaic inscriptions of the *rotunda* of the Dome of the Rock, made with gold tesserae on a background of blue glass tesserae.[50] The copper inscriptions engraved on the external doorways of the edifice were likewise painted blue with golden colored letters standing out against the blue background.[51] In the following generation, epigraphic gold and glass mosaic ornamentation typically characterized the works of Caliph al-Walīd I in Greater Syria and the Hijāz, with little of the original decoration surviving. These works included the Umayyad Mosque of Damascus, the Prophet's Mosque in Medina, and the Ḥarām Mosque in Mecca.[52] Gold and lapis lazuli similarly adorned the mosque erected by al-Walīd's brother Sulaymān (*rg.* 715–717) in Aleppo.[53] The double inscription at the Umayyad market in Baysān, sponsored by the governor Isḥāq b. Qabīsā' during Hishām's reign (724–743) is likewise created in gold and blue glass mosaics.[54] *Litterae aureae* on a blue background are also displayed in the *tabula ansata* inscription placed at eye level in the western aisle of the south wall in the

49 On the social meaning of public texts in Late Antiquity and the Early Middle Ages, see in particular the contributions in Eastmond 2015.

50 Complete color images of the inner octagon in Grabar 1996, figs. 43–49.

51 Color images in Grabar 2006a, 94 (fig. 33) and George 2010, 61 (fig. 37).

52 For a comprehensive overview of al-Walīd I's intense patronage of architecture, see Creswell 1989, 43–126. Deliveries or delivery requests related to the construction of the al-Walīd's Mosque in Damascus are found in *P.Lond.* IV 1334 = *P.Ross.Georg.* IV 3 (709); *P.Lond.* IV 1341 (709); 1342 (709); 1368 (710); 1397, 8 (709); 1411, 3 (709); and 1433 (707). Deliveries or delivery requests related to the construction of the Aqṣā Mosque in Jerusalem are found in *P.Lond.* IV 1334 (709); 1403 (709/710); and 1414 (early VIII).

53 Yaqūt, II, 313.

54 *CIAP* II p. 207 no. 1 (738?).

Umayyad residence of Quṣayr ʿAmra,[55] sponsored by al-Walīd II (*rg.* 743–744). Four other inscriptions in the central niche,[56] the western (above the window)[57] and eastern aisle (above the window)[58] of the south wall, and on the western wall[59] of the same compound are all painted in white letters on a blue background. The inscription on the *khān*'s lintel at Qaṣr al-Ḥayr al-Gharbī patronized by Hishām consisted of cast bronze letters, as evinced by the surviving plugholes.[60] The lasting influence of this design can be seen in later expressions of Islamic art such as the celebrated, possibly 10th-century "Blue Qur'an".[61]

The second overarching graphical framework of reference evidenced by Early Islamic monumental public writing was script. By this time, the first Early Islamic Arabic epigraphic and papyrological testimonies had introduced new orthographic features, different from pre-Islamic testimonies.[62] These betray a concern for the graphic ambiguity of Arabic, possibly as a result of its increased use after the Arab conquest. Epigraphic testimonies of the 670s exhibit a tendency towards a more rigid observance of baselines and text justification, as well as a development of more geometrical letter shapes through straighter vertical lines, and approximations of circular, triangular and rectangular forms, although they lack stable graphic principles.[63] In contrast, monumental epigraphic programs of the late 7th and early 8th century are characterized by the implementation of a highly recognizable standardized script, distinguished by the straightening of the letters' vertical components (with the exception of the group *lām+alif*), governed by principles of equidistance, parallelism, and the justification of lines. The spacing of horizontal baselines (where applicable), in particular, was regimented by a system of interlines regulating letters' extension below and above the base-

55 Imbert 2016, 337, fig. 7.

56 *Ibid.*, 340, fig. 8.

57 *Ibid.*, 334, fig. 5.

58 *Ibid.*, 341, fig. 9.

59 *Ibid.*, 344, fig. 10.

60 Schlumberger 1984, pl. 49d.

61 Cf. however, the stylistic ties of the Blue Qur'an with similarly ornamented "blue books" of the preceding Byzantine and western European tradition. See e.g. Nelson 2005, 72–75. Anecdotal information suggests that the gold and blue color palette was used for prestige correspondence with Abbasid caliphs as well. See, for instance, the description of the letter written in "lapis lazuli highlighted in gold" by a King of India to al-Maʾmūn (*rg.* 813–833) mentioned in *al-Hadāyā*, § 29 (trans. Al-Qaddūmi).

62 Orthographic novelties of Early Islamic Arabic testimonies include the introduction of diacritic signs, the distinct notation of the *tāʾ marbūṭa*, and the notation of <ā> in medial position through an *alif* and in final position through a *yāʾ*. Robin 2006, 343–349 and George 2010, 29–34.

63 Hoyland 2006 and George 2010, 60–61.

line.[64] The codification of this novel monumental script was again heralded by the mosaic and hammered copper inscriptions of the Dome of the Rock,[65] ʿAbd al-Malik's milestones,[66] and all-epigraphic coins and seals. The comparatively high degree of script stability and text justification sets Marwanid official inscriptions apart from both contemporary private epigraphy on graffiti and tombstones, and Sufyanid officially sponsored inscriptions.[67]

On coinage specifically, the progressive introduction of all-epigraphic[68] issues was accompanied by an adjustment of the script(s) to better serve the all-epigraphic format. In particular, the Wāsiṭ mint's coin design from 86 AH onwards distinguished itself by its perfectly straight and horizontal leveling of the script, which was adopted by the Eastern provinces shortly afterwards (Fig. 8).[69] The regimentation of monumental scripts in official epigraphy and coinage further echoes the standardization of late Umayyad and Early Abbasid officially sponsored book culture as demonstrated in Early Qur'anic manuscripts.[70]

Much like the distinctive gold-blue color palette, the preciousness of the surrounding architecture, décor, and materials imbued inscriptions with visual notions of authority and officialdom. While this is most evident in large complexes connected to caliphal patronage, ornamental motifs can also be seen in more mundane official Arabic promulgations. For instance, the Umayyad milestones located on the road between Ludd/Jaffa and Jerusalem[71] are decorated with floral or geometric patterns, and a unique lead seal in the name of ʿAbd al-Malik, produced in *Filasṭīn*, is decorated with depictions of affronté lions, birds, and vines.[72]

In terms of more general aesthetic principles, preserved examples of Arabic monumental epigraphy tend to occupy the writing surface in its entirety. This

64 See in particular George 2007 and 2010, 56–60. Cf. also Grohmann 1967–1971, II, 71–211.

65 On secondary differences between the script styles on display in the different sections of the mosaic running inscriptions of the Dome of the Rock, see George 2010, 60–68 and Milwright 2016, 108–157.

66 The script on the milestones and road inscriptions in the Golan displays fewer standardized features than the group of milestones from the Jerusalem area. Whether this is connected to a chronological succession or a difference in patronage is unclear. See Elad 1999 and George 2010, 69–70.

67 George 2010, 60–61 and Milwright 2016, 120–124. Cf. Grohmann 1967–1971, II, esp. 71–92.

68 On the introduction of all-epigraphic Arabic coinage, see the discussion *infra From Image to Word* with further references.

69 George 2010, 71–74.

70 Déroche 1992; 2002; 2013; 2014; 2018, and George 2010, 74–93.

71 See *supra* p. 92n336.

72 Grabar 1987, 91 and fig. 21.

implies on the one hand, that – in contrast to, for instance, South Arabian monumental epigraphy – [73] a blank surface was perceived as unaesthetic by patrons of Early Islamic Arabic inscriptions.[74] On the other hand, it underscores the careful preparation of the text based on the space at the inscriber's disposal.[75]

The creation of a distinctive visual fashion in a wide array of officially sponsored buildings established an overarching link between architecturally and functionally different edifices.[76] Thus it created a symbolic relationship within imperial geography. In the eyes of culturally mixed audiences, the aesthetic and formal consistency of Arabic public text also constituted a sign of distinction over previous and neighbouring traditions.[77]

The association of Arabic (or at least a certain Arabic)[78] with notions of social prestige is cemented by items of elite material culture. For instance, a pottery bowl found at the Umayyad residence in Jabal Usays (ca. 100 km east of Damascus) bears an inscription mentioning the prince and future caliph (*rg.* 715–717) Sulaymān b. ʿAbd al-Malik. A lidded ivory *pyxis* made in Aden is identified by its Arabic inscription as the commission of the governor of Medina ʿAbd Allāh b. al-Rabīʿ (in office 762–764).[79] Subsequently, Arabic writing filtered down into not only broader segments of coeval society but also into a broader spectrum of written artifacts over the course of the 8th century. An early example is a turban fabric currently housed in Cairo and produced in the Fayyūm in 707. This is decorated with a woven Arabic inscription mentioning its owner – one Sulaymān b. Mūsā.[80] Towards the end of the 8th century, Arabic inscriptions also appeared on precious metal artifacts. The neck of a bird-shaped *aquamanile* by the workshop of a certain Sulaymān dated 797/798 – currently housed in the Hermitage – is

---

73 Stein 2017, 165.

74 On coping with *horror vacui* in Islamic art, see Ettinghausen 1979.

75 Milwright 2016, 119. Cf. *infra* Ch. III, *If the Mountain will not come* (Disposition of Text), and Appendix 2, II.

76 For a synoptic assessment of the standardization of "imperial" architectonic and decorational features of building complexes connected to Marwanid patronage, see Flood 2001, 192–206; cf. also Grabar 2006b, XVIII, 247–252. An indirect reflection of "imperial" style motifs can be seen in the artistic renderings of architectural elements reminiscent of those found in Early Islamic building complexes in illustrations of early Qur'ans such as the so-called "Umayyad codex" from Ṣanʿāʾ. See *i.a.* Bothmer 1987 and George 2018, 49–50 and 57–59.

77 Biermann 1998, 52–53.

78 On the question of formal varieties of Early Islamic documentary Arabic, see Ch. III with further references.

79 Kühnel 1971, no. 18; Ettinghausen/Grabar/Jenkins-Madina 2001, 63 and *ibid.*n162.

80 El-Hawary 1934 and Marzouk 1954.

inscribed in Arabic.[81] Likewise, Arabic inscriptions feature on a late 8th-century bronze ewer in Sasanian style produced in the Baṣran workshop of one Ibn Yazīd.[82] Similar undated inscribed metal objects have surfaced in Mesopotamia and in the Iranian world and Egypt.[83]

Another reflection of the notions of prestige associated with the visual appeal of Arabic can be seen at play in the emergence of pseudo-inscriptions conveying merely a superficial impression of Arabic.[84] The textual dimension of a text could also make more limited concessions to the optisemy[85] of Arabic written artifacts. Luxury textiles embroidered with Arabic inscriptions produced in state sanctioned industries after the 8th century are often characterized by approximate/impressionistic Arabic writings.[86] As already discussed, Arabic protocols on papyrus likewise on occasion display abbreviated writings that reveal the primacy of the referential dimension of the Arabic script over a word-for-word textual meaning.[87] For people already familiar with the spectrum of texts to be found in these media, abbreviations would have sufficed as signifiers of the referenced text or text-segment. Such writings would, however, have remained incomprehensible as textual communication *stricto sensu* to all less proficient Arabic readers.

Arabic official documents on papyrus and parchment had little in the way of the artistic quality of contemporary Arabic public inscriptions and legends on precious metal coinage but were nevertheless not completely devoid of features that operated at an optisemic level. A careful articulation of Early Islamic official documents in layout units (Chapter III) enhanced the visual semantics of the written word. Preserved examples of gubernatorial letters from Early Islamic Egypt distinguish themselves for their large formats, reaching over 90 lines and measuring over two meters in length and 20 cm in width. Despite exhibiting a much greater variety than more centralized corpora, products of official chanceries are distinguished by a greater degree of uniformity of script when compared

---

81 Blair 1998, 103–104.

82 First published by Diakonov 1947 (*non vidi*). The inscribed ewer from Basra bears the date 69 AH (688/689). Grabar 1957, 548 argued that the century had been omitted from the date and that the ewer should be subsequently dated to <1>69 (= 785/786).

83 Fehérvári 1976, 25–38; Baer 1983, and Blair 1998, 104.

84 Aanavi 1968 and *id.* 1969; Ettinghausen 1974; and Blair 1989.

85 On the concept of "optisemy" (visual recognition of a broad category of experience without implying detailed awareness), see Grabar 1992, 172–174.

86 Stillman/Sanders/Rabbat 1999, *s.v.* "Ṭirāz" with further references.

87 See *supra*n42. On the question of abbreviations in Early Islamic Arabic documents, see Kaplony 2018, 338–341.

to private writings.[88] Arabic official hands of the late 7th and early 8th century further show trends of standardization, which share common features with the script style of coeval epigraphy and numismatics.[89] On the text surface, elongated characters were used in justification of the text and to highlight words and text parts.[90] Furthermore, the regular spacing between non-ligated letters often did not differentiate visually between characters belonging to adjacent words.[91] Division of words across lines for the sake of justification is likewise an occasional but by no means uncommon feature.[92] Even spacing and intra-word breaks appear not to have been made out of a concern for word unity but rather for a harmonious placement of the text on the writing surface.[93]

Another end to which text disposition was mobilized in bi- or trilingual documents was the visual establishment of language hierarchy. Unlike the first examples of bilingual papyri from the beginning of Arab rule over Egypt, in Sufyanid and Marwanid bilingual tax demands, requisitions, and orders for deliveries from Egypt and Syria, Arabic is placed above the Greek text.[94] Drawing parallels from numismatics, on Arabo-Sasanian bilingual coinage Arabic legends are placed on the outer margin – a part of the coin usually left blank in the Sasanian period – and written in a bigger script than the Pahlavi field legends. This made the Arabic

88 Sijpesteijn 2007; *ead.* 2013, 230. See also *infra* pp. 181–186. On the development of Early Abbasid documentary scripts, see in particular *infra* pp. 293–294.

89 Abbot 1939, 110; *ead.* 1941, 84; Gruendler 1993, 132–137; Khan 1992, 19–21; Hoyland 2006, 403; Sijpesteijn 2008, *s.v.* "Palaeography".

90 Grob 2010, 188.

91 Abbot 1938, 36. For some revealing examples see *P.DiemGouverneur* (= *P.Ryl.Arab.* I XV 59) (al-Ushmūnayn; 684/685), 6 (والسلم); *P.Cair.Arab.* 154 (= *P.BeckerNPAF* 8) (Ishqawh; 709/710), 16–17 (عبدك), and *Chrest.Khoury* I 90 (= *P.World* p. 124 = *P.Heid.Arab.* I 1) (Ishqawh; 710), 16 (أرضك). As part of the test mentioned *supra* at n39 (Basel, Apr 17, 2016), I asked a group of four students from the University of Basel who had no notion of Arabic to separate "words" based on intra-word spacing in scale black and white images of the following texts: *Chrest.Khoury* I 91 (= *P.Heid.Arab.* I 3), *CPR* III 65, *P.Cair.Arab.* 148 (= *P.World* p. 126 = *P.BeckerNPAF* 2), *P.Cair.Arab.* 160 (= *P.BeckerNPAF* 13), *P.DiemGouverneur* (= *P.Ryl.Arab.* I XV 59) *P.Kratchkovski*, *P.Mird.* 18, *P.MuslimState* 8, *P.Ness.* 60, and *P.SijpesteijnInvitation*. Three participants did not match actual word unities, indicating a perception that the visual surface of the text privileges visual unities over meaning unities. Furthermore, the test revealed that half of the participants were unable to guess the direction of writing. I would again like to thank the participants in this *divertisement* that – needless to say – claims neither representativeness nor scientific accuracy.

92 E.g., *P.Ness.* 64 (Nessana; 674), 3–4 (دينار); *P.Cair.Arab.* 154 (= *P.BeckerNPAF* 8) (Ishqawh; 709/710),16–17 (عبدك); *P.HindsNubia* (Qaṣr Ibrīm; 758), 11–12 (الكف); *P.Khurasan* 3 (Rōb; 765), 8–9 (أكرمه). See Sijpesteijn 2020b, 443 and *ibid.*n30 with further references.

93 On graphic means to articulate text parts in Early Islamic papyri, see Grob 2010, 187–201 with references to previous literature.

94 See *supra* pp. 61–63.

"marks" clearly noticeable as well as making them a visual unit of their own. On bilingual Arabic-Latin Arab-Byzantine coinage minted in North Africa between 715/716 and 720, Arabic legends occupy the coin field while the Latin ones are "relegated" to the margin (Fig. 20).[95] More subtle is the the positional hierarchy of Arabic and Pahlavi legends on one type of transitional Arab-Sasanian copper coins minted in Susa. Here the all-epigraphic reverse is headed by a *basmala* in Arabic while administrative remarks proper follow in Middle Persian.[96]

Returning to papyrology, in bilingual protocols the Greek version is found both above the Arabic[97] and *vice versa.*[98] Interestingly, in all earliest examples of bilingual protocols from the governorship of ʿAbd al-ʿAzīz (685–705) it is the Greek version that takes precedence over the Arabic.[99] Arabic(1st)-Greek(2nd) protocols on the other hand are first attested to after al-Walīd I's accession in 705. Both Greek(1st)-Arabic(2nd) and Arabic(1st)-Greek(2nd) protocols are then documented synchronically until the introduction of monolingual Arabic examples in the 730s.[100] Yet they differed in other respects. In particular, in Greek-Arabic examples (Fig. 1) the religiously inspired phraseology is confined to the *basmala* and to the Qur'anic paraphrases relative to Muḥammad's "mission". Arabic-Greek examples, on the other hand, are the only ones featuring the markedly polemical anti-Christian verses of *Surat-al-Ikhlās*. This suggests that the development of a more articulated imperial ideology corresponded to a new sense of the *mise en scene* of language hierarchy.

On a more general level, the fact that in most bilingual documents the Arabic version was functionally supplementing practical information accessible in other languages, *ipso facto* charged it with a more representational function. As will be explored in further detail later in this study, the phraseology of bilingual documents was not an exact translation either. Rather, non-Arabic translations of the Arabic parallel text almost invariably adapted or excluded formulae of culturally discriminative content (Chapter IV). In other words, language hierarchy corresponded to hierarchy in textual messages, including or excluding readers based on their mastery of Arabic.

---

95 E.g., Walker 1956, pl. XII ns. 184–J.6.
96 *ASCC* 38.
97 Grohmann 1923–1924, XXXVI–XLVIII, types A1–C4.
98 *Ibid.*, XXVII–XXXVI, types 1–12.
99 *P.Gascou* 27a (al-Ushmūnayn; 695); *CPR* III 2 (= *P.Lond.* IV 1412 = *P.BeckerLateinisches* 2) (al-Uqṣur; 685–699); *CPR* III 4 (al-Ushmūnayn; 685–705), 5, (Ihnās; 685–705), 6–7 (Egypt; 685–705), 8 (Fayyūm; 685–705), 9 (Jēme; 685–705), and 10 (Ishqawh; 685–705). Cf. also *P.Ness.* 60a (Nessana; before 674).
100 The earliest dated examples of monolingual Arabic papyrus protocols, *CPR* III 108–109, date back to 114 AH (732/733 CE).

The text, structure, and appearance of official Arabic documents, inscriptions, and coin legends were all conduits of meaningful messages. These had two main parallel but not necessarily overlapping referents: one visual and one textual. Fluent Arabic readership could access the semantic inter-text that connected statements of legitimacy on various media all over the Empire. Throughout the Early Islamic period, however, the textual level of the message remained arguably the most exclusive channel of meaning and one only operative for the minority who were fluent in Arabic – or through the mediation of the latter. For all other viewers, the combined features briefly illustrated above created a visual link to an *optisemic* inter-text bridging Arabic public texts on different media and geographical areas that encoded political, cultural, and ideological meaning through language, script, and text structure.

The Word and the Image: An Arab Late Antiquity

Throughout the period surveyed in this study, the position of Arab-Muslim rulers as leaders of a multifaceted empire conditioned their resort to communicative strategies capable of engaging audiences who were embedded in widely different traditions of expressing authority and legitimacy. A peculiarity of Early Islamic public use of Arabic writing, compared to later periods, is the extent to which public writing intersected with continuous employment of Late Antique symbolism and imagery.

Muslim historical memory makes no secret of Early Islamic rulers' ideological ties to their predecessors and of their attempts to appropriate Late Antique heritage through arts and lifestyle alike. At some point in the first quarter of the 8th century, the Umayyad court poet Jarīr (*fl.* 710s–720s), for instance, dedicated 14 verses of an encomiastic poem about Hilāl b. Aḥwāz al-Māzinī[101] to a highly symbolic reconstruction of the ancestry of the Arab people. In particular, Jarīr emphasizes the Arabs' descent from Abraham through their progenitor Ishmael and lingers on their kinship with other "nobles (*al-ġurr*), sons of Sarah". First, he lays claim to the line of Jacob, under which he names Solomon, Moses, Jesus, and David.[102] He then turns to "the sons of Isaac" as follows:

> The sons of Isaac are lions when they put on the belts of death wearing the coat of armour.
> You see them rejoice in the guidance and the crown bearer is an armed *marzbān*,
> Blazed like a male camel when he returns on the Persian carpet
> Sometimes they have a garment of iron, sometimes you will see them wearing silk and bright cloth.
> If they want to boast, they have but to enumerate among them al-Ṣabahbadh, Kisrā [Chosroes] the family of Hurmuzān [Hormozd] and *qayṣar* [caesar].
> They also had a Book and prophecy and they were kings in Iṣṭakhr and Tustar.
> Al-Waḍḍāḥ fought for the religion and has left resting glory in heritage to the Berbers.[103]

It is notably the two *Shāhānshāhān*, Khusraw (II) and Hormozd (I), together with the Byzantine Emperor (*qayṣar*) that take central stage. Sharing the scene with this illustrious assembly is a horse: Khusraw II's celebrated steed Shabhdez.[104] Curiously enough, the last figure listed in this somewhat eclectic ensemble has nothing of the royal pedigree of his ideal kinsmen: the Berber convert, Umayyad client

101 Jarīr, 104 vv. 27–40.
102 Cf. Q 6: 84 "(. . .) and of his [Jacob's] seed (We guided) David and Solomon and Job and Joseph and Moses and Aaron" (trans. Pickthall); the text in square brackets is mine.
103 Jarīr, 104 vv. 34–40. Translation and text in square brackets are mine.
104 Christensen 1936, 456–457.

https://doi.org/10.1515/9783110740820-017

(*mawlā*), and military commander, al-Waḍḍāḥ.[105] The passage echoes the often-quoted verse by Yazīd II (*rg.* 744): "I am the son of Kisrā; my father is Marwān. One grandfather is *qayṣar*; the other a *khāqān*"[106] – not a completely vain boast as Yazīd was after all the son of a Sasanian princess,[107] herself the great-granddaughter of the Byzantine emperor Maurice[108] and a descendant of a *khāqān*[109] of the Khazars.

Celebratory overtones and poetic license aside, the ideological implications of the passage are clear. Jarīr's patrons saw their symbolic heritage as lying in the cornerstone figures of pan-Abrahamic monotheisms and the great imperial traditions of Late Antiquity, all bound together under the overarching banner of the Muslim "perpetual empire" (*mulk muʿammar*).[110] In turn, this legacy could be claimed by "outsiders" (such as al-Waḍḍāḥ) who had proved their worth through martial virtue and the adoption of elite cultural identifiers (in this case, Islam and an Arabic name).

Genealogy, actual or imputed, did not constitute the only nor perhaps the most immediate channel of appropriation of the repository of late antique heritage. From what one gathers from the combination of literary anecdotes and archeological remains, Umayyad syncretism extended to courtly behavior.[111] To quote but one example, literary descriptions allude to the Islamic continuation

105 Al-Waḍḍāḥ (lit. "the light skinned") was reportedly a commander of a Berber battle unit named after him (*al-waḍḍāḥiya*). Gordon 2001, 152–153, Kennedy 2001, 48 and Hoyland 2015a, 166.

106 Ṭabarī, II, 1874 (trans. Hillenbrand, XXVI, 243) among other places.

107 Shāh-ī-Āfrīd granddaughter of the last Sasanian King of Kings Yazdgerd III, is reported to have been captured by Qutayba b. Muslim in Merv and placed in al-Walīd I's harem; see Ṭabarī, II, 1247 (trans. Hinds, XXIII, 195) and 1874 (trans. Hillenbrand, XXVI, 243). For other possible renderings of the name, see Justi 1963, 272 who, however, erroneously presents Shāh-ī-Āfrīd as the mother of Ibrahīm (*rg.* 744) as well. On Shāh-ī-Āfrīd and the traditions pertaining to her, see in particular Sprengling 1939, 214–217 and Fowden 2004, 240–247 who makes an interesting case for identifying the figure of the bathing princess in the frescos of Quṣayr ʿAmra with her.

108 The marriage of Khusraw II to one Maria, daughter of emperor Maurice, during Khusraw's exile in Constantinople features in no Byzantine chronicle and is possibly a later literary invention or even a confusion with the notorious Persian Christian queen Shīrīn († 628). On the subject, see Baum 2004, esp. 27–28.

109 Khusraw I, the great-great-great-great-great-great-grandfather of Shāh-ī-Āfrīd, is said to have taken in marriage the daughter of the *khāqān* of the Turks to cement an alliance against the Hephthalites in 560. The Turkish princess reportedly bore him the future Hormozd IV (*rg.* 579–590), who is therefore addressed as "Torkzāda" "son of a Turk" in the *Shāh-nāma*. The marriage, however, is impossible on chronological grounds, as Hormozd must already have been born around 540. The incongruity possibly stems from the confusion with the *khāqān* Khazars (often apostrophized as "Turks" in the sources) as some reports suggest. See Shahbazi 2004, *s.v.* "Hormozd IV".

110 Jarīr, 104 v. 28.

111 On Umayyad court life, see *i.a.* Hillenbrand 1982, 3–20; Shaked 1986, 75–87; Grabar 1987, 148–149; Kennedy 2011; Ballian 2012.

of the Sasanian use of hanging crowns[112] as ceremonial objects, both in secular and votive contexts.[113] Decorative renderings of Sasanian- and Byzantine-style hanging crowns intermingled with vegetal elements can furthermore be seen in the mosaics decorating the inner octagon of the Dome of the Rock,[114] and the presence of actual metal crowns at both the Dome of the Rock and the Kaʿba in Mecca is referenced in medieval accounts.[115] Possible remains of a miniaturized Sasanian crown suspended from a stone chain have further been found in the throne apse in the Umayyad complex in Khirbat al-Mafjar.[116]

The planimetry of Umayyad residences and estates reveals a blend of Syrian or more generally Byzantine and Sasanian as well as Central Asian influences.[117] Remains of statuary and pictorial décor that punctuate Umayyad residences and estates scattered across Palestine, Lebanon, Syria, and Jordan similarly exhibit a plethora of motifs and styles of both Sasanian and Byzantine ascendancy, often mixed eclectically within the same building complexes.[118] Byzantine assistance in terms of both materials and laborers is even explicitly stated in the literary sources on the erection of the Umayyad mosques in Damascus[119] and Medina,[120] while it can be assumed that the craftsmen working on the Dome of the Rock belonged to a Christian workshop that used to lay Greek mosaic inscriptions prior to being employed by the Caliph.[121] The presence of Hellenized artisans at the al-Aqṣā Mosque is furthermore indicated by Greek ink-graffiti on wooden beams.[122] Not

112 On the development of Sasanian crowns, see Erdmann 1951; for Sasanian crowns depicted in numismatics in particular, see Göbl 1968, 6–14 and 42–55 and pls. I–XIV. For Byzantine crowns, see Rousseau 2004.

113 For royal attributes in Sasanian art, see Harper 1979.

114 Grabar 1987, 55–56 and *id.* 2006, 85 fig. 29. See also most recently George 2018, 40–47.

115 George 2018, 46n19 and references there.

116 Ettinghausen 1972, 23–39; Hillenbrand 1982, 19; Shaked 1986, 76. Depiction in Hamilton 1959, 91 pl. XII, no. 6. Cf. Ritter 2017, 133.

117 See *i.a.* Creswell 1969 and, more synoptically, *id.* 1989. For a possible political explanation of increasing Sasanian influence on Islamic art and architecture after the failed siege of Constantinople in 717–718, in particular, see Hillenbrand 1981, 63–64 and *ead.* 1999, 29–34.

118 See *i.a.* Grabar 1964; *id.* 1987; *id.* 1993; Ettinghausen 1972; Hillenbrand 1982; Enderlein/Meinecke 1992; Kröger 1999; Ettinghausen/Grabar/Jenkins-Madina 2001; Finster 2001; Talgam 2004; Meinecke 2014; and *ead.* 2016. For a differentiation of "motifs" and "styles" in the context of Early Islamic décor, see in particular Talgam 2004, 1–2.

119 Ibn ʿAsākir († 1175), II, 25–26 (trans. Elisséeff, 40) among other places.

120 Ṭabarī, II, 1194 (trans. Hinds, XXIII, 142) among other places.

121 Milwright 2016, esp. 131–171.

122 Hamilton 1949, 91–92 and pl. XLVIII; for the text translation of the ink-graffiti on wooden beams in the al-Aqṣā, see Schwabe *apud* Hamilton 1949, 93–95. The beams are likely to date back to the repairs made under al-Mahdī (*rg.* 775–785).

surprisingly, the surviving mosaic depictions in the Dome of the Rock (generally floral) and in the Mosque of Damascus (mostly architectural) resonate stylistically with late antique Byzantine imperial architecture.[123] Moreover, late antique motifs characterize the decorative styles of Early Islamic residential complexes that cannot be positively linked to direct royal patronage as well. Stuccos depicting the royal boar hunt in the Sasanian style,[124] for instance, adorn a restored post-conquest estate in Chāl Tarkhān-ʿEshqābād (20 km south of Tehran).[125] The stucco decoration at Chāl Tarkhān-ʿEshqābād demonstrates several parallels with Umayyad residences in Greater Syria, thus hinting at the existence of a common transregional canon of elite artistic expression.[126] Contemporary luxury metalwork from the Iranian world attests to the same proclivity in late antique and particularly Sasanian style and motifs.[127]

Umayyad artistic syncretism is particularly conspicuous in official illustrations of the figure of the ruler. The sculptural and pictorial decoration of Umayyad residences includes depictions of princely figures that can be identified conjecturally as being of both Sasanian and Byzantine ascendancy. The standing statue originally placed over the entrance to the baths of Khirbat al-Mafjar,[128] for instance, depicts a prince dressed in a Sasanian robe.[129] Sasanian style depictions of ruling figures are also to be found in the stuccos of Qaṣr al-Ḥayr al-Sharqī (95 km north-east of Palmyra).[130] Princely figures of Sasanian as well as Byzantine derivation can coexist in the pictorial and sculptural decoration of the same edifice. In particular, a Sasanian prototype served as a model for the standing statue on the façade of Qaṣr al-Ḥayr al-Gharbī.[131] The reclining ruler depicted on the central panel of the eastern aisle of the south wall in the reception hall of Quṣayr ʿAmra also wears Sasanian royal garments.[132] The figure depicted on a

---

123 For the lost mosaic of al-Walīd's mosque in Medina, see Sauvaget 1947.

124 On the fortunes of the Sasanian motif of the "royal hunt" in Islamic art, see Hillenbrand 2009. For an example of the use of this motif in Syrian Umayyad residences, see the painted decoration in the reception hall in the east wing (first floor) at Qaṣr al-Ḥayr al-Gharbī, Schlumberger 1986, pl. 34.

125 Thompson 1976. See also Morony 2004, 283–284.

126 Morony 2004, 283–284; more in detail Thompson 1976, 9–86.

127 Pinder-Wilson 1960 and Orbeli 1981. Cf. also the recently published late Sasanian or Early Islamic silver female bust in hybrid Sasanian-Byzantine style which bears resemblance to female figures depicted in the stucco decoration of Khirbat al-Mafjar, see Rousseau/Northover 2015.

128 Hamilton 1959, pl. 55 ns. 1 and 5.

129 For Sasanian royal garments, see Rose 2001.

130 Genequand 2018.

131 Schlumberger 1986, pl. 64, fig. a.

132 Cf. in particular Khusraw II's robe in the investiture relief in Tāq-i Bostān.

throne in the central aisle of the main hall at Quṣayr ʿAmra and the sculpture of the seated figure in the court of Qaṣr al-Ḥayr al-Gharbī,[133] on the other hand, hint at a "Mediterranean" prototype. Crowned heads of rulers both in Sasanian and Byzantine style are on display on stone capitals in the Umayyad palace-city of ʿAnjar (44 km east of Beirut).[134]

Similarity in style with late antique vocabulary did not *per se* detract from the novelty of Early Islamic artistic synthesis of pre-Islamic elements into new forms and compositions.[135] In fact, the use of Late Antique motifs in Umayyad official art appears to have been part of a conscious artistic amalgamation rather than a random juxtapositioning, as instances of conscious adaptations and harmonization of styles reveal.[136] Nevertheless, Arabic inscriptions and a proportional increase in epigraphical decoration compared to previous and neighbouring cultures constituted a more culturally distinctive and explicit feature of Early Islamic artistic expression.[137]

The fresco decoration of the Umayyad residence in Quṣayr ʿAmra, the best-preserved example of Umayyad pictorial decoration, is emblematic of the use of Arabic to enhance images and connote cultural difference. The central niche on the south wall of the complex is occupied by a figure on a throne sitting beneath a baldaquin with two attendants dressed in the *hymation* and resembling closely in pose and robe the Byzantine depictions of high officials and biblical figures.[138] The baldaquin is adorned with an Arabic inscription that mentions "the heir apparent of the Muslims".[139] The fresco on the southern wall of the western aisle depicts a figure of a reclining man[140] dressed in rich Sasanian-style robes surrounded by a considerable entourage.[141] A panel placed above the scene is inscribed in Arabic and identifies the depicted figure as the future caliph al-Walīd (II) b. Yazīd – probably the

---

133 Schlumberger 1986, pl. 81, fig. b.
134 Finster 2005, 155.
135 Grabar 1987, 130–131 and 196–199.
136 Cf. for instance the "Romanization" of the Sasanian Senmurv motif in the architectural decoration of the façade of the Umayyad palace in Mshatta (30 km to the south of Amman). See Meinecke 2016, 220–221.
137 Cf. e.g. Grabar 1987, 196–197 and Blair 1998, 3–8.
138 Vibert-Guige/Bisheh 2007, pl. 19.
139 Imbert 2016, 340.
140 Fowden 2004, 184 and Vibert-Guige/Bisheh 2007, 37 who examined the frescos of Quṣayr ʿAmra before their most recent restoration in 2012–2013. They mistakenly interpret the figure depicted in the west aisle of the southern wall as a woman. See De Palma *et al.* 2012, 319. For the conservation and cleaning works at Quṣayr ʿAmra, see De Palma *et al.* 2012 and De Palma *et al.* 2013.
141 Vibert-Guige/Bisheh 2007, pl. 26 and de Palma *et al.*, 334 fig. 29 and 339 fig. 34.

patron of the estate.[142] Beneath the fresco a further Arabic inscription in the shape of a *tabula ansata* can be seen.[143] A fresco on the western wall of the main hall depicts six kings paying homage to Walīd, all with Arabic and Greek labels. Whether readily visible or less easy to make out, Arabic writing became an integral component of the iconography of most Early Islamic buildings.[144] Parallels can be drawn between written artifacts of the time. On Early Islamic seals and metalwork excavated in Iraq and Iran, for instance, symbolic animal figures of Sasanian derivation appear flanked by the short *basmala* (*bi-sm allāh*) or similar short formulaic Arabic inscriptions.[145] Arabic was also used to validate Byzantine seals with Christian imagery.[146]

As the figurative language of Early Islamic architectonic decoration was prevalently – if eclectically – derivative, the use of Arabic inscriptions on building complexes represented a device to lend a distinctive and easily identifiable Arab-Muslim overtone to official depictions. Thus, through the signifier of the Arabic written word, culturally ambivalent symbolism of power was organized into the distinctive ideological framework of Early Islamic imperial authority. It is numismatic evidence, however, that has preserved the richest evidence of the interplay of Arabic inscriptions with figurative depictions of Byzantine and Sasanian ascendancy.

Faceless Monarchs and Arabic Inscriptions

The first six decades of "Islamic" numismatics are distinguished by the constant resort to iconography and compositional schemes derived from Byzantine and Sasanian tradition.

The Islamic conquest of the Middle East brought under the same rule several currency zones: the former Sasanian realm, Byzantine Syria, North Mesopotamia, Egypt, and North Africa as well as Visigothic Spain.[147] As in the pre-conquest period, the workhorses of the Early Islamic administration remained the Byzantine gold *solidus* in the Levant and Egypt and the gold *tremissis* in the Maghreb and Spain. In the East, the Islamic fiscus continued to depend on the Sasanian silver *drahm*.

---

142 Imbert 2016, 332.
143 *Ibid.*, 337.
144 See the list *infra* pp. 171–173 (1 and 2).
145 See e.g. Balog 1974, 137–139 and 134 ns. 5, 6a–b, 7, 8a–d, and 9.
146 Miles 1939. Cf. Grabar 1987, 91 (and fig. 21).
147 Heidemann 1998.

While imitative Byzantine coinage was being issued by Arab-controlled mints in Greater Syria, the circulating stocks were supplemented by freshly minted Byzantine copper coins throughout the 640s and the 650s.[148] The import of Byzantine copper coinage began to decline in 655 and came to an end around 658, possibly as a result of a peace treaty between the then governor of Syria Muʿāwiya b. Abī Sufyān and the emperor Constans II (*rg.* 641–668) in the same year.[149] Metrological research has provided further evidence that coppers struck in the Muslim Levant throughout the 650s and 660s closely followed the weight standards of contemporary Byzantine copper coinage.[150]

Furthermore, prior to the end of the 7th century, the visual language of coins produced in the Empire continued to be divided according to the pre-Islamic monetary zones: of Byzantine ascendancy in Egypt, North Africa, and the Levant, and of Sasanian dominance in Iraq and the Iranian world. The first copper coins minted by the Arabs in the Levant mostly followed prototypes of the Byzantine *folles* of Constans II (641–668), to widely varying degrees of accuracy. In Greater Syria, mints of so-called "Umayyad Imperial Image coinage"[151] in the 660s and 670s departed from direct Byzantine prototypes while at the same time maintaining compositional schemes and symbolism (including crosses) of recognizably Byzantine domination. In the eastern regions of the Empire, where the Arab conquest had broken the line of Sasanian kings, mints followed almost unaltered the designs of the coinage of Khusraw II (*rg.* 602–628) and – to a lesser extent – of Yazdgerd III (*rg.* 632–651), generally with only minor iconographic alterations, up to the last decade of the 7th century. Through continuity of use under Arab-Muslim aegis, frozen depictions of Byzantine and Sasanian imperial power devolved into abstract symbols of authority, while at the same time functioning as guarantees of the coins' value.[152] From an early stage, Arab-Muslim minting authorities developed a number of ways of appropriating Byzantine and Sasanian *regalia* through the insertion of distinctive cultural markers.

---

148 Morrison 1972; Phillips/Goodwin 1997; Heidemann 1998, 97–98; Walmsely 1999; Schulze 2007; Foss 2008, 19–20; and Heidemann 2010a, 153–156.

149 For the peace treaty between Muʿāwiya and Constans II, see Kaplony 1996, 33–36 (A 6).

150 Pottier/Schulze/Schulze 2008.

151 Album/Goodwin 2002, 74–75 and Goodwin 2012, 186. Cf. Oddy/Schulze 2012, 187–193.

152 For the progressive standardization of late Sasanian and Early Islamic Arab-Sasanian coinage iconography and legends, see Sears 1997, 26–30 and Heidemann 2010b, 24–25.

In the year 663, Muʿāwiya I became the first Muslim ruler to have coinage issued in his name – if not quite in his image. The coins in question were Arab-Sasanian *drahms* minted in the former Sasanian mint of Darab-gird, the "city of Darius" in Fārs (ca. 210 km south-east of Shiraz). Ironically enough, the portrait itself depicts the late Sasanian King of Kings Khusraw II. On the field legend behind the bust the Sasanian motto *GDH ʾpzwt* (roughly "may (his) glory increase") can also be read. In accordance with late Sasanian formal conventions,[153] the caliph's name and title are inscribed in front of the royal portrait on the obverse side.[154] On the reverse, a more subtle sign of sovereignty was indicated by the use of dating after the *hijra* instead of the Yazdgerd (AY) or post-Yazdgerd era (PYE).[155]

Both devices are well attested in coeval coinage. In the East, *hijrī* dates first appeared on Arab-Sasanian coinage in the early 650s and gradually supplanted AY dates (often a fossilized AY 20) during the 660s and 670s.[156] Almost at the same time, Islamic governors' names began to replace frozen names of the last King of Kings *Khusraw* and *Yazdgerd*, at first unsystematically in the 660s and then consistently from the 670s (Fig. 6).[157]

Yet for all those unable to navigate their way into the legends, governors' and caliphs' names as well as *hijrī* dates remained hidden behind the many ambiguities of the Pahlavi script. From a formal and a strictly visual point of view, however, a third element of rupture distinguished Muʿāwiya's *drahms* from standard Sasanian issues: the short Arabic invocation *bi-sm allāh* ("in God's name") on the outer margin of these coins. Executed in a larger script than the Pahlavi field-legends and placed on the outer margin where no inscription would have been expected in canonical Sasanian coinage, the short Arabic invocation stood out from the rest of the coin. Users able to read Arabic would have recognized in the legend the most common Muslim invocation and a link to its ubiquity in Arabic official and private writerly culture and beyond.[158] For those unfamiliar with Arabic, the different script offered a meta-literate and easily identifiable sign of the distinction of the issuing authority. It furthermore provided the rest of

153 Minting design in the former Sasanian territories was in principle overseen by local governors, though mints formally under the control of the Kufan and Basran super-provinces could show signs of coordination. Sears 1997, 380–385.

154 Göbl 1968, 16–17 and pl. XV and Gaube 1973, 11 (2.2.1.1) and fig. 1.

155 For chronological systems used in Arab-Sasanian coinage, see Sears 1997, 188–262 and Album/Goodwin 2002, 81.

156 Sears 1997, 382; Album/Goodwin 2002, 6; and Heidemann 2010a, 163.

157 Album/Goodwin 2002, 6 and Heidemann 2010a, 163–165.

158 For the cultural influence of the Muslim *basmala* beyond the Arabic documentary tradition, see *infra* Ch. IV.

Sasanian imagery, mottos, and coin design with a new level of meaning under the "umbrella" of the Early Islamic Empire.

Glossing over the occasional and very marginal exchange of figurative motifs across currency zones – such as the appearance of re-emphasized Byzantine and Umayyad imagery on Early Islamic Arab-Sasanian copper coinage – [159] no shared symbol linked regional coinage before the implementation of the epochal monetary reform of ʿAbd al-Malik in 696–698. Short Arabic legends in fact constituted the only *visual* element that linked monetary issues in all three main metals at an empire-wide level throughout the 650s and up to the 690s.

In its earliest decades, derivative Arab-Byzantine coinage sporadically featured Arabic legends[160] or Arabic countermarks.[161] In Greater Syria, a more integrated use of bilingual Greek-Arabic mint names and validating expressions appeared on copper coins following the implementation of more closely regimented minting practices inaugurated in the reign of Muʿāwiya I.[162] In the 690s, monolingual Arabic legends emerged on silver, gold and copper coinage minted in Syrian mints as a result of Marwanid reforms of coin designs.[163] In the Eastern provinces, short validating expressions in Arabic are found on the outer margins of Arab-Sasanian silver coins from 651 onwards.[164] Similar Arabic formulae as well as Arabic countermarks appear on Iraqi and Iranian (mostly undated) Arab-Sasanian copper coins, together with Arabic expressions that have no parallel on precious metal coins.[165] In 667/668, the mints under the authority of the governor of Baṣra (in office 664–670) and Iraq (670–673), Ziyād b. Abī Sufyān, began to issue coins with the motto *bi-sm allāh rabbi* "In the name of God, my Lord".[166] In the following years, other eastern governors followed suit by minting mottos *ad personam* on their coinage (Fig. 6).[167] Furthermore, during the Second Civil War (680–692) all main competing factions issued Arab-Sasanian coinage from the mints under their control and used faction-specific slogans to their propagandistic advantage.

---

159 Gyselen 2000, 31–38. For the *orans* motif, in particular, see *infra* p. 144–145.

160 Foss 2008, 34–35.

161 Schulze/Goodwin 2005.

162 Album/Goodwin 2002, 81–91; Foss 2002 and *id*. 2008, 42–55; Heidemann 2010a, 156–159; and Bacharach 2010, 4–5.

163 See *infra* p. 126–130.

164 Album/Goodwin 2002, 6–9 and Heidemann 2010a, 163.

165 Gyselen 2000, 79 and 83 for Arabic mint names; 92–93 for Arabic legends with parallels in other numismatic media; 96 and 98 for Arabic legends without parallels in other numismatic media; and 20–22 for Arabic countermarks.

166 Album/Goodwin 2002, 9 and Heidemann 2010a, 165.

167 Gubernatorial mottos on Arab-Sasanian coinage could reflect propagandistic aims in response to political friction. See Sears 2003a.

Fig. 6: *ʿAbd al-Raḥmān b. Ziyād,* drahm, *Nahr-Tīrā?, 54 (673/674), 3,7 g (enlarged).* *© Staatliche Münzsammlung, Munich.*

It is against this background that the first explicitly Muslim public inscriptions referring to Muḥammad as God's messenger and proclaiming God's uniqueness saw the light on Zubayrid coinage.[168] At the far western end of the Empire, short-lived Arab-Byzantine copper coins with Arabic marginal legends were issued by the governor, Ḥassan b. al-Nuʿmān al-Ghassānī (in office 698–699/700).[169] After the new governor, Musā b. Nuṣayr (699/700–715) reinstated Latin legends,[170] bilingual Arabic-Latin epigraphic gold coinage was minted in North Africa and southern Spain between 715 and 720 (Fig. 20).[171] Only Egypt's local copper coinage did not include Arabic legends prior to the introduction of epigraphic coinage.[172]

In the early days of interpretative debates on the nature of Islamic art,[173] Ernst Herzfeld wrote of a "negative" and a "positive" discriminative sign of Arab patronage of Umayyad residences: the heterogeneous mix of Byzantine and Sasanian features and the presence of Arabic inscriptions respectively.[174] This combination characterizes very aptly the uses of Arabic public writing examined in this section. In terms of extra-textual meaning, Arabic legends on pre-reform coinage and inscriptions provided a symbolic frame of reference for images of royalty and power from the Sasanian and Byzantine past. If the juxtaposition and adaptation of motifs and styles drawn from all over the conquered lands enabled imperial art to resonate with multiple cultural traditions, Arabic epigraphical decoration infused new blood into the symbols of Late

168 Heidemann 2010a, 167; Foss 2013.
169 See now Jonson 2015, 227–230.
170 Jonson 2015, 224–226 and 230–233.
171 Balaguer 1976; Bates 1992, 281–284; Jonson 2012, 157–158.
172 For the chronology of Early Islamic Egyptian coinage, see *supra* pp. 65–66.
173 On the concept of Islamic art, its development, and its limits in general, see Blair/Bloom 2003.
174 Herzfeld 1910, 107.

Antiquity, while at the same time providing a much-needed modicum of dissociation, cultural self-assertion, and visual coherence to Early Islamic imperial artistic expression. From the point of view of the beholders, the divide between textual and image-based messages was likely to have been blurred. Rather, both aspects operated jointly and in a complementary fashion as integral components of Early Islamic imperial visual rhetoric.

From Image to Word

While Late Antique imagery continued to claim a prominent place in architectonic complexes closely tied to the halls of power and royal patronage, coinage – the amplest source of visual culture in the Early Islamic Empire – registers a gradual but decisive shift towards aniconism, beginning at the close of the 7th century.

Shortly after the Marwanid victory in the Second Civil War, the mint of Damascus 77 AH (696/697) began to issue a novel brand of imperial gold coins, followed by silver ones a year later. These new releases adopted the lighter standard weights of 4,25 g for the *dīnār* and 2,975 g for the *dirham*, compared to the average Byzantine (4,55 g) and Arab-Byzantine *solidi* (4,37–4,38 g) and the Sasanian and Arab-Sasanian drachms (3,6–4,3 and 4,16 g respectively).[175] The second and more conspicuous feature of the new coinage was the elimination of mimetic signs of power in favor of an entirely epigraphic design (Figs. 7 and 8 and Tab. 2). The obverse side of the reformed gold coinage displayed a version of the Muslim testimony of faith in the field legend, reading:

> *lā ilāh illā llāh waḥda-hu lā sharīk la-hu*
>
> "there is no god but God alone, He has no associate"

and the margin legend:

> *muḥammad rasūl allāh* (Q 48: 9) *arsala-hu bi-l-hudā wa-dīn al-ḥaqq li-yuẓhira-hu ʿalā al-dīn kulli-hi* (Q 48: 28)
>
> "Muḥammad is God's Messenger, He has sent Him with the guidance and the religion of truth so that He may proclaim it above all religions".

On the larger silver *dirhams*, the latter legend was displayed on the reverse side and featured the extra line *wa-law kariha al-mushrikūn* " . . . even if the 'associationists' hate it".[176] The reverse of the gold *dīnārs* featured a paraphrase of Sura *al-Ikhlāṣ* (Q 112) in the central legend:

> *allāh aḥad allāh al-ṣamad lam yalid wa-lam yūlad*
>
> "God, One, the Eternal He does not beget nor was begotten"

---

175 For the role of the epigraphic coinage's reduced weight standard in its enduring success based on Gresham's Law, see Bacharach 2010, 19–22.

176 On the determination of the reverse side of silver reformed coinage, see Bacharach 2010, 16.

https://doi.org/10.1515/9783110740820-018

complemented by an administrative legend on the coin's margin:

> *bi-sm allāh ḍuriba hāḏā al-dīnār bi-kadhā fī sanat kadhā*
>
> "in the name of God, this *dīnār* was minted in so-and-so in the year so-and-so".

This abrupt development is accompanied in Muslim historical memory by a wealth of anecdotal information. The narrative sources present the reform as the outcome of an ideological "cold war" with Byzantium and an attempt by the Caliphate to emancipate itself from the import of gold coinage from Byzantium.[177] That the Arabs had already been minting gold coinage for generations by the time of the reform[178] complicates the interpretation of traditional Muslim accounts.

Fig. 7: *Anonymous,* dīnār, *without mint (Damascus), 92 (710/711), 4,252 g (enlarged). © Staatliche Münzsammlung, Munich.*

In fact, the introduction of epigraphic coinage can be interpreted as the crowning of a process that deepened its roots in the Sufyanid period. As we have seen, in the decades leading to ʿAbd al-Malik's reform, Arabic legends with distinctively Islamic overtones had been increasingly featured on Islamic coinage of different political factions. Over time, coins minted under the aegis of the Arab authority had further adopted designs dissociated from Sasanian/Zoroastrian and, espe-

177 According to the main account relating to ʿAbd al-Malik's coinage reform in Baladhurī, 240 (trans. Hitti, 383–384), the Byzantine emperor would have objected to Muslim mottos on imported papyrus rolls and threatened ʿAbd al-Malik with the minting of gold *solidi* featuring anti-Muḥammadan legends in retaliation. In response to the threat, he is supposed to have banished Byzantine gold coins and ordered the minting of new coinage to replace them. A parallel unrelated account of the events is given by Theophanes, 365, 10f. 14–18 (trans. Mango, 509–510); for this passage, see also *infra* p. 146.
178 Miles 1967.

cially, Byzantine/Christian symbolism. Experimentation with epigraphic designs was not a complete novelty either, as attested to by the Arab-Sasanian drachms of the Zubayrid governor of Sistān ʿAbd al-ʿAzīz b. ʿAbd Allāh b. ʿĀmir (in office ca. 685/686–691/692).[179] Despite all this, the innovative potential of the reform was nothing short of radical.

Fig. 8: *Anonymous,* dirham, *Wāsiṭ, 93 (711/712), 2,67 g (enlarged).*
© Staatliche Münzsammlung, Munich.

Ever since symbolic animals made their appearance on Lydian coins in the late 7th century BCE, figurative depictions had been a constant of the coinage of the Near East and the Mediterranean basin and beyond, with textual legends serving mostly as a secondary illustrative feature. In addition to abandoning a figurative model, Umayyad epigraphic coinage also eliminated another common denominator of preceding coinage: the ruler's presence, visual and textual. This latter development was all the more significant as it stood in complete opposition to the trend evidenced by the forerunners of the reform. Significantly, ʿAbd al-Malik b. Marwān had been the first Islamic ruler to mint coinage in his own name in Greater Syria.[180] During the Second Civil War, governors loyal to various contenders had furthermore minted Arab-Sasanian silver coinage in the name of their respective liege.[181]

179 Mochiri 1981.
180 See *infra* pp. 137–138 with further references.
181 Arab-Sasanian silver coinage in the name of Ibn al-Zubayr was issued at the mints of Ardashīr Khurra in 65 (684/685) and 67 AH (686/687), Darab-gird in 53 (684/685), 56–57 (687/688–688/689), and 59 AY (690/691), Jahrom in 54 AY (685/686), Fasā in 54 (685/686) and 56 AY (687/688), Jayy in 63 AH (682/683), the unidentified *GRM-KRMAN* in 69 AH (688/689), Kirmān in 65 (684/685) and 67 AH (686/687), Jiruft in 66–67 AH (685/686–686/687), Iṣṭakhr in 66 AH (685/686), Tawwaj in 67 AH (686/687), and Yazd in 69 AH (688/689); Arab-Sasanian silver coinage in the name of ʿAbd al-Malik b. Marwān was issued at the mints of Ardashīr Khurra in 73 AH (692/693), Darab-gird in 60 (691/692), 63 (694/695), and 67 AY (696/697), Fasā in 60 AY (690/691),

Another striking aspect of the monetary reforms of ʿAbd al-Malik is that by changing the language on the coins to Arabic he *ipso facto* tailored the semantic ideological message to a much more restricted and targeted social group, namely those who had direct or indirect access to Arabic literacy. Importantly, evidence suggests that Zubayrid loyalists had been inclined towards a somewhat different approach just a few years before. When the abovementioned Zubayrid governor ʿAbd al-ʿAzīz b. ʿAbd Allāh issued coins with an all-epigraphic reverse side inscribed with a version of the testimony of faith (*shahāda*), he resorted to Middle Persian in Pahlavi script rather than Arabic.[182] Similarly, coins minted in Kirmān in 688 by the "anti-caliph's"[183] own brother Muṣʿab b. al-Zubayr feature a double *basmala* on the marginal legend, both in Arabic characters and in a Middle Persian translation.[184] Possibly minted during Muṣʿab's tenure, is an Arab-Sasanian issue on which, instead of the minting authority's name, the Pahlavi legend in front of the portrait reads *Mhmt pgtgmy y Dat* "Muḥammad is God's Messenger".[185]

Changing the language from Middle Persian (or Greek) to Arabic limited or, at the very least, retargeted the *textual* reach of the coinage. In fact, the increased use of Arabic legends as well as the evolution of the inscriptional program on Marwanid coinage throughout the years of the Second Civil War, leading up to the all-epigraphic reform has been convincingly interpreted by Bacharach as a response to enduring Khārijite challenges.[186] Yet for all their innovative potential, Islamic monetary issues before 77 AH (696–697) still illustrated, complemented and enhanced (or, rather, appropriated) emblems of suzerainty conveyed by figurative depictions. By substituting figurative imagery with the written word, the reform eliminated arguably the most immediate and reliable vehicle of meaning on the coinage. In fact, literary evidence implies that the new coinage encountered the opposition of both conservative Muslim circles and the non-Arabicized population.[187]

---

and Merv in 76 AH (694/695); Arab-Sasanian silver coinage in the name of Qaṭarī b. al-Fujāʾa was issued at the mints of Ardashīr Khurra, Jahrom, Iṣṭakhr, Tawwaj, and Yazd in 75 AH (694/695), Bīshāpūr in 69 (688/689) and 75 AH (694/695), Darab-gird in 75 (694/695) and 76 AH (695/696), and the unidentified *KRMN-BN* in 77 AH (696/697). Album/Goodwin 2002, 20–21 and 30 and Album 2011, 25 (15–16A)–26 (32–33).

182 Mochiri 1981.

183 On the problematic notion of Ibn al-Zubayr as an "anti-caliph", see McMillan 2011, 70–73. In the referenced paragraph the term "anti-caliph" is used for the sake of readability.

184 *BMC* I p. 102–103.

185 Shams Eshragh 2004.

186 Bacharach 2010, 12–15.

187 Baladhurī 454 (trans. Hitti, II 266); Mawārdī 154 (trans. Yate, 223–224); Ibn al-Athīr IV 416–417. Non-Muslim discontent towards the epigraphic coinage is presented by Baladhurī and

Contemporary sphragistics offers a close comparison. In Egypt, clay seals preserved on the official correspondence of high-ranking Muslim officials dating to the first decades of Muslim rule usually featured animal and even human depictions.[188] There are, however, exceptions such as the all-epigraphic seal of the governor ʿAbd Allāh b. Saʿd (in office 645–655).[189] In the early decades of the 8th century, all-epigraphic seals appeared with increasing consistency on Arabic and Greek official letters, at first coexisting but soon enough supplanting figurative items. The repertoire of about 50 seals associated with Qurra b. Sharīk, in particular, shows trends of transition. The overwhelming majority of seals depict a recurrent animal figure – possibly a wolf, a cheetah, or even a horse – flanked by a star,[190] while single seals depict human subjects – possibly two affronté women and a helmeted figure.[191] A further specimen, however, is inscribed solely with Arabic inscriptions[192] while yet another double seal displays an Arabic inscription on one side and a human figure on the other.[193] Later items of the correspondence

Mawārdī as directed towards their lighter weight standard rather than at their innovative visual language.

188 See the seal of the first Muslim governor of Egypt ʿAmr b. al-ʿĀṣ, depicting a bull (*Nilus* IV 17 = *PERF* 556) and the seal of ʿAbd al-ʿAzīz b. Marwān showing a man with an axe (*Nilus* IV 33 = *PERF* 587). Cf. also the devices on the two seals of *P.Gascou* 27a–b (fig. 2 and 3), likewise issued by the chancery of ʿAbd al-ʿAzīz.

189 Boud'hors *et al.* 2017, 117–118 (ns. 1 and 2 reading *mālik al-mulk* "possessor of the realm").

190 Seals of Qurra b. Sharīk depicting a recurrent animal figure combined with a star are to be found in *P.BeckerNPAF* 12 (709); *P.Heid.Arab.* I 3 (= *Chrest.Khoury* I 91) (710), 4 (709/710), a–l (= *SB* I 5644–5654) (all dated to 709/710), *P.Cair.Arab.* 146 (= *P.BeckerNPAF* 1) (710), 151 (= *P.BeckerNPAF* 5 = *P.BeckerPAF* 14 = *P.Heid.Arab.* I 12) (710), 160 (= *P.BeckerNPAF* 13) (709/710), and 161 (= *P.BeckerNPAF* 14) (709/710); *P.Lond.* IV 1346 (710), 1363 (710), 1374 (711), 1385 (709?), *P.Qurra* 2 (709) and 3 (709/710); *P.Ross.Georg.* IV 2 (710), 4 (710), and 11 (710); *Nilus* IV 18 (= *PERF* 593) (710). Further examples of this typology of seal are to be found in *P.Lond.* IV 1492 (descr.), a collection of 24 detached seals from papyri in the archive of Basileios.

191 *P.Lond.* IV (descr.) 1492.

192 One epigraphical seal of Qurra b. Sharīk is mentioned by Bell in *P.Lond.* IV (descr.) 1492.

193 A fragment of the valediction and date of an Arabic letter in the collection of the University Library of Basel was transcribed by Becker in the Introduction to *P.Bas.* I p. 6–7. The greeting formula used, exclusively reserved for Christian addressees (*wa-l-salām ʿalā man ittabaʿ al-hudā*) and its mention of the year 91 AH (709/710), the date of most of the Qurra correspondence, strongly suggest that we are dealing with a letter from the chancery of Qurra b. Sharīk. A plate of a double seal attached to the letter's fragment can be seen in *P.Bas.* I, pl. I. Of the Arabic portion of the seal only *bi-llāh* "in God" can be clearly read, possibly part of the formula 1 [*āmin fulān* (Qurra?)] 2 *bi-llāh*. During the latest (re- and first) edition of the Basel papyrus collection under the supervision of Sabine Huebner (2015–2017), the double seal and the scraps of papyrus attached could not be located. I thank William Graham Claytor VI for bringing the document to my attention.

of Muslim officials are examples of the transition to all-epigraphic Arabic seals[194] over the course of the 8th and 9th century.[195] Christian officials serving under the Muslim administration, on the contrary, continued to use Christian symbolism on their seals.[196] Fiscal agents found in the Bēk family archive used bullae featuring both astral and animal imagery of Sasanian ascendancy, all-epigraphic Arabic inscriptions, and combinations of figurative and epigraphic motifs.[197]

The gradual adoption of the epigraphic design for coins and seals not only increased radically the presence of Arabic in the public sphere but also reconfigured the way it was experienced. If throughout the period of the 640s to the 690s Arabic writing on coins had operated as an ancillary tool of imperial ideology, it now became its main vehicle – both textually and visually.

A Note on Early Islamic Iconophobia

Scholars have from time to time viewed the general rejection of mimetic representation in Islamic art as the broader cultural matrix of ʿAbd al-Malik's monetary reform – at least as far as its aesthetic dimension is concerned.[198] Dating the emergence of an aniconic vein in Islamic figurative arts is a matter of contention. In particular, while it is generally accepted that Muslim jurisprudential traditions regarding the prohibition on the depiction of living beings deepens their roots in the Umayyad period, determining exactly how far this notion reaches back in time can be controversial.

Van Reenen's extensive study of *ḥadith*-traditions concerned with the Islamic *Bilderverbot* traced the first emergence of iconophobic trends in Muslim litera-

194 See e.g. *Nilus* IV 1 (= *PERF* 577) (718) of Rāshid b. Khālid; *CPR* XXII 9 (729) of Nājid b. Muslim and 13 (VIII) of Ibrahīm b. Yaḥyā; *Nilus* IV 32 (743) of al-Qāsim b. ʿUbayd Allāh; *Nilus* IV 25 (= *PERF* 667) (811) of Ḥassan b. Saʿīd; *Nilus* IV 21 (= *PERF* 670) (812) of Yūnus b. ʿAbd al-Raḥmān; *Nilus* IV 23 (*PERF* 758) (851/852) of ʿAbd al-Malik b. Muḥammad; and *Nilus* IV 30 (= *PERF* 776) (862) of Abū al-Ḥasan Aḥmad b. Muḥammad.

195 Sijpesteijn 2012b, 171–172 and *ead.* 2018, 31.

196 See for instance P.Vind.inv. A. Ch. 1207 (= *PERF* 959), an Arabic tax receipt dated 941 bearing a seal with a cross encircled by Greek letters. This document is currently being prepared for an edition by N. Vanthieghem and A. Martin.

197 Khan 2007, 82–90. For seals and sealing practices in late antique Bactria, see Lerner/Sims-Williams 2011.

198 Most notably Paret 1976–1977, who argued that the emergence of iconophobic attitudes in Islamic art coincided with the coinage reforms at the end of the 7th century.

ture to the 720s–740s, i.e. a generation after ʿAbd al-Malik's reform.[199] Traces of imperially sponsored iconophobic or *proprio sensu* iconoclastic initiatives are even harder to come by and are essentially restricted to historical accounts of the edict against images of Yazīd II (*rg.* 720–724), promulgated possibly in 723.[200] Significantly, chronicles hold that the edict was revoked by Yazīd's brother and successor, Hishām (*rg.* 724–743) upon the former's death.[201] To be sure, trends towards aniconism were in evidence in Islamic art from its very inception. The decoration of Early Islamic sacral architecture such as the Dome of the Rock and the Umayyad Mosque of Damascus in particular, stands out for the absence of figural depictions, other than that of inanimate objects such as architectural or floral motifs.[202] Yet, coeval palatial architecture and numismatics alike are distinguished by a plethora of sculptural and pictorial depictions of animal and human subjects, as most clearly demonstrated in Umayyad complexes in Quṣayr ʿAmra,[203] Khirbat al-Mafjar,[204] and Qaṣr al-Ḥayr al-Gharbī[205] among others. The same applies to figurative decoration in the eastern part of the Empire, as exemplified in the stuccos of the abovementioned post-Sasanian palaces in Chāl Tarkhān-ʿEshqābād.[206]

Turning to numismatics proper, attempts at removing non-Islamic – and specifically Christian – symbols from the surface of coins feature both in the literary and in the documentary record. The anonymous Syriac *Maronite Chronicle* (after 665)[207] states that Muʿāwiya I minted gold and silver coinage that was rejected by the Christian population on account of its lack of crosses.[208] The gold issues mentioned in the passage may be identified with several types of imitation of *solidi* of Phocas and Heraclius, in which crosses have been removed and the reverse cross

---

199 Van Reenen 1990 *contra* Paret 1976–1977. See also previous footnote. Among earlier discussions on the lawfulness of mimic art in Islam, see Arnold 1965, 1–40; Creswell 1946; and Dodd 1969, 38–47.

200 For Yazīd II's edict, its motivations, geographical outreach, and related archaeological and literary evidence, see now Sahner 2017, summarizing previous research on the subject. For the date of the edict in particular, see *ibid.*, 25–27.

201 See *i.a.* Sahner 2017, 33.

202 Cf. the tradition according to which the angel Gabriel refused to enter Muḥammad's home because of the images depicted on its façade, instructing His host to decapitate them "so that they might become like trees". Van Reenen 1990, 33.

203 See especially Vibert-Guigue/Bisheh 2007.

204 See especially Hamilton 1959.

205 See especially Schlumberger 1986.

206 See *supra* p. 134.

207 For a bibliographical overview of the so-called *Maronite Chronicle*, see Teule 2009, 145–147.

208 *Chron. Mar.*, 71 (trans. Palmer, 31).

on steps has been substituted by a T-shaped bar on steps.[209] A more proactive confrontation of Christian and Zoroastrian religious symbolism was heralded by the Marwanid victory in the Second Civil War. Specifically, the Christian cross and the Zoroastrian fire altar disappeared from all gold, silver, and copper coinage minted under direct caliphal control in Greater Syria between 692 and 696.[210] On the Egyptian so-called *ABAZ* copper coins (Fig. 2) – most likely minted under ʿAbd al-ʿAzīz b. Marwān (in office 685–705) – crosses were eliminated as well.

To summarize, all mentioned alterations and adaptations of Byzantine and Sasanian designs appear to have been motivated by a search for an appropriate figurative incarnation of Umayyad imperial ideology rather than by opposition to mimetic representation *per se*. Nor can aniconic tendencies be registered among other political groups within the contemporary Muslim community. In particular, during the Second Civil War, Marwanids, Zubayrids,[211] and Khārijites[212] alike minted Arab-Sasanian coinage in the territories within their respective spheres of influence. All warring groups left the Sasanian iconography on these coins virtually untouched. Rather, political statements were fleshed out by various Arabic slogans inscribed on the outer margin of each faction's coinage, such as the distinctively Khārijite motto *lā ḥukma illā li-lāh* "judgment belongs to God alone". Other late 7th- and early 8th-century coins of Umayyad governors such as the so-called *orans* drahms of Bishr b. Marwān,[213] the so-called radial *drahms* of the "viceroy" of the East, al-Ḥajjāj b. Yūsuf (in office 694–714),[214] and the "standing warrior" trilingual *drahms* of Yazīd b. al-Muhallab (in office 701/702–704/705)[215] introduced extensive modifications to coin imagery, yet never attempted to remove it.

Some atypical "standing caliph" coppers from Palestine and Northern Mesopotamia feature only the legend *muḥammad rasūl allāh* (Muḥammad is God's messenger) flanking the "standing caliph" figure on the obverse. On a rare issue of Arab-Sasanian silver drachms minted in Damascus, presently known through a unique specimen dated 691/692,[216] the name Muḥammad can be read in front of

---

209 Miles 1967, 207–210; Album/Goodwin 2002, 91; Foss 2008, 41–42; Heidemann 2010a, 160–161; and Bacharach 2010, 3–5.

210 See *infra* section "Becoming Word".

211 For Zubayrid coinage, see in particular Foss 2013.

212 For Khārijite coinage during the Second Civil War, see in particular Foss 2002 and Geiser 2010, 172–180.

213 See in particular Treadwell 1999.

214 See in particular Album/Goodwin 2002, 29.

215 Walker 1952, 108–110 (n. 3).

216 Morton & Eden LTB (in Association with Sotheby's), 2012 lot 20 (*muḥammad rasūl allāh*, 691/692, Damascus).

the typical Sasanian royal portrait – the spot reserved for the name of the issuing authority depicted in the field portrait. Since they first appeared on the coinage of the Persian satrap of Lydia and Caria Tyssaphernēs (in office 413–395 BCE), nametags on coins have conventionally referred to the figures depicted on the field. This would imply that the abovementioned coins should be interpreted as depictions of the Prophet Muḥammad.[217] In view of the Islamic aversion to depictions of human figures in general and of religious figures in particular, this interpretation has found little resonance with scholars of Islamic numismatics.[218] Of greater interest to the point at issue, however, is not whether these coins were *intended* as depictions of Muḥammad but rather that they *could* easily be (mis-) interpreted as such – which does not appear to have been much of a deterrent for the minting authorities.

While Islamic attitudes towards images cannot be discounted as one of the influences behind the visual style of ʿAbd al-Malik's coinage reform, they fail to provide sufficient reason for it on their own.

Becoming Word: The Evolution of Coin Design ca. 690–700

While a full appraisal of the reasons behind the introduction of epigraphic coinage during the late 690s and early 700s may continue to elude us, the choice to conceptualize imperial authority in the form of Arabic epigraphy is given some additional context by previous Muslim monetary reforms and their short-term impact.[219]

The formulation of the public ideology of the Early Islamic Empire on coinage drew important input from political frictions within the Muslim community itself. In particular, shorter versions of the *shahāda* were included in the legends of Arab-Sasanian dirhams minted by the Zubayrid governors in Iraq and Iran.[220]

---

217 Foss 2001, 9. Gaube 1973, 36 2.2.3.6, 12 identified the Muḥammad (*MHMT*) occurring in Pahlavi or Arabic on the marginal legend, in front of the portrait, or both in some Arab-Sasanian drachms (so-called "Muḥammad-series") minted in Northern Iran with the homonym Prophet. The figure, however, is probably to be understood as the governor of the region Muḥammad b. Marwān, see Sears, 2003b, 90–97. See also Hoyland 2007, 593–596.

218 Heidemann 2010a, 175–176n71 and *id.* 2010b, 24–25, who argues that by the late 7th century, legends and depictions and text had become separated and independent aspects of coinage, and Treadwell 2015, 86–91.

219 I delve into the relationship between the "standing caliph" and all-epigraphic coinage in Garosi 2022.

220 Bacharach 2010 labels the version of the *shahāda* appearing on Zubayrid coinage as "short" (*bism allāh muḥammad rasūl allāh* "In God's name, Muḥammad is God's Messenger") and "Eastern"

Following the Marwanid victory over the Zubayrids, ʿAbd al-Malik and his subordinates introduced several changes to the coinage. Anonymous and undated solidi were probably minted in Damascus before 74 AH (693/694), based on a Byzantine prototype depicting Heraclius and his sons Heraclius Constantine and Heraclonas on the obverse and a cross on four steps on the reverse.[221] ʿAbd al-Malik's so-called *shahāda* solidi departed from this prototype in three main respects. One was the rather superficial modification of the figures' robes, crowns and facial features. More eye-catching was the removal of crosses from the crowns and scepters held by the obverse figures, and the transformation of the cross on the reverse into a globe on a pole. The third major marker of distinction was the removal of the reverse Greek legend, and its replacement by the Arabic inscription

> *bi-sm allāh lā ilāh illā llāh waḥda-hu muḥammad rasūl allāh,*
>
> "There is no god but God alone, Muḥammad is God's Messenger" (Fig. 9).

Between 72 and 74 AH (690/691–693/694), the same Arabic legend appears on the margin of Arab-Sasanian silver drachms of the Khusraw type issued by the mints of Ḥimṣ (72 AH) and Damascus (72[222]–74 AH).[223]

Fig. 9: *Anonymous,* solidus, *without mint (Damascus?), without date (690–692?).*
© Ashmolean Museum, University of Oxford.

(*bi-sm allāh lā ilāh illā allāh waḥda-hu muḥammad rasūl allāh* "In God's name, there is no god but God alone, Muḥammad is God's Messenger"). In contrast to all-epigraphic coinage, earlier versions of the *shahāda* included the *basmala* as an integral part of the testimony of faith. For different versions of the *shahāda* circulating in Arabic public media, see also Bacharach/Anwar 2012.

221 Miles 1967, 210–211, ns. 6–13; Album/Goodwin 2002, 91; Foss 2008, 65; Bacharach 2010, 9; and Heidemann 2010a, 173–174.

222 Arab-Sasanian drachms minted in Damascus in 72 AH feature a short testimony of faith (*bi-sm allāh muḥammad rasūl allāh* "In God's name, Muḥammad is God's Messenger").

223 Album/Goodwin 2002, 27–28; Foss 2008, 65–66; and Bacharach 2010, 11.

More extensive both in terms of number of sub-types, overall quantitative items and geographical outreach was copper, gold, and silver coinage featuring a bearded standing figure holding a girt with a sword. Unlike previous Arab-Byzantine designs, this iconography – commonly referred to as "standing caliph" – [224] was not based on a identifiable prototype.

The "standing caliph" design possibly appeared first on copper coinage before its adoption on gold coinage in 693/694.[225] Gold coinage of this type (Fig. 10) is characterized by the same globe on a pole on the reverse, and both obverse and reverse images are encircled by Arabic legends. The obverse legend is identical to the one on the *shahāda* solidi while the reverse one reads

bi-sm allāh ḍuriba hādhā al-dīnār sanat kadhā wa-kadhā

"In God's name, this *dīnār* was minted in the year so-and-so."[226]

Fig. 10: *Anonymous,* dīnār, *without mint (Damascus?), 77 (696/697).* *© Ashmolean Museum, University of Oxford.*

Copper "standing caliph" issues from the northern Syrian *junds* (Damascus, Ḥimṣ, and Qinnasirīn) display a reverse symbol resembling the Greek letter Φ – possibly an abbreviation for *ph(ollis)* (< lat. *follis)*[227] (Fig. 11a). In contrast, "standing caliph" copper coinage from *jund Filasṭīn* and *Urdunn* continued to display the Greek numeral *my* (**M** = 40). The figure on the obverse of coins from Palestinian mints furthermore distinguishes itself by a comparatively larger head, adorned

224 On terminology, see Album/Goodwin 2002, 74 and Oddy/Schulze 2012, 193.

225 Cf. for instance Foss 2008, 64.

226 Miles 1967, 212–216, ns. 14–19; Album/Goodwin 2002, 91–94; Foss 2008, 68; Bacharach 2010, 12; and Heidemann 2010a, 175–176.

227 Walker 1956, XXIII.

with a larger headdress (Fig. 11b). On the Palestinian variety, the standing figure further shows raised shoulders and a smaller scabbard while the robe is characterized by a herringbone motif. Copper coinage from the Jazīra depicting the "standing caliph" displays characteristics of both Syrian and Palestinian counterparts in that it features the obverse figure typical of Palestinian mints, combined with the reverse *phi*-shaped object of the northern Syrian issues.

ʿAbd al-Malik is usually credited as the issuing authority on coppers struck by Syrian and Jordanian mints, which bear the usual caliphal titles *ʿabd allāh* and *amīr al-muʾminīn*.[228] In addition to the common type, the mints of Sarmīn (45 km south-west of Aleppo) and Manbij (80 km north-east of Aleppo) also issued anonymous coppers featuring the title *khalīfat allāh* or *khalīfat allāh* and *amīr allāh* (only at Sarmīn). Furthermore, the mint of Maʿarrat Miṣrīn only minted "standing caliph" coinage of the *khalīfat allāh* type. On the other hand, the legend on the obverse of Palestinian and Northern Mesopotamian coinage reads *muḥammad rasūl allāh* (simply *muḥammad* in Ḥarrān), seemingly indicating the figure depicted on the obverse.[229] By contrast, silver and gold "standing caliph" coinage was always anonymous.[230]

Fig. 11a: *ʿAbd al-Malik*, fals, *Ḥalab, without date, 3,29 g (enlarged).*
© Staatliche Münzsammlung, Munich.

228 The mints of Damascus and Amman, in addition to their respective main series, issued also "standing caliph" copper coinage featuring the *shahāda* on both sides of the coin; Foss 2008, 75. Rare issues from the Sarmīn mint also add the name ʿAbd al-Raḥmān, probably a governor; Foss 2008, 80.
229 Cf. *supra* p. 149.
230 For a detailed account of the different subtypes of "standing caliph" copper coinage with regard to iconography and legends, see Album/Goodwin 2002, 91–98 and Foss 2008, 66–81.

Fig. 11b: Muḥammad rasūl allāh, fals, Īlyā Filasṭīn *(Jerusalem), without date.* *© Dumbarton Oaks, Byzantine Collection, Washington, DC.*

A "standing caliph" silver issue is attributed to the mint of Damascus (?) for the year 75 AH (694/695). The obverse features a Sasanian royal bust surrounded by Arabic legends detailing the date, with a margin legend corresponding to the typical reverse legend of the gold series (Fig. 12). On the reverse, the typical Zoroastrian altar is supplanted by a "standing caliph" figure, while the two attendants are replaced by the Arabic legend *khalīfat allāh amīr al-mu'minīn* ("God's Deputy, the commander of the believers"). Silver coins issued in the following year transformed the bust of the Sasanian King of Kings on the obverse into a portrait depicting a caliph holding a sword's scabbard and wearing some sort of conical crown or helmet *en lieu* of the Sasanian winged crown.[231] Possibly in order to avoid the anomaly of having the ruler's depiction on both sides of the coin, the "standing caliph" image on the reverse was substituted with a spear beneath a niche supported by tortile columns (Fig. 13). The niche suggests the Syrian late antique motif of the sacral arch (*sacrum*),[232] which can be seen on Christian and Jewish pilgrim vessels surrounding both the Christian cross and the *menorah*.[233] A cross beneath the *sacrum* also recurs on Axumite coinage.[234] Similar niches, however, can also be seen on Sasanian seals.[235] The substitution of the cross with

231 Cf. the headgear on the obverse bust of rare Arab-Sasanian coppers featuring the name al-Walīd, possibly indicating the caliph al-Walīd I (*rg.* 705–715). The name is flanked by another "illegible" legend in Arabic (according to Gyselen, 2000, 77 and 163) or Pahlavi (according to Album/Goodwin 2002, 48) characters.

232 Miles 1957 interpreted the reverse motif on "*sacrum* and spear" drachms as a *miḥrāb*. For a thorough refutation of this hypothesis, see Treadwell 2005 with reference to other literature.

233 Ravy 1999; for the fortunes of the *sacrum* motif in Islamic art, see Miles 1957, 162–164 and Milwright 2016, 233.

234 Treadwell 2005, 25.

235 See e.g. Gyselen 1994, ns. 10. A. 11–17 and B. 10.

the spear flanked by Arabic inscriptions served as an indication of the issuer's cultural and confessional alterity, while underlining the reverse imagery's sacred dimension.[236] A further referent of the sacral arch (without the spear) can be found in contemporary imperial architecture, where it is used on copper gilded plaques separating the capitals of the octagon in the Dome of the Rock,[237] on stone window-grills[238] and in mosaic decoration[239] in the Congregational Mosque in Damascus, as well as in the wooden decoration of the al-Aqṣā Mosque[240] and stucco balustrade at Qaṣr al-Ḥayr al-Gharbī,[241] among others.

Fig. 12: *Anonymous,* drahm, *75 (694/695), without mint (Damascus?). Image: courtesy of Ryka Gyselen.*

Fig. 13: *Anonymous (frozen Khusraw),* drahm, *without date, without mint (Damascus?), 3.70 g. Reproduced from Treadwell 1999, 268 with permission of the author.*

---

236 Treadwell 2005, 21.
237 Ettinghausen/Grabar/Jenkins-Madina 2001, 60 fig. 85.
238 *Ibid.*, fig. 86.
239 Finster 1970, esp. 113–114 and Förtsch 1993, 185 and pls. 39a–d.
240 Hamilton 1949, pls. L, LIV, LVII, LXIII, and LXXI.
241 Schlumberger 1986, pl. 69, a–b.

The geographical distribution of "standing caliph" mints over Greater Syria and Northern Mesopotamia points to Byzantium as the primary ideological target of this type of coinage. In fact, the striking resemblance in image and wording between "standing caliph" gold coins and Justinian II's Pantokrator (or *servus Christi*[242]) *solidi* suggests a relationship between the two designs, with some scholars even venturing as far as to state that the latter directly inspired the former.[243] Suggestive of a Byzantine connection is also the fact that "standing caliph" issues mark the first official activity of the Northern Mesopotamian mints of the *jund* Qinnasirīn (ancient Chalkis) on the northern frontier with the Byzantine Empire.[244] The relatively inferior quality of the coins minted in this region, in particular, further indicates a hasty production process, possibly linked to military activity in the region.[245]

In spite of the concentration of "standing caliph" coinage in the geographical area of Greater Syria and Northern Mesopotamia, however, the series shows incipient trends that would only come to fulfillment with epigraphic imperial coinage years afterwards. Firstly, "standing caliph" coinage represented the first attempt at establishing a single visual and – to a lesser extent – inscriptional prototype for coinage in all three metals. Specifically, the administrative legend *ḍuriba hādhā* became standard on Umayyad epigraphic coinage in all metals. Secondly, the series exercised a widespread influence as a visual model for contemporary and later coinage, well beyond the boundaries of the Umayyad imperial metropole.

A testament to the wider significance of the "standing caliph" motif beyond the numismatic ambit is offered by one tri-dimensional sculpture originally placed over the main entrance to the Umayyad palace of Khirbat al-Mafjar[246] and a similar depiction on a stucco panel in Qaṣr al-Ḥayr al-Sharqī,[247] which bear a striking resemblance to the "standing caliph" gold coinage image. Rep-

---

242 It has been suggested that the title *servus Christi*/gr. *doulos tou Christou* inspired the Arabic caliphal title *ʿabd allāh* (see Amitai-Preis 2012, 281 and Treadwell 2012b, 147). It must be noted, however, that, to the best of the author's knowledge, *servus Christi*/gr. *doulos tou Christou* was never used in conjuction with imperial titulature prior to Justianian II's time and is only attested as an episcopal title prior to the Arab conquest (see Olister 2006, 68–69). Conversely, *ʿabd allāh* is attested in caliphal titulature since 662. One might thus speculate whether it was not the Islamic use that determined a Byzantine response rather than the other way around.

243 For a recent assessment, see Treadwell 2012b and Humphreys 2013.

244 Album/Goodwin 2002, 80. For a synoptic overview of the "standing caliph" mints, see Album/Goodwin 2002, 121 and Foss 2008, 81–83.

245 Foss 2008, 75–77.

246 Hamilton 1959, pl. 55 ns. 1 and 5. It is noteworthy, however, that the garment of the "standing caliph" statue in Khirbat al-Mafjar is different from those depicted on "standing caliph" coinage.

247 Genequand 2018, 164–168.

resentations of a bearded head with a headgear reminiscent of those of the Syrian "standing caliph" figures also appear on possibly contemporary vessel stamps from the Iranian world.[248]

Furthermore, secondary visual features of Syrian "standing caliph" coinage also exerted an influence on the design of other contemporary and later numismatic series. So-called *ABAZ* copper coins minted in Egypt under the tenure of ʿAbd al-ʿAzīz[249] introduced to Islamic Egypt both the *phi*-shaped object of Syrian and Northern Mesopotamian coins and the numeral **M** of the Palestinian "standing caliph" copper coinage (Fig. 2).[250] A link with Syria is also hinted at by the bust, which resembles the traits of the "falconer" figure that characterizes copper coinage from the so-called Pseudo-Damascus mint in Syria.[251]

Moving eastwards, Arab-Sasanian *drahms* minted in Kufa[252] and Baṣra under the tenure of Bishr b. Marwān (in office 690/691–694 and 692/693–694 respectively) distinguish themselves by their reverse depiction of a frontal figure in a praying position (so-called *orans*[253]), instead of the Zoroastrian fire altar with two attendants.[254] On coins issued in the years 73 AH (Fig. 14) and 74 AH the robe of the reverse figure recalls the one of the "standing caliph" on contemporary gold coinage (Fig. 10).[255]

---

248 Balog 1974, 134 ns. 12a–b. For similar designs found in the Levant, see Whitcomb 1995.

249 See *supra* p. 66 and references there.

250 Foss 2008, 113 and Goodwin 2015, 208.

251 For the so-called "Pseudo-Damascus" mint, see in particular Milstein 1988–1989. For the interpretation of the obverse standing figure on some "Pseudo-Damascus" issues, see Oddy 1991; cf. Album/Goodwin 2002, 87 and Foss 2008, 47–48. For a different interpretation, see Schindel/Hahn 2010b, with a response by Oddy 2012, 109–110.

252 Coins minted in the provincial capital of Kūfa are identified by the mint name *AKWLA* = ʿAqūlā, the Aramaic name of a pre-Islamic settlement to the north of the Islamic Kūfa. See Treadwell 1999, 226–228.

253 For the *orans* motif in Umayyad Arab-Sasanian copper coinage minted in Bīshāpūr, Iṣṭakhr and Susa, see Gyselen 2000, 63–64 and Treadwell 2008, 346–350; 354–355; and 357–358 and *ASCC* 20; 21; 41; 78; and 79.

254 For possible interpretations of the *orans* in Bishr b. Marwān's *drahms*, see Treadwell 1999, 233–240.

255 Treadwell 1999, 238.

Fig. 14: *Bishr b. Marwān,* drahm, *Aqūlā, 73 (692/693).*
Image: courtesy of Luke Treadwell.

To the west, the characteristic pole-on-steps symbol of the "standing caliph" *dīnārs* is found on the obverse side of Arab-Byzantine half *solidi* (or *semisses*, sing. *semissis*) minted in North Africa between 699 and 716 – well after the introduction of all-epigraphic coinage in the Levant. On North African coinage, however, the symbol is not combined with a "standing caliph" obverse but rather with two imperial figures still featuring Christian symbolism.[256] On the third of a *solidus* (or *tremissis*), yet another symbol, a T-shaped bar on steps, is used, possibly as an abbreviation for *T(remissis)*.[257]

Finally, three types of coppers depicting a "standing caliph" figure were minted in the Iranian mint at Susa (ca. 480 km to the south-west of Tehran).[258] These rare issues differed from the rest of the "standing caliph" series as they bore a stylistic elaboration of the "standing caliph" coinage's motifs on the obverse (Fig. 15).[259] In fact, the Susa image and that of contemporary "standing caliph" iconography on Syrian gold, silver, and copper is such that it is debatable whether the die-cutters in Susa used the Syrian coinage as a model.[260] On the reverse side of "standing caliph" coinage from Susa, floral crosses are displayed instead of the recurrent symbols on Syrian and Palestinian "standing caliph" gold (pole on steps), silver (standing caliph figure, *sacrum* and spear), and copper (*phi*-shaped

256 Bates 1995; Album/Goodwin 2002, 108–109; and Jonson 2012.
257 Heidemann 2010b, 33. For the T-shaped pole bar on steps on Sufyanid (?) gold coinage, see *supra* pp. 148–149.
258 Gyselen 2000, 38 and *ASCC* 39a–b and 40 (all from Susa; anonymous; without date/ Umayyad). For Levantine motifs in Islamic coin designs from Iraq and Iran in general, see Gyselen 2000, 33–38.
259 On the notions of "style" and "motif", see *supra*n118.
260 Gyselen 2000, 38 interprets the Susa "standing caliph" copper coins as "Eastern variations on the theme to which Syrian types refer"; Treadwell 2005, 360, on the contrary, maintains that the coins from Susa used Northern Mesopotamian "standing caliph" copper coinage as models.

objects, numeral *my*)[261] coins. Crosses on the Susa "standing caliph" issues reveal close ties to floral motifs that were recurrent in Sasanian figurative traditions, finding their closest parallels in Sasanian sphragistics.[262]

Fig. 15: *Anonymous,* fals, *Shūsh, without date (Gyselen 2000, 146 =* ASCC *39b). Image: courtesy of Ryka Gyselen.*

Whatever the original meaning of the reverse iconography of the Syrian/Northern Mesopotamian "standing caliph" coinage, it was lost on or deemed too unreliable by the Susa minting authorities, to the point that they replaced it with the very symbol it was meant to replace: a cross. Based on the Christian symbolism of the copper coinage from Susa, Gyselen hypothesized that minting was delegated to Christian authorities.[263] Without necessarily implying a Christian connection,[264] an alternative possibility is that the overall conjecturally Byzantine-Syrian composition (a standing figure on the obverse and a sacral symbol on steps on the reverse) of the coins itself led to an association with crosses found on similar coin types.

Another instance of Muslim minting authorities' compliance with pre-Islamic visual-vocabulary is shown by the crown-like headgear on Damascus "*sacrum* and spear" drachms (Fig. 13). The crescent over the headgear worn by the caliph portrait has no parallels with those on Syrian gold and copper coinage nor

261 See *supra* p. 152.
262 Treadwell 2008, 360–361.
263 Gyselen 1984, 241. Cf. *ASCC* 90 depicting a Sasanian-style bust wearing a tiara with a cross on the obverse and a cross encircled by a Pahlavi legend on the reverse. The reverse legend possibly features the term *ʾpskwpws* (< gr. *episkopos*) "bishop". I was able to identify a further specimen of this type not mentioned by Gyselen in the Staatliche Münzsammlung in Munich, (1: 1, 15b, 2; 2,398 g).
264 Treadwell 2008, 360 and *ibid.*n113.

with the Damascus "standing caliph" drachms. In fact, the wearing of crowns is commonly associated with earthly-minded, unjust rule in later Islamic political thought.[265] The crown-like headgear, however, resembles the helmet worn by the obverse portrait and reverse standing figure of rare Arab-Sasanian trilingual Arabic-Middle Persian-Bactrian drachms struck by Yazīd b. al-Muhallab in Anbīr in 703/704,[266] as well as helmets worn by warrior figures represented on ivory panels from the Abbasid family residence of al-Ḥumayma.[267] The depiction on the obverse of the *sacrum* and spear drachms is in many ways emblematic of the limits of the "standing caliph" iconography in terms of associative potential. On one hand, it distances itself from the canons of the standard Sasanian iconography by eliminating the typical winged crown and replacing it with a more culturally distinctive helmet-like headgear. On the other, however, the insertion of a "non-crown" is in itself a visual feature dictated by the distinctively Sasanian-style design of the coin.

This brief overview of the plethora of variables in "standing caliph" coinage over the comparatively limited time span of its production indicates its failure to resonate with widely different geo-cultural realities without extensive iconographic adaptations. In other words, while the "standing caliph" series had imbued Late Antique coinage with new textual and iconographic content, it remained nonetheless bound to the overall regional and support-based compositional schemes and conventions of these earlier designs.

Parallels and *Comparanda*

A close parallel is offered by another iconographic model, which in the years of the Second Civil War (680–692) and those immediately following recurred on coins minted both in Greater Syria and in the Iranian world. As already mentioned, under the governorship of Bishr b. Marwān, the mints of Kūfa (73–75 AH) and Baṣra (75 AH) minted Arab-Sasanian silver drachms inscribed with a short *shahāda* (in the form "In the name of God, Muḥammad is God's messenger") on the obverse marginal legends and characterized by a frontal figure with two attendants with both hands raised – so-called *orans*.[268] Two types of copper coins

265 *I.a.* Crone 2005, 46; Marsham 2009a, 140–141; Bowen Savant 2013, 170–196. Cf. the anecdote according to which Muʿāwiya I refused to wear a crown. For this episode, see Hoyland 1997a, 136.
266 Walker 1952, 108–110 (n. 3).
267 Foote 2012, cat. 153 B. Cf. also the helmet worn by the hunting caliph in a stucco plate in Qaṣr al-Ḥayr al-Sharqī (Genequand 2018, pl. 10).
268 Treadwell 1999.

minted in the *jund* Urdunn (modern day Northern Jordan) show a similar motif, though stylistically considerably different, with one (Type II) or two (Type I) hands raised. Based on stylistic parallels with the *al-wafāʾ li-llāh* and the Pseudo-Damascus coinage it can be tentatively established that Type I was minted around 690, contemporary with or, possibly, slightly before Type II.[269] On both types, the *orans* figure holds a long cross or a *globus cruciger* in one or both hands.[270]

After the Marwanid victory over the Zubayrids, different types of *orans* coppers appeared at the Fārs mints of Bīshāpūr,[271] Susa,[272] and Iṣṭakhr,[273] showing either both or one raised hand.[274] Dated specimens of Iranian *orans* coinage cover the period 692–714. Although the relationship between silver, Syrian and Iranian *orans* coinage is not without some grey areas, stylistic similarities seem to indicate that the Syrian *orans* motif probably served as a model for its later Iranian counterparts.[275] However, Iranian *orans* coppers reveal signs of adaptations. Unlike Syrian *orans* coinage, all Iranian types except *ASCC* 41 (Susa) show the *orans* figure on the reverse, not the obverse. Furthermore, the crosses that characterize both Syrian types of *orans* coinage have been removed. Perhaps more importantly, the *orans* figure on *ASCC* 79 (Bīshāpūr) is depicted in profile, not frontally, with one disproportionally large raised hand. The image differs markedly from coeval *orans* iconography and – similar to the Susa floral cross image – draws inspiration rather from Sasanian sigillographic tradition.[276] Likewise, on the silver *orans* drachms, the two attendants flanking the central standing figure on the obverse are simply a repurposing of the attendants on either side of the Zoroastrian fire altar on Arab-Sasanian coinage (Fig. 14).

The different regional leanings, which characterize both "standing caliph" and *orans* coinage embody the constraints encountered by attempts to implement trans-regional symbols of imperial authority. More particularly, the variant designs of the "standing caliph" and *orans* coinage betray the will or need of the issuing authority to make concessions to regional representational conventions. Elements of Syrian origin such as the *phi*-shaped object(s) and the *orans* image, for instance, were adapted in the Iranian figural tradition by resorting to Sasanian

269 Schulze 2012, 139 suggests that the Syrian *orans* iconography might have originated in anti-Marwanid opposition in Urdunn. For previous links between coinage minted in Urdunn and anti-Marwanid opposition, see Schulze 2010.
270 For a synoptic survey of the Syrian *orans* copper coinage, see Schulze 2012.
271 *ASCC* 78–79; for the attribution of these coins to Bīshāpūr, see Treadwell 2008, 345–346.
272 *ASCC* 41.
273 *ASCC* 20.
274 Cf. also *ASCC* 88 minted at unknown mint.
275 Schulze 2012.
276 Treadwell 2008, 346 and *ibid.*n57.

sigillographic imagery. In much the same way, the Palestinian mints embedded the "standing caliph" image in the local visual vocabulary by keeping the Greek **M** on the reverse. The crown-like element on display in the royal portrait on the Damascus sacrum and spear drachms similarly underscores the need to conform to the Sasanian figurative canon.

To summarize, while Islamic coinage from the period between the years 690–697 reflects trends towards the standardization of imperial propaganda, active attempts by Muslim overlords to implement a trans-regional visual language betray visual vocabulary embedded in different regional representative traditions. This is, I would suggest, where the Arabic epigraphic design came into play. Against the background of representations of power bound to deeply rooted and regionally based artistic and linguistic traditions, an Arabic epigraphic design offered a multi-layered message that was not only operative for all spectators – literate and illiterate – but also transcended the referential constraints of derivative late antique figurative designs and motifs. The universal reach of the Arabic script resided precisely in its exclusivity.

By the time of the reform, the iconic nature of the Arabic script as a visual marker of Muslim imperial rule had in fact been well established through the already almost universal use of Arabic on Islamic coinage over five decades. In this respect, the transition from pre- to post-reform Islamic coinage is a history of continuity. Rather than revolutionizing the coinage's visual language, ʿAbd al-Malik's final reform turned it inside out. Arabic legends already provided pre-reform coinage with a symbolic "umbrella" under which the varied and regionally bound cosmos of Late Antique imagery was infused with new meaning – with the secondary function of expressing the ideological profiles of different groups within the Arab-Muslim community, condensed in group-specific mottos. All-epigraphic coinage did not elevate the Arabic script as the prime visual symbol of Arab imperial authority; rather, it absolutized its role as such.

Those literate in Arabic could appreciate the coins' textual messages in all their layers. This included the polemical charge and the referents of various Qur'anic passages and slogans. At the other end of the spectrum, the elimination of figurative images from imperial coinage left those from all walks of life not literate in Arabic with no meaningful association but the distinctiveness of imperial power signified by the *optisemic* value of the epigraphic design and by the Arabic script. One could say that through the removal of its image, Early Islamic imperial power achieved a more pronounced statement of its presence.

The Eye of the Beholders

In light of the silence of the documentary sources, the assumptions of how Early Islamic Arabic inscriptions were perceived by those who could not read them are admittedly *ipso facto* among the most speculative and anecdotal of the present study. Hints at the considerations that drove perceptions of Arabic official writing by those beholders not literate in Arabic nonetheless punctuate literary accounts.

A passage from the Byzantine historian Theophanes († 818) describes the delivery of a tribute in gold coins from ʿAbd al-Malik to Justinian II in 690/691. According to the account, Justinian finally refused the tribute in view of the coins' peculiar design, which the chronicler describes as "of strange and novel appearance (*neophanes*) the like of which had never been seen before".[277] If the date given by Theophanes is to be believed, the coins referred to could be the so-called *shahāda* solidi discussed above. Interestingly, Theophanes appears more concerned by the coins' overall *visual* impression of awkwardness conveyed *i.a.* by their Arabic inscriptions than by their actual polemical textual content. This is an apt example of how the novelty of the visual component of the Arabic script took primacy over the informative one in the eyes of those not literate in Arabic.

Another, one might say, equal and opposite indicator of the attitude of individuals not literate in Arabic towards the visual language of the Arabic reformed coinage stems from the unlikely environment of late 8th-century England. Sometime after 157 AH (773/774), the King of Mercia, Offa (*rg.* 757–796) issued in his name gold coins that imitated the Spanish *dīnār*s of the Abbasid caliph al-Manṣūr (*rg.* 754–775).[278] The coins in question displayed flawed renderings of the original Arabic legends and were in addition inscribed with the Latin *Offa Rex*, "King Offa", on the (Arabic) reverse field. Notably, the Latin is upside-down when compared to the Arabic field legends. Furthermore, the side with the Latin legend was in all likelihood perceived by the engravers as the obverse side of the coin, whereas – speaking from the perspective of the internal logic of the Arabic alone – that same face was the original reverse.[279] The exact purpose of Offa's imitative *solidus mancusus*[280] still eludes us, with some even venturing as far as

277 Theop. 365, 10f. 14–18 (trans. Mango, 509–510). Cf. also the tradition of the prohibition of Arabic signet rings among Christians quoted in the opening of this study.

278 First published by de Longperier 1841. See also Carlyon-Britton 1908.

279 For the identification of the obverse and reverse side on all-epigraphic Arabic coinage, see Bacharach 2010, 16.

280 The term *mancusus*/*mancosus*, used frequently in Latin sources throughout the 8th and 9th centuries to refer to Arab coins, is in all likelihood a loan from the Arabic *manqūsh* "engraved". The Arabic term occurs in atypical Samanid *dirhams* of 787/788 and 911–913; see Linder-Welin

https://doi.org/10.1515/9783110740820-019

to suggest that these coins were intended as a tribute to the pope.[281] Whatever the case, the interplay of Latin and Arabic (or rather pseudo-Arabic) on Offa's *dīnārs* reveals a purely iconographic approach to the Arabic legends. Accordingly, the coins are designed to convey a non-content related visual impression of the Arabic model, rather than attempting a faithful reproduction (or adaptation) of their phraseology. The insertion of the Latin legend further indicates a purposeful artistic design rather than a straightforward imitation. Offa's imitative *mancusi* inaugurate a rich tradition of pseudo-epigraphic Arabic texts produced in the Mediterranean and Continental Europe.[282]

Similar impressionistic public uses of Arabic writing are implied by decorative pseudo-Arabic inscriptions in Mediterranean and Continental European architecture such as those found on the frieze encircling the 10th-century Byzantine monastery of Hosios Lukas (97 km north-west of Athens)[283] and later uses of Arabic inscriptions in Medieval and Renaissance Italian paintings, sculpture, and decorative arts.[284] Comparable pseudo-inscriptions adorn the façade and doors of the 12th-century cathedral of Notre-Dame in Puy-en-Velay (Auvergne).[285] Pseudo-inscriptions in floral Kufī can be seen on the Bohemond's (*rg.* 1088–1111) mausoleum in Canosa, and there are many more examples.[286] Arabic inscriptions and pseudo-inscriptions on textiles and prized objects, in particular, left an enduring legacy as a visual conduit of social prestige beyond the geographical boundaries of the Muslim world. The most prominent of such instances is represented by the use of Arabic inscriptions on pictorial decorations, vestments, and coinage by the

1965. For a general overview of the so-called *mancusi*, see McCormick 2001, 323–342 and Ilisch 2004, 91–92. On attestations of the term *mancusus* in Latin literature, in particular, see McCormick 2001, 324 and *ibid*.n21 and Annex 2.

281 In a letter by pope Leo III (*rg.* 795–816) to the king of Mercia, Coenwulf (*rg.* 796–821), the latter is reminded of a promise made by king Offa to the *fidelissimi missi* of pope Adrian I (*rg.* 772–795) for sending a tribute of 365 *mancusi* every year. For the passage in question and its possible connection with the Offa *dīnār*, see Carlyon-Britton 1908, 63–66. The "Roman" connection finds partial corroboration from Longperier 1841, 232 that the coin was "procured" in Rome. Contrary to earlier interpretations that viewed the Offa *dīnār* as an exceptional celebrative issue, Ilish 2004, 104 has argued in favour of a larger production of these coins.

282 See e.g. the imitative gold *mancusi* with pseudo-Arabic inscriptions, minted in the County of Barcelona in the 11th century; Balaguer 1999, 70–72.

283 Walker 2015.

284 See e.g. Soulier 1924; Erdmann 1953; Spittle 1953; Tanaka 1989; and Fontana 2002. On Arabic inscriptions on Norman royal robes in particular, see now Dolezalek 2017.

285 Mâle 1923, 323–333 and Fikry 1934.

286 For a survey of Arabic inscriptions in the Latin West, see Erdmann 1953; Spittle 1953; Grabar/Ettinghausen 1974; and Belghagi 1988.

Christian Norman kings.[287] However, Arabic-inscribed textiles and other objects from the Islamic world also found their way to Continental Europe[288] and possibly even to Viking age Scandinavia[289] as trade goods or war spoils.[290] Reproductions of (pseudo-)Arabic-inscribed *ṭirāz* garments were also used in 11th-century continental European sculpture as symbols of exotic opulence.[291]

This selected array of testimonies of impressionistic public use of Arabic epigraphy admittedly differs greatly from the testimonies examined in the previous sections in terms of geographical, political, cultural, and social environment. Yet in its diversity, it underscores the potential of Arabic writing as a meta-literate marker of distinction in societies with a mixed or prevalently non-Arabic cultural profile.

287 For embroidered Arabic inscriptions on Norman royal garments, see Dolezalek 2017; for a synoptic account on Norman and Hohenstaufen coinage in Sicily, see in particular Travaini 1995 and Grierson/Travaini 1998, 76–193; for the Arabic inscriptions in Norman Sicily, see Amari/Gabrieli 1971, Grassi 1992, and Johns 2006; for the Arabic inscriptions in the Cappella Palatina in Palermo in particular, see *i.a.* Johns 2015. On the experience of Islamic art in Norman Sicily in general, see Grabar 2005.

288 *I.a.* Feliciano 2005; Ali-de-Unzaga 2010; Shalem 2007; Ritter 2010 and *id.* 2016b; Rosser-Owen 2015; and Dolezalek 2016. For a synoptic overview, see Dolezalek 2017, 43–50. For the diffusion of the "trend" of Arabic inscriptions through textiles in particular, see Hoffman 2001.

289 Vedeler 2014 and Wärmländer *et al.* 2015. See also the ongoing debate in social media outlets on tablet-woven textile fragments discovered in the 10th-century Viking site of Birka (Sweden) and allegedly bearing the Arabic words *allāh* and *ʿAlī*.

290 For a prominent example, see the "Suaire de Saint-Josse", a 10th-century silk salmite saddle cloth commissioned by the Turkic general and rebel Abū Manṣūr Bukhtegin († 961), brought back from the First Crusade by Étienne de Blois († 1102) and dedicated as a votive gift at the Abbey of Saint-Josse; see Bernus-Taylor/Marchal/Vial 1971.

291 Snyder 2011, esp. 176–180.

Conclusion

On the 2nd of February 1279, the Byzantine emperor Michael VIII Palaelogos (*rg.* 1259–1282) was hosted by the Patriarch John XI Bekkos (in office 1275–1279) to celebrate the Feast of the Presentation of the Christ Child in the Temple. As the ritual *kollyba* was being served to the emperor on a "beautiful and proper" tray engraved with "Egyptian characters", one of the onlookers noted that the name of Muḥammad was engraved on the margin of the platter. After the emperor had one his bodyguards who was skilled in the "Hagarene letters" confirm the presence of Muḥammad's name, something of a diplomatic incident occurred. This was reportedly serious enough to compromise the relations between the *basileus* and the patriarch, who – following the anecdote's narrative – had to resign shortly thereafter.[292]

This episode, recollected by the historian Georgios Pachymeres († ca. 1310), comes from a different time to the one with which the pages above are concerned. It nevertheless illustrates aptly the duality of the visual impression of the Arabic script and the semantic content it conveys that lies at the center of this chapter. While the first is considered "beautiful and proper" to the ceremonial Byzantine court, the second becomes outrageous to the emperor once deciphered. I have suggested that a similar polarity characterized the social practice of Early Islamic Arabic public writing.

Much like the incriminated tray in Pachymeres' account, Early Islamic Arabic writing operated in an environment in which mastery of Arabic was a minority phenomenon. As in the case of the unaware attendants of the Patriarch Bekkos, visual impression was the main access to Arabic characters for the vast majority of the population and the non-Arabized elites of the Early Islamic Empire. I have argued that it was for this reason that Arabic was used by the Arab-Muslim imperial elite to visually articulate its normative public persona.

Arabic official documents addressed to non-Arabs reveal intentionality and could hardly have been expected by their issuer to function primarily as textual messages. Rather, they bear witness to a systematic use of Arabic writing as a symbolic signifier based on the actual absence of textual communication. The public use of the Arabic script secured first and foremost the exclusivity and internal sense of belonging of the Arab Muslim imperial elite. Relevant uses of public Arabic writing in the Early Islamic imperial culture included the appropriation and reinterpretation of symbols and landscapes rooted in the visual world of Late Antiquity. For the imperial elite, Arabic script served as an immediate and

292 For a thorough discussion of the incident of the *kollyba*, see Nelson 2005.

https://doi.org/10.1515/9783110740820-020

easily identifiable *laicorum literatura* of the imperial visual text *vis-à-vis* subordinated segments of the non-Arabicized population.

The effectiveness of the use of public Arabic writing in the imperial visual rhetoric rested in the discriminatory association of the Arabic script with the group of the imperial elite as Arabic was yet to rise to a written *lingua franca*. By their own graphic distinctiveness, Early Islamic Arabic public texts delineated boundaries within mixed audiences. Notions of social hierarchy associated with Arabic were in turn one of the drivers behind the process of Arabization that is perceptible in documentary sources from the second half of the 8th century (Chapters I and IV).

III Shaping Official Umayyad Arabic

Lo sguardo percorre le vie come pagine scritte: la città dice tutto quello che devi pensare, ti fa ripetere il suo discorso, e mentre credi di visitare Tamara non fai che registrare i nomi con cui essa definisce se stessa e tutte le sue parti. Come veramente sia la città sotto questo fitto involucro di segni, cosa contenga o nasconda, l'uomo esce da Tamara senza averlo saputo.

Italo Calvino, *Le Città Invisibili*

Introduction: *Reichsarabisch* or Early Islamic Official Arabic?

The present study has described Imperial Arabic (*Reichsarabisch*) as a broad sociolinguistic framework in which written Arabic was primarily defined by its use in the Early Islamic Imperial administration. The overarching notion of Imperial Arabic thus emphasizes both functional and chronological aspects of Early Islamic Arabic documents; it does not, however, attempt to define the actual variety/-ies of Arabic that appear(s) in "Imperial Arabic" documents. Nor does it differentiate between the variety of Arabic used in *stricto sensu* "imperial" official promulgations and that of coeval private and business-related documents.

Against the background of the similarly *functional* notion of *Reichsaramäisch*, Holger Gzella (2015) coined the term Achaemenid Official Aramaic to describe the highly orthographically, morphologically and lexically peculiar Aramaic idiom used in the Achaemenid official chanceries from the 6th to 4th centuries BCE.[1] This chapter explores the possibility of highlighting the distinctive features of Arabic official documents and delineating what one might define *à la* Gzella as Official Early Islamic Arabic documents within the context of Imperial Arabic.

The issue of singling out a specific linguistic variety in Imperial Arabic documents is neither new nor uncharted. Grob (2010) has advocated a distinction between the language variety on display in Arabic papyri ("documentary standard")[2] in the bosom of Middle Arabic (a historically intermediate state, a linguistically mixed variety, or a sociolinguistically middle register of Arabic).[3] Grob has furthermore underscored the importance of macro-structural patterns in outlining the specific language variety of the documentary standard.[4] Approaching the question from the angle of orthography, Andreas Kaplony (2019) has tackled the quantitative distribution of variant orthographies of selected terms in 7th- to 12th-century Arabic documents, identifying several statistically dominant and minority scribal traditions.[5] Referring to the Early Islamic period in particular,

1 Gzella 2015, 168–177.

2 For graphic and terminological differences between Umayyad and Early Abbasid Arabic documents, see Ch. V with references to further literature.

3 Medjell 2008, Lentin 2008a and *id.* 2008b, and den Heijer 2012; for comprehensive studies on Middle Arabic, see Blau 2002 and Hopkins 1984; for the related Christian and Jewish religiolects, see Blau 1966–1967 and *id.* 1988.

4 For some reflections on the notion of a documentary standard applied to Arabic documentary texts, see Grob 2010, 156–158 and Kaplony 2019.

5 Kaplony 2019.

https://doi.org/10.1515/9783110740820-021

he further postulates an "Umayyad Documentary Arabic" defined by "state" officials as the reference language for writers of pre-800 Arabic documents.

A description of grammatical or orthographical features of a theoretical Early Islamic Official Arabic exceeds the boundaries of this study. Rather, this chapter endeavors to explore *formal* varieties of official Arabic documents. The previous chapter laid the groundwork by examining the use of visual media in conveying social and cultural meaning in officially sponsored Arabic promulgations. I have tried to show that the aesthetics of Imperial Arabic documentary culture were the product and immediate signifier of their *Sitz im Leben*. For people on both sides of the figurative demarcation line drawn by language and script, Arabic symbolized the overarching connection of the different regions of the Early Islamic Empire to the imperial center. The following pages will delve more deeply into the distinctive formulaic and structural features of Imperial Arabic promulgations and their significance in explaining a formal template of official documents.

The distinctive features of an *Official* Documentary Standard can only stand out against the background of one (or several) *Private* Documentary Standard(s). For the purpose of this chapter, "official" refers to the content and/or the production environment and/or technical aspects of Early Islamic Arabic promulgations. Functionally, official promulgations can be further subdivided into representative public statements designed to potentially address an entire community, or those concerned with monopolistic prerogatives of the ruling authority – and most notably those concerned with the collection and management of revenues or the legitimate use of force as a deterrent or repressive measure. Furthermore, official promulgations are those issued in the context of an "office", understood as both the exercise of legitimate authority itself and the place from and in which legitimate authority is exercised. Finally, from a technical viewpoint, "official" indicates promulgations produced by organized bodies of professional writers as opposed to documents that, while possibly striving or even succeeding to conform to the same formal standards, were written outside the framework of formal training. To put it differently, official documents are ideally those produced by actual "scribes", understood as people whose primary profession was writing and who had undergone formal training.[6] In most cases, documents referred to as official in the following pages respond to all or several of the characteristics listed above, although the distinction between private and official items is admittedly fluid at times.[7]

6 On the definitions of "scribe" and "writer", see Mugridge 2010, 575–580.

7 An example of a papyrus of less straightforward repartition is *P.SijpesteijnInvitation* (Egypt; 705–717), a letter issued in the name of the Umayyad prince Sahl b. ʿAbd al-Azīz to the deputy governor ʿUqba b. Muslim. The content of the letter pertains to *stricto sensu* private matters (an invitation to join the sender on the annual Ḥajj pilgrimage). Yet the high degree of formal re-

Interest in the formal structure of Early Islamic Arabic documents has focused mainly on the cataloguing of structuring formulae[8] as well as on laying out the broader cultural trends underlined by the formulaic components of Early Islamic documents.[9] The spectrum of formal typologies of Early Islamic writs, in particular, has recently been thoroughly mapped with full references by Kaplony (2018). Grob's ground-breaking study (2010) has focused further on the documents' internal operational logic.[10] The present chapter approaches the formal structure of Early Islamic promulgations as a distinctive marker of officially sponsored documents. Aspects of lexical choice connected with Early Islamic official Arabic documents will be discussed in Chapter V.

The following analysis is designed to target bodies of evidence that allow for comparisons between texts of official and private provenance as well as between texts produced in different regional contexts. Among the documents on papyrus and related materials, letters represent the largest body of sources. "Letter" in this context is broadly defined as the formal typology of documents explicitly mentioning a sender and an addressee regardless of their functional specifics (e.g., note of demand, decree, tax receipt, business letter etc.).[11] Unlike, for instance, the commensurate body of papyrus protocols, which lack both private counterparts and a broader geographical spectrum, letters represent the only formal category of Early Islamic Arabic sources on soft materials[12] found across multiple geographical contexts both in private and official settings.

The second major body of evidence that lies at the center of the present chapter is official Arabic inscriptions commemorating the foundation, construction, restoration, or enlargement of buildings and monuments. These promulgations not only constitute the bulk of evidence for Early Islamic officially sponsored epigraphy, but are also the inscription type with the most widespread geographical distribution. At the other end of the spectrum, epigraphic testimonies are rich with examples originating outside the channels of official sponsorship, particularly epitaphs and graffiti.

---

finement of the missive, the high profile of the correspondents, the publicity of the occasion, as well as the political background of the exchange (see Sijpesteijn 2014, 185–189) are more akin to official correspondence.

8 Jahn 1937, 157–173, Diem 2004 and *id.* 2008.

9 Frantz-Murphy 1981–1989; Khan 1994; *id.* 2008; and Reinfandt 2015.

10 Grob 2010.

11 Cf., however, Kaplony 2018, 314 who conceptualizes "letter" as a *functional* category.

12 See *supra* Ch. I, *The Rise and Dissolution of "Imperial Arabic"*.

If the Mountain Will Come: Arabic Letters

Early Islamic Arabic letters were written on a variety of materials. Papyrus is the best-represented in the surviving documentary record as well as being the preferred writing support in Egypt and the Levant during the period surveyed in the present study. By contrast, parchment and textiles are dominant in the eastern regions of the Empire – though single items are also found in the western provinces.[13] During the 8th century, documentary Arabic letters on paper also entered the record in Central Asia.[14] A single letter on bone[15] and a handful of scribal exercises on wooden tablets[16] have also been found, dating from the period under examination. Finally, stone tiles were also used in the Early Islamic Empire for epistolary exercises.[17] A distinctive feature of the Arabic epistolary (and, more generally, writing) culture compared to neighbouring cultures is the relative scarcity of ostraca throughout the Early Islamic period.[18]

Early Islamic Arabic documentary culture undoubtedly developed in close contact with the parallel documentary cultures of the former Roman Near East, Egypt, and North Africa, of the Sasanian Middle East, of the kingdoms of late antique Yemen, and of the principalities of Central Asia. Most notably, a few Arabic document types such as protocols and tables are epigones of similar items used by the Byzantine state administration. The highly stylized perpendicular writing of Greek chancery script can be counted among the formative influences on Arabic chancery writing.[19] The preference in Arabic official documents for the *transversa charta* format also finds its roots in the Byzantine scribal tradition.[20] In a similar vein, seals and bullae attached to Arabic documents found in Northern Afghanistan continuate Sasanian figurative imagery[21] and have parallels in contemporary Bactrian documents.[22] On a more general level, the influence of

13 E.g., *P.RagibPlusAncienneLettre* (al-Bahnasā; VII) and *P.BruningSunna* (Egypt; 664/665).

14 *P.HaimPaper* 1–3.

15 *P.Jahn* 2 (= *P.Heid.Arab.* I p. 7) (Egypt; VIII).

16 E.g., P.Cair.EgLib.inv.Gen. 39825 (Egypt; VIII); see also the other examples quoted in Grohmann 1952, 58–60.

17 See *infra* pp. 167–168 with further references.

18 Despite the temptation to assign an earlier date, the first known Arabic ostraca such as those found *en masse* in the excavation of Aswan and Elephantine can be dated paleographically to the 9th and later centuries. For an overview of the writing supports of Arabic documentary texts, see in particular Grohmann 1952, 17–67 and *id.* 1954, 63–83.

19 Grohmann 1960, 246–247.

20 For the adoption of the *transversa charta* format, see Fournet 2009a.

21 Khan 2007, 87.

22 Sims-Williams 2007, 9–10.

https://doi.org/10.1515/9783110740820-022

7th- and 8th-century Pahlavi documentary hands was significant in the process of cursivization of Arabic chancery scripts from the late 8th century onwards.[23] Concurrently, however, the scribal culture underscored by Early Islamic official epistolography is peculiar in terms of both formal structure and *mise en page*.

The most distinctive feature of 7th- and 8th-century Arabic letters is an opening invocation followed by a prescript.[24] Besides the opening invocation, the Early Islamic epistolary prescript comprises up to four formulaic components: (1) an internal address, which is customarily repeated on the *verso*,[25] (2) a salutation, (3) a doxology, and (4) a transitional element introducing the main body of the letter.[26] The closing of the main text is further typically marked by valedictory formulae and/or a date and scribal signatures. Apart from the transitional element and the address, all components of the Early Islamic Arabic prescript consist of Qur'anic paraphrases.[27]

As will be discussed below in greater detail, most of the components of the Early Islamic epistolary prescript in addition show affinities with several pre-Islamic Semitic formulaic usages. Conversely, a similarly articulated prescript is absent from Early Islamic documentary letters penned in languages other than Arabic. Together with external markers such as the use of papyrus as a writing material, the Early Islamic epistolary prescript in turn distinguishes Imperial Arabic letters from later corpora of Arabic documentary epistolography.[28]

23 See in particular Khan 2013a.

24 Cf. Kaplony 2018, 315.

25 The external address of Early Islamic Arabic letters was customarily placed on the visible layer of folded letters on the *verso* side, roughly at the same height of the opening invocation in the inner part on the *recto*. For the folding and rolling of Early Islamic letters, see Grob 2010, 181–182 and *ibid*.n66 and n67. For the sealing of Arabic and bilingual letters, in particular, see *ibid*., 182 and *ibid*.n68 and Sijpesteijn 2012b. For documents from Early Islamic Khurāsān, see in particular Khan 2007, 82–83.

26 Jahn 1937, 158–164; Khan 1992, 126–127; Diem 2008, 856; Grob 2010, 39–42; Sijpesteijn 2013, 223; Reinfandt 2015, 282–284; and Kaplony 2018, 315.

27 Potthast 2019. For the similar formal structure of Suras and Early Islamic official writs, see Kaplony 2018, 316–341.

28 The earliest dated document on paper from Egypt, *P.VanthieghemPlusAncienPapier* (Fusṭāṭ), is dated to 878. Conversely, the latest document on papyrus from the same region, *P.Tyl.Arab.* I 10, is dated to 1087. For the introduction of paper into the Islamicate world, see most recently Rustow 2020, esp. 113–137.

Formulary

The composition of the prescript varies depending on the functional type of individual letters. More specifically, an invocation and internal address are shared features of nearly all Early Islamic Arabic missives. Virtually every Early Islamic Arabic documentary text on papyrus opens with the invocation:

> *bi-sm allāh al-raḥmān al-raḥīm*
> "in the name of God, the Merciful, the Compassionate".

At the core of the formulation lies the juxtaposition of the two theonyms *allāh* and *al-raḥmān*. *ʾlh* is used as a general term for "deity" in various Semitic languages, as attested to in Akkadian, Ugaritic, Hebrew, Phoenician, Aramaic South Arabian, North Arabian, and Nabatean inscriptions.[29] *ʾlh* also features as the designation of the monotheistic God in Late Sabaic as well as Nabatean inscriptions.[30] With the same connotation, *ʾl-ʾlh* appears in the opening invocation of the (Christian) pre-Islamic trilingual Arabic/Greek/Syriac inscription from Zebed (512 CE),[31] as well as in two Christian Arabic epigraphies[32] from the Early Islamic period.[33] Traditionally, Semitists have regarded the Arabic theonym as a loanword from the Syriac *alāh-ā*[34] but more recent scholarship has been more careful with this assumption and has leaned towards considering it as a genuine Arabic word formed as a contraction of the definite article *al* and *ilāh* "god".[35] Clearly of non-Arabic origin is the form *al-raḥmān*.[36] Divine epithets from the root *r-ḥ-m* have a long history in various Semitic languages and have been found in 9th-century BCE Assyrian inscriptions.[37] As a theonym proper, the term *rḥmnʾ* appears in Palmyrene inscriptions,[38] in post-biblical Jewish writings and inscriptions both in Hebrew and Aramaic,[39] and – most prominently – in Jewish as well as Chris-

29 *I.a.* Jeffery 1938, 66; Ambros/Prochàzka 2004, 305.
30 See in particular Gajda 2009, 224.
31 *RCEA* I 2. For a revised edition of the text see Robin 2006, 336–338.
32 Hoyland 2018b and Al-Shdaifat *et al.* 2017.
33 For the use of the theonym *ʾl-ʾlh* and *ʾllh* in pre-Islamic Arabia, see Robin 2020a and b. My gratitude to Christian Robin for generously sending me preliminary drafts of both articles.
34 Jeffery 1938, 66 and references there.
35 See in particular Blau 1972, 175–177 and Ambros 1981.
36 Jeffery 1938, 140–142.
37 Greenfield 2000, 381–384.
38 *ibid.*, 384. In Palmyrene inscriptions *rḥmnʾ* is usually used as an epithet of the god Baʿalshamīn but occasionally occurs in isolation.
39 Sokoloff 1990, 554a *s.v.* *rḥmn* and references there.

tian Late Antique Sabaic (*rḥmn-n*) inscriptions from Yemen.[40] That the term was originally considered a theonym in Arabic as well is made clear by its use in the Qur'an (most emblematically in the homonym Sura 55 *al-Raḥmān*), as well as in the substitution of *allāh* with *al-raḥmān* in some early Islamic graffiti.[41] Similar invocations pairing the two theonyms together are first attested in late Antique ESA epigraphy.[42] The apparently redundant standard Arabic morpheme *raḥīm* can possibly be understood as an apposition "translating" *al-raḥmān*.[43]

By definition, letters always contain an address section. Compared to post-800 epistolography, a distinctive feature of Early Islamic Arabic letters is the presence of an internal address, placed after the opening invocation. The form of the address follows one of several slightly different formulations:

a) *min fulān ilā/li-fulān*
"from N.N. to N.N."
b) *ilā/li-fulān min fulān*
"to N.N. from N.N."

The position of the sender and addressee is usually hierarchically ordered in descending order, with the correspondent with the higher social status appearing in the first position. An internal address is a recurrent standard feature in several letter writing traditions, including Greek, Middle Persian, and Sabaic epistolography among others.[44]

In Early Islamic Arabic official letters proper, the address is commonly introduced by an endophoric reference to the type of document which follows, in the form *hādhā kitāb min* "this is a writ from", *hādhā kitāb barā'a*[45] *min* "this is a writ

40 Beeston 1994, 42; Gajda 2009, 225; Robin 2015, 153–171. For a survey of the monotheistic invocations attested in late Sabaic inscriptions see Gajda 2009, 226–231.
41 For the use of *al-raḥmān* as a theonym in early Islamic graffiti in particular see Imbert 2013a, 118–119; for the use of concurrent theonyms in the Qur'an, see in particular Kaplony 2018, 321–323.
42 See in particular the Sabaic graffito published by Muḥammad ʿAlī al-Ḥājj in 2018 (*non vidi*). Images and the transcription of the text can be viewed on the *Digital Archive for the Study of pre-Islamic Arabian Inscriptions* (*DASI*) database http://dasi.cnr.it/index.php?id=37&prjId=1&corId=0&colId=0&navId=716301928&recId=9996&mark=09996%2C001%2C003 (accessed Apr. 18, 2021). A reedition of the text with a detailed reconstruction of its political and religious context is being prepared by Ahmad al-Jallad.
43 Jomier 2001 and Ambros/Prochàzka 2004, 305. Cf. Kaplony 2018, 319.
44 Stein 2008, 779.
45 Endophoric references utilizing the term *barā'a* are first found in Arabic writs produced in the Eastern provinces in the 760s and occur in Arabic documents from Egypt a decade later. This phenomenon should be contextualized in the broader framework of novel bureaucratic practices

of acquittal from", *hādhihi barā'a min* "this is an acquittal from", or just *barā'a min* "an acquittal from", which is sometimes referred to as a "monumental address".[46] The introduction of the address section through an endophoric demonstrative pronoun features in Achaemenid official Aramaic letters from Egypt and Bactria.[47] Similar endophoric references through the use of demonstrative pronouns are, furthermore, widely used in several Semitic epigraphic traditions, including inscriptions in Hebrew and Aramaic dialects[48] as well as Old Arabic[49] and Nabateo-Arabic[50] testimonies. Early Islamic acquittal deeds (*barā'*), in particular, echo technical terminology found in Hebrew and Nabatean epigraphy, in which verbalized forms of the root *b-r-'* are used.[51] Comparable endophoric references are found in a series of coeval private obligation acts (*dhikr ḥaqq*s), which in turn have parallels in the formulations *ḏkr* "an attestation" and *ḏt tḏkrn* "this attests" in Sabaic legal documents on wooden sticks.[52] In Early Islamic Arabic letters, the short address formula (i.e. without endophoric reference) is repeated on the back of the missives with the sender's and the recipient's names usually being separated by a *vacat*.

Long Prescript

Letters issued by and – to a lesser extent – addressed to Muslim officials and conveying or asking for instructions concerning circumstantial issues are distinguished by a "long" prescript. In discursive official letters, the address section is followed by a salutation in the form:

> *(al-)salām 'alay-ka/-kum* (Q 6:54; 7:46; 13:24; 16:32; 28:55; 39:73)
> "Peace be with you".

---

introduced by the Abbasid takeover. See Khan 2012, 83–84, *id.* 2013a, and *id.* 2014, 17–18; cf. also *infra* pp. 293–294.

46 Khan 2008, 887 and *id.* 2019.

47 See in particular Driver 1957; Grelot 1972; Porten/Yardeni 1986–1999; and Naveh/Shaked 2012. N.b. While the letters of the satrap of Egypt, Arshama, were found in Egypt, they were composed during the latter's stay in Babylon.

48 See in particular Gibson 1971–1975.

49 *RCEA* I 1 (Namāra; 332), 1; for the date, see Robin 2016, 376–377.

50 E.g., Cantineau 1930–1949, II, 38–39, no. IX (Madā'in Ṣāliḥ; 267).

51 Greenfield 1992, 11–17; Khan 2008, 888.

52 X.BSB 48–50 and 52–54.

The greeting *shalōm le-k* is found in the Hebrew text of the Old Testament.[53] Similar salutations were used in neighbouring languages such as Aramaic[54] as well as in Nabatean.[55] In epistolography proper, similar greeting formulae occur across a number of millennial Semitic scribal traditions. Verbalized forms of the root *sh-l-m* are used in Akkadian (and later Assyrian and Babylonian)[56] and Ugaritic[57] letters. *Hshlm ʾt*, *shlm ʾt*, and *wshlm ʾt* were used in the salutation of Hebrew and Canaanite letters in the pre-exilic period (IX–VI BCE).[58] Old and imperial Aramaic letters (V–III BCE) feature the opening greeting *shlm* "Hail to N.N." or similar ones.[59] The same formula (*shlwm*/*shlm*) features in Hebrew and Aramaic letters from Hellenistic and Roman times (II BCE–I–II CE).[60]

In turn, the salutation is customarily followed by a short doxology:

> *fa-innī aḥmadu ilay-ka allāh* (paraphrase of Q 1:2) *alladhī la ilāh illā huwa* (Q 59:22–23) "And I praise God for your sake, there is no other god but He".

Long prescript missives always transition into the main body of the letter through *ammā baʿd fa-* "as for after".

Transitional markers that signal the beginning of the body of the letter are common to several letter writing cultures. The closest parallels to the Early Islamic Arabic *ammā baʿd* are found in the Aramaic *w-kʿt* and *w-kʿn* (and variations thereof).[61] Transitional elements are also found in Coptic epistolography.[62] Similar markers are, by contrast, lacking in Roman and Byzantine documentary Greek epistolography prior to the Muslim conquest.[63]

---

53 See e.g. *Kings* 4:26.
54 Dalman 1905, 244.
55 Cantineau 1978, II, 150 *s.v. shlm l-*; Eksell 2002, 123–125.
56 Hackl/Jursa/Schmidl 2014, 10–12.
57 Kaiser 1970, 15–17. In Ugaritic the formula is found in the verbalized form *yshlm l-k* "may you prosper".
58 Schwiderski 2000, 42–43.
59 Alexander 1978, 162–163; Khan 2008, 891; Doering 2012, 44–54.
60 Schwiderski 2000, 249–250.
61 Schwiderski 2000, 155–164. In Hebrew and Aramaic letters from Hellenistic times, the transitional marker is the relative pronoun *sh* and *dy* respectively. See *ibid.*, 250–252.
62 Biedenkopf-Ziehner 1983, 31–37 and 212–224. See also *infra* pp. 202–203.
63 Luiselli 2008, 697; the use of the transition marker *kai nyn* "and now" in the letters of the Maccabees is in all probability to be understood as a translation from the Hebrew *wᵊ-ʿattā*, which has the same meaning. On this subject, see Doering 2012, 160–161; for the use of transitional markers in Greek and Coptic letters after the Muslim conquest, see also *infra* pp. 197–198 and 202–203.

Long-prescript Arabic letters by or to Arab governors, pagarchs, as well as lower officials contain a valedictory greeting concluding the main text and reading:

> *wa-l-salām ʿalay-ka/-kum* (Q 6:54; 7:46; 13:24; 16:32; 28:55; 39:73) *wa-raḥmat allāh* (Q 11:73) "peace and God's mercy be upon you".

Similar to what was observed with regard to the salutation, the Arabic epistolary valediction must be contextualized in a broader Semitic epistolographic tradition. Valedictory greetings *l-shlm-k* "for your sanity" and *shlm ʿd* "sanity to" occur in Old and Imperial Aramaic letters.[64] Hebrew and Aramaic letters from Hellenistic and Roman times customarily close with the greeting *hwʾ shlwm/hwʾ shlm* "be in good health" and variations thereof.[65] Wishes for both "peace" and "mercy (*rḥmn*)" are occasionally found in extended salutations in Imperial Aramaic letters.[66] In particular, the formulation *rḥmʾ ʾp shlm nhw l-kwn* "Mercy and peace be with you" in the *Epistle of Baruch*[67] resembles the Arabic valediction almost to the letter.

Official Arabic letters with a long prescript first appear in the Nessana dossier in the 680s–690s.[68] Renditions of long prescript components in *Greek* letters by Arab officials that go back as far as the mid-7th century,[69] however, could imply that the distinctive structural features of Early Islamic Arabic epistolography had already become established decades before.[70] In Egypt, Arabic letters with a long prescript first appear in the correspondence of the governors ʿAbd al-ʿAzīz b. Marwān (in office 685–705) and Qurra b. Sharīk (in office 709–715). Throughout the 8th century, and into the Early Abbasid period, official Arabic letters with a long prescript appear in the correspondence of a progressively wider spectrum of Arab officials from Egypt and Syria-Palestine as well as in inter-Arab private

---

64 E.g., *P.Murabbaʿât* 43, 7; 44, 8; 46, 12; and 48, 6 (all from Wādī Murabbaʿāt; ca. 130–134).

65 Schwiderski 2000, 252–254.

66 Doering 2012, 410 and *ibid*.n176; see in particular *TAD* A 4.7, 1–3.

67 2 *Bar.* 78:2; see Doering 2012, 245–247 and 410–412.

68 *P.HoylandDhimma* 1, 1–3 and 2, 1–3 [19–21].

69 For so-called "Arab-style" letters with a full list, see Appendix 3; Greek renditions of parts of the short Arabic prescript are found in Egypt as far back as the 640s, see e.g. *SB* XX 14443 (Ihnās; 643) issued in the name of ʿAmr b. al-ʿĀṣ.

70 A highly controversial, possibly pre-Islamic Arabic letter displaying the typical Arabic prescript is currently being prepared for publication by Fred Donner (Chicago). Preliminary readings were presented at the *7th ISAP Conference* (Berlin 20–23 March 2018).

correspondence.[71] In the Central Asian context, a complete prescript also appears in an unpublished letter from the Bēk family archive,[72] as well as in the letters from Sanjar-Shah.[73] Finally, of particular cultural significance is an official Arabic letter issued by the ruler of Panjakent Dēwāshtīch (*rg.* 706–722) to the governor of Khurāsān al-Jarrāḥ b. ʿAbd Allāh (in office 717–719).[74]

Short Prescript

A short epistolary prescript is characteristic of Arabic and bi- and trilingual receipts and orders for the delivery and transfer of materials, revenues and men, tax demands, and travel permits from 7th- and 8th-century Egypt, bilingual delivery orders from late 7th-century Syria-Palestine, and 8th-century tax receipts from Northern Afghanistan. Short prescript documents are characterized by the juxtaposition of address and main text, and the dispensing with salutation and doxology. They further lack a valedictory section after the main text (Appendix 1B).

In both long and short prescript letters, the main body usually opens with a narration (*expositio*) or a direct order (*dispositio*) introduced by transitional markers. Unlike long prescript Arabic letters, however, short prescript missives lack the marker *ammā baʿd* and transition into the main text with an expository (introduced by the particle *inna-* + a verb in the perfect tense)[75] or dispositive (*fa* + a verb in the imperative)[76] phrase, which is specific to the functional subtype of the documents. Generally speaking, documents with expository phrases express an arguably higher degree of epistolary politeness. Not only do they lack the directness of the imperative tone, but they also have a longer address section, which unlike short prescript letters with dispositive clauses, feature the so-called "monumental address".

The most well represented short prescript letters deal with the collection of taxes or the requisition of *naturalia* and manpower. As explained in the first chapter, orders for deliveries from Sufyanid Palestine (dated specimens 675–

---

71 For a discussion of the formulaic and layout peculiarities of Early Islamic Arabic private and business letters, see *infra* section *Hegemonic and Minority Scribal Traditions in Imperial Arabic* in the present chapter. For some discussion of Early Islamic private and business letters as a genre, see Grob 2010, XIV–XV.

72 Khan 2008, fig. 72.

73 *P.HaimPaper*.

74 *P.Kratchkovski*.

75 Kaplony 2018, § 2.1 (*inna-hu*), 2.2, 2.3, 2.6, and 2.7 (*inn-ī*), 2.4 (*inna-ka*), and 2.5 (*innā*).

76 Kaplony 2018, § 1.1–1.5.

686/687) and Marwanid Egypt (dated specimens 694–714) introduce the main text using the clause *fa-aʿṭū* ("deliver").[77] Bi- and trilingual tax demands from Marwanid and Early Abbasid Egypt (dated specimens 709–753), on the other hand, use the expository clause *inna-hu aṣāba-kum* ("it has befallen you").[78] In Early Abbasid tax receipts from Northern Afghanistan (dated specimens 764–775), the main body of the text is opened and closed by clauses introduced by a few variant forms and combinations of the operative verbs *qabaḍa* "receive" and *addā* "deliver".[79]

Short-prescript letters cover a variety of official demands. A series of orders for the conveyance of messengers by post-mules addressed to an unspecified postmaster (*ṣāḥib al-barīd*) of Ushmūn open with the dispositive phrase *fa-ḥmil* ("transport").[80] In safe-conducts serving as passports for traveling villagers (dated specimens 722–750), the expository section is preceded by the phrase *inn-ī adhintu la-hu* ("that I have authorized him").[81] Finally, short prescript official letters in Arabic include concise orders for the release of resources to a third party. In the specimens published hitherto, the order is introduced either by the dispositive phrase *fa-sarriḥ* ("and release!") or *fa-dfʿa* ("and pay!"), depending on the goods to be transferred.[82] Atypical in this respect is a series of short prescript orders for the delivery of goods that introduce the request with *ʿammā baʿd fa-* + the operative verb in the imperative.[83]

Finally, most official Arabic letters of both the long and the short prescript type contain scribal signatures.[84] These include both scribal signatures proper in the format *wa-kataba fulān* "and has written (this) N.N." or impersonal ones in the form *wa-kutiba* "and it was written".[85] The former are found in discursive

77 Kaplony 2018, § 1.2. Cf. also *P.BeckerPAF* 10 (= *P.Heid.* I 9) (Ishqawh; 709), 2 *fa-arsilū* "and send . . . " not mentioned in Kaplony 2018.

78 *Ibid.*

79 *in-nā qabaḍnā min-ka* (. . .) + *wa-qad qabaḍnā min-ka dhālika*: *P.Khurasan* 1; *in-nā qabaḍnā min-ka* (. . .) + *qabaḍnā-hā min-ka*: *P.Khurasan* 2; *in-nī qabaḍtu min-ka* (. . .) + *qabaḍtu dhālika min-ka*: *P.Khurasan* 3–7 and 19–21; *inna-ka addayta ilay-ya* (. . .) + *qabaḍtu dhālika min-ka*: *P.Khurasan* 9–17, 19–21, and 23; *inna-ka addayta ilay-ya* (. . .) + *wa-qabaḍtu dhālika min-ka*: *P.Khurasan* 8 and 18; *inna-ka addayta ilay-nā* (. . .) + *qabaḍnā dhālika min-ka*: *P.Khurasan* 22.

80 Kaplony 2018, §1.3; add *P.Ryl.Arab.* II 7 (= *P.RagibLettresdeService* 5).

81 Kaplony 2018, § 2.2.

82 *Ibid.*, § 1.4.

83 *Ibid.*; also *P.Christ.Musl.* 21.

84 For Early Islamic Arabic scribes, see Rāġib 1996a, Grob 2010, 86–89, Sijpesteijn 2013, 229–238, *ead.* 2020b, and Reinfandt 2020a; for their coeval Greek and Coptic counterparts, see in particular Bucking 2007 and Cromwell 2017.

85 The formula *wa-kataba* or similar clauses are common in graffiti and official inscriptions al-well, as indicative examples, see *CIAP* III p. 162, no. 2, 3 (graffito) (ʿEin Zureib; VIII?) and *RCEA* I 8* (official inscription) (Fusṭāṭ; 688).

letters with long prescripts, bilingual tax demands, requisition orders, and tax receipts from Egypt and Syria, safe-conducts, and short orders. The impersonal type, however, is preferred in all remaining types of official documents. Furthermore, official Arabic letters are usually dated, and always according to the Islamic era.[86]

Parallel Parameters of Scribal Politesse: Long-Prescript Letters to and from Christians

In terms of formal structure, official Early Islamic Arabic epistolography was susceptible to secondary variations modelled on the targeted addressee. Mention has already been made of the prioritization of either sender or addressee in the address section, based on social rank. Other modifications of the prescript structure were tailored to the addressee's cultural/religious profile.[87] Specifically, letters addressed by Muslim officials to Christian subordinates display different formulae than those that characterize inter-Muslim official correspondence. These variations affect both the general structure of the missive and the phraseology itself. In particular, official *Arabic* letters by Muslims to Christians omit the salutation after the address.[88] In addition, the doxology drops the *ilay-ka*.[89]

In the valedictory section of letters addressed to Christians, the formula *wa-l-salām ʿalā man ittabaʿa al-hudā* (Q 20:47) "peace be upon who follows the Guidance" is furthermore used instead of the standard *(al-)salām ʿalay-ka/-kum*.[90] Two other variants of the valediction to Christian addressees are also encountered in a single letter each, respectively: *wa-l-salām ʿalā muḥammad al-nabiy wa-raḥmat allāh* "Peace and God's mercy be upon the Prophet Muḥammad" in *P.GrohmannQurra-Brief* (Fayyūm; 709) addressed by the governor Qurra to the pagarch of Ihnās, and *wa-l-salām ʿalā awliyāʾ allāh wa-ahl ṭāʿati-hi* "peace be upon the friends of God and those who obey Him", used in the letter of the governor Mūsā b. Kaʿb (in office 758–759) to the Christian ruler of Nubia and Makuria

---

86 For the eras and calendars used in the dating clauses of non-Arabic documents issued in the name of Arab officials, see *infra* p. 202.
87 Adaptations of figures of religious speech in Early Islamic non-Arabic official documents are discussed in Ch. IV.
88 In contrast to their Arabic counterparts, *Greek* letters by Muslim officials from 7th- and 8th-century Egypt and Palestine contain a rendering of the epistolary salutation; see *infra* p. 199–200.
89 Diem 2008, 856; Sijpesteijn 2013, 223.
90 Diem 2008, 860; Sijpesteijn 2013, 223.

(*P.HindsNubia*), both in the salutation and the valediction.[91] While not polemical or anti-Christian *stricto sensu*, the variations in the salutation and valediction used for Christian addressees depart from the more inclusive, interlocutory versions used for Muslims ("I praise God for *your* sake"; "peace and God's mercy be with *you*"), thus stressing the addressee's cultural alterity.

All presently known Early Islamic Arabic letters addressed to recognizably non-Muslim addressees were sent to Christian individuals. It is thus unclear whether the same adaptation of the epistolary formula would have been employed for adherents of other religions as well.[92]

Similarly, the dawning of an inter-Christian Arabic letter writing culture is marked by slight adaptations to the standard Arabic formula. In the letters exchanged between one Father Magnillē and one Ḥabbān b. Yūsuf in the Mird archive (*P.Mird* 45–46) discussed above,[93] the writers resort to a revisited form of the opening invocation in which the trinitarian formula *bi-sm allāh al-ab al-ibn wa-rūḥ al-quds bi-jawhar wāḥid* "In the name of the Father the Son, and the Holy Ghost, in one essence" replaces the *per se* monotheistic but culturally Muslim *basmala*.[94] In contrast, nothing of this nature can be detected in the scant examples of pre-800 Arabic letters written by Jews.[95] Later examples of Arabic letters between Christians may express Christian connotations through secondary markers such as drawings of crosses.[96] These developments are paralleled by the increasing use of Qur'anic quotes in Arabic Muslim epistles dating or datable to the 9th and 10th centuries.[97] These developments are possibly symptomatic of a social environment in which Arabic alone had lost its value as a signifier of cultural belonging, thus prompting the resort to extra-linguistic cultural markers to denote religious affiliations.[98]

---

91 Cf. also the otherwise unattested salutation *wa-al-salām ʿalā al-muʾminīna* ("peace be upon the believers) featuring in P.Michael.inv. Q 5, a 7th/8th-century scribal exercise written in a proficient chancery hand.

92 For non-Arabic letters addressed to non-Muslims by Muslim senders, see *infra* Ch. IV.

93 See *supra* pp. 86–87.

94 For non-Arabic renderings of the *basmala* in Early Islamic Greek, Latin, Middle Persian, Sogdian, and Bactrian documents see *infra* Ch. IV and Appendix 3.

95 For renderings of the *basmala* in post-800 Arabic letters by Jews, see Almbladh 2010, 48–49.

96 See for instance *P.AnawatiPapyrusChretien* (Fusṭāṭ; IX).

97 Potthast 2019. Cf. Sonego 2019 who shows that Qur'anic quotes in legal documents registered an increase in the 9th century.

98 Potthast 2019, 76–77.

Translating Structure into Visuals

The highly standardized scribal framework underscored by official Arabic letters is distinguished as much by formulaic structure as by aesthetic features. Specifically, variations in the composition of the prescript are reflected in a document's layout structure. In particular, long prescript Arabic letters are characterized by a comparatively complex *mise en page*. Typical of long prescript official letters is a tripartite structure corresponding to three semantic units (Appendix 1A).

The key layout feature is the visual separation of the invocation and the rest of the prescript by an *alinea* after the *basmala* and the doxology, respectively. This indicates that the invocation was conceptualized as a semantic unit on its own, while internal address, salutation and doxology were considered parts of the same distinct semantic unit. In official letters, the transitional marker *ammā baʿd* is visually separated from the benediction by an *alinea* and always embedded in the main text. It is therefore, visually speaking, a constituent part of the main body of the latter rather than of the prescript proper.[99] In Arabic letters, the valediction is not singled out visually from the rest of the prescript although it is often located at the beginning of a new line.[100] Moreover, documents produced in specific chanceries occasionally display personalized secondary layout elements. For instance, in official letters by Qurra b. Sharīk, the last line of the missive (when preserved) is usually indented (Fig. 16). Similarly, the official letters issued by the chancery of the pagarch of the Fayyūm Nājid b. Muslim are distinguished by the outdentation of the *basmala* and the following line.[101]

Letter types with a short prescript, on the other hand, are typified by a simplified two-part structure (Appendix 1B). In particular, the *basmala* is separated from the rest of the document by a line break. As salutation, doxology, and (often) transitional marker are missing from short prescript letter types, however, the address is visually embedded in the main text with which it forms a single block. In terms of layout, only short prescript documents with a transitional marker *ammā baʿd* display some sort of visual separation between the address and the main text, with the transition element always marking the beginning of a new line.[102]

---

99 Grob 2010, 40 and 193.

100 Kaplony 2018, § 1.6 and 1.7; on *ibid.*, § 2.2.

101 Sijpesteijn 2013, 227–228 and *ibid.*n59 and *ead.*2020b, 460–461.

102 *Contra* Kaplony 2018, § 1.1, 1.2, 1.3, 1.5, 2.1, 2.2, 2.3, 2.4, 2.5, 2.6, and 2.7 who suggests that in short prescript letters the expository and dispositive phrases (referred to as "*innahu-Kitāb*" and "*fa-Kitāb*" documents respectively) were customarily set at the beginning of a new line. As

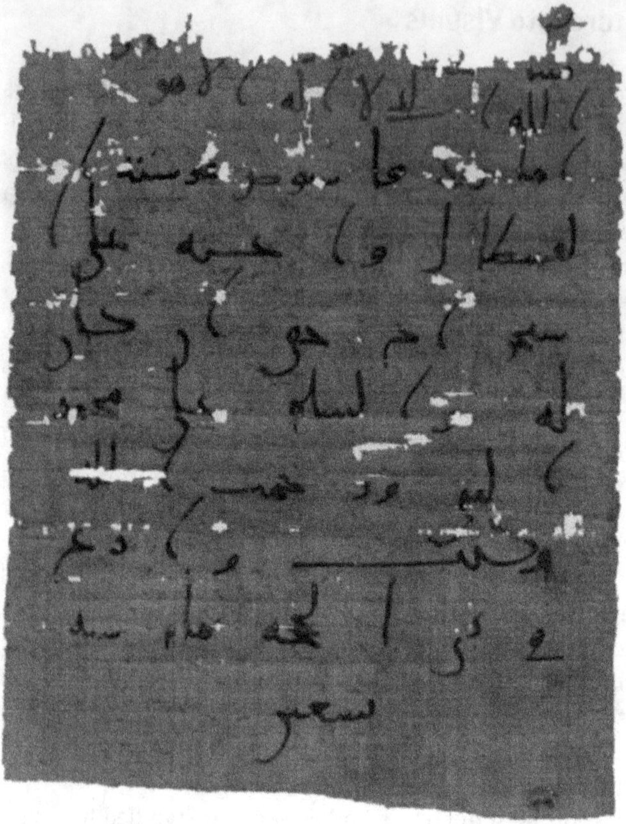

Fig. 16: *P.Vind.inv. A. P. 378 r.*
© Österreichische Nationalbibliothek, Vienna.

The layout structure of Early Islamic Arabic letters notably lacks clear parallels in epistolographic traditions of its neighbors. From the 5th to the 7th century, in Greek, Coptic, Middle Persian, and Sabaic epistolography alike, letters were typically organized visually in one single block.[103] Pre- and Early Islamic letters from the Eastern fringes of the Iranian world display a more articulated layout structure but remain nonetheless distinct from contemporary and later Arabic counterparts. In the Sogdian letters addressed to Dēwāshtīch and other Sogdian

---

it is also evidenced in his registers of references, however, this is almost invariably *not* the case unless the transitional marker *ammā baʿd* is present.

103 For Greek letters, see Luiselli 2008; for Coptic letters, see Richter 2008b; for Middle Persian Pahlavi letters, see Weber 1992, 234–236 and *id.* 2008a; for Sabaic letters, see Stein 2008.

nobles from Mount Mugh, the addressee's name and titles are separated from the sender's by *alinea*. The second half of the address, containing the sender's name and titles and the following line with the opening protocol are further indented.[104] A Bactrian declaration in the Bēk family archive, issued by the *sēr*, displays a similar arrangement.[105] Late Antique Bactrian letters[106] on leather or parchment are usually structured in one to four rectangular layout blocks, arranged perpendicularly to each other on recto and verso.[107] Except for the address placed in the third left quadrant from the top,[108] text blocks are merely juxtaposed and do not overlap with the formulaic articulation of the letter.

The layout of official letters highlighted important parts of the text and formulae. As such, layout belonged to the visual semantics of official documents that operated at a meta-literate level. Formulaic standard phrases, on the other hand, were part of the insider discourse of Early Islamic writings. Both aspects combined to render official Arabic letters not only numerically but also formally the most distinctive typology of Early Islamic Arabic documents when compared to neighbouring and previous scribal traditions.

Striving for Proficiency

The significant degree of standardization evident in the formulaic and layout features of Early Islamic Arabic documents presents us with a reflection of a rigid framework of scribal training and writerly politesse. Looking at the Early Islamic scribal curriculum through the lens of official documents means capturing a series of numerous but ultimately indirect glimpses. By contrast, direct evidence of institutionalized scribal training is scant in the surviving documentation.

The most coherent body of evidence that sheds some light on official scribal training settings is a group of ink inscriptions on marble tiles that were excavated at different residences and building complexes from the Umayyad period in Greater Syria.[109] Two ink writing exercises on bricks and pottery have also

104 Mugh A-14, Nov. 2, B 18, B 16, and B15.
105 *BD* I Y (Rōb; 771); for a discussion of layout features of this document, see *infra* p. 231.
106 *BD* II.
107 Sims-Williams 2007, 15–16 and figs. 1 and 2.
108 *Ibid.*, 16 and fig. 2 (Gi and Gii).
109 Baramki 1939 pl. 34 (= *id.* 1953, 151 = *CIAP* VI 64) and *id.* 1953, 105–117, mostly republished as *CIAP* VI 58–78 (Khirbat al-Mafjar); Schlumberger 1939, 372–373, II–III and fig. 29 = *id.* 1986, 28, II–III (Qaṣr al-Ḥayr al-Gharbī); Grabar *et al.* 1978, I, 191–192 (Qaṣr al-Ḥayr al-Sharqī); Hoyland 2018a, 137–141 (Andarīn); Ritter 2017 p. 49 (Khirbat al-Minya). A further unpublished specimen was

been found at the eastern extremity of the Empire at the site of the palace of the Umayyad governor of Khurasān Naṣr b. Sayyār (in office 738–748) in Samarkand.[110] Later specimens of these tokens from Early Abbasid time have been excavated in the palace-city of Sāmarrāʾ as well as in Caesarea.[111]

These ink inscriptions contain writing-exercises of letters issued in the name of caliphs in both Arabic and Greek.[112] Once their surface had been completely covered, these tiles could be washed and used again. A similar system was found in a trader's shop from Early Islamic Jerash Jordan, where a marble slab was used for temporary annotations.[113]

The presence of scribal training material in officially sponsored residences highlights the relative centralization of scribal training and its vicinity (physical and symbolic) to the halls of power. In comparison, only a few examples of scribal exercises in the coeval papyrological record have been edited hitherto.[114] Some of these can be located in an official setting, either by means of their content or by contextual evidence. For instance, in *P.ShahinSchreibubung* 3 (Egypt; VIII) the writer mentions several times the district of Ihnās and the *kharāj* tax. In P.Vind. inv. A. P. 738 v, a trainee used a financial list from a pagarchal chancery for his practice.[115] The possibly trilingual writer of *P.BerkesTrilingualScribe* (Fayyūm; after 789/790) reused an official list from the pagarchal chancery of the Fayyūm for his practice, hinting at a connection with the latter's milieu. A bilingual clerk was apparently also the writer of the exercise P.Vind.inv. G 39752, which shows a bilingual Greek/Arabic epistolary incipit in the name of one al-Mujālid b. Rābiʿ.

---

found in Bālis, see Sijpesteijn 2013, 232n8. Cf. also the several early Islamic ink inscriptions of the *basmala* on wooden panels from the al-Aqṣā Mosque; see Hamilton 1949: pl. XLIX (2–4).

110 Grenet 2008, 27 and fig. 12. A writing exercise on a brick fragment (*ibid.*, fig. 12, left) contains the *basmala* and single letters in Arabic and is currently being prepared for publication by F. Déroche. One other ostracon (*ibid.*, fig. 12, right, lower part) contains an Arabic writing exercise featuring formulae typical of the early Islamic epistolary prescript: the invocation *bi-sm allāh al-raḥmān al-raḥīm* separated by an *alinea* from an internal address as well as the salutation *salām ʿalay-ka fa-innī aḥmadu i*[*lay-ka allāh*] on the next two lines. This would suggest a dating to the 8th century. The Arabic text appears to be preceded by a Sogdian(?) writing exercise (*ibid.*, fig. 12, right, upper part).

111 *CIAP* II p. 286 no. 19-A (Cesarea) and *P.HerzfeldSamarra* 8 (Sāmarrāʾ).

112 Schwabe 1946, 21–22 (I–II) (Khirbat al-Mafjar). Cf. also the Greek letters (possibly numerals) painted and engraved on stone and marble fragments from Sāmarrāʾ, see Herzfeld 1948, 277 and pl. XXXa.

113 Walmsley *et al.* 2008, 125–126. I thank Kristoffer Damgaard for the reference.

114 For an overview of the *status questionis* on Arabic schooling practices in papyrus documents, see Sijpesteijn 2020b, 435–438.

115 *CPR* XXXIV 22 p. 47–49.

The invocation used in the Greek line, *syn theō* ("with God") is common to writings by Early Islamic pagarchs.[116] The link between Arabic scribal training and imperial patronage might have left a trace in the form of scribal tropes: In a surprising number of Early Islamic writing exercises it is no less than the caliph Hishām (rg. 724–743) who features as the nominal sender or addressee. These include two ink inscriptions on marble tiles from the Umayyad residences of Khirbat al-Mafjar (*CIAP* VI 69) and Qaṣr al-Ḥayr al-Gharbī (*P.SchlumbergerQasr*) and even a private exercise on papyrus (*P.JoySorrow 21*). Whether this is an accident of preservation is not clear. It is possible that at some point after his reign, the figure of the caliph Hishām became part of a standardized model for epistolary writing exercises comparable – *mutatis mutandis* – to the use of the Gracci family names (*Titius, Caius et Sempronius*) in Late Antique and Medieval Latin juristic literature

Exemplars of writing exercises underscore different degrees of proficiency and hence the goals of trainees. Early Islamic Arabic items consist mostly of the repetition of the same epistolary formulae several times over, which indicates that the aim of the practitioner was not to learn letters' shapes or epistolary formulae *per se*, but rather to master proficiency in a chancery hand and, arguably, a suitable *mise en page*.

Interestingly, Early Islamic Arabic writing-exercises reflect an emphasis on epistolary visual articulators in the form of *alineae*, vacats, and *lineae dilatantes*.[117] Overall, Early Islamic scribal exercises of epistolary formulae respect the tripartite structure of official papyrus letters. One writing exercise on a tile found at Khirbat al-Mafjar[118] (Fig. 17) is particularly telling in this regard. The placement of the writing reveals that the tile was broken before being inscribed with the ink. The small area of writing surface at the scribe's disposal forced him to break off the line in the middle of the doxology *fa-innī aḥmadu ilay-ka allāh alladhī lā ilāh | illā huwa* (ll. 4–5). He then broke the line again after the word *huwa*, despite still having almost an entire blank line at his disposal. Similar attention to layout features is also evident in scribal exercises from Central Asia.[119] These and similar instances underscore the insistence on layout in the training setting. They further indicate

116 Morelli 2001, 53–54; see also *infra* p. 200.
117 For the use of the *linea dilatans* as a means for highlighting words and justification of the text in Arabic papyrus letters, see Grob 2010, 188.
118 Baramki 1953, pl. XI and Hamilton 1959, pl. XCV, no. 7.
119 Grenet 2008, 27 fig. 12 (right) (Samarkand; before 820); see in particular the *alinea* after the *basmala*.

that mastery of a proper *mise en page* belonged to the advanced stage of Arabic scribal training.[120]

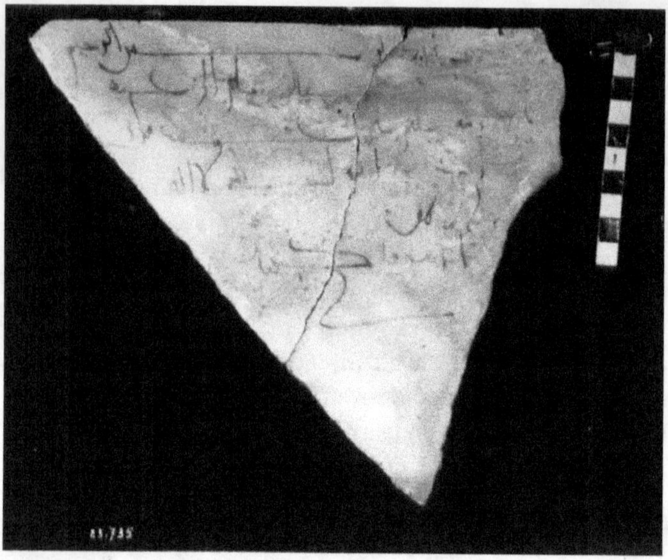

Fig. 17: *Epistolary exercise on a marble tile (Khirbat al-Mafjar). Reproduced from Baramki 1953, pl. XI.*

A meticulous attention to visual structuring features is also implied by the smaller number of examples of writing exercises on papyrus. A fragment containing the incipit of a letter written by one ʿĀṣim b. ʿĀʾib (?) to a certain Muḥammad b. ʿUmar (or ʿAmr), housed in the Denver Public Library, is a poignant example.[121] The arrangement of the writing on the papyrus surface indicates that the piece is complete on both the left and right margins. The small writing surface in fact forced the writer to break the line mid-way through the *basmala* after *al-ra-|-ḥmān*

120 Cf. Vanthieghem 2014b, 403. Vanthieghem sees the practice of epistolary formulae and of *belles lettres* as two stages of proficiency in Arabic writing. It is possible, however, that state-chancery oriented scribal training occurred in a parallel yet distinct environment without intersecting scholarly oriented training practices. The marginality of literary influences on documentary Arabic, especially in the Early Islamic period, also points in this direction. Cf. Sijpesteijn 2020b, 437n13. Cf. also Brockopp 2017, 80–95.

121 The document is part of a portfolio set of 129 "original leaves from rare books and manuscripts" (call number: 094 H629). I thank W. Graham Claytor VI for informing me of the existence of the papyrus and for providing me with a digital image.

al-raḥīm. Despite one half of the second line being at the writer's disposal, he again breaks the line after *al-raḥīm* before passing on to the internal address section. Another illustration is *P.DiemDienstschreiben* d (= *P.David-WeillLouvre* 27a), in which the writer, having at his disposal only a narrow sheet of papyrus, breaks the line in the *basmala* after *al-raḥmān* and then again after *al-raḥīm* on the following line. Such instances clearly reveal that layout was a deeply rooted component of scribal training and of the way in which the visual semantics of official documents were conceptualized.[122] Furthermore, this suggests that the separation of *basmala* from the rest of the letter was considered a layout norm that was to be respected even when space was limited.[123]

122 For the layout of informal Early Islamic Arabic writings, see *infra* p. 184–185; cf. Appendix 1 A.
123 See also *infra* p. 170.

If the Mountain Will Not Come: Official Inscriptions

If letters on papyrus and related materials can be considered the most denotative type of Imperial Arabic documents, official monumental inscriptions signal a similar watershed in the pre-Islamic Arabic epigraphic tradition. Not only do building inscriptions represent the bulk of the evidence of Early Islamic officially sponsored epigraphy, but they also mark a virtually new domain of Arabic writings, compared to only two officially sponsored pre-Islamic inscriptions in the Arabic language.[124] Furthermore, Early Islamic building inscriptions also clearly distinguish themselves from their scant pre-Islamic precursors on a formal level.[125] This stands in contrast to contemporary Arabic graffiti which, to a large extent, were still embedded in the epigraphic culture of pre-Islamic Arabia and the Levant.[126]

Before venturing into the formal specifics of building inscriptions, it is useful to provide a broad functional classification of Early Islamic Arabic officially sponsored inscriptions into the following functional domains:

1. By far the most numerous are building inscriptions commemorating the foundation or restoration of architectural enterprises. This type of text is spearheaded by the Sufyanid dam inscriptions on the Arabian Peninsula (*AI* Z 68 (Ṭā'if; 677/678)) and Hoyland 2006 p. 413 (Medina; 661–680)). The lion's share of items in this category, however, belongs to Marwanid foundation inscriptions in the Dome of the Rock (*RCEA* I 9a (East–Southeast), 10 and 11 (691/692)), the Umayyad Mosque in Damascus (*RCEA* I 18a–b*[127] (705/706)), and the Prophet's Mosque in Medina (Sauvaget 1947 p. 66* (706/707?)). Further foundation inscriptions are found in congregational spaces at the Umayyad *quṣūr* of Qaṣr Burquʿ (*RCEA* I 12 (700/701)), al-Muwaqqar (Mayer 1946 p. 73 (722/723), Qaṣr al-Ḥayr al-Gharbī (*RCEA* I 27 (727)), Qaṣr al-Ḥayr al-Sharqī (*RCEA* I 28 (728/729), Quṣayr ʿAmra (Imbert 2016 p. 337 (735–743)), Khirbat al-Minya (Ritter 2016a p. 65 (743–744?)), and Acre (*CIAP* I p. 30, no. 1 = *RCEA* I 32* (before 743)). Further Umayyad building inscriptions in sectarian spaces include those commemorating the foundation of al-ʿUmayrī Mosque in Bosra (Ory 1999 p. 376 (before 718/719?)) and its successive expansion and restoration

124 *RCEA* I 2 (Zebed; 512) and *RCEA* I 3 (Ḥarran; 568).
125 Cf. Gaube 1982, 213–214.
126 See *supra* p. 89.
127 Two versions extant.

Note: Full references to the present section are given in Appendix 2

https://doi.org/10.1515/9783110740820-023

(Ory 2005 p. 161, no. 1 (720/721) and p. 162, no. 2 (745/746)) as well as the restoration inscription of the mosque of ʿAmr b. al-ʿĀṣ in al-Fusṭāṭ (*RCEA* I 19*[128] (711)). Official inscriptions commemorate the Umayyad patronage of non-sectarian buildings and specifically the construction of the market in Baysān (*CIAP* II p. 207, no. 1 (737/738)), the renovations at the ports of Sidon and Acre (*CIAP* I p. 31, no. 2 = *RCEA* I 37* (before 750)) and the erection of the bridge over the Great Canal in al-Fusṭāṭ (*RCEA* I 8* (688)). Finally, one commemorates the levelling of a street in Fīq (*CIAP* I p. 103, no. 1 (692/703). Early Abbasid building inscriptions primarily celebrate caliphal patronage of the two sanctuaries in Mecca (*MCIA* IV, 1 pp. 40–68, ns. 1–8) and Medina (*RCEA* I 38* (752/753) and *EPI* 14944 and 14941 (768/769)). In addition, single inscriptions commemorate Abbasid caliphal endowments to the urban development in Baysān (*CIAP* II p. 215, no. 1 (753)), Ascalon (*CIAP* I p. 144, no. 1 (771/772)), Ṣanʿāʾ (Mittwoch 1935 p. 235–236 (752/753)), and Djerbent (Gadjev / Shikhsaidov 2002 p. 4 (792/793)). A handful of inscriptions celebrates building enterprises by Abbasid governors in Palestine (*RCEA* V additions and corrections 53 = *RCEA* I 53 (Ramla, 788/789) and *CIAP* II p. 221, no. 3 (Baysān, 794/795)) and in North Africa (*IM* p. 28–29 (Monastir; 797/798)). Finally, the text of a building inscription by the first ruler of the breakaway Idrisid potentate, Idrīs I (*rg.* 788–791), has been reported in the Great Mosque of Tlemcen (*RCEA* I 54*).

2. The second functional category of Early Islamic official inscriptions is benedictory and doxological in nature. As in the case of building inscriptions, these tokens are almost invariably found in architectonic complexes and especially cultic edifices. In fact, benedictory and doxological phrases are a common occurrence in building inscriptions as well. In contrast to building inscriptions proper, however, epigraphies of this type do not contain direct references to construction activities connected to the edifice in which they are placed. Doxological inscriptions usually consist largely of juxtaposed Qur'anic quotes. The interior running mosaic inscriptions of the Dome of the Rock (*RCEA* I 9a and b (691/692) and the lost mosaic inscriptions on the *qibla* wall in the Umayyad Mosque of Damascus[129] and on the southern wall of the Prophet's Mosque in Medina[130] are the best-known examples of this type. Other doxological inscriptions include one found on the outer eastern wall of the Umayyad al-ʿUmayri Mosque in Bosra (Litmann 1949 no. 31 = Ory 1969 no. 3) and an Early Abbasid inscription originally placed in the southern

128 The text of *RCEA* I 19* only survives in the French translation of Pierre Vattier (1666).
129 Flood 2001, 247–251.
130 Sauvaget 1947, 79, no. 4.

porch of the Meccan Ḥarām (*MCIA* IV, 1 p. 46, no. 5). Doxological inscriptions are, however, also to be found in "secular" complexes. The inscription on the Egyptian Gate of Ayla (Whitcomb 1989, p. 168) falls into this category. Benedictory inscriptions, on the other hand, are most common in palatial contexts and consist of prayers for the patron of the building. Once again, eulogies for a building's patron are very common in building inscriptions as well.[131] Setting benedictory inscriptions apart functionally is their lack of direct reference to building activities. Inscriptions of this kind are the fresco inscriptions placed above windows in the western and eastern aisles and in the central niche on the south wall in Quṣayr ʿAmrā (Imbert 2016 p. 342, 340, and 332) and on the abacus of a capital at al-Muwaqqar (Hamilton 1946 p. 70 (722/723)).

3. A third functional typology is represented by official inscriptions that do not fit into any of the abovementioned categories. Excluding inscriptions on small portable objects such as coins, seals, and stamps, these come down to a single land survey in the Nile Delta ordered under the authority of the *ṣāḥib al-kharāj* ʿUbayd Allāh b. al-Ḥabḥāb (in office 724–734).[132]
4. Finally, in a category on their own are inscriptions of a metrological nature. These are primarily represented by the Marwanid milestones in Syria-Palestine (*CIAP* I p. 4, no. 1 (= *RCEA* I 17) (Abū Ghūsh; 685–705); *CIAP* III p. 104, no. 1 (= *RCEA* I 16), p. 104–105 (= *RCEA* I 14) (both from Dayr al-Qalt; 685–705), p. 220, no. 1 and p. 221, no. 2 (both from Fīq; 704); *RCEA* I 15 (Bāb al-Wādī; 685–705); and Silverman 2007 p. 605 (ʿAyn Ḥamad; 685–705) and Early Abbasid ones on the Darb Zubayda (al-Rāshid 1992 p. 138, al-Rāshid 1993 p. 335–336 ns. 1–3 and al-Rāshid 1993 p. 337).

From a formal point of view, the formulaic structure of Early Islamic Arabic building inscriptions (functional domain 1) is both the best documented and most distinctive. The typical structure of building inscriptions comprises four main parts: an invocation, a doxological formula, a dispositive formula (which identifies the authority who ordered the inscriptions), and an executive formula (which identifies those who supervised the actual production of the inscription), in that order. In Early Islamic Arabic building inscriptions, the invocation, doxology, and executive formula are optional, whereas the dispositive formula is compulsory (Appendix 2).[133]

---

131 For some examples, see Hoyland 1997b, 81–82.
132 *CMC* 1 (= *RCEA* I 163) (Upper Manūf; 726/727).
133 For the formulaic features of Early Islamic inscriptions before the Marwanid period cf. also *supra* pp. 90–91.

Formulary

Like contemporary Arabic writings on soft materials, Early Islamic official inscriptions overwhelmingly open with a religious invocation, almost invariably in the form of the complete *basmala*.[134] The use of the short version *bi-sm allāh* "In God's name" is a rare exception.[135] In total, four officially commissioned inscriptions from the Umayyad residences of Qaṣr Burquʿ and Quṣayr ʿAmra feature *allāhumma* in place of the standard *basmala*. This invocation is most notably typical of coeval prayers in Arabic graffiti, the most common being the formula *allāhumma iġfir li-fulān* "O God, forgive N.N.!" Official inscriptions beginning with the invocation *allāhumma* appear to be functionally distinct from those beginning with the *basmala*. On one hand, all of these are interior inscriptions. On the other, fresco inscriptions beginning with *allāhumma* in Quṣayr ʿAmra are all benedictory in nature (functional domain 2) and contain prayers for the patron of the estate without direct links to the actual erection of the residence. Conversely, the building inscription proper on the *tabula ansata* in the western aisle of the southern wall opens with the standard *basmala*.[136]

Umayyad and Early Abbasid inscriptions usually contain a doxological section that follows the opening invocation. Most common in this position is the full testimony of faith, *lā ilāh illā llāh waḥda-hu lā sharīk la-hu muḥammad rasūl allāh*[137] "there is no god but God alone, He has no partner, Muḥammad is God's Messenger".

Distinctive in Early Islamic Arabic building inscriptions is a dispositive clause. From the late 7th century onwards, the clause was almost invariably introduced by the verb *ʾ-m-r* "to order". Almost invariably, the dispositive formula is expressed in the third person perfect form *amara* "(he) ordered", followed by a verbal noun indicating the activity being carried out and the object, commonly introduced by the demonstrative *hādhā*/*-hādhihi*. Alternatively, the object may be put before the dispositive formula, either specified or left undefined. In both cases, *amara* is constructed with the relative pronouns *mā* (or *mimmā*) followed by the verb *amara* and the enclitic reference *bi-hi*/*-hā* (e.g., *hādhā mā amara bi-hi fulān* "This is what N.N. has ordered" or *mimmā amara bi-hi fulān* "This belongs to what has been ordered by N.N.").[138] The dispositive formula ends with the name of the building authority.

---

134 Ritter 2016a, 65; cf. Gaube 1982, 213 (E); Appendix 2, I, A1.

135 Appendix 2, I, A2.

136 Imbert 2016, 335–339 and figs. 6–7.

137 Gaube 1982, 214 (Ea); Ritter 2016a, 65–66; Appendix 2, I, B1; Cf. however Appendix 2, I, B2–3.

138 Gaube 1982, 214 (B); Ritter 2016a, 66; Appendix 2, I, D1–2.

It appears that dispositive formulae were only standardized by the late 7th/early 8th century. In the examples of official epigraphy dated to the reign of Muʿāwiya I, the building authority is introduced by the particle *li-* followed by the caliph's title and name.[139] Both in the portion of the band inscription on the outer octagon of the Dome of the Rock running from east to the south-east side and in the building inscription of Qaṣr Burquʿ, the building authority is not named in an *amara* dispositive formula but rather in an executive clause *banā* "(he) built".[140]

If a clause identifying the supervisor of the activity is provided, it is introduced by the executive formula *ʿalā yaday fulān* "at the hands of N.N.".[141] In the rare instances in which entire communities are credited as the supervisors of the activity, the executive formula *ʿamila* "has made" or even a double formula *ʿamila fulān ʿalā yaday fulān* "it has made (this) N.N. at the hands of N.N." is used.[142] Throughout the Early Islamic period, *banā(-hu) fulān* "N.N. has built (it)" remained a viable – if uncommon – alternative to the executive clause *ʿalā yaday*.[143]

Unusually, 7th-century Umayyad inscriptions also display the scribal note *wa-kataba fulān* "N.N. has written (it)", identifying the actual engraver. A similar hierarchically descending system of dispositive and executive clauses characterizes official epigraphic coinage,[144] weights and stamps[145] as well as papyrus protocols.[146] More generally, uses of the verb *ʾ-m-r* in the perfect tense belong to the standard word choice of Early Islamic official orders on papyrus.[147] Twenty-seven Early Islamic (ca. 40% of the total) official inscriptions still bear a date.[148]

Although functionally different, Umayyad milestones (functional domain 4) are similar to the formal structure of contemporary building inscriptions. They are introduced by the full *basmala* followed by doxology, dispositive, and executive clause.[149] In contrast, the Early Abbasid collection of milestones recovered

---

139 See *supra* p. 90.
140 Appendix 2, I, D3.
141 Gaube 1982, 214 (F); Ritter 2016a, 66; Appendix 2, I, E1.
142 Appendix 2, I, E2 and 4.
143 Appendix 2, I, E3.
144 Balog 1977, 63; see also more in detail Stefan Heidemann's unpublished paper held at the conference *The Measure of Integration – Economic Structures and Resources of the Early Islamic Empire* (Hamburg; Febr. 16–17, 2018).
145 Balog 1976, 4 and Morton 1985, 11–14.
146 Grohmann 1923–1924, XXVII–C.
147 Bsees/Procházka 2015, 295–296.
148 Gaube 1982, 214 (D); Appendix 2, I, G1.
149 Ritter 2016a, 70; see also Appendix 2 I.

from the desert highway of the Darb Zubayda are purely metrological tokens bearing only indications of distance.[150]

Secondary features of Early Islamic official epigraphy were apparently connected to the ruling caliph. From the reign of Hishām onwards, for instance, foundation inscriptions tended to occupy seven lines (Appendix 2, II, A).[151] It may thus be of some significance that all official inscriptions dated to the reign of ʿAbd al-Malik under the latter's direct authority[152] begin with the *basmala*. Likewise, all the official inscriptions from the reign of Yazīd II (*rg.* 720–724) up to the reign of Marwān II (*rg.* 744–750) begin with the invocation. In contrast, none of the official inscriptions recorded in the reign of al-Walīd I (705–715) opens with a *basmala*.

In some instances, secondary formal differences between linked inscriptions can be explained contextually. The twin inscriptions that adorned the lower part of the two columns on either side of the al-Ṣafā gate in the Ḥarām Mosque in Mecca (*MCIA* IV, 1 p. 47, no. 6 = *RCEA* I 51) each bear a second inscription in the upper part (respectively *MCIA* IV, 1 p. 47, no. 7 = *RCEA* I 50 and *MCIA* IV, 1 p. 48, no. 8 = *RCEA* I 52). Of these inscriptions, only the lower ones feature an invocation in the form of the *basmala*. As the lower inscriptions already featured the standard *basmala*, repeating the invocation in the upper inscriptions was possibly deemed by the engravers to be unnecessary. Likewise, among the three inscriptions that commemorate the construction of the Bayʿa Mosque in Mecca, only the one on the exterior wall of the *qibla* (Faʿar 1984 p. 191–192) opens with the *basmala*. If the three inscriptions were conceived as part of one and the same epigraphic work, the *basmala* on the exterior wall of the *qibla* was possibly intended to function as the header of the entire epigraphic cycle.[153] Similar considerations apply to the two pairs of Early Abbasid building inscriptions on the south-eastern and north-western walls of Prophet's Mosque's courtyard in Medina, quoted by Ibn Rustah, where respectively only the longer inscription of each pair displays the *basmala*.[154]

150 Of the Abbasid milestones along the Darb Zubayda route, only al-Rāshid 1993 p. 336 no. 3 (before 785) has a dispositive formula (*hādhā mā amara bi-hi al-mahdī ʿabd allāh ʿabd allāh amīr al-mūʾminīn ʿalā yaday yaqṭīn b. mūsā* "This is what has ordered the Servant of God al-Mahdī, ʿAbd Allāh Commander of the Believers at the hands of Yaqṭīn b. Mūsā").

151 Ritter 2016a, 70 and Appendix 2, II.

152 Cf. *RCEA* I 8 sponsored by ʿAbd al-Azīz b. Marwān, which does not include the *basmala*.

153 A third one-line building inscription on a stone slab in the Bayʿa Mosque is known to me only through the fiche in the *EPI* (labelled "Coll. G. Wiet"). I am unaware of where in the mosque the inscription was originally located or whether it is presently *in situ*.

154 Sauvaget 1947 p. 56, A (114 words, with *basmala*) and B (56 words, without *basmala*) and 58, D (117 words, with *basmala*) and E (37 words, without *basmala*). For the placement of the inscriptions, see *ibid.*, 63–64 and fig. 2.

Disposition of Text

The most common physical shape of Umayyad and Early Abbasid official building inscriptions is quadrangular and rectangular.[155] Noticeable exceptions are the running mosaic inscriptions in the inner and outer octagon in the Dome of the Rock. In addition, just under a third of Early Islamic Arabic inscriptions are enclosed by a linear frame.[156]

While Early Islamic Arabic chancery documents strive for a harmony between formulaic and visual articulation of a document's sections, nothing of the kind is on display in contemporary epigraphic testimonies. Without exception, Umayyad and Early Abbasid officially sponsored inscriptions are written in *scriptio continua*. Only in inscriptions longer than three lines does the *basmala* usually – but not invariably[157] – occupy the entire first line (Appendix 2, II, A and B), thereby forming a semantic and visual unit on its own.

The underlying aesthetic principle of officially sponsored Arabic inscriptions – when a frame is provided – is the perfect correspondence between text and writing surface.[158] Even when a frame is not provided, lines on official inscriptions tend to be exactly the same length.[159] This *horror vacui* of sorts suggests that blank spaces were not considered aesthetic. It also implies that significant preparatory work with regard to measurement had to be done before the actual engraving.

---

155 Ritter 2016a, 70.

156 Sharon 2018 p. 101 (Jerusalem; 652/653); Silverman 2007 p. 605 (ʿAyn Ḥamad; 685–705); *CIAP* I p. 4 no. 1 (= *RCEA* I 17) (Abū Ghūsh; 685–705); *CIAP* II, p. 5 no. 1 (= *RCEA* I 15) (Bāb al-Wādī; 685–705); Ory 1999 p. 376 (Bosra; 718/719); Ory 1969 no. 3 (Bosra; 720/721); Mayer 1946 p. 73 (Qaṣr al-Muwaqqar; 722/723); Hamilton 1946, 70 (Qaṣr al-Muwaqqar; related to 722/723); *RCEA* I 28 (Qaṣr al-Ḥayr al-Sharqī; 728/729); *CIAP* II p. 207 no. 1 (Baysān; 737/738); Imbert 2016 p. 337 (Quṣayr ʿAmra; 735–743); Imbert 2016 p. 340 (Quṣayr ʿAmra; 735–743); Sauvaget 1944 no. 1 (= *RCEA* I 25) (Bouar; 742/743); *CIAP* I p. 144 no. 1 (Ascalon; 771/772); *MCIA* IV, 1 p. 44 no. 4 (= *RCEA* I 49) (Mecca; 783/784); *MCIA* IV, 1 p. 46 no. 5 (Mecca; related to 783/784); *MCIA* IV, 1 p. 47 no. 6 (= *RCEA* I 51) (Mecca; 783/784); *RCEA* V additions and corrections 53 (= *RCEA* I 53) (Ramla, 788/789); Gadjev/Shikhsaidov 2002 p. 4 (Djerbjent; 792/793); *IM* p. 28–29 (Monastir; 797/798).

157 E.g., *CIAP* I p. 103 no. 1 (Fīq; 692–702): (1) *bi-sm allāh al-raḥmān*|(2) *al-raḥīm*.

158 Ritter 2016a, 70.

159 See for instance the foundation inscription in Khirbat al-Minya in Ritter 2016a, 64–66 and figs. 7, 9, and 10.

Umayyad Official Documentary Standard as Early Islamic Documentary Standard

Going back to the question at the beginning of this chapter, the evidence examined in the previous pages clearly delineates a cluster of formulaic and layout features that regulated Imperial Arabic official epistolography and epigraphy. More regimented Arabic scribal practices become tangible in the environment of Umayyad imperial chanceries in Greater Syria between the 670s and 690s. While evidence points to Umayyad Greater Syria as the probable origin of Early Islamic Arabic official formal features, the comparison between papyrus documents and inscriptions from different corners of the Early Islamic world underscores an essential homogeneity of formulaic and layout components in the Imperial metropole and its appendices.

Diachronically, the establishment of official formal templates in the Umayyad period marks a *caesura* in the scant evidence of pre-Islamic Arabic writing. Official letters and public inscriptions signal the appearance of new documentary types in the Arabic text culture. The epistolary prescript and the hierarchical system of clauses in official epigraphy, in particular, represent an original synthesis of pre-Islamic formal features among which Old Arabic is only one and not the most prominent influence.

Evidence indicates that the formal templates codified in the Umayyad period remained the norm throughout the 8th century, bridging the political watershed of the Abbasid revolution (750). Only around the turn of the 9th century do papyri bear witness to the implementation of new parameters of scribal etiquette. In particular, the internal address, salutation, doxology, and transitional marker typical of the Umayyad prescript fell out of favor. At the same time, the benediction *aṭāla allāh baqāʾ-hu/ka*[160] "may God prolong his/your life" – probably a reflection of Abbasid court ceremonial protocol[161] – came to be the standard feature of official epistolary writing.[162] These formulaic innovations were accompanied by the increasing cursivization of Arabic documentary scripts,[163] together

160 For the use of the blessings *aṭāla allāh baqāʾ-hu* and *aṭāla allāh baqāʾ-ka* based on the rank of the addressee, see Khan 2013b, 207 and Reinfandt 2015, 285.

161 Khan 2008, 895 cf. *id.* 2013b, 208.

162 Khan 2008, 893–894; Grob 2010, 42; and Reinfandt 2015, 283–284. Cf. Jahn 1937, 166–167 and Diem 2008, 856.

163 Khan 2008, 896–897; for parameters of cursiveness in Arabic documentary scripts in particular, see Grob 2013.

https://doi.org/10.1515/9783110740820-024

with a few changes in the domain of orthography.[164] An Umayyad Official Documentary Standard thus established itself as the hegemonic formal frame of reference for both the Umayyad and Early Abbasid official documentary culture.

Having defined the broad formal framework that characterized the main corpora of politically hegemonic Early Islamic Arabic writings, we can now turn to examining the extent to which official promulgations differed from Arabic documents produced in private settings.

Hegemonic and Minority Scribal Traditions in Imperial Arabic

Considering the territorial expansion of Early Islamic imperial polity and the different materials and social *loci* that Early Islamic Arabic documents represent, it is hardly surprising that the coexistence of a plurality of writing traditions left a trace on the cumulative body of Early Islamic documentary evidence. A Christian Arabic graffito mentioning the caliph Yazīd I (rg. 680–683) found at Qaṣr Burquʿ suggests the existence of a separate Christian Arabic scribal tradition running parallel to coeval Muslim epigraphy.[165] The graffito's opening invocation *dhkr ʾl-ʾlh* "may God be mindful" is otherwise not found in contemporary Arabic graffiti. Rather, it is reminiscent of the formula *dkyr* N.N. "may N.N. be remembered", which is typical of pre-Islamic Nabatean and of Nabateo-Arabic graffiti, and has an exact parallel in the Old Arabic inscription from Zebed (near Aleppo).[166] Likewise, the orthography of the term "God", *ʾl-ʾlh*, with the unassimilated definite article diverges from the standard *ʾllh*.[167] More specifically, the first orthography of the theonym resonates with pre-Islamic Christian Old Arabic orthography as well as with some other examples of Early Islamic Christian Arabic writings;[168] the second orthography, on the other hand, is overwhelmingly dominant in Islamic age writings.

Furthermore, the anonymous Christian Arab writer addresses Yazīd I as *malik* "king". Islamic Medieval tradition notably stigmatizes the concept of kingship (*mulk*) as the sign of worldly temporal rule and it is often used in a derogatory way as the polar opposite of well-guided rule.[169] Conversely, the title was deeply

164 Kaplony 2019, 317–319.
165 Al-Shdaifat *et al.* 2017, 322–323.
166 *RCEA* I 2 (512) with corrections by Robin 2006, 337.
167 See *supra* p. 176 and references there.
168 Cf. in particular the Arabic lintel inscription in Early Islamic Christian monastic complex in Kilwa (ca. 170 km north-east of Tabūk), Farès 2010.
169 E.g., Ayalon 2005, Crone 2005, 41, and Marsham 2009a, 140–141.

rooted in pre-Islamic Near Eastern Arab potentates active in the "barbarian plain" (Fowden 2004) between Northern Arabia, Syria, and Southern Iraq. The Ghassānid phylarch al-Ḥārith (*rg.* 528/529–568/569) bears the title *malik* in a pre-Islamic Old Arabic graffito from Jabal Usays,[170] as does his ancestor Thaʿlaba, named in a Nabateo-Arabic graffito near Elat.[171] Imruʾ al-Qays (b. ʿAmr?) styles himself *mlk* in his epitaph in Namāra[172] and a "king (Aramaic ideogram *MLK*) of Lakhm" is mentioned in the Middle Persian inscription of Paikuli.[173] The Ḥujrid client kings of the Himyarite kingdom in Yemen likewise bear the title *mlk* in the group of inscriptions[174] for which they were patrons or which mentioned them.[175] To sum up, the engraver of the Qaṣr Burquʿ graffito appears to envisage Arab rulers according to pre-Islamic Levantine categories and to associate Umayyad kingship with the Christian phylarchs of Late Antiquity.[176] This cultural perspective is reflected in the formulaic, orthographical, and terminological peculiarities of his writing, all of which are embedded in a Syrian Christian Arabic epigraphic tradition.

A parallel but opposing process is underscored by the abovementioned *P.Mird.* 45 and 46: Here, the markedly Christian invocation "in the name of the Father, the Son and the Holy Ghost" betrays the will to create a separate scribal framework by modifying a characteristic element of Muslim Arabic epistolography, while maintaining its overall formal structure. Against this background, it may be of some relevance that *P.Jahn* 10, one of the few letters of arguably Jewish authorship in the cumulative body of Early Islamic Arabic epistolography, lacks the entire prescript, with the exception of the opening invocation.[177]

---

170 Al-Ushsh 1964, 302.
171 Avner/Nehne/Robin 2013; for the identity of "Thaʿlaba the king" (*tʿlbh ʾl-mlk*) in particular, see *ibid.*, 243–249.
172 *RCEA* I 1.
173 Humbach/Skjærvø 1983.
174 Robin 2012, esp. 70–82.
175 For the use of the title *mlk* for pre-Islamic Arabian potentates in general, see Avner/Nehne/Robin 2013, 249–253.
176 Andreas Kaplony (LMU, Munich) kindly pointed out to me that *malik* is a common Arabic translation of the Greek title *basileus*, reserved since the early 7th century for the Byzantine emperor; the intention of the Christian writer of the graffito in Qaṣr Burquʿ might thus have been to underline the imperial dignity of Yazīd I. The "dignity of king" (*axiōma basileōs*), however, had also been bestowed by Justinian on the 6th-century Ghassānid phylarch al-Ḥārith; see Shahid 1995–2009, I, 95–98. For the role played by Christian Arab tribes in early "Muslim" armies, see al-Qāḍī 2016, 88–93.
177 See *supra* p. 48n54.

Cases in which distinctive formulaic features can be located in clearly defined cultural matrixes are comparatively rare. Within the broader spectrum of confessionally unmarked or explicitly Muslim writings, recurrent formal divides nonetheless mark documents created in official and private settings.

Plurality within the Same Standard: Private Letters on Papyrus and Related Materials

The documentation on papyrus and related materials reflects permeable structural boundaries between letters produced in official and unofficial settings. Specifically, Early Islamic Arabic private letters conform to the formal template of what has been defined above as long prescript letters.[178] The main distinctive scribal feature of official and private epistolography is the "monumental" – to borrow Khan's terminology – address section introduced by the endophoric reference *hādhā* ("This is a (. . .))", which is absent from all items of private and business correspondence.[179] Furthermore, and contrary to official missives, private and business letters are rarely dated.

While operating in virtually the same formal framework, letters related to business and private exchanges are, nonetheless, differentiated from their official counterparts through a comparatively less scrupulous articulation of the prescript in a formulaic and visual structure. The most significant of these is the occasional omission or alteration of virtually any component of the prescript.

In principle, Arabic letters from all denominations always open with the complete *basmala* – when preserved. Highly exceptional, and in fact found only in *P.World* p. 162, is the use in private letters[180] of the short variant *bi-sm allāh* instead of the more common *bi-sm allāh al-raḥmān al-raḥīm*. An extra-epistolary parallel is provided by a Sufyanid private obligation deed, *P.BruningSunna*. More

---

178 Cf. Kaplony 2018, 344–345.

179 *Ibid.* Early Islamic private and business letters can contain internal references to the document such as the often-encountered locution *kitābī hādhā* "this letter of mine"; these, however, are never found in the opening address section. The introductory endophoric reference is found in private legal documents.

180 An exercise on a marble tile from Qaṣr al-Ḥayr al-Gharbī features the short invocation *bi-sm allāh*; see Schlumberger 1986, 28 (II).

common is the omission of the salutation[181] and/or the doxology.[182] A handful of private and business letters, finally, lacks the transitional element *ammā baʿd*.[183]

Occasionally, in private and business letters, non-standard variations of salutation,[184] doxology,[185] and transition formula[186] are also encountered. In *P.Khalili* I 21, for instance, a textile-merchant salutes his business partner with the formula *salām ʿalay-ka* ***wa-raḥmatu-hu*** "peace and His (i.e. God's) mercy upon you" and omits the doxology altogether. In particular, the variation of the valediction *wa-l-salām ʿalay-ka wa-raḥmat allāh wa-barakātu-hu* "peace, God's mercy and His blessing be upon you" is found exclusively in private or business correspondence.[187] Some of these features may reach back to pre-Islamic uses. The salutation *silm anta* (or *sālim anta/salām anta*) "you are at peace" used by the writer of *P.JoySorrow* 38, in particular, is attested in letters attributed to Muḥammad and ʿUthmān and transmitted in literary sources.[188]

---

181 *P.Hamb.Arab.* II 65 (Egypt; vii/viii); *P.David-WeillLouvre* 30 (Egypt; viii); *P.Khalili* I 24 (Egypt; viii); *P.JoySorrow* 38 (Egypt; viii); *P.World* p. 162 (Egypt; viii) and 182 (Egypt; viii); *P.Mird* 51 (Khirbat al-Mird; viii); and *P.Jahn* 10 (Fayyūm; late VIII). Cf. Khan 1992, 126, who, however, conflates short prescript (which *systematically* lack the salutation) and long prescript missives.

182 *P.Hamb.Arab.* II 65 (Egypt; vii/viii); *P.Khalili* I 21 (Egypt; viii); *P.JoySorrow* 38 (Egypt; viii); *P.DiemRemarkableDocuments* 1 (Egypt; vii) (draft); *P.World* p. 162 (Egypt; viii); and *P.Jahn* 10 (Fayyūm; late VIII).

183 *P.Hamb.Arab.* II 65 (Egypt; vii/viii); *P.Khalili* I 24 (Egypt; viii); *P.JoySorrow* 4 (Egypt; viii); and 30 (Egypt; viii).

184 *P.DiemRemarkableDocuments* 1, r 2 and v 4 (Egypt; VII; *salām ʿalay-ka* ***wa-raḥmat allāh***) (draft); *P.Khalili* I 21, 2 (Egypt; VIII; *salām ʿalay-ka* ***wa-raḥmatu-hu***); *P.Mird* 57, 2 (Khirbat al-Mird; VIII; [. . .] ***wa-salāma***).

185 *P.RagibLettres* 10, v 3 (Egypt; VIII; *fa-inn-ī aḥmadu ilay-ki allāh*); P.Vind.inv. A. P. 8181, 4 (Egypt; VII; *fa-innī aḥmadu ilay-ka allāh*); and *P.Khalili* I 14, 2–3 (Egypt; VIII; *fa-innī aḥmadu ilay-ka allāh alladhī lā ilāh illā huwa* ***taʿālā***).

186 *P.JoySorrow* 5, 7 (*ammā* ***ʿalā ithr dhālika***)and 17, 7 (*ammā* ***ʿalā ithr dhālika***) (both from Egypt; viii). N.b. the use of the transition *ammā* ***ʿalā ithr dhālika*** "as for what comes after" is always additional to that of *ammā baʿd* and is used to open a further section of the letter.

187 *CPR* XVI 18 (Egypt; viii); *P.Berl.Arab.* II 75 (= *P.Loth* 2), r 8 (Fayyūm; viii); *P.Jahn* 5, r 11 (Egypt; viii); *P.MuslimState* 25 (Fayyūm 730–743), 9; *P.RagibLettreFamiliale* (Egypt; 721), 14; *P.Younes-DeuxLettres* 1 (= *P.MarowExchanges* 1), 14 (Egypt; viii); and *P.World* p. 186, r 13 (Egypt; 786/787). N.b. the occurrences in *P.Berl. Arab.* II 23, r 12 and 73, r 8 (both from Egypt; viii) are integrated by the editor and it is just as possible or even probable that the original line reads *wa-l-salām ʿalay-ka wa-raḥmat allāh*, as noted by the editor in the commentary. The translation of *P.Muslim-State* 13 (Fayyūm; 730–743), 10–11 reads "peace be upon you and the *blessings* of God" (emphasis is mine) despite the Arabic text reading [*wa-l-salām*] *ʿalay-ka wa-raḥmat allāh*.

188 Diem 2008, 860–861 and Younes 2013, 22.

Overall, Early Islamic Arabic official letters rarely contain long verbatim Qur'anic quotes,[189] but draw from a standard and recurrent pool of Qur'anic paraphrases instead.[190] The use of figures of religious speech by writers in private correspondence is more varied than that by contemporary professional scribes. A recent survey of Qur'anic quotations in first millennium Arabic letters by Daniel Potthast (2019) shows marked differences between the use of Qur'anic quotes in official and private correspondence. In particular, despite their low numbers compared to official correspondence, Early Islamic private and business-related letters exhibit a wider variety of Qur'anic quotes, a trend that characterizes 9th- and 10th-century documentation as well.[191] Furthermore, different variants of the same quotes can occur in official and private or business correspondence.

The predominant form of the so-called *ḥamdala* (*al-ḥamdu li-llāh rabb al-ʿālamīn* "praise to God, lord of (all) living", Q 1:2), for instance, is the verbalized version *aḥmadu (ilay-ka) allāh,* most notably used in the first segment of the epistolary doxology. While official correspondence only features the verbalized *ḥamdala*, however, the non-verbalized form is occasionally found in business and private correspondence dated or datable to the 7th and 8th centuries.[192] Furthermore, in one private letter, the *ḥamdala* is written in an alternative verbalized form using the perfect tense (*ḥamidtu*), not found elsewhere in official correspondence.[193] Similarly, in another, possibly business-related letter the writer expands the second part of the doxology with a series of divine attributes that find no parallel in coeval official letters.[194] As I have already pointed out, a similar pattern pertains to the use of the valediction *wa-l-salām ʿalay-ka* (Q 6:54, 7:46, 13:24, 16:32, 28:55, and 39:73) *wa-raḥmat allāh* ***wa-barakātu-hu*** (Q 11:73), which is used exclusively in private and business letters.[195]

---

189 On the use of Qur'anic technical *vocabulary* in Early Islamic documents, see Donner 2011; for judicial documents in particular, see Tillier 2013, 25–29 and *id.* 2015, 141–151; for taxation, see Sijpesteijn's commentary on *P.MuslimState* 8 (Fayyūm; 730–743).

190 Potthast 2019.

191 *Ibid.*, 3.1–3.3.

192 *P.Berl.Arab.* II 25 (Fayyūm; VIII), r 5 (*al-ḥamdu li-llāh*); *P.Jahn* 10 (Fayyūm; VIII), 5 (*fa-l-ḥamdu li-llāh*); *P.MuslimState* 38 (Fayyūm; 730–743), 4 (*bi-ḥamdi allāh*); *P.RagibLettreFamiliale* (Egypt; 721), 7 (*bi-ḥamdi allāh*); *P.RagibLettres* 9b (Egypt; VIII), 4 (*bi-ḥamdi allāh*); and *P.SijpesteijnTravel* (Fayyūm; 735), 7 (*al-ḥamdu li-llāh*).

193 *CPR* XVI 8 (Egypt; VII/VIII), r 6 (*wa-ḥamidtu allāh*).

194 *P.MuslimState* 33 (Fayyūm; 730–743), 3–4 (*aḥmadu ilay-ka allāh alladhī lā ilah illā huwa* | ***al-laṭīf al-khabīr al-qādir ʿalā mā yurīdu*** "I praise for you God, besides Whom there is no god but He, **the Kind, the Knowing, the One who is able to do what he wants**).

195 See *supra* n187.

It is, however, at the level of layout that official letters differ most from their private counterparts. Early Islamic private and business letters abide in principle by the tripartite structure, with the three obligatory layout blocks separated by the *alinae* that characterize official long prescript epistolography: (1) invocation, (2) address + salutation + doxology, and (3) main text introduced by the transitional marker *ammā baʿd*. Nonetheless, a handful of private and business letters features a single layout block with the *basmala* visually embedded into the rest of the prescript.[196] Much more widespread, however, is the omission of the *alinea* between the doxology and the transitional element.[197] This results in the contraction of the typical tripartite structure to a bi- or even a monopartite one. There are, however, also forms of "hypercorrection". In *P.Jahn* 5 for instance, an 8th-century private letter, a certain Abū Ismāʿīl singles out the *ammā baʿd* as a layout block on its own, separated from both the prescript and the main body.[198] In parallel, throughout the 8th century, long-prescript letters from the chanceries of Arab officials show a progressive standardization of script features and the development of a more rounded and slenderer chancery style characterized by the use of a thin-cut *kalamos*. This process eventually gave rise to a distinctive official epistolary style, which differed not only from coeval private correspondence and epigraphic as well as literary scripts, but also from the thicker and more angular hands in which other types of official documents such as bilingual demands and receipts and protocols were penned.[199]

Patterns of difference are clearest when formal differences occur within the few examples of Arabic archives or dossiers comprising both official and private documents. In the dossier of Arabic documents from Nessana, *P.Ness.* 56, a bilingual release from an obligation, is the only Arabic item of written exchange between

196 *P.JoySorrow* 1 (Egypt; VIII), 1; *P.DiemRemarkableDocuments*, 1 (Egypt; VII), 1; *P.RagibLettres* 10 (Egypt; VIII), 1; *P.TillierFustat* 2 (Fusṭāṭ; 785–793), 1; *P.Khurasan* 28 (Rōb; 766), 1. Cf. *P.Ragib-Juridiction* 1 (Egypt; 662/663), 7, 12; *P.BruningSunna* (Egypt; 664/665), 1; P.Vind.inv. A. P. 11163 (Egypt; VII), 1.

197 *CPR* XVI 27 (Egypt; VII/VIII), 2; *P.Berl.Arab.* II 49 (Egypt; VIII), r 3; *P.David-WeillLouvre* 12–13 (Madīnat al-Fāris; VIII), 3; *P.JoySorrow* 21 (Egypt; after 724), 4; *P.Khalili* I 21 (Egypt; VIII), 2; *P.Mird* 61 (Khirbat al-Mird; VIII), 5; *P.RagibLettres* 9b (Egypt; VIII) v, 3; *P.RagibLettres* 10 (Egypt; VIII), v 3; *P.RagibLettres* 11 (Egypt; VIII) r, 3–4; *P.RagibLettreFamiliale* (Egypt; 721), 6; *P.ReinfandtLeinen-haendler* (Ihnās; early VIII) r, 3; and *P.YounesCondolence* 3 (probably Fayyūm; VIII), 3; *P.Youne-sCondolence* 4, 3 (Fusṭāṭ; VIII); and *P.YounesCondolence* 5 (= *P.JoySorrow* 20), 2 (Egypt; VIII). Cf. also the documents discussed *infra* at p. 185 and references there. Letters omitting the doxology altogether are not included in this list.

198 *P.Jahn* 5, r 3.

199 Gruendler 1999, 131–139 summarizing her conclusions. For a more recent assessment, see now Sijpesteijn 2020b, 455–467.

private parties – or at least parties not serving in their official capacity.[200] Compared to the other testimonies in the Nessana dossier, *P.Ness.* 56 is set apart by a comparatively rudimentary layout. In particular, the initial invocation is attached to the main body of the document in a single layout block without the customary articulating *alinea*. Furthermore, compared to official Nessana Arabic items – and indeed compared to the well-practiced hand of the Greek version – [201] the Arabic *ductus* of *P.Ness.* 56 is quite irregular with an especially imprecise observance of the baseline.

In the archive of ʿAbd Allāh b. Asʿad (ca. 730–743),[202] the overwhelming majority of documents are official letters by the pagarch of the Fayyūm and ʿAbd Allāh's superior Nājid b. Muslim. A smaller group of items, however, comprises ʿAbd Allāh's half official, half business-related correspondence with lowlier officials and with business partners[203] as well as a few letters not involving ʿAbd Allāh directly.[204] It can hardly be a coincidence that these more private items in ʿAbd Allāh's archive are differentiated by the thickness of the writing *vis-à-vis* the "slender" and more regular script executed with a sharper *kalamos* that characterizes correspondence from the pagarch's chancery.[205] A further marker of difference in the incoming correspondence from the pagarchal office is a more closely followed layout. In particular, seven business letters addressed to ʿAbd Allāh lack a graphic separation between the doxology and the transition formula.[206] In contrast, this layout feature is always present in documents issued in Nājid's name.

Among the 33 Arabic documents from the Bēk family archive (755–777), six pertain to private legal and economic matters. Within this small group, *P.Khurasan* 28 (766) is set apart by its lack of *alinea* between the opening invocation and the endophoric reference (*hādhā mā . . .*) introducing the main text of the document.[207] Official receipts from this archive further distinguish themselves by

200 One Yazīd b. Fāʾid, acting as a witness in *P.Ness.* 56 appears in *P.HoylandDhimma* 1 among the group of persons who have wronged the people of Nessana, and he is the addressee of *P.HoylandDhimma* 2 in which he seems to be involved in the collection of taxes.
201 For a discussion of the layout structure of *P.Ness.* 56, see *infra* p. 230.
202 *P.MuslimState* 1–23, 35, and 37.
203 *P.MuslimState* 24–34.
204 *P.MuslimState* 38–39.
205 Sijpesteijn 2013, 230 and *ead.* 2020b, 460–462.
206 *P.MuslimState* 24, 3; 25, 3; 28, 3; 31, 3; 32, 3; 34, 3; and 38, 4 (all from the Fayyūm; 730–743).
207 Cf. however, *P.Khurasan* 16 (772), 1 that lacks an *alinea* after the opening introduction and displays an overall atypical structure by having the addressee's name placed after the invocation and before the endophoric reference.

their script, exhibiting more cursive features compared to the more archaic letter shapes featured in legal documents from the same cache.[208]

To be sure, missives promulgated by official chanceries are not immune to occasional "transgressions" from the standard epistolary formulae and layout. Such instances are, however, comparatively few and can in many cases be explained contextually. These include the Arabic petition addressed by Dēwāshtīch to the *amīr* Jarrāḥ b. ʿAbd Allāh, where the scribe has used the valedictory formula *wa-l-salām ʿalāy-ka wa-raḥmat allāh* both in the valediction and in the salutation. This is possibly the result of the agency of an overzealous bilingual Sogdian-Arabic scribe, or because the document is likely a draft.[209] Similarly, two letters between Arab officials from the Nessana dossier (*P.HoylandDhimma* 1 and 2) lack an *alinea* between the doxology section and the main text. The fact that both letters are written on the same sheet of papyrus and on the re-used verso of a Greek account, however, suggests that they are to be considered drafts or, possibly, copies for safekeeping.

Multiple Parallel Formal Standards: Private Epigraphy

Unlike 7th- and 8th-century Arabic letters, items of Early Islamic official epigraphy lack direct counterparts in the private domain. Formal comparisons between officially sponsored inscriptions and private epigraphic testimonies can therefore be based only on the use of shared examples of religious speech and general considerations of aesthetic principles.

A first formulaic divide applies to the different roles of the *basmala* in Early Islamic official and private epigraphy. In the realm of Early Islamic official epigraphy, the *basmala* is structural in every inscription longer than three lines. Conversely, the use of the *basmala* is unsystematic or entirely absent from private graffiti. Notably, several graffiti conform to pre-Islamic writing conventions, especially in the use of the header *anā fulān* "I am N.N.". Furthermore, while Early Islamic Arabic epitaphs from Egypt and Iraq open with the full *basmala*, examples from Syria[210] and the Arabian Peninsula[211] often drop the complete

208 Khan 2007, 66–71.

209 See *supra* p. 89.

210 *CIAP* III p. 230–233 ns. 13–16, (all from Fīq; VII/VIII); Ory 1969 ns. 22, 23, 28, and 79a (all from Bosra; VIII).

211 Al-Faqīh 1992 p. 118, no. 2, 366–368 no. 1–2, 456, no. 4 (all from ʿAsham and its hinterland; VIII).

basmala while displaying both a variety of alternative invocations and the shortened form *bi-sm allāh*.[212]

On a more general note, private devotional tokens underline the use of competing theonyms. In official inscriptions, Allāh is the only theonym used – as is indeed the case in the overwhelming majority of private writings. A handful of graffiti from the western Arabian Peninsula, however, show evidence of the substitution of Allāh by al-Raḥmān.[213] In addition, Early Islamic Arabic graffiti exhibit a plethora of God's attributes that are otherwise not present in contemporary official epigraphy.[214]

Formulations of the Muslim testimony of faith (or *shahāda*) are a common component of official Arabic inscriptions but also appear on a variety of items of private epigraphy, most commonly in funerary contexts. The oldest example of Early Islamic private epigraphy occurs on a tombstone of one ʿAbbāsa bt. Jurayj from Aswan, dated 691.[215] Significantly, the composition and wording of the Aswan testimony of faith differs from the version(s)[216] circulating on contemporary official inscriptions and coins in two main aspects. In official building inscriptions, the *shahāda* is juxtaposed with the *basmala* to the point that the two formulae may be considered a single semantic entity.[217] On the tombstone from Aswan, on the other hand, the *basmala* and the *shahāda* are separated by nine lines and are therefore demarcated as two independent semantic units. This is also the case in several examples of 8th-century private graffiti.[218] Furthermore,

---

212 Ory 1969 ns. 21, 24, and 27 (all from Bosra; VIII); cf. also the variant *bi-sm allāh al-raḥmān* in *WS004* (Wādī Shīreh; related to 727/728). I thank Julia Maczuga for the reference.

213 Imbert 2013a, 118–119; for "hegemonic" and minority theonyms in the Qur'an, see in particular Kaplony 2018, 321–323.

214 For an overview of some of God's epithets frequently encountered in Early Islamic Arabic graffiti and stelae, see Hoyland 1997b, 83–84 and Nevo 1994, 121–125.

215 El-Hawary 1932 (= *CG* IX 3201). There is, however, a distinct possibility that the date of ʿAbbāsa's tombstone should be understood as <1>71 AH (= 788). This is suggested by both the script style and phraseology of the stele, which are more akin to early 9th-century epitaphs. See Hoyland 1997b, 87n65.

216 Bacharach 2010 classifies the versions of the *shahāda* circulating at the end of the 7th century as: "short" (*bi-sm allāh muḥammad rasūl allāh* "In God's name, Muḥammad is God's Messenger), "Eastern" (*bi-sm allāh* ***lā ilāh ilā allāh waḥda-hu*** *muḥammad rasūl allāh* "In God's name, there is no god but God alone, Muḥammad is God's Messanger), "Syrian" (*lā ilāh ilā allāh waḥda-hu* ***lā sharīk la-hu*** *muḥammad rasūl allāh* "In God's name, there is no god but God alone, He has no partner, Muḥammad is God's Messenger"), and "Jerusalem" (*bi-sm allāh* ***al-raḥmān al-raḥīm lā ilāh ilā allāh waḥda-hu lā sharīk la-hu*** *muḥammad rasūl allāh* "In the name of God, the Merciful the Compassionate, there is no god but God alone, He has no partner, Muḥammad is God's Messenger").

217 Bacharach 2010, 7–8.

218 E.g., *AI* Y 287 (Wādī Māsil; VIII).

the testimony of faith found on ʿAbbāsa's tombstone is positioned after the date, which conversely always belongs in the closing section of official epigraphies.

Secondly, the formulation of the testimony of faith encountered in official inscriptions (appendix. 2, B1):

> *lā ilāh illā llāh waḥda-hu lā sharīk la-hu muḥammad rasūl allāh*
>
> "There is no god but God, Muḥammad is God's messenger"

differs slightly from the verbalized one reproduced on ʿAbbāsa's funerary stele:

> ***fa-hiyā tashhadu anna*** *lā ilāh illā llāh waḥda-hu lā sharīk la-hu muḥammad* ***ʿabdu-hu wa-rasūlu-hu***
>
> "and she testifies that there is no god but God, Muḥammad is His servant and His messenger".

The latter version of the *shahāda*, dubbed "Egyptian" by Bacharach,[219] is found in several 8th-century funerary steles from Egypt[220] as well as on a contemporary tombstone from Jerusalem.[221] The same version of the testimony of faith also appears on an 8th-century papyrus fragment containing instructions for prayers.[222] Finally, the so-called Egyptian formulations recur in graffiti from the Judean Desert,[223] the Arabian Peninsula,[224] and Libya.[225]

Other tombstones from Egypt[226] and the Levant[227] present another variant of the *shahāda*, paraphrasing the text of Q 3:18:

> ***shahida allāh anna-hu*** *lā ilāh illā llāh* ***wa-l-malāʾika wa-ūlūʾ al-ʿilm qāʾiman bi-l-qisṭ*** *lā ilāh illā huwa* ***al-ʿaẓīm al-ḥakīm***
>
> "Allah bears witness that there is no god but God, and (so do) the angels and those possessed of knowledge, maintaining His creation with justice; there is no god but He, the Mighty, the Wise." (trans. Shakir)

---

219 Bacharach 2010, 2.
220 *CG* I 2 (= *RCEA* I 55) (790/791), 3 (= *RCEA* I 56) (795/796), 4 (= *RCEA* I 58) (796/797), and 7 (= *RCEA* I 61) (798/799), VIII 3187 (VIII), IX 3203 (799/800), X 3977 (VIII), *RCEA* I 57 (796/797), 63 (799/800), Randall 1933 p. 328 (744/745), and *EPI* 43922 (762/763). Cf. Bacharach 2010, 2 and Bacharach/Anwar 2012, 64.
221 Schick/Salameh 2004 no. 1 (VIII).
222 *P.MalczyckiInstructions* (Egypt; VIII), v 6.
223 *PoI* 1.25 (780/781).
224 al-Kilābī 1995 (*non vidi*) no. 163 (Badā; 794/795).
225 Bartoccini 1964 no. B-1630 (Ṣabrātha; VIII).
226 *CG* VII 2466 (VIII).
227 Ory 1967 no. 55 (VIII).

A number of other formulations of the testimony of faith can be found among surviving Early Islamic graffiti. For instance, one Saʿīd, leaving a graffito in the Negev Desert in the year 786, phrased his testimony by paraphrasing Q 112 heavily:

> *wa-yashhadu li-llāh wa-kafā bi-llāh shahīdan anna-hu aḥadan aḥadan* (sic) *ṣamad lā wālida wa-lā walada*[228]
>
> "And he testifies unto God – and God suffices as witness – the He is One, One, Eternal, He is no begetter and no begotten".

In general, in Arabic private epigraphy of the 7th and 8th century, verbalized forms of the testimony of faith are preferred over the non-verbalized style of official inscriptions.

Overall, items of religious speech in Early Islamic funerary texts show an asymmetrical development when compared to coeval public epigraphy. In his study of Early Islamic funerary practices, Halevi (2007) hypothesizes the development of funerary formulae on Islamic Arabic tombstones as falling into four main stages: (1) without distinctive Muslim confessional references (until 690), (2) with distinctive Muslim confessional references but without Qur'anic quotations (after 690), (3) with unsystematic use of Qur'anic quotations (after ca. 720s), and finally (4) with a recurrent semi-standardized set of Qur'anic quotes and paraphrases.[229] According to Halevi's classification, a set of recurrent, relatively standardized formulae of devotion on Early Islamic tombstones only developed in the last decade of the 8th century and the beginning of the 9th century.[230] This stands in stark contrast to the process of standardization of official documentary culture a century before and shows a significant difference in the pace of development of a formulaic "canon" in the official and private writing culture.[231] Furthermore, while a standardized collection of Qur'anic paraphrases had already been established in public life by the end of the 7th century, the slow permeation of Qur'anic

228 *PoI* 1.26.

229 Halevi 2007, 14–32; Halevi's milestone of 690 is, however, heavily reliant on the contested dating of *CG* IX 3201, on which see *supra*n215. Cf. Lindstedt's (2019) repartition of 7th and 8th-century Arabic inscriptions into an "earliest" (up to ca. 690) and a "distinctively Muslim" layer.

230 *Ibid.*, 32. A more consistent use of Qur'anic quotes on epitaphs is heralded by the tombstone of one Rabīʿa b. Maslama, *CG* I 3 (= *RCEA* I 56) (Egypt; 795).

231 Cf. Brockopp 2017, 50–58 and 80–83 who points out that an organized Islamic scholarly community evolved at a much slower rate than and independently of Arabic state-oriented bureaucracy and only formed over the course of the 9th century.

phraseology into epitaphs suggests that it was not until about a century later that the Qur'an came to play a formalized role in Muslim devotion to the dead.[232]

One should avoid dismissing the items of religious speech found in Early Islamic private epigraphy too hastily as the fruit of free individual expression. In fact, the phraseology, language, themes, and style of Arabic graffiti are remarkably homogeneous across different regions.[233] The use of parallel variants of the *shahāda* – some occurring in several regions – in private epigraphy is rather evidence of forms of private religious devotion and belief transmitted within the minority Arab Muslim community. It further cemented in private writing culture without being translated into the formulation of imperial ideology in official media or being impacted by the latter.[234]

Comparing officially sponsored inscriptions to commissioned funerary steles also reveals two different types of preparation. As stated above, official engravers went to great lengths to ensure that an epigraphic text occupied the entire surface provided. Less painstaking attention to detail by contrast characterized the relation between text and surface in contemporary funerary steles, in which blank spaces often occur at the bottom of the frame.[235]

232 Halevi 2007, 25–30; for the "consumption" of Qur'anic text in daily practices of piety and apotropaic uses, see Bsees 2019.
233 Hoyland 1997b, 90–91.
234 Cf. Brockopp 2017, 66–67.
235 See e.g., *CG* I 1 (= *RCEA* I 6) (Aswān?; 652) and 2 (= *RCEA* I 55) (Fusṭāṭ; 790), *CIAP* III p. 230, no. 14 (Fīq; 699/700?), p. 232, no. 15 (Fīq; VIII) and p. 233, no. 16 (Fīq; VIII); Ory 1969, no. 55 and 56 (ʿAyn al-Jarr; VIII); and *CG* I 7 (Egypt; 798).

Conclusion

Overall, the Imperial Arabic documentary culture is one that, while borrowing from its past and its neighbouring environment, was generally characterized by distinctive features both diachronically – when compared to the pre-Islamic epigraphic text tradition – and synchronically – when compared to contemporary private Arabic writing.

The formulaic and layout structuring features of the documents surveyed in the previous pages illustrate the Official Umayyad Arabic scribal culture postulated in the opening of this chapter. The official documents that make up the majority of Early Islamic writing reveal that (1) from the late 7th century at the latest onwards, the imperial administration functioned as an agent of standardization of scribal practices through organized bodies of trained bureaucrats; (2) The systematic trans-regional implementation of formal and layout norms set by Umayyad secretaries singled out the Umayyad Official Documentary Standard as the hegemonic scribal tradition within the sociolinguistic framework of Imperial Arabic; (3) Secondary aspects of the formulaic and layout structure of official documents varied depending on the document's function but were consistent within a particular sub-type; (4) Where linguistic and scriptic boundaries were fluid, the norm of formal parameters set by state bureaucrats extended to areas of private writing – despite the occasional inability of private writers to comply with them, or their choice not to comply; (5) Contemporaneously, the politically hegemonic Official Umayyad scribal culture coexisted with underlying pre-Islamic Arabic and Arabian formal conventions that survived in private practice of Arabic literacy – and most notably in private epigraphy. For literacy practices outside the agency of trained bureaucrats, such as funerary epigraphy, the influence of organized agents of standardization began to have an impact on the documentary record only over a century later; (6) Similarly, and still during the Early Islamic period, distinct minority scribal cultures (e.g., Christian scribal culture) can be discerned within the bosom of Imperial Arabic.

If Imperial Arabic was shaped by the political expansion of the Early Islamic Empire in the 7th and 8th centuries, the formal framework of Official Umayyad Arabic was the area in which the Empire's agency was most deeply and widely reflected *within* Imperial Arabic. By the late 7th century, the consolidation of a professional bureaucratic apparatus had produced a split in Arabic text culture: in the domain of official chanceries, a fairly uniform trans-regional formal framework defined by professional scribes emerged from pre-Islamic Arabic (and Arabian) epigraphic texts. ʿAbbāsa's tombstone from Aswān, Saʿīd's graffito in the Negev, and the Christian Arabic letter of Anbā Magnillē from Khirbat al-Mird

https://doi.org/10.1515/9783110740820-025

represent as many writing (sub-)cultures coexisting in the bosom of Imperial Arabic. The first two examples underscore writing practices within the Arab demographic minority and under the homogenizing mantle of the Umayyad Official Standard: these were the relics of an Arabian (rather than merely Arabic) pre-Islamic written tradition and an independent inner Arab Islamic parallel text tradition respectively. In the case of the third example, one is faced in contrast with a distinctive pattern *within* the Official Umayyad Documentary Standard, through the adaptation of the formal official template.

To conclude, private and official Arabic promulgations by the Early Islamic Arab-Muslim minority betray – as Hoyland puts it – a group "united by a shared ideology and common religious idiom". It was through strict scribal norms that official imperial papyri and inscriptions introduced a distinctive note into official imperial documents *vis à vis* private promulgations.

IV A Culture of Ambivalence

E come i piacevoli modi e gentili hanno forza di eccitare la benivolenza di coloro co' quali noi viviamo, così per lo contrario i zotichi e rozzi incitano altrui ad odio et a disprezzo di noi

Giovanni della Casa, *Galateo ovvero de' costumi*

Negotiating "Arab Style"

Commenting on the latent tensions that shine through the letters of Qurra b. Sharīk to Basileios, Arietta Papaconstantinou remarks that "in a sense, the local elites were key actors who formed the main articulation of the system and in many ways defined the form in which power was exerted".[1] In every imperial system, the establishment of provincial rule entails the formation and maintenance of relations between the transregional ruling elite and ethnically and culturally diverse entities, or, in more general terms, between the imperial hegemonic center and the more peripheral areas, which become subjugated to the center. While power and authority remain crucial attributes of the center, the transregional imperial ruling elite does not hold a monopoly of power over the whole territory under its nominal authority, but rather shares control with local intermediate governing bodies (local elites, religious entities etc.) that mediate the ruling elite's relation to the local population. This set of relations is hierarchical and structurally weighted in favour of the center but nonetheless subject to negotiation over the degree of autonomy enjoyed by the intermediaries.[2] The Early Islamic government's need to obtain the compliance of a multitude of regional elites, to whom they delegated administrative tasks at various levels, allowed for negotiations over the degree of autonomy of those groups.[3] Language and cultural expertise, in particular, were a natural bargaining chip of the local elites *vis-à-vis* their Arab Muslim masters.[4] Literary reports give a sense of the social and practical implications at stake.

According to an often-quoted account, when the chief secretary of the *dīwān* of Iraq, the Iranian Zādān Farrūkh, was confronted with the prospect of being removed from office by al-Hajjāj b. Yūsuf, he replied "do not imagine that, for he (al-Hajjāj) is more in need of me than I am of him. There is nobody except me who

---

1 Papaconstantinou 2015, 280.
2 Tilly 1997; Motyl 2001; and Barkey 2004.
3 Papaconstantinou 2015, *passim* who interprets the early decades of Muslim rule over Egypt in light of a system of conflicting loyalties swinging between the obeisance to the central authority and the local power base of the non-Islamized landed aristocracy; cf. Sijpesteijn 2013, 91–113 on the increasing involvement of Arab officials in provincial administration as a means of strengthening Arab control over the extraction and management of revenues at the expense of the local landed aristocracy over the first century of Muslim rule; for a case study of these developments, see Legendre 2016.
4 Reinfandt 2020a; for the agency of Christian physicians as cultural mediators between the Christian and Muslim communities in particular, see Zaborowski 2010; for cultural mediators at the Abbasid court, see Drews 2013.

https://doi.org/10.1515/9783110740820-026

is satisfactory for keeping his records". When shortly thereafter the convert Ṣāliḥ b. ʿAbd al-Raḥmān did manage to translate the state registers into Arabic, Zādān's son supposedly scolded him for "cutting off the basis of the Persians".[5] Similar accounts are reported for contemporary Syria. For instance, Ibn ʿAsākir indicates ʿAbd al-Malik b. Marwān's dissatisfaction with the dependence of Muslim administration on Christian secretaries as the main catalyzer behind the translation of the state registers from Greek into Arabic.[6] According to a different account of the same event, when news of the caliph's design spread, the chief secretary Sarjūn b. Manṣūr was supposed to have remarked bitterly that the Greek scribes should find a new livelihood.[7] The other side of the coin can be seen in a passage from the *Chronography* by Theophanes. Here we read of an attempt to remove Christian secretaries from Islamic chanceries as late as 758/759 only for them to be reintegrated shortly thereafter owing to the Arab scribes' inability "to write numbers".[8] Undoubtedly, these and similar accounts are imaginative reconstructions of much more complex historical realities. I quote them to emphasize that throughout the Umayyad and Early Abbasid period, the performance of the Arab Imperial administrative machinery rested on institutionalized communication between ethnically and culturally distinct social milieus and between practitioners of different languages.

The preceding chapter has touched on one side of this encounter, by discussing Arabic official letters addressed to Christians. Notably, the formulaic structure of Arab-Muslim official correspondence with Christian subordinates underscores different – and comparatively discriminatory – norms of scribal politesse compared to contemporary intra-Muslim letters.[9] The present chapter examines the other side of readership: it delves into the formal peculiarities that characterize the correspondence of Arab-Muslim officials in languages other than Arabic. As these documents typically show several of the distinctive formal and formulaic features that characterize Umayyad letters written in Arabic, they will be referred to – for want of a more stringent term – as "Arab-style" documents.[10] In particular, the focus will linger on the parameters of social behavior and the communica-

5 Balādhurī, 300–301 (trans. Hitti, 455–456) and Ibn al-Nadīm, 242 (trans. Dodge, II, 581–582). On bilingual administrators in early Islamic Iraq and Iran in general, see Frye 1975.

6 Ibn ʿAsākir, XXII, 320–322; I thank Luke Yarbrough for the reference.

7 Balādhurī, 193 (trans. Hitti, 301).

8 Theophanes, 596 (trans. Mango, 431).

9 For a discussion of strategic epistolary politesse with particular reference to Arabic letters on papyrus, see Grob 2010, 121–123.

10 The label "Arab style" was coined by Luiselli (2008) to refer to epistolary formulae displaying Arabic influences in 7th- and 8th-century Greek epistolography.

tive strategies that governed the relationship of Arab-Muslim officials with the non-Arabized regional elites of the conquered lands.

Greek Arab-Style Letters

The body of Greek language papyrological evidence on the Early Islamic administration includes a wealth of official letters, orders, receipts and the like issued in the name of both Arab-Muslim and Christian officials. In terms of formal structure, 7th and 8th century Greek correspondence by Christian civil officials and members of the clergy resonates with pre-conquest 5th-, 6th-, and early 7th-century Byzantine conventions and lacks an epistolary prescript.[11] However, a number of formal novelties surfaces in Greek letters issued by Arab officials in 7th- and 8th-century Egypt and Palestine. Specifically, these documents show a similar prescript to Umayyad official letters in Arabic language.

Correspondence by Arab officials in Greek includes both longer missives and short demand notes for the delivery (or acquittal) of goods and tax money. By analogy with contemporary Arabic official epistolography, these two types correspond to Arabic long-prescript letters with a five-part prescript (invocation, internal address, salutation, benediction, and transitional marker[12]) plus valediction, and short prescript (invocation and internal address) notes respectively (Chapter III). In structural terms, the latter are less distinctive. The use of Christian invocations in official acts before the regnal formulae were sanctioned by a decree of the emperor Mauricius, as reflected by 6th- and 7th-century Greek and Coptic legal documents.[13] Furthermore, the internal address is a common feature of disparate ancient letter-writing cultures.[14]

As for longer Greek letters, the Greek prescript in Arab style is organized into the same five components as contemporary Arabic official letters. In particular, when the header is preserved, all Greek letters by Arab officials open with the invocation

a) *en onomati tou theou*, "In God's name"

---

11 Luiselli 2008, 696 and *ibid*.n127.

12 My scrutiny has identified 45 Greek Arab-style official letters with a long prescript dated before 800 CE. A fully annotated list of the Greek documents analyzed in this chapter is given in Appendix 3. I thank Lajos Berkes for sharing with me a preliminary edition of P.Berol.inv. 2791, an Arab-style Greek letter from the Fayyūm assigned to the late 7th century based on paleography (not included in Appendix 3). See Berkes (forthcoming).

13 Bagnall/Worp 1981 and *id*. 2004, 99–100. For a list and discussion of the Christian invocations used in 6th- and 7th-century legal documents see *ibid*., 100–109.

14 See *supra* p. 177.

CPR XXII 52 (Ishqawh; 709–714); *P.Apoll.* 4 (Edfū; VII/VIII); *P.Apoll.* 7–8 (Edfū; VII/VIII); *P.Gascou* 27b (Fayyūm; 695); *P.Lond.* IV 1350–1 (Ishqawh; both 710); *P.Lond.* IV 1353 (Ishqawh; 710); *P.Lond.* IV 1356 (Ishqawh; 710); *P.Lond.* IV 1359–60 (Ishqawh; both 710); *P.Lond.* IV 1362 (Ishqawh; 710); *P.Lond.* IV 1368–70 (Ishqawh; all 710); *P.Lond.* IV 1374–6 (Ishqawh; both 710); *P.Lond.* IV 1378–80 (Ishqawh; all 710); *P.Lond.* IV 1381 (Ishqawh; 708–710); *P.Lond.* IV 1394 (Ishqawh; 708–709); *P.Lond.* IV 1401 (Ishqawh; 709–714); *P.Ross.Georg.* IV 2 (Ishqawh; 710); *P.Ross.Georg.* IV 13 (Ishqawh; 709–710); *P.Ross.Georg.* IV 14 (Ishqawh; 710); *SB* I 4826 (Fayyūm; VII); *SB* VIII 9748 (Fayyūm; VII); *SB* VIII 9752 (Fayyūm; VII); *SB* X 10459 (Ishqawh; 709–714); *SB* XVI 12575 (Fayyūm; VII/VIII); *SB* XVIII 13771 (Ihnās; 707); and *SPP* VIII 1198 (Ihnās; 709).

or

b) *en onomati tou theou tou pantokratoros*, "In the name of God Almighty"

P.Ness. 63 (Nessana; 675); *P.Ness.* 71 (Nessana; late VII); *P.Ness.* 72 (Nessana; 684); *P.Ness.* 73 (Nessana; 683); and *PSI* XV 1570 (Edfū; 667 or 682).

Short Greek and Coptic demand notes issued in the name of Muslim pagarchs usually open with the invocation *syn theō* "with God" instead.[15] All Greek letters by Muslim officials – when preserved – feature an internal address according to the format *o deina tō deini* "N.N. to N.N." or *para deinos pros deina*[16] "from N.N. to N.N."

15 The *syn theō* invocation is attested in tax demands and scribal exercises from the chanceries of the pagarchs of the Fayyūm ʿAwf b. Nāfiʿ (in office end of VII) (*CPR* XXII 11–12), Nājid b. Muslim (in office ca. 730–743) (*CPR* XIX 27, *CPR* XXII 8–10, *SB* I 5130, XVI 12857, XVIII 13247, and *SPP* VIII 1184), Yaḥyā b. Hilāl (in office ca. 744–760) (*CPR* XXII 18, *P.Christ.Musl.* 15, *SB* XVIII 13247, *SPP* III 260 and VIII 1199–1200), Maymūn b. Kaʿb (in office 762–763) (*P.Christ.Musl.* 17 and *SPP* X 64), Khālid b. Yazīd (in office 777–778) (*CPR* XXII 20 and P.Heid.inv.Arab. 856), ʿAbd al-Malik b. Salāma (in office 789–790) (*CPR* XXII 20), Ibrahīm b. Yaḥyā (*CPR* XXII 13 and *SB* VIII 9760), of the pagarch of the Fayyūm (in office in 694) and later duke of Arcadia and Thebaid (in office 696–703) ʿAṭiya b. Juʿayd (*CPR* IV, 3–4 and 6, VIII 74–76, 79–81 and 84, *P.Gascou* 28, *SB* III 7240 and XXIV 16219, and *SB Kopt.* 1783 and 1785) of the pagarch of Ihnās ʿAbd al-Malik b. Yazīd (in office ca. 750) (*CPR* XXII 7) of the pagarch of Ihnās (718–723) and Ushmūnayn (710–716 or 725–731) Rāshid b. Khālid (*CPR* II 123, IV 5, XIX 26, *SB* XVIII 13870, *SPP* VIII 1083 and 1194–1195 and X 197), of the pagarchs of Ihnās ʿAbd Allāh b. ʿAbd al-Raḥmān (*SB* XVIII 13247 and 13249) ʿAmr b. ʿUbayd (*SB* XXVI 16754), Muḥammad b. Abī al-Qāsim (in office in 714–716) (*SB* VI, 9262 and XX 14234), of the pagarch of Ushmūnayn Ṣāliḥ(?) b. Abī Rāshid (in office in 723–724) (*SB* XXVIII 17257). A pagarch is, however, the already mentioned Rāshid b. Khālid whose pagarchial heading features in a Greek writing exercise following the invocation *en onomati tou deou* (sic!) (*CPR* XXII 18, 42). The invocation *en onomati tou theou* also features in two Arabic-Greek (*P.StoetzerSteuerQuittungen* 2 = *SB* XVIII 13771 and *P.BaranskiArabisation* = *SPP* VIII 1198) tax receipts issued by the (tax?) official ʿAbd al-Raḥmān b. Abī ʿAwf (in office early VIII). On ʿAbd al-Raḥmān, see Barański 2019, 26–30.

16 *P.Apoll.* 7 and 8 (both Edfū; VII/VIII); *PSI* XV 1570 (Edfū; 667 or 682); *SB* VIII 9748 (Fayyūm; VII); *SB* VIII 9752 (Fayyūm; VII); *SB* XVI 12575 (Fayyūm; VII/VIII).

Following the address section, a number of Arab-style Greek letters display a greeting in the form

eirenē soi/hymin "peace be with you"

PSI XV 1570 (Edfū; 667 or 682); *SB* I 4826 (Fayyūm; VII); *SB* VIII 9748 (Fayyūm; VII); *SB* VIII [9752] (Fayyūm; VII).

Most Arab-style Greek letters contain a doxological utterance in the form

eucharistō/ eucharistoumen tō theō, "I /we thank God"

CPR XXII 52 (Ishqawh; 709–714); *P.Lond.* IV 1350–3 (Ishqawh; all 710); *P.Lond.* IV 1356 (Ishqawh; 710); *P.Lond.* IV 1359–60 (Ishqawh; both 710); *P.Lond.* IV 1362 (Ishqawh; 710); *P.Lond.* IV 1368–70 (Ishqawh; all 710); *P.Lond.* IV 1374–6 (Ishqawh; both 710); *P.Lond.* IV 1378–80 (Ishqawh; all 710); *P.Lond.* IV 1381 (Ishqawh; 708–710); *P.Lond.* IV 1394 (Ishqawh; 708–709); *P.Lond.* IV 1399 (Ishqawh; 709–714); *P.Lond.* IV 1401 (Ishqawh; 709–714); *P.Ness.* 72 (Nessana; 684); *P.Ness.* 73 (Nessana; 683); *P.Ross.Georg.* IV 2 (Ishqawh; 710); *P.Ross.Georg.* IV 14 (Ishqawh; 710); *SB* V 7520 (Ishqawh; 710); *SB* X 10459 (Ishqawh; 709–714).

The main text of Greek letters by Arab officials from Egypt is typically marked by the transitional element

a) *kai meta tauta*, "and after this"

CPR XXII 52 (Ishqawh; 709–714); *P.Lond.* IV 1350–3 (Ishqawh; all 710); *P.Lond.* IV 1356 (Ishqawh; 710); *P.Lond.* IV 1359–60 (Ishqawh; both 710); *P.Lond.* IV 1362 (Ishqawh; 710); *P.Lond.* IV 1368–70 (Ishqawh; all 710); *P.Lond.* IV 1374–6 (Ishqawh; all 710); *P.Lond.* IV 1378–80 (Ishqawh; all 710); *P.Lond.* IV 1381 (Ishqawh; 708–710); *P.Lond.* IV 1394 (Ishqawh; 708–709); *P.Lond.* IV 1399; (Ishqawh; 709–714); *P.Lond.* IV 1401 (Ishqawh; 709–714); *P.Ross.Georg.* IV 2 (Ishqawh; 710); *P.Ross.Georg.* IV 13 (Ishqawh; 709–710); *P.Ross.Georg.* IV 14 (Ishqawh; 710); *PSI* XV 1570 (Edfū; 667 or 682); *SB* V 7520 (Ishqawh; 710); *SB* VIII 9748 (Fayyūm; VII); *SB* VIII 9752 (Fayyūm; VII); *SB* X 10459 (Ishqawh; 709–714); *SB* XVI 12575 (Fayyūm; VII/VIII).

In Arab-style Greek letters from Syria-Palestine, the main body of the letter is introduced by the particle

b) *epeita* "afterwards"

P.Ness. 72 (Nessana; 684); *P.Ness.* 73 (Nessana; 683).

After the main body of the text, Arab-style Greek official letters usually display a valedictory greeting, reading

a) *eirenē soi/hymin* "peace be upon you"

P.Apoll. 5 (Edfū; VII/VIII); *P.Apoll.* 8 (Edfū; VII/VIII); *P.Ness.* 70 (Nessana; 685); *P.Ness.* 74 (Nessana; 685); *PSI* XV 1570 (Edfū; 667 or 682).

or

b) *eirenē soi/hymin apo tou theou* "peace from God be upon you"

P.Apoll. 7 (Edfū; VII/VIII); *P.Lond.* V 1892 (VII/VIII); *P.Ness.* 68 (Nessana; 680); *SB* VIII 9748 (Fayyūm; VII); P.Vind.inv. G 44498.

Scribal remarks – when provided – are introduced in Arab-style Greek letters by the clause *egraphē* "it was written" and a date according to the Egyptian (in Egypt) or Roman (in Syria-Palestine) calendar and an indiction year. In bilingual requisition orders from Nessana, the dating clause is completed by an indication of the corresponding Islamic year.[17]

The form of the prescript in evidence in the Greek correspondence of Arab-Muslim officials is unparalleled in pre-conquest Greek epistolography. There can hardly be any doubt that the prescript of Greek letters by Arab officials is a transposition of the characteristic formulae of Early Islamic *Arabic* official letters.[18] Despite the obvious similarities, however, the Arabic and Arab-style Greek formulary are phrased differently. On closer examination, formulations of the epistolary prescript in Arabic and Greek outline a precise pattern of adaptation.

Both Greek versions of the *basmala* stand out for omitting the characteristic succession of theonyms (*allāh* + *al-raḥmān*)[19] that characterizes the Arabic version, instead using the standard Greek term for "God", *theos*, alone:[20]

(Arabic) *bi-sm allāh* ***al-raḥmān al-raḥīm*** "In the name of God, the Merciful the Compassionate"

(Greek) -a *en onomati tou theou* "In the name of God"

(Greek) -b *en onomati tou theou* ***tou pantokratoros*** "in the name of God Almighty"

The variant *en onomati tou theou tou pantokratoros* (b), in particular, features an element unrelated to the Arabic model. In itself, the concept of an omnipotent god is common to all Abrahamic religions and is certainly not specifically Christian. The corresponding Arabic expression, *allāh ʿalā kull shayʾ qādir*, for instance, is a frequent occurrence in the Qur'an (e.g., Q 2:107). The term *pantokratōr*, however, also has strong biblical overtones as it is used as a *nomen sacrum* both in the Greek Old and New Testament, as well as in both Christian and Jewish papyri to translate

---

17 Cf. Kraemer 1958, 176.

18 Luiselli 2008, 696–697 and Reinfandt 2015, 282–283.

19 See *supra* pp. 176–177.

20 For the use of the formula *en onomati tou theou* in early Islamic writing exercises, see Berkes 2017b, 32–33.

the Hebrew *Sebaoth*.[21] The invocation *en onomati tou theou tou pantokratoros* is in fact the only element of the Arab-style Greek prescript that features in private correspondence of the Arab period as well.[22] Similar considerations apply to the use of the formula *syn theō* in short prescript demand notes by Arab officials. Although the use of the phrase as an opening invocation can be traced back to the influence of the Arabic *basmala*, the formula per se is attested in Christian and even pre-Christian writings.[23] The Arab-style Greek formulae thus introduce terminology resonating with Christian use behind the façade of Muslim administrative jargon.[24]

Official Arabic letters can feature an endophoric reference, in the format *hādhā kitāb min* "this is a writ from", *hādhā kitāb barā'a min* "this is a writ of acquittal from", *hādhihi barā'a min* "this is an acquittal from", or just *barā'a min* "an acquittal from" after the opening invocation.[25] By contrast, in the address section of Arab-style Greek letters endophoric references are unattested.[26]

The formulation of the Greek salutation perfectly mirrors *salām ʿalay-ka*.

(Arabic) *salām ʿalay-ka/-kum* "peace be upon you"

(Greek) *eirēnē soi* or *hymin* "peace to you"

However, in almost all known examples of Arabic letters addressed to Christians, the salutation is omitted,[27] whereas it is found in 7th-century Arab-style letters, only to disappear in 8th-century examples.[28] When Arabic official letters addressed to Christians do contain a salutation, this may appear in forms not attested in inner-Muslim correspondence. In the already mentioned letter addressed to the Christian king of Makuria by the governor Mūsā b. Kaʿb, the salutation section reads *salām ʿalā* ***awliyā' allāh wa-ahl ṭāʿati-hi*** "peace be upon **the friends of God and those who obey Him**". By contrast, Arab-style Greek letters do not feature formulae specifically tailored to Christians.

The deepest formal divide between 7th- and 8th- century Arabic and Arab-style Greek letters surfaces in the doxological section of the prescript.

---

21 Montevecchi 1956 and *ead.* 1988, 283 and Naldini 1968, 22–23.

22 *P.Ross.Georg.* V 11 (Egypt; VIII), see Luiselli 2008, 698. The invocation *hᵉn pᵉ-ran ᵉm-pᵉ-noute pantōkratōr* is also attested in Coptic private letters; see *P.Laur.* V 204 (Oxyrhyncite; VII).

23 Naldini 1968, 13.

24 Johannes Thomann came up with the ingenious suggestion that the Greek *en onomati tou theou tou pantokratoros* may have been intended to recreate the metrical effect of the Arabic *bi-sm allāh al-raḥmān al-raḥīm* (p.c. Jan. 24, 2018).

25 See *supra* pp. 177–178 with further references.

26 See however *infra* p. 254 for an Arab-style endophoric reference in Greek legal documents.

27 See *supra* p. 183.

28 *PSI* XV 1570; *SB* I 4826; *SB* VIII 9748; *SB* VIII [9752].

(Arabic) *aḥmadu allāh* ***allādi la ilāh illā huwa*** "I praise God, there is no god but He"

(Greek) *eucharistoumen/eucharistō tō theō* "we/I thank God"

The Greek version of the doxology noticeably lacks the Muslim anti-trinitarian profession of the unicity of God. Through the omission of the only *explicitly* Muslim cultural identifier from the formulary, the Arab-style Greek phraseology thus departs from the Islamic religious milieu of the Arabic original and locates itself in a non-definitional-monotheistic one.

As regards the valedictory section, Arab-style Greek correspondence does not feature the formulae typically used in contemporary Arabic letters addressed to Christians.

(Arabic) -a *wa-l-salām ʿalā* **man ittabaʿa al-hudā** "peace be upon who follows the guidance"

(Arabic) -b *wa-l-salām ʿalā* ***muḥammad al-nabiy wa-raḥmat allāh*** "Peace and God's Mercy be upon the Prophet Muḥammad"

(Greek) -a *eirēnē soi/hymin*[29]

(Greek) -b *eirēnē soi/hymin* ***apo tou theou***[30]

Both Arab-style variants of the valedictory greeting are based on the Arabic formula used in contemporary intra-Muslim Arabic official correspondence *wa-l-salām ʿalay-ka (wa-raḥmat allāh)* "peace (and God's mercy) be upon you". The phrase *apo tou theou* is not found in pre-Islamic Greek documentary letters on papyrus[31] and is thus to be considered an innovation of the Early Islamic period. Yet it does not correspond precisely to the Arabic valediction either. *Apo tou theou* may have been intended to render the second half of the Arabic valedictory phrase (*wa-raḥmat allāh*) although it differs from it in its wording.

To summarize, in terms of epistolary etiquette, Arab-style Greek letters can be considered a sort of buffer zone between parallel administrative hierarchies of different cultural and ethnic belonging. In itself, the transposition of the Arab prescript into Greek entails a statement of cultural distinctiveness by the Arab-Muslim elite. At the same time, however, the Greek prescript systematically softens the religious overtones of the Arabic epistolary formulae. Compared to

29 *P.Apoll.* 5 (Edfū; VII/VIII), 3 (*eirēnē hymin*); *P.Apoll.* 8 (Edfū; VII/VIII), r 5 (*eirēnē soi*); *P.Ness.* 70 (Nessana; 685), r 9 (*eirēnē soi*); *P.Ness.* 74 (Nessana; 685), r 10 (*eirēnē soi*); *PSI* XV 1570 (Edfū; 667 or 682), r 13 (*eirēnē hymin*).

30 *P.Apoll.* 7 (Edfū; VII/VIII), r 4; *P.Lond.* V 1892; *P.Ness.* 68 (Nessana; 680), r 6; *SB* VIII 9748 (Fayyūm; VII), r 5; a further unpublished letter (P.Vind.inv. G 44498) only contains the segment *apo tou theou*, see Morelli 2010a, 42.

31 Based on an automatic search in the *papyri.info* database (data extracted on Mar. 5, 2018).

Arabic letters addressed to Christians, Greek Arab-style formulaic structure is more inclusive and mitigates the potential for cultural friction: while the first ostensibly stresses cultural difference between the (Muslim) sender and the (Christian) addressee, the vaguely monotheistic figures of speech of Arab-style Greek missives emphasize common cultural traits.

Arab-Style Coptic Letters

In parallel with the Arab-style Greek epistolographic tradition, a handful[32] of 8th-century Coptic letters[33] also displays a long prescript structure that can be traced back to Arabic formal influences.[34] Regarding the formulae themselves, the renderings of the Arabic epistolary prescript into Coptic are essentially consistent with those observed in Arab-style Greek missives. The invocation is rendered in the shortened form

> *h^{e}m-p^{e}-ran ^{e}m-p^{e}-noute* "in the name of God"[35]
>
> *O.CrumVC* 116 (Fayyūm; VII?); *P.Fay.Copt.* 26 (Fayyūm; VIII/IX); *P.Mich.Copt.* 12 (Fayyūm; VII); *P.Ryl.Copt.* 321 (Egypt; VIII); *SB Kopt.* I 280[36] (Fayyūm; VIII/IX).

and the salutation

> *t-irene ne-k* "peace to you"
>
> *P.Bal.* 214 (Deir el-Balā'izah; VII/VIII); *P.Bal.* 262 (Deir el-Balā'izah; VII/VIII); *P.Heid.* XI 490 (al-Ushmūnayn; VIII); *P.Ryl.Copt.* 321 (Egypt; VIII).
>
> *t-irene ^{e}n-p^{e}-noute ne-k* "God's peace to you"
>
> *CPR* II 225 (Fayyūm; VIII/IX); *P.Fay.Copt.* 26 (Fayyūm; VIII/IX); *P.Mich.Copt.* 12 (Fayyūm; VII); *SB Kopt.* I 280 (Fayyūm; VIII/IX).[37]

---

32 Applying the criteria evidenced *supra* at p. 219, my scrutiny has identified ten Arab-style Coptic letters dated or datable before 800. A full list of the Coptic letters analyzed in this chapter is given in Appendix 3. See also the documents quoted by Berkes (forthcoming) with less restrictive criteria.
33 Research in Coptic epistolography has been conducted without the help of automated search engines. Furthermore, only documents dated (whether paleographically or absolutely) by their respective editors have been included.
34 Richter 2008b, 763. Cf. Berkes (forthcoming).
35 In *O.CrumVC* 116 (Fayyūm; VII?) the invocation *h^{e}m p^{e}-ran ^{e}m-p^{e}-noute* and the salutation *t-eirene nēt^{e}n* are not located in the prescript but on the *verso* together with the address.
36 See the new edition by Garel 2019.
37 In *SB Kopt.* 280 courtesy titles of the addressee are embedded in the salutation. See Garel 2019.

or

> *t-irēnē nak ebol hit*^{e}*n-p*^{e}*-noute* "Peace unto you from God"
>
> *P.Heid.* XI 491 (al-Ushmūnayn; VIII); *P.Lond.Copt.* I 1165 (al-Ushmūnayn; VII/VIII) *P.Ryl.Copt.* 321 (Egypt; VIII).

The transition element *menesa nei* "after this" further divides the prescript from the body of the letter. At the close,

> *tirene ne-k* "Peace to you"

is repeated in the valediction

> *O.CrumVC* 116 (Fayyūm; VII/VIII); *P.Bal.* 256 (Deir el-Balā'izah; VII/VIII); *P.Bal.* 277 (Deir el-Balā'izah; VII/VIII).

Some of the aforementioned formulaic features are not entirely particular to Early Islamic Coptic writing. Christian religious invocations especially were used as headers on Coptic legal documents datable before the Islamic conquest. Probably under the influence of the Arabic *basmala*, Coptic legal documents dated after the Arab conquest increasingly display monotheistic invocations like *h*^{e}*n p*^{e}*-ran* ^{e}*n-p*^{e}*-noute* at the expense of Trinitarian ones.[38] The former were likely preferred under Early Islamic rule on account of their religious neutrality.[39] Pre-conquest Coptic letters also feature transitional markers. The phrases *epeidē čē* "and after" and *menesa nei* "after this", in particular, are common in Coptic letters both before and after the Islamic conquest of Egypt.[40] Of interest, however, is that whenever transitional markers occur in combination with other epistolary features listed above, only the form *menesa nei* is in use. Overall, the simultaneous occurrence of multiple elements of the epistolary prescript can only be interpreted as a result of the influence of Arabic epistolography.

When compared to Greek Arab-style letters, their Coptic counterparts evidence two main differences. The first pertains to the environment of their emergence. As already illustrated, known examples of Arab-style Greek letters not only strongly belong in the sphere of the imperial administration but also are invariably issued in the name of Muslim officials. By contrast, the identity of the

---

38 For a list of religious invocations used in Coptic documents, see Richter/Schmeltz 2010, 201–203.

39 Berkes 2017b, 33. For the use of invocations influenced by the Muslim *basmala* in Early Islamic Greek private letters and legal documents, see *supra* p. 206 and *infra* p. 254–255 respectively.

40 Biedenkopf-Ziehner 1983, 31–38 and pl. IV.

authors of the Arab-style *Coptic* missives and the context of their production are more opaque.

Most Arab-style Coptic letters do indeed contain indications that the sender was acting in an official administrative capacity. As much is inferred from, for instance, the letter by one Zacharias to "his true friend" the *amīr* Rāshid and pertaining to tax administration.[41] Three exemplars of Arab-style Coptic letters are the reused backs of Arabic missives[42] or contain transcriptions of Arabic words,[43] which would suggest a degree of familiarity with Arabic whether in written or oral form. *P.Bal.* 277 (Deir el-Balā'izah; VII/VIII), in particular, a fragmentary letter mentioning "watchmen" of some sort and written on the back of an earlier Arabic letter, contains a number of mistakes, which possibly suggests that Coptic was not the unnamed writer's first language.[44] Three Arab-style Coptic letters open with the two oblique strokes // instead of a cross.[45] The use of the symbol is, however, indistinctive per se to the authors' cultural milieu as it is used in Coptic letters between adherents of different confessions and even between Christian correspondents.[46] At the other end of the spectrum, some missives unmistakably belong in a private context[47] and hint at a Christian origin.[48] An Arab-style prescript and valediction, for instance, features in a letter written by one Gabriel to the monk Phiēou asking for the delivery of some vinegar.[49]

The second major difference between Arabic and Arab-style Coptic official correspondence pertains to the formulary itself. To begin with, Coptic renderings of the Muslim doxology cannot be found in any of the surviving examples of Early Islamic Coptic letters. Nor does the Arab-style Coptic formulary presuppose a direct translation of the Arabic original. It may in fact have been the result of the translation of 8th-century Arab-style Greek epistolographic formulae. This possibility may even be hinted at by the variant of the greeting *t-irēnē nak ebol h^{e}n-*

---

41 *P.Ryl.Copt.* 285 (Hermopolite; VIII).

42 *CPR* II 225 (Fayyum; VIII/IX); *P.Bal.* 262 and *P.Bal.* 277 (both from Deir el-Balā'izah; VII/VIII).

43 *P.Fay.Copt.* 26 (Fayyum; VIII/IX), 6–7.

44 For Arabs writing in Coptic, see Boud'hors 2016.

45 *P.Mich.Copt.* 12 (Fayyum; VII) and *P.Ryl.Copt.* 321 (Egypt; VIII).

46 Richter 2003, 228 (IV); cf. also *infra Shifting Boundaries between Scribal Cultures in the Umayyad Empire*.

47 In *P.Mich.Copt.* 12 (Fayyum; VII), for instance the unnamed sender confronts the equally anonymous recipient about an unsettled business-affair concerning cattle.

48 *P.Bal.* 214 (Deir el-Balā'izah; VII/VIII), is a fragmentary letter concerning the collection of gold for the *dēmosion* tax addressed by one Kollouthas to the monks of the Apa Apollo and Apa Jeremias monasteries. Both the onomastics and the figures of speech (e.g., l. 2 ^{e}*n-e-n-panagion* ^{e}*n-eiote* "your all-holy fathers") suggest an inner Christian context.

49 *P.Fay.Copt.* 12 (= *P.Lond.Copt.* 551 r).

p^e-*noute*, which corresponds closely to the Greek *eirēnē soi/hymin apo tou theou* discussed above.

Coptic evidence offers a broader context for the related Arab-style Greek correspondence. Overall, the appearance of the Arab epistolary prescript in Coptic epistolography postdates the rise of a Greek Arab-style epistolographic tradition by several decades, as all published Coptic examples can be assigned to the 8th century based on paleography. This overlaps with the gradual process of tightening Arab control over the lower ranks of administration in Egypt during the 8th century. At the same time, the appearance of the "Arab" epistolary prescript in Coptic letters by Christians indicates a double process of downgrading. On one hand, the Arab-style prescript appears to have become disenfranchised from immediate *Muslim* connotations and to have become fashionable even among Christian circles at some point during the 8th century. On the other, Arab-style formulae lost their *official* character over time and – through prestige or sheer habit – permeated private scribal practices.[50]

The "Arabic" Letters from Sogdia

Non-Arabic documents issued by Muslim authorities outside Egypt are exceedingly rare and circumscribed to single findings. Evidence for correspondence of Early Islamic Muslim officials in Sogdian has been preserved in the quadrilingual (Sogdian, Chinese, Old Turkish, and Arabic) Umayyad archive from the fortress of Mount Mugh.[51]

Mugh 1.1, the first document to be unearthed at the site,[52] is a Sogdian letter sent by the Muslim military commander ʿAbd al-Raḥmān b. Sulḥ to the "king of Sogdia and sovereign of Samarkand" Dēwāshtīch (*rg*. 706–722) around 720. The letter exhibits a close resemblance to the formal structure of Arabic epistles. The missive opens with the invocation *pr-n'm βyy δ'mδn'k* "in the Name of God,[53] the creator"[54] followed by the address and the benediction *'sp's ZKn βy* "thanks to God". By contrast, Sogdian letters from the same archive issued in the name of

50 Similar conclusions are drawn by Berkes (forthcoming).

51 For the archive of Dēwāshtīch, see *supra* pp. 101–102.

52 For the turbulent history of Mugh 1.1 and of its edition, see Livshits 2015, 15–16 and Yakubovich 2002, 232–234.

53 For the use of *βy-* as a theonym in Sogdian documents, see Henning 1965. On the Sogdian religious panorama in general, see Shenkar 2017.

54 The translation follows Yakubovich 2002 *contra* Livshits 2015. On the reading, cf. also Livshits 2015, 92 comm. l. 1.; see also Henning 1965, 249.

or addressed to Dēwāshtīch and/or other local notables lack the invocation and doxology and open with an address and an endophoric reference to the type of missive (e.g., “a report”, “a message” etc.) instead.[55] This implies that the structure of Mugh 1.I reflects scribal conventions that were introduced in the region by the Arabs.[56] Unlike coeval Arabic official letters, Mugh 1.I contains no transition element linking the prescript to the body of the letter. The lower part of the document is lost so that it is impossible to ascertain whether the missive featured a valediction.

A second missive by an Arab official in the Mugh archive has surfaced in scraps of paper used to line a dagger’s scabbard (today in the Topkapı Museum).[57] The very fragmentary document contains the *incipit* of a letter by the *amīr* of Khurāsān Saʿīd b. ʿAbd al-ʿAzīz (in office 720–721) to one *Wxshw-*(. . .),[58] likely a “chief scribe ((*δ*)[*p’yr*]*ptw*) of Samarkand”.[59] Like in Mugh 1.I, the missive opens with the invocation [*pr*]*-n’m βyy δ’mδ*(*n’*)[*k*] “in the name of the Creator”.

The figures of religious speech employed in the Arab-style Sogdian letters from Mount Mugh betray a distinct local coloring. The Sogdian transposition of the *basmala* in particular, not only expunges the distinctive Muslim binomial *allāh*/*al-raḥmān al-raḥīm* of the Arabic original but also reformulates the invocation by resorting to locally rooted religious vocabulary. More specifically, the theonym *δ’mδn’k* “Creator”, corresponding to the Middle Persian *dādār* “creator”, is one of the most recurrent attributes and theonyms of Ahura Mazdā in Zoroastrian literature.[60] The Middle Persian invocation *pad nām ī dādār* “in the name of the creator” is, in fact, a recurrent opening formula in Zoroastrian texts preserved in Middle Persian.[61] Similar appellations like *δ’mδ’r’k* “creator”, “master of creation” are furthermore used as divine epithets in Sogdian Buddhist texts.[62]

The use of a shortened doxology *’sp’s ZKn βy* “thanks to God” in Mugh 1.I further de-Islamicizes the religious overtones of the document. The Sogdian

55 E.g., Mugh A-14.
56 See Huseini (forthcoming).
57 Text partially edited by Livshits 1962, 221. An image of the document is provided by Lurje 2008, 38 (fig. 2) and Livshits 2015, 204–205.
58 Livshits 1962, 221, l. 2.
59 Lurje 2008, 40n1. The addressee of the Sogdian letter by Saʿīd b. ʿAbd al-ʿAzīz was originally understood by Livshits as a “priest” ([*βyn*]*ptw*).
60 Nyberg 1974, 60 *s.v.* “dātār”; cf. Kellens 1989.
61 Nyberg 1964, 1 and 18; Malandra 1996 *s.v.* “Day”. The rarer variant *pad nām ī dādār weh abzōnīg* “in the name of Creator, the Beneficent, the Bountiful” is probably a later rendering of the Arabic *bi-sm allāh al-raḥmām al-raḥīm*; Nyberg 1974, 26.
62 *TSP* 8: 61, 71, 75, and 190 and *TSP* 8 bis: 5 and 9. On the role of sacred texts in Sogdia, see de la Vaissière/Riboud/Grenet 2003, esp. 128–133.

translation, moreover, shows an almost identical word choice to the Greek *eucharistō tō theō*. The culturally ambiguous social etiquette of ʿAbd al-Raḥmān b. Sulḥ's and Saʿīd b. ʿAbd al-ʿAzīz's letters, stands out more clearly if compared with the formulary of the only Arabic document in the archive (Tab. 1). At some point between 717 and 719, Dēwāshtīch addressed an Arabic petition in epistolary form (*P.Kratchkovski* (Mount Mugh)) to the *amīr* al-Jarrāḥ b. ʿAbd Allāh (in office 717–719).[63] The letter conforms overall with the formal structure of coeval epistles from other regions of the Empire.[64]

Tab. 1: Arabic and Arab-style Formularies in the Mugh Archive.

	Standard Arabic official letters (7th–8th)	***P.Kratchkovski***	**Mugh 1.I**
Invocation	*bi-sm allāh al-raḥmān al-raḥīm* "In the name of God, the Merciful, the Compassionate"	*bi-sm allāh al-raḥmān al-raḥīm* "In the name of God, the Merciful, the Compassionate"	*pr-nʾm βγy* ***δʾmδnʾk*** "In the name of God, the Creator"
Address	*li-fulān min fulān* "to N.N. from N.N."	*li-l-amīr al-jarrāḥ b. ʿabd allāh min mawlā-hu dīwāstī*[65] "To the *amīr* al-Jarrāḥ b. ʿAbd Allāh from his client Dēwāshtīch"	*MN xmyr ʾʾβtrxwmʾn pwn swpx ʾt sγwδy-k MLKʾ sʾmrknδc MRYʾ δy-wshtc* "From the *amīr* ʿAbd al-Raḥmān b. Sulḥ to Dēwāshtīch, King of Sogdia and ruler of Samarkand"
Salutation	*al-salām ʿalay-ka/-kum* "Peace be upon you	*al-salām ʿalay-ka wa-raḥmat allāh* Peace and God's mercy be upon you	/

63 On *P.Kratchkovsky*, see *supra* p. 102.
64 *P.Kratchkovsky* is one of the few Arabic petitions surviving from the Umayyad period. For a formal analysis of the document, see Khan 1990, 8–9. For an explanation of the formal peculiarities of the document, see *supra* p. 103 and 181; for the use of titles in particular, see *infra* p. 239.
65 Both the positioning of the sender's name after that of the addressee and the qualification of "client" in *P.Kratchkovski* (line 2) indicate the lower social standing of Dēwāshtīch before al-Jarrāḥ; cf. *supra* p. 177.

Tab. 1 (continued)

	Standard Arabic official letters (7th–8th)	***P.Kratchkovski***	**Mugh 1.I**
Doxology I	*aḥmadu ilay-ka allāh . . .* “I praise God to you . . .”	*aḥmadu ilay-ka allāh . . .* “I praise God to you . . .”	*ʾspʾs ZKn βγ* “Thanks to God”
Doxology II	*alladhī lā ilāh ʾillā huwa* “there is no other god but He”	*alladhī lā ilāh ʾillā huwa* “there is no other god but He”	/
Transition	*ammā baʿd* “as for after”	*ammā baʿd* “as for after”	/
Valediction	*wa-l-salām ʿalay-ka wa-raḥmat allāh* “peace be upon you and the mercy of God”	*wa-l-salām ʿalay-ka wa-raḥmat allāh* “peace be upon you and the mercy of God”	n.d.

Most conspicuously, in *P.Kratchkovski* the doxology section features the complete Muslim proclamation of faith (lines 4–5), signaling Dēwāshtīch’s recognition – at least *de iure* – of Islam. Both the complete testimony of faith in *P.Kratchkovski* and its omission in Mugh 1.I are best understood outside a framework of religious allegiances *stricto sensu* but rather as elements of epistolary politesse[66] across cultural boundaries.

The emergence of an official Arab-style epistolary tradition in Sogdia was apparently characterized by similar communicative strategies – down to terminology – as its counterparts from faraway Egypt and Syria. In particular, Arab-style Sogdian letters show a tendency to mitigate or omit explicitly Muslim phrases and an effort to incorporate elements of the local religious speech which compare well to the formulary of Greek and Coptic official correspondence by Arab Muslims.

66 Eighth-century Arabic letters written by (arguably) Christian officials to their Muslim superiors feature the same prescript as official letters written by Arab-Muslims; Sijpesteijn 2013, 223 and *ibid.*, 223n31.

Arab-Style Middle Persian letters

Some years back, Dieter Weber published a highly remarkable Middle Persian Pahlavi business letter on papyrus. The document is supposedly housed at the British Museum or at the British Library (to which the Manuscript Collection was transferred in 1973); however, the editor was unable to locate the object at either location and edited the text based on a photograph (BL 065541?).[67] Of particular cultural significance is the header *pṭ' ŠM Y yzdṭ'* = *pad nām ī yazd* "in God's name" featured in the letter.

The formula closely resembles the Zoroastrian invocation *pad nām ī yazdān* "in the name of the gods" first found in the 3rd-century Mazdean inscription of Paikuli[68] and in the 4th-century Zoroastrian inscription of Meshkinshahr.[69,70] However, pre-Islamic Pahlavi letters on papyrus, parchment, and textiles typically open with the address and greeting formulae and not with an invocation.[71] Furthermore, *pad nām ī yazd* is a well-known translation of the Arabic *basmala* in the Pahlavi legends of Arab-Sasanian coins which will be discussed in the next paragraphs. These considerations induced the editor to assign the undated letter to the early Islamic period and to understand the invocation *pad nām ī yazd* as influenced by the Arabic *basmala*.[72] This conclusion is corroborated by the peculiar *ductus* of the letter which has affinities with other Early Islamic Pahlavi hands from the Pahlavi Archive.[73]

In fact, three – likely 8th-century – letters from the Pahlavi Archive housed at Berkeley (Berk. 187, 188, and 197)[74] open with the same invocation, *pad nām ī yazd*, otherwise unattested in the earlier phases of the archive.[75] None of the letters known to date reveal further structural influences by Arabic models.

The Middle Persian rendering of the Arabic parallels the Greek *en onomati tou theou* in that it expunges the distinctive binomial *allāh/al-raḥmān* of the Arabic

---

67 Weber 2005, 226 fig. 1, the photograph bears the number 065541 on the back while the number 1303 is written in pencil on the front, see *ibid.*, 225.

68 Humbach/Skjærvø 1983.

69 Frye/Skjærvø 1996.

70 For the use of *yazdān* in Sasanian epigraphy, see the references in Gignoux 1972, *s.v. yazd'n*.

71 Weber 2008c, 804–805 and Gignoux 2008, 830–832. For Middle Persian epistolography, cf. also the formulae contained in the short treaty *nāmak-nipēsishnīh* "How to write letters", see Zaehner 1937.

72 For further considerations on the layout of the letter published by Weber 2005, see *infra* p. 213.

73 *Ibid.*, 225.

74 Berk. 187 is edited by Weber 2008b, 219 and *id.* 2014, 180–181. Transcriptions of the *incipits* of Berk. 188 and 197 are given by Weber 2014, 180.

75 Weber 2008b, 216 and *id.* 2014, 180.

original in favor of the more locally rooted *yazd* "god". The variant featuring in Berk. 187 *pad nām ī yazd* ***ī kardakkar***[76] "in the name of God who is powerful", in particular, is semantically strikingly similar to the Greek/Coptic Arab-style *pantokratōr*-invocation and provides a further instance of adaptation of the Muslim *basmala* in a culturally ambivalent manner.[77] Berk. 187 is a note from a further unspecified "surveillance of the mosques" (*pēshānīg ī mazgitān*) to the *ostāndār* and is arguably the only document of those discussed above of official pertinence and is likely of Muslim authorship.[78] As in the case of the Coptic and Greek documentation, also in the evidence from the Pahlavi Archive, the *basmala* (or rather its adapted versions) proves the most versatile element of the Arabic prescript in terms of outreach in private writing practices.[79]

Several decades ago, Gignoux (1979) indicated the Middle Persian *pad nām ī yazdān* as one of the possible sources of the Arabic *bi-sm allāh*.[80] The evidence surveyed in this chapter both contradicts and – in a manner – corroborates Gignoux's thesis. While the Arabic *basmala* likely developed independently of the Zoroastrian *pad nām ī yazdān*;[81] the latter possibly influenced the Arab-style *pad nām ī yazd*. Contextualized in the broader framework of Early Islamic Arab-style promulgations, the form *pad nām ī yazd* might have embodied the will of Arab-Muslim authorities to find a formulation that could resonate with both Arab and Iranian religious speech.

Trading Rank Identifiers

The use of non-denominational religious speech and of Christian or Zoroastrian religious jargon by Early Islamic Arab officials is an indication of a policy of compromise. Official documents issued by Arab authorities in a variety of languages in fact attest to further strategies in which the Early Islamic Arab Muslim attempt

76 Weber 2014, 181 revising the previous reading *ī kard man* "who made me" in *id.* 2008b, 219.
77 Cf. Weber 2005, 225. I disagree, however, with Weber's interpretation that the writer's intent was to *disguise* his Zoroastrian affiliation by using a religiously ambiguous formula. The writer, whether a convert or a Zoroastrian, may in fact quite on the contrary have wished to display his mastery of a "fashionable" Arabic formulary.
78 Berk. 197 is addressed by the accountant Yazd to the *ostāndār* while Berk. 188 is sent by an anonymous writer to his "most beloved brother Pōzōy".
79 For the influence of the *basmala* outside the Early Islamic Empire, see *infra* pp. 231–233.
80 Gignoux 1979 and Gignoux/Algar 1990, 172 *s.v.* "besmāllah". The Persian origin of the *basmala* had been independently postulated already by Blochet 1898, 40.
81 For the origin of the *basmala*, see Goldziher 1926 *s.v.* "Bismillāh" and Shaked 1993, 152–153 and *ibid.*n53–63 with further references, see also Moubarac 1957, 58–61. Cf. also *supra* pp. 176–177.

to capitalize on Late Antique concepts of authority and legitimacy.[82] The most evident of such cases is the use of titles by Arab officials.

Notably, naming titles of office and in particular epithets of rank was not part of the formal address of Arab officials in Early Islamic Arabic documents.[83] The only systematic exceptions to this rule are the use of the caliphal titulature with mentions of caliphs from the Sufyanid period onwards,[84] as well as the use of the identifier *mawlā* for clients of Muslim notables.[85] Overall, however, Arabic official promulgations from the 8th and later centuries show the use of a hierarchical set of eulogies and pious invocations attached to names – instead of titles of office proper – to identify an official's function and rank.[86]

By contrast, when at the receiving or issuing end of correspondence in Greek and Coptic, Arab officials are typically addressed with titles of office and honorifics, which are occasionally Arabic loanwords. For instance, in Greek administrative documents one frequently encounters the term *amira*/*amiras* (< arab. *amīr* "commander") to identify various Arab officials.[87] Greek translations of Arabic terms are also encountered. Arab pagarchs of the 8th century, for example, are referred to as *epikeimenos pagarchias*, possibly a translation of the corresponding Arabic expression *ṣāḥib al-kūra*.[88] Finally, some of the designations of Early Islamic officials such as the title *symboulos* used for provincial governors of Early Islamic Egypt and Syria[89] are documentary neologisms.[90]

At the other end of the spectrum, rank designations used in Greek, Coptic and Middle Persian documents both issued by and addressed to Arab officials are always rooted in Roman and Sasanian protocol. Despite avoiding systematic patterns, the use of Roman rank epithets by Arab officials followed hierarchical rules which are broadly consistent with pre-conquest Roman use.[91] Specifically, *endoxotatos*

---

82 Cf. the discussion on the appropriation of late antique heritage in Early Islamic art in Ch. II.
83 Kaplony 2016, 393–394 and 397–398. For a comparison with the use of titles in pre-Islamic Arabic and Greek inscriptions sponsored by Arabs, see *ibid.*, 391. For the absence of titles as identifiers of Arab officials on seals, see in particular Sijpesteijn 2018, 131–132.
84 For the caliphal titulature, see *supra* pp. 90–91 and 153 and references there.
85 Balog 1977, 61.
86 *Ibid.*, 63–68 and *id.* 1976, 5–9 .
87 For the function of *amīr*s in the administration of Early Islamic Egypt, see *supra* p. 96n368; for similar officials featuring in the Pahlavi Archive, see *supra* p. 96; for *amīr*s in Early Islamic Central Asia, see *supra* p. 106.
88 Gonis 2004, 190.
89 In the Nessana dossier, the title *symboulos* is used for the district governor of Ghaza. See Papaconstantinou 2009, 452n28.
90 For *symboulos* and its origin see Morelli 2010b; cf. Papaconstantinou 2009, 452.
91 For an overview of late Roman rank epithets and honorifics, see Koch 1903.

(*gloriosissimus*), a rank epithet reserved for high officials in late Roman Egypt, is used for Arab pagarchs, *amīrs*, and dukes both in the documents issued by and addressed to them.[92] Arab *amirs*, dukes, and pagarchs are addressed as *eukleestatos*.[93] The rank epithets *paneuphēmos* (*famosissimus*) and *hyperphyestatos* (*excellentissimus*), which in the late Roman period denoted the highest dignity, are reserved for Arab governors in missives addressed to them.[94] A further "*paneuphēmos amir* Apulase" mentioned in a Coptic inscription from the hinterland of Aswan was most likely a duke.[95] Unclear is instead the exact capacity of an otherwise unknown *paneuphēmos* ʿAbd al-ʿAzīz b. Mundhir, to whom a Coptic letter by a priest "from the village of Arsinoe" is addressed.[96] Other uses of Roman honorifics are quite arbitrary, however. Both Atias son of Goedos (ʿAṭīya b. Juʿayd)[97] and Ioseph son of Abeid (Yūsuf b. ʿUbayd) style themselves as *Flavius* in Greek and Coptic documents issued in their name. Already in the 5th and 6th century, the Roman *Flavius* was used as a status marker rather than a *gentilicium proprio sensu*.[98] Two other Coptic documents mention a Flavius Saal son of Abdella (Sahl b. ʿAbd Allāh).[99] Similar, rather arbitrary, use of pre-Islamic titulature is shown by numismatic evidence from the East. On Arab-Sasanian copper coinage minted in the Iraq and Iran, Arab governors occasionally bear the royal Sasanian honorific *pērōz* "victorious".[100]

In stark contrast, Byzantine and Sasanian status identifiers – either in the form of loanwords or translations – are not found in the Early Islamic *Arabic* official documents. From this, it can be inferred that Arab officials' attitude towards the non-Arabized/Islamized elites of the Empire was essentially janiform: abiding

---

92 For the use of *endoxotatos* for Arab officials, see Morelli 2001, 21 comm. l. 1, *id.* 2010a, 17–18 and Papaconstantinou 2009, 453 and *ibid.*n35 with further references. For the use of *endoxotatos* in Greek papyri in general, see Hörnikel 1930, 8–11; for Coptic, see Förster 2002 *s.v.* "*endoxotatos*". For the use of *endoxotatos* for the *symbloulos* of the Nessana papyri, see Papaconstantinou 2009, 452n28.

93 For the use of *eukleestatos* for Arab officials, see Morelli 2001, 21 comm. l. 1 and Papaconstantinou 2009, 453 and *ibid.*n31 with further references. For the use of *eukleestatos* in Greek papyri in general, see Hörnikel 1930, 13 for Coptic, see Förster 2002 *s.v.* "*eukleestatos*".

94 Papaconstantinou 2009, 452.

95 Bruning 2018a, 99–102; cf. *O.Crum* 356 (Dayr al-Baḥrī; VI/VII), featuring an anonymous *eukleestatos* [*paneu*]*phēmos doux*.

96 *BKU* III 481 (Fayyūm; VIII); see the new edition by Berkes 2018, 415–417.

97 See *supra* pp. 63–64.

98 For the development of "Flavius" as an honorific title, see Keenan 1973–1974.

99 For the use of Flavius by Arab officials, see Gonis/Morelli 2000, 194; Papaconstantinou 2009, 453–454; and Sijpesteijn 2013, 202.

100 Gyselen 2000, 94–95. On instances in which *pērōz* may be understood as either a title or a personal name, see *ibid.*, 77. For the use of Sasanian mottos on Arab-Sasanian coinage in general, see *supra* p. 139.

by Late Antique notions of status where language barriers did not exist while adopting a more culturally defensive stance while writing in Arabic. Posing as Roman and Sasanian aristocrats was less of a process of cultural assimilation than a pragmatic ad hoc strategy to lend Arab imperial power a more familiar face and strike the right chord with members of local elites.

Arab-Style Epistolography: *mise en page*

Chapter II has evidenced how the layout of Early Islamic Arabic official letters constituted a crucial component of the visual semantics of official documents. The scribes of Arabic official documents utilized *alinae*, vacats, but also elongation (*linea dilatans*) of characters to organize a text's functional parts as well as to highlight certain words. The same aesthetic principles are not shared by most Arab-style Greek and Coptic missives from Egypt, which are organized in a single continuous text-block, with the prescript graphically indistinguishable from the main text.

Bilingual documents, in particular, provide a handy ground for comparison between layout features occurring in the Arabic and twin non-Arabic text. Most notably, in bilingual requisition orders and tax demands[101] from the dossiers of the governors ʿAbd al-ʿAzīz b. Marwān and Qurra b. Sharīk, the Arabic text presents the bipartite layout structure of short prescript Arabic letters with a visually distinguished invocation (Appendix 1B). In the Greek versions, on the other hand, the invocation is embedded in the main text of the document. Clerical practices appear to have been slightly different in coeval Palestine, as in the requisition orders from Nessana[102] the invocation builds a separate layout block, thus abiding by the bipartite *mise en page* of the Arabic version.[103] The same layout is displayed only by two examples from Egypt.[104]

In the East as well, the influence of the Arabic layout structure is evidenced in both Mugh 1.1 and the Pahlavi papyrus letter from the British Library. In particular, the initial invocation builds a distinct layout block, separated from the main body of the letter by a line break.[105] As far as one can determine from the fragmen-

---

101 For the difference between what I label "tax demands" and "requisition orders" based on their respective operative clauses, see *supra* p. 80; on the visual relationship between the Arabic and Greek text of bilingual tax demands and requisition orders, see *supra* pp. 128–129.
102 *P.Ness.* 60, 63, 66 and 67 (Nessana; all dated between 674 and 690).
103 Cf. *supra* pp. 181–182 and Appendix 1 B; for the layout structure of Arab-style Greek legal documents from Nessana, see *infra* p. 255.
104 *P.Heid.Arab.* I h (= *SB* I 5651) and *P.Heid.Arab.* I f (= *SB* I 5649) (Ishqawh; 709–710).
105 Livshits 2015, 90 fig. 24 and Weber 2005, 226 fig. 1.

tary status of the document, the same applied to the fragmentary Sogdian letter by Saʿīd b. ʿAbd al-ʿAzīz.[106] Arab-style letters from the Pahlavi Archive, on the other hand, have little in the way of distinctive layout features.

A peculiar visual feature of the Greek correspondence of Arab-Muslim officials is the continuation of the Byzantine custom of using crosses <†> as beginning and end markers.[107] Eventually, on 8th-century long-prescript Greek letters, crosses were frequently replaced by two oblique strokes <//> or – less often – by the two symbols <ϵ> and <ⲗ>. These are commonly used in both Arabic letters and in Greek and Coptic documents issued by Muslims. T. S. Richter, however, has convincingly shown that the use of the symbols transcended religious affiliation. Rather, it was part of an epistolary etiquette employed by Christians as well when addressing Muslims and even – albeit rarely – in missives between (arguably) Christian correspondents.[108] The precise meaning of the two strokes is unknown. Scholars have interpreted the symbol as a substitute for the Christian cross (a “non-cross”).[109] Possibly, the use of the two oblique strokes deepens its roots in pre-Islamic documentary traditions. Sabaic documents on wooden sticks utilize a similar trilinear item <\//>[110] as an end and paragraph marker, especially – but not exclusively – in documents with legal character in a manner that resembles the use of the double strokes in later Arabic and Arab-style documents. Substitutions of Christian symbols using double strokes or other symbols in Muslim official promulgations appear to have been far from systematic. On Greek short-prescript demand notes issued by Muslim officials, in particular, crosses and Christograms are found well into the 8th century.[111,112]

106 Cf. Livshits 1962, 221, l. 1.
107 E.g., *SB* XX 14443 (Ihnās; 643) issued in the name of ʿAmr b. al-ʿĀṣ, *CPR* VIII 78 (Egypt; VII/VIII) issued in the name of ʿAṭiya b. Juʿayd and *P.StoezerSteuerquittung* (al-Ushmūnayn; 709) issued in the name of Sufyān b. Ghunaym. For a general overview on the use of graphic signs and symbols in late antique documents, see Internullo's (2019–2020) overview with further references.
108 Richter 2003, 223–230.
109 *Ibid.*, 224 with reference to previous literature and Berkes 2014, 192.
110 For this symbol, see Stein 2010a, 31, *id.* 2010b, 306, *id.* 2013, I, 34 (1.2.3), and Drewes/Ryckmans 2016, XV (2.3.3.).
111 Examples of 8th-century Greek documents issued in the name of Arab officials and displaying crosses and/or Christograms are *CPR* XIX 27 (Fayyūm; 730–743) from the chancery of Nājid b. Muslim (in office c. 730–743) and *SPP* III 260 (Madīnat al-Fayyūm; 753) from the chancery of Yaḥyā b. Hilāl (in office 745–761?). On Nājid, see *supra* p. 73; on Yaḥyā, see *supra* p. 74 and references there.
112 The use of crosses in official promulgations sponsored by Arab officials is not particular to papyrology. The already mentioned Greek inscription of Muʿāwiya I is opened by a cross; see di Segni 1997, no. 54.

To summarize, in the absence of secondary markers such as specific religious symbols, Arab-style letters in principle abided by the overall appearance of other official documents in the same language. Distinctive layout features were limited to the occasional visual emphasis on the opening invocation. Even within one language, however, the *mise en page* of the text seemingly depended on the clerical system dominant for each region, document type, and period.

Shifting Boundaries between Scribal Cultures in the Umayyad Empire

In its essence, the emergence of an Arab-style epistolary prescript in non-Arabic letters was a distinctive expression of Arab-Muslim officials.[113] Its use in private Coptic and Middle Persian letters, however, suggests that the non-denominational character of Arab-style formulae was a conduit for elements of the Arabic letter-writing culture to infiltrate 8th-century private epistolography outside the administrative sphere as well.

Documentary evidence in both Arabic and other languages provides a broader context for the adoption of Arab cultural identifiers by the non-Arab elites of the Early Islamic Empire. Some attempts at assimilation into the Arab imperial culture are rather superficial or even opportunistic. In his Arabic letter to the governor of Khurāsān al-Jarrāḥ b. ʿAbd Allāh, for instance, Dēwāshtīch styles himself "*mawlā* ("client") of the *amīr*", a denomination usually reserved for converts. Nothing indicates that Dēwāshtīch himself had actually mastered Arabic nor that he had converted to Islam. Quite the contrary is implied by his public persona. Bronze coinage minted during Dēwāshtīch's reign features invocations to the Iranian goddess "Nanā[114] lady of Panj".[115] Depictions of Nanā are also preserved in Dēwāshtīch's palace in Panjakent.[116] Rather than a statement of religious allegiance, the "title" *mawlā* should be understood as part of a general tone of *captatio benevolentiae*.[117] Other public statements by Dēwāshtīch ostentate a positive disposition towards the Arab conquerors. The fresco depictions in his palace in Panjakent possibly celebrate the Arab storming of Samarkand in 712 and depict a peaceful conversation between a local ruler (in all likelihood Dēwāshtīch himself) and an Arab.[118]

Somewhat similar considerations apply to a graffito left by one Georgios at the monastery of Apa Apollo in Bāwiṭ. Georgios presents himself as a *mawlā*

---

113 Luiselli 2008, 697; Reinfandt 2015, 282–283; and Garosi 2020.

114 For the attributes and iconography of the goddess Nanā and her function in the Bactrian and Sogdian pantheon, see *i.a.*, Henning 1965, 252 and n67 and 68, Shenkar 2014, 116–128, and *id.* 2017, 197–199; On the iconography of Nanā's representations in Central Asia, see Azarpay 1981, 132–139.

115 Smirnova 1963, no. 356–363 and Grenet 1989, 176 and *ibid.*n34.

116 Azarpay 1981, 132–139.

117 Notably, in Mugh 1.1 which is datable after *P.Kratchkovski* Dēwāshtīch is never referenced as a client of the Arabs. See also Yarbrough 2016, 196 pointing at the role of the scribe in determining the letter's formulae.

118 *Ibid.*, 64–67 and figs. 28–31.

https://doi.org/10.1515/9783110740820-027

(*maulē*) of one ʿAbd Allāh b. ʿAmr. Fournet (2009b) has suggested that the ʿAbd Allāh of the graffito should be identified with the homonymous son of the first governor of Egypt ʿAmr b. al-ʿĀṣ. Further hints at Georgios' familiarity with the Arab establishment are his statement that he was accompanied to the monastery by an Arab, a Moager son of Ēglan (arab. Muhājir b. Hajlān/or ʿAjlā). Nonetheless, the staurogram and the Christian invocation exclude the author from being a convert. More likely, Georgios' claim to the status of *mawlā* is to be understood as a social rather than religious declaration:[119] Georgios apparently took pride in his acquaintance with the milieu of the Arab imperial elite.

Over the course of the 8th century, however, one increasingly encounters in papyri and related media individuals born into a substrate language, who had more thoroughly assimilated into the superstratal Arabic writing culture. The *simmāk* (< gr. *symmachos*) Georgios addressing his superior ʿAbd Allāh b. Asʿad, for instance, adopted Arabic and the norms of scribal etiquette that went with it.[120] Coeval bi- and trilingual scribal exercises hint at structural changes in the clerical system of the Islamic administration in Egypt. While evidence from the 7th and early 8th century indicates that Arabic was practiced in isolation from a Greek and Coptic scribal milieu, 8th-century multilingual documents attest to the rise of bureaucrats with multilingual expertise who mastered both the Arabic and the substrate scribal conventions.[121] While the advantages that employment in the Arab chanceries had to offer for Copts skilled in Arabic in terms of economic gains are self-explanatory, documentary evidence suggests that mastery of Arabic was also a conduit to social advancement.

As previously discussed, Arab officials' correspondence with Christian subordinates was governed by slightly different guidelines of scribal politesse.[122] The formal structure of a few 8th-century Arabic documents suggests that different parameters of epistolary etiquette were also reserved for Christians who practiced written Arabic. In 8th-century Hermopolis/al-Ushmūnayn, one Yazīd b. Aslam addressed an Arabic letter (*CPR* XVI 4) to a "scribe/secretary" (arab. *kātib*)[123] by

---

119 For the institution of *walāʾ* in the absence of religious conversion during the Umayyad period, see Crone 1987, 49 and *ibid*.n358.

120 *P.MuslimState* 24 (Fayyūm; 730–743).

121 Berkes/Younes 2012 and Reinfandt 2020a, 146–149.

122 See *supra* pp. 183–184.

123 Grohmann 1964, 132. *Kātib* seems to have designated an official since pre-Islamic times. In fact, in the 5th-/6th-century inscription of Umm al-Jimāl (Jordan) featuring an otherwise unknown "ʿUlayh son of the secretary (*kātib*) of the cohort Augusta Secunda Philadelphiana" *kātib* is seemingly used to translate the Latin *librarius*. The reading of the inscription, however, is not unanimous. The version cited here is based on Bellamy's revision of Littmann's first 1929 edition.

the name of Petosiris.[124] From the content of the letter – discussing the collection of taxes from the district of Ihnās – as well as from Petosiris' qualification as "scribe", it can be inferred that both sender and addressee hold posts in the administration. It is furthermore heavily implied that Petosiris was a Christian, as the sender used the doxology *aḥmadu allāh alladhī lā ilāh illā huwa* (i.e. without the *ilay-ka*).[125] However, the valedictory formula employed by Yazīd, *wa-l-salām ʿalay-ka wa-raḥmat allāh*, is the one usually reserved for Muslim addressees.[126]

Similar instances are in evidence in coeval items of private epistolography. Sometime in the 8th century, a certain Umm al-Ḥakam bt. al-Ḥakam addressed an Arabic letter to an agent of hers, by the name of Mēnas Pečōš (*Mīnā Bajūsh*).[127] Judging by his name and the lack of the *ilay-ka* from the doxology, Mēnas was a Christian, who was able to read and possibly write Arabic. As observed in the Arabic letters addressed to the scribe Petosiris, the sender bids Mēnas farewell with the formula *al-salām ʿalay-ka*, instead of the variant *wa-l-salām ʿalā man ittabaʿ al-hudā*, "peace upon whom follows the Guidance", which might have been expected for a Christian addressee. The hybrid formulary of Arabic used in the letters sent to the Christians Petosiris and Mēnas reflects the liminal cultural status of the recipient. Furthermore, it indicates that Muslim writers, when addressing Arabicized Christians, applied different and more inclusive figures of scribal politesse.[128]

The rise of biliterate clerks indicates a deeper process of assimilation into the Arabic documentary culture than merely the use of Arab-style features in private letters by non-Arabicized Christians and Zoroastrians. These two phenomena can even be interpreted as successive stages of Arabicization: the substitution of local elites through Arab or Arabized personnel during the 8th century, de facto stripped the Arab-style scribal culture of its function. Indeed, the appearance of multiliterate scribes in the Islamic chanceries overlaps chronologically with the disappearance of official Arab-style documents.

For the comparison between the two readings and the discussion of the inscription's date, see Bellamy 1988, 372–377.

124 For the figure of Petosiris, see Reinfandt 2020a.

125 See *supra* p. 183.

126 See *supra* p. 180.

127 *P.Jahn* 12 (Egypt; late VIII).

128 Cf. the lack of the valediction in an Arabic safe-conduct from Saqqāra, *P.PiletteSauf-Conduit* (729) issued by an *ʿāmil* carrying the Christian name ʿĪsā.

Parallel Scribal Traditions: Numismatics

The evidence so far examined in this chapter pertains to epistolary forms and is thus related to a targeted endeavor by the Arab authorities to reach out to members of various groups. Further light on the encounter between the Arab and the local scribal traditions is shed in official promulgations through which Arab authorities engaged with their subjects on a more general scale. With the notable exception of the Greek inscription of Hammat Gader,[129] non-papyrological evidence for officially sponsored non-Arabic texts rests entirely with pre-reform Arab-Byzantine and Arab-Sasanian coins and seals.

The Pahlavi Precursors

Since the first appearance of Arabic phrases on Arabo-Sasanian *drahms* in 651 up to the progressive implementation of all-epigraphic Arabic coinage in the 8th century, coins minted by the Arab governors in Iraq, Iran, and Central Asia were characterized by a functional and positional language divide. Much like under Sasanian rule, administrative remarks proper (name of the issuing authority, mint and date) as well as Sasanian royal mottos like *GDH ʾpzwt* "may kingship increase" continued to be inscribed in Middle Persian on the obverse and reverse field legends.[130] Arabic was typically used on the margins for short invocations, countermarks and personal mottos of the Arab governors (Fig. 6).[131]

Interference between the Arabic and Middle Persian on legends of Arab-Sasanian coinage was exceptional. A rendering of the *basmala* in Pahlavi characters *PWN ŠM Y*[132] *yazdt = pad nām ī yazd* "in God's name" can be seen on "standing

129 See *supra* p. 18.

130 For Middle Persian mottos that only feature in Arab-Sasanian copper coinage, see Gyselen 2000, 97–98.

131 In Arab-Sasanian copper coinage, because of the limited writing surface, positional divides between Arabic and Pahlavi legends are less pronounced than in silver coins; see Gyselen 2000, esp. 105–111.

132 For the use of "Arameograms" (ideographic spellings of originally Aramaic terms) in Pahlavi, see MacKenzie 1986, xii and Toll 1990.

https://doi.org/10.1515/9783110740820-028

caliph"[133] coppers from the mint of Susa,[134] as well as on the Kirmān *dirham* issues of Muṣʿab b. al-Zubayr between 688 and 691.[135] The same Middle Persian legend is found on a bilingual Arabic/Middle Persian all-epigraphic *dirham* weight.[136] In the weight under discussion, the phrase "in God's name this drachm weighs 7/10 (. . .) of the standard of Jayy" is found in Arabic and Middle Persian (*pad nām ī yazd*) on the obverse and reverse legend respectively.[137] The entire Middle Persian legend is in fact a straight rendition of the well-attested Arabic administrative legend *bi-sm allāh ḍuriba hādhā al-dirham* etc. = *pad nām ī yazd ēn darhm* etc. "in God's name this *dirham* was etc.".[138]

Similar to the opening invocation of Mugh 1.1 and to those found on Arab-style Greek, Coptic and Middle Persian letters, the rendering of the *basmala* on Arab-Sasanian coins is shortened in relation to the Arabic original. The distinctive binomial *allāh*/*al-raḥmān* is once more expunged, here substituted by the more locally rooted *yazd* "god".[139] The considerations on the adaptation of the *basmala* in Arab-style epistolography do not necessarily apply to numismatics, however, where the shortened version *bi-sm allāh* and not the complete *bi-sm allāh al-raḥmān al-raḥīm* is the standard form of the invocation.

The use of the languages of the Byzantine and Sasanian administration in Islamic coinage came to an end with the gradual implementation of all-epigraphic Arabic issues under ʿAbd al-Malik and his successors.[140] Qur'anic paraphrases on the field legends on the obverse and reverse side of the coins display

---

133 On the definition "standing caliph", see *supra* p. 152 and references there; for a possible explanation of the visual peculiarities of "standing caliph" coinage minted in Iran in particular, see *supra* pp. 159–160.

134 *ASCC* 40. Gyselen 2000, 98 however notes that the second half of the legend is very difficult to read.

135 *BMC* I p. 103–104.

136 Curiel/Gignoux 1976, 165–169.

137 *Ibid.*, 165–166; curiously the item weighs 2,83 grams and therefore falls short of the ideal 7/10 ratio between reformed *dirhams* (2,97g) and a *mithqāl* (4,25 g), indicating that the "standard of Jayy" must have been lighter than a standard *mithqāl*. See Curiel/Gignoux 1976, 166. The parallel use of different weight standards possibly indicates that the weight was produced shortly after the monetary reforms of ʿAbd al-Malik. A similar situation is attested in early 8th-century Egypt, where weight standards modelled on the Byzantine *solidus* (4,55 g) were still produced in parallel with reformed *dīnār* weights (4,25 g) during the governorate of Qurra b. Sharīk. See *UAT* 3 (4, 43 g) and 4 (4,24 g).

138 For administrative legends on reformed coinage, see *supra* p. 143.

139 Cf. *supra* p. 232.

140 The use of Greek in Islamic coinage comes to an end around the close of the 7th century. The use of Middle Persian was more resilient on the last coins with illiterate legends in Pahlavi script surviving in the so-called "later Sistān" series until 142 AH (759/760); see Album/Goodwin 2002,

the full proclamation of faith. The obverse side of reformed gold coins embraces the central legend and the marginal legend, while the reverse displays the text of Sura *al-Ikhlāṣ* (Q 112) in the central legend and the executive marginal legend (Tab. 2).

Tab. 2: Legends on post-Reform Arabic Gold Coinage.

	Field	Margin
Obverse[141]	*lā ilāh illā llāh waḥda-hu lā sharīk la-hu* "there is no god but God alone, He has no associate"	*muḥammad rasūl allāh* (Q 48:9) *arsala-hu bi-l-hudā wa-dīn al-ḥaqq li-yuẓhira-hu ʿalā al-dīn kulli-hi* (Q 48:28) "Muḥammad is God's Messenger, He has sent him with the guidance and the religion of truth so that He may proclaim it above all religions."[142]
Reverse	*allāh aḥad allāh al-ṣamad lam yalid wa-lam yūlad* (Q 112) "God, One, the Eternal He does not beget nor was begotten"	*bi-sm allāh ḍuriba hādā al-dīnār bi-kadhā fī sanat kadhā wa-kadhā* "in the name of God, this *dīnār* was minted in so-and-so in the year so-and-so"[143]

The all-epigraphic format with Arabic Quranic paraphrases represented one of the most enduring legacies of the Marwanid dynasty well beyond its overthrow in 750. It is therefore somewhat ironic that its first recorded use occurs in a Pahlavi Arab-style issue minted by Zubayrid loyalists opposing the Marwanid house during the second *fitna*. Right before the end of the second civil war in 72 AH (691/692 CE), the Zubayrid[144] governor of Sistān ʿAbd al-ʿAzīz b. ʿAbd Allāh b. ʿĀmir minted Arab-Sasanian coins which eliminated the typical Zoroastrian fire altar on the reverse of Sasanian coinage in favor of a Middle Persian legend in Pahlavi script:

43–45 from the mint of Jayy dated 113 AH (731/732). For Arab-Byzantine Latin coinage, see the *infra* section *Early Islamic Latin Coinage and the Arab-style Bible*.

141 For the determination of the obverse side on Islamic reformed coinage, see Bacharach 2010, 16.

142 For reformed dirhams this legend is displayed on the reverse side and encompasses the extra bit *wa-law kariha al-mushrikūn* "(. . .) even if the 'associators' hate it".

143 On reformed dirhams, the legend *bi-sm llāh ḍuriba hādā al-dirham bi-kadhā fī sanat kadhā wa-kadhā* is displayed on the obverse side; see Bacharach 2010, 16.

144 For Zubayrid propaganda, see Lynch 2015 and Foss 2013. Cf. Treadwell 2012a. For the different strategies of language use in Zubayrid and Marwanid propaganda in particular, see *supra* p. 145.

(1) *dōaftād* (2) *yazd-ew bē oy* (3) *any yazd nēst* (4) *Muhammad paygāmbar ī yazd* (5) *SK*

(1) Seventy-two. (2) One God but He (3) Another God does not exist (4) Muhammad (is) the Messenger of God (5). *SK* (= Sagastan)[145]

The main characterizing aspects of the subsequent Marwanid reformed coinage are in evidence in this issue. This includes not only the *ante litteram* transposition of the complete *shahāda*, but also the all-epigraphic design of the future reformed coinage. Even the disposition of the legends heralds the layout of the all-epigraphic coinage whereby the administrative information encloses the field legend (lines 1 and 5). While the emission of ʿAbd al-ʿAzīz b. ʿAbd Allāh b. ʿĀmir's coins actually predates the introduction of the Muslim testimony of faith in the Syrian coinage, there can be no doubt that the Pahlavi testimony of faith was based on the formulation circulating in the Arab-Muslim community. In fact, similar doxological statement appears on a tombstone in Aswān dated 690.[146]

Early Islamic Latin Coinage and the Arab-Style Bible

An Arab-style tradition in the Greek language does not exist in pre-reform Arab-Byzantine coinage. The bilingual validating expressions (e.g., *ṭayyib/kalon* "good") and mint names on so-called "Umayyad Imperial Image coinage"[147] minted in Greater Syria between the 660s and 690s[148] do not betray clear influences from one language on the other. Only occasionally do more complex Arabic invocations appear, such as in the so-called *al-wafāʾ li-llāh* "obeisance belongs to God" coins.[149] In no such instance, however, are Greek legend translations of the Arabic formulae provided.

The divides between Arabic and substratal languages are more fluid when it comes to Arab-Byzantine coinage from the westernmost provinces of the Islamic Empire. Unlike the Levant and the Iranian world, where Arab authorities adopted pre-conquest coin designs and inscriptions as early as the 640s and 650s, by the time of the Arab conquest of the Maghreb, the language reforms of ʿAbd al-Malik

145 The first specimen of this kind was published by Mochiri 1981 from whom I reproduce both the Middle Persian text and the translation; "does not" is my translation (Mochiri 1981 has "doesn't").
146 *CG* IX 3201 (= el-Hawary 1932); cf., however, *supra* p. 208n215. For the version of the *shahāda* featuring on ʿAbbāsa bt. Jurayj's tombstone in particular, see Bacharach/Anwar 2012; see also *supra* p. 209.
147 For the definition "Umayyad Imperial Image coinage", see *supra* p. 81.
148 For a synoptic periodization of pre-reform Umayyad coinage, see Heidemann 2010a.
149 For the *al-wafāʾ li-llāh* coinage, see Foss 2008, 35 and Milstein 1988–1989; for a related legend (*amara allāh bi-l- wafāʾ wa-l-ʿadl* "God ordered honesty and justice") being used in Arab-Sasanian copper coinage, see Gyselen 2000, 93 (*ASCC* 17 and 36).

were already gaining ground in the rest of the Empire. Coinage issued by Arab authorities in North Africa and Spain between 698 and 716[150] reflects this liminal situation in that it displays Latin transpositions of the Arabic coin legends in use in contemporary Syria.

This hybrid nature is already apparent on visual grounds. Some of the gold issues are entirely epigraphic, adopting the aniconic outlook of the reformed coinage introduced in the Levant in 697 and in the East in the following year (Fig. 18).

Fig. 18: *Anonymous,* solidus, *Spania, Ind. XI (712/713), 4, 465 g (enlarged).*
© Staatliche Münzsammlung, Munich.

Concomitantly, however, image-based gold coins with Byzantine iconography were also in circulation (Fig. 19). All Early Islamic issues from North Africa before the Arab invasion of Spain in 711 are undated. In his seminal study of the Arab-Byzantine coinage, the late John Walker suggested that the repartition between figurative and all-epigraphic coinage in the region mirrored a chronological sequence and, *in speciem*, that the figurative issues preceded the aniconic ones.[151]

Based on the fact that both all-epigraphic and figurative Arab-Byzantine Latin coinage displays the same legends as well of the peculiarities of the script used in the two series, Bates has convincingly argued that all-epigraphic and figurative Arab-Byzantine Latin coins were minted at the same time at different mints. He further suggested that figurative coins were issued in Carthage, one of the two functioning Byzantine mints inherited by the Arabs upon the conquest (the second being Alexandria). In parallel, aniconic coins were possibly issued by a newly established North African mint[152] after the model of the reformed Syrian series.[153]

150 Balaguer 1976; Bates 1992; *id.* 1995; and Jonson 2015.
151 Walker 1956, XLVI–XLVII.
152 Walker 1956, XLVIII, Bates 1995, 13 and Jonson 2015, 219.
153 Bates 1995, 13.

Fig. 19: *Anonymous,* semissis, *no mint, no date, 2,1o g (enlarged).*
© Staatliche Münzsammlung, Munich.

The precise location of this mint is unknown, and it has also been hypothesized that it was an itinerant rather than a proper urban establishment.[154] This supposition is corroborated by the fact that the "North African mint" was apparently transferred to Spain when Mūsā crossed the Strait of Gibraltar to bring his former protégé Ṭāriq b. Ziyād back into the fold in 711.[155]

Overall, the Latin legends can be repartitioned into doxological statements, invocations and administrative remarks (Tabs. 3 and 4).

Tab. 3: Latin Arab-style Legends on Copper Coinage from North Africa.[156]
(Adapted from Jonson 2015)

Type	Obverse	Reverse
TIB, anonymous (Ibn al-Nuʿmān), no mint (North Africa mint).	a) *DEVS NON EST ALIVS DEVS N(on est)* "There is no god except for God" b) *NON EST D(ev)S NIS(i) IPSE SOL(vs) (so)C(io)S ET NON (h) ABETV(r)* "There is no god but He alone, and He has no partner"	(a; c; and d) *DEVS IN NOMINE TVO VNVS* "O God in Thy name alone" (c) *DEVS NON EST ALIUS DEVS N(on est)* "There is no god except for God"

154 Jonson 2015, 219 cf. Bates 1995,15.
155 Bates 1995, 15.
156 The tables provided in this study do not reproduce some of the graphic peculiarities of the Arab-Byzantine coinage from North Africa and Spain. Islamic Latin bronze as well as gold coins use a mixture of Latin and Greek script. In particular, Greek signs for the letters *alpha*, *delta*, *tau*, *kappa*, and *lambda* are occasionally used instead of their Latin equivalents. The letter *thēta* is also used as a numeral for 9. Furthermore, letters or even entire words are frequently inverted or retrograde. Cf. Bates 1995, 12–13.

Tab. 3 (continued)

Type	Obverse	Reverse
	c) *DEUS IN NOMINE TVO VNVS* "O God in Thy name alone"	(b) *D(eus) D(ominus) N(oster) CIAS MA(gnus) ET(ernus) OMN(ia) N(oscens ?)* "O God, our Lord ??? Great, Eternal, All-knowing"
	d) *D(e)VS T(v)VS D(e)VS ET ALIVS NON E(st)* "Thy god is God and there is no other"	(d) *D(e)US T(v)VS D(e)VS ET ALIVS NON E(st)* "Thy god is God and there is no other"
TIB, Mūsā b. Nuṣayr, no mint.	*I(n) N(omine) DOMINI VNVS DSEV* (for *DEVS*) "In the name of the Lord, God Alone."	*MVSE F(ilius) NVSIR*[157] *AMIR A(fricae)* "Mūsā son of Nuṣayr *amīr* of Africa"
TIB, Mūsā b. Nuṣayr, Tripoli.	*D(o)MIN(i) NUM(mus) IN TRIP(o)Li FAKT(us)* (*sic*!) *XVX* "O Lord! (This) *numus* (was) made in Tripoli"	*IN N(omine) D(omi)NI IUS(si)T MVSE AMIR A(fricae)* "In the name of the Lord, Mūsā *amīr* of Africa ordered (this)"

The phrasing of the formulae and their absence from pre-conquest local coinage leave no doubt that the Early Islamic Latin coin legends were modeled on the formulae featured in coeval Arabic all-epigraphic coinage minted in the Levant, Mesopotamia, and Iran (Tabs. 3 and 4; cf. Tab. 2). At the same time, the Latin renditions exhibit both novelties and extensive modifications when compared to their Arabic counterparts.

One of the structural peculiarities of the Latin legends on North African and Spanish Arab-Byzantine coinage pertains to the positional arrangement. In

157 Jonson 2015, 225 has *NUSIaR*. Little is known about early Islamic Arabic orthography in Latin characters. Even if *NUSIR* is to be understood as an abbreviation, the integration *NUSIaR* seems unlikely. In 7th- and 8th-century Greek transcriptions of Arabic terms, the diphthong <ay> is never rendered as [ia]; it is, however, often rendered in Greek as [ī]. See Kaplony 2015, 9. In the Latino-Arabic letter BL 3124 the Arabic diphthong <ay> is likewise rendered in Latin script as [i]. See Internullo/D'Ottone Rambach 2018, 67–68 [15–16]. It is therefore more probable that Arabic <Nuṣayr> would have been rendered as [Nusīr] or possibly [Nusair] rather than as [Nusiar] as Jonson postulates. To the best of the author's knowledge only three Arabic words (two of which personal names) are transcribed in Latin characters in Islamic Latin coinage, all three of which appear in the same legend: arab. *mūsā* = lat. *muse*, arab. *nuṣayr* = lat. *nusir*, and arab. *amīr* = lat. *amir*. As both *mūsā* and *amīr* are transcribed *in pleno* in Latin, it stands to reason that this was done with *nuṣayr* too. To understand *NUSIR* as a complete spelling rather than an abbreviation seems therefore the most plausible option.

Tab. 4: Latin Arab-style Legends on Gold Coinage from North Africa and Spain. (Adapted from Walker 1956 and Bates 1995)

Type	Obverse	Reverse
Images I	*D(e)VS TV(v)S D(e)VS ET A(li)VS NON E(st)* "Your God is God and there is no other"	*IN NOMINE TVO D(eus) VVIECTIM* (?) "In Thy name, God (. . .)"
Images II	*NON EST D(ev)S NISI IPSE SOLVS C(v) I S(ocivs) N(on est).* "There is no god but He alone who has no associate similar unto Him"	*D(eus) D(ominus) NO(ster) MA(gnus) ET(ernus) OMN(i)A N(oscens)* "God is our Lord, the Great the Eternal, the All-knowing"
Ind. II–IV	*D(ev)S ETERN(v)S MAGN(v)S OMNI(vm) CR(e)A(tor)* "God, the Eternal, the Great, God the Creator of all things"	*IN N(omine) D(omi)NI MIS(e)R(i) C(ordis) S(o)L(idus) FE(ritus) IN (af)R(i)C(a) IND(ictione) II–III* "In the name of the merciful Lord, this *solidus* was minted in Africa on the 2nd–4th indiction"
Ind. VII–IX, Africa	*IN N(omine) D(omi)NI N(on) D(eu) S N(isi) VN(vs)C(ui) N(o)N SoC(ivs) ALius SIMIL(i)S* "In the name of the Lord, there is no god but the only God, no other god is similar unto him"	*IN N(omine) D(omi)NI MIS(e)R(i) C(ordis) S(o)L(idus) FE(ritus) IN AFR(i)C(a) IND(ictione) VII–Θ* "In the name of the merciful Lord, this *solidus* was minted in Africa on the 7th–9th indiction"
Ind. X–XII, Spain	*IN N(omine) D(omi)NI N(on) D(eu)S N(isi) D(eus) S(o)L(u)S N(o)N D(eus) ALius (SIMILIS)* "In the name of the Lord, there is no god but the only God, no other god (is similar unto him)"	*H(i)C S(oli)D(us) F(e)R(i)T(us) (i)N SP(a)N(ia) ANN(o) XCIII–XCV IND(ictione) X–XII* "In the name of the merciful Lord, this *solidus* was minted in Spain in the year 93–95 in the 10th–12th indiction"
Ind. XII–XIII, Africa	*IN N(omine) D(omi)NI N(on) D(eu) S N(i)SS(i) D(eus) S(o)L(u)S N(o)N D(eus) ALius SIMILIS* "In the name of the Lord, there is no god but the only God, no other god is similar unto him"	*S(o)L(i)D(us) F(e)R(i)T(us) (i)N AF(ri)C(a) ANN(o) XCV–XCVI IND(ictione) XII–XIII* "In the name of the merciful Lord, (this) *solidus* was minted in Africa in the year 95–96 in the 12th–13th indiction"

reformed Arabic *dīnārs*, the *basmala* recurs only in the administrative legend, *bi-sm allāh ḍuriba hādā al-dīnār bi-kadhā fī sanat kadhā wa-kadhā* "in the name of God this *dīnār* was minted in so-and-so in the year so-and-so" placed on the reverse. On the Arab-Byzantine Latin copper and gold emissions, adaptations of the *basmala* occur both alone[158] and combined with renderings of the *shahāda*,[159] which is never the case in reformed Arabic emissions.[160] As pertains to the administrative legend proper, only types Ind. II–IV and VII–IX include the *basmala* as in the Arabic model formulary. Finally, while Arabic reformed *dīnārs* are dated only by *hijrī* years, Arab-Byzantine Latin emissions are dated by both *hijrī*- and indiction year.[161]

More meaningful, however, are incongruities in terms of phrasing choices. As regards the wording of the *basmala*, in Arabic coinage it invariably appears in the shortened form *bi-sm allāh* "in the name of God". Latin renderings, however, display both the shortened form *in nomine Domini* and the complete ones

in nomine domini misericos
"In the name of the Merciful Lord" or "In the name of the Lord, the merciful"

and

in nomine tuo deus ***vivificans*** *et misericordis*
"In Thy name o life-giving and merciful God".

Likewise, the first segment of the Muslim proclamation of faith is rendered in the Latin in a number of different versions. The truest to the standard Arabic version reads

non est deus nisi ipse solus cui socius non est
"There is no God but He (Himself) alone, Who has no associate"

or slight variations thereof. Other Latin renderings of the *shahāda* take more liberties with the Arabic model and show some unease with the anti-trinitarian vein of the Muslim proclamation of faith such as

non est deus nisi deus solus ***non deus similis***
"In the name of the Lord, there is no god but the only God, **no god is similar** (unto Him)/ **a similar god does not exist**"

158 Type TIB (Ibn al- Nuʿmān); legends ov. c) and rv. a).
159 Types TIB, Mūsā b. Nuṣayr (no mint) and Ind. VII–IX and Ind. X–XII. On gold coins, the invocation plus testimony of faith is always found in the obverse legend.
160 *Basmala* and *shahāda* (both in shortened and complete form) occur together on "standing caliph" gold coinage as well as on pre-reform Zubayrid and Umayyad Arab-Sasanian coinage from 685 onwards. See in particular Bacharach 2010, 3–15 and Heidemann 2010a, 166–184.
161 Walker 1956, XLVII and Bates 1995, 13–15.

Which features a freer rendering of the Arabic *lā sharīk la-hu* through the interpretative periphrasis,[162] or

> *non deus nisi deus* ***omnium creator***
> "There is no God but God, **the Creator of all things**"

which substitutes the *lā sharīk la-hu* segment with the more generic monotheistic expression.

A further way in which Arab-style Latin legends differ systematically from the phraseology of epigraphic Arabic coinage is through what appears to be calculated omissions. The most macroscopic deviation from the Arabic model phraseology pertains to the second section of the Muslim profession of faith focusing on Muḥammad's prophetic mission. The Muḥammad formula is in fact on display on the bilingual Arabic-Latin series introduced in North Africa and Spain between 716 and 719. On those coins, the testimony of God's unicity features both in the Arabic obverse field legend and the Latin reverse marginal legend. Very noticeably, however, only the *Arabic* reverse field legend contains the reference to Muḥammad. By contrast, this section is never translated into Latin (Fig. 20).[163]

Fig. 20: *Anonymous,* solidus, *Africa, 98 (716/717), 4,288 g (enlarged).*
© Staatliche Münzsammlung, Munich.

162 One could speculate whether the Latin legend *non deus similis* "no god is similar (unto Him)/a similar god does not exist" was modelled on the Qur'anic quotation *lam yakun la-hu kufuʾan aḥad* "no one is similar unto Him" rather than of *lā sharīk la-hu* "He has no partner". Cf. the Greek translation on Arabic-Greek protocols *ouk egeneto (autō) omotimos* (*CPR* III 65, 6; 72, 6; and 73, 6). The formula is not, however, encountered on Early Islamic epigraphic coinage on which Arab-Byzantine Latin coins were modelled.
163 Bates 1992; *BMC* II 184-J. 6; Miles 1950, no. 1 (a–f).

The reverse of standard reformed *dīnār*s displays the markedly anti-Christian text of Sura *al-Ikhlāṣ* (Q 112) in the field legend: *allāh aḥad allāh al-ṣamad lam yalid wa-lam yūlad* "God, One, the Eternal He does not beget nor was begotten". The legend is not to be found in any recognizable form in the Latin. The only element of the wording of the Sura that can possibly be recognized in some Latin legends is the divine attribute *eternus* (= arab. *al-ṣamad*) appearing in some of the legends which consist of lists of divine epithets and are otherwise unrelated to the text of Sura 112:

> *deus eternus* ***deus magnus omnium creator***
> "God is Eternal, God is Great, is the Creator of all things"
> *deus* ***dominus noster magnus*** *eternus* ***omnia noscens***
> "God is our Lord, is Wise, is Great, is Eternal, is All-knowing"
> *deus eternus* ***deus magnus omnium creator***
> "God is Eternal, God is Great, is the Creator of all things".

Finally, some of the Latin phraseology is almost entirely unrelated in wording to the original Arabic model. This includes the case invocations:

> ***Deus tuus Deus***
> "Your god is God"
> *deus* ***dominus noster magnus eternus omnia noscens***
> "God is our Lord, is Wise, is Great, is Eternal, is All-knowing"

and

> ***domine deo quis tibi similis***
> "O lord God, who is similar unto You?"

Overall, the figures of religious speech employed in the Early Islamic Latin and bilingual Arabic-Latin coinage resonate with a non-denominational pan-Abrahamic religious milieu. The referential dimension of the vocabulary remains therefore ambiguous and likely changed depending on the readership. Notably, the array of God's attributes used on Arab-Byzantine Latin coinage parallels both biblical and Quranic usage.[164] The phrasing of the Latin legends, however, frequently betrays biblical influences. The legend *Deus tuus Deus* in particular, echoes Deuteronomy 7:9 *Deus tuus ipse est Deus*. The invocation *in nomine tuo* has no parallel in Arabic coinage.[165] By contrast, it is often encountered in passages

---

164 A list of the Qur'anic parallels to the theonyms and attributes used in Islamic Latin coinage is provided by Walker 1956, c.

165 The invocation *bi-smi-ka allāhumma* "in Thy name, o God" is used as the introductory invocation in the *textus receptus* of the treaty of al-Ḥudaybiya (628). For Muslim traditions pertaining to this treaty, see Wensinck 1927, *s.v.* "Hudaibiya".

from both the Old and New Testament.[166] The legend *domine deo quis tibi similis* is in fact a direct quote from the Psalms.[167]

In other terms, while the phraseology of Early Islamic Latin coinage displays a decisively monotheistic imprint, it avoids explicit Muslim statements. In view of the linguistic and geographical circumstances surrounding the emergence of Arab-Byzantine Latin coinage, biblical vocabulary would have been much more recognizable for local users of the coins. Verbatim quotes from the Latin *Vulgata* further operated within a biblical rather than Qur'anic intertextual milieu.

Though the legends of Arab-Byzantine Latin coins will continue to puzzle the specialists of Early Islamic coinage,[168] the comparison with Arab-style documents provides a broader interpretative framework. The Latin adaptations of Muslim phraseology outline a common pattern and a community of intent with their Greek, Coptic, Middle Persian, and Sogdian counterparts. Early Islamic Arab Muslim authorities utilized the omission of explicitly Muslim-Arab elements from the *shahāda* and *basmala* to create an ambiguous or rather ambivalent trans-cultural non-definitional monotheistic framework.

---

166 E.g., in Ps 43:9; Ps 53:3; Ps 88:17 Ps 115:17 etc. and in Matt 7:22 etc.

167 Ps 44:10 (*Domine, quis similis tibi*?); 70:19 (*Deus, quis similis tibi*?); and 88:9 (*Domine, Deus virtutum, quis similis tibi*?).

168 Cf. Bates 1995, 15 "It is interesting to observe the difficulty that these *provincial* early Muslims had in composing an adequate Latin version of the Muslim *shahāda* as found on the coins of Damascus. (...) Arabs and 'Romans' in Ifriqiya *worked out, on the spot*, a new coinage for the new regime by combining vague knowledge of what was happening in Damascus with pre-existing local practices" (emphasis is my own).

Parallel Scribal Traditions: Independent Arab-Style Scribal Practices

An outline of the fortunes of Arab-style features in non-Arabic scribal traditions would not be complete without discussing a handful of texts apparently far removed from the channels of Arab official promulgations. These either developed seemingly in the absence of official precedents or were issued outside the area of direct Arab political control.

Arab-Style Greek Legal Documents

Early Islamic Greek documents of private, business and legal character generally do not display structural features ascribable to Arabic scribal influences.[169] A unique exception to this rule is a bilingual papyrus in the Nessana dossier pertaining to the assessment of debt of some sort, *P.Ness.* 56 (Nessana; 687).[170] Both the Arabic and Greek versions of the document are completed by two independent lists of witnesses.[171] One of the witnesses in the Arabic version, one Yazīd b. Fā'id, is mentioned in two official letters, *P.HoylandDhimma* 1–2 (ca. 680–690), in which he acts as a minor fiscal official.[172]

As for the formulary, the Greek version of the agreement starts with the invocation *en onomati tou theou* followed by the opening formula *tauta ta* "these are what . . . ". To the best of my knowledge, the opening *tauta ta* is unparalleled in Greek contracts from the preceding as well as later periods. Most likely the Greek opening of *P.Ness.* 56 is modeled on the Arabic endophoric reference *hādhā mā* "this is what . . . ", the typical opening clause of Arabic legal documents – which can be seen also in the Arabic version.[173]

---

169 For legal deeds, see Khan 1994, 193–211 and *id.* 2008, 887–889; for letters, see Luiselli 2008, 692–696 and Reinfandt 2015, esp. 287–289.

170 For a discussion of the content of *P.Ness.* 56, see *supra* p. 83n292.

171 See *infra*n172.

172 On Yazīd b. Fā'id, see Hoyland 2015b, 55.

173 The clause *hādhā mā* followed by a verb in the 3rd person perfect is attested in Egypt for contracts of sale (*hādhā mā ishtarā*) *Chrest.Khoury* I 48 (Egypt; VII) *Chrest.Khoury* II 17 (= *P.Vente* 14) (Fayyūm; VIII) *Chrest.Khoury* II 22 (Fusṭāṭ; VIII), and *P.Vente* 15 (Egypt; 767–776), official receipts (*hādhā mā akhadha*) *P.GrohmannMuhadara* II p. 12 (Ihnās; 643), receipts *P.GrohmannPapyrusprotokoll* 1 (Egypt; VII), leases (*hādhā mā akrā*) *Chrest.Khoury* I 64 (Fayyūm; 796) and *P.KhanLegalPapyrus* (Egypt; 796), divorce agreements (*hādhā mā iṣṭalaḥa*) *Chrest.Khoury* I 19 (Madīnat al-Fayyūm;VIII), and deeds of surety (*hādhā mā ḥamala*) *CPR* XXVI 36 (Egypt; VII) and in the

https://doi.org/10.1515/9783110740820-029

In terms of layout structure, *P.Ness.* 56 further presents us with a curious incongruence. As mentioned in the previous chapter, the Arabic version of the document distinguishes itself by its somewhat crude execution with no visual separation between the invocation and the rest of the text, a comparatively rudimentary *ductus*, and neglect of baselines.[174] By comparison, the Greek version is redacted in a more proficient hand by one archdeacon Georgios s. of Viktor who also features among the witnesses of a contemporary divorce agreement (*P.Ness.* 57). In fact, in the Greek text the invocation-header *is* separated visually from the opening protocol of the document by an *alinea*.[175] Ironically, the layout of the Greek version is in a way more "Arabic" than the actual Arabic text. This underscores further the Greek scribe's familiarity with "Arab" scribal conventions.

In terms of cultural trends, *P.Ness.* 56 confirms the impression of a pronounced influence of Arabic scribal features on the local clerical practices which is already inferred from the official documents of the Nessana dossier.[176]

The Arab Style on the Eastern Frontier

The last evidence for Arab formal influences to be discussed in this section concerns the scribal panorama *outside* the Arab domains. A Bactrian edict in the form of an open letter by one Kēra Tonga[177] "governor of the renowned *qaġan* (. . .), king of the Kadgan people",[178] and "Lord *sēr*"[179] opens with the invocation *pido namo yezidaso* "In the name of God".[180] Other Islamic period documents of legal pertinence in the Bēk family archive open invariably with a protocol sum-

Khurasān for slave emancipations (*hādhā mā aʿtaqa*) *P.Khurasan* 29 (Rōb; 755) and manumission (*hādhā mā kātaba*) *P.Khurasan* 32 (Rōb; 765).

174 See *supra* p. 206.

175 See *supra* p. 185 and 236. Despite the affinities, the Greek and Arabic texts of *P.Ness.* 56 otherwise differ markedly in wording as well as in structural and formal features: each version of the document was redacted by a different scribe; the more detailed Greek one is dated after the Roman calendar, indiction cycle, and the provincial era by day, month, and year; the Arabic version is dated after the Muslim era by year only. Both versions of the agreement further include a set of witnesses; the Arabic version records four witness clauses all bearing Arab names and none of which are autographed; the Greek version, by contrast, shows only one witness clause by one Sergios son of Georgios, who signs in his own hand.

176 See *supra* pp. 80–84.

177 On Kēra Tonga Spara, see Sims-Williams 2010, 78 *s.v.* "κηραυο τογγαυο {τογγαυο} σπαραυο".

178 On the emendations to the original reading of *BD* I Y, see Sims-Williams 2008, 98–99.

179 For the title *sēr*, see Khan 2007, 16–17.

180 For the double administrative hierarchy of Northern Afghanistan during the Early Islamic period, see *supra* pp. 105–106 and references there.

marizing the date, type and place of the transaction, as well as the names of the parties involved.[181] The cultural background of the Bactrian legal documents from this archive underscores essential continuity with pre-Islamic local scribal traditions. In particular, local deities are called upon as guarantee of the document's validity.[182]

The invocation of *BD* I Y is unparalleled in Bactrian materials dated to before the advent of Islam and rather betrays the influence of the Arabic *basmala*.[183] The edict contains a transition element (*misido* "further"), which, however, is rather undistinctive as it is employed in Bactrian legal documents as well as letters both before and after the establishment of an Arab presence in the region.[184] The visual appearance of the document, while peculiar, is also undistinctive. Legal documents in the Bēk family archive are always written in a continuous text block (more precisely in two independent continuous text blocks as the documents are redacted in two copies on the same sheet).[185] The text of letters, on the other hand, is either organized in a single vertical layout-block or – more frequently – distributed on two to four layout blocks turned at 90° to each other.[186] The *mise en page* of *BD* I Y is peculiar within the archive in that an *alinea* separates the prescript from the main text of the edict in correspondence with the transition element (lines 3–4).[187] The layout of the document is reminiscent of the Sogdian official letters in the Mount Mugh archive,[188] and thus seemingly embedded in a Middle Iranian documentary tradition.

Nonetheless, the use of a translated version of the *basmala* in a promulgation by a local ruler who was not subject to Arab authority, nor addressing Arab parties,[189] adds a further political layer to the use of Arabic documentary conventions. This is not an isolated case. On the other side of the Hindu Kush, renditions of the *basmala* appear on the silver coinage minted by the *rutbīl*s of Zābulistān. In particular, a few issues of silver drachms of Spūr *martān shāh* feature the rendering of the *basmala* in Pahlavi characters *PWN ŠM ZY yazdt spwl bg hwtʾp*

181 *BD* I and Sims-Williams 2001.
182 Khan 2007, 17.
183 *I.a.* Sims-Williams 2002b, 236.
184 Sims-Williams 2007, 233 *s.v.* "*misido*".
185 *BD* III pl. 1–101 corresponding to the documents *BD* I A–Y; Sims-Williams 2000, 9–10 and *id.* 2001, 10.
186 See *supra* p. 187.
187 *BD* III pl. 102.
188 See *supra* pp. 186–187.
189 In *BD* I Y the *sēr* vouchsafes Mīr b. Bēk and his properties against liability for the debts of Mīr's estranged brother Bāb; none of the individuals mentioned in the document bears an Arabic name.

whm'n'c mrt'n MLK' "in God's name, Spur, His Majesty, the Lord, Wahmānāz, King of Men".[190]

The appearance of Middle Iranian versions of the Arabic *basmala* on official promulgations of independent rulers is usually interpreted as a sign of cordial relations with the Arabs or even nominal submission to Arab rule.[191] The same argument has been put forward for the use of the Arabic *basmala* in the marginal legends of Arab-Hephthalite[192] drachms issued in the name of Zhulād, in nearby Gōzgān in the late 7th century.[193]

The evidence discussed in this and the previous chapter indicates that the spread of Arab documentary fashions transcended a framework of clear-cut religious and/or political allegiance. Copts and Zoroastrians living under Muslim rule used "Arab" prescripts in their private correspondence. The influence of the Arabic *basmala*, with its vague monotheistic connotation, in particular, induced an increase in monotheistic invocations in 7th- and 8th-century Greek, Coptic, and Middle Persian official and private documents alike.[194] Furthermore, already in the earliest Arabic letters by Christians from 9th- and later century Egypt and 8th-century Palestine, the *basmala* or adapted forms thereof are used.[195] The Early Islamic potentates of Zābulistān and Gōzgān took over and adapted Arab-Sasanian coin designs, just as their predecessors had done with Sasanian coinage for centuries before. In fact, on the silver coinage of Spūr and Zhulād the Sasanian

190 NumH 211–216 (Zābul; after 688). See Humbach 1966, 60 47 (*contra* Göbl 1967, ns. 211–216); Gyselen 2009, esp. 149 and *ead.* 2010, 238; Vondrovec 2014, 549–550. For an overview of Spur's coinage, see Gyselen 2009, 143–156 and Vondrovec 2014, 549–550. Further "Arab" influences on Spur's coinage can be inferred from the minting of copper coins with an all-epigraphic reverse, *ASCC* 86; for the attribution of these coins to Spur, see Gyselen 2008.

191 Sims-Williams 2002b, 236; Gyselen 2008, 126–127 and *ead.* 2009, 238. I disagree with Sims-Williams 2002b, 236 who accepts that the presence of an Arab-style invocation in *BD* I Y indicates "that its writer was, at least nominally, a Muslim"; the evidence discussed in this chapter demonstrates that the use of Arab-style formulae transcended "walled-off" categories of religious affiliation.

192 On the label Arab-Hephthalite, see Walker 1941, LXV–LXIX; Göbl 1967, 186–193, and Album/Goodwin 2002, 40–42. It refers to the (usually) trilingual Arabic, Middle Persian (in Pahlavi script) and Bactrian (in Graeco-Bactrian script) coinage of independent rulers of Gōzgān between the 680s and 690s and to coins struck by Arab governors at Anbīr in 682/683 (ʿAbd Allāh b. Khāzim), 695/696 (Umayya b. ʿAbd Allāh), and 703/704 (Yazīd b. al-Muhallab). For a synoptic overview of Arab-Hephthalite coinage, see Sims-Williams 2008, 115–123.

193 Sims-Williams 2008, 116–123.

194 See *supra Negotiating "Arab Style"*, passim.

195 See *supra* p. 86; for the use of the *basmala* among Christian and Jews in the Medieval period, see Almbladh 2010 and Potthast 2019.

motto *GDH ʾpzwt* "may kingship increase" can be read right next to the *basmala*. Against this background, one may wonder whether the likes of Kēra Tonga, Spūr, and Zhulād did not see the *basmala* as just another fashionable and culturally relevant documentary design. I would merely pose this as a question; I will not attempt to address it here.

Conclusion

The making of an official Arab-style scribal culture represents the point of encounter of the sub- and superstrate cultures and languages, social layers and political resources that defined the Umayyad and Early Abbasid Empire. As long as Hellenized, Persianized, Latinized etcetera local elites retained key posts as intermediate governing bodies in the Islamic imperial pyramid, the languages as well as the social etiquette of the Byzantine and Sasanian society shaped the way Umayyad power was exerted. At its core, the hybrid nature of the documentary material reviewed in this chapter embodies this need to balance cultural "soft power" with negotiation and cooperation.

Overall, the rhetorical strategies underscored by the documents analyzed above can be described as the dissociation of the distinctive Arab formal structure – characterizing both Arabic and Arab-style promulgations – on the one hand, from the Arabic language and a distinctively Muslim content – confined to statements in Arabic – on the other. Through formula structure and secondary visual features, the non-Arabic promulgations of Early Islamic Arab-Muslim officials demarcated a line that was in equal measure social and cultural. At the other end of the bargain, the removal of the cultural barrier put up by the Arabic language and script went hand in hand with the reception of symbols (such as honorifics) of Byzantine and Sasanian imperial power that transcended language.

Furthermore, Greek, Coptic, Sogdian, and Latin official promulgations by Umayyad Arab officials and the respective substratal cultural traditions shared more than a common language; they shared a common non-definitional monotheistic *religious* language. This tendency to de-Islamicize took the double form of omitting explicitly Muslim/Qur'anic statements and incorporating elements of local religiolects and even sacral literature. If this course of action were deemed advantageous or even necessary by the Arab minority in culturally alien environments, it remained nonetheless a one-sided process: an Umayyad Greek, Coptic, or Middle Persian "style" scribal tradition in Arabic was never to be.

If we accept that the Arab authorities' ambivalent cultural stance was driven by the resilience of Late Antique societal and religious values in the conquered societies, what does this imply with regard to the subsequent processes of Islamization[196] and Arabization? The appeal of the culturally hybrid, non-denominational imperial culture nurtured by the Arab-Muslim imperial elite was not lost on local elites. Throughout the Early Islamic Empire, we encounter cases of individuals for whom the fascination with the Umayyad imperial culture preceded the

196 On the concept of Islamization as different from conversion to Islam, see Mikhail 2014, 107.

https://doi.org/10.1515/9783110740820-030

assimilation into the Arabic language and distinctively Islamic values. For individuals like the abovementioned Gabriel and Georgios s. of Viktor it was likely the social ascendancy of an Arab – not necessarily Islamic (nor Arabic) – imperial *Leitkultur* that induced them to adopt Arab-style formulae in their own private writings.

Fittingly, the twilight of an official Arab-style scribal tradition is signaled by the emergence of another phenomenon that functioned as a buffer between different cultures and languages: the emergence of non-Arab clerks with Arabic language expertise. The gradual assimilation of the regional elites into the Arabic language and scribal etiquette or their replacement with multilingual clerks, progressively emptied the ambivalent Arab-style documentary culture of its purpose. For the likes of Petosiris and Mēnas, the assimilation into the Arabic language and documentary standard was a conduit to the income and social advancement that awaited them in the service of the imperial administration.

V An Empire of Words

Tant d'histoire, dit le duc d'Auge au duc d'Auge, tant d'histoire pour quelques calembours, pour quelques anachronismes. Je trouve cela misérable.

R. Queneau, *Les Fleurs Bleues.*

Regional Idiolects in the Use of Administrative Loanwords in Documentary Arabic

A precise assessment of the cultural influxes which intermingled in and imprinted the progressive re-elaboration of the pre-Islamic epigraphic Arabic textual tradition of the 4th to 6th century into the Arab-Muslim imperial culture of the 7th and 8th century has proved an elusive issue in the field of Islamic studies. Much like early Islamic coinage, fine arts and architecture (Chapter II), distinctive features of the Umayyad Imperial Arabic scribal culture show continuities with pre-Islamic traditions. This is particularly evident with regard to the usage of formulae and terminology rooted in first-millennium writings in Aramaic, Hebrew, Nabatean, and Sabaic as well as other Semitic languages – though often blended together in rather eclectic ways (Chapter III). Chancery practices provide glimpses in the relation of the early Islamic scribal tradition with its formative environment but offer little insight into the quality of this relation or, in other terms, on how the peculiarity of the early Islamic imperial rule affected the way elements of late antique scribal cultures were selected, re-shaped, and incorporated into 7th- and 8th-century Arabic imperial documentary culture.

On a general level, the high degree of formal coherence of 7th- and 8th-century Arabic official writings across the different corners of the Muslim world indicates a high degree of centralization in scribal training and practices.[1] However, this is not *per se* indicative of "vertical" power relations between the Islamic imperial core-lands, the *rāshidūns*' Western Arabia, Umayyad Syria, and Abbasid Iraq and the provinces of the empire nor of how these relations mutated diachronically. The opacity of the evidence to this regard is aggravated by its asymmetrical nature, with relative plentifulness of documentary textual sources stemming from peripheral areas of the Muslim world (and especially Egypt) and comparatively few testimonies from the imperial core-land(s) of the Muslim empire.

This chapter investigates formal and terminological features of the early Islamic documentary sources as indicators of hierarchical power-relations. Specifically, the following discussion completes the trajectory of chapter 4 by investigating the contribution of pre-Islamic scribal traditions in shaping the word selection of official Arabic documents. In particular, this section endeavors to

1 Even the use of diacritical dots shows significant affinities between papyrological and epigraphical sources across Egypt, Syria and Khurāsān. On this subject, see Kaplony 2008.

Note: Ch. V is a revised, expanded and fully annotated version of a paper submitted for publication in the Proceedings of the Workshop *Egypt Incorporated* (Leiden; Dec. 12–15, 2016)

https://doi.org/10.1515/9783110740820-031

highlight both "horizontal" and "vertical" cross-cultural influences based on regional idiolectic patterns, or lack thereof, in the use of technical loanwords in early Islamic official administrative documents. On one hand, this approach is aimed at addressing the influence of distinctive regional elements in determining standard Arabic administrative language on a *trans-regional* scale or their failure to do so. On the other, it delves into the role of Islamic administrators from the centers of imperial power in Umayyad Greater Syria[2] and early Abbasid Iraq as agents of standardization and propagation of an Arabic imperial bureaucratic jargon. Concomitantly, the analysis of the regional and transregional patterns in the use of loanwords serves the purpose of problematizing the degree of integration of Egypt's administrators within the broader context of the early Islamic imperial system.

In general terms, a loanword can be defined as a term that is transferred from a language (donor language) to another (receiving language).[3] Loanwords *stricto sensu*, i.e. words which have been assimilated to the receiving language's morphology and phonology[4] (e.g., eng. "clerk" < gr. *klērikos*) further distinguish themselves from unassimilated words that retain the donor language's spelling and pronunciation, thus staying recognizably foreign in the receiving language (e.g., ger. *Palais* < fr. *palais*).[5] The process of lexical borrowing is rarely random. The primary function of loanwords is to fill a recipient language's expressive incapacity. It is a truism that lexical borrowings cluster more often in technical ambits and in newly introduced concepts and technologies than in items of vernacular language. Expressive *manco*s alone, however, are not a sufficient reason for lexical borrowings as languages possess the creative potential to supply new terms for new concepts.[6] Loanwords are instead commonly driven by factors like status and prestige ("social dominance")[7] or even cultural pressure[8] associated with one language.[9] This is most evident in the case of borrowings which superimpose native equivalents by providing an additional semantic nuance or degree of sophistication.[10] Loanwords are thus the most immediate and superficial indicator of linguistic interference.[11] The semantic domains in which lexical borrow-

2 Henceforth referred to as Syria.
3 *I.a.* Haspelmath 2009, 36–38 and Winford 2010, 171.
4 Winford 2010, 173–175.
5 *Handbuch der Linguistik* 1977, 250–251; Thomason/Kaufman 1988, 21.
6 Haspelmath 2009, 46–48.
7 Van Coetsem 2000, 57 and 229–233.
8 Thomason/Kaufman 1988, 77; Winford 2010, 180–181.
9 Winford 2010, 171.
10 Haspelmath 2009, 48–49 and Thomason 2001, 66–77.
11 Thomason 2001, 10–11 and Versteeg 2001, 477–480.

ings cluster further illustrate the nature of the contact between languages as well as the context in which it occurs.[12]

Throughout the 7th and 8th centuries Arabic was at the receiving end of the borrowing process from a number of substratal languages. Besides providing glimpses of the incorporation of previous administrative traditions into the Islamic rule and *vice versa*,[13] the foreign vocabulary of documentary Arabic also hints at more general cultural trends. Regional idiolectic[14] use of administrative loanwords, in particular, illustrates the extent of "horizontal" influences of regional administrative practices on the Arabic culture. Conversely, transregional consistency in the use of "foreign" technical terms sheds light on the quality of "vertical" cultural influences exercised by Umayyad and Abbasid imperial style on the more peripheral regions of the early Islamic Empire.

12 Examining Middle Iranian borrowings in the Qur'an, Cheung 2017, 332 for instance noted that these tend to cluster in luxury and military items, which accords well with the historical information on the contacts between pre-Islamic Arabs and the Sasanians. For some general consideration on the relationship between loanwords and semantic domains, see Tadmor 2009, 64–65.

13 For Arabic terms borrowed or transcribed into early Islamic non-Arabic documents, see in particular Behnstedt 2006 for items in Coptic and the glossary in Kaplony 2015, 13–77 with a linguistic analysis by al-Jallad 2016 for items in Greek. See also Richter 2010, 209–211 on the Qurra dossier.

14 In its technical acceptation, "idiolect" (Bloch 1948, 7, § 1.7) describes the features of grammar, pronunciation, vocabulary, and orthography unique to an individual. Here and in the rest of the chapter the term is used *lato sensu* to describe the terminological features unique to administrative documents produced in the same geographical area.

The Loanwords in Imperial Arabic (640–800)

Since the late 17th century, philologists began to champion the utility of Arabic for understanding the Hebrew text of the Bible.[15] In their eyes, the geographical isolation of the pre-Islamic Arabian Peninsula had preserved the Arabic idiom from outside interferences so that it came to "exceed in purity not only the Chaldean and Syrian, but even the Hebrew language".[16] From its earliest days, Arabic literature contradicts this romantic view. To give an emblematic example, even the totemic name of Muḥammad's own tribe, the Quraysh, is a derivative of *qirsh* "shark", a borrowing from aram. *krsh'* < gr. *karcharias*.[17] Furthermore, linguistic borrowings were a constituent component of Arabic vocabulary since before the rise of Islam. The engraver of the previously mentioned Arabic inscription, commemorating the construction of a church in honour of Saint John in the Syrian town of Ḥarrān at the hands of the Arab phylarch Sharaḥīl b. Ẓālim, resorted to the term *marṭūl*, a loan from Greek *martyrion*, to refer to the erected sanctuary.[18] When, almost 90 years after Sharaḥīl's time, the Muslim armies marched into the Near East the exposure of Arabic to terminological interferences by other languages increased dramatically and a large number of foreign terms flocked into the new language of power.[19] By the early 12th century, the Muslim grammarian al-Jawālīqī († 1144) could list more than 700 terms he considered Arabicized words of foreign origin (*al-mu'arrab*). By this time Arabic had become the idiom of choice of a large proportion of the population of the Islamic commonwealth and a language of long-term communication, culture and science even among non-Muslim segments of society.[20]

On the contrary, up to the 9th century, Arabic had been a *Verkehrssprache* of a tiny minority of mostly native Arabic speakers while the vast majority of the population of the Early Islamic empire experienced Arabic as the high-prestige language of the imperial administration and of public promulgations (Chapter I).

---

15 Barr 1968, 67–70.

16 Schultens 1739, 2. Cf. Fück 1955, 105–107.

17 Jeffery 1938, 237.

18 See *supra* p. 46.

19 For a brief overview, see Versteegh 2010, 635–639.

20 For the emergence of Arabic as a *lingua franca* and the first attestations of Arabic being used by non-Muslims in documentary sources, see *supra* pp. 52–54.

Note: Research for Ch. v was carried out with the help of the *Arabic Papyrology Database* (data extracted on Febr. 27, 2018), the *Thesaurus d'épigraphie Islamique* (data extracted on Febr. 25, 2018) and *papyri.info* (data extracted on Jan. 5, 2018).

https://doi.org/10.1515/9783110740820-032

The pool of loanwords encountered in 7th- and 8th-century documentary sources reflects this intermediate phase in the historical development of Arabic. Overall, the terminological contribution of substratal languages to Arabic appears to have been limited at this stage.[21] To be sure, loanwords are already attested in multiple semantic categories. These includes *inter alia* toponyms[22] (e.g., *Miṣr*[23] < sab. *mṣr*[24] in *P.DiemFruehеUrkunden* 1 r, 4), individual names (e.g., *al-Iṣbahbadh* < MP *spāhbed* in *P.Khurasan* 5, 3), commodities (e.g., *māʾida* < et. *māʾĕdd* < gr. *magis* in *P.GrohmannWirtsch.* 17, 4), professions (e.g., *bayṭār* < gr. *ippiatros* in *P.L.Bat.* XXXIII 65, 17), flora[25] (e.g., *qurṭ* < gr. *chortos* in *P.Cair.Arab.* 231, 4) and fauna (e.g., *birdhaun* < gr. *bourdon* in *P.MuslimState* 7, 7 and 10), structures (e.g., *iṣṭabl* < gr. *stablon* in *P.L.Bat.* XXXIII 65, 4) etc. Loanwords covering the aforementioned areas, however, occur only sporadically in early Islamic Arabic documents. In particular, more private 7th- and 8th-century Arabic testimonies (mostly graffiti and private letters on papyrus) rarely employ loanwords at all.[26]

Consistent, systematic use of loanwords is attested, conversely, only in documents pertaining to the sphere of imperial administration and finances. Unsurprisingly, most borrowings are semantically restricted to "technical" terminology.[27] Providing a comprehensive survey of the loan-vocabulary in Early Islamic documentary Arabic is beyond the scope and limits of this study.[28] This chapter

21 My first cursory scrutiny of the surveyed corpus yielded a poll of about 130 loanwords. Of these, fewer than half are discussed in this chapter.

22 For the list of the main Arabic Egyptian toponyms with their equivalent in Greek and Coptic, see Legendre 2013, 286.

23 Not to be confused with the homologous *miṣr*, which denotes the garrison-cities established by the Arabs in the provinces conquered by them. The latter term, however, never occurs in this acceptation in 7th- and 8th-century Arabic documents.

24 *Miṣr* cognates are attested in several Semitic languages. See Bosworth 1993 *s.v.* "*Miṣr*" (B.) Only in Ge'ez and in South Arabian languages does the term occur without a final ending indicating a transmission through South Arabia. See Jeffery 1938, 266.

25 For the discussion of several Arabic plant-name etymologies, see Löw 1881.

26 My preliminary survey of loanwords in early Islamic Arabic graffiti has yielded only a handful of loanwords, mostly circumscribed to Qur'anic quotations; see e.g *ṣirāṭ* (< gr. *strata*/lat. *strata* through Aramaic) in *CIAP* III p. 179 l. 2 (cf. Q 48:2). Forthe etymology of *ṣirāṭ*, see in particular Jeffery 1938, 196 and *ibid.*nn1–3.

27 Cf. Richter 2010, 209 with particular regard to Arabic letters in the Basileios' archive.

28 Scholarly information on foreign vocabulary in the Arabic language is scattered across encyclopaedia and lexicon entries, journal articles, and collected volume contributions, a few of which (e.g., Grohmann 1932) are concerned with documentary materials. More comprehensive are Fraenkel's (1886) seminal work on Aramaic loanwords and Asbaghi's (1988) and Siddiqi's (1919) studies on Persian loanwords. Further studies on single oeuvres (or collections of oeuvres) which merit notice include Fraenkel's on the Qur'an and pre-Islamic poetry (1880), Jeffery's on the Qur'an (1938) further refined by Zammit (2002) and Hebbo's on Ibn Isḥāq's († 767) *Sīra*.

focuses on the particular semantic domain of administrative *termini technici*, i.e., elements of administrative vocabulary that cannot be stringently translated without a loss of meaning.

Suspect of being loanwords are principally those terms lacking an Arabic verbal root, having a corresponding Arabic verbal root but not being used in the original sense of the root (e.g., *kharāj*), having more than 3 radicals (e.g., *qanqal*), or exhibiting unusual morphological types (e.g., the *fāʿal* form), and different possible vocalizations (e.g., *khātam* vs. *khātim*).[29] In what follows, technical loanwords encountered in early Islamic Arabic documents are divided by geographical area of their (attested) use in 7th- and 8th-century documentary sources, by ambit of pertinence, and listed in alphabetical order. Loanwords occurring in 7th- and 8th-century *non*-Arabic documents have only been discussed in the case of transcriptions of Arabic terms (e.g., gr. *masgida* = arab. *masjid* < aram. *masgḏā*).

Loanwords only Attested in Documents from Egypt (640/641–800)

a) Fiscal Administration

balad, "town", "country"[30] < gr. *palation*/lat. *palatium* (literally "palace").[31] Possibly to be understood as an administrative unit.[32] Except for one instance of fiscal pertinence,[33] however, the term occurs in the examined documents in the general sense of "land". This lemma appears multiple times in the Qur'an[34] suggesting a pre-Islamic loan.

A comprehensive lexicon of Greek loanwords in Arabic is currently under preparation by Nikolai Serikoff.

29 For a more detailed discussion on the topic of loanwords' morphology in Arabic, see Fraenkel 1886, XI–XVII; Siddiqi 1919, 17–74; Spitaler 1955, 211–213 and Schall 1982, 143–150. For more general considerations on recognizing loanwords, see Haspelmath 2009, 43–45.

30 Cf. It. "paese."

31 Nöldeke in Fraenkel 1886, 28; Vollers 1887–1897, 312; Jeffery 1938, 82–83; Schall 1982, 147; and Hebbo 1984, 50.

32 Sijpesteijn 2013, 144–145.

33 *P.MuslimState* 36 (Fayyūm; 730–743), 6; the document is a note on the collection of a tax instalment addressed to the pagarch Nājid b. Muslim.

34 E.g., in Q 2:126, 7:57, 7:58, 14:35, 16:7 etc. cf. also *balda* "region, land" in Q 25:49, 27: 91 etc.

In Arabic papyri from the 8th century:

CPR XVI 7 (Egypt; VII/VIII), 6; *P.HindsNubia* (Qaṣr Ibrīm; 758), 12, 16 and 28; *P.MuslimState* 36 (Fayyūm; 730–743), 6.

nā'iba, an extraordinary tax for the maintenance of canals and dams < gr. *naubion* < dem. *nb*.[35]

In Arabic papyri from the 8th century:

CPR XXI 1 (= *Chrest.Khoury* I 72 = *P.Loth* 1) (Madīnat al-Fayyūm; 785), 4 and 8.

ṣadaqa, literally "alms", by extension "alms-tax"[36] < aram.[37] *ṣəḏaqtā* "sincerity, alms".[38]

In Arabic papyri from the 8th century:

P.MuslimState 8 (Fayyūm; 730–743), 9, 21, 30 and 31; *P.Cair.Arab.* 197, 5 (Egypt; 765–766); *P.Christ.Musl.* 7 (Fayyūm; 743–744), 3; *P.Christ.Musl.* 11 (Fayyūm; 743–749), 5; P.Heid. inv. Arab. 28.[39]

sijill, "register" or simply "document" < gr. *sigillon*/lat. *sigillum*.[40] The term *sigillion* is attested in Greek and Coptic documents from the Islamic period as a denomination for a "safe-conduct".[41] The use of *sijill* in the same meaning and context is to date attested in Arabic only through literary evidence though it has been identified in two unedited 8th-century Arabic papyri.[42] The only Qur'anic passage (Q 21: 104) in which the term occurs may suggest that the term originally denoted a book-scroll in Arabic.[43]

---

35 Frantz-Murphy 2001, 155–156.
36 For an extensive discussion of *ṣadaqa* in the early Islamic fiscal context, see Sijpesteijn 2013, 181–199.
37 Those terms are classified as "aram." (= Aramaic) that are attested across multiple Aramaic dialects and pre-eminently in the historical stage labelled by Creason (2004, 391–393) as "Late Aramaic" (200–700) and as "Middle Aramaic" by Beyer (1986, 43).
38 Fraenkel 1880, 20; Jeffery 1938, 194 and Sijpesteijn 2013, 184 and *ibid*.n376, cf. Sokoloff 1992, 952; *id*. 2002, 458 and *id*. 2009, 348.
39 Sijpesteijn 2013, 189 and *ibid*.n397; for other documents possibly related to *ṣadaqa*, see *ibid*. 188–189.
40 Fraenkel 1886, 251–252; Nöldeke 1910, 27–28; Jeffery 1938, 163–164. Cf. Daris 1971, 104. The etymology is controversial, however; see Carter 2006, 137–138. *Sijill* occurs in the sense of "register" for example in *P.Khalili* I 2, 6, 7, 12, 13, and 15 (Dalāṣ; VIII).
41 Rāġib 1997, 146 and Sijpesteijn 2013, 311–312.
42 MS. Copt. b 7 (1) and MS. Copt. b e 35 (2)/Bodleian Library. Sijpesteijn 2012a, 708–709. Cf. also Vanthieghem's remarks 2014a, 267–268n7.
43 De Blois 1997, *s.v.* "*Sidjill*".

ṭabl, "(tax) instalment" < gr. *tablon*/lat. *tabula*.[44] Regarding the exact meaning of the word there has been some disagreement among scholars about whether it describes a tax-instalment, a register, or both.[45]

In Arabic papyri from the 8th century:

> *CPR* XXI 3 (= *P.Cair.Arab.* 77) (Egypt; 794), 5; *CPR* XXI 4b (= *Chrest.Khoury* II 26 = *P.GrohmannBeziehung* p. 339) (Madīnat al-Fayyūm; 796), 8; *P.Berl.Arab.* II 24 (Egypt; VIII), 13; *P.Cair.Arab.* 169 (al-Ushmūnayn; 752), 5; *P.Clackson* 45 (Bāwiṭ; 753), 7; *P.DiemFrüheUrkunden* 3 (Fayyūm; 779), 4; *P.GrohmannProbleme* 5 (Ihnās; VIII), 2 (x2) and 4; *P.MuslimState* 2, 9; *P.MuslimState* 3, 7; *P.MuslimState* 13, 10; *P.MuslimState* 20, 16; *P.MuslimState* 23, 14; *P.MuslimState* 36, 6 (all from the Fayyūm; 730–743); *P.World* p. 162 (Egypt; VIII), 13.

ūsiya, a land enjoying privileged fiscal conditions[46] < gr. *ousia*.[47] The term is encountered quite often but only in papyri from 9th- and later centuries Egypt as a definition for an "estate" or "domain".[48] Grohmann, noted an occurrence in an unpublished 8th-century papyrus housed in Berlin possibly referring to a caliphal estate.[49]

zakāt < aram. *zāḵūṯā*[50] "merit". Used interchangeably with *ṣadaqa* in a single document.[51] The somewhat enigmatic ending in *āt* has been interpreted by Brockelmann as formed to rhyme with *ṣalāt*.[52] Alternatively, one could think of a transmission through the Sabaic form *zkt* "grace", "favour".[53]

In Arabic papyri from the 8th century:

> *P.MuslimState* 8 (Fayyūm; 730–743), 11, 12, 16, and 18.

---

44 Grohmann 1932, 277. Cf. Daris 1971, 111.

45 A useful synoptic overview of the different positions and debates is given by Sijpesteijn 2013, 281–283.

46 Kremer (von) 1883, 12 [190].

47 Grohmann 1932, 281.

48 Legendre 2018, 411–412.

49 P.Berl.inv.Arab. 15014⅔, reported from Grohmann 1932, 281–282. Cf. *CPR* VIII 82 (= *SB* VI 9460) (Fayyūm; 699/700), 5, mentioning "estates of the caliph" (*ousias tou prōtosymboulou*). For caliphal estates in Egypt, see now Legendre 2018, 404.

50 Fraenkel 1880, 23; Jeffery 1938, 153; Sijpesteijn 2013, 184 and *ibid*.n376 cf. Sokoloff 1992, 176 and *id.* 2002, 412–413. For the Qur'anic Arabic spelling *zkwẗ* for <zakāt>, see Spitaler 1960 and cf. al-Jallad 2017b.

51 Sijpesteijn 2013, 181–199.

52 Brockelmann 1927, 14.

53 Beeston 1994, 42 [25].

b) Institutions and Officials

biyāq, "deacon" < copt. *piakou*, the Fayyumic for m of *p*^{e}-*diakonos* < gr. *diakonos*.[54]

In Arabic papyri from the 8th century:

CPR XXVI 37 (Egypt; VIII/IX), 8; *P.DiemAmtlicheSchreiben* 1 (Ihnās; 729–743), 5.[55]

dīwān, "official register", "office" < syr. *dīwān* "book" "treasury", "chancery" < MP *dēwān* "archive", "collected writings".[56] In Muslim literary sources, ʿUmar I (*rg.* 634–644) is generally credited with the establishment of the first *dīwān*, an office charged with the regularized redistribution of the wealth accumulated during the first Islamic conquests among the Muslim troops.[57] Seventh and 8th-century papyrological sources have yielded information compatible with this institution.[58] The term *dīwān* itself, however, is first attested in the early Abbasid period.

In Arabic papyri from the 8th century:

P.Berl.Arab. I 2 (Fayyūm; 761), 4.

duks, "duke"[59] < gr. *doux*/lat. *dux*.[60] Although literarily documented, is not attested in any Arabic document published to date. A few years ago, however, Sijpesteijn observed the occurrence of the term in an unpublished official Arabic papyrus from the 8th century housed in the Bodleian Library.[61]

furāniq, "courier" < JBA *parwanqā* < MP *parwānag* "guide".[62]

In Arabic papyri from the 8th century:

P.DiemRemarkableDocuments 2 r, (al-Ushmūnayn; 751), 5; *P.RagibLettresdeService* 2 (= *P.MargolioutℎSelectPapyri* 2 = *P.Ryl.Arab.* I IV 2) (al-Ushmūnayn; 751), 5; *P.RagibLettresde-*

---

54 Berkes/Vanthieghem 2020, 157 with further references.
55 For this reading and the dating of the document, see *ibid.*, 154–157.
56 Asbaghi 1988, 130; Ciancaglini 2008, 151 and Sokoloff 2009, 294.
57 Duri 1965, *s.v.* "*dīwān*" (i.) and Kennedy 2001, 60–73.
58 For the *dīwān* and documents related to this institution, see Sijpesteijn 2011, 252–265.
59 For the office of the "duke" in Early Islamic Egypt, see Grohmann 1964, 123–124, Sijpesteijn 2013, 86–87, and Legendre 2016.
60 Cf. Grohmann 1932, 279–280.
61 MS. Copt. d. 23, reported from Sijpesteijn 2012, 710 and *ead.* 2013, 119 and *ibid.*n15.
62 Hebbo 1984, 273–274; Asbaghi 1988, 206; Siddiqi 1919, 71; Silverstein 2007, 20; Cf. Sokoloff 2002, 929 and Ciancaglini 2008, 237–238.

Service 3 (= *P.Ryl.Arab.* I IV 1) (al-Ushmūnayn; 751), 5; *P.RagibLettresdeService* 4 (= *P.MargoliouthSelectPapyri* 3 = *P.Ryl.Arab.* I IV 4) (al-Ushmūnayn; 752), 6; *P.Ryl.Arab.* II 6 (= *P.MargoliouthSelectPapyri* 1 = *P.Ryl.Arab.* I IV 3 = *P.RagibLettresdeService* 1) (al-Ushmūnayn; 745), 5.

qahramān, "superintendent", "majordomo"[63] < JBA *qāharmānā* < MP *kārframān*.[64]

In Arabic papyri from the 8th century:

P.YounesGovernors 3 (Egypt; 769–773), 8.

qusṭāl (also ***jusṭāl***) an official involved in the collection and quittance of taxes < gr. *augoustalis*/ lat. *augustalis*.[65] Two other etymologies from Greek have also been hypothesized, from gr. *kouaistor* /lat. *quaestor*[66] and gr. *zygotatēs*[67] "mint ward" (possibly mediated through syr. *sagāsṭrā*)[68] respectively.

In Arabic papyri from the 8th century:

P.Cair.Arab. 149 (= *P.BeckerNPAF* 3) (Ishqawh; 709–714), 27 (*jusṭāl*); *P.GrohmannQorraBrief*, (Fayyūm; 709), 6 (*qusṭāl*).[69]

simmāk, an official assisting and supervising the tax collection[70] < gr. *symmachos* "helper".

In Arabic papyri from the 8th century:

P.MuslimState 14, 5; *P.MuslimState* 15, 5, 11 and 13; *P.MuslimState* 24r, 2, 6 and v, 1 (all from the Fayyūm; 730–743); *P.YounesGovernors* 2, 5 (Fayyūm; 798).

---

63 For *qahramān* as a title, see *infra* in this chapter.

64 Henning 1958, 49n2 and Sokoloff 2002, 989 *contra* Asbaghi 1988, 222 who derives the term from pers. *kuhramān*.

65 Kaplony in Richter 2010, 209. Cf. Daris 1971, 31–32. For this office, see Preisigke 1925–1931, III, 204.

66 Fraenkel 1886, 187 who postulates a transmission through the Aramaic; Karabacek 1886, 6–7 and Grohmann 1932, 276–277.

67 Becker 1911, 255 and Frantz-Murphy 2001, 121.

68 Kameya 2017, 142–146.

69 The attestation of *qusṭāl* in *P.World* p. 130 (Ishqawh; 709–710), 3 has been emended by W. Diem. Cf. *P.DiemAfrodito* p. 261, 2.

70 For this office, see Grohmann 1964, 123 and Sijpesteijn 2013, 130–132 and *ibid*.n89. Cf. Preisigke 1925–1931, III, 166.

tarjumān, "interpreter" < aram. *targmānā*. In Arabic papyri from the 8th century:

P.JoySorrow 43 (Egypt; VIII), 2.

In Coptic papyri from the 8th century:

P.Ryl.Copt. 214 (Hermopolite; VIII), 8.

c) Infrastructure[71]

hury, "granary" < gr. *horrion* (also *horeion/hōreion*) /lat. *horreum*.[72]

In Arabic papyri from the 8th century:

Chrest.Khoury I 91 (Ishqawh; 710), 8, 34, 77, and 79; *P.BeckerPAF* 10 (= *P.Heid.Arab.* I 9) (Ishqawh; 709), 2 and 4; *P.Christ.Musl.* 1 (= *P.Cair.Arab.* 286 = *P.BeckerPAF* 16 = *SPP* VIII 1345) (Ishqawh; 706), 3; *P.Heid.Arab.* I 13 (Ishqawh; 709–714), 4; *P.MuslimState* 23 (Fayyūm; 730–743), 20.

sijn, "prison" < gr. *signon* /lat. *signum* "insignia".[73] Originally denoting the emblem of the Roman legions, the term *signa* came to indicate the inner segment of a military camp (where a legion's *signa* were kept). In Late Antique usage, the part of the camp labelled *signa* was often used as an improvised prison, which explains the transfer of meaning.[74]

In Arabic papyri from the 8th century:

P.MuslimState 19 (Fayyūm; 730–743), 7; *P.Khalili* I 14 (Egypt; VIII), 11.

---

71 Various loanwords denominating edifices (e.g., *iṣṭabl* < gr. stablon and *sūq* < aram. *sūqā* in *P.L.Bat.* XXXIII 65 (Fusṭāṭ; VIII), 4 and 7 architectonic elements (e.g., *bāb* < aram. *bābā* in *P.BeckerPAF* 10 (= *P.Heid.Arab.* I 9) (Ishqawh; 709), 3 and *qanṭara* < lat. *cantherius* (?) in *RCEA* I 8* (Fusṭāṭ; 688), 1 and even larger conglomerates (e.g., *madīna* < aram. *madīnṯā* in is *P.StoetzerSteuerquittung* (al-Ushmūnayn; 709) are encountered in early Islamic Arabic documents. Here I have discussed only terms that feature prominently in official administrative documents.

72 Fraenkel 1886, 136 and Grohmann 1932, 277. Cf. Daris 1971, 80.

73 Hebbo 1984, 181–182; Cf. Bevan 1922; 71. Surprisingly, the term is not included in Jeffery's (1938) list despite its occurrance in Sura 12.

74 For the semantic transformation of the term *signa*, see Niehoff-Panagiotidis 1996.

d) Coinage

ṭābiʿ, "seal" < aram. *ṭaḇʿā* "stamp".[75] Rather than being the *fāʿil* form of the denominative verb *ṭ-b-ʿ* to "impress", "to stamp" – often used for the minting of seals and weights,[76] it stems directly from Palestinian Aramaic *ṭāḇʿā* "stamp".[77] In Arabic papyri from the 8th century:

P.MuslimState 8 (Fayyūm; 730–743), 19.

e) Metrology

kayl[78] ***al-dīmūs***, a measure of unclear value < gr. *metron dēmosion*.[79]

In Arabic papyri from the 8th century:

Chrest.Khoury I 91 (Ishqawh; 710), 42; *P.BeckerPAF* 10 (= *P.Heid.Arab.* I 9) (Ishqawh; 709), 6.

faddān, a square measure for lots of land < aram. *paddānā*.[80]

In Arabic papyri from the 8th century:

Chrest.Khoury I 66 (= *P.GrohmannBeziehung* p. 338) (Fayyūm; 795), 1, 8, and 9; *CPR* XVI 9 (Egypt; VIII), 8 and 10; *CPR* XXI 2a (= *P.Cair.Arab.* II p. 70 = *P.GrohmannApercu* p. 85 = *P.GrohmannProbleme* III p. 143) (Fayyūm; 792), 1 and 3; *CPR* XXI 3 (= *P.Cair.Arab.* 77) (Egypt; 794), 11; *CPR* XXI 4b (= *Chrest.Khoury* II 26 = *P.GrohmannBeziehung* p. 339) (Madīnat al-Fayyūm; 796), 6 and 11; *CPR* XXI 5 (= *P.Ryl.Arab.* II 4 = *P.Ryl.Arab.* I IX 6 = *P.MargoliouthSelectPapyri* p. 413–414) (al-Ushmūnayn; 798/799), 5 and 13; *P.BruningDevelopments* (= *P.Khalili* II 5) (Fusṭāṭ; 753), v (e) 4 and (j) 10; *P.DiemFrueheUrkunden* 4 (Fayyūm; 793), 7; *P.Khalili* I 2 (Dalāṣ; late VIII), 5, 6, 7, 8, 11, 12, and 13; *P.MuslimState* 23 (Fayyūm; 730–743), 34; *P.Philad. Arab.* 7 (Egypt; 794), 4; *P.SijpesteijnTravel* (Fayyūm; 734), 13.

---

75 Fraenkel 1886, 192–194. Cf. Sokoloff 1992, 220 and *id.* 2009, 144.
76 Amitai-Preiss 2012, 281–282.
77 Fraenkel 1886, 192–194. Cf. Sokoloff 1992, 220 and *id.* 2009, 144.
78 See *infra s.v.* "*kayl*".
79 Becker 1906, 31; Grohmann 1932, 276; Kreuzsaler 2007, XXXII.
80 Fraenkel 1886, 129; Sokoloff 2002, 888 and *id.* 2009, 1157. For the value of the measure, see Grohmann 1954, 178–180 and Hinz 1970, 65. For the value of Islamic measures and their fluctuations over the centuries, see also the dedicated section of the *Measuring Medieval Islamic Economy* database http://www.medievalislamiceconomy.uwo.ca/measures/index.html (accessed Febr. 2, 2021).

kharrūba, literally "kernel of the carob tree's fruit (carob being itself a derivative of arab. *kharrūb*)", a small weight unit (ca. 0,196 g)[81] often used for coins < aram. *krwb'*.[82]

In Arabic standard-weights from the 8th century:

BM 4 (734–742); *BM* 5 (737); *BM* 7 (734–742); *BM* 11 (751–753 or 755–758); *BM* 12 (759–760); *CAM* 25; *CAM* 29; *CAM* 30; *CAM* 31 (all 725–734); *CAM* 49–50 (734–742); *CAM* 51 (737); *CAM* 52 (734–742); *CAM* 90 (749–750); *CAM* 100; *CAM* 101 (both 751–753 or 755–758); *CAM* 145–146; *CAM* 151–152 (all 762–774); *CAM* 155–159; *CAM* 160 (769–774); *CAM2 BM* 7; *CAM2 BM* 8 (both 725–734); *CAM2 BM* 11–12 (737); *CAM2 BM* 27 (751–753 or 755–758); *CAM2 BM* 42–43 (769–774); *CAM2 PRC* 9 (725–734); *CAM2 PRC* 24 (762–774); *EAG* I 15–16 (725–734); *EAG* I 30 (737); *EAG* I 31 (734–742); *EAG* I 45–46 (734–745); *EAG* I 49 (749–750); *EAG* I 64; *EAG* I 65–66 (all 751–753 or 755–758); *EAG* I 71; *EAG* I 73; *EAG* I 74 (all 759–760); *EAG* II 8 (734–742); *EIGS* 33–35; *EIGS* 37–39; *EIGS* 40; *EIGS* 41; *EIGS* 43 (all 725–734); *EIGS* 73; *EIGS* 77 (both 734–742); *EIGS* 78–81 (737); *EIGS* 82 (738/739); *EIGS* 83–84 (739/740); *EIGS* 117 (721–726); *EIGS* 148; *EIGS* 149 (749–750); *EIGS* 174; *EIGS* 175–176; *EIGS* 177; *EIGS* 178–180 (all 751–753 or 755–758); *EIGS* 217; *EIGS* 218; *EIGS* 223 (all 759–760); *EIGS* 248 (762–769); *EIGS* 273; *EIGS* 274–277 (all 769–774); *EIGS* 314 (779–780); *EIGS* 333 (781–784 or 792); *EPV* 45–47; *EPV* 50; *EPV* 52–53; *EPV* 54–56; (all 725–734); *EPV* 92–93; *EPV* 95; *EPV* 96–98; *EPV* 99–101 (all 734–742); *EPV* 137–140 (749–750); *EPV* 169–172; *EPV* 173; *EPV* 174–175 (all 751–753 or 751–758); *EPV* 180; *EPV* 181; *EPV* 184 (all 759–760); *EPV* 222–224 (778/779); *EPV* 230; *EPV* 231–232 (both 782–784); *EPV* 240; *EPV* 241; *EPV* 242 (all 793–794); *GSW* 100; *GSW* 101; *GSW* 102 (all 735–734); *GSW* 94 (> 750); *GSW* 112; *GSW* 115; *GSW* 116 (all 734–742); *GSW* 140 (749–150); *GSW* 144 (751–753 or 755–758); *GSW* 188; *GSW* 193 (both 762–774); *GSW* 195 (779–780); *GWVS* 4 (725–734); *GWVS* 15 (734–742); *GWVS* 20 (751–753 or 755–758); *GWVS* 33 (759–760); *UAT* 76; *UAT* 77; *UAT* 79–80; *UAT* 81–82; *UAT* 86 (all 725–734); *UAT* 152–155; *UAT* 156–157 (all 734–742); *UAT* 260; *UAT* 261; *UAT* 262–264 (all 749–750); *UAT* 282–284 (>750); *UAT* 296–297 (750–751 or 753–755); *UAT* 317–318; *UAT* 319–321; *UAT* 322–325 (all 751–753 or 755–758); *UAT* 347 (781–786); *UAT* 383 (758–759); *UAT* 387; *UAT* 388 (both 759–760); *UAT* 460–462 (762–774); *UAT* 496; *UAT* 497 (both 769–774); *UAT* 533–534 (773–775); *UAT* 598; *UAT* 599 (both 787–806).

irdabb, a dry measure for grains corresponding to ca. 38,8 l. in Early Islamic Egypt[83] < gr. *artabē*.[84] The Greek *artabē* has been identified since Herodotus' time as an originally Persian measure, the use of which in Egypt is documented in the papyri since the Ptolemaic period.[85]

---

81 For the value of a *kharrūbā*, see Miles/Matson 1948, 9; Grohmann 1954, 147; and Hinz 1970, 14.

82 Löw 1881, 176, no. 132 and Fraenkel 1886, 141.

83 Bagnall 2009, 186–187; Morelli 2019, 14; cf. Rathbone 1983, 270–272. For the value of the *irdabb* in Islamic times, see Hinz 1970, 39–40.

84 Grohmann 1954, 156 and Ashtor 1991, *s.v.* "*Makāyil*" (A. 1.).

85 Schmidt 1971, 100–102. Alternatively, an Egyptian origin of the term has also been hypothesized; Cf. Vollers 1887–1897, 653 and Ciancaglini 2008, 116 and references there.

In Arabic papyri from the 7th and 8th centuries:

Chrest.Khoury I 66 (= *P.GrohmannBeziehung* p. 338) (Fayyūm; 795), 1 (x2); *Chrest.Khoury* I 91 (Ishqawh; 710), 12, 28, and 29; *Chrest.Khoury* I 98 (= *P.Jahn* 12)(Fayyūm; late VIII), r 17; *CPR* XXVI 17 (= *P.ThungWrittenObligations* 2) (Madīnat al-Fayyūm; 795), 4 (x2); *P.BeckerPAF* 10 (= *P.Heid.Arab.* I 9 (left)(Ishqawh; 709), 4 and 6; *P.BruningDevelopments* (= *P.Khalili* II 5), v 4 and 9; *P.Cair.Arab.* 160 (= *P.BeckerNPAF* 13) (Ishqawh; 709/710), 7 (*P.BeckerNPAF* 13, 6); *P.Christ.Musl.* 1 (= *P.Cair.Arab.* 286 = *P.BeckerPAF* 16 = *SPP* VIII 1345) (Ishqawh; 709), 2, 3, and 15; *P.Cair.Arab.* 371; *P.David-WeillLouvre* 12–13 (Madīnat al-Fāris; VIII), 6 and 14; *P.DelattreEntagion* (Anṣinā; 694), 9; *P.DiemFruehеUrkunden* 1 (Fayyūm; 698), 6 and 7; *P.Heid.Arab.* I 5, 6 (x2); *P.Heid.Arab.* I a (= *SB* I 5644), 7 (x2); *P.Heid.Arab.* I c (= *SB* I 5646), 7; *P.Heid.Arab.* I e (= *SB* I 5648), 3 (x2); *P.Heid.Arab.* I g, 6; *P.Heid.Arab.* I k (= *SB* I 5653), 3 (x2); *P.Heid.Arab.* I l (= *SB* I 5654), 7 (x2) (all from Ishqawh; 709/710); *P.MuslimState* 23 (Fayyūm; 730–743), 13, 17, 19, 33(x2), 34, 37, 38, and 39; *P.YounesGovernors* 1 (= *P.World* p. 171 = *P.Ryl.Arab.* I I 5) (Fusṭāṭ; 797), 10 (*P.World* p. 171 and *P.Ryl.Arab.* I I 5, 8).

kayl, "measure" < aram. *kaylā*.[86]

In Arabic papyri from the 8th century:

Chrest.Khoury I 91 (= *P.Heid.Arab.* I 3) (Ishqawh 710), 9, 38, 50, and 59; *P.BeckerPAF* 10 (= *P.Heid.Arab.* I 9) (Ishqawh 709), 6.

In Arabic standard weights from the 8th century:[87]

EAG I 53; *EAG* I 54; *EAG* I 55; *EAG* I 57; *EAG* I 60 (all 754–775); *EAG* I 61 (750–751 and 753–755); *EIGS* 192; *EIGS* 199; *EIGS* 200–204 (all 754–775); *EPV* 151–154; *EPV* 155–157 (both 754–775); *EPV* 167–168 (751–753 or 751–758); *GWS* 150 (750–751 or 751–753); *GWS* 151 (754–775); *UAT* 293–294 (753–755); *UAT* 349; *UAT* 350–351; *UAT* 352; *UAT* 354; *UAT* 365; *UAT* 366–370 (all 754–775).

mithqāl, a unit of weight corresponding to a gold *dīnār* = 4,25 g[88] < aram. *maṯqālā*.[89] The term also occurs in the Qur'an.[90]

In Arabic papyri from the 8th century:

CPR XXI 3 (= *P.Cair.Arab.* 77) (Egypt; 794), 4.

---

86 Fraenkel 1886, 204 and Jeffery 1938, 252.
87 On weights, *kayl* only occurs as a part of a quotation from Q 25:181. Much more frequent on weights and stamps are, however, the attestations of its derivatives *mikyāl* and *mikyala*.
88 Grohmann 1954, 140–143 and Hinz 1970, 1–2.
89 Fraenkel 1886, 202; Jeffery 1938, 258.
90 Q 4:40, 10:61, 21:47, 31:16, 34:3 and 22 and 99:7 and 8.

In Arabic standard weights from the 8th century:

BM 1 (717–720 or 721–722); *BM* 3; *BM* 3g (both 725–734); *BM* 4 (734–742); *BM* 5 (737); *BM* 6 (743–749); *BM* 7; *BM* 9 (both 734–742); *BM* 10; *BM* 11 (both 751–753 or 755–758); *BM* 12; *BM* 13 (both 759–760); *BM* 14–15; *BM* 16–17 (all 762–769); *BM* 19 (769–774); *BM* 20; *BM* 21; *BM* 22 (all 775–777); *BM* 23 (775–785); *BM* 24; *BM* 24g (both late VII); *BM* 25g (781–784 or 792); *BM* 26 (785–786); *BM* 27 (784–785 or 805–806); *BM* 57 (754–775); *EAG* I 10 (717–720 or 721–722); *EAG* I 12; *EAG* I 13; *EAG* I 14; *EAG* I 15–16 (all 725–734); *EAG* I 27 (734–742); *EAG* I 28 (737); *EAG* I 29 (734–742); *EAG* I 30 (737); *EAG* I 31 (734–742); *EAG* I 39; *EAG* I 40 (both 743–749); *EAG* I 43; *EAG* I 44 (both 734–745); *EAG* I 49 (749–750); *EAG* I 59; *EAG* I 60 (both 754–775); *EAG* I 62–63; *EAG* I 64; *EAG* I 65–66 (all 751–753 or 755–758); *EAG* I 68 (751–758 or 781–786); *EAG* I 69 (758–759); *EAG* I 70; *EAG* I 71; *EAG* I 73; *EAG* I 74 (all 759–760); *EAG* I 76; *EAG* I 79; *EAG* I 80 (all 762–769); *EAG* I 85; *EAG* I 86; *EAG* I 87; *EAG* I 88; *EAG* I 89; *EAG* I 90; *EAG* I 92–93 (all 775–785); *EAG* I 95–96 (775–778); *EAG* II 3 (725–734); *EAG* II 8 (734–742); *EAG* II 18 (749–769); *EAG* II 26 (775–785); *EIGS* 31; *EIGS* 33–35; *EIGS* 36; *EIGS* 37–39; *EIGS* 40; *EIGS* 41; *EIGS* 42; *EIGS* 43 (all 725–734); *EIGS* 66; *EIGS* 67; *EIGS* 68 (all 734–742); *EIGS* 69–70 (737); *EIGS* 71 (734–742); *EIGS* 72 (737); *EIGS* 73; *EIGS* 74–76; *EIGS* 77 (all 734–742); *EIGS* 78–81 (737); *EIGS* 82 (738/739); *EIGS* 83–84 (739/740); *EIGS* 112–113; *EIGS* 114–116 (all 721–726); *EIGS* 129; *EIGS* 130 (both 742–745); *EIGS* 136; *EIGS* 137; *EIGS* 138–139; *EIGS* 140 (all 743–749); *EIGS* 148; *EIGS* 149 (both 749–750); *EIGS* 162; *EIGS* 163–164 (both > 750); *EIGS* 171–172; *EIGS* 173; *EIGS* 174; *EIGS* 175–176; *EIGS* 177; *EIGS* 178–180 (all 751–753 or 755–758); *EIGS* 192; *EIGS* 193; *EIGS* 194–195; *EIGS* 196; *EIGS* 197 (all 754–775); *EIGS* 215; *EIGS* 216; *EIGS* 217; *EIGS* 218; *EIGS* 221; *EIGS* 222; *EIGS* 223 (all 759–760); *EIGS* 236; *EIGS* 237–239; *EIGS* 240; *EIGS* 241–243; *EIGS* 244; *EIGS* 248 (all 762–769); *EIGS* 257; *EIGS* 258; *EIGS* 259; *EIGS* 273 (all 769–774); *EIGS* 284; *EIGS* 289; *EIGS* 290–291; *EIGS* 292–293; *EIGS* 294; *EIGS* 295; *EIGS* 296; *EIGS* 297; *EIGS* 298; *EIGS* 299; *EIGS* 300–301; *EIGS* 302–303; *EIGS* 304; *EIGS* 305 (all 775–785); *EIGS* 314 (779–780); *EIGS* 327; *EIGS* 328; *EIGS* 331; *EIGS* 332; *EIGS* 333; *EIGS* 336; *EIGS* 337 (all 781–784 or 792); *EIGS* 338 (785–786); *EIGS* 340 (795); *EPV* 45–47; *EPV* 48; *EPV* 49; *EPV* 50; *EPV* 52–53; *EPV* 54–56; *EPV* 57; *EPV* 58–59 (all 725–734); *EPV* 86; *EPV* 87–88; *EPV* 89–91; *EPV* 92–93; *EPV* 94; *EPV* 95; *EPV* 96–98; *EPV* 99–101 (all 734–742); *EPV* 105 (742–745); *EPV* 126–127; *EPV* 129; *EPV* 130–131; *EPV* 132–133 (all 739–749); *EPV* 134; *EPV* 135 *EPV* 136; *EPV* 137–140 (all 749–750); *EPV* 144; *EPV* 145; *EPV* 146; *EPV* 147 (all >750); *EPV* 155–157 (754–775); *EPV* 167–168; *EPV* 169–172; *EPV* 173; *EPV* 174–175 (all 751–753 or 751–758); *EPV* 180 (759–760); *EPV* 186; *EPV* 187; *EPV* 188 (all 760); *EPV* 193–196; *EPV* 197–200; *EPV* 201–202; *EPV* 203 (all 762–769); *EPV* 207; *EPV* 208; *EPV* 209 (all 769–774); *EPV* 210–211; *EPV* 212–216; *EPV* 218–219 (all 775–785); *EPV* 221 (775/776); *EPV* 222–224 (778/779); *EPV* 231–232 (782–784); *EPV* 233 (785–786); *EPV* 234; *EPV* 235; *EPV* 236 (all 791/792); *EPV* 236_{bis} and $_{\text{ter}}$ (792/793); *EPV* 237–239 (784–785 or 805–806); *EPV* 240; *EPV* 241; *EPV* 242 (all 793–794); *GSW* 94 (> 750); *GSW* 98; *GSW* 99; *GSW* 100; *GSW* 101; *GSW* 102; *GSW* 103 (all 725–734); *GSW* 111; *GSW* 112; *GSW* 113; *GSW* 114; *GSW* 115; *GSW* 116; *GSW* 117; *GSW* 125; *CSW* 126 (all 734–742); *GSW* 128 (742–745); *GSW* 131 (759–769); *GSW* 133; *GSW* 134 (both 743–749); *GSW* 139 (749); *GSW* 140 (749–150); *GSW* 144; *GSW* 145; *GSW* 146 (all 751–753 or 755–758); *GSW* 156 (759–760); *GSW* 161; *GSW* 162; *GSW* 165; *GSW* 166; *GSW* 167; *GSW* 168 (all 762–769); *GSW* 188 (762–774); *GSW* 195 (779–780); *GSW* 196; *GSW* 197; *GSW* 198; *GSW* 199; *GSW* 201; *GSW* 202; *GSW* 206 (all 785–786); *GWVS* 2; *GWVS* 3; *GWVS* 4 (all 725–734); *GWVS* 15 (734–742); *GWVS* 20 (751–753 or 755–758); *UAT* 67; *UAT* 70; *UAT* 71–73; *UAT* 75; *UAT* 76; *UAT* 77; *UAT* 78; *UAT* 79–80; *UAT* 81–82; *UAT* 83; *UAT* 84; *UAT* 85 (all 725–734); *UAT* 127–129; *UAT* 130; *UAT* 131 (all 742–745); *UAT* 145; *UAT* 146–147; *UAT* 148–150; *UAT* 151; *UAT* 152–155; *UAT*

156–157 (all 734–742); *UAT* 218–220 (734–745); *UAT* 241; *UAT* 242; *UAT* 243–244; *UAT* 245 (all 743–749); *UAT* 259; *UAT* 260; *UAT* 261; *UAT* 262–264 (all 749–750); *UAT* 277; *UAT* 279–281; *UAT* 282–284 (all >750); *UAT* 296–297 (750–751 or 753–755); *UAT* 314; *UAT* 315–316; *UAT* 317–318; *UAT* 319–321; *UAT* 322–325 (all 751–753 or 755–758); *UAT* 343–346; *UAT* 347 (all 751–758 or 781–786); *UAT* 353; *UAT* 354; *UAT* 355–356; *UAT* 357; *UAT* 358; *UAT* 3579–360; *UAT* 361–364 (all 754–775); *UAT* 383 (758–759); *UAT* 388; *UAT* 403–404 (all 759–760); *UAT* 411 (760–762); *UAT* 420; *UAT* 421; *UAT* 422–423; *UAT* 424; *UAT* 425–426; *UAT* 427–428; *UAT* 429; *UAT* 430–431; *UAT* 432–433; *UAT* 434 (all 762–769); *UAT* 460–462 (762–774); *UAT* 476–477; *UAT* 478; *UAT* 479; *UAT* 480; *UAT* 481; *UAT* 482–485 (all 769–773); *UAT* 505; *UAT* 506; *UAT* 507–508; *UAT* 509–511; *UAT* 512–513; *UAT* 514; *UAT* 515; *UAT* 516; *UAT* 517–519; *UAT* 520–521 (all 775–785); *UAT* 522–523; *UAT* 524–525; *UAT* 527 (all 780); *UAT* 565; *UAT* 566 (both 778 or 784–787); *UAT* 578; *UAT* 579; *UAT* 580 (all 784–785); *UAT* 584 (786–787); *UAT* 590 (791–792 or 795–796); *UAT* 596; *UAT* 597; *UAT* 598; *UAT* 599 (all 787–804); *UAT* 609 (789–790); *UAT* 613; *UAT* 614; *UAT* 615; *UAT* 616 (791–792 or 795–796); *UAT* 624; *UAT* 625 (both 798 or 802).

qanqal, a measure of capacity of unclear value < gr. *kagkellon*.[91] The Greek term is commonly considered a loanword from Latin *cancellus* "gate", which leaves open more than one problem as to how the word came to be used as a unit of measure.[92] This is, however, a false etymology. As rightly recognized by Becker, the Greek lemma is a rendering of the Persian measure *kankal* and was imported into Egypt at a very early stage.[93] The use of the *kagkellon* is documented as early as the first century and greatly increases in Byzantine times.

In Arabic papyri from the 8th century:

Chrest.Khoury I 91 (Ishqawh; 710), 44 and 46.

qinṭār, "centner" (a unit of weight corresponding to 100 *raṭls*)[94] < syr. *qnṭr*ʾ (shortened form of *qanṭīnārā*) < gr. *kentēnarion*/lat. *centenarium*.[95] This measure is referred to both in pre-Islamic poetry[96] and in the Qur'an,[97] suggesting an early loan.[98]

91 For the value of the *kangkellon*, see Mayerson 2003, 179–180. For the limits of Mayerson's reconstruction of the measure's value, see Kreuzsaler 2007, XXXIIn39.
92 See e.g. Fraenkel 1886, 208; Daris 1971, 48; and Mayerson 2003, 179.
93 Becker 1906, 31; Hebbo 1984, 305; and Kreuzsaler 2007, XXXI. Cf. Nöldekle 1879, 221n2.
94 Hinz 1970, 24–27.
95 Fraenkel 1886, 203; Sokoloff 2002, 1014. Cf. Krauss 1898–1899, II, 553 and Sokoloff 1992, 491 (*s.v.* "Targum Neofiti"). Cf. also Daris 1971, 53–54.
96 Fraenkel 1880, 13.
97 Q 3:14 and 75 and 4:20.
98 Fraenkel 1880,13; *id.* 1886, 203; and Jeffery 1938, 243–244.

In Arabic papyri from the 8th century:

P.BruningDevelopments (Fusṭāt?; 753), 4(x2) and 9 (x2); *P.KarabacekPapiergeschichte* p. 107 (al-Bahnasā; VIII), 7; *P.MuslimState* 23 (Fayyūm; 730–743), 35 and 36; *P.Christ.Musl.* 7 (Fayyūm; 743–744), 8; *P.Khalili* I 7 (Egypt; VIII), 2 and 4.

qisṭ,[99] a measure of capacity corresponding to ca. 0.54 l.[100] < aram. *qīṣṭā*[101] < gr. *xestēs*[102]/lat. *sextarius*.[103]

In Arabic papyri from the 7th and 8th centuries:

P.DelattreEntagion (Anṣinā: 694), 9 and 10 (x2); *P.Cair.Arab.* 342, 4; *P.Cair.Arab.* 343, 4 (both from Egypt; VIII); *P.KarabacekKuenstler* p. 67 (Fayyūm; VIII), 6; *P.VanthieghemMiel* 1 (Fusṭāṭ; 761), 4; *P.VanthieghemMiel* 2, 4; *P.VanthieghemMiel* 3, 5, and 9 (both from Fusṭāṭ; 772); *P.World* p. 141 a (Madīnat al-Fayyūm; 776), 4.

In Arabic standard weights from the 8th century:

CAM 3 (709–714); *CAM* 8–9; *CAM* 10–11 (all 714–717 or 720–721); *CAM* 12; *CAM* 13; *CAM* 14; *CAM* 15; *CAM* 16 (all 720–721); *CAM* 18; *CAM* 19–22 (all 720–724); *CAM* 33; *CAM* 34; *CAM* 35; *CAM* 36 (all 725–734); *CAM* 37 (729/730); *CAM* 38–41; *CAM* 42–43 (all 725–734); *CAM* 46 (742–746); *CAM* 55; *CAM* 56–57; *CAM* 58; *CAM* 59; *CAM* 60; *CAM* 61 (all 734–742); *CAM* 68–69; *CAM* 70; *CAM* 71; *CAM* 72–73 (all 734–745); *CAM* 81–82; *CAM* 83 (all 743–749); *CAM* 92 (749–750); *CAM* 97–98 (749–769); *CAM* 102–103 (751–753 or 755–758); *CAM* 104–105 (750/751 or 753–755); *CAM* 111; *CAM* 112; *CAM* 113–115 (all 754–775); *CAM* 127 (758–759); *CAM* 129–130; *CAM* 132–133 (all 759–760); *CAM* 136; *CAM* 137–139 (all 759–769); *CAM* 143 (762–769); *CAM* 163; *CAM* 167–169; *CAM* 170–171 (all 769–774); *CAM* 181 (779); *CAM2 BM* 13; *CAM2 BM* 14 (both 739/740); *CAM2 BM* 15 (737); *CAM2 BM* 19; *CAM2 BM* 20 (both 734–745); *CAM2 BM* 25 (749/750); *CAM2 BM* 29 (751–753 or 755–758); *CAM2 BM* 31 (754–755); *CAM2 BM* 50 (775–778); *CAM2 PRC* 1 (714–717 or 720–721); *CAM2 PRC* 4; *CAM2 PRC* 5 (all 717–720); *CAM2 PRC* 8; *CAM2 PRC* 9 (both 725–734); *CAM2 PRC* 16 (734–745); *EAG* I 3 (709–714); *EAG* I 5; *EAG* I 6; *EAG* I 7 (all 714–717 and 720–721); *EAG* I 9; *EAG* I 10 (both 717–720 or 721–722); *EAG* I 18; *EAG* I 19; *EAG* I 20; *EAG* I 21 (all 720–732); *EAG* I 26 (742–746); *EAG* I 42 (743–749); *EAG* I 51 (749–750); *EAG* I 55; *EAG* I 56; *EAG* I 57 (all 754–775); *EAG* I 67; *EAG* I 72; *EAG* I 75 (both 759–760); *EAG* I 103; *EAG* I 104 (both 780–781);

99 Not to be confused with the homologous Arabic word for “justice”; for that etymology, see Fraenkel 1886, 206, Jeffery 1938, 237–238, and Hebbo 1984, 296.
100 Bagnall 2009, 187; Morelli 2019, 13. For the value of the *qisṭ* in Islamic times, see Hinz 1970, 50.
101 Not to be confused with the homologous *qīṣṭā* “chest” < lat. *cista*.
102 The term *qisṭās* “balance” occurring in Q 17:35 and 26:182 is possibly a parallel form preserving the original ending of the Greek source-term. Cf. Jeffery 1938, 238–239. I thank Andreas Kaplony for bringing the term to my attention.
103 Fraenkel 1886, 205; Grohmann 1954, 167. Cf. Krauss 1898–1899, II, 535. Cf. Daris 1971, 77–78. A direct derivation from Greek or through mediation of copt. as hypothesized by Vorderstrasse 2015, 209.

EAG II 4 (725–734); *EAG* II 7 (720–724 or 744); *EAG* II 10; *EAG* II 11 (both 737); *EAG* II 14 (734–745); *EAG* II 20–21 (749–769); *EAG* II 22 (759–769); *EAG* II 27; *EAG* II 28 (both 775–778); *EIGS* 6; *EIGS* 7–10; *EIGS* 13; *EIGS* 14 (all 714–717 or 720–721); *EIGS* 18–19; *EIGS* 20–21; *EIGS* 22–23; *EIGS* 24; *EIGS* 26; *EIGS* 27; *EIGS* 28; *EIGS* 51–53 (725–734); *EIGS* 54 (729/730); *EIGS* 55; *EIGS* 57–58; *EIGS* 59–60; *EIGS* 61–62; *EIGS* 63 (all 725–734); *EIGS* 92 (734–742); *EIGS* 93–96 (737); *EIGS* 97; *EIGS* 98 (both 739/740); *EIGS* 99–100 (740/741); *EIGS* 101; *EIGS* 102; *EIGS* 103; *EIGS* 104; *EIGS* 110 (all 734–742); *EIGS* 120–123; *EIGS* 124–125; *EIGS* 128 (all 721–726); *EIGS* 132; *EIGS* 133–134 (all 742–745); *EIGS* 142–143; *EIGS* 144 (743–749); *EIGS* 153–154; *EIGS* 155 (all 749–750); *EIGS* 165 (>750); *EIGS* 182–185; *EIGS* 186–187; *EIGS* 191 (all 751–753 or 755–758); *EIGS* 200–204; *EIGS* 205 (all 754–775); *EIGS* 226; *EIGS* 228; *EIGS* 232 (759–760); *EIGS* 234; *EIGS* 235 (both 760–762); *EIGS* 248 (762–769); *EIGS* 265–270; *EIGS* 271 (769–774); *EIGS* 287 (774–776); *EIGS* 308 (775–778); *EIGS* 311; *EIGS* 312–313 (both 778–779); *EPV* 6; *EPV* 8–9 (all 714–717 or 720–721); *EPV* 14 (720–724); *EPV* 17; *EPV* 18 (both 717–720); *EPV* 20–27; *EPV* 31–38; *EPV* 40; *EPV* 43 (all 724–734); *EPV* 69–72; *EPV* 73–75; *EPV* 78; *EPV* 83; *EPV* 85 (all 734–742); *EPV* 102; *EPV* 103 (both 742–745); *EPV* 106–109; *EPV* 113 (both 743–749); *EPV* 116–118; *EPV* 119 (both 739–749); *EPV* 135 (749–750); *EPV* 151–154 (754–775); *EPV* 158–160 (750–751 or 753–755); *EPV* 161–162; *EPV* 163–166 (both 751–753 or 751–758); *EPV* 183 (759–760); *EPV* 189_{bis}; *EPV* 203_{bis} (both 762–769); *EPV* 204; *EPV* 205–206 (both 769–774); *EPV* 225–227 (777/778); *EPV* 228 (781–782); *GSW* 86 (720–724); *GSW* 87 (709–714); *GSW* 89; *GSW* 90; *GSW* 91 (all 714–717 or 720–721); *GSW* 93 (739–749); *GSW* 95 (>750); *GSW* 105; *GSW* 106; *GSW* 107; *GSW* 108 (all 725–734); *GSW* 120 (740); *GSW* 122; *GSW* 123; *GSW* 124 (all 734–742); *GSW* 135 (743–749); *GSW* 141 (749–750); *GSW* 147 (751–753 or 751–758); *GSW* 152; *GSW* 155 (both 754–775); *GSW* 157 (759–760); *GSW* 187 (759–769); *GSW* 206 (796); *GWVS* 8 (725–734); *GWVS* 10; *GWVS* 11 (both 721–726); *GWVS* 13; *GWVS* 14; *GWVS* 16 (all 734–742); *GWVS* 21; *GWVS* 22 (both 751–753 or 755–758); *GWVS* 27; *GWVS* 30 (both 769–774); *UAT* 6; *UAT* 7; *UAT* 8; *UAT* 9; *UAT* 10–13 (all 709–713); *UAT* 19; *UAT* 20–21; *UAT* 22; *UAT* 23; *UAT* 24; *UAT* 25–26; *UAT* 27; *UAT* 28; *UAT* 29–30 (all 714–717 or 720–721); *UAT* 40–43; *UAT* 46–51; *UAT* 52; *UAT* 54; *UAT* 55–57; *UAT* 58 (all 717–720 or 721–722); *UAT* 62 (720–724); *UAT* 89; *UAT* 90–96; *UAT* 98; *UAT* 99–105; *UAT* 115; *UAT* 116; *UAT* 117–123 (all 725–734); *UAT* 132 (742–745); *UAT* 172; *UAT* 177–181; *UAT* 182–189; *UAT* 191–192; *UAT* 196–197; *UAT* 198; *UAT* 204; *UAT* 206; *UAT* 208 (all 734–742); *UAT* 222–223; *UAT* 224–226; *UAT* 227–232; *UAT* 236 (all 734–745); *UAT* 246–247; *UAT* 248; *UAT* 249; *UAT* 250–251 (all 743–749); *UAT* 266 (749–750); *UAT* 285–287 (>750); *UAT* 298; *UAT* 299–300; *UAT* 301 (all 750–751 or 753–755); *UAT* 303–313; *UAT* 326–328; *UAT* 329–331 (all 751–753 or 755–758); *UAT* 334–335; *UAT* 336–338 (750–763); *UAT* 365; *UAT* 366–370; *UAT* 371 (all 754–775); *UAT* 389 (758–759); *UAT* 405–406 (759–760); *UAT* 438–439 (760–762); *UAT* 445; *UAT* 446–447; *UAT* 448–451 (759–769); *UAT* 469 (762); *UAT* 486; *UAT* 487; *UAT* 488–494 (all 769–773); *UAT* 535 (773–775); *UAT* 541–542; *UAT* 544 (all 775–785); *UAT* 545; *UAT* 546–547 (all 775–777); *UAT* 557–558 (777–778); *UAT* 585 (786–787).

qulla, "jar" (a measure of capacity corresponding to ca. 120 *raṭls*)[104] < aram. *qulləṯā*.[105]

104 Grohmann 1954, 171.

105 Fraenkel 1886, 170. Vorderstrasse 2015, 211 postulates a loan from the Coptic root *kelōl*.

In Arabic papyri from the 8th century:

P.MuslimState 28 v, 1; *P.MuslimState* 29, 11 (both from the Fayyūm; 730–743); *P.Khalili* I 7 (Egypt; VIII), 5.

tillīs, literally "sack" (a measure of capacity)[106] < syr. *tlyṣʾ* < gr. *thyllis*.[107] The alternative derivation from the Latin *trilicium* suggested by de Goeje[108] presents both semantic and morphological difficulties.[109]

In Arabic papyri from the 8th century:

P.Prag.Arab. 55, (Egypt; VIII), 1.

satl, attested only once in *Chrest.Khoury* I 48, 5 (Egypt; ca. 641[110]) and believed by the first editor to be a parallel form of the standard ***sayṭl*** and ***saṭl*** (< pal. aram. *ṣiṭlā* < gr. *sitla*/ lat. *situla*)[111] has been proved to be a ghost word by M. Tillier and N. Vanthieghem.[112]

f) Military

jaysh, "military" < aram. *gaysā* "troop", "band".[113]

In Arabic papyri from the 7th and 8th centuries:

Chrest.Khoury I 90 (= *P.World* p. 124 = *P.Heid.Arab.* I 1) (Ishqawh; 710), 9; *P.BeckerPAF* 8 (= *P.Heid.Arab.* I 7), 3; *P.BeckerPAF* 9 (= *P.Heid.Arab.* I 8), 7 (both from Ishqawh; 709); *P.BeckerPapyrusstudien* (Anṣinā; 713/714), 4; *P.DelattreEntagion* (Anṣinā; 694), 5; *P.DiemFrueheUrkunden* 1 (Fayyūm; 698), r 4; *P.DiemFrueheUrkunden* 5 (Fayyūm; 776–778), v 3; *P.GascouQurra* (= *Chrest.Khoury* I 92 = *P.RagibQurra* 1), (Fayyūm; 709), 15 and v 2.

106 Hinz 1970, 51–52.
107 Payne Smith 1879–1901, 4448; Sokoloff 2009, 1649.
108 De Goeje 1866, 19 (glossary) and Dozy 1881, II, 150.
109 Fraenkel 1886, 197–198.
110 For the date of *Chrest.Khoury* I 48, see Tillier/ Vanthieghem 2019, 168.
111 Fraenkel 1886, 67.
112 Tillier/ Vanthieghem 2019, 168 and 171–172. The authors read *Chrest.Khoury* I 48, 5 as *fī madī[nati-hi] [sanat] ʿishrīn sana[t]*.
113 Fraenkel 1886, 238. De Lagarde, however, considers the Aramaic term to be a loanword from the Bactrian; de Lagarde 1866, 28.

jund, litt. "army" < JBA *gwnd*'[114] (= gr. *gounda*) < MP *gund*.[115] *Jund* historically denotes the districts in which the early Muslim garrisons were settled and one of the sub-provinces into which Umayyad Syria was originally divided.[116] In 8th-century Arabic documents, however, the term occurs only in the general sense of "troops."

In Arabic papyri from the 8th century:

Chrest.Khoury I 90 (= *P.World* p. 124 = *P.Heid.Arab.* I 1), 8 and 24; *Chrest.Khoury* I 91, 14 (both from Ishqawh; 710); *P.Cair.Arab.* 148 (= *P.World* p. 126 = *P.BeckerNPAF* 2) (Ishqawh; 708–710), 4 and 22; *P.Cair.Arab.* 150 (= *P.BeckerNPAF* 7 = *P.BeckerPAF* 12) (Ishqawh; 709), 6.

nūtī (*nawtī*?)[117] "sailor" < gr. *nautēs*[118] rather than from JPA *nawṭ*.[119]

In Arabic papyri from the 7th and 8th century:

Chrest.Khoury I 96 r (= *P.Heid.Arab.* II 1 = *P.Jahn* 1) (Egypt: VII/VIII), 4; *P.BeckerPapyrusstudien* (Anṣinā; 713/714), 5 (x2) and 6; *P.Cair.Arab.* 152 (= *P.BeckerNPAF* 10) (Ishqawh; 709), 4; *P.DelattreEntagion* (Anṣinā; 694), 1 and 7; *PERF* 614 (Fusṭāṭ?; 778/779), r 7, 8 and v 9, 18 and 20; *P.Heid.Arab.* II 1 v (Egypt: VII/VIII), 3 and 4; *P.Khalili* I 7 (Egypt; VIII), 2 and 5.

nawbaj, "ship carpenter" < gr. *naupēgos*.

In Arabic papyri from the 8th century:

P.BeckerPAF 8 (= *P.Heid. Arab.* I 7), 5; *P.Cair.Arab.* 152 (= *P.BeckerNPAF* 10), 4[120] (both from Ishqawh; < 709).

qādis, a type of ship < syr. *qadsā* < gr. *kados* "vessel", "basin".[121]

---

114 Fraenkel 1880, 13; *id.* 1886, 238–239; Jeffery 1938, 104–105; Hebbo 1984, 79–80; Sokoloff 2014, 269; and Cheung 2017, 323.
115 The word *gund* is of Parthian origin, see MacKenzie 1971, 38. It is unclear, however, whether the term is originally of Iranian or Semitic origin; see Ciancaglini 2008, 135. For the controversy surrounding the etymology of the Middle Iranian *kund*, see Rossi 2015.
116 For the early Islamic institution of the *jund, see* Bouderbala 2008 with particular respect to the Egyptian context.
117 For the issue of the original pronunciation of the term *nwty*, see Kaplony 2015, 72.
118 For the connotations of the term *nautēs* in Greek papyri from the Early Islamic period, see Christides 1999, 57.
119 Cf. Krauss 1898–1899, II, 355.
120 See Diem's 1984a emendation, 258.
121 Fraenkel 1886, 219; Sokoloff 2009, 1319.

In Arabic papyri from the 8th century:

P.BeckerPAF 8 (= *P.Heid.Arab.* I 7), 1; *P.BeckerPAF* 9 (= *P.Heid.Arab.* I 8), 6 (both from Ishqawh; 709).

safīna, "ship" < aram. *spīntā* < MP *apsān*;[122] already occurs in the Qur'an.[123]

In Arabic papyri from the 7th and 8th centuries:

Chrest.Khoury I 96 (= *P.Heid.Arab.* II 1 r = *P.Jahn* 1) (Egypt; VII/VIII), r 3; *P.BeckerPapyrusstudien* (Anṣinā; 713/714), 3; *P.DiemDienstschreiben* d (= *P.David-WeillLouvre* 27a) (Fusṭāṭ; 720), 5; *P.DelattreEntagion* (Anṣinā; 694), 3; *P.DiemFrueheUrkunden* 1 (Fayyūm; 698), r 4; *PERF* 614 (Fusṭāṭ?; 778/779), r 3, 7,[8] and v 2, 6, 9, 10, 18, 20, and 21; *P.Heid.Arab.* II 1 v (Egypt; VII/VIII), 4 and 5 (x2); *P.Heid.Arab.* I 22 (Ishqawh; 709–714), 3(x2); *P.JoySorrow* 9 (Egypt; VIII), 10; *P.Khalili* I 7 (Egypt; VIII), 1, 2, and 5; *P.GascouQurra* (= *Chrest.Khoury* I 92 = *P.RagibQurra* 1), (Fayyūm; 709), 7 and 8; *P.ReinfandtLeinenhaendler* (Ihnās; VIII), r 20, 22(x2), and 23; *P.Ross.Georg.* IV 10 (Ishqawh; 709/710), r 1; *P.World* p. 113 (= *P.GrohmannApercu* p. 41 = *P.GrohmannMuhadara* II p. 12) (Ihnās; 643), r 7.

Loanwords Attested in Documents from Egypt and other Regions (640/641–800)

a) Fiscal Administration

kharāj "finances", "tax in money", or "land-tax"[124] < JBA *kragā* "poll-tax" or MP *harag* ultimately derives from Old Babylonian through a millennial history of borrowings.[125] The defective form of the term which occurs in Q 18:94 (*kharj*) is a subtle hint at a derivation from the Middle Persian.[126] The word is used in two instances in the Qur'an in the general sense of "tribute" or "reward".[127] A more technical connotation of the term is first attested in late 8th-century

---

122 Fraenkel 1886, 216–217 (cf. *ibid.*, 292); Jeffery 1938, 171–172; Hebbo 1984, 190–191 and Asbaghi 1988, 162.

123 Q 18:71 and 79 and 29:15.

124 For the early Islamic acceptation(s) of *kharāj*, see Legendre/Younes 2015, 2b, Sijpesteijn 2013, 177, *ibid.*n337 and *ibid.*, 190–193, and Legendre 2018, 409–410; Cf. Frantz-Murphy 2001, 141–142.

125 Nöldeke 1879, 241n1; Fraenkel 1886, 283; Khan 2007, 43–44; Asbaghi 1988, 105; Khan 2014, 24; cf. Abbot 1938, 93 and Sokoloff 2002, 599. Cahen 1990, *s.v.* "*Kharādj*" (I.) derives *kharāj* from Greek *chōregia* "military."

126 Cf. Azarpay *et. al.* 2003, 26.

127 The term *kharāj* surprisingly does not appear among the loanwords listed by Jeffery. In the Qur'an, *kharāj* occurs in Q:18: 94 (*kharj*) and 23:72 (*kharāj*).

papyri from Khurāsān and Egypt in this chronological order.[128] In the late 7th/early 8th century, Middle Persian documents housed at Berkeley the MP forerunner *harg* occurs as part of the compound name *harg-gar-īd* denoting a tax inspector.[129] In the 4th century BCE Aramaic documents from Bactria the AOA corresponding variant of the term (*hlk*') is attested.[130] In 7th-century Bactrian documents from the Bēk family archive, the variant of the term *yargo* (also in *composita*) is used to denote "duties" or "corvée".[131]

In Arabic papyri from 8th-century Egypt:

Chrest.Khoury I 66 (= *P.GrohmannBeziehung* p. 338) (Fayyūm; 795/796), 5 and 11; *CPR* XXI 1 (= *Chrest.Khoury* I 72 = *P.Loth* 1) (Madīnat al-Fayyūm; 785), 1 and 8; *CPR* XXI 2a (= *P.Cair. Arab.* II p. 70 = *P.GrohmannApercu* p. 85 = *P.GrohmannProbleme* III p. 143), 1; *CPR* XXI 2b (= *P.World* p. 116 = *P.GrohmannApercu* p. 50), 3 (6) (both Fayyūm; 792); *CPR* XXI 3 (= *P.Cair. Arab.* 77) (Egypt; 794), 3; *CPR* XXI 4b (= *Chrest.Khoury* II 26 = *P.GrohmannBeziehung* p. 339) (Madīnat al-Fayyūm; 796), 2 and 8; *CPR* XXI 5 (= *P.Ryl.Arab.* II 4 = *P.Ryl.Arab.* I IX 6 = *P.MargoliouthSelectPapyri* p. 413–414) (al-Ushmūnayn; 799), 7 and 8 (*P.MargoliouthSelectPapyri* p. 413–414, 6 and 7); *P.Berl.Arab.* II p. 20–21 (= *P.DiemFrueheUrkunden* 6 = *P.GrohmannProbleme* 17) (Egypt; 796), 5; *P.Berl.Arab.* II 26 (Egypt; VIII), r 4 and 8; *P.David-WeillLouvre* 16 (Egypt; 773), 9; *P.Christ.Musl.* 24 (Fayyūm; 798–803), [5]; *P.DiemFrueheUrkunden* 3 (Fayyūm; 779), 4; *P.DiemFrueheUrkunden* 4 (Fayyūm; 793), 4; *P.DiemFrueheUrkunden* 5 (Fayyūm; 776–778), v 2; *P.DiemFrueheUrkunden* 7 (Egypt; 784), 3 and 8; *P.JoySorrow* 43 (Egypt; VIII), 15; *P.Ryl.Arab.* I XV 14 b (Egypt; 795/796), 2; *P.ShahinSchreibubung* 3 (Egypt; VIII), v 3 and 4; *P.VanthieghemRecu* (Fayyūm; 787/788), 3 and 5; *P.YounesGovernors* 1 (= *P.World* p. 171 = *P.Ryl. Arab.* I I 5) (Fusṭāṭ; 797), 16, 17, and 18 (*P.World* p. 171 = *P.Ryl.Arab.* I I 5, 15, 16, and 17).

In Arabic parchments from 8th-century Khurāsān:

P.Khurasan 1 (Rōb; 764), 5 and 6; *P.Khurasan* 2 (Rōb; 765), 6; *P.Khurasan* 4 (Rōb; 766), 6; *P.Khurasan* 5 (Rōb; 766), 6; *P.Khurasan* 6 (Rōb; 766), 9 and 14; *P.Khurasan* 7 (Rōb; 767), 6; *P.Khurasan* 9 (Rōb; 769), 6 and 7; *P.Khurasan* 10 (Rōb; 769), 3 and 4; *P.Khurasan* 11 (Rōb; 771), 5; *P.Khurasan* 12 (Rōb; 768), 7; *P.Khurasan* 13 (Rōb; 769), 5 and 6; *P.Khurasan* 14 (Rōb; 769), 4; *P.Khurasan* 15 (Rōb; 771), 4 and 5(x3); *P.Khurasan* 16 (Rōb; 772), 5; *P.Khurasan* 17 (Rōb; 771), 5 and 7; *P.Khurasan* 18 (Rōb; 771), 5; *P.Khurasan* 19 (Rōb; 774), 5 and 8; *P.Khurasan* 20 (Rōb; 774), 4 and 5; *P.Khurasan* 21 (Rōb; 775), 10; *P.Khurasan* 23 (Rōb; 770), 5.

---

128 The first dated occurrence in the Khurāsān is *P.Khurasan* 1 (Rōb; 764), 5 and 6, in Egypt *P.David-WeillLouvre* 16, 9 (Egypt; 773). This fact has been interpreted as an indicator that the institute of the *kharāj* originated in the Eastern administrative tradition and was introduced in the rest of the Islamic empire as a corollary of the pervasive Iranian cultural influence which accompanied the Abbasid revolution. See e.g. Khan 2012, 80–83 and *id.* 2007, 25; Sijpesteijn 2013, 177 and *ibid.*n337. Cf. Reinfandt 2015, 286–289.

129 Berk. 27 (Qom; 673/674), 3 and 14.

130 Naveh/Shaked 2012, 30.

131 Sims-Williams 2007, 228. See e.g. *BD* I Q (Rōb; 671), 23.

jizya, "money tax", "poll-tax" (*jizyat al-raʾs*), or "land tax" (*jizyat al-arḍ*)[132] < JBA, syr. *gzīṯā* "capitation".[133] *Jizya* is attested once in the Qur'an; given the "technical sense" of the word in the passage at issue (Q 9: 29), however, Jeffery holds the Quranic verse for a later interpolation.[134]

In Arabic papyri from 8th-century Egypt:

Chrest.Khoury I 90 (= *P.World* p. 124 = *P.Heid.Arab.* I 1) (Ishqawh; 710), 7, 12, and 27; *Chrest.Khoury* I 93 (= *P.Heid.Arab.* I 5), 4; *Chrest.Khoury* I 94 (= *P.Heid.Arab.* I 6), 5 (both from Ishqawh; 709/710); *P.Berl.Arab.* II 23 (Egypt; VII), r 8; *P.Cair.Arab.* 149 (= *P.BeckerNPAF* 3) (Ishqawh; 709–710), 10, 19, 22, and 23; *P.Cair.Arab.* 153 (= *P.BeckerPAF* 13 = *P.BeckerNPAF* 6) (Ishqawh; 710), 10 (*P.BeckerPAF* 13 and *P.BeckerNPAF* 6, 7); *P.Cair.Arab.* 160 (= *P.BeckerNPAF* 13) (Ishqawh; 709/710), 5 (*P.BeckerNPAF* 13, 4); *P.Cair.Arab.* 161 (= *P.BeckerNPAF* 13) (Ishqawh; 709/710), 5 (*P.BeckerNPAF* 14, 4); *P.Cair.Arab.* 162 (= *P.BeckerNPAF* 15) (Ishqawh; 709/710), 5 (*P.BeckerNPAF* 15, 4); *P.Cair.Arab.* 163 (= *P.BeckerNPAF* 16), 5 (*P.BeckerNPAF* 16, 4); *P.Cair.Arab.* 169 (al-Ushmūnayn; 752), 8; *P.Cair.Arab.* 174 (al-Ushmūnayn; 722), 6; *P.Cair.Arab.* 175 (= *P.GrohmannApercu* p. 55 = *P.BeckerPAF* 17) (Ishqawh; 731), 6; *P.Cair.Arab.* 180 (al-Ushmūnayn; 731/732), 5 and 7; *P.Clackson* 45 (Bāwiṭ; 753), 5 and 9; *P.DiemFruehe Urkunden* 7 (Egypt; 784), 10; *P.DiemFrueheUrkunden* 8 (Egypt; 734), 6; *P.DiemFrueheUrkunden* 9 (Egypt; 730/731), 10; *P.DonnerFragments* 3 (Egypt; 731–734), 11; P.Gen.inv. 713;[135] *P.Giss.Arab.* 6 (Egypt; VIII), 2; *P.Giss.Arab.* p. 33 a (= *P.RagibSauf-conduits* 4) (Egypt; 734), 2 and 7 (*P.RagibSauf-conduits* 4, 1 and 6); *P.GrohmannProbleme* 5 (Ihnās; VIII), 4 and 5(x3); *P.GrohmannProbleme* 6 (Egypt; 735), 3(x2); *P.Heid.Arab.* I a (= *SB* I 5644), 5; *P.Heid.Arab.* I b (= *SB* I 5645), 5; *P.Heid.Arab.* I c (= *SB* I 5646), 5; *P.Heid.Arab.* I d (= *SB* I 5647), 5; *P.Heid.Arab.* I e (= *SB* I 5648), 3 (x2); *P.Heid.Arab.* I f (= *SB* I 5649), 4; *P.Heid.Arab.* I g (= *SB* I 5650), 5; *P.Heid.Arab.* I h (= *SB* I 5651), 5; *P.Heid.Arab.* I i (= *SB* I 5652), 5; *P.Heid.Arab.* I k (= *SB* I 5653), 1; *P.Heid.Arab.* I l (= *SB* I 5654), 5 (all from Ishqawh; 709/710); *P.Mil.Vogl.* I 8 a–b (Egypt; 734), a r 2, 3, and 10 and b r 2; *P.MuslimState* 22, 11; *P.MuslimState* 23, 25, and 26; *P.MuslimState* 35, 5(x2) (all from the Fayyūm; 730–743); *P.Qurra* 4 (Ishqawh; 709), 14; *P.Qurra* 5 (Ishqawh; 708–710), 3, 6, 10, and 19; *P.RagibLettres* 2a (= *P.RogersNotice* p. 15 bottom) (Fayyūm; VIII), r 8; *P.RagibSauf-conduits* 1 (Saqqāra; 717–719), 4; *P.RagibSauf-conduits* 4 (= *P.Giss.Arab.* p. 33 a) (Egypt; 734), 1 and 6 (*P.Giss.Arab.* p. 33 a 2 and 7); *P.RagibSauf-conduits* 5 (= *P.SilvestrePaléographie* p. 84) (Saqqāra; 750), 5; *P.RagibSauf-conduits* 6 (Saqqāra; 751), 5; *P.RagibSauf-conduits* 7 (= *P.SilvestredeSacyPapyrus* A) (Saqqāra; 751), 6; *P.RagibSauf-conduits* 8 (= *P.SilvestredeSacyPapyrus* B) (Saqqāra; 751), 5; *P.SijpesteijnQurra* (Ishqawh; 710), 5.

---

132 For the early Islamic acceptation(s) of *jizya* and the different taxes it describes, see Legendre/Younes, https://www.universiteitleiden.nl/en/research/research-projects/humanities/formation-of-islam-topics (accessed Jan. 15, 2021), 1b; Legendre 2013, 220–221; and Sijpesteijn 2013, 173–174 and *ibid.*n311.

133 Nöldeke 1879, 241n1; Fraenkel 1886, 283; Jeffery 1938, 101–102; Bosworth 1969, 131–132; Sokoloff 1992, 275 *id.* 2009, 225.

134 Jeffery 1938, 101.

135 The piece is unpublished and will soon appear as *P.Gen.* V 3. I thank the editor, Khaled Younes, for the information and for providing me with the preliminary edition of the text (p.c. Febr. 14, 2018).

In Bactrian parchments from Khurāsān:

BD I W7 (Rōb; 747), 8.

That the Bactrian term *gazito* may be a transposition of the Arabic *jizya* is suggested by the mention on the same line of *barito*, another loanword from the Arabic (< arab. *barīd* "post") and by the specification "an Arab *gazit*" (*taziimaggoo*[136] *gazito*).

In Arabic coins from Khurāsān:

Walker 1952 p. 108, no. 3 ov, mg (Anbīr; 703/704).[137]

kūra, "district" < aram. *kōrā* < gr. *chōra* "region".[138]

In Arabic papyri from 7th- and 8th-century Egypt:

Chrest.Khoury I 66 (= *P.GrohmannBeziehung* p. 338) (Fayyūm; 795/796), 5; *Chrest.Khoury* I 91 (= *P.Heid.Arab.* I 3) (Ishqawh; 710), 23; *Chrest.Khoury* I 93 (= *P.Heid.Arab.* I 5), 3; *Chrest.Khoury* I 94 (= *P.Heid.Arab.* I 6), 4 (both from Ishqawh; 709/710); *CPR* XXI 2b (= *P.GrohmannApercu* p. 50 = *P.World* p. 116) (Fayyūm; 792), 3; *CPR* XXI 4b (= *P.GrohmannBeziehung* p. 339 = *Chrest.Khoury* II 26) (Madīnat al-Fayyūm; 796), 3; *CPR* XXI 5 (= *P.Ryl.Arab.* II 4 = *P.Ryl.Arab.* I IX 6 = *P.MargoliouthSelectPapyri* p. 413–414) (al-Ushmūnayn; 798/799), 4 and 10; *P.BeckerPAF* 1 (Ishqawh; 709/710), 6; *P.BeckerPAF* 9 (Ishqawh; 709), 2 and 3; *P.Berl.Arab.* II 26 (Egypt; VIII), r 4; *P.Cair.Arab.* 149 (= *P.BeckerNPAF* 3) (Ishqawh; 709–714), 5, 10, 19, and 27; *P.Cair.Arab.* 150 (= *P.BeckerPAF* 12) (Ishqawh; 709), 13; *P.Cair.Arab.* 154 (= *P.World* p. 129 = *P.BeckerNPAF* 8) (Ishqawh; 709–714), 8 (*P.World* p. 129 and *P.BeckerNPAF* 8, 6); *P.Cair.Arab.* 155 (= *P.BeckerNPAF* 9) (Ishqawh; 709/710), 8 (*P.BeckerNPAF* 9, 6); *P.Cair.Arab.* 160 (= *P.BeckerNPAF* 13), 4 (*P.BeckerNPAF* 13, 3); *P.Cair.Arab.* 161 (= *P.BeckerNPAF* 14), 4 (*P.BeckerNPAF* 14, 3); *P.Cair.Arab.* 163 (= *P.BeckerNPAF* 16), 4 (*P.BeckerNPAF* 16, 3) (all from Ishqawh; 709/710); *P.Cair.Arab.* 167 (= *P.GuestPapyrus*) (Akhmīm; 757/758), 96; *P.Cair.Arab.* 169 (al-Ushmūnayn; 752), 2; *P.Cair.Arab.* 180 (al-Ushmūnayn, 731/732), 3; *P.Christ.Musl.* 11 (Fayyūm; 743–749), 3; *P.Christ.Musl.* 23 (Fayyūm; 772–778), 3; *P.Christ.Musl.* 24 (Fayyūm; 798–803), [5]; *P.David-WeillLouvre* 16 (Egypt; 773), 5; *P.David-WeillLouvre* 30 (Egypt; VIII), 9; *P.DelattreEntagion* (Anṣīnā; 694), 3; *P.DiemFrueheUrkunden* 1 (Fayyūm; 698), r 3; *P.DiemFrueheUrkunden* 2 (Egypt; 685–705), r 3; *P.DiemFrueheUrkunden* 4 (Fayyūm; 793), 4; *P.DiemFrueheUrkunden* 5 (Fayyūm; 776–778), r 2 and 3, and v 1 and 6; *P.DiemFrueheUrkunden* 6 (= *P.GrohmannProbleme* 17) (Egypt; 796), 5; *P.DiemFrueheUrkunden* 7 (Egypt; 784), 8; *PERF* 614 (Fusṭāṭ?; 778/779), r 6, 7, 8 and v 5, 9, 17, and 21; *P.Heid.Arab.* I a (= *SB* I 5644), 4; *P.Heid.Arab.* I c (= *SB* I 5646), 4; *P.Heid.Arab.* I d (= *SB* I 5647), 4; *P.Heid.Arab.* I 4, 14; *P.Heid.Arab.* I f (= *SB* I 5649), 4; *P.Heid.Arab.* I g (= *SB* I 5650), 4; *P.Heid.Arab.* I h (= *SB* I 5651), 4; *P.Heid.*

---

136 For the use of *tazig*- for "Arab", see Sundermann 1993.

137 Walker misread the mint-name as *HURA* (Khurāsān), cf. Album/Goodwin 2002, 41.

138 Freytag 1830–1837, IV, 70; Hebbo 1984, 326–327; Schall 1960, 184; and Sokoloff 2009, 612. Grohmann postulated a South Arabian derivation of the term (Grohmann 1959, 34).

Arab. I i (= *SB* I 5652), 4; *P.Heid.Arab.* I k (= *SB* I 5653), 4*P.Heid.Arab.* I l (= *SB* I 5654), 4; *P.Heid.Arab.* I 4, 14; *P.Heid.Arab.* I 10 (all from Ishqawh; 709/710), 7; *P.KarabacekBemerkungenMerx* (= *P.MerxDocuments* p. 55) (Fayyūm; 685–705), 3; *P.JoySorrow* 42 (Dalāṣ; VIII), 11; *P.Khalili* I 2 (Dalāṣ; late VIII), r 3, 5, and 14; *P.Lond.* 1356 (Ishqawh; 710), 1; *P.MuslimState* 2, 6; *P.MuslimState* 4, 5; *P.MuslimState* 7, 8; *P.MuslimState* 11, v 2 (all from the Fayyūm; 730–743); *P.PiletteSauf-Conduit* (Saqqāra; 729), 4; *P.Qurra* 1 (Ishqawh; 709), r 7; *P.Qurra* 3 (Ishqawh; 709/710), r 7; *P.Qurra* 5 (Ishqawh; 708–710), 18; *P.RagibLettreFamiliale* (Egypt; 721), 15; *P.RagibQurra* 3 (Ishqawh; 710), r 6; *P.RagibSauf-conduits* 1 (Saqqāra; 719), 1 and 3; *P.RagibSauf-conduits* 3 (Armant; 734), 3 and 5; *P.RagibSauf-conduits* 5 (= *P.SilvestrePalaeography* p. 84) (Saqqāra; 750), 3 and 4; *P.RagibSauf-conduits* 6 (Saqqāra; 751), 3 and 4; *P.RagibSauf-conduits* 7 (= *P.SilvestredeSacyPapyrus* A) (Saqqāra; 751), 3 and 5; *P.RagibSauf-conduits* 8 (= *P.SilvestredeSacyPapyrus* B) (Saqqāra; 751), 3 and 4; *P.ShahinSchreibubung* 3 (Egypt; VIII), v 2; *P.Steuerquittungen* 1 (Ihnās; 764/765), 2; *P.StoetzerSteuerquittungen* 2 (Ihnās; 707),[139] 4; *P.TillierDebts* 1 (= *Chrest.Khoury* I 48) (Asyūṭ; related to 640/641), 4; *P.VanthieghemRecu* (Fayyūm; 787/788), 3; *P.VanthieghemSaufConduit* (Egypt; 717), 5; *P.World* p. 132 (Egypt; 793), 4 and 6; *P.YounesGovernors* 1 (= *P.World* p. 171 = *P.Ryl.Arab.* I I 5) (Fusṭāṭ; 797), 13 (*P.World* p. 171 = *P.Ryl.Arab.* I I 5, 11); *P.YounesGovernors* 2 (Fayyūm; 798), 4.

In Arabic papyri from 7th- and 8th-century Syria:

P.Mird 19 (Khirbat al-Mird; VII), 3; *P.Mird* 95 (Khirbat al-Mird; VIII), 5; *P.Ness.* 60 (Nessana; 674), 3; *P.Ness.* 61 r (Nessana; 675), 3; *P.Ness.* 62 (Nessana; 675), 3.

In Arabic seals and standard weights from 8th-century Syria:

APS 12 ov (Bulunyās; VIII?), 2; *APS* 16 fl (unknown provenance; 771–772), 2; Amitai-Preiss 2007 10 ov (Ascalon; VIII?), 2; Amitai-Preiss 2007 11 ov (ʿAmwās; VIII?), 2; Amitai-Preiss 2000 p.104. ov (Tiberias; VII/VIII), 2.

In Arabic inscriptions from 8th-century Syria:

Hoyland 2018a p. 137 (Andarīn; VIII), 5.

In Arabic parchments from 8th-century Khurāsān:

P.Khurasan 1 (Rōb; 764), 3.

qarya, literally "village" but also denoting the fiscal unit of a village and its surroundings[140] < aram. *qiryəṯā* (but the term has a long history in different Semitic languages).[141] *Qarya* often occurs in the Qur'an.[142]

139 For the date of *P.StoetzerSteuerquittungen* 2, see *supra* p. 57.

140 Sijpesteijn 2013, 144.

141 Zimmern 1915, 9; Jeffery 1938, 236; Hebbo 1984, 292.

142 57 attestations, see e.g. in Q 2:58, 4:72, 6:123, 7:88, 9:92 etc.

In Arabic papyri from 8th-century Egypt:

Chrest.Khoury I 91 (= *P.Heid.Arab.* I 3) (Ishqawh; 710), 48; *CPR* XVI 9 (Egypt; VIII), 8 and 11; *P.AbbottUbaidAllah* (Egypt; 724), 1; *P.BeckerPAF* 2 (Ishqawh; 709), 6; *P.Berl.Arab.* II 23 (Egypt; VII), r 6; *P.Berl.Arab.* II 75 (= *P.Loth* 2) (Madīnat al-Fayyūm; VIII), r 7; *P.Cair.Arab.* 149 (= *P.BeckerNPAF* 3) (Ishqawh; 709–714), 28; *P.Cair.Arab.* 150 (= *P.BeckerPAF* 12) (Ishqawh; 709), 7, 13, 15, 17, and 19; *P.Cair.Arab.* 153 (= *P.BeckerNPAF* 6) (Ishqawh; 710), 8 (*P.BeckerNPAF* 6, 5); *P.Cair.Arab.* 154 (= *P.World* p. 129 = *P.BeckerNPAF* 8) (Ishqawh; 709–714), 12 (*P.BeckerNPAF* 8, 10); *P.Cair.Arab.* 162 (= *P.BeckerNPAF* 15) (Ishqawh; 709/710), 4 (*P.BeckerNPAF* 15, 3); *P.Cair.Arab.* 169 (al-Ushmūnayn; 752), 6 and 8; *P.Clackson* 45 (Bāwiṭ 753), 6 and 8; *P.DiemAmtlicheSchreiben* 3 (= *P.DiemFrueheUrkunden* p. 150 = *P.GrohmannProbleme* III p. 148, no. 3 = *P.GrohmannApercu* p. 90, no. 2) (Egypt; VIII), 6; *P.DiemFrueheUrkunden* 6 (= *P.GrohmannProbleme* 17) (Egypt; 796), 7; *P.Heid.Arab.* I 4, 16; *P.Heid.Arab.* I 11, 2 and 5 (both from Ishqawh; 709/710); *P.JoySorrow* 16 (Fusṭāṭ; VIII), 12; *P.Khalili* I 2 (Dalāṣ; late VIII), r 3, 10, 14, and r 1; *P.Khalili* I 14, 10; *P.Khalili* I 24, r 5 (both from Egypt; VIII); *P.MuslimState* 2, 8; *P.MuslimState* 4, 10 and 12; *P.MuslimState* 5, 7; *P.MuslimState* 8, 26, 29, 30, 31, and 33; *P.MuslimState* 10, 4, 7, and 9; *P.MuslimState* 11, v 2; *P.MuslimState* 12, 2; *P.MuslimState* 14, 7 and 21; *P.MuslimState* 18, 8, and 10; *P.MuslimState* 21, 8, and 11; *P.MuslimState* 23, 7, 10, 16, and 27(x2) (all from the Fayyūm; 730–743); *P.RagibLettres* 2a (= *P.RogersNotice* p. 15 bottom) (Fayyūm; VIII), r 4; *P.YounesGovernors* 2 (Fayyūm; 798), 7.

In Arabic papyri from 7th-century Syria:

P.HoylandDhimma 2 (Nessana; 680–690), 22; *P.Mird* 19 (Khirbat al-Mird; VII), 3.

maks, "custom dues"[143] < aram. *maḵsā* "toll, tribute,[144] impost".[145]

In Arabic papyri from 8th-century Egypt:

P.Cair.Arab. 147 (= *P.BeckerNPAF* 4 = *P.BeckerPAF* 7 (left part)) (Ishqawh; 710), 3 and 6 (*P.BeckerNPAF* 4, 2 and 5); *P.Heid.Arab.* I 2 (Ishqawh; 710), 24.

In Coptic papyri from 8th-century Egypt:

P.Gascou 24 (= *CPR* II 228), 31 (?).

---

143 For the institution of *maks*, see Forand 1966.

144 In the so-called bilingual (Palmyrene/Greek) "tariff" of Palmyra (137 CE) the term *maqəṣā* (line 3 *et seq.* in the Palmyrene version) is translated in the Greek as *telos*. Both the Greek and Palmyrene text are edited by Chabot in *CIS* II 3, no. 3913 and by Cooke 1903, 313–340 (n. 147) who provides a translation and commentary of the Palmyrene version. I thank Stefanie Schmidt for calling my attention to the inscription.

145 Fraenkel 1886, 283.

In Arabic inscriptions from 8th-century Syria:

Hoyland 2018a p. 137 (Andarīn; viii), 4.

rizq (*ruzq*?)[146] < JBA, syr. *rōziqā*[147] "daily ration" or "stipendium" < MP *rōzig* "daily bread".[148] Both the word and the denominative verbal root are frequently used in the Qur'an with the religious connotation "(God's) provision",[149] which suggests an early loan. The use of *rizq* in a more technical sense is first attested in the Arabic and Greek[150] papyri from Syria[151] and Egypt.[152] The term (*rōsigo*) furthermore occurs in Bactrian documents with a seemingly administrative nuance, though not in connection with the Muslim occupation.[153] Contemporarily, the archetypal Middle Persian term seems to have retained its original meaning as coeval Pahlavi documents[154] employ it in the sense of a "daily ration" and not as a denomination for an institutionalized tax.[155]

In Arabic papyri from 8th-century Egypt:

Chrest.Khoury I 91 (= *P.Heid.Arab.* I 3) (Ishqawh; 709), 14 and 39; *P.AbbottUbaidAllah* (Egypt; 724), 4; *P.DietrichTopkapi* 1 (= *P.BeckerNPAF* 12), 8 (*P.BeckerNPAF* 12, 4) (Ishqawh; 709); *P.David-WeillLouvre* 26 (Egypt; viii), r 7 and 8; *P.Gascou* 27b (al-Ushmūnayn; 695), 6; *P.GascouQurra* (= *Chrest.Khoury* I 92 = *P.RagibQurra* 1) (Ishqawh; 709), r 9 and v 2; *P.Heid.Arab.* I 13 (Ishqawh; 709–714), 7; *P.JoySorrow* 43 (Egypt; viii), 12; *P.KarabacekBemerkungenMerx* (= *P.MerxDocuments* p. 55) (Fayyūm; 685–705), 6; *P.Khalili* I 15 (Egypt; viii), r 6; *P.Lond.* 1375 (Ishqawh; 711), 1 (right).

---

146 For the issue of the original pronunciation of the term *rizq*, see Kaplony 2015, 10.

147 Ciancaglini 2008, 255; Sokoloff 2002, 1063 and *id.* 2009, 1445.

148 Rückert 1856, 279; de Lagarde 1866, 81 (210); Nöldeke 1876, 768–769; Siddiqi 1919, 56; Jeffery 1938, 142–143; Hebbo 1984, 140–141; Asbaghi 1988, 135; Kaplony 2015, 10; and Cheung 2017, 326. The lemma is surprisingly overlooked by Fraenkel in both cited oeuvres.

149 About 120 attestations, see e.g. in Q 2:20, 7:32 and 20:131.

150 For the occurrence and connotation of *rhouzikon* (= arab. *rizq*) in early Islamic Greek papyri, see Mayerson 1994 and *id.* 1995.

151 *P.Ness.* 60, 5 (Nessana; 674); *P.Ness.* 61 r, 6 (Nessana; 675); *P.Ness.* 62, 6 (Nessana; 674); *P. Ness.* 69 (Nessana; 680/681); *P.Ness.* 93 (Nessana; late VII), 2, 3, 6, 13, 14, 17, 24, 36, and 38.

152 35 attestations in 19 documents (including Greek materials). The earliest (surely) dated attestation is *P.Gascou* 27b (al-Ushmūnayn; 695), 6.

153 Cf. *BD* I al (Rōb; 459–484?), 6 concerning a monthly allowance for the "Hephthalites and the Persians". For the date of the document, see De Blois/Sims-Williams 2018, 66–67.

154 See e.g. Gignoux 2003, no. 4 (Qom; 680), 3.

155 For the connotations of *rūzig* in 6th and 7th-century Pahlavi documents, see Weber 2008a, xxix–xxxi.

In Greek papyri from 8th-century Egypt:

P.Apoll. 49 (Edfū; related to 675/676 or 660/661), 5; *P.Apoll.* 94 (Edfū, second half of VII), 6; *P.Apoll.* 95 (Edfū, second half of VII), B 2; *P.Lond* IV 1335 (Ishqawh; 709), 5; *P.Lond* IV 1404 (Ishqawh; 709–714), 7; *P.Lond* IV 1407 (Ishqawh; 709), 2; *P.Lond* IV 1434 (Ishqawh; 716), 165; *P.Lond* IV 1435 (Ishqawh; 716), 122.

In Arabic Papyri from 7th-century Syria:

P.Ness. 60 (Nessana; 674), 5; *P.Ness.* 61 r (Nessana; 675), 6; *P.Ness.* 62 (Nessana; 674), 6.

In Greek papyri from 7th century Syria:

P.Ness. 69 (Nessana; 680/681), 1; *P.Ness.* 93 (Nessana; late VII), 2, 3, 6, 13, 14, 17, 24, 36, and 38.

b) Institutions and Officials

barīd "post", "messenger", "post station", and a distance measure (= 24 km)[156] possibly from < gr. *beredos*/lat. *veredus* "postal horse". There is, however, no consensus regarding the origin of the term. Among the other proposed etymologies the most accredited are those which would derive the term from Middle Persian *buride-ye dum* "dock tailed" and from Akkadian *puridu* "courier" and *beru* respectively.[157] Whatever the case, *barīd* seems a quite ancient loan and appears not to have been borrowed through Aramaic.[158] Literary evidence hints at the Arabs' knowledge of the *barīd* in pre-Islamic time[159] and the term *brdn* "courier"[160] is attested in a late Sabaic monumental inscription of king Abraha inscription dated 548.[161]

In Arabic papyri from 8th-century Egypt:

P.Cair.Arab. 153 (= *P.BeckerNPAF* 6) (Ishqawh; 710), 7 (*P.BeckerNPAF* 6, 6); *P.Christ.Musl.* 5 (Fayyūm; 717–720), r 5; *P.DiemRemarkableDocuments* 2 (al-Ushmūnayn; 751), r 2 and 4 and v 1; *P.Ryl.Arab.* II 6 (*P.RagibLettresdeService* 1 = *P.Ryl.Arab.* I IV 3 = *P.MargolliouthSelectPapyri* 1) (al-Ushmūnayn; 745), r 2 and 4 and v 1; *P.RagibLettresdeService* 2 (= *P.Ryl.Arab.* I IV 2 = *P.MargolliouthSelectPapyri* 2) (al-Ushmūnayn; 751), r 2 and 4 and v 1; *P.RagibLettresdeService* 3 (= *P.Ryl.Arab.* I IV 1 (al-Ushmūnayn; 751), r 2 and 5 and v 1; *P.RagibLettresdeService* 4 (= *P.Ryl.Arab.* I IV 4 = *P.MargolliouthSelectPapyri* 3) (al-Ushmūnayn; 751), r 2 and 5 and v 1 (*P.Ryl.Arab.*

156 Hinz 1970, 55.
157 For a survey of the debate and of the different possible etymologies, see Ullmann 1997, 5–14 and Silverstein 2001, 92–94.
158 Cf. Fraenkel 1886, 283.
159 Silverstein 2007, 47–48.
160 Beeston 1994, 43 [39], who interprets *brdn* as a loanword from Persian *bardhūn*.
161 *CIH* 541 (Ma'rib), 48.

I IV 4 and *P.MargolioutbSelectPapyri* 3, r 1 and 4); *P.Ryl.Arab.* II 7 (= *P.RagibLettresdeService* 5 = *P.Ryl.Arab.* I IV 5) (al-Ushmūnayn; 759), r [2] and [4] and v 1 P.

In Greek papyri from 8th-century Egypt:

CPR XIV 33 (al-Ushmūnayn; vii), 2 (*bered*); *P.Apoll.* 27 (Edfū; 667/668 or 682/683), 1–2 (*bereda*); *P.Apoll.* 33 (Edfū; second half of vii), 13 (*beredos*); *P.Apoll.* 64 (Edfū; second half of vii), r 2 (*beredos*); *P.Lond.* IV 1336, 15 (*ber*); *P.Lond.* IV 1351, 15 (*ber*^{d}); *P.Lond.* IV 1353, 29 (*ber*^{d}); *P.Lond.* IV 1356, 41 (*ber*^{d}); *P.Lond.* IV 1362, 24 (*ber*^{d}); *P.Lond.* IV 1368, 12 (*ber*^{d}); *P.Lond.* IV 1370, 19 (*ber*^{d}) (all from Ishqawh; 710); *P.Lond.* IV 1380 , 33 (*ber*^{d}) (Ishqawh; 711); *P.Lond.* IV 1383 (Ishqawh; 708–710), v 16 (*berid*); *P.Lond.* IV 1401 (Ishqawh; 709–714), 15 ([*b*]*er*^{d}); *P.Lond.* IV 1403(Ishqawh; 709–714), 7 ([*b*]*er*^{d}); *P.Lond.* IV 1416 (Ishqawh; 732/733), F 51 (*ber*[^{d}]); *P.Lond.* IV 1419 (Ishqawh; 716/717), 1358 ([*b*]*er*^{d}); *P.Lond.* IV 1433 (Ishqawh; 707), Fol. 1 45 (*ber*^{d}), Fol. 4a 122 (*ber*^{d}), Fol. 4b 143, Fol. 6 193 (*ber*^{d}), Fol. 8n 312 (*ber*^{d}), Fol. 9b 350, and Fol. 10b 368 (*ber*^{d}); *P.Lond.* IV 1434 (Ishqawh; 716), Fol. 4a 17 (*ber*^{d}) and 25 (*ber*^{d}), Fol. 5 44 (*berē*^{d}), Fol. 10 2, 254 (*beri*^{d}), and Fr. 2, r 328 (*beri*^{d}); *P.Lond.* IV 1440 (Ishqawh; 709), 4 (*beri*^{d}); *P.Lond.* IV 1441 (Ishqawh; 706), Fol. 8 80 (*ber*^{d}) and 84 (*ber*^{d}) and Fol. 8b 89 (*beri*^{d}); *P.Lond.* IV 1443 (Ishqawh; early viii), v Col. 1 35 (*ber*^{d}) and Col. 2 48 (*ber*[^{d}]) and 56 (*ber*^{d}); *P.Lond.* IV 1463 (Ishqawh; early viii), v 1 ([*b*]*er*[^{d}]); *P.Lond.* IV 1464 (Ishqawh; early 709–714), v 3 (*ber*^{d}); *P.Ross.Georg.* IV 13 (Ishqawh; 709/710), v 2 (*ber*^{d}); *P.Ross.Georg.* IV 15 (Ishqawh; 710), Fr. I v 1 (*bered*); *P.Ross. Georg.* IV 27; *SB* XX 15100 (Ishqawh; 710), v 15 (*ber*^{d}).

The attestations of *barīd* cognates in the Greek documents from Egypt further merit some attention. Unlike their Arabic counterparts, the lemma in these latter occurs exclusively in the meaning of "letter carrier". The term is rendered in a number of different spellings, which include *bered, berēd, berid, bereda*[162] and the abbreviated form *ber*^{d}.[163] Implicitly accepting the Latin/Greek derivation of the term, editions of Greek papyri invariably render the lemma as an abbreviation of *bered(arios)*. Neither *beredos* nor *beredarios* are attested in Greek papyri before the Islamic conquest.[164] The insecurity of the Greek scribes with regard to the orthography of the term, combined with the fact that there is not a single instance in which the word *beredarios* is written *in pleno*, suggests that the form *bered* (and its variations) may just be a transliteration of the Arabic *barīd* rather than a Greek abbreviation for *beredarios*.[165] The fact that all the letter carriers identified as *bered(arios?)* in early Islamic Greek papyri all carry Arab names further hints at the predominantly Arab dimension of the *barīd* in this time.[166]

162 For the issue of the original pronunciation of the Arabic term, see Kaplony 2015, 19.

163 See e.g. *P.Lond.* IV 1434, 17 (*ber*^{d}), 26, 44 (*berē*^{d}), 256 (*beri*^{d}) (Ishqawh; 716).

164 Cf. Silverstein 2007, 29–30. The form *oueredarios* is attested in *P.Oxy.* LIV 3758 (dated to 325), 120; I thank Jelle Bruning for the reference.

165 Cf. Chrystides 1999, 55.

166 Cf. Fantoni 1989, 74. For the early Islamic istitution of the *barīd*, see in particular Ullmann 1997; Silverstein 2007, *id.* 2012; and Bruning 2018b.

In Arabic parchments from 8th-century Khurāsān:

P.Kratchkovski (Mount Mugh; 717–719), 13; *P.Khurasan* 6 (Rōb; 766), 7, 8, 12, and 13.

In Sogdian parchments from 8th-century Khurāsān:

Mugh Б-15 (Mount Mugh; before 722), 10?.[167]

In Bactrian parchments from 8th-century Khurāsān:

BD I W (Rōb; 747), 7, 8, 6′, and 7′.[168]

In Arabic Epigraphies from 8th-century Ḥijāz:

al-Rāshid 1992 p. 138 (al-Rabada; late VIII), 3; *DZ* II p. 430 (Darb Zubayda; 775–785).

kitāb, "(piece of) writing" (epigraphies included)[169] "letter", "writ" is possibly not built from the root *k-t-b* but directly borrowed from aram. *kṯāḇā*.[170] The original Arabic meaning of the root ***k-t-b*** "to write" is "to bind together"[171] while the additional semantic aspect of "writing" is derived from the Aramaic cultural milieu.[172] Both *kitāb* and the verbal root *k-t-b* occur several times in the Qur'an.[173] The impression of an early loan is finally corroborated by an attestation of the verbal root in a Sabaic[174] and a Dadanitic[175] inscription respectively.[176]

In Arabic papyri from 7th- and 8th-century Egypt:

Chrest.Khoury I 66 (= *P.GrohmannBeziehung* p. 338) (Fayyūm; 795/796), 4; *Chrest.Khoury* I 90 (= *P.World* p. 124 = *P.Heid.Arab.* I 1), 11; *Chrest.Khoury* I 91 (= *P.Heid.Arab.* I 3), 84 (Ishqawh; 710); *Chrest.Khoury* I 93 (= *P.Heid.Arab.* I 5), 2; *Chrest.Khoury* I 94 (= *P.Heid.Arab.* I 6), 3 (both from Ishqawh; 709/710); *CPR* III 1, 2 p. 107 (Egypt; 749), 2; *CPR* XVI 4 (Egypt; VII/VIII), r 4; *CPR*

---

167 Lurje 2008, 44–45 (19).

168 De Blois/Sims-Williams 2018, 131.

169 E.g., *CG* I 1 (= *RCEA* I 6) (Aswān?; 652). Cf. the use of *sfr* (< aram. *ṣifrā*) in Safaitic inscriptions, al-Jallad 2015a, 340 *s.v.* *S¹FR*.

170 Fraenkel 1886, 249; Jeffery 1938, 248–249; Hebbo 1984, 311; Brünnow/Fischer 2008, 93.

171 Lane 1863–1893, 2590 a.

172 Fraenkel 1886, 249; Jeffery 1938, 248–249; Hebbo 1984, 311.

173 *Kitāb* attested some 261 times in the Qur'an e.g. in Q 2:2. As a verb, *k-t-b* occurs 51 times e.g. in Q 2:79.

174 Most interestingly the verb occurs in a scribal-clause almost identical to those discussed above: 1 *w-**kt(b)** ḏn m-2-s³ndn ʾlzʾd* "and ʾlzʾd wrote this inscription" (Robin/Gajda 1994, 129).

175 JSLih 279 (al-ʿUlà; date unknown).

176 For a survey of Aramaic loanwords pertaining to the ambit of writing in pre-Islamic literature, see Maraqten 1998, *passim*.

XVI 7 (Egypt; VII/VIII), 4; *CPR* XVI 18 (Egypt; VII/VIII), r 6; *CPR* XVI 27 (Egypt; VII/VIII), 3, 7, 9, and 10; CPR XVI 33 (Egypt; VII), 8; *CPR* XXI 2b (= *P.GrohmannApercu* p. 50 = *P.World* p. 116) (Fayyūm; 792), 2; *CPR* XXI 4b (= *P.GrohmannBeziehung* p. 339 = *Chrest.Khoury* II 26) (Madīnat al-Fayyūm; 796), 2; *CPR* XXI 5 (= *P.Ryl.Arab.* II 4 = *P.Ryl.Arab.* I IX 6 = *P.MargoliouthSelectPapyri* p. 413–414) (al-Ushmūnayn; 798/799), 2; *P.BeckerPAF* 1 (Ishqawh; 709/710), 8; *P.BeckerPAF* 2 (Ishqawh; 710), 8; *P.BeckerPAF* 4 (Ishqawh; 709/710), 9; *P.BeckerPAF* 5 (Ishqawh; 710), 4; *P.BeckerPAF* 11 (Ishqawh; 709–714), 2; *P.Berl.Arab.* I 2 (Fayyūm; 760/761), 4; *P.Berl. Arab.* I 3 (Fusṭāṭ; late VIII), 7; *P.Berl.Arab.* II 23 (Egypt; VII), r 7 (x2), and 10; *P.Berl.Arab.* II 24 (Egypt; VII/VIII), 10, and 11; *P.Berl.Arab.* II 25 (Egypt; VIII), r 5 and 6; *P.Berl.Arab.* II 26 (Egypt; VIII), r 10; *P.Berl.Arab.* II 49 (Egypt; VIII), r 5 and 8; *P.Berl.Arab.* II 50 (Egypt; VIII), 2, 4, and 6; *P.Berl.Arab.* II 72 (Egypt; VIII), 7 and 10 (x2); *P.Berl.Arab.* II 75 (= *P.Loth* 2) (Egypt; VIII), r 11 (x2) and 16; *P.Cair.Arab.* 146 (= *P.BeckerNPAF* 1) (Ishqawh; 710), 31; *P.Cair.Arab.* 148 (= *P.World* p. 126 = *P.BeckerNPAF* 2) (Ishqawh; 708–710), 11 (*P.World* p. 126 and *P.BeckerNPAF* 2, 7); *P.Cair.Arab.* 149 (= *P.BeckerNPAF* 3) (Ishqawh; 714), 8, 15, and 20; *P.Cair.Arab.* 150 (= *P.BeckerPAF* 12) (Ishqawh; 709), 12, 18, and 20; *P.Cair.Arab.* 151 (= *P.BeckerNPAF* 5 = *P.BeckerPAF* 14 = *P.Heid.Arab.* I 12) (Ishqawh; 710), r 12 and v b; *P.Cair.Arab.* 153 (= *P.BeckerNPAF* 6 = *P.BeckerPAF* 13) (Ishqawh; 710), 11 (= *P.BeckerNPAF* 6 = *P.BeckerPAF* 13, 8); *P.Cair.Arab.* 154 (= *P.World* p. 129 = *P.BeckerNPAF* 8) (Ishqawh; 709/710), 13 (*P.World* p. 129 = *P.BeckerNPAF* 8, 11); *P.Cair.Arab.* 155 (= *P.BeckerNPAF* 9) (Ishqawh; 709/710), 11 (*P.BeckerNPAF* 9, 9); *P.Cair.Arab.* 156 (= *P.BeckerNPAF* 11), 4; *P.Cair.Arab.* 157, 4 (both from Ishqawh; 709); *P.Cair. Arab.* 159, 4 and 15; *P.Cair.Arab.* 160 (= *P.BeckerNPAF* 13), 3 (*P.BeckerNPAF* 13, 2); *P.Cair. Arab.* 161 (= *P.BeckerNPAF* 14), 3 (*P.BeckerNPAF* 14, 2); *P.Cair.Arab.* 162 (= *P.BeckerNPAF* 15), 3 (*P.BeckerNPAF* 15, 2); *P.Cair.Arab.* 163 (= *P.BeckerNPAF* 16), 3 (*P.BeckerNPAF* 16, 2) (all from Ishqawh; 709/710); *P.Cair.Arab.* 167 (= *P.GuestPapyrus*) (Akhmīm; 757/758), 99; *P.Cair. Arab.* 169 (al-Ushmūnayn; 752), 2; *P.Cair.Arab.* 174 (al-Ushmūnayn; 722), 2; *P.Cair.Arab.* 175 (= *P.GrohmannApercu* p. 55 = *P.BeckerPAF* 17) (Ishqawh; 731), 2; *P.Cair.Arab.* 180 (al-Ushmūnayn; 731/732), 2; *P.Cair.Arab.* 260 (Egypt; VIII), 1; *P.Clackson* 45 (Bāwiṭ; 753); *P.DiemAphrodito* p. 261–264 (= *P.World* p. 130) (Ishqawh; 709/710), 2; *P.DiemCair.Arab.* V 317 (= *P.Cair. Arab.* 317) (Egypt; VIII), 1; *P.DiemDienstschreiben* b (Fusṭāṭ; 720), 13; *P.DiemFruehеUrkunden* 4 (Fayyūm; 793), 2; *P.DiemFruehеUrkunden* 5 (Fayyūm; 776–778), r 1; *P.DiemFrueheUrkunden* 6 (= *P.GrohmannProbleme* 17) (Egypt; 796), 2; *P.DiemFrueheUrkunden* 7 (Egypt; 784), 2; *P.DiemFrueheUrkunden* 8 (Egypt; 734), 2; *P.DiemFrueheUrkunden* 9 (Egypt; 730/731), 9; *P.DiemGouverneur* (= *P.Ryl.Arab.* I XV 59) (al-Ushmūnayn; 684–695), 3; *P.GascouQurra* (= *Chrest.Khoury* I 92 = *P.RagibQurra* 1) (Ishqawh; 709), 11; *P.HanafiTwoPaperDocuments* 3 (Egypt; 762/763), 2; *P.HanafiWill* (Egypt; 721), 6; *P.Heid.Arab.* I a (= *SB* I 5644), 3; *P.Heid.Arab.* I b (= *SB* I 5645), 3; *P.Heid.Arab.* I c (= *SB* I 5646), 3; *P.Heid.Arab.* I d (= *SB* I 5647), 3; *P.Heid.Arab.* I f (= *SB* I 5649), 3; *P.Heid.Arab.* I g (= *SB* I 5650), 3; *P.Heid.Arab.* I h (= *SB* I 5651), 3; *P.Heid. Arab.* I i (= *SB* I 5652), 3; *P.Heid.Arab.* I l (= *SB* I 5654), 3; *P.Heid.Arab.* I 2, 36; *P.Heid.Arab.* I 4 (all from Ishqawh; 709/710), 3 and 15; *P.Heid.Arab.* I 13, 2; *P.Heid.Arab.* I 18, 3 (both from Ishqawh; 709–714); *P.Heid.Arab.* II 1 v (Egypt; VII/VIII), 3; *P.Heid.Arab.* II 24, 15; *P.Heid.Arab.* II 25, 12; *P.Heid.Arab.* II 42, 3 (all from Egypt; VIII); *P.Horak* 85 (Egypt; VIII), r 5 and 6; *P.Jahn* 5 (Egypt; late VIII), r 7; *P.JoySorrow* 3, 5; *P.JoySorrow* 4, 4 and 9; *P.JoySorrow* 5, 8 and 11; *P.JoySorrow* 9, 4 (all from Egypt; VIII); *P.JoySorrow* 10, 5; *P.JoySorrow* 11, 8 (both from Alexandria; VIII); *P.JoySorrow* 12, 5; *P.JoySorrow* 13 (both from Egypt; VIII), 7 and 12; *P.JoySorrow* 14 (Fusṭāṭ; VIII), 7 and 13; *P.JoySorrow* 15 (Egypt; VIII), 8; *P.JoySorrow* 23 (Fusṭāṭ; VIII), 6, 10, 31, and 32; *P.JoySorrow* 24, 7, 15, and 17; *P.JoySorrow* 25, 7 and 9(x2); *P.JoySorrow* 26, 8 and 9;

P.JoySorrow 27, 5, 7, and 9(x2); *P.JoySorrow* 28, 6; *P.JoySorrow* 30, 8; *P.JoySorrow* 31, 5; *P.JoySorrow* 34, 3; *P.JoySorrow* 35, 4; *P.JoySorrow* 36, 5 (all from Egypt; VIII); *P.JoySorrow* 39 (Alexandria; VIII), 5 and 8; *P.JoySorrow* 41 (Fusṭāṭ; VIII), 9; *P.JoySorrow* 43 (Egypt; VIII), 9, 15, and 18; *P.Khalili* I 2 (Dalāṣ; late VIII); *P.Khalili* I 14, 6; *P.Khalili* I 15, v 5; *P.Khalili* I 24, r 3 and 7 (all from Egypt; VIII); *P.KhanLegalPapyrus* (Egypt; 796), 7; *P.MuslimState* 5, 10; *P.MuslimState* 6, 5 and 9; *P.MuslimState* 8, 23; *P.MuslimState* 12, 11; *P.MuslimState* 14, 11; *P.MuslimState* 15, 7, 11, and 12; *P.MuslimState* 17, 5; *P.MuslimState* 18, 11, and 16; *P.MuslimState* 19, 5; *P.MuslimState* 23, 27; *P.MuslimState* 24, 5; *P.MuslimState* 26, 9, and 12; *P.MuslimState* 29, 11; *P.MuslimState* 31, 9; *P.MuslimState* 32, 10; *P.MuslimState* 33, 11; *P.MuslimState* 34, 7; *P.MuslimState* 35, 4; *P.MuslimState* 38, 6, 8, 11, 12, and 23 (all from the Fayyūm; 730–743); *P.PalauRib.Arab.* 2 (Fayyūm; 789/790), 1; *P.PiletteSauf-Conduit* (Saqqāra; 729), 2; *P.Qurra* 3 (Ishqawh; 709/710), r 10; *P.Qurra* 4 (Ishqawh; 709), 13; *P.Qurra* 5 (Ishqawh; 708–710), 13, 14, 15, 25, and 32; *P.RagibLettres* 2a (= *P.RogersNotice* p. 15 bottom) (Fayūm; VIII), r 8; *P.RagibLettres* 4 (Egypt; VIII), 7 and 8; *P.RagibLettres* 9a (Egypt; VIII), r 7; *P.RagibLettres* 11 (Egypt; VIII), r 11; *P.RagibPlusAncienneLettre* (al-Bahnasā; VII), 2; *P.RagibLettreFamiliale* (Egypt; 721), 15; *P.RagibQurra* 3 (Ishqawh; 710), 6; *P.RagibSauf-conduits* 1 (Saqqāra; 719), 1; *P.RagibSauf-conduits* 3 (Armant; 734), 2; *P.RagibSauf-conduits* 5 (= *P.SilvestrePalaeography* p. 84) (Saqqāra; 750), 2; *P.RagibSauf-conduits* 6 (Saqqāra; 751), 2; *P.RagibSauf-conduits* 7 (= *P.SilvestredeSacyPapyrus* A) (Saqqāra; 751), 2; *P.RagibSauf-conduits* 8 (= *P.SilvestredeSacyPapyrus* B) (Saqqāra; 751), 2; *P.ShahinScheltbrief* (Egypt; late VIII), r 4 and 7; *P.ShahinSchreibubung* 1b (Egypt; VIII), 7; *P.SijpesteijnTravel* (Fayyūm; 735), 16; *P.VanthieghemCorrespondance* II (= *P.BeckerPAF* 3) (Ishqawh; 709), 3; *P.VanthieghemRecu* (Fayyūm; 787/788), 2; *P.World* p. 132 (Egypt; 793), 2 and 12; *P.YounesCondolence* 3 (Fayyūm; VIII), 8; *P.YounesGovernors* 1 (= *P.World* p. 171 = *P.Ryl.Arab.* I I 5) (Fusṭāṭ; 797), 7, 15, and 18 (*P.World* p. 171 = *P.Ryl.Arab.* I I 5, 5, 14, and 17); *P.YounesGovernors* 2 (Fayyūm; 798), 2.

In Arabic epigraphies from 7th-century Egypt:

CG I 1 (= *RCEA* I 6) (Aswān?; 652), 4 and 6.

In Arabic epigraphies from 8th-century Ḥijāz:

Ghabban 2011 p. 500, no. 1, 7; *NI* p. 73, no. 6, 6 (both from al-Wujayriyya; 709/710); *NI* p. 107, no. 33 (Wādī al-Burayka; VIII), 1); *NI* p.156, no. 79 (Qāʿal-Muʿtadil; VIII), 3; *RCEA* I 38* (Medina; 752/753) (x2).

In Arabic papyri from 7th- and 8th-century Syria:

P.DiemStelle (= *P.KisterLetter* = *P.Mird* 47) (Khirbat al-Mird; VII), 5; *P.HoylandDhimma* 1 (Nessana; 680–690), 13; *P.Mird* 10 (Khirbat al-Mird; VIII), 2; *P.Mird* 23 (Khirbat al-Mird; VIII), 8 and 14; *P.Mird* 25 (Khirbat al-Mird; VII/VIII), 4, 5, and 10; *P.Mird* 43 (Khirbat al-Mird; 744/745), v 3; *P.Mird* 44 (Khirbat al-Mird; VIII), 2; *P.Mird* 53 (Khirbat al-Mird; VII/VIII), 3; *P.Mird* 55 (Khirbat al-Mird; VIII), 1; *P.Mird* 68 (Khirbat al-Mird; VII/VIII), 4.

In Arabic epigraphies from 8th-century Syria:

CIAP VI 59 (Khirbat al-Mafjar; 724–743), 5; *CIAP* VI 69 (Khirbat al-Mafjar; 724–743), 6; *EIA* no. 67 (Wādī Salma; 758/759), 4; *EIA* no. 82 (Wādī Salma; 767/768), 9; *PoI* 1.22 (Negev Desert; VII/VIII), 3; Jumʿa/al-Maʿānī 1999 p. 247–248 (Karak; VIII), 13.

In Arabic parchments from 8th-century Khurāsān:

P.Khurasan 1 (Rōb; 764), 2; *P.Khurasan* 2 (Rōb; 765), 2; *P.Khurasan* 3; *P.Khurasan* 5 (Rōb; 766), 2; *P.Khurasan* 6 (Rōb; 766), 2; *P.Khurasan* 7, 2; *P.Khurasan* 8, 2 (both from Rōb; 767); *P.Khurasan* 9 (Rōb; 769), 2; *P.Khurasan* 10 (Rōb; 769), 2; *P.Khurasan* 12 (Rōb; 768), 2; *P.Khurasan* 13 (Rōb; 769), 2; *P.Khurasan* 14 (Rōb; 769), 2; *P.Khurasan* 24 (Rōb; 771), 2; *P.Khurasan* 25 (Rōb; 762), 2; *P.Khurasan* 26 (Rōb; 765), 2; *P.Khurasan* 27 (Rōb; 766), 2; *P.Khurasan* 30 (Rōb; 777), 2.

In Arabic epigraphies from 7th-century Iraq:

Al-Ṣandūq 1955 p. 213 (Ḥafnat al-Abyaḍ; 683/684), 11.

māzūt, a village headman[177] < gr. *meizoteros/meizōn*.[178]

In Arabic papyri from 8th-century Egypt:

P.BeckerPAF 9 (= *P.Heid.Arab.* I 8) (Ishqawh; 709), 3; *P.BeckerPAF* 2 (Ishqawh; 710), 6, 12; *P.Cair.Arab.* 149 (= *P.BeckerNPAF* 3) (Ishqawh; 709–710), 28; P.*Cair.Arab.* 158 (Ishqawh; 710), 7; *P.David-WeillLouvre* 16 (Egypt; 773), 9; *P.MuslimState* 31 (Fayyūm; 730–743), 5; *P.Qurra* 5 (Ishqawh; 708–710), 21?.[179]

c) Infrastructure

masjid, "mosque" < aram. *masgḏā* "place of worship". The Aramaic term is documented in papyri and inscriptions centuries before the Arab conquest.[180] The use of *masjid* in Arabic had in all probability crystallized before the Islamic era as the numerous occurrences in the Qur'an suggest.[181]

177 For the office of the *māzūt*, see Grohmann 1964, 129–131; Frantz-Murphy 2001, 118; Sijpestein 2013, 144. Cf. F. Preisigke 1925–1931, III, 133.

178 Grohmann 1932, 280–281; Richter 2010, 209. For an extensive study of the office of the *meizōn/-oteros* and its evolution from the 4th to the 7th century, see Berkes 2017a, 53–82. To the best of the author's knowledge, the only attestation of the term outside Egypt in the early Islamic empire is Muʿāwiya's Greek inscription of Hammat Gader (Israel). There, the term possibly appears in abbreviated form; see di Segni 1997, 239–240.

179 For doubts concerning this reading, see Diem's 1984, 261 remarks.

180 Nöldeke 1908 *s.v.* "Arabs (ancient)", 666–667; Jeffery 1938, 163 and 263–264. Cf., however, Sima 2004, 23 who rightly points out, that *masgḏā* is only attested once in *P.Cowley* 44, 3 (Aswān; 412 BCE?) and that the term *msgd* in Nabatean may well reflect Arabian rather than Aramean influences. He therefore considers *masjid* originally Arabic and, consequently, interprets the late Sabaic *ms¹gd* as a loanword from Arabic rather than from Aramaic.

181 Attested 28 times e.g. in Q 2:114, 144, 149, etc.

In Greek papyri from 8th-century Egypt (*masgida*):

CPR XXII 43 (Egypt; 715/716 or 716/717), 1; *CPR* XXII 53 (Ishqawh; 714–716), 9; *P.Lond* IV 1341 (Ishqawh; 709), [5], *P.Lond* IV 1368 (Ishqawh; 710), 1, 6, and 12; *P.Lond* IV 1397 (Ishqawh; 709), 8; *P.Lond* IV 1403 (Ishqawh; 709/710), 4; *P.Lond* IV 1411 (Ishqawh; 709), 3; *P.Lond* IV 1414 (Ishqawh; early VIII), [24], 76, [118], [149], [176], 198, and 218; *P.Lond* IV 1433 (Ishqawh; 707), 40, 81, 111, 238, 272, 299, 333, 334, 367, 407, 441, 462, 524, and 557; *P.Lond* IV 1435 (Ishqawh; 716), 15 and 76; *P.Lond* IV 1439 (Ishqawh; early VIII), 4; *P.Lond* IV 1441 (Ishqawh; 706), 99; *P.Lond* IV 1451 (Ishqawh; early VIII), 75 and 152; *P.Ross.Georg.* IV 3 (= *P.Lond* IV 1334) (Ishqawh; 709), 4 and 16; *SB* X 10454 (Ishqawh; 709), 4.

In Arabic inscriptions from 8th-century Syria:

CIAP I p. 4, no. 2 (Abū Ghūsh; viii), 4; *CIAP* I p. 144, no. 1 (ʿAsqalān; 771/772), 4; *RCEA* I 18* (Damascus; 705/706), a and b; *MI* 14 (Bosra; vii/viii), 2; *WS001*, 4; *WS003*, 7 (both from Wādī Shīreh; related to 727/728).

In Arabic inscriptions from 8th-century Arabia:

EPI 14944 (Medina; 778/779); *EPI* 14993 (Mecca; related to 761/762); *EPI* 14941 (Medina; 768/769); Sauvaget 1947 p. 56 B* (= *RCEA* I 47*) (Medina; 785/786); Sauvaget 1947 p. 58 D* (= *RCEA* I 46*) (Medina; 781/782) (x2); Sauvaget 1947 p. 66* (Medina; 706/707); Sauvaget 1947 p. 58 E* (= *RCEA* I 46*) (Medina; 749/750); *MCIA* IV, 1 p. 40, no. 1* (= *RCEA* I 40*) (Mecca; 757/758) (x2); *MCIA* IV, 1 p. 44, no. 3* (= *RCEA* I 48*) (Mecca; 783/784); *MCIA* IV, 1 p. 47, no. 7 (= *RCEA* I 50) (Mecca; 783/784) (x2); *MCIA* IV, 1 p. 48, no. 8 (= *RCEA* I 52) (Mecca; 783/784); *TKN* p. 191–192 (Mecca; related to 761/762), 3, 4, and 10; *TKN* p. 194 (Mecca; related to 761/762), 3.

qaṣr, "castle", "citadel", "palace" < CPA *qsrʾ* < gr. *kastron*/lat. *castrum*.[182] Often encountered in pre-Islamic poetry[183] and in the Qur'an.[184] The loan apparently pre-dates the rise of Islam and possibly goes back to the Roman occupation of Arabia.

In Arabic papyri from 8th-century Egypt:

P.LiebrenzQuittung (Luxor; viii), 2, 16, and 17; *P.RagibSauf-conduits* 3 (Luxor; < 734), 4.

In Arabic parchments from 8th-century Khurāsān:

P.Khurasan 11 (Rōb; 771), 4; *P.Khurasan* 16 (Rōb; 772), 5; *P.Khurasan* 17 (Rōb; 772), 5; *P.Khurasan* 18 (Rōb; 772), 5; *P.Khurasan* 19 (Rōb; 774), 5; *P.Khurasan* 20 (Rōb; 774), 4; *P.Khurasan* 21 (Rōb; 775), 6; *P.Khurasan* 22 (Rōb; 774/775), 5; *P.Khurasan* 24 (Rōb; 771), 5.

---

182 Fraenkel 1880, 14; *id.* 1886, 234; Jeffery 1938, 240; Schall 1982, 147. Cf. Sokoloff 2014, 378.
183 Fraenkel 1880, 14.
184 Q 7:74, 22:45, 25:10, and 77:32.

In Arabic inscriptions from 8th-century Syria:

EPI 40352 (1) (= Mayer 1946 p. 73?) (Qaṣr al-Muwaqqar; 722/723), 1.

In Arabic inscriptions from 8th-century North Africa:

IM p. 28–29 (Monastir; 797/798), 5.

d) Coinage

Due to the plentifulness of surviving early Islamic coinage and its structural repetitiveness, to list single occurrences of the Arabic definitions for gold, silver and copper currency (namely *dīnār*, *dirham*, and *fals*) would have been a task of gigantic proportions and limited significance.[185] In addition, occurrences on coins are difficult to evaluate since the circulation of a coin (particularly precious metal-coinage) is largely independent from its minting place. I have instead opted to list all occurrences of terms referring to coinage in non-numismatic evidence. I have, however, catalogued occurrences of the lemmata under consideration in a less extensive and more territorially bound selected corpus of seals, weights and stamps.

dīnār,[186] the standard gold coin of ca. 4,25 g after ʿAbd al-Malik's reform in 696/697[187] < aram. *dīnārā* < gr. *dēnarios*/lat. *denarius*.[188] An early loan, the term occurs in the Qur'an[189] and in pre-Islamic poetry[190] and in early Islamic time is already used as a personal name.[191] Furthermore, the occurrence of

185 The type of coin is usually specified on the reverse legend, normally reading *bi-smillāh ḍuriba hādhā al-fals/dirham/dīnār bi* + mint name *fī sanat* + number "In the name of God this *fals/dirham/dīnār* was minted in nom. loc. in the year so-and-so", see *supra* Tab. 2.

186 Based on *P.RagibAn22* (= *P.DiemAphrodito* p. 272), 2 (Egypt; 642/643) where a diacritical dot is to be seen on the first hook of the word *dīnār* (*d{n}yr*), Rāġib suggested that the 7th-century pronunciation of the term was *danīr*. This is very unlikely as it is confirmed by the morphology of the term in Greek, Aramaic, and Syriac. In all probability the writing in *P.RagibAn22*, 2 is a scribal error.

187 Hinz 1970, 1–2. Cf. the metrological analysis of early Islamic *dīnār* weights from Egypt in Miles 1963, 79–82. Additionally, on the metrological conversion of early Islamic measures, see dedicated section in the *Measuring Medieval Islamic Economy* database http://www.medievalislamiceconomy.uwo.ca/money_coinage/coinage/index.html (accessed Febr. 2, 2021); for prices in early Islamic Egypt, see now Morelli 2019.

188 Fraenkel 1880, 13; *id.* 1886, 191–192; Krauss 1888–1889, II, 207–208; and Jeffery 1938, 133–134.

189 Q 3:75.

190 Fraenkel 1880, 13; *id.* 1886, 192.

191 See e.g. *AI* 60 (Z72), 1 (Tā'if; VII).

dnrt in two 5th-century Sabaic documents[192] bears witness to the early use of the term in the region. Furthermore, the lemma is found on virtually every gold *dīnār* of the "standing caliph" (692–696) and all-epigraphic series (since 696–697). All-epigraphic gold coinage was minted in Syria, al-Andalus, and Ifrīqiya in Umayyad times and in Iraq and Egypt[193] under the Abbasids. Moreover, the minting of coins continued in Spain under the Umayyad independent emirate.

In Arabic papyri from 7th- and 8th-century Egypt:

Chrest.Khoury I 19 (Madīnat al-Fayyūm; VIII), 4; *Chrest.Khoury* II 22 (Fusṭāṭ; VIII), 11; *Chrest.Khoury* I 64 (Egypt; 796), 5; *Chrest.Khoury* I 91 (= *P.Heid.Arab.* I 3), (Ishqawh; 710), 54; *Chrest.Khoury* I 93 (= *P.Heid.Arab.* I 5), 4 and 5; *Chrest.Khoury* I 94 (= *P.Heid.Arab.* I 6), 5 (both form Ishqawh; 709/710); *CPR* XVI 4 (Egypt; VII/VIII), r 1 and 12; *CPR* XXI 2a (= *P.Cair.Arab.* II p. 70 = *P.GrohmannApercu* p. 85 = *P.GrohmannProbleme* III p. 143) (Fayyūm; 792), 1; *CPR* XXI 3 (= *P.Cair.Arab.* 77) (Egypt; 794), 4 and 11; *CPR* XXI 4b (= *P.GrohmannBeziehung* p. 339 = *Chrest.Khoury* II 26) (Madīnat al-Fayyūm; 796), 6; *CPR* XXI 5 (= *P.Ryl.Arab.* II 4 = *P.Ryl.Arab.* I IX 6 = *P.MargoliouthSelectPapyri* p. 413–414) (al-Ushmūnayn; 798/799), 5 and 13; *CPR* XXVI 16 (= *P.ThungWrittenObligations* 1) (Egypt; 789), 3 and 4; *P.BeckerPAF* 1 (Ishqawh; 709/710), 5; *P.BeckerPAF* 8 (= *P.Heid. Arab.* I 7), 5 and 6(x2); *P.BeckerPAF* 9 (= *P.Heid.Arab.* I 8), 8(x2); *P.BeckerPAF* 10 (= *P.Heid.Arab.* I 9), 6 (all from Ishqawh; 709) *P.BeckerPapyrusstudien* (Anṣinā; 713/714), 6(x2); *P.BruningSunna* (Egypt; 664/665), 4; *P.Berl.Arab.* II 49 (Egypt; VIII), r 16; *P.Cair.Arab.* 149 (= *P.BeckerNPAF* 3) (Ishqawh; 714), 24; *P.Cair.Arab.* 152 (= *P.BeckerNPAF* 10) (Ishqawh; 709), 1 and 6 (x2); *P.Cair.Arab.* 154 (= *P.World* p. 129 = *P.BeckerNPAF* 8) (Ishqawh; 709/710), 9(x2) (*P.World* p. 129 and *P.BeckerNPAF* 8, 7); *P.Cair.Arab.* 155 (= *P.BeckerNPAF* 9) (Ishqawh; 709/710), 7 (*P.BeckerNPAF* 9, 5); *P.Cair.Arab.* 160 (= *P.BeckerNPAF* 13), 5 and 6(x2) (*P.BeckerNPAF* 13, 4 and 5); *P.Cair. Arab.* 161 (= *P.BeckerNPAF* 14), 6 (*P.BeckerNPAF* 14, 5); *P.Cair.Arab.* 162 (= *P.BeckerNPAF* 15), 5 and 6 (*P.BeckerNPAF* 15, 4 and 5); *P.Cair.Arab.* 163 (= *P.BeckerNPAF* 16), 6(x2) (*P.BeckerNPAF* 16, 5) (all from Ishqawh; 709/710); *P.Cair.Arab.* 180 (al-Ushmūnayn; 731/732), 6 and 8; *P.Cair.Arab.* 260 (Egypt; VIII), 1; *P.Cair.Arab.* 274 (al-Ushmūnayn; VIII), 1(x3) and 4(x3); *P.Clackson* 45 (Bāwiṭ; 753), 6; *P.David-WeillLouvre* 12–13 (Madīnat al-Fāris; VIII), 11, 12, 13, and 14 (x2); *P.David-WeillLouvre* 16 (Egypt; 773), 3, 4, 5, and 8; *P.David-WeillLouvre* 24 (Egypt; 741), r 2; *P.DiemAphrodito* p. 261–264 (= *P.World* p. 130) (Ishqawh; 709/710), 4; *P.DiemCair.Arab.* V 317 (= *P.Cair.Arab.* 317) (Egypt; VIII), 5; *P.DiemFrueheUrkunden* 3 (Fayyūm; 779), 2; *P.DiemFrueheUrkunden* 4 (Fayyūm; 793), 8; P.*DiemFrueheUrkunden* 7 (Egypt; 784), 10 and 13; *P.DiemMauleselin* (Egypt; VIII), 2 and 6; *P.DiemRemarkableDocuments* 1 (Egypt; VII), r 3, 4(x3), 5(x2), 6(x3), 6–7 (x2), 7(x2), 8, 9, 10 and v 2(x2) and 4–5; *P.DietrichTopkapi* 1 (= *P.BeckerNPAF* 12) (Ishqawh; 709), 14 (= *P.BeckerNPAF* 12, 10); *P.GrohmannProbleme* 5 (Ihnās; VIII), 6(x5); *P.GrohmannProbleme* 6 (Egypt; 735), 4(x4); *P.GrohmannSteuerpapyrus* (al-Ushmūnayn; VIII), 3; *P.HanafiBusinessLetter* (Egypt; VIII), 4; *P.HanafiCairoCopenhagen*

---

192 X.BSB 62, 2 (unknown provenance; 480;); X.BSB 145, 2, 3 and 5 (unknown provenance; V). See Stein 2010b, 318–319.

193 Starting with ʿAlī b. Sulaymān's governorate (in office 786–787).

1 (Egypt; VIII), 4 and 9; *P.HanafiTwoPaperDocuments* 3 (Egypt; 762/763), 6; *P.Heid.Arab.* I a (= *SB* I 5644), 5 and 6; *P.Heid.Arab.* I b (= *SB* I 5645), 5 and 6 (x2); *P.Heid.Arab.* I c (= *SB* I 5646), 5 and 6; *P.Heid.Arab.* I d (= *SB* I 5647), 6(x2); *P.Heid.Arab.* I e (= *SB* I 5648), 1 and 2; *P.Heid.Arab.* I f (= *SB* I 5649), 4(x2); *P.Heid.Arab.* I g (= *SB* I 5650), 5; *P.Heid.Arab.* I h (= *SB* I 5651), 5 and 6; *P.Heid.Arab.* I i (= *SB* I 5652), 6(x2); *P.Heid.Arab.* I k (= *SB* I 5653), 2(x2); *P.Heid.Arab.* I l (= *SB* I 5654), 5 and 6(x2) (all from Ishqawh; 709/710); *P.Heid.Arab.* I 10 (Ishqawh; 710), 6; *P.Heid. Arab.* I 11 (Ishqawh; 709/710), 2; *P.Heid.Arab.* II 5, v 4; *P.Heid.Arab.* II 24, 14 (both from Egypt; VIII); *P.HindsNubia* (Qaṣr Ibrīm; 758), 50 and 61; *P.JoySorrow* 4, 11; *P.JoySorrow* 31, 24 and 28; *P.JoySorrow* 34, 4 and 6; *P.JoySorrow* 35, 8; *P.JoySorrow* 37, 6 (all from Egypt; VIII); *P.Khalili* I 1 (al-Bahnasā; early VIII), 3, 6, 9, 17, and 20; *P.Khalili* I 9b (Egypt; 723), 7; *P.Khalili* I 14 (Egypt; VIII), 12; *P.KhanLegalDocument* (Egypt; 707), 3; *P.KhanLegalPapyrus* (Egypt; 796), 5(x2); *P.LiebrenzQuittung* (al-Uqṣur; VIII), 2 and 7; *P.Mil.Vogl.* I 8a-b (Egypt; 731–734), a v 1, 2, and 3 and b r 2 and v 1, 2, and 3; *P.MuslimState* 8, 22; *P.MuslimState* 20, 8 and 13; *P.MuslimState* 23, 33 (x2), 34 (x2), 35(x2), 36, 37, 38, and 39 (x3); *P.MuslimState* 24, 4; *P.MuslimState* 26, 5, and 8; *P.MuslimState* 27, 7, and 10; *P.MuslimState* 28, 12; *P.MuslimState* 29, 12, 14, 16, and 17 (x2); *P.MuslimState* 30, 6 (all from the Fayyūm; 730–743); *P.Philad.Arab.* 7 (Egypt; 794), 4; *P.Prag.Arab. Beilage* VII (Egypt; VIII), 9; *P. Qurra* 3 (Ishqawh; 710), r 8; *P. Qurra* 5 (Ishqawh; 708–710), 16 and 30; *P.RagibAn22* (= *P.DiemAphrodito* p. 272) (Egypt; 642/643), 2(x2); *P.RagibJuridiction* 1 (Egypt; 662/663), 10; *P.RagibLettres* 8 (Saqqāra; 757), r 15; *P.RagibPlusAncienneLettre* (al-Bahnasā; VII), 2, 5, and 8; *P.RagibQurra* 2 (Fayyūm; 709/710), r 14 and 16; *P.ReinfandtLeinenhaendler* (Ihnās; VIII), r 21 and v 10; *P.Ryl.Arab.* I XV 14 b (Egypt; 795/796), 2; *P.Ryl. Arab.* I XV 56 a (Egypt; VIII), 1; *P.Ryl.Arab.* II 9 (Egypt; 703/704), r 1 and 4; *P.SijpesteijnTravel* (Fayyūm; 734), 5; *P.StoetzerSteuerquittung* (al-Ushmūnayn; 709), 12; *P.StoetzerSteuerquittungen* 2 (Ihnās; 707), 14; *P.TillierDebts* 1 (= *Chrest.Khoury* I 48) (Asyūṭ; related to 640/641), 6; *P.TillierDebts* 2 (= *P.RagibJuridiction* 2) (Fusṭāṭ; 676/677), 6; *P.TillierFustat* 2 (Fusṭāṭ; 785–793), 4 and 8; *P.TillierFustat Annexe* (Fusṭāṭ; VIII), 1, 10, 13, and 14 (x2); *P.Vente* 14 (= *Chrest.Khoury* II 17) (Fayyūm; VIII), 3 and 4; *P.Vente* 15 (Egypt; 767–776), 3; *P.World* p. 160, 2, 3, 4, 5, 6, 7, 8, and 10; *P.World* p. 162, 14 (both from Egypt; VIII); *P.World* p. 186 (Egypt; 786/787), r 6, 7, and 11.

In Arabic standard weights from 8th-century Egypt:

BM 1 (717–720 or 721–722); *BM* 6d (743–749); *BM* 10 (751–753 or 755–758); *BM* 13; *BM* 14–15 (762–769); *BM* 19 (769–774); *BM* 23 (775–785); *BM* 24; *BM* 24g (both late VII); *BM* 26 (785–786); *BM* 27 (784–785 or 805–806); *BM* 57 (754–775); *CAM* 99 (751–753 or 755–758); *CAM* 120–121; *CAM* 124 (all 754–775); *CAM* 128; *CAM* 131 (both 759–760); *CAM* 140 (762–769); *CAM* 162 (769–774); *CAM* 172; *CAM* 173 (both 775–785); *CAM* 180 (779); *CAM2 BM* 16 (741–746); *CAM2 PRC* 22 (760–762); *CAM2 PRC* 27 (769–774); *CAM2 PRC* 32 (775–778); *CAM2 PRC* 35 (785–786); *EAG* I 27 (734–742); *EAG* I 39 (743–749); *EAG* I 59 (754–775); *EAG* I 70 (759–760); *EAG* I 76 (762–769); *EAG* I 90; *EAG* I 92–93 (all 775–785); *EAG* I 95–96 (775–778); *EAG* II 3 (725–734); *EAG* II 18 (749–769); *EIGS* 2 (709–714); *EIGS* 3 (714–717 or 720–721); *EIGS* 17 (717–720 or 721–722); *EIGS* 29; *EIGS* 30; *EIGS* 31; *EIGS* 32 (all 725–734); *EIGS* 67; *EIGS* 71 (both 734–742); *EIGS* 72 (737); *EIGS* 129; *EIGS* 130; *EIGS* 136; *EIGS* 138–139 (all 742–745); *EIGS* 162 (>750); *EIGS* 188 (751–753 or 755–758); *EIGS* 241–243 (762–769); *EIGS* 259 (769–774); *EIGS* 284 (774–776); *EIGS* 298; *EIGS* 299; *EIGS* 300–301; *EIGS* 302–303; *EIGS* 304; *EIGS* 305 (all 775–785); *EIGS* 327; *EIGS* 331; *EIGS* 332 (all 781–784 or 792); *EIGS* 338 (785–786); *EIGS* 340 (795); *EPV* 2 (709–714); *EPV* 11; *EPV* 12–13 (all 714–717 or 720–721); *EPV* 51 (725–734); *EPV* 87–88 (734–742); *EPV* 105 (742–745); *EPV* 114; *EPV*

115 (both 743–749); *EPV* 132–133 (739–749); *EPV* 134; *EPV* 135 (both 749–743); *EPV* 144; *EPV* 145 (both >750); *EPV* 155–157 (754–775); *EPV* 167–168 (751–753 or 751–758); *EPV* 187; *EPV* 188 (both 760); *EPV* 201–202; *EPV* 203 (both 762–769); *EPV* 207; *EPV* 209 (both 769–774); *EPV* 210–211 (775–785); *EPV* 221 (775/776); *EPV* 234; *EPV* 235; *EPV* 236 (all 791/792); *EPV* 236$_{\text{bis}}$ and $_{\text{ter}}$ (792/793); *GSW* 99 (725–734); *GSW* 134 (743–749); *GSW* 139 (749); *GSW* 145 (751–753 or 755–758); *GSW* 156 (759–760); *GSW* 161 (762–769); *GSW* 196 (785–786); *UAT* 4 (709–714); *UAT* 14; *UAT* 15 (both 714–717 or 720–721); *UAT* 67 (720–724); *UAT* 127–129; *UAT* 130 (all 742–745); *UAT* 145; *UAT* 151 (both 734–742); *UAT* 241 (743–749); *UAT* 277 (>750); *UAT* 314 (751–753 or 755–758); *UAT* 353; *UAT* 355–356 (all 754–775); *UAT* 403–404 (759–760); *UAT* 411 (760–762); *UAT* 420; *UAT* 421; *UAT* 422–423 (all 762–769); *UAT* 476–477; *UAT* 478 (all 769–773); *UAT* 565 (778 or 786–787); *UAT* 584 (786–787); *UAT* 590 (all 791–792 or 795–796); *UAT* 596; *UAT* 597 (787–804); *UAT* 609 (789–790); *UAT* 613; *UAT* 614; *UAT* 615; *UAT* 616 (all 791–792 or 795–796); *UAT* 624; *UAT* 625 (798–802).

In Arabic papyri from 7th-century Syria:

P.Ness. 56 (Nessana; 686/687), 2, and 3(x2); *P.Ness.* 64, 4(x2), 20, and 21; *P.Ness.* 65 (both from Nessana; 676), 2 and 17(x2).

dirham, the standard silver coin of 2,97 g = 7/10 of a *dīnār* after ʿAbd al-Malik's reform in 698/699[194] < MP *drahm* or syr. *draḵmā* < gr. *drachmē*. On coins, the lemma appears in all standard post-reform silver issues which in early Islamic times were minted in virtually every province of the Islamic empire in over 30 mints. Like *dīnār*, this lemma is attested both in the Qur'an[195] and pre-Islamic poems,[196] which hints at an early borrowing.[197]

In Arabic papyri from 8th-century Egypt:

Chrest.Khoury I 98 (= *P.Jahn* 12), r 6 (x2); *P.HanafiCairoCopenhagen* 1 (Egypt; VIII), 10 and 11; *P.Horak* 85 (Egypt; VIII), r 6 and 8; *P.Jahn* 9, r 6; *P.Jahn* 10, 8(x2) (both from Madīnat al-Fayyūm; late VIII); *P.Khalili* I 1 (al-Bahnasā; early VIII), 12; *P.JoySorrow* 17 (Egypt; VIII), v 5; *P.JoySorrow* 33 (Dimyāṭ; VIII), 8 and 12(x2); *P.JoySorrow* 34 (Egypt; VIII), 7; *P.Khalili* I 21 (Egypt; VIII), 3; *P.Prag.Arab. Beilage* VII (Egypt; VIII), 8(x2), 9, and 12; *P.TillierFustat Annexe* (Fusṭāṭ; VIII), 1 and 10.

194 Hinz 1970, 2 For the metrology of the (rare) early Islamic *dirham* weights from Egypt, see Miles 1963, 82–83.

195 Q 12:20.

196 Spitaler 1955, 216 and *ibid.*n10.

197 Fraenkel 1880, 13; *id.* 1886, 191; Jeffery 1938, 129–130; Spitaler 1955, 216; and Hebbo 1984, 117–118.

In Arabic standard weights from 8th-century Egypt:

BM 6 (743–749); *BM* 11 (751–753 or 755–758); *CAM* 78 (743–749); *CAM* 89 (749–750); *CAM* 101 (751–753 or 755–758); *CAM* 164 (769–774); *EIGS* 140 (743–749); *EIGS* 163–164 (>750); *EIGS* 174; *EIGS* 175–176; *EIGS* 177 (all 751–753 or 755–758); *EIGS* 244 (762–769); *EPV* 94 (734–742); *EPV* 129 (739–749); *EPV* 136; *EPV* 146 (both 749–750); *EPV* 186 (760); *GSW* 94 (> 750); *GSW* 117 (all 734–742); *GSW* 128 (742–745); *GSW* 133 (743–749); *UAT* 131 (742–745); *UAT* 243–244; *UAT* 245 (all 743–749); *UAT* 282–284 (>750); *UAT* 296–297 (750–751 or 753–755); *UAT* 322–325 (751–753 or 755–758); *UAT* 357; *UAT* 358 (both 754–775); *UAT* 388 (759–760); *UAT* 434 (762–769).

In Arabic papyri from 8th-century Syria:

P.Mird 36, 3, 4 and 5; *P.Mird* 83 v, 1 (both Khirbat al-Mird; VIII).

In Arabic ink inscriptions from 8th-century Syria:

Walmsley *et al.* 2008: 125–126 (Jerash; VIII).[198]

In Arabic parchments from 8th-century Khurāsān:

P.Khurasan 1 (Rōb; 764), 6 and 7; *P.Khurasan* 2 (Rōb; 764/765), 8; *P.Khurasan* 3 (Rōb; 765), 7(x2), 9, and 10; *P.Khurasan* 4, 8; *P.Khurasan* 5, 10; *P.Khurasan* 6, 10, 12, and 16 (all from Rōb; 766); *P.Khurasan* 7, 7; *P.Khurasan* 8, 6 (both from Rōb; 767); *P.Khurasan* 9, 9; *P.Khurasan* 10, 4 (both from Rōb; 769); *P.Khurasan* 11 (Rōb; 771), 6 and 7; *P.Khurasan* 12 (Rōb; 768), 9; *P.Khurasan* 13, 7; *P.Khurasan* 14, 4 (both from Rōb; 769); *P.Khurasan* 15 (Rōb; 771), 7; *P.Khurasan* 16, 6 and 7; *P.Khurasan* 17, 6 and 7(x2); *P.Khurasan* 18, 6 (all from Rōb; 772); *P.Khurasan* 19, 7 and 8(x2); *P.Khurasan* 20, 5, and 6 (both from Rōb; 774); *P.Khurasan* 23 (Rōb; 770), 7; *P.Khurasan* 26 (Rōb; 765), 4 and 8; *P.Khurasan* 27 (Rōb; 766), 5; *P.Khurasan* 28 (Rōb; 767), 6; *P.Khurasan* 31 (Rōb; 763), 2; *P.Khurasan* 32 (Rōb; 765), 4(x2), 5 and 6.

fals (also *fuls*)[199] < JBA, syr. *pūlsā* < gr. *follis*/ lat. *follis*.[200] In numismatics, *fals* represents the standard denomination for reformed copper coinage and is found on coins minted from Spain to Afghanistan.

---

198 It is most interesting that debts are noted in *dirhams* in an area in which the fiscal apparatus at the time operated in gold currency.

199 See *supra* p. 268.

200 Fraenkel 1886, 192. For the Late Antique Byzantine *follis*, see Maresch 1994, 44; for the *follis*' equivalence in gold, see Morelli 1996, 142 and *ibid*.n23.

In Arabic papyri from 8th-century Egypt:[201]

P.David-WeillLouvre 12–13 (Madīnat al-Fāris; VIII), 6; *P.JoySorrow* 17 (Egypt; VIII), v 5; *P.TillierFustat Annexe* (Fusṭāṭ; VIII), 1 and 10; *P.World* p. 186 (Egypt; 786/787), r 8(x2).

In Arabic standard weights from 8th-century Egypt:

BM 3 (725–734); *BM* 4 (734–742); *BM* 5 (737); *BM* 7 (734–742); *BM* 12 (759–760); *CAM* 6 (714–717 or 720–721); *CAM* 24; *CAM* 25; *CAM* 26; *CAM* 27; *CAM* 29; *CAM* 30 (all 725–734); *CAM* 48; *CAM* 49–50 (all 734–742); *CAM* 51 (737); *CAM* 52 (734–742); *CAM* 90 (749–750); *CAM* 100 (751–753 or 755–758); *CAM* 106 (751–758 or 781–786); *CAM* 151–152 (762–774); *CAM* 160 (769–774); *CAM2 BM* 3 (714–717 or 720–721); *CAM2 BM* 7; *CAM2 BM* 8 (both 725–734); *CAM2 BM* 11–12 (737); *CAM2 BM* 27 (751–753 or 755–758); *CAM2 PRC* 24 (762–774); *EAG* I 12; *EAG* I 13; *EAG* I 14 (all 725–734); *EAG* I 30 (737); *EAG* I 43; *EAG* I 44; *EAG* I 45–46 (all 734–745); *EAG* I 49 (749–750); *EAG* I 64; *EAG* I 65–66 (all 751–753 or 755–758); *EAG* I 68 (751–758 or 781–786); *EAG* I 71; *EAG* I 73; *EAG* I 74 (all 759–760); *EAG* II 8 (734–742); *EIGS* 4 (714–717 or 720–721); *EIGS* 36; *EIGS* 37–39; *EIGS* 40; *EIGS* 41; *EIGS* 42; *EIGS* 43; *EIGS* 64 (all 725–734); *EIGS* 73; *EIGS* 74–76; *EIGS* 77 (all 734–742); *EIGS* 78–81 (737); *EIGS* 82 (738/739); *EIGS* 83–84 (739/740); *EIGS* 114–116; *EIGS* 117; *EIGS* 126; *EIGS* 127 (all 721–726); *EIGS* 148; *EIGS* 149 (both 749–750); *EIGS* 178–180 (all 751–753 or 755–758); *EIGS* 217; *EIGS* 218; *EIGS* 223 (all 759–760); *EIGS* 248 (762–769); *EIGS* 273 (769–774); *EIGS* 328; *EIGS* 333 (both 781–784 or 792); *EPV* 45–47; *EPV* 48; *EPV* 49; *EPV* 52–53; *EPV* 54–56; *EPV* 57 (all 725–734); *EPV* 92–93; *EPV* 95; *EPV* 96–98; *EPV* 99–101 (all 734–742); *EPV* 128; *EPV* 130–131 (both 739–749); *EPV* 137–140 (749–750); *EPV* 169–172; *EPV* 173; *EPV* 174–175 (all 751–753 or 751–758); *EPV* 180; *EPV* 181; *EPV* 184 (all 759–760); *EPV* 231–232 (782–784); *EPV* 237–239 (784–785 or 805–806); *EPV* 240; *EPV* 241; *EPV* 242 (all 793–794); *GSW* 98; *GSW* 100 (725–734); *GSW* 112; *GSW* 115; *GSW* 116; *GSW* 125; *GSW* 126 (all 734–742); *GSW* 140 (749–150); *GSW* 144 (751–753 or 755–758); *GSW* 188; *GSW* 193 (both 762–774); *GWVS* 2; *GWVS* 3; *GWVS* 4 (all 725–734); *GWVS* 15; *GWVS* 16 (both 734–742); *GWVS* 20 (751–753 or 755–758); *UAT* 18 (714–717 or 720–721); *UAT* 75; *UAT* 76; *UAT* 77; *UAT* 78; *UAT* 79–80; *UAT* 81–82; *UAT* 83; *UAT* 84; *UAT* 85 (all 725–734); *UAT* 152–155; *UAT* 156–157 (all 734–742); *UAT* 218–220 (734–745); *UAT* 260; *UAT* 261; *UAT* 262–264 (all 749–750); *UAT* 317–318; *UAT* 319–321 (all 751–753 or 755–758); *UAT* 343–346; *UAT* 347 (all 751–758 or 781–786); *UAT* 387 (759–760); *UAT* 460–462 (762–774); *UAT* 533–534 (773–775); *UAT* 566 (778 or 786–787); *UAT* 598; *UAT* 599 (787–804).

In Arabic seals from 8th-century Syria:

Amitai-Preiss / Farhi 2009–2010 5 (Syria; VIII?).

201 The root *kh-t-m* is attested in the Arabic parchments from Khurāsān, see for example *P.Khurasan* 25 (Rōb; 762), 12.

khātam (also *khātim*),[202] "seal" < aram. *ḥātmā* (though the root is attested in different Semitic languages).[203] The loan appears to be quite ancient as the term is attested in the Qur'an[204] and in pre-Islamic poetry.[205]

In Arabic papyri from 8th-century Egypt:

P.Clackson 45 (Bāwiṭ; 753), 7.

In Arabic seals from 8th-century Egypt:

EIGS 318–319 (781–784 or 792).

In Arabic seals from 8th-century Syria:

Amitai-Preiss 10 ov (Ascalon; VIII?), 1; Amitai-Preiss 11 ov (ʿAmwās; VIII?), 1; Amitai-Preiss 2000 p. 104 ov (Tiberias; VII/VIII), 1; *SA* 2 (Syria; VIII?), 1.

e) Metrology

dānaq, 1/6 of the *dirham*-weight[206]< JBA, syr. *dānqā* < gr. *danakē* < elam. *da-na-kash*.[207]

In Arabic papyri from 8th-century Egypt:

P.HanafiCairoCopenhagen 1 (Egypt; VIII), 11; *P.Prag.Arab. Beilage* VII (Egypt; VIII), 3 and 5 (x4).

In Arabic papyri from 8th-century Syria:

P.Mird 36 (Khirbat al-Mird; VIII), 2 and 3.

In Arabic parchments from 8th-century Khurāsān:

P.Khurasan 3 (Rōb; 765), 5, 9, and 10; *P.Khurasan* 5, 10; *P.Khurasan* 6, 10, 12, and 16 (both from Rōb; 766); *P.Khurasan* 9, 10; *P.Khurasan* 10, 4 (both from Rōb; 769); *P.Khurasan* 11 (Rōb; 771), 6 and 7; *P.Khurasan* 12 (Rōb; 768), 9 and 10; *P.Khurasan* 13, 8; *P.Khurasan* 14, 5 (both from Rōb; 769); *P.Khurasan* 16, 6 and 7; *P.Khurasan* 17, 8; *P.Khurasan* 18, 6 and 7 (all from Rōb; 772); *P.Khurasan* 19, 7 and 8(x2); *P.Khurasan* 20, 5(x2) (both from Rōb; 774); *P.Khurasan* 21, 11(x2); *P.Khurasan* 22 (both form Rōb 775), 8.

202 The regular Arabic form *khātim* is secondarily developed from the root. See also *supra* p. 268.
203 Nöldeke 1875, 112; Fraenkel 1880, 17; *id.* 1886, 252; Jeffery 1938, 120–121; and Hebbo 1984, 98–99.
204 Q 33:40.
205 Fraenkel 1880, 17 and Jeffery 1938, 121.
206 For the value of the *dānaq*, see Hinz 1970, 11.
207 Eilers 1957, 332–333; Grohmann 1954, 145–146; and Asbaghi 1988, 117.

iqnīz, literally "small cup" (a measure of unknown value usually used for liquids and particularly for wine) < gr. *knidion*.[208]

In Arabic papyri from 7th- or 8th-century Egypt:

P.KarabacekBemerkungenMerx (= *P.MerxDocuments* p. 55) (Egypt; 685–705), 9.

In Arabic papyri from 8th-century Syria:

P.Mird 41 (Khirbat al-Mird; VIII), 1.

qīrāṭ (also in the defective form ***qirāṭ***), "carat"[209] (1/24 of a *dīnār* weight)[210] < aram. *qīrāṭā* < gr. *keration*/ lat. *ceratium* (1/24 of the gold *solidus*).[211]

In Arabic papyri from 8th-century Egypt:

P.Cair.Arab. 180 (al-Ushmūnayn; 731/732), 7 and 9; *P.World* p. 153a (= *P.GrohmannWirtsch.* 11) (Egypt; VIII), r 3; *P.HanafiCairoCopenhagen* 1 (Egypt; VIII), 2 and 6(x2); *P.Khalili* I 1 (al-Bahnasā; early VIII), 17; *P.Prag.Arab. Beilage* VII (Egypt; VIII), 8; *P.SijpesteijnTravel* (Fayyūm; 734), 5; *P.StoetzerSteuerquittungen* 2 (Ihnās; 707), 14.

In Arabic standard weights from 8th-century Egypt:

CAM 6 (714–717 or 720–721); *CAM* 24; *CAM* 26; *CAM* 27 (all 725–734); *CAM* 48 (734–742); *CAM2 BM* 3 (714–717 or 720–721); *CAM2 PRC* 6 (720–721); *EAG* I 12; *EAG* I 13; *EAG* I 14 (all 725–734); *EIGS* 4 (714–717 or 720–721); *EIGS* 36; *EIGS* 42; *EAG* I 43; *EAG* I 44 (all 734–745); *EIGS* 114–116 (721–726); *UAT* 18 (714–717 or 720–721); *EPV* 48; *EPV* 57 (both 725–734); *EPV* 128; *EPV* 130–131 (both 739–749); *GSW* 125 (734–742); *GWVS* 2; *GWVS* 3 (both 725–734); *UAT* 75; *UAT* 78; *UAT* 83; *UAT* 84; *UAT* 85 (all 725–734); *UAT* 218–220 (734–745).

In Arabic papyri from 8th-century Syria:

P.Mird 36 (Khirbat al-Mird; VIII), 1.

In Arabic seals from 8th-century Syria:

Amitai-Preiss 2007 6 ov, 4; Amitai-Preiss 2007 7 ov, 2; Amitai-Preiss / Fahri 2009–2010 3, 3 (all from Syria; VIII?).

---

208 Grohmann 1954, 170 and *ibid*.n4.
209 Carats are usually classified under coinage. As, to the best of my knowledge, there is no early Islamic *qīrāṭ* coin, I have preferred to list the term under the more vague label "metrology".
210 For a detailed reconstruction of a *qīrāṭ*'s value on the basis of Egyptian glass coin-weights, see Miles 1963, 83–87. For the difference between the Islamic *qīrāt* and the Roman carat, see in particular *ibid*., 86. Cf. Hinz 1970, 27 and Bruning 2018a, 70–71.
211 Fraenkel 1886, 200; Grohmann 1954, 146–147.

raṭl, "pound"[212] < aram. *rṭl'* (shortened form of *rṭyl*) < gr. *litron.*[213]

In Arabic papyri from 7th- or 8th-century Egypt:

P.BeckerPAF 9 (= *P.Heid.Arab.* I 8) (Ishqawh; 709), 3, 4, and 5; *P.Berl.Arab.* II 50 (Egypt; VIII), 5 and 6; *P.DiemFrüheUrkunden* 1 r (Fayyūm; 698), 8; *P.HanafiBusinessLetter* (Egypt; VIII), 2; *P.HanafiCairoCopenhagen* 1 (Egypt; VIII), 2.

In Arabic standard weights from 8th-century Egypt:

BM 25g (781–784 or 792); *CAM* 2 (709–714); *CAM* 53 (737); *CAM* 54 (740/741); *CAM* 79 (743–749); *CAM* 108–110 (754–7775); *CAM* 166 (769–774); *CAM* 182 (784–785); *CAM* 188 (796–806); *CAM2 BM* 17 (741–746); *CAM2 BM* 23 (738–747); *CAM2 BM* 28 (751–753 or 755–758); *CAM2 BM* 37 (762–769); *CAM2 BM* 47; *CAM2 BM* 48; *CAM2 BM* 49 (all >750); *CAM2 PRC* 3 (717–720); *CAM2 PRC* 7 (725–734); *CAM2 PRC* 34 (both 781–784 or 792); *EAG* I 2 (709–714); *EAG* I 17 (725–734); *EAG* I 24 (732/733); *EAG* I 25 (742–746); *EAG* I 32; *EAG* I 33 (both 734–742); *EAG* I 34 (740/741); *EAG* I 35 (734–742); *EAG* I 41 (743–749); *EAG* I 50 (749–750); *EAG* I 52; *EAG* I 53; *EAG* I 54 (all 754–775); *EAG* I 81 (762–769); *EAG* I 84 (769–774); *EAG* I 94 (773–776); *EAG* I 97; *EAG* I 98 (both 775–778); *EAG* II 9 (734–742); *EAG* II 19 (749–769); *EIGS* 5; *EIGS* 12 (both 714–717 or 720–721); *EIGS* 44; *EIGS* 44; *EIGS* 46–47; *EIGS* 48; *EIGS* 49 (all 725–734); *EIGS* 87 (734–742); *EIGS* 88 (736/737); *EIGS* 90 (740/741); *EIGS* 91 (734–742); *EIGS* 131 (741/742); *EIGS* 145 (743–749); *EIGS* 150; *EIGS* 151; *EIGS* 152 (all 749–750); *EIGS* 168; *EIGS* 169 (both 753–755); *EIGS* 199; *EIGS* 208–209 (all 754–775); *EIGS* 225; *EIGS* 229; *EIGS* 231 (all 759–760); *EIGS* 233 (760–762); *EIGS* 260; *EIGS* 261; *EIGS* 262–264 (all 769–774); *EIGS* 286 (774–776); *EIGS* 306; *EIGS* 307 (both 775–778); *EIGS* 309; *EIGS* 310 (both 778–779); *EIGS* 315 (779–780); *EIGS* 320; *EIGS* 321–322; *EIGS* 323; *EIGS* 324; *EIGS* 325–326; *EIGS* 327; *EIGS* 330 (all 781–784 or 792); *EIGS* 339 (789); *EIGS* 341; *EIGS* 342 (both 798–802); *EPV* 1 (709–714); *EPV* 150 (754–775); *GWS* 96 (725–734); *GWS* 109 (737); *GWS* 137 (749); *GWS* 150 (750–751 or 751–753); *GWS* 151; *GWS* 152 (both 754–775); *GWS* 159; *GWS* 160 (both 762–769); *GWVS* 5; *GWVS* 6; *GWVS* 7; *GWVS* 9 (all 725–734); *GWVS* 12 (734–742); *GWVS* 17 (742); *GWVS* 18 (734–742); *GWVS* 23 (759/760); *GWVS* 25 (760–762); *GWVS* 28; *GWVS* 29 (both 769–774); *GWVS* 34 (779); *GWVS* 36 (781–786 or 805–806); *GWVS* 41 (795/796); *UAT* 1; *UAT* 2 (both 709–714); *UAT* 14 (714–717 or 720–721); *UAT* 34; *UAT* 35 (both 717–720 or 721–722); *UAT* 64; *UAT* 65; *UAT* 66 (all 725–734); *UAT* 124–125; *UAT* 135; *UAT* 136; *UAT* 137; *UAT* 138–139; *UAT* 140; *UAT* 144; *UAT* 158; *UAT* 171; *UAT* 190 (all 734–742); *UAT* 215–216 (734–745); *UAT* 237–238; *UAT* 239 (all 743–749); *UAT* 256; *UAT* 257; *UAT* 258 (all 749–750); *UAT* 293–294 (753–755); *UAT* 302 (all 751–753 or 753–758); *UAT* 349; *UAT* 350–351; *UAT* 352 (all 754–775); *UAT* 382 (758–759); *UAT* 384; *UAT* 397–398; *UAT* 400; *UAT* 401 (all 759–760); *UAT* 408–409 (760–762); *UAT* 415–16 (762–769); *UAT* 440; *UAT* 441 (both 759–769); *UAT* 470–471; *UAT* 472; *UAT* 473–474; *UAT* 475 (all 769–773); *UAT* 528; *UAT* 531; *UAT* 532 (all 773–775); *UAT* 536–537 (775–785); *UAT* 556 (777–778); *UAT* 567 (780); *UAT* 572 (= *CAM2 PRC* 33); *UAT* 573–574 (both 781–784 or 792); *UAT* 582; *UAT* 583 (both 786–787); *UAT* 587; *UAT* 588; *UAT* 589 (all 791–792 or 795–796); *UAT* 604 (787–796); *UAT* 608 (792); *UAT* 611; *UAT* 612 (both 792–796); *UAT* 617 (793–794); *UAT* 620; *UAT* 621 (both 798–802).

212 For the value of the *raṭl*, see Hinz 1970, 27–33.
213 Fraenkel 1886, 202; Krauss 1898–1899, II, 578–579; Hebbo 1984, 142–143. Cf. Sokoloff 2009, 1461.

In Arabic papyri from 8th-century Syria:

P.Mird 35 (Khirbat al-Mird; early VIII), 2, 3, 6, 8, 10, 11, and 14.

In Arabic seals from 8th-century Syria:

Ettinghausen 1939 p. 73 (Syria?; 743/744), 6.

ūqiya, "ounce", (1/12 of a *raṭl*)[214] < aram. *'wqy'* < gr. *ougkia*/lat. *uncia.*[215]

In Arabic papyri from 8th-century Egypt:

P.MuslimState 23 (Fayyūm; 730–743), 37.

In Arabic standard weights from 8th-century Egypt

BM 18 (762–769); *CAM* 32 (725–734); *CAM* 91 (749–750); *CAM* 96 (749–769); *CAM* 135 (759–769); *CAM2 BM* 24; *CAM2 BM* 25 (both 749/750); *CAM2 BM* 30 (751–758 or 781–786); *CAM2 BM* 36 (759–769); *CAM2 BM* 45–46 (769–774); *CAM2 BM* 50 (775–778); *CAM2 PRC* 30; *CAM2 PRC* 31 (both 773–776); *EAG* I 25 (742–746); *EAG* I 69 (758–759); *EAG* I 82 (762–769); *EIGS* 11 (714–717 or 720–721); *EIGS* 89 (739/740); *EIGS* 135 (742–745); *EIGS* 181; *EIGS* 189–190 (all 751–753 or 755–758); *EIGS* 198 (754–775); *EIGS* 214 (758–759); *EIGS* 224; *EIGS* 226 (both 759–760); *EIGS* 245 (762–769); *EIGS* 272 (769–774); *EIGS* 285 (774–776); *EIGS* 316 (780/781); *EIGS* 329; *EIGS* 335 (both 781–786 or 792); *GWVS* 39 (786–806); *UAT* 36 (717–720 or 721–722); *UAT* 126; *UAT* 143 (both 734–742); *UAT* 295 (>750); *UAT* 333 (750–763); *UAT* 339–342 (751–758 or 781–786); *UAT* 386; *UAT* 407 (both 759–760); *UAT* 410 (760–762); *UAT* 442–443 (759–760); *UAT* 538 (775–785); *UAT* 554–555 (777–778); *UAT* 564 (778); *UAT* 568 (780); *UAT* 575 (781–784 or 792); *UAT* 577 (781–784 or 790–791); *UAT* 592; *UAT* 603 (both 787–804); *UAT* 607 (787–796); *UAT* 619 (793–794); *UAT* 623 (798–802).

In Arabic standard weights from 8th-century Syria:

Miles 1939 p. 4 (Syria?; original weight: V–VI/ validation: 705–715), mg.

214 Hinz 1970, 34–35; Cf. Grohmann 1954, 147–149.
215 Fraenkel 1886, 201–202; Vollers 1887–1897, 312; Krauss 1898–1899, II, 22; Hebbo 1984, 40 and *ibid.*n1. Cf. Daris 1971, 80–81.

f) Military

qamīṣ "shirt",[216]< gr. *kamision*/lat. *camisia*[217] possibly through eth. *qamīs*.[218] Likely an early borrowing, its use occurring both in the Qur'an and in pre-Islamic poetry.[219] The requisition of *kamisia* destined to Arab troopers for a price fixed by the central administration is referenced in the Basileios archive.[220]

In Arabic papyri from 7th-century Syria:

P.Mird. 82 (Khirbat al-Mird; VII), 4.

In Arabic papyri from 7th- or 8th-century Egypt:

P.BeckerPAF 5 (Ishqawh; 710), 4 and 7; *P.JoySorrow* 5 (Egypt; VII/VIII).

Loanwords Attested only Outside Egypt (640/641–800)

a) Fiscal Administration

iqlīm, a subdivision of a *kūra* < syr. *qlīmā* < gr. *klima*.[221]

In Arabic papyri from 7th-century Syria:

P.Ness. 60 (Nessana; 674), 3; *P.Ness.* 61 r (Nessana; 675), 3; *P.Ness.* 62 (Nessana; 675), 4; *P.Ness.* 67 (Nessana; 689), 2.

In Arabic inscriptions from 8th-century Syria:

Hoyland 2018a p. 137 (Andarīn; VIII), 4.

---

216 Morelli 2019, 24 "camicie, tuniche aderenti (. . .) si è già osservato però che le tuniche conservate sono sempre molto larghe. È possibile che un termine di significato e di origine diverso sia stato applicato agli indumenti effettivamente in uso in Egitto nel periodo bizantino" and *ibid*.n66 with further references. See also Younes' commentary to *P.JoySorrow* 5 l. 8–9 and *ibid*.n282.
217 Fraenkel 1886, 44–45; Jeffery 1938, 243; Hebbo 1984, 303.
218 Jeffery 1938, 243.
219 *Ibid.*
220 *CPR* XXII 55 (706), 3 and *P.Lond.* IV 1356 (710), r 4 and 10 and v 1b. For documents in Arabic, see the references in the main text. For the Arab administration's control on the prices of *kamisia*, see Morelli 2019, 24–25. A reference to *kamisia* acquired on behalf of the Arab administration is possibly also found on *P.Rein.Cent.* 57 (Egypt; VII); for the date and function of the document, see Morelli 2019, 25 and *ibid*.n72. On requisitions of items of clothing on behalf of Early Islamic Arab authorities in general, see Sijpesteijn's commentary to *P.MuslimState* 3, l. 8.
221 Schall 1982, 148. Cf. *id.* 1960, 77 and Sokoloff 2009, 1371.

A brief Christian Arabic inscription discovered on a cell's lintel in the ruins of a monastery in Kilwa[222] (close to the present-day border between Saudi Arabia and Jordan in the province of Tabuk) paleographically datable to the early Islamic period[223] also utilizes the term.

In Arabic seals from 8th-century Syria:

APS 12 ov, 1 (Bulunyās; VIII?); *APS* 16 (fd) (Syria?; 771–772), 1; Amitai-Preiss 2007 10 rv, 1 (Ascalon; VIII?); Amitai-Preiss 2007 11 rv, 1 (ʿAmwās; VIII?).

b) Institutions and Officials

sīr,[224] the title carried by a local ruler in the documents from early Abbasid Khurāsān[225] < bact. *sēro*.[226]

In Arabic parchments from 8th-century Khurāsān:

P.Khurasan 25 (Rōb; 762), 3.

c) Metrology

jarīb, a measure of capacity corresponding to *7 qafīzs*[227] < aram. *grīḇā* < MP *grīw*.[228]

In Arabic parchments from 8th-century Khurāsān:

P.Khurasan 24 (Rōb; 771), 10.

mīl, "mile", "milestone" < aram. *mīlā* < gr. *milion*/lat. *milium*. The term is already attested in pre-Islamic poetry.[229]

---

222 For the archaeological context of the Kilwa monastery, see Farès 2011.
223 The inscription of Kilwa was originally assigned to around 1000 by Savignac (see Farès 2011, 251). In light of the striking similarity of the script to that of 7th-c. Arabic epigraphies, it suggests rather a dating before the 8th century; see Farès 2010, 245.
224 For the reading *sīr* instead of the homographic *shīr, see* Khan 2007, 16–17.
225 See *supra* p. 105.
226 Cf. Sims-Williams 2010, 128 *s.v.* "σηρο". The title occurs on various Bactrian documents and Hunnic coins; see Göbl 1967, 165–166 (n. 241, 242, and 243); *BD* I W (Rōb; 747), 10 abd Y (Rōb; 771), 11 (cf. *BD* I R (Bactria; 674), 18 and S (Bactria; 692), 3, 6, and 11) and Khan 2007, 16–17.
227 Hinz 1970, 38. Cf. Grohmann 1954, 161–162.
228 De Lagarde 1866, 29; Asbaghi 1988, 85; Cf. Nöldeke 1879, 242n2.
229 Fraenkel 1880, 13; *id.* 1886, 282–283; Vollers 1887–1897, 317.

In Arabic inscriptions from 7th- and 8th-century Syria:

CIAP I p. 4, no. 1 (= *RCEA* I 17) (Abū Ghūsh; 685–705), 1 and 5; *CIAP* II p. 5, no. 1 (= *RCEA* I 15) (Bāb al-Wādī; 685–705), 1 and 5; *CIAP* III p. 104, no. 1 (= *RCEA* I 16), 1, 5, and 6; *CIAP* III p. 105, no. 2, 3, 7(x2) (both from Dayr al-Qalt; 685–705); *CIAP* III p. 220, no. 1, [2], and 6; *CIAP* III p. 221, no. 2, 3 and 5 (both from Fīq; 704); Silverman 2007 p. 605 (ʿAyn Ḥamad; 685–705), [6] and 9.

In Arabic inscriptions from 8th-century Ḥijāz:

al-Rāshid 1992 p. 138, (al-Rabada; late VIII), 2; *DZ* I p. 229, no.1, 1–2; *DZ* II p. 487, 7 (both from the Darb Zubayda; datable 775–785).

In Arabic inscriptions from 8th-century Caucasus:

Kračkovskaja 1952 p. 89 (Tiblisi?; VIII), 3.

mudy, a measure of capacity[230] < aram. *mōdī* < gr. *modion*/lat. *modius*.[231]

In Arabic papyri from 7th- and 8th-century Syria:

P.Mird 27 (Khirbat al-Mird; 744/745), 2; *P.Mird* 38 (Khirbat al-Mird; VIII), 1; *P.Ness.* 60 (Nessana; 674), 7 and 17; *P.Ness.* 61, r 7 and 16; *P.Ness.* 62, 8 and 18; *P.Ness.* 63, 1 and 12 (all from Nessana; 675); *P.Ness.* 64, 2 and 19; *P.Ness.* 65, 15 (both from Nessana; 676); *P.Ness.* 66 (Nessana; 677), 2 and 11; *P.Ness.* 67 (Nessana; 689), 6.

qafīz, a measure of capacity[232] < JBA, syr. *qp̄īzā* (= gr. *kapetis*) < MP *kawīz*.[233]

In Arabic parchments from 8th-century Khurāsān:

P.Khurasan 24, 6(x2), 7, 8, 9, and 10 (Rōb; 771).[234]

230 For the theoretical value values of a *mudy* in Islamic times, see Grohmann 1954, 156.
231 Fraenkel 1886, 206–207. Cf. Daris 1971, 74.
232 For the value of a *qafīz*, see Hinz 1970, 48–50. Cf. Grohmann 1954, 161.
233 Fraenkel 1886, 207; Asbaghi 1988, 220 and Sokoloff 2002, 1032.
234 For the use of *qafīz* in post-800 Arabic documents, see *infra* p. 295.

Regional Diversity in the Use of Administrative Loanwords in Early Islamic Documentary Arabic

Before putting the results in a broader context, a few *caveats* should be introduced. In particular, the number of loanwords and tokens is heavily influenced by the uneven distribution of the sources. As most of our knowledge of 7th- and 8th-century Arabic technical administrative terminology derives from fiscal papyri from Egypt, it is only natural that the bulk of the evidence for the use of technical loanwords should stem from that region. This not only affects which and how frequently loan-terms are attested, but also influences which and to what extent donor languages are represented. Assessment of regional idiolectic uses can therefore be ascertained only in those (few) semantic domains that offer reasonable grounds for comparison between the relatively over-represented testimonies from Egypt and the under-represented evidence from other regions. These can be categorized into three main semantic domains: metrology, currency, and administrative institutions.

The use of regional idiolects is at its most macroscopic in metrological terminology and particularly in the use of capacity measures. Clear regional terminological divides are evidenced not only between regions of different linguistic substrates but also within areas sharing a similar linguistic background. The geographical area of use of a metrological loanword invariably shows continuity with the pre-conquest archetypal term. The principal capacity-measure used for larger fiscal revenues in goods in Egypt is the *irdabb*, as had been the case since the first Persian conquest. In the same functional context, in fiscal documents from Syria the *mudy* is attested instead.[235] In 8th-century documents, the use of the Iranian measures *qafīz* and *jarīb* is confined to Central Asia.[236] The use of other metrological loanwords stretches across more regions sharing the same administrative background. This is the case with the originally Greek *qīrāṭ*, *qisṭ*, *raṭl*, and *ūqiya*[237] attested in areas of Byzantine administrative tradition but not in the former Sasanian domains.

Based on the existence of parallel regional metrological idiolects mirroring the respective pre-conquest regional usage, one can assume that these terms were loaned into Arabic for fiscal purposes in the years following the Islamic conquest. This is corroborated by the fact that none of the named units of measure is attested in pre-Islamic materials. This phenomenon bears witness to the *laissez*

---

235 In Nessana, the use of the *modios* is attested in papyri datable to pre-Islamic times. See e.g. *P.Ness.* 89 (VI/VII).

236 For the geographical distribution of the use of Iranian loanwords, see *infra* p. 295.

237 N.b. trans-regional terminological consistency does not imply trans-regional metrological consistency.

https://doi.org/10.1515/9783110740820-033

faire attitude of the early Islamic imperial authorities in keeping the centuries' old system of regional metrological nomenclatures (or rather to the impossibility of substituting them with a unitary trans-regional system). The use of *mīl* can be considered the exception that proves the rule. The latter lemma is the only metrological term whose use is attested in pre-Islamic literature, and the metrological loanword with the largest area of documented use stretching between the Caucasus and Western Arabia.

At the other end of the spectrum, loanwords falling into the domain of money and currency display an almost total absence of regionally diversified uses. This does moreover not reflect pre- or post-conquest practice in other languages. The Byzantine and Sasanian nomenclature for currency persists alike in non-Arabic private and official documents throughout the 7th to 9th century. During this timespan and beyond, gold coins continue to be referred to as *nomisma* in Greek documents from Egypt and Syria, as *holokottinos* in Coptic documents from Egypt and as *solidus* on Latin coins from North Africa and Spain. Greek papyri from Nessana refer to silver currency as *miliarēsion*.[238] In two Bactrian purchase contracts from the Balkh region, *BD* I V (729), 10 and *BD* I W (747), 10 and 31, the reference to reformed Arabic silver coins is specified more strongly to avoid terminological ambiguities: "good, locally current Arab (*tazago*) silver drachms (*ddrachmo*)".[239] Arabic terminology for currency on the other hand is not only consistent across the lands of the Islamic empire but also irrespective of cultural and linguistic boundaries. The originally Latin, Aramaic-coloured, Arabic *fals*, for instance, is used for coppers minted in Latin-writing North Africa, in Greek- and Coptic-writing Egypt and Middle Persian- and Bactrian-writing Khurāsān. The originally Greek, but morphologically Iranian-Aramaic *dirham* is used for silver coins minted in Arabic/Greek-writing Syria[240] and in Greek/Coptic-writing Egypt as well as in reformed coinage from the ex-Sasanian territories. The only currency label whose use is confined to one geographical area in the surveyed time span is the fraction of the silver *dirham* referred to as *dānaq*[241] which is only attested in the Khurāsān where – unlike in the ex-Byzantine domains – the local administration operated on silver currency.

Accounting for this homogeneity are multiple factors. Borrowed definitions for currency notably differ from their strictly metrological counterparts in that the

238 *P.Ness.* 73 (683) and 158 (VII/VIII).

239 The Arabic *dirham* and the Persian *drahm* are homographic in most Iranian scripts, which do possess signs for short vowels. As Bactrian documents employ the Greek script, the two terms are graphically distinguishable.

240 Bacharach 2010, 17–18; Foss 2008, 110.

241 For the geographical distribution of the use of *dānaq*, see *infra* p. 295.

former are documented in Arabic even in non-technical contexts before the rise of Islam. The term *dīnār* in particular, even came to be used as a personal name by the time of the Arab takeover.[242] The Arabs' familiarity with these lemmata doubtlessly smoothed their employment in the early Islamic administrative machinery. The Islamic conquest had furthermore merged together three major currency zones: the silver-based Iranian world, the gold- and copper-based Byzantine Levant and North Africa, and gold- and copper-based Visigothic Spain.[243] The reforms of ʿAbd al-Malik further unified the Islamic monetary system by issuing the standard coin types of the silver *dirham* and the gold *dīnār*.[244] These factors made a unitary nomenclature for money highly desirable. The reliance on native (if borrowed) terminology for the new institutionalized coinage issued by dozens of mints was but a facet of the claim of cultural hegemony[245] and self-awareness[246] that permeated ʿAbd al-Malik's reform from the beginning.

The third semantic domain allowing for comparison between corpora of different regional provenance concerns bureaucratic and institutional terminology. In this respect ambivalent trends are evidenced which loosely correspond to the different administrative layers concerned. The institution of the *barīd*, for instance, is referred to in all main corpora of administrative sources and as such is clearly an example of trans-regionally implemented technical jargon. Arabic labels for standard taxes are also used consistently on a trans-regional level. The occurrence of *rizq* (7th century), *jizya* (7th–8th century), and *kharāj* (8th century) in documents scattered across different regions signals institutional contiguity between geographical contexts as far apart as Egypt and Sijistān passing through Syria.[247] The occurrence of *rizq* and *kharāj*[248] in the Qur'an in non-technical acceptations suggests that they were borrowed into Arabic before the rise of Islam with

242 See e.g. *AI* Z 72, (al-Tamallaqī; VII), 1.
243 Heidemann 1998.
244 On the subject of Umayyad policies concerning money, see Shatzmiller 2017, 19–25.
245 For the political tensions with Byzantium playing in the background of Abd al-Malik's reform, see for instance Kaplony, 1996, 141–160; for the numismatic aspect, in particular, see Treadwell 2012b. On the internal ideological challenges to the Umayyad caliphate as reflected in the coinage of their opponents, see Foss 2013; Geiser 2010; and Foss 2002.
246 For the development and ideological significance of an Arab Muslim iconography on coinage, see Heidemann 2010a and Bacharach 2010.
247 Consistency in terminology does not, of course, automatically imply homogeneity of institutions. There is in fact little evidence to prove that the *kūra* mentioned in *P.Khurasan* 1 from the region of Balkh is compatible with the homonymous administrative units mentioned in Egypt and Syria or that the *gazito* of the Early Islamic Bactrian documents is analogous to the *jizya* levied in coeval Egypt.
248 For the technical acceptation of the term *jizya* in the Qur'an, see Jeffery 1938, 101.

the conquest adding an additional technical connotation to both terms. Eminently regional terminology (that is not only attested in one region alone but also rooted in the linguistic substratum of that region) occurs only for less ordinary allowances like the *nāʾiba*.

Labels for territorial administrative sub-divisions show a similar pattern. The main sub-provincial administrative territorial unit, the *kūra* is ubiquitous in our documentation. Regional terminological discrepancies are discernible only in the lower levels of provincial administration. *Iqlīm* in particular appears to have been used as a technical term for a territorial subdivision of the *kūra* only in the Levantine area but not in neighboring Egypt nor in distant Khurāsān. Finally, the use of foreign terminology to designate civil offices seems to have been circumstantial and bound to a specific geo-cultural context. *Duks*, *simmāk*, and *māzūt* are never attested in pre-Islamic materials and were borrowed into Arabic directly from Greek. This strongly suggests that borrowing occurred already in Islamic times[249] and mirrored circumstantial realities since, as far as one can tell, their use was restricted to Egypt. The use of *sīr* in the Arabic documents from Bactria shows a similar instance from the Eastern cultural substratum.

To summarize, in the use of technical loanwords two tendencies can be discerned. Loanwords pertaining to the highest administrative layers tend to be used consistently on a trans-regional scale and more clearly display the normalizing influence of the central government. Documents pertaining to lower or more contextual administrative ambits, on the other hand, reveal a more circumstantial and regionally bounded use of loanwords. The regional diversity in the use of administrative loanwords most clearly evidenced by metrological terminology in particular, reflects the plurality of the administrative contexts and traditions incorporated in the early Islamic rule. Unsurprisingly, loanwords borrowed into Arabic before the time of the Islamic conquest are less bound to distinctive geographical areas and are *ipso facto* less indicative of regional influences on the early Islamic Arabic administrative jargon.

249 Cf. Schall 1982, 148–149.

Terminology and Regional Settings: The Role of Umayyad Syria and the Looming Shadow of Abbasid Iraq

The peculiarities of the use of loanwords in documentary Arabic entail inferences on the type of cultural influences exercised by the imperial centers of Umayyad Damascus and Abbasid Baghdad on the scribal practices of the provinces.

The first macroscopic peculiarity of the foreign technical vocabulary in early Islamic Arabic administrative documents is the prominent role of the Aramaic cultural milieu in the transmission of foreign concepts and definitions to Arabic. Forty-one (66 %) of the 62 analyzed technical loanwords are borrowed either from or through an Aramaic dialect, 24 (c. 39 % of the total) are common to both so-called Western and Eastern dialects,[250] 16 (c. 26 % of the total) stem from Eastern dialects (Babylonian Aramaic and Syriac), and a final 1 (c. 2 % of the total) is exclusively attested in Western dialects (Jewish Palestinian Aramaic and Christian Palestinian Aramaic).[251] These figures are all the more significant considering that the bulk of the analyzed evidence stems from Egypt, a non-Aramaic speaking or writing region.[252] The use in Egypt of the fiscal, metrological, and military Aramaic technical terms *faddān, jaysh, jizya, kharrūba, kayl, maks, mithqāl, qarya, qulla, ṣadaqa, safīna* (< MP), *tillīs, ūsiya*, and *zakāt* transcends the local administrative and linguistic substratum and indicates that the technical jargon imported by the Arabs had formed outside Egypt's geographical boundaries, most likely in Umayyad Syria.

These data must, however, be taken with a grain of salt. Linguistic interferences between Aramaic and Arabic speakers deepen their roots in pre-Islamic times, and Aramaic-Arabic bilingualism was a widespread phenomenon along

250 For a brief overview of the Aramaic dialects, see Creason 2004, 391–393 and Stempel 1998, 12–13; for a more extensive overview, see Beyer 1986.

251 For comparison with early Islamic literary sources, Hebbo's analysis of the loanwords in the biography of the Prophet written by Ibn Isḥāq but heavily redacted by Ibn Hishām († 833) has revealed Aramaic (dialects) to be the most featured language yielding 84 out of 226 loanwords (37 %) and more than doubling the relative share of the second-most featured language, Persian with 42 terms (18,5 %). Hebbo 1984, 371. Among the corpus of 256 loanwords (excluding proper names) identified by Jeffery in the Qur'an, 61,3 % are borrowed from or through Aramaic dialects (including Syriac); about 60 % of the 66 proper names listed by Jeffery are also borrowed from an Aramaic dialect; see Zammit 2002, 58–59.

252 The rare examples of Syriac papyri connected to the activity of Syriac monks in late antique Egypt (Brashear 1998 and Berkes/McLaughlin 2018) are but few exeptions confirming the rule.

https://doi.org/10.1515/9783110740820-034

the frontier between Syria, Arabia, and southern Iraq – though the number of Arabic borrowings from Aramaic that can be securely dated to pre-Islamic times is slim.[253] The boundaries between Nabatean Aramaic and Arabic in particular appear to have been – in both spoken and written form – highly permeable.[254]

A directional pattern mirroring distinctively early Islamic geopolitical axes of power is discernible in the use of the term *kūra*. Some light on the loan history (or the implementation) of this lemma is shed by a terminological comparison between the bilingual Arabic/Greek and Arabic/Bactrian documents and dossiers from Syria, Egypt, and Central Asia. Greek documents from Egypt and Bactrian documents from Khurāsān display a terminological discrepancy with their Arabic *pendants*. In papyri from Egypt, the administrative unit defined in Arabic as *kūra* corresponds in Greek to either *pagarchia* "pagarchy" or *dioikēsis* "district"[255] (the latter term is mainly attested for Afroditō/Ishqawh).[256] In the Arabic documents from the Bēk family archive the district referred to as *kūra* comprises the jurisdiction over Rōb, Samangān, and a third locality whose identification remains obscure.[257] Bactrian legal documents from the same archive report in the opening protocol[258] the district in which a legal agreement or transaction was performed. Three 7th-century legal agreements also mention the "district of Samgān" for which the Bactrian term *ōdigo* "district" is used. In Middle Persian documents from the Pahlavi Archive, the largest provincial units carry the name of *ōstān* ("province" or "district")[259] and are further subdivided in *rōstāg*s ("districts") and *deh*s ("villages").[260]

Things are different in the 7th-century bilingual requisition orders from the Syrian town Nessana. In all bilingual documents the Greek and Arabic terminol-

253 Retso 2006 *s.v.* "Aramaic/Syriac Loanwords"; Hoyland 2004, 189–190; Tannous 2008; Knauf 2009, 245–247. Cf. Fück 1950, 46.

254 Nehmé 2017b. For Arabic loanwords in Nabatean, see O'Connor 1986 and Greenfield 1992.

255 For an indicative example compare e.g. *P.Lond* IV 1334, 2 (Greek) (Ishqawh; 709) and *P.Qurra* 3 r,7 (Arabic) (Ishqawh; 709/710) both addressed by the governor Qurra b. Sharīk (in office 709–714) to Basileios *dioikētēs* of Afroditō and *CPR* XIX 27, 2 (Greek) (Fayyūm; 730–743) and *P.MuslimState* 2, 6 (Arabic) (Fayyūm; 730–743), both produced in the chancery of the pagarch of the Fayyūm Nājid b. Muslim.

256 I thank Isabelle Marthot-Santaniello for calling my attention to this phenomenon.

257 For the identification of these localities, see Khan 2007, 20.

258 For the formal structure of the Bactrian legal documents in the archive of the family of Bēk, see *supra* pp. 255–256.

259 For the use of *kūra* and *ōstān* as synonyms in Islamic Iraq, see Løkkegaard 1950, 164 and Frye 1977, 10–11 and *ibid.*n10.

260 Gignoux 2004, 37.

ogy mirror each other using *chōra* and *kūra* respectively.[261] The Arabic term (or at least its technical acceptation) seems therefore to have been modelled on the administrative terminology current in Syria at the time of the conquest. From here, it was apparently imported into other regions of the empire through the influx of the central Arab administration. This case thus bears direct witness to the implementation of a term (*kūra*) grounded in the Syrian administrative idiolect in the whole Islamic empire, without direct connections to the local administrative (or even linguistic) backgrounds.[262] Like *kūra*, *iqlīm* is translated in bilingual documents from Nessana with its Greek archetype *klima*.[263] The documents from Umayyad Syria thus show a closer correspondence between the Arabic technical jargon and the Greek substratal administrative jargon than documents produced in other regions of the empire.

Spelling is a final element to take into account in assessing regional influences on early Islamic documentary Arabic. Further clues of a "Syrian" matrix behind Umayyad administrative jargon are provided by the morphology of some of the loanwords used in Arabic documents from Egypt. The Aramaicizing spellings[264] for the originally Greek metrological terms *raṭl*, *qīrāṭ*, *qisṭ*, and *qinṭār*[265] (Greek *litron*, *keration*, *xestēs*, and *kentēnarion*) in Arabic documents produced in

261 For an illustrative example, compare e.g. *P.Ness.* 60 (Nessana; 674), 3 (Arabic) and 10 (Greek).

262 Løkkegaard 1950, 164, followed by Morony 2005, 129, postulates that use of the term *kūra* in the Arabic administrative nomenclature of Islamic Iraq goes back to Seleukid administrative practice. He bases this claim on two accounts by al-Maqdisī (x) and Yāqūt († 1229) who report that *kūra* was introduced by the Persians and by Alexander respectively. To the best of the author's knowledge, *chōra*/*kūra* is never attested as a technical denomination for an administrative subdivision in Seleukid, Arsacid, and Sasanian documentary sources. *Chōra*/*kūra* is furthermore not to be found among the territorial subdivisions mentioned in the likely early 7th-century *Mādayām ī hazār dādestān* (*Book of a Thousand Judjments*). It might be added that the term is not attested in Middle-Iranian languages. In view of this, Løkkegaard's theory of a continuity of use of *chōra*/*kūra* throughout the Seleukid to the Early Islamic period is an *interpretatio difficilior*. For the Seleukid administration, see Aperghis 2004, 263–285 and Capdetry 2007, 229–275. For administrative terminology in the *Mādayām ī hazār dādestān*, see Lukonin 1983, 732–733. Commenting on the use of *kūra* in Arabic papyri from Egypt, Løkkegaard *loc. cit.* further remarks "if the term should prove to have been transferred from Egypt to Iraq, the loan would be quite unique in its kind, as in all other respects it is rather Iraq which is the model for the rest of the provinces". The use of *chōra*/*kūra* in the Nessana papyri (unknown to Løkkegaard) provides the missing link between Egypt and Iraq. I thank Irene Soto Marin for her helpful advice on matters regarding the Seleukid administration.

263 Cf. Kaplony 2016, 395. For an illustrative example, see *P.Ness.* 61 r, 3 (Arabic) and 10 (Greek) (Nessana; 675).

264 The use of Semitic measures in Greek documents is also frequently attested in pre-Islamic Syria throughout the 2nd to 7th century. See introduction to *P.Petra* 3–5, 77.

265 For *qinṭār* cf. also the form *qnṭn* in Sabaic. Beeston 1994, 43 [35].

a region of a preponderantly Greek administrative tradition like Egypt, points at the central administration in Syria as the reference cultural model.[266] The spelling of administrative loanwords used in Umayyad Syria indicates that they were mostly not borrowed directly from the local pre-Islamic administrative language, Greek, but rather *via* Aramaic. The language contact constellation in Umayyad Syria as reflected by the use of loanwords thus takes the shape of an interaction between two groups of bilingual practitioners: Greek-Aramaic and Aramaic-Arabic practitioners respectively. It appears therefore that local variants of spoken Aramaic functioned as a linguistic bridge between the Greek and Arabic language milieu without direct contact between the two. By comparison, the model of language contact in coeval Egypt is radically different. Not only is a significant component of the regional administrative idiolect made up by direct borrowings from Greek (*duks*, *hury*, *māzūt*, *nā'iba*, *nawbāj*, *nūtī*, *qusṭāl*, *simmāk*, *ṭabl*, and *ūsiya*) but also contacts between the substratal vernacular Coptic and Arabic are almost non-existent.[267]

Syro-Palestinian influences are evidenced in the vocabulary of Greek papyri from 7th- and 8th- century Egypt as well. Specifically, administrative texts from this period feature a number of neologisms and variant spellings, replacing technical terms attested in the region prior to the conquest. Part of these terminological novelties can be linked to Syrian inputs. Following the Arab conquest, *chōrion* becomes the standard designation for the fiscal unit of the village supplanting the previous technical term *kōmē*.[268] This can be explained with the import of administrative jargon from Syria, where *chōrion* was used in this technical sense already in the pre-conquest period.[269] The use of the form *gonachion* "blanket" (< aram. *gunkha*) in administrative documents from the early Arab period, instead of the earlier spellings attested in Egypt before the conquest *gaunakēs*/*kaunakēs*, also possibly reflects a Syrian orthography and is similarly indicative of a broader cultural trend.[270] That multilingual Syro-Aramean experts formed part of a mobile entourage that followed Marwanid governors finds some confirmation in anecdotal reports as well. Most notably, the polyglot Edessine entrepreneur and tax-of-

266 There is of course no conclusive argument to prove administrative loanwords attested in Early Islamic Arabic documents were not borrowed long before the Arab conquest.

267 Richter 2010, 211. A substantial increase in Arabic loanwords in Coptic is first discernible in the 11th and later centuries as significant parts of Egypt's population began to adopt Arabic. See Richter 2009, 422–426.

268 Morelli 2001, 22–23; Sijpesteijn 2013, 70 and *ibid.*n155 and references there.

269 Gascou 2013, 672.

270 For this subject, see Morelli 2002, 76–77. For a more extensive survey of the terminological novelties in Greek and Coptic documents from early Islamic Egypt, see Sijpesteijn 2013, 69–71.

ficial Athanasios br. Gumōyē is said to have been appointed as chief secretary to ʿAbd al-ʿAzīz b. Marwān when the latter became governor of Egypt.[271]

In conclusion, in Umayyad Imperial Arabic a trans-regional set of technical loanwords existed which overlapped the several regional administrative idiolects modelled on different local realities. This trans-regional "foreign" technical terminology bears the traces of an Aramaic or rather Aramaicizing imprint, reflecting the bureaucratic language defined by imperial officials in Umayyad Syria. Conversely, the direct lexical borrowings from other languages (e.g., Greek and Middle Persian) tend to be circumscribed by distinctive geographical contexts or confined to pre-Islamic loanwords.

Abbasid imperial officials played a similar role in shaping the imperial Arabic administrative jargon of their time. Again, this phenomenon must be contextualized in a broader framework with particular respect to the structural changes in the formulary, graphic, and terminological features undergone by Arabic documentary sources in the late 8th and in particular the early 9th century (Chapter III). As already discussed, from the second half of the 8th century the Umayyad epistolary prescript undergoes substantial changes with the removal of the address from the main body of the letter, the dropping of the transition formula and the disappearance of the doxology (*ḥamdala* + *shahāda*). Some of the formal novelties in post-750 Arabic documents point at an Iranian origin and reflect the increasing presence of Iranian officials in the imperial chanceries favoured by the Abbasid takeover.[272] The graphic features of the late 8th-century Khurāsān parchments, for instance, bear the marks of Pahlavi scribal practices (and particularly a tendency towards a cursivity of the script) which become characteristic of documents from Egypt only in the 9th century.[273] Arabic tax receipts from the Bēk family archive further utilize the operative clause *addā fulān* "N.N. has delivered". This latter will become a standard operative clause in tax receipts from Egypt only decades later.[274]

Over the course of the 9th and 10th centuries, the shifts in the formulary are mirrored by an increasing use of Iranian technical loanwords in fiscal contexts. Though they fall outside the time span surveyed in this study, they will be dis-

271 On Athanasios, see Debié 2016, 53–64. For the identification with the homonymous *endoxotatos chartoularios* mentioned in *P.Lond.* IV 1447 (Ishqaw; 685–705) see Naïm Vanthieghem's paper held at the *ISAP VIII Online Conference* (Mar. 15–18, 2021); cf. also Bell 1910, xxin2.

272 For a survey of the Iranian influences on Abbasid Arabic documentary culture, see Khan, 2008, 888–889 and 896–897; Grob 2010, 42 and Reinfandt 2015, 286–288.

273 For Iranian graphic influxes on 9th-century Arabic papyri, see Khan 2013a, 234–245.

274 *Ibid.*, 231–232. For a survey of the formularies used in Arabic tax receipts from 8th–11th-century Egypt, see Frantz-Murphy 2001, 64–68.

cussed briefly. Arabized Persian technical terms like *daftar* "register", "account book" < MP *daftar*[275] of the same meaning first appear in Arabic papyri from Egypt in the early 9th century.[276] This further coincides with the falling out of use of technical terms typical of Umayyad administrative jargon. The Iranian word *jahbadh* "cashier" < MP *gāhbad* "treasurer"[277] is introduced in the 9th century and supplants the semantically equivalent *qusṭāl* at the dawning of the following century.[278] Over the course of the 9th century, *jāliya*[279] replaces *jizya* (or *jizya al-rā's* respectively) as the standard denomination for the poll-tax.[280] Arabic juristic literature suggests that *jāliya* was used in this technical acceptation in Iraq before it was introduced in Egypt.[281] Another Iranian loanword which is attested both in early-Islamic poetry and in the Qur'an,[282] but becomes a designation of an official office only in Abbasid time, *wazīr* "(chief) minister" < MP *wičīr*,[283] is also first encountered in papyri from Egypt from the 9th century onwards.[284] This cultural shift coincides with the appointment of members of the royal family and descendants of Arab families settled in the Eastern provinces and – after the death of Hārūn al-Rashīd (809) – of officials of Turkish and eastern Iranian descent to governors and other high posts in the regional administration during the reign of of the Abbasids.[285]

---

275 Frantz-Murphy 2001, 81; Asbaghi 1988, 124.

276 The first dated attestation of *daftar* is *P.GrohmannUrkunden* 9, 3 (Ihnās; 838). A potentially earlier attestation is further found in *P.Cair.Arab.* 285 (Egypt) paleographically assigned by the editor to the late 8th/early 9th century.

277 Khan 2012, 83; *id.* 2014, 27; Frantz-Murphy 2001, 81; Asbaghi 1988, 95; Kameya 2017, 146–148.

278 The last dated attestation of *qusṭāl* in Arabic fiscal documents is P.Vind.inv. A. P. 13986 (= *PERF* 896) (Egypt; 918/919), v 6 though the term occurs in later Geniza materials. The first dated attestation of *jahbadh* is *P.GrohmannProbleme* 14, 3 (Egypt; 863). Kameya (2017, 148–155) contends that the transition from *qusṭāl*s to *jahbadh*s reflected a change in the tax-farming procedure and particularly the substitution of government-appointed tax officials with contractors elected from the ranks of the local population, in an attempt to ease tensions during tax collection.

279 The term *jāliya* is used in early 8th-century Umayyad papyri in its literal meaning of "fugitives". How the word came to designate the poll-tax is not entirely clear. Cf. Fattal 1958, 265.

280 The term is first attested as a tax designation in *P.DiemFrueheUrkunden* 7, 8 (Egypt; 784).

281 Morimoto 1981, 176 quoting Abū Yūsuf's († 798) *Kitāb al-Kharāj*. The passage refers to the reign of Harūn al-Rashīd (*rg.* 786–809).

282 Goitein 2010, 170–17.

283 Jeffery 1938, 287–288; Asbaghi 1988, 271–272.

284 First attested in *CPR* III 170 (al-Ushmūnayn; 858/859), 7.

285 Kennedy 1981, 31–38 and *id.* 1998; Sijpesteijn 2017 and *ead.* 2020b, 399–404; Reinfandt 2020b, esp. 230–232. For the integration of Central Asian elites into the Abbasid empire, see in particular de la Vaissière 2007. Cf. also Crone 1984, 173–189.

The occurrence of technical loanwords stemming from an Iranian linguistic substratum in 8th-century Arabic documents offers a glimpse into the process playing out in the background of the cultural watershed of the 9th century. A comparison of the early Abbasid Arabic documents from Khurāsān with their counterparts from Egypt shows that transregional standard administrative terms of the 9th century still belonged to the distinctive administrative idiolect of the Eastern provinces in the 8th century. The archetypal term for *kharāj*, the MP *harg*, is already attested during the 7th century in early Islamic fiscal documents in Middle Persian from Iran.[286] The Arabic *kharāj* as a denomination for money taxes in turn is attested in the Khurāsān corpus decades before its first recorded occurrence in papyri from Egypt.[287] By the time of the introduction of the term *kharāj* in early Abbasid papyri from Egypt, the Umayyad specific designation for the land-tax in money, *jizyat al-arḍ* had disappeared from the record.[288] Around the same time *kharāj* is attested in a paper document from Iran.[289] In the second half of the 8th century, the use of the measures of Iranian origin *dānaq* and the *qafīz* is circumscribed to documents from Central Asia. Both make their appearance in papyri from Egypt and Syria dated or datable to the late 8th/early 9th centuries.[290] *Furāniq* and *dīwān*, two other technical terms stemming from an Iranian substratum, also first occur in documents from Egypt around the turn of the mid-8th century anticipating other terminological innovations in the decades to follow. Once again, lexical evidence is substanciated by information on the migration of Iranian administrative personel into Egypt described in the literary sources.[291] Clerks of Iranian and Turkic descent likewise punctuate the prosopography of 9th-century administrative papyri.[292] Much like in the documents from coeval Khurāsān, some members of this new class of administrators can be identified as descendants of families of post-Sasanian administrators. This is the case for insance for Abū ʿAmr *al-qahramān*, superintendent of the Abbasid governor

286 See *supra* p. 284.
287 See *supra ibid.*
288 The latest datable attestation of the *jizyat al-arḍ* is *P.MuslimState* 35, 5 (Fayyūm; 730–743).
289 *P.KhanBerkeley* 5, 4 (Qom?; VIII–IX). The paper is one of five very fragmentary Arabic documents most probably belonging to the same archive of the early Islamic Pahlavi documents discussed at pp. 95–98. For the dating of the archive, see Weber 2008b; cf. Khan 2003, 33.
290 Both *dānaq* and *qafīz* occur in several 9th-century papyri none of which, however, bears an absolute date, see for example *P.Cair.Arab.* 420, 4 (Egypt; late VIII to the early IX) for the former and *P.World* p. 168 (= *P.GrohmannWirtsch.* 2), r, 8 (Egypt; IX) for the latter.
291 See in particular the lists compiled by Guest 1922 and Yarshater 1998.
292 Reinfandt 2020, 230–232 with further references.

Muḥammad b. Saʿīd[293] (in office 769–773)[294] and for one (. . .) al-Raḥmān b. al-Dibīr (< MP *dibīr* "scribe") featured in the already mentioned potsherd from Panjakent.[295]

To summarize, one distinguishes two layers in the usage of administrative loanwords in Arabic documents from Umayyad Egypt: a regionally idiolectic one, most clearly visible in the semantic domains of metrology and offices rooted in the regional administrative context and a "foreign" one most evident in overlapping administrative institutions. This latter layer distinguishes itself both in vocabulary and morphology for a strong, conjecturally Aramaic component. In coeval papyri from Syria, by contrast, the difference between the first and second layer is more difficult to discern. In documents from the Abbasid period, a third layer superimposes the other two and partially supplants elements of the second (Umayyad) transregional layer. This transition is marked by increasing "Iranization" of the technical terminology which reflects a cultural shift at the highest echelons of the imperial administration.

293 *P.YounesGovernors* 3 (Egypt; 769–773), 8. On the term *qahramān*, see *supra The Loanwords in Imperial Arabic s.v.* "*qahramān*" in this chapter.
294 On Muḥammad b. Saʿīd, see Younes 2018: 33–35.
295 Belenitsky/Isakov 1969.

Conclusion

As far as lexical borrowings are indicative of the extent of penetration of one language by another, the influence by substratal languages on early Islamic Arabic vocabulary was, overall, limited. Borrowability was generally restricted to terms of technical character. Arguably, the loanwords examined in this chapter did not belong to an average vernacular lexical choice. Rather they were elements of a bureaucratic language defined by state officials. Technical vocabulary *per se* indicates special knowledge based on specialized training and qualifications and entails an implicit claim to superior status and authority.

A question that has yet to be addressed is that of intentionality or, in other terms, whether the use of loanwords in Arabic official documents mirrored a purposeful and conscious employment of foreign technical terminology. As most of today's English speakers would not necessarily recognize the word "belt" as a loan from the Latin (though possibly of Etruscan origin) *baltus*, one is left asking to what extent Arab officials were aware of the foreign component of the Arabic they employed. Further, one could wonder whether the conscious use of loan- and foreign words constituted an element of scribal finesse and cultural prestige for 7th- and 8th-century Arabic officials. For a scribe of the Umayyad age, was using an Aramaic loanword, for instance, a sign of status distinction, much as using a French term would be for an 18th-century Russian literate?[296] Medieval Arab lexicographers were not unaware of the existence of foreign terms in Arabic and even developed methods to identify and explain them.[297] The etymologies provided by those later lexicographers and their ascription of loanwords to one language or the other are to be taken with a grain of salt and are at times even ideologically biased.[298] The attitude of medieval Muslim scholars towards loanwords in Arabic sacred literature in particular ranges from acceptance to outright rejection.[299] Independently of all this, the learned considerations of later religious scholars can hardly account for the perceptions and purposes of imperial officials in the early days of the Islamic empire.

296 Fraenkel (1880, 1–2) for example suggested that the use of foreign vocabulary in pre-Islamic Arabic poems constituted an element of literary finesse; cf. Cheung 2017, esp. 332.

297 Prominent examples of this genre are al-Jawālīqī's († 1144) *Kitāb al-muʿarrab min al-kalām al-aʿjamī* and al-Suyūṭī's († 1505) *al-Muzhir fī-ʿulūm al-lugha.*

298 Rippin 2008, 257–260; *id.* 2002 *s.v.* "Foreign Vocabulary"; Zammit 2002, 60–61; and Jeffery 1938, 31–32.

299 For a brief account on the commentators' opinions on the foreign vocabulary in Islamic sacred texts and the Qur'an in particular, see Cheung 2017, 317–318; Carter 2006, 121–124; and Zammit 2002, 53–55. For a more exhaustive synopsis, see Jeffery 1938, 2–11.

https://doi.org/10.1515/9783110740820-035

The use of technical loanwords in 7th- and 8th-century Arabic documents certainly responded to the concrete needs of the ever-developing early Islamic administration. At the same time, the lexical choice of borrowed vocabulary shifted in tandem with more general developments of the formal features of the early Islamic official scribal culture. At different times, and in response to different geopolitical circumstances, lexical elements of the substratal regional scribal culture associated with the center of imperial power became culturally hegemonic in Arabic writings within the early Islamic Empire. This indicates expressive choices transcending concerns for semantic stringency, oriented to some extent along reasons of social and symbolic prestige. For Early Islamic scribes operating in Egypt, the use of culturally hegemonic technical vocabulary provided a marker of inclusion and a signifier of their status as members of a broader imperial elite.

Summary and Conclusions

The "Elephant in the Dark"

Whoever has taken an interest in Oriental folklore, is likely familiar with the popular proverb of the seven blind men and the elephant. As the story goes, seven blind men attempt to determine what an elephant is by touching each one of the animal's extremities. As each of them senses a different limb, every blind man ends up reaching a different understanding of what *the* elephant is. The rise of Arabic as a written language during the 7th and 8th centuries is both sudden and fragmented. The documentary evidence, which appears scattered across far-flung territories and typologies of sources, may in fact appear not unlike the isolated limbs of this metaphorical "elephant". As this study nears its end, I hope to have demonstrated that by jointly considering this heterogeneous textual material there are many insights to be gained. In some versions of the story, the endeavor of the seven blind men to piece together each person's insights fails spectacularly – each one of them is so entangled in his own subjective grasp of the elephant that they distrust the others. By focusing on the context of emergence, formal features, and terminological choice, I have attempted to illustrate the meaningful ties connecting the *disiecta membra* of Early Islamic textual evidence in a cohesive narrative.

Brief Outline of Research Outputs

The present research is the first study dedicated to the rise, spread, and social connotations of written Arabic based on the appraisal of virtually the whole spectrum of published papyrological, epigraphic, as well as numismatic sources dated or datable before the 9th century. Its most substantial contribution to these fields lies in its application of the socio-cultural model of "empire" – understood as a hierarchical configuration of power – to the context of the emergence and development of documentary Arabic.

The work proposes a periodization of the development of Arabic as a written language into a pre-800 "imperial language" stage and a post-800 "*lingua franca*" stage. The former stage, which has been defined as *Imperial Arabic,* is characterized by relatively few Arabic documents and a typological preponderance of official texts. Characteristic of the former phase is further the resilience of local languages in official and private ambit. By contrast, the latter period is marked by the quantitative and typological proliferation of Arabic documents, as well as by a progressive increase of the relative share of Arabic documents of "private"

https://doi.org/10.1515/9783110740820-036

emergence. The exponential spread of Arabic documents corresponds to the disappearance of documentary texts in Greek from Egypt and Syria, in Middle Persian from Iran, and in Bactrian from Afghanistan. The changes in the documentary record of the 9th and later centuries mark a loosening of the ties between the Arab-Muslim minority and the Arabic language, which increasingly develops into a language of communication – and eventually science and knowledge – beyond religious and ethnic boundaries. In documents from the periphery of the Empire (Egypt, Iran, and Central Asia), trends of transition only appear in the late 8th century, with the first spread of Arabic among Christians and Zoroastrians, and the general permeation of Arabic terms and formulaic uses into neighbouring documentary cultures. In regions with a large indigenous native Arabic population like the Arabian Peninsula and Syria-Palestine, in contrast, these phenomena surface up to two generations before.

The initial survey in Chapter I further detected two main periods of acceleration in the development of Arabic documentary practices during the Umayyad period: a first one in the 660s and a second, more incisive one, starting from the 690s. Noticeably, these correspond to the rise to power of the Sufyanid and the Marwanid branch of the Umayyad clan, both dynastic changes born out of periods of civil strife within the Muslim community. In the short term, both the First and the Second Muslim Civil Wars exposed the need for tighter caliphal control over provincial administration and for more solid formulations of imperial legitimacy.[300]

From the point of view of the documents, the centralizing efforts of the Umayyad ruling elite took the shape of a quantitative increase in Arabic documents as well as the normalization of the latter's formal guidelines. Around the close of the 7th century, in particular, official uses of Arabic became more systematic in the context of the Marwanid administrative reforms resulting in *i.a.* the ousting of Greek and Middle Persian from public statements on inscriptions and coinage. This increase in official promulgations in Arabic can largely be explained with a culturally defensive stance of the Umayyad imperial minority triggered by the confrontation with inside and outside adversaries in a generally culturally alien environment. The genesis of the all-epigraphic Arabic coinage of

300 While the centralizing spirit of ʿAbd al-Malik's reforms has found wide acceptance among scholars, the degree of centralization is widely debated; for a critical view, see in particular Morimoto 1981, Robinson 2000, esp. 166, and Johns 2003. However, more recent scholarship has increasingly brought to light trends of centralization – if not a centralized polity – visible under Muʿāwiya's reign; see in particular Hoyland 2006, Foss 2009, Legendre 2016, and Bruning 2018a, esp. 155–160. A testimony of Muʿāwiya's direct involvement in provincial administration is a lead ring-seal sanctioning the dismissal of ʿAbd Allāh b. ʿĀmir b. Kurayz al-Ḥaḍramī (664) from the post of governor of Baṣra; see Baldwin & Sons 2012, Lot. 5.

ʿAbd al-Malik, in particular, is the crowning effort of decades of confrontations with representative standards of previous empires and of anti-Umayyad Muslim groups during the Second Civil War. The main argument advanced in Chapter II is that the mediality of the Arabic language and script was used as a signifier of socio-political hierarchies. Through Arabic public writing, the imperial elite could engage different audiences on multiple levels: the Arabic language and script granted the Arab-Muslim imperial elite an easily accessible sense of identity. The formulation of the cornerstones of the Islamic creed on public statements further provided the symbolic glue for the unity of the Islamic peoples. At the other end of the spectrum, aesthetic and graphic peculiarities of Arabic imperial promulgations operated as iconic illustrations of authority *vis-à-vis* subordinated segments of the imperial polity. Official documents on papyrus addressed to non-Arabic native writers can also be interpreted as forms of symbolic communication conveyed through the visual impression of a text's graphic and visual features: pragmatic bi- and trilingualism persisted in the provincial administration of Egypt, Iran, and Central Asia until the end of the 8th century.

Contextually, the structural features of official papyri, inscriptions, and coins underwent a process of normalization. The official templates which surface in late 7th-century papyri from Egypt resulted from the standardization of documentary practices of the Umayyad domestic administration in Syria. Similarly, the codification of an official Arabic epigraphic text selected, re-organized, and normalized the elements found *in nuce* in 7th-century Sufyanid epigraphy from the Arabian Peninsula. Reformed epigraphic coinage incorporated suggestions of the Zubayrid coinage mixed with novelties coming from the imperial capital. The underlying structural principle of *Umayyad Official Arabic* documents is a fixed succession of formulaic components, usually opened by the *basmala* invocation. In terms of layout, the common concept of all Early Islamic official texts is a functional division of text-parts through the *mise-en-page*: in chancery documents, a repartition into layout blocks visually set off the preamble from the informative section of the text. In contemporary reformed coinage, religious utterances were sectionally separated from administrative content by the latter being placed in the reverse margin. Official epigraphy strove for a fixed number of lines and correspondence between writing-surface and written text with the invocation visually set off by occupying the first line. The common genetic background of Umayyad Official Arabic is further signaled by formulaic links between all the corpora examined. The endophoric reference introduced by the pronoun *hādhā*, and the operative clause *amara bi-*, for instance, are common features in official writs, inscriptions as well as seals, coins, and papyrus protocols. The institutional skeleton behind this imperial culture is shown by scribal exercises found in Umayyad papyri from Egypt and ink inscriptions and ostraca from Syria and Central Asia.

Already in the 7th and 8th centuries, the standardization of professional scribal practices of Arabic resulted in a situation of diglossia or – more to the point of the present study – "dimorphia". The formal features of Arabic texts authored by private writers appear to have been both more influenced by regional practices and less systematic compared to scribal promulgations. Arabic graffiti and private letters on papyrus preserve formulaic conventions that either date back to the pre-Islamic period, such as the *anā fulān* formula, or that developed in parallel to official ones such as the salutation *salām ʿalay-ka wa-raḥmatu-hu*. Differences between official and private texts extended also to uses of religious speech. A standardized official *Vulgata* of Qur'anic paraphrases dominated ideological statements on official papyri, coinage, and inscriptions. Notably, religious formulae that characterized private expressions of piety in Arabic private letters, funerary epigraphy, and graffiti are often unattested in official documents or have different wording, as in the case of the so-called "Egyptian" proclamation of faith. Our analysis of private epigraphy and private letters has further shown that these latter texts did not abide by the same aesthetic conventions as their official counterparts. These outputs advocate upholding a distinction of the evidence according to "private" and "official" provenance as analytic categories despite the occasional difficulty of determining clear boundaries.

Official formal templates also offer insights into the brokered character of Early Islamic imperial governance. Greek, Coptic, Middle Persian, and Sogdian letters by Arab officials of Egypt, Palestine, Central Iran, and Central Asia were modeled on the formulaic structure of contemporary Arabic official missives. The religious formulae of these *Arab-style* promulgations, however, were stripped of specifically Islamic (or Arabian) content and adapted to fit local monotheistic religious undertones. De-Islamization was coupled with the adoption of Roman and Sasanian status identifiers. The pattern of adaptation to specific local realities indicates awareness of the Arab ruling elite for the cultural circumstances of the provinces and the need to compromise with local interests. These findings are confirmed by similar adaptations of Muslim formulae in Early Islamic Latin and Middle Persian coinage. Reciprocally, late 8th-century Arabic letters by Muslims "react" to the emergence of Arabized Christians in Egypt by doing away with discriminatory social behavior, which had characterized Arabic letters to Christians during the previous two generations.

A last way in which the reach of the Early Islamic Empire informs *Official Arabic* is terminology. The distribution of loanwords in the administrative idiolects of Arabic sources from Egypt, Syria-Palestine, and Central Asia reveals the existence of layers of terminology, which respond to different cultural dynamics. The influence of substratal languages on the Early Islamic administrative idiolects is at its strongest in highly "localized" functional domains. The domains closer to the administration, on the contrary, exhibit a set of technical terms which are used uniformly in disparate regions. Finally, the results shed new light on the diachrony and political dimension of the official varieties of Imperial Arabic. The transregional component of Umayyad official technical terminology is represented by borrowings from Aramaic (with a significant contribution by Western dialects). The official Abbasid technical jargon, on the other hand, registers an increase of Persian and Eastern Aramaic borrowings.

While remaining in its essence an analysis of documentary practices, the results of this work further tie into a number of questions of general significance for the understanding of the social geography and cultural stratification of the Early Islamic Empire, as well as its relationship with the pre-Islamic past.

Re-orienting Egypt

A first way in which the conclusions reached in this study open new prospects for the research of the Early Islamic Empire, pertains to the agency of the imperial metropole in the periphery. The structural and formulaic aspects of Arabic papyrological evidence excavated in Egypt clearly show that the designs of those documents looked eastwards – to Syria and Damascus, and later to Iraq and Baghdad. In other words, by examining the Early Islamic documentary Arabic culture in Egypt, we are looking at its beginnings rather than its origins. This is *per se* neither an unexpected nor a previously unremarked insight. The developments of Arabic coinage and official epigraphy in the late 7th century are in fact unanimous in pointing to Greater Syria – and Damascus more specifically – as the source of administrative innovations that spread concentrically throughout the Umayyad Empire.

What the analysis of the use of loanwords in Umayyad Official Arabic (Chapter V) adds to our understanding of the reach of imperial power is a qualitative element. Umayyad Syria/Damascus was not merely a gateway for innovations brought by the Arabs to the conquered lands, to be spread at an imperial level, but even contributed to Umayyad Official Arabic itself by giving it a Syrian cultural imprint.[301,302] The documents' terminology further suggests that

301 Cf. for instance Khan 2008, 898 "The formulaic structure of both Arabic legal documents and Arabic letters in the Umayyad period were brought by the Arabs to the conquered territories. Some features of the formulae can be shown to have parallels in the pre-Islamic Semitic formula traditions (. . .)" and Reinfandt 2015, 288 "Thus the Arab tradition stood on the shoulders of a longer – *conjecturally Semitic or Near Eastern* – tradition that had been submerged during Greek, Roman, and Byzantine rule but reappeared in the 7th century" (emphasis is mine).

302 The presence of distinctively Syrian influences in the realm of Umayyad residential art can be inferred from the presence of Palmyran-style sculptures in the palace of Qaṣr al-Ḥayr

the Arabic secretaries operating in Egypt were drawn from the ranks of clerical personnel trained in Greater Syria. The rise of Iranian elements in the papyri from Early Abbasid Egypt underscores a similar convergence of imperial geography, ideology, and documentary fashions.

These reflections of course mostly concern our understanding of Early Islamic texts in Arabic. However, the same considerations apply to a smaller extent to neighbouring disciplines as well. If titles, terms, and epistolary formulae surfacing in the Early Islamic Greek and Coptic administrative idiolect of Egypt were "imported" from Umayyad Syria (Chapters III–V), then looking at an Islamic imperial context should be taken into account for the development of Greek and Coptic papyrology. Furthermore, the number of Greek loanwords transferred to Arabic through the intermediary of Aramaic dialects suggests that an otherwise invisible class of multilingual Aramaic clerks functioned as the mediators between the Greek and Arabic writing milieu.

The accidents of preservation determined that we see more vividly how much of the East the Arabs brought to the West. Yet, our evidence offers a sense of the extent to which imperial documents from the Iranian world and Central Asia looked west to Umayyad Syria. Thus, for instance, the old Roman *castrum* lives on, in a fashion, in the parchments from 8th-century Bactria in its late epigone *qaṣr*. In the same way, Judeo-Christian formulae influenced the use of invocations among Zoroastrians through the mediation of the Muslim *basmala*. The cross on pole of Byzantine coinage made inroads in Iran, modified into the floral cross of "standing caliph" coppers minted in Susa. Put in a different perspective, this is as much a matter of re-orienting Egypt as it is one of re-centering Umayyad Syria.

I have underscored in the introduction that the choice to focus my analysis on formal features was in response to the limits imposed by the fragmentation of textual evidence. While this remains true, the expanding documentary evidence from the Eastern regions of the Early Islamic Empire will in the future hopefully lead to a more organic understanding of the development of Early Islamic economic, administrative, and legal institutions as well. The still largely unpublished documents from the "Pahlavi Archive" in particular, show promise of providing historians with a much-needed term of comparison for the papyrological evidence from the Egyptian countryside. The orders delivered to the *bun* by a distant nameless *amīr* in the Berkeley parchments, for instance, echo requests of the equally anonymous *amiras* working in the background of the Senouthios

al-Gharbī; see Hillenbrand 2018, 88 and *ibid.*n18 with further references. Cf. also Meinecke 2020, 113–114.

archive.[303] The mention of taxes referred to as *kharāj* in the documents from Qom three generations before its first dated occurrence in Arabic in Central Asia and four generations before its introduction into Egypt shows that Greek, Coptic, and Arabic evidence should be considered in tandem with the Pahlavi one.

An Implosion of Late Antiquity

The nature of the connection between the Umayyad imperial metropole and the periphery is related to the question of the relationship of the Early Islamic Empire to the heritage of previous cultural traditions. Throughout the study, I have touched upon a broad array of "strings" attaching the Early Islamic documents to their antecedents of the 5th- to 7th-century Middle East; some very tenuous and likely unconscious, such as single lexical borrowings, other structural such as the "Semitic" epistolary prescript.

I have avoided trying to address the question of whether the Early Islamic Empire should be considered a part of Late Antiquity with capital letters as virtually every aspect of the Early Islamic culture originated in *one* late antiquity or the other.[304] While numismatics, architecture, and fine arts indicate most prominently Sasanian and Byzantine[305] artistic influxes (Chapter II), chancery documents underscore more vividly the "Semitic" contribution to Umayyad culture (Chapter III).

By emphasizing this, what point are we making? On one hand, that the merger of Roman, Persianate, Central Asian, and Arabian cultural regions into the Islamic Empire risks fitting very quickly into a paradigm of what has been referred to by scholars as an "explosion of Late Antiquity";[306] on the other, that the question of change and continuity between the Early Islamic and the previous world is to an

---

303 *CPR* XXX 12 (Egypt; VII).

304 The question of whether the Umayyad Empire should be considered as part of a Long Late Antiquity is debated among modern historians. For an overview of general questions on the periodization and competing notions of Late Antiquity, see *i.a.* James 2008, Marcone 2008, and Johnson 2012; for Early Islam's connection to the world of Late Antiquity, see especially Brown 1971, Fowden 1993, Kennedy 2001 and *id.* 2004b, Robinson 2003, and Marsham 2009b.

305 E.g., Hoyland 2015a, 230 "The Arabs were (. . .) not only heirs to Rome (. . .) but also heirs to Persia".

306 The expression "Explosion of Late Antiquity" (it. *esplosione di tardoantico*) was coined by Giardina 1999 as a critical assessment of the progressive chronological expansion of the concept of Late Antiquity (see also Marcone 2008, 17 and *ibid.*n53); with particular reference to the Early Islamic civilization, I use the term "explosion of Late Antiquity" to emphasize the merger of pre-Islamic practices from different cultural areas brought about by the Islamic conquest.

extent a matter of emphasis. Indeed, in the Arabic documentary evidence change and continuities are not only simultaneous but often also inextricably intermingled. Thus, for instance, the appearance of royal figures in Sasanian robes in Umayyad palaces of Syria and Palestine constitutes both an advancement of Sasanian royal imagery and a break with local iconographic tradition. The policy of cultural ambiguity that governed the relationship of the Muslim imperial elite with local elites further gives a measure of the extent in which resorting to the values of pre-Islamic late antique societies could be an ad hoc social strategy (Chapter IV). This is true for much of the heritage of previous cultures synthetized by the Umayyads into new forms and directions.

Without underplaying aspects of diversity, the discussion of formal templates and technical loanwords has put forward a pattern to navigate "late antique" traits of Imperial Arabic texts, or, in metaphorical terms, to make the Islamic Late Antiquity "implode". The high degree of trans-regional uniformity characterizing practices of Official Arabic (that is, by extension, of the cultural influences that shaped Official Arabic) indicates that for as long as the Islamicate world remained under the effective political rule of one imperial authority, imperial sponsorship was the driving force behind the selection and advancement of cultural traditions in the Caliphate – which tended to be those with which the metropole identified itself more closely. This is most clearly exemplified by the Syria-centric Aramaicizing imprint of Umayyad Official Arabic and the Iraq-centric Persianizing imprint of Early Abbasid Official Arabic.

Conversely, the influence of traditions which persisted, were adapted, were reshaped, and advanced outside the agency of imperial institutions, remained confined to a regional basis (Chapter III). This is not only true for the cultures the Islamic Empire superseded but also for the culture of origin of the Arab-Muslim elites. For instance, the theonym of South Arabian monotheists, *al-raḥmān*, enjoyed global resonance in the Islamicate world due to the influence of the Arab administration. At the other end of the spectrum, pre-Islamic Arabic formulae which did not make the cut for Umayyad Official Arabic, like the *anā fulān* opening, remained an essentially Arabian phenomenon throughout the 7th and 8th century.

Imperial Arabic as a Mirror of Early Islamic Society

The parallel existence of formal features that bear the mark of a private or official environment lead us to the plurality of social circumstances in which Imperial Arabic was practiced. The status of Arabic as a superstratal language in most regions of the Empire, together with the historically determined ideological matrix of the Umayyad language policy, laid the groundwork for the remarkable formal uniformity of official varieties of Imperial Arabic.

In many ways, the progressive Arabization of the populations of the Empire in the 9th and later centuries broke the ties between Arabic and the Islamic imperial administration, and marks a natural end of Imperial Arabic (Chapter I). As Arabic made its way into the conquered societies, the normative force of top-down regulations dwindled progressively and the responsiveness of private documentary practices slowed down. For instance, while the Umayyad epistolary prescript had gradually disappeared from Early Abbasid official documents during the late 8th century, it can still be found in private letters well into the 9th century.[307] Preliminary studies further suggest that post-Umayyad Arabic orthography became progressively less uniform with the passing of the centuries and dynasties.[308]

By contrast, aspects of polyphony within Imperial Arabic are the fruit of more circumscribed social configurations. Specifically, differences between private and official practices of Imperial Arabic can be connected to three main sources: (I) parallel writing traditions, (II) degree of formality/tone, (III) transformative trends.

Diversity *vis-à-vis* official scribal standards in terms of the parallel existence of fleshed-out writing traditions primarily concerns private epigraphy and represents the conjunction point of multiple social factors. In geographic terms, Early Islamic graffiti and epitaphs emerged in regions in which practice of Arabic literacy were rooted in the pre-Islamic time. Graffiti in particular give voice to semi-nomadic groups that are scarcely represented in other documentary sources.[309] Furthermore, a significant portion of these texts operate with a comparatively low degree of literacy and do not underscore a system of formal training (Chapter III). This in turn explains both the comparatively low incidence of official scribal practices on Early Islamic private epigraphy and the more conservative attitude of Arabic graffiti compared to official inscriptions in preserving the epigraphic tradition of old North Arabian languages.

307 E.g., *P.RagibLettres* 12, *P.David-WeillLouvre* 11, *P.Ryl.Arab.* II 8 (= *P.Ryl.Arab.* I VI 12), and *P.YounesCondolence* 1b (all from Egypt; all paleographically assigned to the 9th century).

308 See in particular the case-studies presented by Kaplony 2019 comparing spellings of selected terms and grammatical features in Umayyad, Abbasid, Fatimid Arabic, and Fatimid Judeo-Arabic documents. For the use of diacritical dots in Umayyad and Early Abbasid documents; see Kaplony 2008. Greek scribes also operated within relatively standardized norms for the transcription of Arabic terms; see Kaplony 2015.

309 Hoyland 1997b, 92. For the acquisition and purpose of literacy in a nomadic and semi-nomadic environment, see MacDonald 2009, IV who emphasizes the ludic aspect of literacy.

While it is clear that some private formulaic uses carried on from pre-Islamic Arabia, others reveal a distinctively Islamic tone. The occurrence of common religious expressions in private letters, graffiti, and epitaphs suggests that individual Arabic writers were exposed to a richer variety of religious traditions than those codified by official documents. Judging from the distribution of religious formulae in graffiti and epitaphs, some of these "private" traditions circulated across a significant geographical area. Throughout this study, I have argued that throughout the 7th and 8th centuries, the connection between Arabic and the milieu of the imperial elite was a key social drive behind the process of Arabization (as distinct from Islamization and conversion to Islam) of the regional elites of the Early Islamic Empire and, eventually, of broader strata of its population. The related phenomenon of the adoption of Arab-style scribal conventions in the writings of Christians and Zoroastrians within the Empire and by Central Asian rulers beyond its borders certainly corroborate this view. However, unofficial networks constituted a transformative factor of Early Islamicate societies in their own right. The variant of the Muslim testimony of faith used in the epitaph of ʿAbbāsa bt. Jurayj, for instance, indicates that her conversion was occasioned in contact with circles in which private practices of Arabic exerted a decisive influence.

In the formal peculiarities of private documents, we further discern elements of tone and register. The negligence of layout features in private letters on papyrus suggests lower standards of formality compared to official communications. Likewise, formulae only attested in private letters like the valediction *wa-l-salām ʿalay-ka wa-raḥmat allāh wa-barakātu-hu* possibly represent figures of politesse that belonged in a less formal, more familiar tone of letter-writing rather than an independent formulaic tradition altogether.

A last source of plurality within Imperial Arabic are "break-off" writing practices. As long as Arabic remained the native language of insular Muslim communities, its use strongly implied affiliation to the Arab-Muslim milieu.[310] Conversely, the adoption of the Arabic language by non-Muslims entailed the need to emphasize distinctive cultural traits. In Palestine, a distinctive Christian Arabic writing culture had detached itself from Umayyad Official Arabic as early as the 8th century. From Umayyad Official Arabic, Early Islamic Christian Arabic letters adopted the overall structure but adapted the formulae to express a distinct Christian identity. An urge for religious distinction also transpires from the use of the

310 Post 800, Arabic letters register an increase of the use of the – Muslim-connoted – so-called *taṣliya* (*ṣallā allāh ʿalā muḥammad/ʿalay-hi wa-sallama* "may God bless Muḥammad and give him peace"). This phenomenon can be interpreted as the will of the writer to mark his Muslim identity in a time in which Arabic had lost its quality as a signifier of religious boundaries. See Potthast 2019, 73.

spelling *al-ilāh* for "God" in dissociation with the coeval Muslim connoted *allāh*. Furthermore, the use of *al-ilāh* indicates that Early Islamic Christian Arabic writings from the Near East still looked to pre-Islamic Christian Arabic epigraphy.

The discussion on formal varieties of Imperial Arabic has not ventured into a linguistic categorization. A systematic linguistic and orthographical analysis based on the formal varieties of Early Islamic Arabic laid out in this study is the natural complement to the present research.[311] It may confirm or reject the preliminary categorizations laid out in the present work. Either way, if this study were to serve as the first step towards more thorough investigations, it would have fulfilled its purpose.

Concluding Note

Recent restorations have revealed that the figure depicted to the left of the future Umayyad caliph al-Walīd II in the frescos of Quṣayr ʿAmra is a scribe. Holding a sheet of papyrus or parchment, a stylus, and an inkpot,[312] he resembles his colleagues who populated the halls of the Neo-Assyrian royal palaces 1500 years ago. From the direction followed by the stylus on the sheet (from right to left),[313] it is heavily implied that he is writing in Arabic. Likely, a document written by a real-life scribe in al-Walīd's entourage would have been far from what today's Arabists would consider the most accomplished fruits of Arabic writing. It would rather have been of the kind historians would find more intriguing. We can only approximate what subject such a document was most likely to address. We can, however, be fairly sure of what formulae would have been used, how sections would have been divided and what the *mise-en-page* would have looked like. We could be about equally as confident for texts written in contemporary North Africa, Iraq, or Yemen – where no Early Islamic papyri and parchments have survived. Starting from formalized conventions of "Imperial" Arabic texts, it is my hope that this study has shown how these documents, for all their pragmatic and stereotypical nature, also carried "the dreams of men, the seed of commonwealths, the germs of empires" (J. Conrad, *Heart of Darkness*).

311 A study on linguistic variation in Arabic documentary papyri is currently being prepared by Fokelien Kootstra. On orthography, see Sijpesteijn 2020b (esp. 464–465), showing that 8th-century Arabic administrative documents display a more closely regimented orthography than coeval private and commercial ones.

312 De Palma *et al.* 2012, 334–335.

313 *Ibid.*, figs. 20 and 29.

Appendices

Appendix 1: Formal and Layout Structure of Early Islamic Arabic Official Letters

A) Long prescript (Official)/tripartite structure

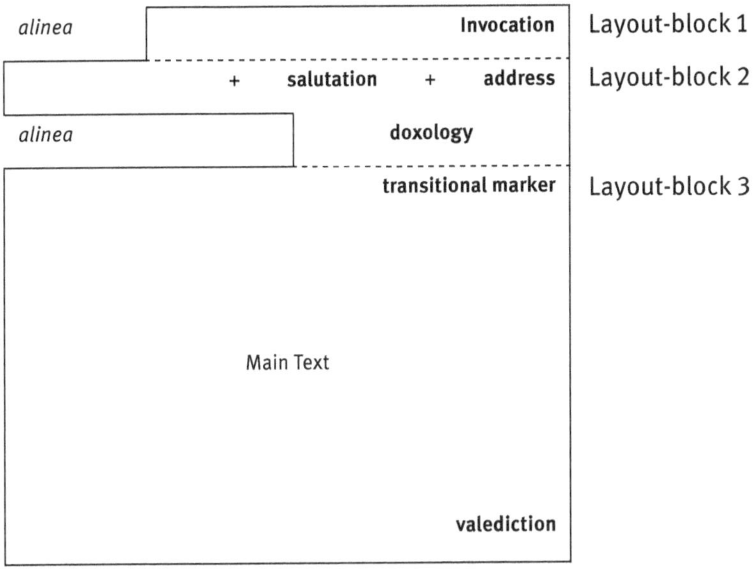

B) Short prescript (Official)/bipartite structure

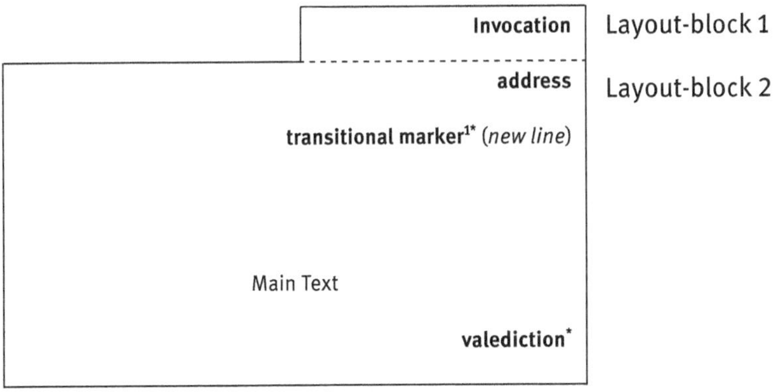

* Exceptional

https://doi.org/10.1515/9783110740820-037

Appendix 2: Formal and Layout Structure of Early Islamic Official Inscriptions

I

A Invocation

A1 *bi-sm allāh al-raḥmān al-raḥīm*

Sharon 2018 p. 101 (Jeruslem; 652/653); Hoyland 2006 p. 413 (Medina; 661–680); Silverman 2007 p. 605 (ʿAyn Ḥamad; 685–705); *CIAP* I p. 4, no. 1 (= *RCEA* I 17) (Abū Ghūsh; 685–705); *CIAP* I p. 103, no. 1 (Fīq; 692–702); *CIAP* II p. 5, no. 1 (= *RCEA* I 15) (Bāb al-Wādī; 685–705); *CIAP* III p. 104, no.1 (Abū Ghūsh; 685–705); Sharon 1966 (Fīq; 692); *CIAP* III p. 105, no. 2 (Khān al-Ḥathrūra; 685–705); *RCEA* I 12 (Qaṣr Burquʿ; 700/701); *CIAP* III p. 220, no.1 (Fīq; 704/705); *CIAP* III p. 221, no. 2 (Fīq; 704/705); *RCEA* I 9a (Jerusalem; 691/692) (x 5); *RCEA* I 9b (Jerusalem; 691/692); *RCEA* I 10 (Jerusalem; 691/692); *RCEA* I 11 (Jerusalem; 691/692); *RCEA* I 26* (Mecca; 719/720); Ory 1969 no. 3 (Bosra; 720/721); Mayer 1946 p. 73 (Qaṣr al-Muwaqqar; 722/723); *RCEA* I 27 (Qaṣr al-Ḥayr al-Gharbī; 727); *RCEA* I 28 (Qaṣr al-Ḥayr al-Sharqī; 728/729); *CIAP* II p. 207, no. 1 (Baysān; 737/738) (x 2); Imbert 2016 p. 337 (Quṣayr ʿAmra; 735–743?); Sauvaget 1944 p. 100 (= *RCEA* I 25) (Bouar; 742/743); Ritter 2016a p. 65 (Khirbat al-Minya; 743–744?); Ory 2005 no. 2 (Bosra; 745/746); *CIAP* II p. 215, no. 2 (Baysān; 752/753); Mittwoch 1935 p. 235–236 (Ṣanʿāʾ; 753/754); *MCIA* IV, 1 p. 40, no. 1* (= *RCEA* I 40*) (Mecca; 757/758); Faʿar 1984 p. 189–192 (Mecca; 761/762); *CIAP* I p. 144, no. 1 (Ascalon; 771/772); *MCIA* IV, 1 p. 43, no. 2 (Mecca; 776/777); *MCIA* IV, 1 p. 44, no. 4 (= *RCEA* I 49 (Mecca; 783/784); *MCIA* IV, 1 p. 46, no. 5 (Mecca; related to 783/784); *MCIA* IV, 1 p. 47 no. 6 (= *RCEA* I 51 (Mecca; 783/784) (x2); *RCEA* V additions and corrections 53 (= *RCEA* I 53) (Ramla, 788/789); *RCEA* I 54* (Tilmisān; 790/791); Gadjev/Shikhsaidov 2002 p. 4 (Djerbjent; 792/793); Zbiss 1960 II p. 28–29 (Monastir; 797/798); Abdeljaouad 2001 p. 43, no. 2 (Monastir; related to 797/798).

A2 *bi-sm allāh*

Kračkovskaja 1952 p. 89 (VIII; Tblisi); *CIAP* II p. 221, no. 3 (Baysān; 794/795).

A3 *allāhumma*

RCEA I 12 (Qaṣr Burquʿ; 700/701); Hamilton 1946 p. 70 (Qaṣr al-Muwaqqar; related to 722/723); Imbert 2016 p. 332 (Quṣayr ʿAmra; 735–743); Imbert 2016 p. 340 (Quṣayr ʿAmra; 735–743); Imbert 2016 p. 342 (Quṣayr ʿAmra; 735–743).

https://doi.org/10.1515/9783110740820-038

B Doxology

B1 *lā ilā illā allāh waḥda-hu lā sharīk la-hu muḥammad rasūl allāh*

CIAP I p. 4, no. 1 (= *RCEA* I 17) (Abū Ghūsh; 685–705); *CIAP* II p. 5, no. 1 (= *RCEA* I 15) (Bāb al-Wādī; 685–705); *CIAP* III p. 104, no. 1 (Abū Ghūsh; 685–705); *CIAP* III p. 105, no. 2 (Khān al-Ḥathrūra; 685–705); Silverman 2007 p. 605 (ʿAyn Ḥamad; 685–705) – addition of *ṣallā allāh ʿalay-hi wa-sallama*; *RCEA* I 9a (Jerusalem; 691/692) (x 5) – no *muḥammad rasūl allāh* (x2/5); no *lā sharīk la-hu muḥammad rasūl allāh* (x1/5); *RCEA* I 9b (Jerusalem; 691/692) – no *muḥammad rasūl allāh*; Sharon 1966 (Fīq; 692); *CIAP* III p. 220, no. 1 (Fīq; 704/705); *CIAP* III p. 221, no. 2 (Fīq; 704/705); Sauvaget 1944 no. 1 (= *RCEA* I 25) (Bouar; 742/743) – addition of *arsala-hu bi-l-hudā wa-dīn al-ḥaqq li-yuẓhira-hu ʿalā al-dīn kulli-hi wa-law kariha al-mushrikūn*; Ory 1969 no. 3 (Bosra; 720/721) – no *muḥammad rasūl allāh*; *RCEA* I 27 (Qaṣr al-Ḥayr al-Gharbī; 727)) – no *muḥammad rasūl allāh*; *RCEA* I 28 (Qaṣr al-Ḥayr al-Sharqī; 728/729); *CIAP* II p. 207, no. 1 (Baysān; 737/738) – addition of *ṣallā allāh ʿalay-hi wa-sallama*: *CIAP* II p. 215, no. 2 (Baysān; 752/753) – addition of *ṣallā allāh ʿalay-hi wa-sallama*; Mittwoch 1935 p. 235–236 (Ṣanʿāʾ; 753/754) – addition of *arsala-hu bi-l-hudā wa-dīn al-ḥaqq li-yuẓhira-hu ʿalā al-dīn kulli-hi*; *CIAP* I p. 144, no. 1 (Ascalon; 771/772) – addition of *ṣallā allāh ʿalay-hi wa-sallama*; Abdeljaouad 2001 p. 43, no. 2 (Monastir; related to 797/798) – addition of *ṣallā allāh ʿalay-hi wa-sallama*.

B2 *al-ḥamdu li-llāh alladhī lā illā huwa*

RCEA I 9a (Jerusalem; 691/692) – no *alladhī lā illā huwa*; *RCEA* I 10 (Jerusalem; 691/692); *RCEA* I 11 (Jerusalem; 691/692).

B3 *baraka min allāh*

CIAP II p. 221, no. 3 (Baysān; 794/795).

C Endophoric Reference Alone (VII c.)

C1 *hādhā al-kadhā li-fulān*

AI Z 68 (Ṭāʾif; 677/678); Hoyland 2006 p. 413 (Medina; 661–680).

D Dispositive Clause

D1 *amara bi-*

Silverman 2007 p. 605 (ʿAyn Ḥamad; 685–705); *CIAP* I p. 4, no. 1 (= *RCEA* I 17) (Abū Ghūsh; 685–705); *CIAP* I p. 103, no. 1 (Fīq; 692–702); *CIAP* II p. 5, no. 1 (= *RCEA*

I 15) (Bāb al-Wādī; 685–705); *CIAP* III p. 104, no. 1 (Abū Ghūsh; 685–705); *CIAP* III p. 105, no. 2 (Khān al-Ḥathrūra; 685–705); *RCEA* I 8* (Fusṭāṭ; 688) – *hādhihi* (. . .) *amara bi-hā*; Sharon 1966 (Fīq; 692); *CIAP* III p. 220, no. 1 (Fīq; 704/705); *CIAP* III p. 221, no. 2 (Fīq; 704/705); *RCEA* I 18*[1] (Damascus; 705/706); Sauvaget 1947 p. 66* (Medina; 706/707); Ory 1999 p. 376 (Bosra; 717/718); *RCEA* I 26* (Mecca; 719/720); Mayer 1946 p. 73 (Qaṣr al-Muwaqqar; 722/723); *RCEA* I 27 (Qaṣr al-Ḥayr al-Gharbī; 727); *RCEA* I 28 (Qaṣr al-Ḥayr al-Sharqī; 728/729); *CIAP* II p. 207, no. 1 (Baysān; 737/738); Sauvaget 1944 no. 1 (= *RCEA* I 25) (Bouar; 742/743); Ritter 2016a p. 65 (Khirbat al-Minya; 743–744?); *RCEA* I 46* (Medina; 749/750); *CIAP* I p. 31, no. 2* (= *RCEA* I 37 (Sidon and Acre; before 750)) – *mā amara bi-*(. . .)*/-hi*; Mittwoch 1935 p. 235–236 (Ṣanʿāʾ; 753/754); *EPI* 14993 (Mecca; 761/762); al-Faʿar 1984 p. 189–192 (Mecca; 761/762); al-Faʿar 1984 p. 194 (Mecca; 761/762) – *hādhā amara* (sic) (. . .) *bi-*; *EPI* 14941 (Medina; 768/769); *CIAP* I p. 144, no. 1 (Ascalon; 771/772); *MCIA* IV, 1 p. 43 no. 2 (Mecca; 776/777); *MCIA* IV, 1 p. 44, no. 3* (= *RCEA* I 48*) (Mecca; 783/784); *MCIA* IV, 1 p. 44, no. 4 (= *RCEA* I 49) (Mecca; 783/784); *MCIA* IV, 1 p. 47, no. 7 (= *RCEA* I 50) (Mecca; 783/784); *MCIA* IV, 1 p. 47, no. 6 (= *RCEA* I 51) (Mecca; 783/784) x 2; *MCIA* IV, 1 p. 48, no. 8 (= *RCEA* I 52) (Mecca; 783/784); Gadjev/Shikhsaidov 2002 p. 4 (Djerbjent; 792/793).

D2 *mimmā amara*

RCEA I 10 (Jerusalem; 691/692) – *mimma amara-hu* (sic); Ory 2005 no. 2 (Bosra; 745/746); *CIAP* II p. 215, no. 2 (Baysān; 752/753); *EPI* 14944 (Medina; 778/779); *RCEA* V additions and corrections 53 (= *RCEA* I 53) (Ramla, 788/789); *CIAP* II p. 221, no. 3 (Baysān; 794/795); *IM* p. 28–29 (Munastir; 797/798); Abdeljaouad 2001 p. 43, no. 2 (Munastir; related to 797/798).

D3 *mā banā* (sic)

RCEA I 12 (Qaṣr Burquʿ; 700/701).

E Executive Clause 1

E1 *ʿalā yaday fulān*

RCEA I 10 (Jerusalem; 691/692); Sharon 1966 (Fīq; 692) – *ʿumilat ʿalā yaday*; *CIAP* I p. 103, no. 1 (Fīq; 692–702) – *ʿumilat ʿalā yaday*; *CIAP* III p. 220, no.1 (Fīq; 704/705); *CIAP* III p. 221, no. 2 (Fīq; 704/705); *RCEA* I 10 (Jerusalem; 691/692); Mayer 1946 p. 73

1 Two versions extant.

(Qaṣr al-Muwaqqar; 722/723) – *buniyat ʿalā yaday*; *RCEA* I 27 (Qaṣr al-Ḥayr al-Gharbī; 727) – *ajra-hu ʿumila* (?) *ʿalā yaday*; *CIAP* II p. 207, no. 1 (Baysān; 737/738); Ritter 2016a p. 65 (Khirbat al-Minya; 743–744?); *CIAP* I p. 31, no. 2* (= *RCEA* I 37* (Sidon and Acre; before 750)) – *wa-jarā ʿalā yaday*; Ory 1969 no. 15 (Bosra; VIII); *CIAP* II p. 215, no. 2 (Baysān; 752/753); Mittwoch 1935 p. 235–236 (Ṣanʿāʾ; 753/754); al-Faʿar 1984 p. 194 (Mecca; 761/762); *CIAP* I p. 144, no. 1 (Ascalon; 771/772); *MCIA* IV, 1 p. 43 no. 2 (Mecca; 776/777); *MCIA* IV, 1 p. 44, no. 4 (= *RCEA* I 49) (Mecca; 783/784); *RCEA* V additions and corrections 53 (= *RCEA* I 53) (Ramla, 788/789); Gadjev/Shikhsaidov 2002 p. 4 (Djerbjent; 792/793); *CIAP* II p. 221, no. 3 (Baysān; 794/795).

E2 *mimmā faʿala fulān ʿalā yaday fulān*

CIAP I p. 30, no. 1* (= *RCEA* I 32*) (Acre; before 743) – *mimmā jarā ʿalā yaday* Ory 1969 no. 15 (Bosra; VIII) – *mimmā jarā ʿalā yaday*; *RCEA* I 28 (Qaṣr al-Ḥayr al-Sharqī; 728/729) – *mimmā ʿamila* (. . .) *ʿalā yady*.

E3 *banā*

Hoyland 2006 p. 413 (Medina; 661–680) – *banā-hu*; *RCEA* I 9a (Jerusalem; 691/692) – *banā hādhihi al-qubba*.

E4 *ʿamila fulān*

EPI 14944 (Medina; 778/779) – *mimmā ʿamila*; *MCIA* IV, 1 p. 47, no. 6 (= *RCEA* I 51) (Mecca; 783/784) x2; *MCIA* IV, 1 p. 44, no. 4 (= *RCEA* I 49) (Mecca; 783/784) – *mimmā ʿamila*.

F Supervisory Clause

F1 *wa-qāma bi-hi/ʿalay-hi fulān*

Hoyland 2006 p. 413 (Medina; 661–680); *RCEA* I 8* (Fusṭāṭ; 688); Ory 1969 no. 1 (Bosra; 720/721); Sauvaget 1944 no. 1 (= *RCEA* I 25) (Bouar; 742/743).

G Signature

G1 (wa-)*kataba fulān*

AI Z 68 (Ṭāʾif; 677/678); Ory 1969 no. 1 (Bosra; 720/721).

II

A) Official Inscriptions (7 lines)

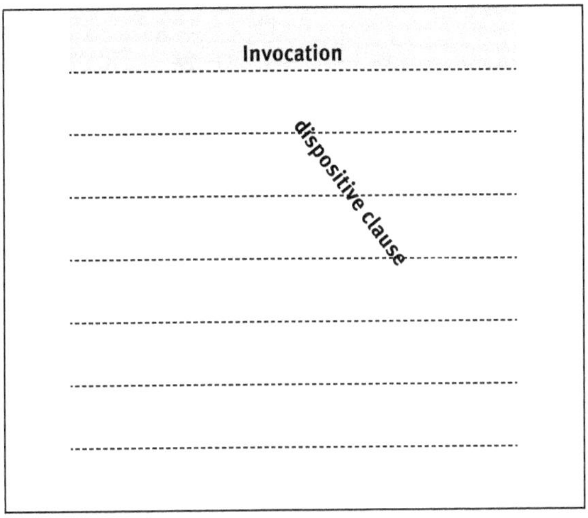

B) Official Inscriptions (3 lines)

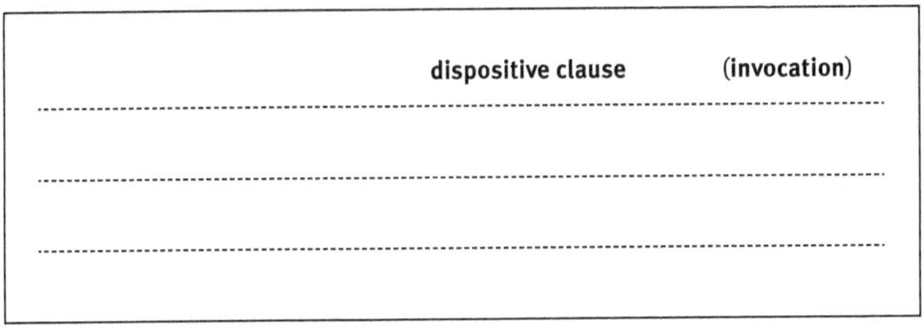

Appendix 3: Comparative Table of Early Islamic Arab-style Letters

https://doi.org/10.1515/9783110740820-039

	Arabic to Muslim addressees	Arabic to Christian addressees	Arab-style Greek	Arab-style Coptic	Arab-style Sogdian	Arab-style Middle Persian
Invocation	*bi–sm allāh al-raḥmān al-raḥīm* "In the name of God, the Merciful, the Compassionate"	*bi–sm allāh al-raḥmān al-raḥīm* "In the name of God, the Merciful, the Compassionate"	/	/	/	/
			en onomati tou theou "In God's name" *CPR* XXII 52 (Ishqawh; 709–714) *P.Apoll.* 4 (Edfū; VII/VIII) *P.Apoll.* 7–8 (Edfū; VII/VIII) *P.Lond.* IV 1350–1 (Ishqawh; both 710) *P.Lond.* IV 1353 (Ishqawh; 710) *P.Lond.* IV 1356 (Ishqawh; 710) *P.Lond.* IV 1359–60 (Ishqawh; both 710) *P.Lond.* IV 1362 (Ishqawh; 710) *P.Lond.* IV 1368–70 (Ishqawh; all 710) *P.Lond.* IV 1374–6 (Ishqawh; both 710) *P.Lond.* IV 1378–80 (Ishqawh; all 710) *P.Lond.* IV 1381 (Ishqawh; 708–710) *P.Lond.* IV 1394 (Ishqawh; 708–709) *P.Lond.* IV 1401 (Ishqawh; 709–714) *P.Ross.Georg.* IV 2 (Ishqawh; 710) *P.Ross.Georg.* IV 13 (Ishqawh; 709–710) *P.Ross.Georg.* IV 14 (Ishqawh; 710) *SB* I 4826 (Fayyūm; VII) *SB* VIII 9748 (Fayyūm; VII)	*Hᵉm pᵉ-ran ᵉm-pᵉ-noute* "In God's name" *O.CrumVC* 116 (Fayyūm; VII?) *P.Fay.Copt.* 26 (Fayyūm; VIII/IX) *P.Mich.Copt.* 12 (Fayyūm; VII) *P.Ryl.Copt.* 321 (Egypt; viii)	/	*pad nām ī yazd* "In God's name" Weber 2005 Berk. 188 Berk. 197

			SB VIII 9752 (Fayyūm; VII) *SB* X 10459 (Ishqawh; 709–714) *SB* XVI 12575 (Fayyūm; VII/VIII)			
	/	/	b) *en onomati tou theou* ***tou pantokratoros*** "In the name of God Almighty" *P.Ness.* 63 (Nessana; 675) *P.Ness.* 71 (Nessana; late VII) *P.Ness.* 72 (Nessana; 684) *P.Ness.* 73 (Nessana; 683) *P.Ross.Georg.* V 11 (Egypt; VIII) PSI XV 1570 (Edfū; 667 or 682)	/	/	*pad nām ī yazd* ***ī kardakkar*** "in the name of God who is powerful" Berk. 187
	/	/	/	/	*pr n'm βyy* ***δ'mδn'k*** "in the name of God, the creator" Mugh 1.I (Mount Mugh; 720–1)	/
Address	*min fulān ilā fulān* "from X to Y"	*min fulān ilā fulān* "from X to Y"	a) *para deinos pros deina* "From X to Y" *P.Apoll.* 7–8 (Edfū; VII/VIII) *PSI* XV 1570 (Edfū; 667 or 682) *SB* VIII 9748 (Fayyūm; VII) *SB* VIII 9752 (Fayyūm; VII) *SB* XVI 12575 (Fayyūm; VII/VIII)	/	*MN* X *'t* Y "From X to Y" Mugh 1.I (Mount Mugh; 720–1)	

(continued)

(continued)

	Arabic to Muslim addressees	Arabic to Christian addressees	Arab-style Greek	Arab-style Coptic	Arab-style Sogdian	Arab-style Middle Persian
			b) *o deina tō$_i$ deini$_i$* "X to Y" *CPR* XXII 52 (Ishqawh; 709–714) *P.Lond.* IV 1350–3 (Ishqawh; all 710) *P.Lond.* IV 1356 (Ishqawh; 710) *P.Lond.* IV 1378–80 (Ishqawh; all 710) *P.Lond.* IV 1381 (Ishqawh; 708–710) *P.Lond.* IV 1394 (Ishqawh; 708–709) *P.Lond.* IV 1399 (Ishqawh; 709–714) *P.Lond.* IV 1401 (Ishqawh; 709–714) *P.Ness.* 72 (Nessana; 684) *P.Ness.* 73 (Nessana; 683) *P.Ross.Georg.* IV 2 (Ishqawh; 710) *P.Ross.Georg.* IV 13 (Ishqawh; 709–710) *P.Ross.Georg.* IV 14 (Ishqawh; 710)			
Salutation	*salām ʿalay-ka/ ʿalay-kum* "peace be upon you"	*salām ʿalay-ka/ ʿalay-kum* "peace be upon you" (exceptional)	*eirenē soi/hymin* "peace be upon you" (VII c.) *PSI* XV 1570 (Edfū; 667 or 682) *SB* I 4826 (Fayyūm; VII) *SB* VIII 9748 (Fayyūm; VII) *SB* VIII 9752 (Fayyūm; VII)	a) *T-eirene nak / nēt^{e}n* "peace unto you" *P.Bal.* 214 (Deir el-Balā'izah; VII/VIII) *P.Bal.* 262 (Deir el-Balā'izah; VII/VIII) *P.Heid.* XI 490 (al-Ushmūnayn; VIII)	/	/

/	/	/		b) *T-irēnē* ^{e}*n-p*^{e}*-noute ne-k/* *T-irēnē nak ebol hit*^{e}*n-p*^{e}*-noute* "God' peace to you/ Peace unto you from God" *CPR* II 225 (Fayyūm; VIII/IX) *P.Fay.Copt.* 26 (Fayyūm; VIII/IX) *P.Heid.* XI 491 (al-Ushmūnayn; VIII) *P.Lond.Copt.* I 1165 (al-Ushmūnayn; VII/VIII) *P.Mich.Copt.* 12 (Fayyūm; VII) *P.Ryl.Copt.* 321 (Egypt; VIII) *SB Kopt.* 280 (Fayyūm; VIII/IX)	/	/

(continued)

(continued)

	Arabic to Muslim addressees	Arabic to Christian addressees	Arab-style Greek	Arab-style Coptic	Arab-style Sogdian	Arab-style Middle Persian
Doxology (1) *ḥamdala*	*aḥmadu ilay-ka allāh . . .* "I praise God for your sake . . . "	*aḥmadu allāh . . .* "I praise God . . . "	*eucharistō/ eucharistoumen tō theō* "I/we thank God" *CPR* XXII 52 (Ishqawh; 709–714) *P.Lond.* IV 1350–3 (Ishqawh; all 710) *P.Lond.* IV 1356 (Ishqawh; 710) *P.Lond.* IV 1359–60 (Ishqawh; both 710) *P.Lond.* IV 1362 (Ishqawh; 710) *P.Lond.* IV 1368–70 (Ishqawh; all 710) *P.Lond.* IV 1374–6 (Ishqawh; both 710) *P.Lond.* IV 1378–80 (Ishqawh; all 710) *P.Lond.* IV 1381 (Ishqawh; 708–710) *P.Lond.* IV 1394 (Ishqawh; 708–709) *P.Lond.* IV 1399 (Ishqawh; 709–714) *P.Lond.* IV 1401 (Ishqawh; 709–714)	/	*sp's ZKn βγ* "Thanks to God" Mugh 1.I (Mount Mugh; 720)	/
Doxology (2) (*shahāda*)	*. . . alladhī lā ilāh illā huwa* " . . . there is no other god but He"	*alladhī lā ilāh illā huwa* " . . . there is no other god but He"	/	/	/	/

Transition	*ammā baʿd* "as for after"	*ammā baʿd* "as for after"	a) *kai meta tauta* (Egypt) "and after" *CPR* XXII 52 (Ishqawh; 709–714) *P.Lond.* IV 1350–3 (Ishqawh; all 710) *P.Lond.* IV 1356 (Ishqawh; 710) *P.Lond.* IV 1359–60 (Ishqawh; both 710) *P.Lond.* IV 1362 (Ishqawh; 710) *P.Lond.* IV 1368–70 (Ishqawh; all 710) *P.Lond.* IV 1374–6 (Ishqawh; both 710) *P.Lond.* IV 1378–80 (Ishqawh; all 710) *P.Lond.* IV 1381 (Ishqawh; 708–710) *P.Lond.* IV 1394 (Ishqawh; 708–709) *P.Lond.* IV 1399 (Ishqawh; 709–714) *P.Lond.* IV 1401 Ishqawh; 709–714) *P.Ross.Georg.* IV 2 (Ishqawh; 710) *P.Ross.Georg.* IV 13 (Ishqawh; 709–710) *P.Ross.Georg.* IV 14 (Ishqawh; 710) *PSI* XV 1570 (Edfū; 667 or 682) *SB* V 7520 (Ishqawh; 710) *SB* VIII 9748 (Fayyūm; VII) *SB* VIII 9752 (Fayyūm; VII) *SB* X 10459 (Ishqawh; 709–714) *SB* XVI 12575 (Fayyūm; VII/VIII) b) *epeita* (Syria) "afterwards" *P.Ness.* 72 (Nessana; 684) *P.Ness.* 73 (Nessana; 683)	*Menesa nai* "thereafter" *CPR* II 225 (Fayyūm; VIII/IX) *P.Fay.Copt.* 26 (Fayyūm; VIII/IX) *P.Ryl.Copt.* 321 (Egypt; VIII)	/	/

(continued)

(continued)

	Arabic to Muslim addressees	Arabic to Christian addressees	Arab-style Greek	Arab-style Coptic	Arab-style Sogdian	Arab-style Middle Persian
Valediction	*wa-l-salām ʿalay-ka wa-raḥmat allāh* "peace be upon you and the mercy of God"	/	a) *eirenē soi/hymin* "peace be upon you" *P.Apoll.* 5 (Edfū; vii/viii) *P.Apoll.* 8 (Edfū; vii/viii) *P.Ness.* 70 (Nessana; 685) *P.Ness.* 74 (Nessana; 685) *PSI* XV 1570 (Edfū; 667 or 682)	*T–eirene nak / nēt^{e}n* "peace be with you" *O.CrumVC* 116 (Fayyūm; vii/viii) *P.Bal.* 256 (Deir el–Balā'izah; vii/viii). *P.Bal.* 277 (Deir el–Balā'izah; vii/viii)	n.d.	/
	/	/	b) *eirenē soi/hymin* ***apo tou theou*** "peace from God be upon you" *P.Apoll.* 7 (Edfū; vii/viii) *P.Lond.* V 1892 (vii/viii) *P.Ness.* 68 (Nessana; 680) *SB* VIII 9748 (Fayyūm; vii) P.Vind.inv. G. P. 44498	/	n.d.	/
	/	*wa-l-salām ʿalā man ittabaʿa al-hudā* "peace be with him who follows the Guidance"	/	/	n.d.	/

Legend

Omission

Adaptation

Bibliography

Primary Sources

Abbreviations of Quoted Editions

Arabic, Greek and Coptic Documents

Editions of Greek and Coptic papyri are quoted according to the abbreviations of J. F. Oates *et. al.* *Checklist of editions of Greek, Latin, Demotic and Coptic papyri, Ostraca and Tablets*, 5th edition (Bulletin of the American Society of Papyrologists Suppl. 9) (Oxford: Oxbow, 2001). The up-to-date electronic version is accessible at http://papyri.info/docs/checklist (accessed Apr. 30, 2021). Editions of Arabic papyri are quoted according to the abbreviations of P.M. Sijpesteijn, J. F. Oates and A. Kaplony "Checklist of Arabic Papyri", *Bulletin of the American Society of Papyrologists* 42 (2005), 127–166. The up-to-date electronic version is accessible at http://www.naher-osten.uni-muenchen.de/forschung/papyrologie/apb/index.html (accessed Apr. 30, 2021).

Aramaic Documents

TAD = Porten, Bezalel / Yardeni, Ada, *Textbook of Aramaic documents from ancient Egypt I: Letters*, Winona Lake: Eisenbrauns, 1986.

Middle Iranian Documents

Berk. = Pahlavi Documents, Berkeley CA, mostly unedited.

BD = Sims-Williams, Nicholas, *Bactrian Documents from Northern Afghanistan*

I: *Legal and Economic Documents*. London: The Nour Foundation, 2000.

II: *Letters and Buddhist Texts*. London: The Nour Foundation, 2007.

III: *Plates*, London: The Nour Foundation, 2012.

CII = *Corpus Inscriptionum Iranicarum, Part III: Pahlavi Inscriptions, Vol. IV, Ostraca, Vol. V, Papyri*

Plates: Menasce (de), Jean, *Ostraca and Papyri*, London: Lund Humphries, 1957.

Text: Weber, Dieter, *Ostraca, Papyri und Pergamente*, London: School of Oriental and African Studies, 1992.

Mugh = Sogdian documents from the Mugh archive, mostly edited by Vladimir A. Livshits, *Sogdian Epigraphy of Central Asia and Semirech'e. Corpus Inscriptionum Iranicarum. Part II: Inscriptions of the Seleucid and Parthian Periods and of Eastern Iran and Central Asia vol. III* (ed. Nicholas Sims-Williams, trans. Tom Stableford), London, 2015.

Tab. = Pahlavi Documents from the Ṭabaristān Archive.

TSP = Emile Benveniste, *Textes Sogdiens édités, traduits et commentés par E. Benveniste* Paris: Librairie Orientaliste Paul Geuthner, 1940.

https://doi.org/10.1515/9783110740820-040

Sabaic Documents and Inscriptions

CIH = *Corpus Inscriptionum Semiticarum. Pars Quarta, Inscriptiones Himyariticas et Sabaeas continens*, 3 vols., Paris: E. Republicae Typographeo, 1889–1931.

X.BSB = Stein, Peter, *Die altsüdarabischen Minuskelinschriften auf Holzstäbchen aus der Bayerischen Staatsbibliothek in München*, 2 vols., Tübingen: Wasmuth, 2010.

Arabic Epigraphy

N.b. Inscriptions known only through literary reports have been marked with an asterisk (e.g., *RCEA* I 8*).

AI = Grohmann, Adolf, *Arabic Inscriptions. Expedition Philby-Ryckmans-Lippens en Arabie* 2,1m Louvain: Publications Universitaires, Inst. Orientaliste, 1962.

CIAP = Sharon, Moshe, *Corpus Inscriptionum Arabicarum Palaestinae*

I: Leiden/New York/Cologne: Brill, 1997.

II: Leiden/Boston: Brill, 1999.

III: Leiden/Boston: Brill, 2004.

CG = Wiet, Gaston, el-Hawary Hassan, M., and Rached Hussein, eds., *Catalogue Général du Musée Arabe du Caire. Stèles Funéraires*

I: *Tome Premier*, Cairo: Institut Français d'Archéologie Orientale, 1932.

VII: *Tome Septième*, Cairo: Institut Français d'Archéologie Orientale, 1940.

VIII: *Tome Huitième*, Cairo: Institut Français d'Archéologie Orientale, 1941.

IX: *Tome Neuvième*, Cairo: Institut Français d'Archéologie Orientale, 1941.

X: *Tome Dixième*, Cairo: Institut Français d'Archéologie Orientale, 1942.

CMC = Wiet, Gaston, *Catalogue général du Musée de l'art islamique du Caire. Inscriptions historiques sur pierre*, Cairo: Institut Français d'Archéologie Orientale, 1971.

DZ = al-Rāshid, Saʿd b. Abdulaziz

I: *Darb Zubaydah, the Pilgrim Road from Kufa to Mecca*, Riyadh: Riyadh University Libraries, 1980.

II: "Darb Zubayda: La Route de Pèlerinage de Kûfa à la Mecque", in: Ali I. al-Gahbban *et al.*, eds., *Routes d'Arabie: Archéologie et Histoire du Royaume d'Arabie Saoudite*, Paris: Somogy, 2010, 425–431.

EIA = Jbour (al), Khaled Suleman, *Etudes des inscriptions arabes dans le désert Nord-Est de la Jordanie*, 2 vols. Ph.D. thesis, Aix-Marseille, 2006.

IM = Zbiss, Slimane M., *Inscriptions de Monastir. Corpus des Inscriptions Arabes de Tunisie, 2ème partie*, Tunis: La Presse, 1960.

MCIA = *Matériaux pour un Corpus inscriptionum Arabicarum*

I: *Égypte*:

Max van Berchem, *Fascicule premier*, Paris: Leroux, 1894.

Gaston Wiet, *Tome deuxième*, Cairo: Imprimerie de l'institut français d'archéologie orientale, 1930.

IV: el-Hawary, Ḥasan M. / Wiet, Gaston, *Arabie: inscriptions et monuments de la Mecque Ḥaram et Kaʿba*, revu et mis au point par Nikita Elisséeff, Cairo: Imprimerie de l'institut français d'archéologie orientale, 1984.

MI = Ory, Solange, *Monuments et inscriptions des époques Umayyade et Salǧukide à Buṣrā*, Ph.D. thesis, Paris, 1969.

NI = al-Kilābī, Ḥayāt (2009), *Al-nuqūsh al-islāmiyya ʿalā ṭarīq al-ḥajj al-shāmī bi-shamāl ġarb al-Mamlaka al-ʿArabiya as-saʿūdiyya (min al-qarn al-awwal ilā al-qarn al-khāmis al-hijrī)*, Riyadh: King Fahd National Library
PoI = Nevo Yehuda D., "Towards a prehistory of Islam", *Jerusalem Studies in Arabic and Islam* 17 (1994), 101–141.
RCEA = Combe Etienne *et al.*, eds., *Répertoire Chronologique d'Épigraphie Arabe*
I: *Tome Premier*, Cairo: Institut Français d'Archéologie Orientale, 1931.
V: *Tome Cinquième*, Cairo: Institut Français d'Archéologie Orientale, 1934.
XV: *Tome Quinzième*, Cairo: Institut Français d'Archéologie Orientale: Cairo, 1956.
TKN = al-Faʿar, Muḥammad Fahd ʿAbd Allāh, *Taṭawwur al-kitābāt wa l-nuqūsh fī l-Ḥijāz mundhu fajr al-islām ḥattā muntaṣaf al-qarn as-sābiʿ al-hijrī, coll. Asāʾil jāmiʿiyya*, Mecca: Umm al-Qurā, 1984.
WS = al-Bqāʿīn, Firas / Corbett, Glenn J. / Khamis, Elias, "An Umayyad Era Mosque and Desert Waystation from Wadi Shīreh, Southern Jordan", *Journal of Islamic Archaeology* 2 (2015), 93–126.

Arabic Numismatics and Sigillography

APS= Porter, Venetia, *Arabic and Persian Seals and Amulets in the British Museum*, London: British Museum Press, 2011.
BM= Lane Poole, Stanley, *Catalogue of Arabic Glass Weights in the British Museum*, London: Longmans & co., 1891.
BMC = Walker, John, *A Catalogue of the Muhammadan Coins in the British Museum*
I: *A Catalogue of the Arab-Sassanian Coins*, London: British Museum, 1941.
II: *A Catalogue of the Arab-Byzantine and post-Reform Umaiyad Coins*, London: British Museum, 1956.
CAM = Miles, George C., *Contributions to Arabic Metrology: Early Arabic Glass Weights and Measure Stamps Acquired by the American Numismatic Society 1951–1956*, New York: The American Numismatic Society, 1958.
CAM2 = Miles, George C., *Early Arabic Glass Weights and Measure Stamps in the Benaki Museum, Athens (= CAM2 BM), and the Peter Ruthven Collection, Ann Arbor (= CAM2 PRC)*, New York: The American Numismatic Society, 1963.
DOC = Foss, Clive, *Arab-Byzantine Coins. An Introduction, with a Catalogue of the Dumbarton Oaks Collection* (Dumbarton Oaks Byzantine Collection Publications 12), Washington: Dumbarton Oaks Research Library and Collection, 2008.
EAG = *Early Arabic Glass Weights and Stamps*
I: Miles George C. / Frederick R. Matson, *With a Study of the Manufacture of Eighth-Century Egyptian Glass Weights and Stamps* (Numismatic Notes and Monographs 111), New York: The American Numismatic Society, 1948.
II: Miles George C. *Early Arabic Glass Weights and Stamps. A Supplement* (Numismatic Notes and Monographs 120), New York: The American Numismatic Society, 1951.
EIGS = Morton, Alexander H., *A Catalogue of Early Islamic Glass Stamps in the British Museum*, London: British Museum Publications, 1985.
EPV = Launois, Aimée, "Estampilles et poids faibles en verre omeyyades et abbasides au Musée Arabe du Caire", *Mélanges islamologiques* 3 (1956), 1–83.

GWS = Petrie, Flinders W. M., *Glass Stamps and Weights Illustrated from the Egyptian Collection in University College, London*, British School of Archaeology in Egypt University College, London, 1926.
GWVS= Eldada, Katharina, "Glass Weights and Vessel Stamps", in: Jere L. Bacharach, ed., *Fustat Finds. Beads, Coins, Medical Instruments, Textiles and other Artifacts from the Awad Collection*, Cairo: The American University in Cairo Press, 2004, 112–166.
SICA = *Sylloge of Islamic Coins in the Ashmolean*
I: Album, Stephen / Goodwin, Tony, *Pre-Reform Coinage of the Early Islamic Period*, Oxford: Ashmolean Museum, 2002.
UAT = Balog, Paul, *Umayyad, ʿĀbbasid and Ṭūlūnid Glass Weights and Vessel Stamps*, New York: The American Numismatic Society, 1976.

Literary Sources

Alvarus = Paulus Alvarus, *Indiculus luminosus* in: Juan Gil, ed., *Corpus scriptorum Muzarabicorum I*, Madrid: Inst. "Antonio de Nebrija", 1973, 270–314. Partial English translation: Colbert, Edward P., *The Martyrs of Córdoba (850–859): A Study of the Sources*, Washington: Catholic University of America Press, 1962.
Balādhurī = Aḥmad b. Jābir al-Balādhurī, *Liber expugnationis regionum* [*Futūḥ al-buldān*], 2 vols., Michael J. de Goeje, ed., reprint, Frankfurt: Institute for the History of Arabic-Islamic Science at the Johann Wolfgang Goethe University, 1992 [1866]. English Translation: *Origins of the Islamic State, Being a Translation from the Arabic Accompanied with Annotations, Geographic and Historic Notes of the Kitâb Futûḥ Al-Buldân of al-Imâm abu-l ʿAbbâs Aḥmad ibn-Jâbir al-Balâdhuri*, Philip Khûri Ḥitti (trans.), New York: Columbia University Press, 1916–1924.
Bīrūnī = Muḥammad b. Aḥmad al-Bīrūnī, "Das Vorwort zur Drogenkunde [*Kitāb al-ṣaydala fī al-ṭibb*] des Bīrūnī eingeleitet, übersetzt und erläutert von Max Meyerhof", *Quellen und Studien zur Geschichte der Naturwissenschaften und der Medizin* 3, 3, [157–208].
Chron. Mar. = *Chronicon Maroniticum*, in: E. W. Brooks, ed., *Chronica Minora*, II (Corpus Scriptorum Christinorum Orientalium, *Scriptores Syri* 3), Paris: Louvain: Secrétariat du CorpusSCO, 1904, 43–74. Partial English translation: Palmer, Andrew, *The Seventh Century in West Syrian Chronicles*, Liverpool: Liverpool University Press, 1993 at 29–35.
Jahshiyārī = Ṃuhammad b. ʿAbdūs, *Kitāb al-wuzarāʾ wa-al-kuttāb*, Muṣṭafā as-Saqqā *et al.*, eds., reprint, Cairo: Sharikat Maktabat wa-Maṭbaʿat Muṣṭafā al-Bābī al-Ḥalabī, 1981 [1938]. Partial German Translation: *Das Buch der Wezire und Staatssekretäre von Muḥammad Ibn ʿAbdūs al-Ǧahshiyārī: Anfänge und Umaiyadenzeit*, Josef Latz, ed., Bonn: University of Bonn, 1958.
al-Hadāyā: *Kitāb al-dhakhāʾir wa-at-tuḥaf li-al-Rashīd ibn al-Zubayr*, Muḥammad Ḥamīdullāh, ed., Kuwait: Maṭbaʿat Ḥukūmat al-Kuwayt, 1959. English Translation: *Book of Gifts and Rarities* (Kitāb al-Hadāyā wa al-Tuḥaf). *Selections Compiled in the Fifteenth Century from an Eleventh-Century Manuscript on Gifts and Treasures*, Ġāda al-Ḥijjāwī al-Qaddūmī (trans.), Cambridge, MA: Harvard University Press, 1996.
HP = *History of the Patriarchs of the Coptic church of Alexandria I: Saint Mark to Theonas (300) II: Peter I to Benjamin I (661) III: Agathon to Michael I (766) IV: Mennas I to Joseph (849)*, Basil T. A. Evetts, ed. and trans., reprint, Paris: Firmin-Didot, 1948–1959 [1904–1913].

Ibn ʿAsākir = ʿAlī b. Ḥassan b. Hibat Allāh b. ʿAbd Allāh b. al-Ḥusayn al-Dimashqī, *Tāʾrīkh madīnat Dimashq*, 80 vols, ʿAli Shīrī, ed., Beirut: Dār al-Fikr, 1995–201. Partial French translation: *La description de Damas d'Ibn Asakir historien mort à Damas en 571/1176*, 2nd edition, Nikita Elisséef (trans.), Damascus: IFPO, 2008.
Ibn al-Dunyā = ʿAbd Allāh b. Muḥammad b. ʿUbayd b. Sufyān, *Kitāb ḥilm Muʿāwiya*, Ibrāhīm Ṣāliḥ (trans.), Damascus: Dār al-bashāʾir li-al-ṭibāʿa wa-n-nashr wa-t-tawzīʿ, 2003.
Ibn al-Nadīm = Muḥammad b. Ishāq al-Nadīm, *Kitāb al-fihrist*, 2 vols., Gustav Flügel, ed., reprint, Beirut: Khayats, 1964 [1871–1872]. English Translation: *The Fihrist of al-Nadīm: A Tenth-Century Survey of Muslim Culture* (Records of Civilization: Sources and Studies 83), 2 vols, Bayard Dodge (trans.), New York/London: Columbia University Press, 1970.
Jarīr = Jarīr b. ʿAṭīya, *The Naḳāʾiḍ of Jarīr and al-Farazdaḳ*, 3 vols., Anthony A. Bevan, ed., Leiden: Brill, 1905–1912.
Muqaddasī = Shams al-Dīn Abū ʿAbd Allāh Muḥammad b. Aḥmad b. Abī Bakr al-Bannā al-Muqaddasī, *Descriptio imperii moslemici* [*Aḥsan at-taqāsīm fī maʿrifat al-aqālīm*] (*Bibliotheca Geographorum Arabicorum* III), Michael J. de Goeje, ed., 3rd edition, Leiden: Brill, 1967. English translation: *The Best Divisions for Knowledge of the Regions: A Translation of* 'Ahsan al-taqasim fi maʿrifat al-aqalim', Basil Anthony Collins (trans.), Reading: Garnet Publishing, Centre for Muslim Contribution to Civilization, 1994.
Ṭabarī = Muḥammad b. Jarīr al-Ṭabarī, *Tārīkh al-Rusul wa al-Mulūk*, 3 vols., Michael J. de Goeje, ed., Leiden: Brill, 1879–1901. English translation: *The History of al-Ṭabarī*, 40 vols., Ehsan Yar-Shater (general ed.), Albany: State University of New York Press, 1985–2007.
Theophanes = Theophanes Confessor, *Theophanis chronographia*, Carl de Boor, ed., 2 vols., reprint, Hildesheim: G. Olms, 1980 [repr. 1883–1885]. English Translation: *The Chronicle of Theophanes Confessor: Byzantine and Near Eastern history, AD 284–813*, Cyril Mango (trans.), Oxford: Clarendon Press, 2006 [repr. 1997].
Yāqūt = Shihāb al-Dīn b. ʿAbd Allāh al-Rūmī al-Hamawī, *Jacut's geographisches Wörterbuch* [*Kitāb muʿjam al-buldān*], 6 vols., Ferdinand Wüstenfeld, ed., Leipzig: Brockhaus, 1866–1873.

Secondary Sources

Aanavi, Don (1968), "Devotional Writing: 'Pseudoinscriptions' in Islamic Art", *The Metropolitan Museum of Art Bulletin* 26, 353–358.
Aanavi, Don (1969), *Islamic Pseudo Inscriptions*, Ph. D. Thesis, Columbia University.
Abbott, Nabia (1938), *The Ḳurrah Papyri from Aphrodito in the Oriental Institute* (Studies in Ancient Oriental Civilization 15), Chicago: Chicago University Press (= *P.Qurra*).
Abbot, Nabia (1941), "Arabic Paleography", *Ars Islamica* 8, 65–104.
Abbot, Nabia (1957–1972), *Studies in Arabic Literary Papyri*, 3 vols., Chicago: University of Chicago Press (= *P.AbbottLiteraryPapyri*).
Abdeljaouad, Lotfi (2001), *Inscriptions arabes des monuments islamiques des grandes villes de Tunisie: Monastir, Kairouan, Sfax, Sousse et Tunis*, Ph.D. thesis, Aix-Marseille.
Adams, James N. (2003), *Bilingualism and the Latin Language*, New York: Cambridge University Press.
Adamska, Anna (2013), "Latin and Three Vernaculars in East Central Europe from the Point of View of Social Communication", in: Mary Garrison, Arpad P. Orbán, and Marco Mostert, eds., *Spoken and Written Language: Relations between Latin and the Vernacular*

Languages in the Earlier Middle Ages (Utrecht studies in medieval literacy 24), Turhout: Brepols, 325–364.

Album, Stephen (2011), *Checklist of Islamic Coins*, 3rd edition, Santa Rosa: Stephen Album Rare Coins.

Album, Stephen / Goodwin, Tony (2002), *Sylloge of Islamic Coins in the Ashmolean 1: the Pre-Reform Coinage of the Early Islamic Period*, Oxford: Ashmolean Museum (= *SICA* I).

Alexander, Philip S. (1978), "Remarks on Aramaic Epistolography in the Persian Period", *Journal of Semitic Studies* 23, 155–170.

Ali-de-Unzaga, Miriam (2010), "Qur'anic Inscriptions on the So-Called 'Pennon of Las Navas de Tolosa' and Three Marinid Banners", in: Fahmida Suleman, ed., *Word of God, Art of Man. The Qur'an and Its Creative Expressions: Selected Proceedings from the International Colloquium, London, 18–21 October 2003* (Qur'anic Studies Series 4), Oxford: Oxford University Press, 239–270.

Almbladh, Karin (2010), "The 'Basmala' in Medieval Letters in Arabic Written by Jews and Christians", *Orientalia Suecana* 59, 45–60.

Alram, Michael (2016), *Das Antlitz des Fremden: die Münzprägung der Hunnen und Westtürken in Zentralasien und Indien* (Schriften des Kunsthistorischen Museums 17), Vienna: Verlag der Österreichischen Akademie der Wissenschaften.

Amari, Michele / Gabrieli, Francesco (1971), *Le epigrafi arabiche di Sicilia: Trascritte, tradotte e illustrate* (a cura di Francesco Gabrieli), Palermo: S. F. Flaccovio.

Ambros, Arne (1981), "Zur Entstehung der Emphase in Allāh", *Wiener Zeitschrift für die Kunde des Morgenlandes* 73, 23–32.

Ambros, Arne A. / Procházka, Stephan (2004), *A Concise Dictionary of Koranic Arabic*, Wiesbaden: Reichert.

Amitai-Preiss, Nitzan (2000), "A Poll Tax Seal of Tiberias", in: Moshe Dotham, ed., *Hammath Tiberias II: Late Synagogues* (Ancient Synagogues Studies), Jerusalem: Israel Exploration Society, 2000, 104–105.

Amitai-Preiss, Nitzan (2007), "Islamic Lead Coins, Weights, and Seals in the Israel Museum", *Israel Museum Studies in Archeology* 6, 13–20.

Amitai-Preiss, Nitzan (2012), "Umayyad Vocabulary on Administrative Objects from Palestine", in: Bruno Callegher and Arianna D'Ottone, eds., *3rd Simone Assemani Symposium on Islamic Coins* (Numismatica antica e medievale, Studi 3), Trieste: EUT, 280–287.

Amitai-Preiss, Nitzan / Farhi, Yoav (2009–2010), "A Small Assemblage of Lead Sealings", *Israel Numismatic Journal* 17, 233–237.

ʿAmr, Abdel-Jalil (1986), "More Islamic Inscribed Pottery Lamps from Jordan", *Berytus* 34, 161–168.

ʿAmr, Abdel-Jalil (1988), "Two Early Abbasid Inscribed Pottery Lamps from Ğeraš", *Zeitschrift des Deutschen Palästina-Vereins* 104, 146–149.

ʿAmr, Abdel-Jalil / Khairy, Nabil I. (1986), "Early Islamic Inscribed Pottery Lamps from Jordan", *Levant* 18, 143–153.

Anthony, Sean W. (2014), *Crucifixion and Death as Spectacle: Umayyad Crucifixion in Its Late Antique Context* (American Oriental Series 96), New Haven: American Oriental Society.

Anthony, Sean W. (2015), "Fixing John Damascene's Biography: Historical Notes on His Family Background", *Journal of Early Christian Studies* 23, 607–627.

Aperghis, Gerassimos G. (2004), *The Seleukid Royal Economy: The Finances and Financial Administration of the Seleukid Empire*, Cambridge: Cambridge University Press.

Arnold, Sir Thomas W. (1965), *Painting in Islam. A Study of the Place of Pictorial Art in Muslim Culture*, 2nd edition with a new introduction by B. W. Robinson, New York: Dover Publications.

Asbaghi, Asya (1988), *Persische Lehnwörter im Arabischen*, Wiesbaden: Harrassowitz.
Ashtor, Eliyahu (1969), *Histoire des prix et des salaires dans l'Orient médiéval* (Monnaie, prix, conjoncture 8), Paris: S.E.V.P.E.N.
Ashtor, Eliyahu (1991), "*Makāyil* (A. 1.)", *Encyclopaedia of Islam*, 2nd ed., 6, 117–121.
Avigad, Nahman (1976), *Beth She'arim III*, Jerusalem: Massada Press.
Avner, Uzi / Nehmé, Laïla / Robin, Christian J. (2013), "A Rock Inscription Mentioning Thaʿlaba, an Arab King from Ghassān", *Arabian Archaeology and Epigraphy* 24, 237–256.
Awad, Henri A. (1972), "Seventh Century Arab Imitations of Alexandrian Dodecanammia", *Museum Notes (American Numismatic Society)*, 18, 113–117.
Awad, Henri A. / Bacharach, Jere (1981), "Rare Early Egyptian Islamic Coins and Coin Weights: The Awad Collection", *Journal of the American Research Center in Egypt* 18, 51–56.
Azarnoush, Samra / Grenet, Frantz (2007), "Where Are the Sogdian Magi?", *Bulletin of the Asia Institute* 21, 159–177.
Azarpay, Guitty (1981), *Sogdian Painting: The Pictorial Epic in Oriental Art*, Berkeley *et al.*: University of California Press.
Azarpay, Guitty / Martin, Kathleen / Schwartz, Martin / Weber, Dieter (2003), "New Information on the Date and Function of the Berkeley MP Archive", *Bulletin of the Asia Institute* 17, 17–29.
al-Azmeh, Aziz (2001), *Muslim Kingship: Power and the Sacred in Muslim, Christian, and Pagan Polities*, London: I.B. Tauris. 2001.
Bacharach, Jere (1996), "Marwanid Umayyad Building Activities: Speculations on Patronage", *Muqarnas* 13, 27–44.
Bacharach, Jere (2010), "Signs of Sovereignty: the 'Shahāda,' Quraʾanic Verses, and the Coinage of ʿAbd al-Malik", *Muqarnas* 27, 1–30.
Bacharach, Jere / Anwar, Sherif (2012), "Early Versions of the *Shahāda*: A Tombstone from Aswan of 71 A.H., the Dome of the Rock, and Contemporary Coinage", *Der Islam* 89, 60–69.
Baer, Eva (1983), *Metalwork in Medieval Islamic Art*, Albany: State University of New York Press.
Bagatti, Bellarmino (1947), *I Monumenti di Emmaus el-Qubeibeh e dei dintorni Risultato degli scavi e sopralluoghi negli anni 1873, 1887–90. 1900–2. 1940–44* (Pubblicazioni dello Studium Biblicum Franciscanum 4), Jerusalem: Tipografia dei PP. Francescani.
Bagnall, Roger S. (2009), "Practical Help: Chronology, Geography, Measures, Currency, Names, Prosopography, and Technical Vocabulary", in: Roger S. Bagnall, ed., *The Oxford Handbook of Papyrology* (Oxford Handbooks), New York: Oxford University Press, 179–196.
Bagnall, Roger S. / Worp, Klaas A. (1981), "Christian Invocations in the Papyri", *Chronique d'Egypte* 56, 112–133 and 362–365.
Bagnall, Roger S. / Worp, Klaas A. (2004), *Chronological Systems of Byzantine Egypt*, Leiden/Boston: Brill, 2004.
Balaguer, Ana M. (1976), *Las Emisiones Transicionales Arabe-Musalmanas de Hispania*, Barcelona: Instituto Antonio Agustín de Numismática.
Balaguer, Ana M. (1999), *Història de la moneda dels comtats catalans*, Barcelona: Institut d'Estudis Catalans.
Baldwin & Sons Ltd. (2012), *Classical Rarities of Islamic Coinage*, Baldwin's Islamic Coin, London, Auction 19 (Wednesday 25th April 2012).
Ballian, Anna (2012), "Country Estates, Material Culture, and the Celebration of Princely Life: Islamic Art and the Secular Domain", in: Brandie, Ratcliff and Helen C. Evans, eds., *Byzantium and Islam: Age of Transition 7th–9th Century*, New York: The Metropolitan Museum of Art, 200–208.

Balog, Paul (1974), "Sasanian and Early Islamic Ornamental Glass Vessel-Stamps", in: Dickran K. Kouymjian, ed., *Near Eastern Numismatics, Iconography, Epigraphy, and History. Studies in Honor of George C. Miles*, Beirut: American University, 131–140.

Balog, Paul (1976), *Umayyad, Abbasid and Tulunid Glass Weights and Vessel Stamps* (Numismatic Studies 13), New York: American Numismatic Society (= *UAT*).

Balog, Paul (1977), "Pious Invocations probably Used as Titles of Office or as Honorific Titles in Umayyad and ʿAbbasid Times", in: Myriam Rosen-Ayalon, ed., *Studies in Memory of Gaston Wiet*, Jerusalem: Institute of Asian and African Studies, 61–68.

Baramki, Dimitri C. (1939), "Excavations at Khirbet al-Mefjer III", *Quarterly of the Department of Antiquities in Palestine* 8, 51–53.

Baramki, Dimitri C. (1953), *Arab Culture and Architecture of the Umayyad Period: A Comparative Study with Special Reference to the Results of the Excavations of Hisham's Palace*, Ph.D. thesis, London.

Baramki, Dimitri (1964), "al-Nuqūsh al-ʿarabiyya fī al-bādiya as-sūriya", *al-Abḥāth* 17, 317–346.

Barański, Tomasz (2019), "The Arabic Text of SPP VIII 1198 and Its Significance for the Study of Arabisation of the Egyptian Administration", *Journal of Juristic Papyrology* 49, 17–30 (= *P.BaranskiArabisation*).

Bardtke, Hans (1962), *Die Handschriftenfunde in der Wüste Juda*, Berlin: Evangelische Haupt-Bibelgesellschaft.

Barkey, Karen (2008), *Empire of Difference. The Ottomans in Comparative Perspective*, Cambridge: Cambridge University Press.

Barr, James (1968), *Comparative Philology and the Text of the Old Testament*, Oxford: Clarendon Press.

Bartoccini, Renato (1964), "Il tempio Antoniniano di Sabratha", *Libya Antiqua* 1, 21–65.

Barton, David (2007), *Literacy: An Introduction to the Ecology of Written Language*, Malden: Blackwell.

Bashear, Suliman (1991), "Qibla Musharriqa and Early Muslim Prayer in Churches", *The Muslim World* 81, 267–282.

Bates, Michael (1992), "The Coinage of Spain under the Umayyad Caliphs of the East, 711–750", in: Carmen A. Asìns, ed., *III Jarique de Numismatica hispano-arabe*, Madrid: Museo Arqueológico Nacional, 271–289.

Bates, Michael (1995), "Roman and Early Muslim Coinage in North Africa", in: Mark Horton and Thomas Wiedemann, eds., *North Africa from Antiquity to Islam: Papers of a Conference Held at Bristol, October 1994*, Bristol: Centre for Mediterranean Studies, 12–15.

Baum, Wilhem (2004), *Shirin: Christian – Queen – Myth of Love. A Woman of Late Antiquity: Historical Reality and Literary Effect*, Piscataway: Gorgias Press.

Becker, Carl H. (1906), *Papyri Schott-Reinhardt I* (Veröffentlichungen aus der Heidelberger Papyrussammlung 3), Heidelberg: Carl Winters (= *P.Heid.Arab.* I).

Becker, Carl H. (1911), "Neue Arabische Papyri des Aphroditofundes", *Der Islam* 2, 245–268 (= *P.BeckerNPAF*).

Beckwith, Christopher I. (2009), *Empires of the Silk Road: A History of Central Eurasia from the Bronze Age to the Present*, Princeton: Princeton University Press, 2009.

Beeston, Alfred F. L. (1994), "Foreign Loanwords in Sabaic", in: Norbert Nebes, ed., *Arabia felix: Beiträge zur Sprache und Kultur des vorislamischen Arabien: Festschrift Walter W. Müller zum 60. Geburtstag*, Wiesbaden: Harrassowitz, 1994, 39–45.

Behnstedt, Peter (2006), "Coptic Loanwords", *Encyclopedia of Arabic Language and Linguistics*, 1, 501–505.

Belenitsky, Alexandr Markovič / Isakov, Abdullo (1969), "Rannyaya arabskaya nadpis' na čerepke iz Pjenžikenta", *Epigrafika Vostoka* 19, 38–41.
Belghagi, Moncef (1994), *Schrift und Bild: die Rezeption islamischer Kufimotive in der abendländischen Kunst vom 11. bis zum 20. Jahrhundert*, Tehran: Soroush Press.
Bell, Harold I. (1910), *Greek Papyri in the British Museum Catalogue with Texts IV: the Aphrodito Papyri with an Appendix of Coptic Papyry ed. by W.E. Crum*. London: British Museum (= *P.Lond.* IV).
Bell, Harold I. (1945), "The Arabic Bilingual Entagion", *Proceedings of the American Philosophical Society* 89, 531–542.
Bellamy, James A. (1985), "A New Reading of the Namārah Inscription", *Journal of the American Oriental Society* 105, 31–48.
Bellamy, James A. (1988), "Two Pre-Islamic Arabic Inscriptions Revised: Jabal Ramm and Umm Al-Jimal", *Journal of the American Oriental Society* 108, 369–372.
Bellamy, James A. (1990), "Arabic Verses from the First/Second Century: The Inscription of 'En 'Avdat", *Journal of Semitic Studies* 35, 73–79.
Berkel (van), Maaike (2014), "Reconstructing Archival Practices in Abbasid Baghdad", *Journal of Abbasid Studies* 1, 7–22.
Berkes, Lajos (2014), "Schreibübungen mit einem Psalm-Zitat: Neues aus der Verwaltung des Fayums im 8. Jh.", *Zeitschrift für Papyrologie und Epigraphik* 188, 241–244.
Berkes, Lajos (2017a), *Dorfverwaltung und Dorfgemeinschaft in Ägypten von Diokletian zu den Abbasiden* (Philippika 104), Wiesbaden: Harrassowitz.
Berkes, Lajos (2017b), "Writing Exercises from Early Islamic Bawit (with an Appendix by Alain Delattre)", in: Sohbi Bouderbala, Silvie Denoix, and Matt Malczycki, eds., *New Frontiers of Arabic Papyrology. Arabic and Multilingual Texts from Early Islam* (Islamic History and Civilization 144), Leiden/Boston: Brill, 28–40.
Berkes, Lajos (2018), "On Arabisation and Islamisation in Early Islamic Egypt. I. Prosopographic Notes on Muslim Officials", *Chronique d'Egypte* 93, 415–420.
Berkes, Lajos (2019), "The Latest Identified Greek Documentary Text from Egypt: A Papyrus from 825 AD (*SPP III2* 577 Reconsidered)", *Zeitschrift für Papyrologie und Epigraphik* 209, 110–115.
Berkes, Lajos (2020), "Requisitions for the Conquering Arabs: Two More Letters from Hypatios to Senouthios", *Zeitschrift für Papyrologie und Epigraphik* 216, 251–257.
Berkes, Lajos (forthcoming), "'Peace be upon you': Arabic Greetings in Greek and Coptic Letters Written by Christians in Early Islamic Egypt", in: Edmund P. Hayes and P. M. Sijpesteijn, eds., *The Ties that Bind*, Cambridge: Cambridge University Press.
Berkes, Lajos / Claytor, William G. VI (2017), "Hypatios, Kulyab, and the Requisiton of Milk: a Letter from the Senouthios Archive", *Zeitschrift für Papyrologie und Epigraphik* 203, 223–226.
Berkes, Lajos / McLaughlin, Alexandra T. E. (2018), "A Syriac Letter Reused for a Greek Tax Receipt from the Early Islamic Period", *Bulletin of the American Society of Papyrologists* 55, 59–69.
Berkes, Lajos / Vanthieghem, Naïm (2020), "Notes on the Careers of Nāǧid b. Muslim and ʿAbd al-Malik b. Yazīd", *Chronique d'Égypte* 95, 154–161.
Berkes, Lajos / Younes, Khaled (2012), "A Trilingual Scribe from Abbasid Egypt? A Note on CPR XXII 17", *Archiv für Papyrusforschung* 58, 97–100.
Bernus-Taylor, Marthe / Marchal, Henri / Vial, Gabriel (1971), "Le Suaire de Saint-Josse, Musée du Louvre: Dossier et recensement", *Bulletin de liaison du Centre international d'étude des textiles anciens* 33, 22–57.

Bevan, Anthony, A. (1922), "Some Contributions to Arabic Lexicography", in: Thomas W. Arnold and Reynold A. Nicholson, eds., *A Volume of Oriental Studies Presented to Edward G. Browne on his 60th Birthday (7 February 1922)*, Cambridge: Cambridge University Press, 1922, 51–93.

Beyer, Klaus (1986), *The Aramaic Language: its Distribution and Subdivisions* (trad. John F. Healy), Göttingen: Vandenhoeck & Ruprecht.

Biedenkopf–Ziehner, Anneliese (1983), *Untersuchungen zum koptischen Briefformular unter Berücksichtigung ägyptischer und griechischer Parallelen* (Koptische Studien 1), Würzburg: Gisela Zauzich.

Biermann, Irene A. (1989), "The Art of the Public Text: Medieval Islamic Rule", in: Irving Lavin, ed., *World Art. Themes of Unity in Diversity: Acts of the XXVIth International Congress of the History of Art*, 2 vols., University Park: The Pennsylvania State University Press, 283–290.

Biermann, Irene A. (1998), *Writing Signs: The Fatimid Public Text*, Berkley *et al.*: University of California Press.

Blair, Rebecca / Savage, Robert (2006), "Name Writing but not Environmental Print Recognition Is Related to Letter-Sound Knowledge and Phonological Awareness in Pre-Readers", *Reading and Writing* 19, 991–1016.

Blair, Sheila S. (1989), "Legibility Versus Decoration in Islamic Epigraphy: The Case of Interlacing", in: Irving Lavin, ed., *World Art. Themes of Unity in Diversity: Acts of the XXVIth International Congress of the History of Art*, 2 vols., University Park: The Pennsylvania State University Press, 329–334.

Blair, Sheila (1992), "What Is the Date of the Dome of the Rock", in: Julian Raby and Jeremy Johns, eds., *Bayt al-Maqdis: ʿAbd al-Malik's Jerusalem* (Oxford Studies in Islamic Art 9, 2), Oxford: Oxford University Press, 59–87.

Blair, Sheila S. (1998), *Islamic Inscriptions*, Edinburgh: Edinburgh University Press.

Blair, Sheila S. (2006), *Islamic Calligraphy*, Edinburgh: Edinburgh University Press.

Blair, Sheila S. / Bloom, Jonathan M. (2003), "The Mirage of Islamic Art: Reflections on the Study of an Unwieldy Field", *The Art Bulletin* 85, 152–184.

Blau, Joshua (1966–1967), *A Grammar of Christian Arabic Based Mainly on South-Palestinian Texts from the First Millennium*, 3 vols. (Corpus Scriptorum Christianorum Orientalium 267–269), Louvain: Secrétariat du CSCO.

Blau, Joshua (1972), "Arabic Lexicographical Miscellanies", *Journal of Semitic Studies* 17, 173–190.

Blau, Joshua (1982), "The Transcription of Arabic Words and Names in the Inscription of Mu'āwiya from Ḥammat Gader", *Israel Exploration Journal* 32, 102.

Blau, Joshua (1988), *Studies in Middle Arabic and Its Judaeo-Arabic Variety*, Jerusalem: Magnes Press Hebrew University.

Blau, Joshua (2002), *A Handbook of Early Middle Arabic* (Max Schloessinger Memorial Series Monographs 6), Jerusalem: Max Schloessinger Memorial Foundation.

Bloch, Bernard (1948), "A Set of Postulates for Phonemic Analysis", *Language* 24, 3–46.

Blochet, Edgar (1898), "Études sur l'histoire religieuse de l'Iran I", *Revue de l'histoire des religions* 38, 26–63.

Blois (de), François C. (1997), "*Sidjill*", *Encyclopaedia of Islam*, 2nd ed., 9, 538a–545a.

Blois (de), François C. (2000), "A Persian poem lamenting the Arab conquest", in: Ian Richard Netton, ed., *Studies in honour of Clifford Edmund Bosworth*, Leiden/Boston: Brill, 82–95.

Blois (de), François C. (2006), "Du nouveau sur la chronologie bactrienne post-hellénistique: l'ère de 223–224 ap. J.-C.", *Comptes rendus des séances de l'Académie des Inscriptions et Belles-Lettres* 150, 991–997.

Bodel, John (2001), *Epigraphic Evidence. Ancient History from Inscriptions*, London: Routledge.

Bolle, Katharina (2019), "Inscriptions between Text and Texture: Inscribed Monuments in Public Spaces – A Case Study at Ostia", in: Andrej Petrovic, Ivana Petrovic, and Edmund Thomas, eds., *The Materiality of Text – Placement, Perception, and Presence of Inscribed Texts in Classical Antiquity* (Brill Studies in Greek and Roman Epigraphy 11), Leiden/Boston: Brill, 348–379.

Booth, Phil (2013), "The Muslim Conquest of Egypt Reconsidered", in: Constantin Zuckerman, ed., *Constructing the Seventh Century* (Travaux et mémoires 17), Paris: Association des Amis du Centre d'Histoire et Civilisation de Byzance, 639–670.

Borrut, Antoine (2011), *Entre mémoire et pouvoir l'espace syrien sous les derniers Omeyyades et les premiers Abbassides (v. 72–192/692–809)*, Leiden/Boston: Brill.

Bosworth, Clifford E. (1969), "Abū ʿAbdallāh al-Khwārazmī on the Technical Terms of the Secretary's Art: Contribution to the Administrative History of Mediaeval Islam", *Journal of the Economic and Social History of the Orient* 12, 113–164.

Bosworth, Clifford E. (1993), "*Miṣr* (A.–B.)", *Encyclopaedia of Islam*, 2nd ed., 7, 146.

Bothmer (von), Hans-Caspar (1987), "Architekturbilder im Koran. Eine Prachthandschrift der Umayyadenzeit aus dem Yemen", *Pantheon* 45, 4–20.

Bouderbala, Sobhi (2008), Ǧund Miṣr*: Etude de l'administration militaire dans l'Égypte des débuts de l'Islam 21/642–218/833*, Ph.D. thesis, Paris, 2008.

Boud'hors, Anne (2007), "L'apport de papyrus postérieurs à la conquête arabe pour la datation des ostraca coptes de la tombe TT29", in: Petra M. Sijpesteijn *et al.*, eds., *From al–Andalus to Khurasan: Documents from the Medieval Muslim World* (Islamic History and Civilization 66), Leiden/Boston: Brill, 115–129.

Boud'hors, Anne (2016), "Degrés d'arabisation dans l'Egypte du VIIIe siécle: CPR II 228 revisité", in: Jean-Luc Fournet and Arietta Papaconstantinou, eds., *Mélanges Jean Gascou: textes et études papyrologiques* (Travaux et Mémoires 20/1), Paris: Association des Amis du Centre d'Histoire et Civilisation de Byzance, 71–90 (= *P.Gascou* 24).

Boud'hors, Anne (2020), "Situating the Figure of Papas, Pagarch of Edfu at the End of the Seventh Century: the Contribution of Coptic Documents", in: Sabine R. Huebner *et al.*, eds., *Living the End of Antiquity – Individual Histories from Byzantine to Islamic Egypt* (Millennium Studien/Millennium Studies 84), Berlin: De Gruyter, 63–72.

Boud'hors, Anne / Delattre, Alain / Berkes, Lajos / Chang, Ruey-Lin / Garel, Esther / Gascou, Jean / Marthot-Santaniello, Isabelle / Ochała, Grzegorz / Vanthieghem, Naïm (2018), "Un nouveau départ pour les archives de Papas. Papyrus coptes et grecs de la jarre d'Edfou", *Le Bulletin de l'Institut français d'archéologie orientale* 117, 87–124.

Bowen Savant, Sarah (2013), The *New Muslims of Post-Conquest Iran: Tradition, Memory, and Conversion* (Cambridge Studies in Islamic Civilization), Cambridge: Cambridge University Press.

Böwering, Gerhard (2002), "God and His Attributes", *Encyclopaedia of the Qurʾān*, 2, 316b–331b.

Brashear, William M. (1998), "Syriaca", *Archiv für Papyrusforschung und verwandte Gebiete* 44, 86–127.

Bravmann, Meir (2012) [repr. 1968], "The State Archives in the Early Islamic Era", in: Fred Donner, ed., *The Articulation of Early Islamic State Structures* (The Formation of the Classical Islamic World 6), Ashgate: Franham, 183–185.

Brock, Sebastian (1982), "Syriac Views of Emergent Islam", in: Gautier H., A., Juynboll, ed., *Studies on the First Century of Islamic Society*, Carbondale: Southern Illinois University Press, 9–21.

Brockelmann, Carl (1927), "Semitische Reimwortbildungen", *Zeitschrift für Semitistik und Verwandte Gebiete* 5, 6–38.

Brockopp, Jonathan E. (2015), "Interpreting Material Evidence: Religion at the 'Origins of Islam'", *History of Religions* 55, 121–147.

Brockopp, Jonathan E. (2017), *Muhammad's Heirs: The Rise of Muslim Scholarly Communities, 622–950* (Cambridge Studies in Islamic Civilization), Cambridge: Cambridge University Press.

Brown, Peter (1971), *The World of Late Antiquity from Marcus Aurelius to Muhammad* (Library of European Civilization), London: Thames and Hudson.

Bruning, Jelle (2015), "A Legal Sunna in Dhikr Ḥaqqs from Sufyanid Egypt", *Islamic Law and Society* 22, 352–374.

Bruning, Jelle (2018a), *The rise of a Capital: Al-Fusṭāṭ and Its Hinterland, 18/639–132/750* (Islamic History and Civilization 153), Leiden/Boston: Brill.

Bruning, Jelle (2018b), "Developments in Egypt's Early Islamic Postal System (with an Edition of P.Khalili II 5)", *Bulletin of the School of Oriental and African Studies* 81, 25–40.

Brünnow, Rudolf E. / Fischer, August (2008), *Klassisch-arabische Chrestomatie aus Prosaschriftstellern*, 8th edition (Porta Linguarum Orientalium: Neue Serie17), Wiesbaden: Harrassowitz.

Bsees, Ursula (2019), "Qurʾān Quotations in Arabic Papyrus Amulets", in: Andreas Kaplony and Michael Marx, eds., *Qurʾān Quotations Preserved on Papyrus Documents, 7th–10th Centuries and the Problem of Carbon Dating Early Qurʾāns* (Documenta Coranica 2), Leiden/Boston: Brill, 112–138.

Bsees, Ursula / Procházka, Stephan (2015), "Performatives in Arabic Administrative Speech", in: Stephan Procházka, Lucian Reinfandt, and Sven Tost, eds., *Official Epistolography and the Language(s) of Power. Proceedings of the First International Conference of the Research Network* imperium & officium*: Comparative Studies in Ancient Bureaucracy and Officialdom, University of Vienna, 10–12 November 2010* (Papyrologica Vindobonensia 8), Vienna: Österreichische Akademie der Wissenschaften, 293–300.

Bucking, Scott (2007), "On the Training of Documentary Scribes in Roman, Byzantine, and Early Islamic Egypt", *Zeitschrift für Papyrologie und Epigraphik* 159, 229–247.

Bulliet, Richard W. (1994), *Islam: The View from the Edge*, New York: Columbia University Press.

Burt, Roland S. (2005), *Brokerage and Closure: An Introduction to Social Capital*, Oxford: Oxford University Press, 2005.

Cahen, Claude (1990), "*Kharādj* (I.)", *Encyclopaedia of Islam*, 2nd ed., 4, 1030–1034.

Canard, Marius (1964), "Les relations politiques et sociales entre Byzance et les Arabes", *Dumbarton Oaks Papers* 18, 33–56.

Cantineau, Jean, ed., (1930–1949), *Inventaire des inscriptions de Palmyre*, 10 vols. (Publications du Musée National Syrien de Damas 1, 1–10), Beyrouth: Imprimerie Catholique.

Cantineau, Jean (1978), *Le nabatéen*, Osnabrück: Otto Zeller.

Capdetrey, Laurent (2007), *Le pouvoir séleucide: territoire, administration, finances d'un royaume hellénistique (312–129 avant J.-C.)*, Rennes: Presses universitaires de Rennes.

Carlyon-Britton, Philip W. P., (1908), "The Gold Mancus of Offa, King of Mercia", *British Numismatic Journal* 5, 55–72.

Carter, Michael (2006), "Foreign Vocabulary", in: Andrew Rippin, ed., *The Blackwell Companion to the Qur'an* (Blackwell Companions to Religion), Malden: Blackwell, 120–139.

Caskel, Werner (1930), Aijām al-ʿArab. *Studien zur altarabischen Epik* (Islamica III, 5), Leipzig: Asia Major.

Castrizio, Daniele (2010), *Le Monete della Necropoli Nord di Antinoupolis (1937–2007)* (Scavi e Materiali 2), Florence: Istituto papirologico "G. Vitelli".
Chattopadhyaya, Brajadulal (1998), *Representing the Other? Sanskrit Sources and the Muslims 8th–14th Century*, New Dehli: Manohar.
Cheung, Johnny (2017), "On the Middle–Iranian Borrowings in Qurʾānic (and pre–Islamic) Arabic", *in: Ahmad al–Jallad, ed., Arabic in Context. Celebrating 400 Years of Arabic at Leiden University* (Studies in Semitic Languages and Linguistics 89), Leiden/Boston: Brill, 317–336.
Choat, Malcom (2010), "Early Coptic Epistolography", in: Arietta Papaconstantinou, ed., *The Multilingual Experience in Egypt, from the Ptolemies to the Abbasids*, Burlington: Ashgate, 153–178.
Christensen, Arthur (1936), *L'Iran sous les Sassanides*, Copenhagen: Munksgaard.
Christides, Vassilios (1999), "Continuation and Change in Early Arab Egypt as Reflected in the Termsand Titles of the Greek Papyri", *Graeco-Arabica* 4, 53–62.
Ciancaglini, Claudia A. (2008), *Iranian Loanwords in Syriac* (Beiträge zur Iranistik 28), Wiesbaden: Ludwig Reichert.
Clermont-Ganneau, Charles (1900a), "Deux nouveaux lychnaria grec et arabe", *Recueil d'Archeologie Orientale* 3, 41–47.
Clermont-Ganneau, Charles (1900b), "Nouveau lychnarion a inscription coufique", *Recueil d'Archeologie Orientale* 3, 283–285.
Cline, Erich H. / Graham, Mark H. (2011), *Ancient Empires: From Mesopotamia to the Rise of Islam*, Cambridge: Cambridge University Press, 2011.
Coetsem (van), Frans (2000), *A General and Unified Theory of the Transmission Process in Language Contact* (Monographien zur Sprachwissenschaft 19), Heidelberg: C. Winter.
Cole, Juan (2019), "Paradosis and Monotheism: a Late Antique Approach to the Meaning of *Islām* in the Quran", *Bulletin of the School of Oriental and African Studies* 83, 405–425.
Colt, Dunscombe H. (ed) (1962), *Excavations at Nessana* I, London: British School of Archaeology in Jerusalem.
Cooke, George A. (1903), *A Text-Book of North-Semitic Inscriptions: Moabite, Hebrew, Phoenician, Aramaic, Nabataean, Palmyrene, Jewish*, Oxford: Clarendon Press.
Corriente, Federico (2007), "The Psalter Fragment from the Umayyad Mosque of Damascus: A Birth Certificate of Nabaṭī Arabic", in: Juan P. Monferrer Sala, ed., *Eastern Crossroads: Essays on Medieval Christian Legacy* (Georgias Eastern Christian Studies 1), Piscataway: Gorgias Press, 303–320.
Costa, Paolo M. (1994), *Studies in Arabian Architecture* (Collected Studies Series 455), Aldershot: Variorum.
Creason, Stuart (2004), "Aramaic", in: Roger D. Woodard, ed., *The Cambridge Encyclopedia of the World's Ancient Languages*, Cambridge: Cambridge University Press, 391–426.
Creisher, Michelle / Goren, Yuval / Artzy, Michal / Cvikel, Deborah (2019), "The Amphorae of the Ma'agan Mikhael B Shipwreck: Preliminary Report", *Levant* 51, 105–120.
Creswell, Keppel A. C. (1946), "The Lawfulness of Painting in Early Islam", *Ars Islamica* 11/12, 159–166.
Creswell, Keppel A. C. (1969), *Early Muslim Architecture: Umayyads, A.D. 622–750*, 2 vols., Oxford: Clarendon Press.
Creswell, Keppel A. C. (1989), *A Short Account of Early Muslim Architecture*, revised and supplemented by James W. Allan, Aldershot: Scolar Press.
Cromwell, Jennifer (2013), "Coptic Texts in the Archive of Flavius Atias", *Zeitschrift für Papyrologie und Epigraphik* 184, 280–288.

Cromwell, Jennifer (2017), *Recording Village Life: A Coptic Scribe in Early Islamic Egypt* (New Texts from Ancient Cultures), Ann Arbor: University of Michigan Press.

Crone, Patricia (1984), *Slaves on Horses: The Evolution of the Islamic Polity*, Cambridge: Cambridge University Press.

Crone, Patricia (1987), *Roman, Provincial and Islamic Law: The Origins of the Islamic Patronate* (Cambridge Studies in Islamic Civilization), Cambridge *et al.*: Cambridge University Press.

Crone, Patricia (1994), "The First Century Concept of *hijra*", *Arabica* 41, 352–387.

Crone, Patricia (2004), *God's Rule: Government and Islam*, New York: Columbia University Press.

Crone, Patricia (2005), *Medieval Islamic Political Thought* (The New Edinburgh Islamic Surveys), Edinburgh: Edinburgh University Press.

Crone, Patricia (2012), *The Nativist Prophets of Early Islamic Iran*, Cambridge: Cambridge University Press.

Crone, Patricia / Cook, Michael (1977), *Hagarism: The Making of the Islamic World*, Cambridge: Cambridge University Press.

Crone, Patricia / Hinds, Martin (1986), *God's Caliph: Religious Authority in the First Centuries of Islam* (University of Cambridge Oriental Publications 37), Cambridge *et al.*: Cambridge University Press.

Crum, Walter E. / Bell, Harold I. (1922), *Wadi Sarga Coptic and Greek Texts from the Excavations Undertaken by the Byzantine Research Account*, with an introduction by Reginald Campbell Thompson (Coptica 3), Hauniae: Gyldendal (= *P.Sarga*).

Curiel, Raôul / Gignoux, Philippe (1976), "Un poids arabo-sasanide", *Studia Iranica* 5, 165–169.

Dalman, Gustaff (1901), *Aramäisch-Neuhebräisches Wörterbuch zu Targum, Talmud und Midrasch*, Frankfurt: Kauffmann.

Daniel, Robert /al-Jallad, Ahmad / al-Ghul, Omar (2013), "The Arabic toponyms and oikonyms in 17", in: Ludwig Koenen, Maarit Kaimio, and Robert Daniel, eds., *The Petra Papyri* II (American Center of Oriental Research Publications 7), Amman: American Center of Oriental Research, 23–48.

Daris, Sergio (1971), *Il lessico latino nel greco d'Egitto* (Estudis de Papirologia i Filologia Biblica 2), Barcelona: Papyrologica Castroctaviana.

Day, Florence E. (1942), "Early Islamic and Christian Lamps", *Berytus* 7, 65–79.

Day, Florence E. (1952), "The Tirāz Silk Of Marwān", in: George C. Miles, ed., *Archaeologica Orientalia in Memoriam Ernst Herzfeld*, Locust Valley: J. J. Augustin, 39–61.

Debié, Muriel (2016), "Christians in the Service of the Caliph: Through the Looking Glass of Communal Identities", in: Antoine Borrut and Fred Donner, eds., *Christians and Others in the Umayyad State* (Late Antique and Medieval Islamic Near East 1), Chicago: The Oriental Institute of the University of Chicago, 53–71.

De Jong, Janneke (2017), "Arabia, Arabs, and 'Arabic' in Greek Documents from Egypt", in: Sohbi Bouderbala, Silvie Denoix, and Matt Malczycki, eds., *New Frontiers of Arabic Papyrology: Arabic and Multilingual Texts from Early Islam* (Islamic History and Civilization 144), Leiden/Boston: Brill, 3–27.

Delattre, Alain (2007), *Papyrus coptes et grecs du monastère d'apa Apollô de Baouît conservés aux Musées royaux d'Art et d'Histoire de Bruxelles* (Mémoire de la Classe des Lettres 3/43), Bruxelles: Académie royale de Belgique (= *P.Brux.Bawit*).

Delattre, Alain (2015), "Remarques sur la taxation au monastère de Baouît au début de l'époque arabe", in: Andreas Kaplony, Daniel Potthast, and Cornelia Römer, eds., *From Bāwīṭ to Marw. Documents from the Medieval Muslim World* (Islamic History and Civilization 66), Leiden/Boston: Brill, 83–93.

Delattre, Alain (2018), "Checkpoints, sauf-conduits et contrôle de la population en Égypte au début du VIIIe siècle", in: Alain Delattre, Marie Legendre, and Petra Sijpesteijn, eds., *Authority and Control in the Countryside: From Antiquity to Islam in the Mediterranean and Near East (6th-10th Century)* (Leiden Studies in Islam and Society 9), Leiden/Boston: Brill, 531–546.

Delattre, Alain / Liebrenz, Boris / Richter, Tonio S. / Vanthieghem, Naïm (2012), "Écrire en arabe et en copte. Le cas de deux lettres bilingues", *Chronique d'Egypte* 87, 170–188 (= *P.DelattreEcrire*).

Delattre, Alain / Pintaudi, Rosario / Vanthieghem, Naïm (2013), "Un entagion bilingue du gouverneur ʿAbd al-ʿAzīz ibn Marwān trouvé à Antinoé", *Chronique d'Egypte* 88, 363–371 (= *P.DelattreEntagion*).

Delattre, Alain / Vanthieghem, Naïm (2016), "*Un ensemble archivistique trilingue* à Strasbourg: un protocole et deux ordres de réquisition de la fin du VIIe siècle", in: Jean L. Fournet and Arietta Papaconstantinou, eds., *Mélangés Jean Gascou: textes et études papyrologiques* (Travaux et Mémoires 20/1), Paris: Association des Amis du Centre d'Histoire et Civilisation de Byzance, 109–129 (= *P.Gascou* 27a–b).

Derda, Tomasz / Wipszycka, Ewa (1994), "L'emploi des titres abba, apa et papas dans l'Egypte byzantine", *The Journal of Juristic Papyrology* 24, 23–56.

Déroche, François (1987–1989), "Les manuscrits arabes datés de IIIe/IXe siècle", *Revue des Études Islamiques* 55–57 and 343–379.

Déroche, François (1992), *The Abbasid Tradition, Qurʾans of the 8th to the 10th Centuries* (The Nasser D. Khalili Collection of Islamic Art 1), London/New York: Azimuth Editions, Oxford University Press, 1992.

Déroche, François (2002), "New Evidence for Umayyad Book Hands", in: *Essays in Honour of Ṣalāḥ al-Dīn al-Munajjid* (al-Furqān publication 70), London: al-Furqān, 2002, 611–642.

Déroche, François (2009), *La transmission écrite du Coran dans les débuts de l'islam. Le codex Parisinopetropolitanus* (Texts and Studies on the Qurʾān 5), Leiden/Boston: Brill.

Déroche, François (2013), "Contrôler l'écriture. Sur quelques caractéristiques de corans de la période omeyyade", in: Azaiez, Mehdi and Sabrina Mervin, eds., *Le Coran: nouvelles approches*, Paris: Centre National de la Recherche Scientifique, 39–55.

Déroche, François (2014), *Qurʾans of the Umayyads: A First Overview* (Leiden Studies in Islam and Society 1), Leiden/Boston: Brill, 2014.

Déroche, François (2018), "A Qur'anic Script from Umayyad Times: Around the Codex of Fustat", in: Alain George and Andrew Marsham, eds., *Power, Patronage, and Memory in Early Islam: Perspectives on Umayyad Elites*, New York: Oxford University Press, 3–38.

Diakonov, M. M. (1947), "Ob odnoy rasmey arabskoy nadpisi", *Epigrafika Vostoka* 1, 5–8.

Diem, Werner (1979–1983), "Untersuchungen zur frühen Geschichte der arabischen Orthographie. 1: Die Schreibung der Vokale. 2: Die Schreibung der Konsonanten. 3: Endungen und Endschreibungen. 4: Die Schreibung der zusammenhängenden Rede, Zusammenfassung", *Orientalia* Part 1: 48 (1979), 207–257; Part 2: 49 (1980), 67–106; Part 3: 50 (1981), 322–383; Part 4: 52 (1983), 357–404.

Diem, Werner (1983), "Der Gouverneur an den Pagarchen. Ein verkannter arabischer Papyrus vom Jahre 65 der Hijra", *Der Islam* 60, 104–111 (= *P.DiemGouverneur*).

Diem, Werner (1984a), "Philologisches zu den arabischen Aphrodito-Papyri", *Der Islam* 61, 251–275.
Diem, Werner (1984b), "Einige frühe amtliche Urkunden aus der Sammlung Papyrus Erzherzog Rainer (Wien)", *Le Muséon* 97, 109–158 (= *P.DiemFrueheUrkunden*).
Diem, Werner (2004), ""katabtu ilayka" "Ich schreibe Dir" und Verwandtes: Ein Beitrag zur Phraseologie des arabischen Briefes unter besonderer Berücksichtigung des Briefperfekts", *Zeitschrift der Deutschen Morgenländischen Gesellschaft* 154, 285–345.
Diem, Werner (2008), "Arabic Letters in Pre–modern Times: A Survey with Commented Selected Bibliographies", in: Eva M. Grob and Andreas Kaplony, eds., *Documentary Letters from the Middle East: The Evidence in Greek, Coptic, South Arabian, Pehlevi, and Arabic (1st–15th c CE)* (Asiatische Studien/Etudes asiatiques 62, 3), Bern *et al.*: Peter Lang, 843–883.
Diethart, Johannes / Feissel, Dennis / Gascou, Jean (1994), "Les *prôtokolla* des papyrus byzantins du ve au viie siècle. Edition, prosopographie, diplomatique", *Tyche* 9, 9–40.
Dodd, Erica C. (1969), "The Image of the Word: Notes on the Religious Iconography of Islam", *Berytus* 18, 35–73.
Dodd, Erica C. / Khairallah, Shereen (1981), *The Image of the Word. A Study of Quranic Verses in Islamic Architecture*, 2 vols., Beirut: American University.
Doering, Lutz (2012), *Ancient Jewish Letters and the Beginnings of Christian Epistolography* (Wissenschaftliche Untersuchungen zum Neuen Testament 298), Tübingen: Mohr Siebeck.
Dolezalek, Isabelle (2016), "Comparing Forms, Contextualising Functions: Arabic Inscriptions on Textiles of the Norman King William II and Fatimid ṭirāz", in: Juliane von Fircks and Regula Schorta, eds., *Oriental Silks in Medieval Europe* (Riggisberger Berichte 21), Riggisberg: Abegg-Stiftung, 80–91.
Dolezalek, Isabelle (2017), *Arabic Script on Christian Kings. Textile Inscriptions on Royal Garments from Norman Sicily* (Das Mittelalter – Beihefte 5), Berlin: De Gruyter.
Domaszewicz, Lidia / Bates, Michael L. (2002), "Copper Coinage of Egypt in the Seventh Century", in: Jere L. Bacharach, ed., *Fustat Finds: Beads, Coins, Medical Instruments, Textiles, and Other Artifacts from the Awad Collection*, Cairo/New York: The American University in Cairo Press, 88–111.
Donner, Fred M. (1998), *Narratives of Islamic Origins: The Beginnings of Islamic Historical Writing* (Studies in Late Antiquity and Early Islam 14), Princeton: Darwin Press.
Donner, Fred M. (2002–2003), "From Believers to Muslims: Confessional Self-Identity in the Early Islamic Community", *Al-Abhath* 50–51, 9–53.
Donner, Fred M. (2010), *Muhammad and the Believers: At the Origins of Islam*, Cambridge, MA: The Belknap Press of Harvard University.
Donner, Fred M. (2011), "Qur'ânicization of Religio-Political Discourse in the Umayyad Period", *Revue des mondes musulmans et de la Méditerranée* 129, 79–92.
Donner, Fred M. (2012) [repr. 1986], "The Formation of the Islamic State", in: Fred Donner, ed., *The Articulation of Early Islamic State Structures* (The Formation of the Classical Islamic World 6), Franham: Ashgate, 1–14.
Doyle, Michael W. (1986), *Empires* (Cornell Studies in Comparative History), Ithaca: Cornell University Press.
Dozy, Reinhardt (1881), *Supplément aux Dictionnaires Arabes*, 2 vols., Leiden: Brill.
Drechsler, Andreas (1999), *Die Geschichte der Stadt Qom im Mittelalter (650–1350): politische und wirtschaftliche Aspekte* (Islamkundliche Untersuchungen 224), Berlin: Klaus Schwarz.

Drewes, Abraham J. / Higham, Thomas F. C. / MacDonald, Michael C. / Bronk Ramsey, Christopher (2013), "Some Absolute Dates for the Development of the Ancient South Arabian Minuscule Script", *Arabian Archaeology and Epigraphy* 24, 196–207.
Drewes, Abraham J. / Ryckmans, Jacques (2016), *Les inscriptions sudarabes sur bois dans la collection de l'Oosters Instituut conservée dans la bibliothèque universitaire de Leiden, texte révisé et adapté par Peter Stein*, ed. by Peter Stein and Harry Stroomer, Wiesbaden: Harrassowitz.
Drews, Wolfram (2013), "The Emergence of an Islamic Culture in Early Abbasid Iraq: The Role of non-Arab Contributions", in: Nikolas Jaspert *et al.*, eds., *Cultural Brokers at Mediterranean Courts in the Middle Ages* (Mittelmeerstudien 1), Paderborn: Wilhelm Fink, Ferdinand Schöning, 47–62.
Driver, Godfrey R. (1957), *Aramaic Documents of the Fifth Century B.C*, Oxford: Clarendon Press.
Duri, Abd al-Aziz (1965), "*Dīwān* (i.)", *Encyclopaedia of Islam*, 2nd ed., 2, 323–327.
Eastmond, Anthony, ed (2015), *Viewing Inscriptions in the Late Antique and Medieval World*, Cambridge: Cambridge University Press.
Eck, Werner / Gronke, Monika / Hesberg (von), Henner (2007), "Die Stimme der Bauten – Schrift am Bau", in: Dietrich Boschung and Hansgerd Hellenkemper, eds., *Kosmos der Zeichen. Schriftbild und Bildformel in Antike und Mittelalter: Begleitbuch zur Ausstellung des Lehr- und Forschungszentrums für die antiken Kulturen des Mittelmeerraumes der Universität zu Köln und des Römisch-Germanischen Museums der Stadt Köln* (Schriften des Lehr- und Forschungszentrums für die antiken Kulturen des Mittelmeerraumes 5), Wiesbaden: Reichert, 211–234.
Edwards, Holly (1991), "Text, Context, Architext: The *Qur'an* as Architectural Inscription", in: Carol G. Fisher, ed., *Brocade of the Pen: The Art of Islamic Writing*, East Lansing: Kresge Art Museum, 63–75.
Edwell, Peter *et al.* (2015), "Arabs in the Conflict between Rome and Persia, AD 491–630", in: Greg Fisher, ed., *Arabs and Empires before Islam*, Oxford: Oxford University Press, 276–372.
Eickelman, Dale F. (1978), "The Art of Memory: Islamic Education and Its Social Reproduction", *Comparative Studies in Society and History* 20, 485–516.
Eilers, Wilhelm (1957), "Akkad. kaspum 'Silber, Geld' und Sinnverwandtes", *Die Welt des Orients* 2, 322–337.
Eisenstadt, Shmuel N. (1969), *The Political Systems of Empires: The Rise and Fall of the Historical Bureaucratic Societies*, 2nd edition, New York: The Free Press.
Eksell, Kerstin (2002), *Meaning in Ancient North Arabian Carvings* (Acta Universitatis Stockholmiensis 17), Stockholm: Almquist and Wiksell.
Elad, Amikam (1995), *Medieval Jerusalem and Islamic Worship. Holy Places, Cerimonies, Pilgrimage* (Islamic History and Civilization 8), Leiden/Boston/Köln: Brill.
Elad, Amikam (1999), "The Southern Golan in the Early Muslim Period. The Significance of Two Newly Discovered Milestones of ʿAbd al-Malik", *Der Islam* 76, 33–88.
Elad, Amikam (2002), "Community of Believers of 'Holy Men' and 'Saints' or Community of Muslims? The Rise and Development of Early Muslim Historiography", *Journal of Semitic Studies* 47, 241–308.
Enderlein, Volkmar / Meinecke, Michael (1992), "Graben, Forschen, Präsentieren. Probleme der Darstellung vergangener Kulturen am Beispiel der Mschatta-Fassade", *Jahrbuch der Berliner Museen* 34, 137–172.

Erdmann, Kurt (1951), "Die Entwicklung der sasanidischen Krone", *Ars Islamica* 15–16, 87–123.
Erdmann, Kurt (1953), "Arabische Schriftzeichen als Ornamente in der abendländischen Kunst des Mittelalters", *Abhandlungen der Akademie der Wissenschaften und der Literatur in Mainz, Geistes- und sozialwissenschaftliche Klasse* 9, 467–513.
Ettinghausen, Richard (1939), "An Umaiyad Pound Weight", *Journal of the Walters Art Gallery* 2, 73–76.
Ettinghausen, Richard (1972), *From Byzantium to Sasanian Iran and the Islamic World: Three Modes of Artistic Influence* (The L. A. Mayor Memorial Studies in Islamic Art and Archaeology), Leiden: Brill.
Ettinghausen, Richard (1974), "Arabic Epigraphy: Communication or Symbolic Affirmation", in: Dickran K. Kouymjian, ed., *Near Eastern Numismatics, Iconography, Epigraphy, and History. Studies in Honor of George C. Miles*, Beirut: American University, 297–317.
Ettinghausen, Richard (1979), "The Taming of the Horror Vacui in Islamic Art", *Proceedings of the American Philosophical Society* 123, 15–28.
Ettinghausen, Richard / Grabar, Oleg / Jenkins-Madina, Marilyn (2001), *Islamic Art and Architecture 650–1250* (Pelican History of Art), New Haven: Yale University Press.
al-Faʿar, Muḥammad Fahd ʿAbd Allāh (1984), *Taṭawwur al-kitābāt wa l-nuqūsh fī l-Ḥijāz mundhu fajr al-islām ḥattā muntaṣaf al-qarn as-sābiʿ al-hijrī, coll. Asā'il jāmi'iyya*, Mecca: Umm al-Qurā (= *TKN*).
Fantoni, Georgina (1989), *Griechische Texte X: Greek Papyri of the Byzantine Period* (Corpus Papyrorum Raineri 14), Vienna: Hollinek (= *CPR* XIV).
al-Faqīh, Ḥassan (1992), *Mikhlāf ʿasham* (Mawāqiʿ athariyya fī Tihāma 1), Riyadh: n.d.
Farès, Saba (2010), "L'inscription de Kilwa: nouvelle lecture", *Semitica Classica* 3, 241–248.
Farès, Saba (2011), "Christian Monasticism on the Eve of Islam: Kilwa (Saudi Arabia) – New Evidence", *Arabian Archaeology and Epigraphy* 22, 243–252.
Fattal, Antoine (1958), *Le statut légal des non-Musulmans en pays d'Islam* (Recherches de l'Institut de Lettres Orientales 10), Beirut: Imprimerie Catholique.
Fehérvári, Géza (1976), *Islamic Metalwork of the Eighth to the Fifteenth Century in the Keir Collection with a foreword by Ralph Pinder-Wilson*, London: Faber & Faber.
Feliciano, María-Judith (2005), "Muslim Shrouds for Christian Kings? A Reassessment of Andalusi Textiles in Thirteenth-Century Castilian Life and Ritual", in: Cynthia Robinson and Leyla Rouhi, eds., *Under the Influence: Questioning the Comparative in Medieval Castile* (Medieval and Early Modern Iberian World 22), Leiden/Boston: Brill, 101–131.
Ferguson, Carl (1971), "Contrasting Patterns of Literacy Acquisition in a Multilingual Society", in: Wilfred H. Whiteley, ed., *Language Use and Social Change: Problems of Multilingualism with Special Reference to Eastern Africa*, London: International African Institute, 234–253.
Fiema, Zbigniew T. *et al.* (2015), "*Provincia Arabia*: Nabatea, the Emergence of Arabic as a Written Language, and Graeco-Arabica", in: Greg Fisher, ed., *Arabs and Empires before Islam*, Oxford: Oxford University Press, 373–433.
Fikry, Ahmad (1934), *L'art roman du Puy et les influences islamiques* (Études d'Art et d'Archéologie), Paris: Leroux.
Finster, Barbara (1970), "Die Mosaiken der Umayyadenmoschee", *Kunst des Orients* 7, 83–141.
Finster, Barbara (2001), "Probleme der Antikenrezeption in der Umayyadischen Kunst", in: Dieter Kuhn and Helga Stahl, eds., *Die Gegenwart des Altertums: Formen und Funktionen des Altertumsbezugs in den Hochkulturen der Alten Welt*, Heidelberg: Forum, 373–389.

Finster, Barbara (2005), "'Vine Ornaments and Pomegranates as Palace Decoration in ʿAnjar", in: Bernard O'Kane, ed., *The Iconography of Islamic Art: Studies in Honour of Robert Hillenbrand*, Edinburgh: Edinburgh University Press, 143–158.

Fisher, Greg (2011), *Between Empires Arabs, Romans, and Sasanians in Late Antiquity* (Oxford Classical Monographs), Oxford: Oxford University Press.

Flood, Finbarr B. (2001), *The Great Mosque of Damascus: Studies on the Makings of an Umayyad Visual Culture* (Islamic History and Civilization 33), Leiden/Boston/Köln: Brill.

Folz, Robert (1953), *L'idée d'Empire en Occident du Ve au XIVe siècle* (Collection Historique), Paris: Aubiers.

Fontana, Maria-Vittoria (2002), "The Pseudo-Epigraphic Arabic Characters", in: Marco Ciatti and Max Seidel, eds., *Giotto: The Santa Maria Novella Crucifix*, Florence: Edifir, 217–225.

Foote, Rebecca M. (2012), "An Abbasid Residence at al-Humayma", in: Ratcliff Brandie and Helen C. Evans, eds., *Byzantium and Islam: Age of Transition 7th–9th Century*, New York: The Metropolitan Museum of Art, 221–222.

Forand, Paul G. (1966), "Notes on ʿUšr and Maks", *Arabica* 13, 137–141.

Förster, Hans (2002), *Wörterbuch der griechischen Wörter in den koptischen dokumentarischen Texten* (Texte und Untersuchungen zur Geschichte der altchristlichen Literatur 148), Berlin/New York: De Gruyter.

Förtsch, Reinhard (1993), "Die Architekturdarstellungen der Umaiyadenmoschee von Damaskus und die Rolle ihrer antiken Vorbilder", *Damaszener Mitteilungen* 7, 177–212.

Foss, Clive (2001), "Anomalous Byzantine Coins. Some Problems and Suggestions", *Oriental Numismatic Society Newsletter* 166, 5–12.

Foss, Clive (2002), "The Kharijites and Their Coinage", *Oriental Numismatic Society Newsletter* 171, 24–34.

Foss, Clive (2008), *Arab-Byzantine Coins. An Introduction, with a Catalogue of the Dumbarton Oaks Collection* (Dumbarton Oaks Byzantine Collection Publications 12), Washington: Dumbarton Oaks Research Library and Collection (= *DOC*).

Foss, Clive (2009), "Egypt under Muʿāwiya Part. I: Flavius Papas and Upper Egypt. Part II: Middle Egypt, Fusṭāṭ and Alexandria", *Bulletin of the School of Oriental and African Studies* 72, 1–24 and 259–278.

Foss, Clive (2013), "ʿAbdallah ibn al-Zubayr and his Coinage", *Journal of the Oriental Numismatic Society* 216, 11–17.

Fournet, Jean-Luc (2009a), "Esquisse d'une anatomie de la lettre antique tardive d'après les papyrus", in: Roland Delmaire, Janine Desmuliez, and Pierre-Louis Gatier, eds., *Correspondances. Documents pour l'histoire de l'Antiquité tardive. Actes du colloque, Lille, novembre 2003* (Collection de la maison de l'Orient et de la Méditerranée 40: Série littéraire et philosophique 13), Lyon: Maison de l'Orient et de la Méditerranée, 23–66.

Fournet, Jean-Luc (2009b), "Conversion religieuse dans un graffito de Baouit? Revision de SB III 6042", in: Anne Boud'hors, James Clackson, Catherine Luis, and Petra Sijpesteijn, eds., *Monastic Estates in Late* Antique *and Early Islamic Egypt. Ostraca, Papyri, and Essays in Memory of Sarah Clackson* (American Studies in Papyrology 46), Cincinnati: American Society of Papyrologists, 141–147.

Fowden, Garth (1993), *Empire to Commonwealth: Consequences of Monotheism in Late Antiquity*, Princeton: Princeton University Press.

Fowden, Garth (2004), *Quṣayr ʿAmra. Art and the Umayyad Elite in Late Antique Syria* (The Transformation of the Classical Heritage 36), Berkeley: University of California Press.

Fraenkel, Siegmund (1880), *De Vocabulis in Antiquis Arabum Carminibus et in Corano Peregrinis*, Leiden: Brill.

Fraenkel, Siegmund (1886), *Aramäische Fremdwörter im Arabischen*, Leiden: Brill.

Frantz-Murphy, Gladys (1981–1989), "A Comparison of Arabic and Earlier Egyptian Contract Formularies. 1: The Arabic Contracts from Egypt (3rd/9th–5th/11th centuries). 2: Terminology in the Arabic Warranty and the Idiom of Clearing/Cleaning. 3: The Idiom of Satisfaction. 4: Quittance Formulas. 5: Formulaic Evidence", *Journal of Near Eastern Studies*, Part 1: 40 (= Arabic and Islamic Studies in Honor of Nabia Abbott 2), 203–225; 355–356; Part 2: 44, 99–114; Part 3: 47 105–112; Part 4: 47, 269–280; Part 5: 48, 97–107 (= *P.FrantzMurphyComparison*).

Frantz-Murphy, Gladys (2001), *Arabic Agricultural Leases and Tax Receipts from Egypt* (Corpus Papyrorum Raineri 21), Vienna: Hollinek (= *CPR* XXI).

Frantz-Murphy, Gladys (2007), "Economics of State Formation in Early Islamic Egypt", in: Petra M. Sijpesteijn *et al.*, eds., *From al–Andalus to Khurasan. Documents from the Medieval Muslim World* (Islamic History and Civilization 66), Leiden/Boston: Brill, 101–114.

Freytag, Georg W. (1830–1837), *Lexicon Arabico–Latinum*, 4 vols., Halle: C. A. Schwetschke und Sohn.

Friedman, Hannah / Vorderstrasse, Tasha / Mairs, Rachel / Adams, Russell (2017), "Fragments of an Early Islamic Arabic Papyrus from Khirbet Hamrā Ifdān", *Arabian Archaeology and Epigraphy* 28, 285–296.

Frye, Richard N. (1975), "A Note on Bureaucracy and School in Early Islamic Iran", *Islamic Quarterly* 19, 86–89.

Frye, Richard N. (1977), *The Golden Age of Persia: The Arabs in the East* (History of Civilization), London: Weidenfeld & Nicolson.

Frye, Richard N. / Skjærvø, Prods O. (1996), "The Middle Persian Inscription from Meshkinshahr", *Bulletin of the Asia Institute* 10, 53–61.

Fück, Johann (1950), *ʿArabiya: Untersuchungen zur arabischen Sprach- und Stilgeschichte* (Abhandlungen der Sächsischen Akademie der Wissenschaften zu Leipzig, Philologisch-historische Klasse 45,1), Berlin: Akademie-Verlag, 1950.

Fück, Johann (1955), *Die arabischen Studien in Europa bis in den Anfang des 20. Jahrhunderts*, Leipzig: Harrassowitz.

Gadjiev, Murtazali S. / Shikhsaidov, Amri R. (2002), "The Darband-nama on Harun Al-Rashid and a Newly Discovered Arabic Inscription from A. H. 176", *Manuscripta Orientalia* 8, 3–10.

Gajda, Iwona (2009), *Le royaume de Ḥimyar à l'époque monothéiste l'histoire de l'Arabie du Sud ancienne de la fin du IVe siècle de l'ère chrétienne jusqu'à l'avènement de l'Islam* (Mémoires de l'Académie des inscriptions et belles–lettres 40), Paris: De Boccard.

Garel, Esther (2018), "Une demande de recensement du pagarque Rāšid b. Khālid; *CPR IV* 1 revisité", *Chronique d'Egypte* 93, 187–199.

Garel, Esther (2019), "Relire une lettre fayoumique. L'exemple de SB Kopt. I 280", *Journal of Coptic Studies* 21, 63–71.

Garel, Esther / Vanthieghem, Naïm (2022), "Nouveaux textes sur les pagarques du Fayoum au viiie siècle", in: Lajos Berkes, ed., *Christians and Muslims in Early Islamic Egypt* (American Studies in Papyrology 56), Ann Arbor: University of Michigan Press, 87–126 (= *P.Christ.Musl.* 6–24).

Garosi, Eugenio (2020), "Cross–Cultural Parameters of Scribal Politesse in the Correspondence of Arab–Muslim Officials from Early Islamic Egypt", in: Sabine R. Huebner *et al.*, eds.,

Living the End of Antiquity – Individual Histories from Byzantine to Islamic Egypt (Millennium Studien/Millennium Studies 84), Berlin: De Gruyter, 73–94.

Garosi, Eugenio (2022), "Imperial Arabic: Some Notes on Visual Symbolism", in: Lajos Berkes, ed., *Christians & Muslims in early Islamic Egypt* (American Studies in Papyrology 56), Ann Arbor: University of Michigan Press, 13–32.

Gascou, Jean (2013), "Arabic Taxation in the Mid-Seventh-Century Greek Papyri", in: Constantin Zuckerman, ed., *Constructing the Seventh Century* (Travaux et Mémoires 17), Paris: Association des Amis du Centre d'Histoire et Civilisation de Byzance, 2013, 671–677.

Gascou, Jean / Worp, Klaas A. (1982), "Problèmes de documentation Apollinopolite", *Zeitschrift für Papyrologie und Epigraphik* 49, 83–95.

Gatier, Pierre-Luis (2015), "Les Jafnides dans l'épigraphie grecque au Vie siècle", in: Denis Genequand and Cristian J. Robin, eds., *Les Jafnides: rois arabes au service de Byzance (VIe siècle de l'ère chrétienne). Actes du colloque de Paris, 24–25 novembre 2008* (Orient et Mediterraneé 17), Paris: De Boccard, 193–222.

Gaube, Heinz (1973), *Arabosasanidische Numismatik* (Handbücher der mittelasiatischen Numismatik 2), Braunschweig: Klinkhardt und Biermann.

Gaube, Heinz (1979), "Die syrischen Wüstenschlösser. Einige wirtschaftliche und politische Gesichtspunkte zu ihrer Entstehung", *Zeitschrift des Deutschen Palästina-Vereins* 95, 182–209.

Gaube, Heinz (1982), "Epigraphik", in: Wolfdietrich Fischer and Helmut Gätje, eds., *Grundriss der arabischen Philologie I: Sprachwissenschaft*, Wiesbaden: Reichert, 210–225.

Geertz, Clifford (1960), "The Javanese Kijaji: The Changing Role of a Cultural Broker", *Comparative Studies in Society and History* 2, 228–249.

Geiser, Adam R. (2010), "What Do We Learn About the Early Khārijites and Ibāḍiyya from Their Coins?", *Journal of the American Oriental Society* 130, 167–187.

Genequand, Denis (2018), "Two Possible Caliphal Representations from Qaṣr al-Ḥayr al-Sharqī and Their Implication for the History of the Site", in: Alain George and Andrew Marsham, eds., *Power, Patronage, and Memory in Early Islam: Perspectives on Umayyad Elites*, New York: Oxford University Press, 147–174.

George, Alain (2007), "The Geometry of Early Qur'anic Manuscripts", *Journal of Qur'anic Studies* 9, 78–110.

George, Alain (2010), *The Rise of Islamic Calligraphy*, London: Saqi.

George, Alain (2018), "Paradise or Empire? On a Paradox of Umayyad Art", in: Alain George and Andrew Marsham, eds., *Power, Patronage, and Memory in Early Islam: Perspectives on Umayyad Elites*, New York: Oxford University Press, 39–67.

Ghabban, Ali (2008), "The Inscription of Zuhayr, the Oldest Islamic Inscription (24 AH/AD 644–645), the Rise of the Arabic Script and the Nature of the Early Islamic State", *Arabian Archaeology and Epigraphy* 19, 210–237.

Ghabban, Ali (2011), *Les deux routes syrienne et égyptienne de pèlerinage au nord-ouest de l'Arabie Saoudite*, 2 vols. (Textes arabes et études islamiques 44/1–2), Cairo: Institut Français d'Archéologie Orientale.

al-Ghul, Omar (2006), "Preliminary Notes on the Arabic Material in the Petra Papyri", *Topoi* 14, 139–169.

Giardina, Andrea (1999), "Esplosione di tardoantico", *Studi Storici* 40, 157–180.

Gibson, John C. L. (1971–1975), *Textbook of Syrian Semitic Inscriptions, I: Hebrew and Moabite Inscriptions, II: Aramaic Inscriptions, Including Inscriptions in the Dialect of Zenjirli*, Oxford: Clarendon.

Gignoux, Philippe (1972), *Glossaire des inscriptions pehlevies et parthes* (Corpus inscriptionum Iranicarum, Supplementary series 1), London: Humphries.

Gignoux, Philippe (1979), "Pour une origine Iranienne du *bi'smillah*", in: Philippe Gignoux, Raôul Curiel, Rika Gyselen, and Clarisse Herrenschmidt, eds., Pad nām i yazdān. *Études d'épigraphie, de numismatique et d'histoire de l'Iran ancien* (Travaux de l'Institut d'études iraniennes 9), Paris: Klincksieck, 159–163.

Gignoux, Philippe (1991), "Une nouvelle collection de documents pehlevi cursif du début du septième siècle de notre ère", *Comptes rendus des séances de l'Académie des Inscriptions et Belles-Lettres* 135, 683–700.

Gignoux, Philippe (1996), "Six documents pehlevis sur cuir du California Museum of Ancient Art, Los Angeles", *Bulletin of the Asia Institute* 10, 63–72.

Gignoux, Philippe (2001), "Nouveaux documents pehlevis sur soie", in: Maria G. Schmidt and Walter Bisang, eds., *Philologica et linguistica: Historia, pluralitas, universitas. Festschrift Helmut Humbach zum 80. Geburtstag am 4. Dezember 2001*, Trier: WVT Wissenschaftlicher Verlag, 281–301.

Gignoux, Philippe (2003), "Sept documents économiques en pehlevi", in: Aloïs van Tongerloo, ed., *Iranica selecta: Studies in Honour of Professor Wojciech Skalmowski on the Occasion of His Seventieth Birthday* (Silk Road Studies 6), Turnhout: Brepols, 79–89.

Gignoux, Philippe (2004), "Aspects de la vie administrative et sociale en Iran du 7ème siècle", in: Ryka Gyselen, ed., *Contibutions à l'histoire et la géographie historique de l'empire sassanide* (Res Orientales 16), Bures-sur-Yvette: Groupe pour l'étude de la civilisation du Moyen-Orient, 37–48.

Gignoux, Philippe (2008), "Lettres privées et lettres d'affaires dans l'Iran du VIIe siècle", in: Eva M. Grob and Andreas Kaplony, eds., *Documentary Letters from the Middle East: The Evidence in Greek*, Coptic, *South* Arabian, Pehlevi, and Arabic (1st–15th c CE) (Asiatische Studien/Etudes asiatiques 62, 3), Bern *et al.*: Peter Lang, 827–842.

Gignoux, Philippe (2009), "Les documents économiques de Xwarēn", in: Philippe Gignoux and Ryka Gyselen, eds., *Trésors d'Orient: Mélanges offerts à Rika Gyselen* (Studia Iranica, Cahier 5), Paris: Association pour l'Avancement des Études Iraniennes, 81–102.

Gignoux, Philippe (2010), "La collection de textes attribuables à Dādēn-vindād dans l'Archive pehlevie de Berkeley", in: Ryka Gyselen, ed., *Sources for the History of Sasanian and Post-Sasanian Iran* (Res Orientales 19), Bures-sur-Yvette: Groupe pour l'étude de la civilisation du Moyen-Orient, 11–134.

Gignoux, Philippe (2012), "Une archive post-sassanide du Tabaristan (I)", in: Rika Gyselen, ed., *Objets et documents inscrits en parsïg* (Res Orientales 21), Bures-sur-Yvette: Groupe pour l'Etude de la Civilisation du Moyen-Orient, 29–96.

Gignoux, Philippe (2014), "Une archive post-sassanide du Tabaristan (II)", in: Rika Gyselen, ed., *Argenterie,documents et monnaies de tradition sassanide* (Res Orientales 22), Bures-sur-Yvette: Groupe pour l'Etude de la Civilisation du Moyen-Orient, 29–71.

Gignoux, Philippe (2016), "Une archive post-sassanide du Tabaristan (III)", in: Rika Gyselen, ed., *Words and Symbols: Sasanian Objects and the Tabarestān Archive* (Res Orientales 24), Bures-sur-Yvette: Groupe pour l'Etude de la Civilisation du Moyen-Orient, 171–184.

Gignoux, Philippe / Algar, Hamid (1990), "Besmellāh", *Encyclopaedia Iranica*, 4, 172–174.

Göbl, Robert (1967), *Dokumente zur Geschichte der Iranischen Hunnen in Baktrien und Indien*, vol. 1, Wiesbaden: Harrassowitz.

Göbl, Robert (1968), *Sasanidische Numismatik* (Handbücher der mittelasiatischen Numismatik 1), Braunschweig: Klinkhardt und Biermann.

Goeje (de), Michael J. (1866), *Liber expugnationis regionum, auctore Imámo Ahmed ibn Jahja ibn Djábir al-Beládsorí: quem e codice Leidensi et codice Musei Brittannici*, Leiden: Brill.
Goitein, Shelomo D. (2010) [repr. 1966], *Studies in Islamic History and Institutions with an Introduction of Norman A. Stillman* (Brill Classicsin Islam 5), Leiden/Boston: Brill.
Goldziher, Ignaz (1889–1890), *Muhammedanische Studien*, 2 vols., Halle: Max Niemeyer.
Goldziher, Ignaz (1926), "Bismillah", *Encyclopaedia of Religion and Ethics*, 2, 666–668.
Gonis, Nikolaos (2001), "Reconsidering Some Fiscal Documents from Early Islamic Egypt", *Zeitschrift für Papyrologie und Epigraphik* 137, 225–228.
Gonis, Nikolaos (2004), "Another Look at Some Officials in Early ʿAbbāsid Egypt", *Zeitschrift für Papyrologie und Epigraphik* 149,189–195.
Gonis, Nikolaos (2022), "Rāshid b. Khālid: An Amīr in Middle Egypt under the Umayyads", in: Lajos Berkes, ed., *Christians and Muslims in Early Islamic Egypt* (American Studies in Papyrology 56), Ann Arbor: University of Michigan Press, 127–134.
Gonis, Nikolaos / Morelli, Federico (2000), "A Requisition for the 'Commander of the Faithful'", *Zeitschrift für Papyrologie und Epigraphik* 132, 193–195.
Goody, Jack (ed) (2005) [repr. 1968], *Literacy in Traditional Societies*, Cambridge: Cambridge University Press.
Goodwin, Tony (2012), "The Standard Terminology in SICA 1", in: Tony Goodwin, ed., *Arab Byzantine Coins and History. Papers Presented at the 13th Seventh Century Syrian Numismatic Round Table Held at Corpus Christi College, Oxford, on 11th and 12th September 2011*, London: Archetype, 185–186.
Goodwin, Tony (2015), "The Egyptian Arab-Byzantine Coinage", in: Andrew Oddy, Ingrid Schulze, and Wolfgang Schulze, eds., *Coinage and History in the Seventh Century Near East 4*, London: Archetype.
Gordon, Matthew S. (2001), *The Breaking of a Thousand Swords: A History of the Turkish Military of Samarra (A.H. 200–275/815–889 C.E.)* (SUNY Series in Medieval Middle East History), Albany: State University of New York Press.
Grabar, Oleg (1957), "Review of *Epigrafika Vostoka* I–VIII", *Ars Orientalis* 1, 547–560.
Grabar, Oleg (1959), "The Umayyad Dome of the Rock", *Ars Orientalis* 3, 33–62.
Grabar, Oleg (1964), "Islamic Art and Byzantium", *Dumbarton Oaks Papers* 18, 67–88.
Grabar, Oleg (1977), "Notes sur les cérémonies Umayyades", in: Myriam Rosen-Ayalon, ed., *Studies in Memory of Gaston Wiet*, Jerusalem: Institute of Asian and African Studies, 51–60.
Grabar, Oleg (1987), *The Formation of Islamic Art*, Revised and enlarged edition, New Haven/London: Yale University Press.
Grabar, Oleg (1992), *The Mediation of Ornament* (A.W. Mellon Lectures in the Fine Arts, Bollingen Series, 35: 38), Washington/Princeton: Princeton University Press.
Grabar, Oleg (1993), "Umayyad Palaces Reconsidered", *Ars Orientalis* 23, Pre-Modern Islamic Palaces, 93–108.
Grabar, Oleg (1996), *The Shape of the Holy: Early Islamic Jerusalem*, Princeton: Princeton University Press.
Grabar, Oleg (2005), "The Experience of Islamic Art", in: Irene A. Bierman, ed., *The Experience of Islamic Art on the Margins of Islam*, Reading: Ithaca, 11–60.
Grabar, Oleg (2006a), *The Dome of the Rock*, Cambridge, MA: Harvard University Press.
Grabar, Oleg (2006b), *Islamic Art and Beyond* (Variorum Collected Studies Series 809), Aldershot/Burlington: Variorum.
Grabar, Oleg / Ettinghausen, Richard (1974), "Art and Architecture", in: Joseph Schacht and Clifford E. Bosworth, eds., *The Legacy of Islam*, Oxford: Clarendon Press, 244–317.

Grabar, Oleg / Holod, Renata / Knustad, James / Trousdale, William (1978), *City in the Desert: Qasr al-Hayr East*, 2 vols. (Harvard Middle Eastern Monographs 23–24), Cambridge, MA: Harvard University Press.

Graham, Abigail S. (2013), "The Word is Not Enough: A New Approach to Assessing Monumental Inscriptions. A Case Study from Roman Ephesos", *American Journal of Archaeology* 117, 383–412.

Grassi, Vincenza (1992), "Le iscrizioni normanne in caratteri arabi in Sicilia", *Studi Magrebini* 24, 29–38.

Greenfield, Jonas (1992), "Some Arabic Loanwords in the Aramaic and Nabatean Texts from Naḥal Ḥever", *Jerusalem Studies in Arabic and Islam* 15, 10–21.

Greenwood, Timothy (2004), "Corpus of Early Medieval Armenian Inscriptions", *Dumbarton Oaks Papers* 58, 27–91.

Grelot, Pierre (1972), *Documents araméens d'Egypte* (Littératures anciennes du Proche-Orient, 5), Paris: Ed. du Cerf.

Grenet, Frantz (1989), "Les « Hunes » dans les documents Sogdiens du mont Mugh", in: Charles-Henri de Fouchécour and Philippe Gignoux, eds., *Études irano-aryennes offertes à Gilbert Lazard* (Studia Iranica, Chaier 7), Paris: Association pour l'Avancement des Études Iraniennes, 165–184.

Grenet, Frantz (2008), "Le palais de Nasr ibn Sayyar à Samarkand (années 740)", in: Étienne de La Vaissière, ed., *Islamisation de l'Asie centrale. Processus locaux d'acculturation du VIIe au XIe siècle* (Studia Iranica, Cahier 39), Paris: Association pour l'Avancement des Études Iraniennes, 11–28.

Grenet, Frantz / de la Vaissière, Étienne (2002), "The Last Days of Panjikent", *Silk Road Art and Archaeology* 8, 155–196.

Grierson, Philip / Travaini, Lucia (1998), *The Medieval European Coinage with a Catalogue of the Coins in The Fitzwilliam Museum, Cambridge 14 – Italy III: South Italy, Sicily, Sardinia*, Cambridge: Cambridge University Press.

Griffith, Sidney, H. (1986), "Greek into Arabic: Life and Letters in the Monasteries of Palestine in the 9th Century: The Example of the *Summa Theologiae Arabica*", *Byzantion* 56, 117–38.

Griffith, Sidney H. (1997), "From Aramaic to Arabic: The Languages of the Monasteries of Palestine in the Byzantine and Early Islamic Periods", *Dumbarton Oaks Papers* 51, 11–31.

Griffith, Sidney H. (2012), "The Melkites and the Muslims: The Qur'ān, Christology, and Arab Orthodoxy", *al-Qanṭara* 33, 413–443.

Griffith, Sidney H. (2016), "The Manṣūr Family and Saint John of Damascus: Christians and Muslims in Umayyad Times", in: Antoine Borrut and Fred Donner, eds., *Christians and Others in the Umayyad State* (Late Antique and Medieval Islamic Near East 1), Chicago: The Oriental Institute of the University of Chicago, 29–50.

Grob, Eva M. (2010), *Documentary Arabic Private and Business Letters on Papyrus: Form and Function, Content and Context* (Archiv für Papyrusforschung und verwandte Gebiete – Beihefte 29), Berlin: De Gruyter.

Grob, Eva M. (2013), "A Catalogue of Dating Criteria for Undated Arabic Papyri with 'Cursive' Features", in: Anne Regourd, ed., *Documents et histoire. Islam, VIIe-XVIe s. Actes des journées d'études Musée du Louvre/EPHE,mai 2008* (Ecole pratique des hautes études. Scienceshistoriques et philologiques II. Hautes études orientales – Moyen etProche-Orient, 5/51), Geneva: Droz, 123–143.

Grohmann, Adolf (1923–1924), *Protokolle. I: Einleitung und Texte. Mit einer Schrifttafel und vier Abbildungen im Texte. II: Tafeln* (Corpus Papyrorum Raineri 3), Vienna: Burgverlag Ferdinand Zöllner (= *CPR* III).

Grohmann, Adolf (1932), "Griechische und lateinische Verwaltungstermini im arabischen Ägypten", *Chronique d' Egypte* 13–14, 275–284.

Grohmann, Adolf (1952), *From the World of Arabic Papyri* (Royal Society of Historical Studies), Cairo: al-Maaref (= *P.World*).

Grohmann, Adolf (1954), *Einführung und Chrestomathie zur arabischen Papyruskunde. I: Einführung* (Monografie Archivu Orientálního 13, 1), Prague: Státní Pedagogické Nakladalství.

Grohmann, Adolf (1957), *Greek Papyri of the Early Islamic Period in the Collection of Archduke Rainer*, Cairo: Institut français d'archéologie orientale.

Grohmann, Adolf (1959), *Studien zur historischen Geographie und Verwaltung des frühmittelalterlichen Ägypten* (Denkschriften der Österreichischen Akademie der Wissenschaften, Philosophisch-historische Klasse 77,2), Vienna: Verlag der Österreichischen Akademie der Wissenschaften.

Grohmann, Adolf (1962), *Expédition Philby-Ryckmans-Lippens en Arabie II, Textes épigraphiques I: Arabic Inscriptions* (Bibliothèque du Muséon 50), Louvain: Publications Universitaires (= *AI*).

Grohmann, Adolf (1963), *Arabic Papyri from Ḫirbet el-Mird* (Bibliothèque du Muséon 52), Louvain: Institut orientaliste (= *P.Mird*).

Grohmann, Adolf (1964), "Der Beamtenstab der Arabischen Finanzverwaltung in Ägypten in früharabischen Zeit", in: Horst Braunert, ed., *Studien zur Papyrologie und Wirtschaftsgeschichte: Friedriech Oertel zum achtzigsten Geburtstag gewidmet*, Bonn: Habelt, 120–134.

Grohmann, Adolf (1967–1971), *Arabische Paläographie*, 2 vols. (Denkschriften der Österreichische Akademie der Wissenschaften, Philosophisch-historische Klasse 95), Vienna, *et al*: Böhlau.

Gruendler, Beatrice (1993), *The Development of the Arabic Scripts: From the Nabatean Era to the First Islamic Century According to the Dated Texts* (Harvard Semitic studies 43), Atlanta: Scholars Press.

Gruendler, Beatrice (2006), "Arabic Alphabet: Origin", *Encyclopedia of Arabic Language and Linguistics*, 1, 148–165.

Guest, Rhuvon (1922), "Relations Between Persia and Egypt Under Islam up to the Fāṭimid Period", in: Thomas A. Walker and Reynold A. Nicholson, eds., *A Volume of Oriental Studies, Presented to Edward G. Browne on his 60th Birthday (7 February 1922)*, Cambridge: Cambridge University Press, 163–174.

Guidetti, Mattia (2013), "The Contiguity between Churches and Mosques in the Early Islamic Bilad al-Sham", *Bulletin of the School of Oriental and African Studies* 76, 229–258.

Guidetti, Mattia (2017), *In the Shadow of the Church. The Building of Mosques in Early Medieval Syria* (Arts and Archaeology of the Islamic World 8), Leiden/Boston: Brill.

Gyselen, Rika (1983), "De quelques ateliers monétaires sasanides. I. Un prétendu atelier de Gurgan", *Studia Iranica* 12, 235–238.

Gyselen, Rika (1984), "Le monnayage de cuivre umayyade a legendes pehlevies de Suse", *Cahiersde la Delegation Archeologique Franraise en Iran* 14, 237–245.

Gyselen, Rika (1994), *Catalogue des sceaux, camées et bulles sassanides de la Bibliothèque nationale et du Musée du Louvre I: Collection générale*, Paris: Bibliothèque nationale.

Gyselen, Rika (2000), *Arab-Sassanian Copper Coinage* (Veröffentlichungen der numismatischen Kommission 34), Vienna: Österreichische Akademie der Wissenschaften (= *ASCC*).

Gyselen, Rika (2008), "Notes numismatiques sassanide et arabosassanide", *Studia Iranica* 37, 119–128.

Gyselen, Rika (2009), "Two Notes on post Sassanian Coins", in: Ryka Gyselen, ed., *Sources pour l'histoire et la géographie du monde iranien (224–710)* (Res Orientales 18), Bures-sur-Yvette: Groupe pour l'étude de la civilisation du Moyen-Orient, 143–171.

Gyselen, Rika (2010), "'Umayyad' Zāvulistān and Arachosia: Copper Coinage and the Sasanian Monetary Heritage", in: Michael Alram, ed., *Coins, Arts and Chronology II: The First Millenium C.E. in the Indo-Iranian Borderlands* (Denkschriften der Österreichischen Akademie der Wissenschaften, Philosophisch-historischen Klasse 412), Vienna: Verlag der Österreichischen Akademie der Wissenschaften, 219–241.

Gzella, Holger (2015), *A Cultural History of Aramaic from the Beginnings to the Advent of Islam* (Handbuch der Orientalistik 1, 111), Leiden/Boston: Brill.

Hackl, Johannes / Jursa, Michael / Schmidl, Martina (2014), *Spätbabylonische Privatbriefe* (Alter Orient und Altes Testament 414), Münster: Ugarit-Verlag.

Hadad, Shulamit / Khamis, Elias (1998), "Inscribed Pottery Lamps from the Early Islamic Period at Beth Shean", *Israel Exploration Journal* 48, 66–76.

Haim, Ofir / Shenkar, Michael / Kurbanov, Sharof (2016), "The Earliest Arabic Documents Written on Paper: Three Letters from Sanjar-Shah (Tajikistan)", *Jerusalem Studies in Arabic and Islam* 43, 141–189 (= *P.HaimPaper*).

Halevi, Leor (2007), *Muhammad's Grave: Death Rites and the Making of Islamic Society*, New York: Columbia University Press.

Hamidullah, Muḥammad (1939), "Some Arabic Inscriptions of Medinah of the Early Years of the Hijrah", *Islamic Culture* 13, 427–439.

Hamilton, Robert W. (1946), "An Eighth Century Water-Gauge at al-Muwaqqar", *Quarterly of the Department of Antiquities in Palestine* 12, 70–72.

Hamilton, Robert W. (1949), *The Structural History of the Aqsa Mosque: A Record of Archaeological Gleanings from Repairs of 1938–1942*, London and Jerusalem: Oxford University Press.

Hamilton, Robert W. (1959), *Khirbat al Mafjar: An Arabian Mansion in the Jordan Valley* (Palestine Archeological Museum), Oxford: Clarendon Press.

Hardt, Michael / Negri, Antonio (2001), *Empire*, Cambridge, MA: Harvard University Press.

Harper, Prudence (1979), "Thrones and Enthronement Scenes in Sasanian Art", *Iran* 17, 49–64.

Haspelmath, Martin (2009), "Lexical Borrowing: Concepts and Issues", in: Martin Haspelmath and Uri Tadmor, eds., *Loanwords in the World's Languages: A Comparative Handbook*, Berlin: De Gruyter Mouton, 35–54.

Hasson, Isaac (1982), "Remarques sur l'inscription de l'époque de Mu'āwiya à Ḥammat Gader", *Israel Exploration Journal* 32, 97–101.

Haug, Robert (forthcoming), "Local, Regional, and Imperial Politics: Ṭabaristān and the Early Empire, Struggle and Integration on Multiple Levels", in: Stefan Heidemann and Katharina Mewes, eds., *The Reach of Empire -The Early Islamic Empire at Work Volume 2* (Studies in the History and Culture of the Middle East 37), Berlin/Boston: De Gruyter.

Haugen, Einar (1972), "The Ecology of Language", in: *The Ecology of Language. Essays by Einar Haugen Selected and Introduced by Anwar S.Dil*, Stanford: Stanford University Press, 325–339.

el-Hawary, Ḥasan M. (1930), "The Most Ancient Islamic Monument Known Dated A.H. 31 (A.D. 652), from the Time of the Third Calif 'Uthman", *Journal of the Royal Asiatic Society* 2, 321–333.
el-Hawary, Ḥasan M. (1932), "The Second Oldest Islamic Monument Known, Dated A.H. 71 (A.D. 691). From the Time of the Omayyad Calif 'Abd-el-Malik ibn Marwān", *The Journal of the Royal Asiatic Society of Great Britain and Ireland* 2, 289–293.
el-Hawary, Ḥasan M. (1934), "Un tissu abbaside de Perse", *Bulletin de l'Institut d'Egypte* 16, 61–71.
el-Hawary, Ḥasan M. / Rached Husein (1932), *Catalogue général du Musée arabe du Caire III: Stèles funéraires*, Cairo: Institut français d'archéologie orientale (= *CMC* I).
Hawting Gerald R. (1999), *The Idea of Idolatry and the Emergence of Islam: From Polemic to History* (Cambridge Studies in Islamic Civilization), Cambridge: Cambridge University Press.
Hebbo, Ahmed I (1984), *Die Fremdwörter in der Arabischen Prophetenbiographie des Ibn Hischām (gest. 218/834)*, Frankfurt: Peter Lang.
Heidemann, Stefan (1998), "The Merger of Two Currency Zones in Early Islam. The Byzantine and Sasanian Impact on the Circulation in Former Byzantine Syria and Northern Mesopotamia", *Iran* 36, 95–112.
Heidemann, Stefan (2010a), "The Evolving Representation of the Early Islamic Empire and Its Religion on Coin Imagery", in: Angelika Neuwirth, Nicolai Sinai, and Michael Marx, eds., *The Qurʾan in Context, Historical and Literary Investigations into the Qurʾanic Milieu* (Texts and Studies on the Qurʾān 6), Leiden *et al.*: Brill, 149–195.
Heidemann, Stefan (2010b), "The Standing Caliph Type – the Object on the Reverse", in: Andrew Oddy, ed., *Coinage and History in the Seventh Century Near East 2. Proceedings of the 12th Seventh Century Syrian Numismatic Round Table Held at Gonville and Caius College, Cambridge on 4th and 5th April 2009*, London: Archetype, 23–34.
Heijer (den), Johannes (2012), "Introduction: Middle Arabic and Mixed Arabic, A New Trend in Arabic Studies", in: Liesbeth Zack and Arie Schippers, eds., *Middle Arabic and Mixed Arabic: Diachrony and Synchrony* (Studies in Semitic Languages and Linguistics 64), Leiden/Boston: Brill, 1–25.
Henning, Walter B. (1958), "Mitteliranisch", in: Karl Hoffmann *et al.*, eds., *Iranistik* (Handbuch der Orientalistik 4, 1), Leiden: Brill, 120–126.
Henning, Walter B. (1965), "A Sogdian God", *Bulletin of the School of Oriental and African Studies* 28, 242–254.
Herzfeld, Ernst (1910), "Die Genesis der islamischen Kunst und das Mshatta-Problem", *Der Islam* 1, Part 1: 27–63, Part 2: 105–144.
Hillenbrand, Robert (1981), "Islamic Art at a Crossroad: East versus West at Mshatta", in: Abbas Daneshvari, ed., *Essays in Islamic Art and Architecture* (Islamic Art and Architecture 1), Malibu: Undena Publications, 63–87.
Hillenbrand, Robert (1982), "La Dolce Vita in Early Islamic Syria: The Evidence of Later Umayyad Palaces", *Art History* 5, 1–35.
Hillenbrand, Robert (1999), *Islamic Art and Architecture*, London: Thames and Hudson.
Hillenbrand, Robert (2009), "What Happened to the Sasanian Hunt in Islamic Art?", in: Vesta S. Curtis and Sarah Stewart, eds., *The Rise of Islam* (The Idea of Iran 4), London: I.B. Tauris, 84–101.
Hillenbrand, Robert (2018), "Hishām's Balancing Act: The Case of Qaṣr al-Ḥayr al-Gharbī", in: Alain George and Andrew Marsham, eds., *Power, Patronage, and Memory in Early Islam: Perspectives on Umayyad Elites*, New York: Oxford University Press, 83–132.

Hinz, Walther (1970), *Islamische Masse und Gewichte umgerechnet ins metrische System* (Handbuch der Orientalistik, Ergänzungsband 1), 2nd edition, Leiden/Köln: Brill.

Hirschler, Konrad (2012), *The Written Word in the Medieval Arabic Lands. A Social and Cultural History of Reading Practices*, Edinburgh: Edinburgh University Press.

Hoffman, Eva (2001), "Pathways of Portability: Islamic and Christian Interchange from the Tenth to the Twelfth Century", *Art History* 24, 17–50.

Hopkins, Simon (1984), *Studies in the Grammar of Early Arabic Based upon Papyri Datable to before 300 A.H./912 A.D* (London Oriental Series 37), London *et al.*: Oxford University Press.

Hörnickel, Otto (1930), *Ehren- und Rangprädikate in den Papyrusurkunden: ein Beitrag zum römischen und byzantinischen Titelwesen*, Borna-Leipzig: Noske.

Howard-Johnson, James (2010), "The Rise of Islam and Byzantium's Response", in: Andrew Oddy, ed., *Coinage and History in the Seventh Century Near East 2. Proceedings of the 12th Seventh Century Syrian Numismatic Round Table held at Gonville and Caius College, Cambridge on 4th and 5th April 2009*, London: Archetype, 1–9.

Hoyland, Robert G. (1997a), *Seeing Islam as Others Saw It: A Survey and Evaluation of Christian, Jewish and Zoroastrian Writings on Early Islam* (Studies in Late Antiquity and Early Islam 13), Princeton: Darwin Press, 1997.

Hoyland, Robert G. (1997b), "The Content and Context of Early Arabic Inscriptions", *Jerusalem Studies in Arabic and Islam* 21, 77–102.

Hoyland, Robert G. (2004), "Language and Identity: The Twin Histories of Arabic and Aramaic", *Scripta Classica Israelica* 23, 183–199.

Hoyland, Robert G. (2006), "New Documentary Texts and the Early Islamic State", *Bulletin of the School of Oriental and African Studies* 69, 395–416.

Hoyland, Robert G. (2007), "Writing the Biography of the Prophet Muhammad: Problems and Solutions", *History Compass* 5, 581–602.

Hoyland, Robert G. (2009a), "Arab Kings, Arab Tribes and the Beginnings of Arab Historical Memory in Late Roman Epigraphy", in: Hannah M. Cotton, Robert G. Hoyland, Jonathan J. Price, and David Wasserstein, eds., *From Hellenism to Islam: Cultural and Linguistic Change in the Roman Near East*, Cambridge/New York: Cambridge University Press, 374–400.

Hoyland, Robert G. (2009b), "Late Roman Provincia Arabia, Monophysite Monks and Arab Tribes: a Problem of Centre and Periphery", *Semitica et Classica* 2, 117–139.

Hoyland, Robert G. (2010), "Mount Nebo, Jabal Ramm, and the Status of Christian Palestinian Aramaic and Old Arabic in Late Roman Palestine and Arabia", in: Michael MacDonald, ed., *The Development of Arabic as a Written Language. Papers from the Special Session of the Seminar for Arabian Studies held on 24 July, 2009* (Supplement to the Proceedings of the Seminar for Arabian Studies 40), Oxford: Archaeopress, 29–45.

Hoyland, Robert G. (2015a), *In God's Path: The Arab Conquest and the Creation of an Islamic Empire* (Ancient Warfare and Civilization), Oxford: Oxford University Press.

Hoyland, Robert G. (2015b), "The Earliest Attestation of the *Dhimma* of God and His Messenger and the Rediscovery of P. Nessana 77 (60s AH/680 CE)", with an appendix by Hannah Cotton, in: Behnam Sadeghi *et al.*, eds., *Islamic Cultures, Islamic Contexts. Essays in Honor of Professor Patricia Crone* (Islamic History and Civilization 114), Leiden/Boston: Brill, 51–71 (= *P.HoylandDhimma*).

Hoyland, Robert G. (2018a), "Khanāṣira and Andarīn (Northern Syria) in the Umayyad Period and a New Arabic Tax Document", in: Alain George and Andrew Marsham, eds., *Power, Patronage, and Memory in Early Islam: Perspectives on Umayyad Elites*, New York: Oxford University Press, 133–146.

Hoyland, Robert G. (2018b), “Two New Arabic Inscriptions: Arabian Castles and Christianity in the Umayyad Period”, in: Laïla Nehmé and Ahmad al-Jallad, eds., *To the Madbar and back again Studies in the Languages, Archaeology, and Cultures of Arabia Dedicated to Michael C.A. Macdonald* (Studies in Semitic Languages and Linguistics 92), Leiden/Boston: Brill, 327–337.

Huehnergard, John (2017), “Arabic in Its Semitic Context”, in: Ahmad al-Jallad, ed., *Arabic in Context. Celebrating 400 Years of Arabic at Leiden University* (Studies in Semitic Languages and Linguistics 89), Leiden/Boston: Brill, 3–34.

Humbach, Helmut (1966), *Baktrische Sprachdenkmäler*, Wiesbaden: Harrassowitz.

Humbach, Helmut (1967), “Zu den Legenden der hunnischen Münzen”, *Münchener Studien zur Sprachwissenschaft* 22, 39–56.

Humbach, Helmut / Skjærvø, Prods O. (1983), *The Sassanian Inscription of Paikuli Part 3: Restored Text and Translation*, Wiesbaden/Tehran: Ludwig Reichert, The Iranian Culture Foundation.

Humphreys, Michael (2013), “The ‘War of Images’ Revisited, Justinian II’s Coinage Reform and the Caliphate”, *The Numismatic Chronicle* 173, 229–244.

Huseini, Said R. (in press), “Thinking in Arabic, Writing in Sogdian: Arab Sogdian Diplomatic Relation in the early eight Century”, in: Andreas Kaplony and Matt Malczycki, eds., *From the Ruler of Samarqand to the Andalusian “Law of the Muslims”: Sogdian, Greek and Arabic Documents and Manuscripts from the Islamicate World and Beyond*, Leiden/Boston: Brill.

Ilisch, Lutz (2004), “Die imitativen solidi mancusi: „Arabische” Goldmünzen der Karolingerzeit”, in: Reiner Cunz, ed., *Fundamenta Historiae. Geschichte im Spiegel der Numismatik und ihrer Nachbarwissenschaften: Festschrift für Niklot Klüßendorf zum 60. Geburtstag am 10. Februar 2004* (Veröffentlichungen der urgeschichtlichen Sammlungen des Landesmuseums zu Hannover 51), Hannover: Niedersächsisches Landesmuseum, 91–106.

Imbert, Frédéric (1996), *Corpus des inscriptions arabes de Jordanie du Nord*, Ph.D. thesis, Aix-Marseille.

Imbert, Frédéric (2000), “Le Coran dans les graffiti des deux premiers siècles de l’hégire”, *Arabica* 47, 381–390.

Imbert, Frédéric (2011), “L’Islam des pierres: l’expression de la foi dans les graffiti arabes des premiers siècles”, *Revue des mondes musulmans et de la Méditerranée* 129, 57–78.

Imbert, Frédéric (2013a), “Le Coran des pierres: statistiques épigraphiques et premières analyses”, in: Mehdi Azaiez and Sabrina Mervin, eds., *Le Coran: nouvelles approches*, Paris: Centre National de la Recherche Scientifique, 99–124.

Imbert, Frédéric (2013b), “Graffiti Arabes De Cnide Et De Kos: Premières Traces Épigraphiques De La Conquête Musulmane En Mer Égée”, in: Constantin Zuckerman, ed., *Constructing the Seventh Century* (Travaux et Mémoires 17), Paris: Association des Amis du Centre d’Histoire et Civilisation de Byzance, 731–758.

Imbert, Frédéric (2015), “Califes, princes et poètes dans les graffiti du début de l’Islam”, *Romano-Arabica* 15, 59–78.

Imbert, Frédéric (2016), “Le prince al-Walīd et son bain: itinéraires épigraphiques à Quṣayr ʿAmra”, *Buletin d’études orientales* 64, 321–363.

Internullo, Dario (2016), “Un unicum per la storia della cultura. Su un papiro latinoarabo della British Library (P.Lond. inv. 3124)”, *Mélanges de l’Ecole française de Rome. Moyen Âge* 128, https://journals.openedition.org/mefrm/3233 (accessed Sept. 5, 2020).

Internullo, Dario (2019–2020), "«Magis intellegi quam legi». Segni e simboli grafici cristiani nel Mediterraneo tardoantico e altomedievale", *Storicamente* 15–16, 1–28.

Internullo, Dario / D'Ottone Rambach, Arianna (2018), "One Script for Two Languages: Latin and Arabic in an Early Allographic Papyrus", in: Arianna D'Ottone Rambach, ed., *Palaeography between East and West. Proceedings of the Seminar on Arabic Palaeography held at Sapienza, University of Rome* (Supplementi alla Rivista degli Studi Orientali 1), Pisa: Fabrizio Serra, 53–72.

Jahn, Karl (1937), "Vom frühislamischen Briefwesen. Studien zur islamischen Epistolographie der ersten drei Jahrhunderte der Hiğra auf Grund der arabischen Papyri", *Archiv Orientální* 9, 153–200 (= *P.Jahn*).

al-Jallad, Ahmad (2014), "On the Genetic Background of the Rbbl bn Hfʿm Grave Inscription at Qaryat al-Fāw", *Bulletin of the School of Oriental and African Studies* 77, 445–465.

al-Jallad, Ahmad (2015a), *An Outline of the Grammar of the Safaitic Inscriptions* (Studies in Semitic Languages and Linguistics 80), Leiden/Boston: Brill.

al-Jallad, Ahmad (2015b), "New Epigraphica from Jordan I: a Pre-Islamic Arabic Inscription in Greek Letters and a Greek Inscription from North-Eastern Jordan", *Arabian Epigraphic Notes* 1, 51–70.

al-Jallad, Ahmad (2015c), "Echoes of the Baal Cycle in a Safaito-Hismaic Inscription", *Journal of Ancient Near Eastern Religions* 15, 5–19.

al-Jallad, Ahmad (2017a), "The Arabic of the Islamic Conquests: Notes on Phonology and Morphology based on the Greek Transcriptions from the First Islamic Century", *Bulletin of the School of Oriental and African Studies* 80, 419–39.

al-Jallad, Ahmad (2017b) "Was it *sūrat al-baqárah*? Evidence for Antepenultimate Stress in the Quranic Consonantal Text and its Relevance for صلوه Type Nouns", *Zeitschrift der Deutschen Morgenländischen Gesellschaft* 167, 81–90.

al-Jallad, Ahmad (2018a), "What is Ancient North Arabian", in: Daniel Birnstiel and Na'ama Pat-El, eds., *Re-Engaging Comparative Semitic and Arabic Studies* (Abhandlungen für die Kunde des Morgenlandes 115), Wiesbaden: Harrassowitz.

al-Jallad, Ahmad (2018b), "The Arabic of the Petra Papyri", in: Antti Arjava, Jaakko Frösén, and Jorma Kaimio, eds., *The Petra Papyri V* (American Center of Oriental Research Publications 8), Amman: American Center of Oriental Research, 35–55.

al-Jallad, Ahmad (2020a), "ʿArab, ʾAʿrāb, and Arabic in Ancient North Arabia: The first attestation of (ʾ)ʿrb as a group name in Safaitic", *Arabian Archaeology and Epigraphy* 31, 422–435.

al-Jallad, Ahmad (2020b), *The Damascus Psalm Fragment: Middle Arabic and the Legacy of Old Ḥigāzī* (Late Antique and Medieval Islamic Near East 2), Chicago: The Oriental Institute of the University of Chicago.

al-Jallad, Ahmad / al-Manaser, Ali (2015), "New Epigraphica from Jordan I: a pre-Islamic Arabic Inscription from North-East Jordan", *Arabian Epigraphic Notes* 1, 51–70.

James, Edward (2008), The Rise and Function of the Concept 'Late Antiquity'", *Journal of Late Antiquity* 1, 20–30.

al-Jbour, Khaled S. (2006), *Etudes des inscriptions arabes dans le désert Nord-Est de la Jordanie*, Ph.D. thesis, Aix-Marseille.

Jeffery, Arthur (1938), *The Foreign Vocabulary of the Qurʾān* (Gaekwad's Oriental Series 79), Baroda: Oriental Institute.

Jezewski Mary A. (1995), "Evolution of a Grounded Theory: Conflict Resolution through Culture Brokering", *Advances in Nursing Science* 17, 14–30.

Johns, Jeremy (2003), "Archaeology and the history of early Islam: the first 70 years", *Journal Economic and Social History of the Orient* 46, 411–436.
Johns, Jeremy (2006), "The Arabic Inscriptions of the Norman Kings of Sicily. A Reinterpretation", in: Maria Andaloro, ed., *Nobiles Officinae: Perle, filigrane e trame di seta dal Palazzo Reale di Palermo (Palermo, Palazzo Reale, December 2003–March 2004)*, Catania: Maimone, 324–337.
Johns, Jeremy (2015), "Arabic Inscriptions in the Cappella Palatina: Performativity, Audience, Legibility and Illegibility", in: Anthony Eastmond, ed., *Viewing Inscriptions in the Late Antique and Medieval World*, Cambridge: Cambridge University Press, 99–123.
Johnson, Scott F. (2012), "Preface: On the Uniqueness of Late Antiquity", in: Scott F. Johnson, ed., *The Oxford Handbook of Late Antiquity* (Oxford Handbooks), New York/Oxford: Oxford University Press, xi–xxx.
Jomier, Jacques (2001), "The divine name "al-Raḥmān" in the Qur'ān", in: Andrew Rippin, ed., *The Qur'an: Style and Contents* (The Formation of the Classical Islamic World 24) (trad. Andrew Rippin), Aldershot: Ashgate, 197–213.
Jones, Alan (1992–1996), *Early Arabic Poetry*, 2 vols. (Oxford Oriental Institute Monographs 14–15), Oxford: Ithaca Press.
Jonson, Trent (2012), "The Earliest Dated Islamic Solidi from North Africa", in: Tony Goodwin, ed., *Arab–Byzantine Coins and History. Papers presented at the Seventh Century Syrian Numismatic Round Table held at Corpus Christi College, Oxford on 10th and 11th September 2011*, London: Archetype, 157–168.
Jonson, Trent (2015), "The Earliest Islamic Copper Coinage of North Africa", in: Andrew Oddy, Ingrid Schulze, and Wolfgang Schulze, eds., *Coinage and History in the Seventh Century Near East 4. Proceedings of the 14th Seventh Century Syrian Numismatic Round Table held at The Hives, Worcester on 28th and 29th September 2013*, London: Archetype, 217–240.
Jumʿa, Maḥmūd K. / al-Maʿānī, Sulṭān A. (1999), "Naqsh shāhiday li-aḥad umarāʾ al-bayt al-marwānī min Miḥnā – al-Karak", *Majallat jāmiʿat Dimashq* 15, 240–250.
Justi, Ferdinand (1963), *Iranisches Namenbuch*, Hildesheim: Georg Olms.
Kaiser, Otto (1970), "Zum Formular der in Ugarit gefundenen Briefe", *Zeitschrift des Deutschen Palastina-Vereins* 86, 10–23.
Kameya, Manabu (2017), "From Qusṭāl to Jahbadh: An Aspect of Transition on the Egyptian Tax-Collecting System", in: Sobhi Bouderbala, Sylvie Denoix, and Matt Malczycki, eds., *New Frontiers of Arabic Papyrology: Arabic and Multilingual Texts from Early Islam* (Islamic History and Civilization 144), Leiden/Boston: Brill, 141–160.
Kaplony, Andreas (1996), *Konstantinopel und Damaskus. Gesandtschaften und Verträge zwischen Kaisern und Kalifen 639–750: Untersuchungen zum Gewohnheits-Völkerrecht und zur interkulturellen Diplomatie* (Islamkundliche Untersuchungen 208), Berlin: Klaus Schwarz.
Kaplony, Andreas (2008), "What Are Those Few Dots for? Thoughts on the Orthography of the Qurra Papyri (709–710), the Khurāsān Parchments (755–777) and the Inscription of the Jerusalem Dome of the Rock (692)", *Arabica* 55, 91–112.
Kaplony, Andreas (2015), "The Orthography and Pronunciation of Arabic Names and Terms in the Greek Petra, Nessana, Qurra and Senouthios Letters (Sixth to Eighth Centuries CE)", *Mediterranean Language Review* 22, 1–81.

Kaplony, Andreas (2016), "Die Arabisierung der frühislamischen Verwaltung Syrien–Palästinas und Ägyptens im Spiegel der zweisprachigen griechisch–arabischen Dokumente (550–750): ein Plädoyer für einen regionalen Ansatz", in: Nora Schmidt, Nora K. Schmid, and Angelika Neuwirth, eds., *Denkraum Spätantike. Szenarien der Reflexion von Antiken im Umfeld des Koran* (Episteme in Bewegung 5), Wiesbaden: Harrassowitz, 387–404.

Kaplony, Andreas (2018), "Comparing Qur'ānic Suras with pre-800 Documents (with an Appendix on Subtypes of pre-800 kitāb Documents)", *Der Islam* 95, 312–366.

Kaplony, Andreas (2019), "Scribal Traditions in Documentary Arabic: From the One Imperial Standard Language to the One (Jewish) Language for Transnational Communication (7th–12th Centuries)", in: Jessica L. Goldberg and Eve Krakowski, eds., *Documentary Geniza Research in the 21st Century* (Jewish History 32), Haifa: Haifa University Press, 311–333.

Karabacek (von), Joseph (1886), "Der Mokaukis von Aegypten", *Mitteilungen aus der Sammlung der Papyrus Erzherzog Rainer* 1, 1–11.

Karev, Yury (2015), *Samarqand et le Sughd à l'époque ʿabbāside: histoire politique et social* (Studia Iranica, Cahier 55), Paris: Association pour l'Avancement des Études Iraniennes.

Keegan, Peter / Laurence, Ray / Sears, Gareth (eds.) (2013), *Written Space in the Latin* West, *200 BC to AD 300*, London: Bloomsbury Academic.

Keenan, James (1973–1974), "The Names Flavius and Aurelius as Status Designations in Later Roman Egypt", *Zeitschrift für Papyrologie und Epigraphik*, Part 1: 11, 33–63, Part 2: 13, 283–304.

Kellens, Jean (1989), "Ahura Mazdā n'est pas un dieu créateur", in: Charles-Henri de Fouchécour and Philippe Gignoux, eds., *Études irano-aryennes offertes à Gilbert Lazard* (Studia Iranica, Chaier 7), Paris: Association pour l'Avancement des Études Iraniennes, 217–228.

Kennedy, Charles A. (1963), "The Development of the Lamp in Palestine", *Berytus* 14, 67–115.

Kennedy, Hugh (1981), "Central Government and Provincial Élites in the Early 'Abbāsid Caliphate", *Bulletin of the School of Oriental and African Studies* 44, 26–38.

Kennedy, Hugh (1998), "Egypt as a Province in the Islamic Caliphate 641–868", in: Carl F. Petry, ed., *The Cambridge History of Egypt*, vol. 1, New York: Cambridge University Press, 62–85.

Kennedy, Hugh (2001a), *The Armies of the Caliphs: Military and Society in the Early Islamic State*, London: Routledge.

Kennedy, Hugh (2001b), "Islam", in: Glen W. Bowersock, Peter Brown, and Oleg Grabar, eds., *Interpreting Late Antiquity: Essays on the Postclassical World*, Cambridge, MA: The Belknap Press of Harvard University Press, 219–237.

Kennedy, Hugh (2004), "The Decline and Fall of the First Muslim Empire", *Der Islam* 81, 3–30.

Kennedy, Hugh (2011), "Great Estates and Elite Lifestyles in the Fertile Crescent from Byzantium and Sasanian Iran to Islam", in: Albrecht Fuess and Jan-Peter Hartung, eds., *Court Cultures of the Muslim World* (SOAS-Routledge Studies on the Middle East 13), London: Routledge, 54–79.

Key-Fowden, Elizabeth (2004), "Christian Monasteries and Umayyad Residences in Late Antique Syria", in: José M. Blázquez Martínez and Antonio González Blanco, eds., *Sacralidad y arqueología. Homenagje al Prof. Thilo Ulbert al cumplir 65 años* (Antigüedad y cristianismomonografías históricas sobre la antigüedad tardía 21), Murcia: Universidad de Murcia, 565–581.

Khamis, Elias (2001), "Two Wall Mosaic Inscriptions from the Umayyad Market Place in Bet Shean/Baysān", *Bulletin of the School of Oriental and African Studies* 64, 159–176.

Khan, Geoffrey (1990), "The historical development of the structure of medieval Arabic petitions", *Bulletin of the School of Oriental and African Studies* 53, 8–30.

Khan, Geoffrey (1992), *Arabic Papyri, Selected Material from the Khalili Collection* (Studies in the Khalili Collection 1), Oxford: Nour Foundation in association with Azimuth Editions and Oxford University Press (= *P.Khalili* I).

Khan, Geoffrey (1993), *Bills, Letters and Deeds. Arabic Papyri of the 7th to 11th Centuries* (The Nasser D. Khalili Collection of Islamic Art 6), London/New York: Azimuth Editions and Oxford University Press (= *P.Khalili* II).

Khan, Geoffrey (1994), "The Pre–Islamic Background of Muslim Legal Formularies", *Aram* 6, 193–224.

Khan, Geoffrey (2003), "The Arabic Paper Fragments from Berkeley", *Bulletin of the Asia Institute* 17, 31–34 (= *P.KhanBerkeley*).

Khan, Geoffrey (2007), *Arabic Documents from Early Islamic Khurasan* (Studies in the Khalili Collection 5) London: The Nour Foundation (= *P.Khurasan*).

Khan, Geoffrey (2008), "Remarks on the Historical Background and Development of the Early Arabic Documentary Formulae", in: Eva M. Grob and Andreas Kaplony, eds., *Documentary Letters from the Middle East: The Evidence in Greek*, Coptic, *South* Arabian, Pehlevi, and Arabic (1st–15th c CE) (Asiatische Studien/Études Asiatiques 62, 3), Bern *et al.*: Peter Lang, 885–906.

Khan, Geoffrey (2012), "The Khurasan Corpus of Arabic Documents", in: Teresa Bernheimer and Adam Silverstein, eds., *Late Antiquity: Eastern Perspectives*, Cambridge: Gibb Memorial Trust, 71–86.

Khan, Geoffrey (2013a), "The Development of Early Arabic Documentary Script", in: Robert M. Kerr and Thomas Milo, eds., *Writings and Writing from Another World and Another Era (Festschrift J.J. Witkam)*, Cambridge: Archetype, 229–247.

Khan, Geoffrey (2013b), "The Historical Development of Early Arabic Documentary Formulae", in: Esther-Miriam Wagner, Ben Outhwaite, and Bettina Beinhoff, eds., *Scribes as Agents of Language Change* (Studies in Language Change 10), Boston: De Gruyter, 199–215.

Khan, Geoffrey (2014), *Arabic Documents from Early Islamic Khurāsān* (Einstein Lectures in Islamic Studies 3), Berlin: Freie Universität Berlin.

Khoury, Raif G. (1986), "Die arabischen Inschriften", in: Thilo Ulbert, ed., *Resafa II: Die Basilika des Heiligen Kreuzes in Resafa-Sergiupolis*, Mainz: Philipp von Zabern, 179–180.

al-Kilābī, Ḥayāt (1995), *Al-āthār al-islāmiya bi-baldat Badā, muḥāfaẓat al-Wajh, shamāl ġarb al-Mamlaka al-ʿArabiyya as-saʿūdiya*, Ph.D. thesis, Riyadh.

al-Kilābī, Ḥayāt (2009), *Al-nuqūsh al-islāmiyya ʿalā ṭarīq al-ḥajj al-shāmī bi-shamāl ġarb al-Mamlaka al-ʿArabiya as-saʿūdiyya (min al-qarn al-awwal ilā al-qarn al-khāmis al-hijrī)*, Riyadh: King Fahd National Library (= *NI*).

Kilpatrick, George D. (1964), "Dura-Europos: The Parchments and the Papyri", *Greek, Roman and Byzantine Studies* 5, 215–225.

King, Geoffrey R. D. (1983), "Two Byzantine Churches in Northern Jordan and their Re-use in the Islamic Period", *Damaszener Mitteilungen* 1, 111–136.

King, Geraldine M. (1990), *Early North Arabian Hismaic: A Preliminary Description Based on a New Corpus of Inscriptions from the* Ḥismā *Desert of Southern Jordan and Published Material*, Ph.D. thesis, London.

Kirk, George E. / Welles, Bradford C. (1962). "The Inscriptions", in: Dunscombe H. Colt, ed., *Excavations at Nessana (Auja Hafir, Palestine) I*, Princeton: Princeton University Press, 131–197.

Kister, Menahem (2018), "*Islām* – Midrashic Perspectives on a Quranic Term", *Journal of Semitic Studies* 63, 381–406.

Knauf, Ernst A. (2010), "Arabo-Aramaic and ʿArabiyya: From Ancient Arabic to Early Standard Arabic, 200 CE–600 CE", in: Angelika Neuwirth, Nicolai Sinai, and Michael Marx, eds., *The Qur'an in Context, Historical and Literary Investigations into the Qur'anic Milieu* (Texts and Studies on the Qur'ān 6), Leiden *et al.*: Brill, 197–254.

Koch, Paul (1903), *Die byzantinischen Beamtentitel von 400 bis 700*, Jena: G. Neuenhahn.

Kračkovskaja, Vera A. (1952), "Pamjatniki arabskogo pis'ma v Srjednjej Azii i Zakavkaz'je do IX v.", *Epigrafika Vostoka* 6, 81–84.

Kraemer Casper J. (1958), *Excavations at Nessana Volume III: Non-literary Papyri*, Princeton: Princeton University Press (= *P.Ness.*).

Krauss, Samuel (1898–1899), *Griechische und Lateinische Lehnwörter im Talmud, Midrasch und Targum*, 2 vols., Berlin: Calvary.

Kremer (von), Alfred (1883), *Beiträge zur arabischen Lexikographie*, Vienna: C. Gerold's Sohn.

Kreuzsaler, Claudia (2007), *Griechische Papyrusurkunden kleineren Formats – Neuedition. SPP III2 449–582: Quittungen* für *die Getreidesteuer* (Papyrologica Vindobonensia 6) Vienna: Österreichische Akademie *der Wissenschaften* (= *SPP* III_2).

Kröger, Jens (1999), "Vom Flügelpaar zur Flügelpalmette. Sasanidische Motive in der islamischen Kunst", in: Barbara Finster, Christa Fragner, and Herta Hafenrichter, eds., *Bamberger Symposium Rezeption in der Islamischen Kunst* (Beiruter Texte und Studien 61), Stuttgart: Franz Steiner, 193–204.

Kropp, Manfred (2017), "The ʿAyn ʿAbada Inscription Thirty Years Later: A Reassessment", in: Ahmad al-Jallad, ed., *Arabic in Context. Celebrating 400 years of Arabic at Leiden University* (Studies in Semitic Languages and Linguistics 89), Leiden/Boston: Brill, 53–74.

Kubitschek, Wilhelm (1897), "Beiträge zur frühbyzantinischen Numismatik 2: Verzeichniss der im Wiener Münzcabinet befindlichen byzantinischen Zwölfer aus Münzstätte Alexandria", *Numismatische Zeitschrift* 29, 192–196.

Kühnel, Ernst (1971), *Die islamischen Elfenbeinskulpturen: VIII.-XIII. Jahrhundert* (Elfenbeinskulpturen, Ergänzungsband), Berlin: Deutscher Verlag für Kunstwissenschaft.

Kurvers, Jeanne / van Hout, Roeland / Vallen, Ton (2009), "Print Awareness of Adult Illiterates: A Comparison with young Pre-readers and low-educated adult Readers", *Reading and Writing* 22, 863–888.

Lagarde (de), Paul (1866), *Gesammelte Abhandlungen*, Leipzig: Brockhaus.

Landwehr, Achim (2013), "Über den Anachronismus", *Zeitschrift für Geschichtswissenschaft* 61, 5–29.

Lane, Edward W. (1863–1893), *An Arabic-English Lexicon Derived from the Best and most Copious Eastern Sources*, 8 vols., London: Williams and Norgate.

Leatherbury, Sean V. (2019), "Framing Late Antique Texts as Monuments: The *Tabula Ansata* between Sculpture and Mosaic", in: Andrej Petrovic, Ivana Petrovic, and Edmund Thomas, eds., *The Materiality of Text – Placement, Perception, and Presence of Inscribed Texts in Classical Antiquity* (Brill Studies in Greek and Roman Epigraphy 11), Leiden/Boston: Brill, 380–404.

Legendre, Marie (2013), *Pouvoir et territoire L'administration islamique en Moyenne-Égypte pré-ṭūlūnide (642–868)*, Ph.D. thesis, Leiden.

Legendre, Marie (2016), "Neither Byzantine nor Islamic? The Duke of the Thebaid and the Formation of the Umayyad State", *Historical Research* 89, 1–18.

Legendre, Marie (2019), "Landowners, Caliphs and State Policy over Landholdings in the Egyptian Countryside: Theory and Practice", in: Alain Delattre, Marie Legendre, and Petra Sijpesteijn, eds., *Authority and Control in the Countryside: From Antiquity to Islam in the Mediterranean and Near East (6th-10th Century)* (Leiden Studies in Islam and Society 9), Leiden/Boston: Brill, 392–419.

Legendre, Marie / Younes, Khaled (2015), "The Use of the Terms *ǧizya* and *kharāǧ* in the First 200 years of hiǧra in Egypt" https://www.universiteitleiden.nl/en/research/research-projects/humanities/formation-of-islam-topics (accessed Jan. 15, 2021).

el-Leithy, Tamer (2011), "Living Documents, Dying Archives: Towards a Historical Anthropology of Medieval Arabic Archives", *al-Qanṭara* 32, 389–434.

Lentin, Jérôme (2008a), "Middle Arabic", *Encyclopaedia of the Arabic Language and Linguistics*, 3, 215–226.

Lentin, Jérôme (2008b), "Moyen arabe et variétés mixtes de l'arabe: premier essai de bibliographie", in: Jérôme Lentin and Jacques Grand'Henry, eds., *Moyen arabe et variétés mixtes de l'arabe à travers l'histoire: actes du premier colloque international (Louvain-la-Neuve, 10–14 mai 2004)* (Publications de l'Institut Orientaliste de Louvain 58), Louvain: Peeters, XXV–LXXXVII.

Lerner Judith A. / Sims-Williams, Nicholas (2011), *Seals, Sealings, and Tokens from Bactria to Gandhara (4th to 8th century CE) with Contributions by Aman ur Rahman and Harry Falk* (Denkschriften der Österreichischen Akademie der Wissenschaften, Philosophisch-historische Klasse 421: Veröffentlichungen zur Numismatik 52), Vienna, Österreichische Akademie der Wissenschaften.

Levy-Rubin, Milka (2009), "The Pact of ʿUmar", in: David Thomas and Barbara Roggema, eds., *Christian-Muslim Relations: A Bibliographical History. Volume I (600–900)* (The History of Christian-Muslim Relations 11), Leiden/Boston: Brill, 360–364.

Liebrenz, Boris (2020), "An Archive in a Book: Documents and Letters from the Early-Mamluk Period", *Der Islam* 97, 120–171.

Lilie, Ralf-Johannes (1976), *Die Byzantinische Reaktion auf die Ausbreitung der Araber* (Miscellanea Byzantina Monacensia 22), Munich: Beck.

Linder-Welin, Ulla S. (1965), "Some Rare Samanid Dirhams and the Origin of the Word Mancusus", in: *Congresso internazionale di numismatica Roma, 11–16 settembre 1961*, vol. 2, Roma: Istituto italiano di numismatica, 499–508.

Lindstedt, Ilkka (2015), "*Muhājirūn* as a Name for the First/Seventh Century Muslims", *Journal of Near Eastern Studies* 74, 67–73.

Lindstedt, Ilkka (2019), "Who is in, Who is out? Early Muslim Identity through Epigraphy and Theory", *Jerusalem Studies in Arabic and Islam* 46, 147–246.

Livshits, Vladimir A. (1962), *Sogdijskie dokumenty s gory Mugh II: Juridicheskie dokumenty i pisʾma*, Moskow: Izd. vostočnoj lit.

Livshits, Vladimir A. (2015), *Sogdian Epigraphy of Central Asia and Semirech'e* (Corpus Inscriptionum Iranicarum Part III: Inscriptions of the Seleucid and Parthian Periods and of Eastern Iran and Central Asia) (trad. Nicholas Sims–Williams), London: SOAS (= Mugh).

Livshits, Vladimir A. / Raspopova, Valentina I. (2015), "Sogdijskaâ epigrafika Pendžikenta", in: Valerii P. Nikonorov and Vadim A. Alyokshin, eds., *Akademicheskoye vostokovedeniye v Rossii i stranakh bližnego zarubež'ya (2007–2015)* (Proceedings of the Institute for the History of Material Culture of the Russian Academy of Sciences 45), St. Petersburg: Contrast, 327–343.

Løkkegaard, Frede (1950), *Islamic Taxation in the Classic Period with Special Reference to Circumstances in Iraq* (Studies in Islamic History 10), Copenhagen: Branner & Korch.

Longperier (de), Adrien (1841), "Remarkable Gold Coin of Offa", *The Numismatic Chronicle* 4, 232–234.

Löw, Immanuel (1881), *Aramäische Pflanzennamen*, Leipzig: Wilhelm Engelmann.

Ludwig, Ralph (2016), *Linguistic Ecology and Language Contact* (Cambridge Approaches to Language Contact), Cambridge: Cambridge University Press.

Luiselli, Raffaele (2008), "Greek Letters on Papyrus: First to Eighth Century", in: Eva M. Grob and Andreas Kaplony, eds., *Documentary Letters from the Middle East: The Evidence in Greek*, Coptic, *South* Arabian, Pehlevi, and Arabic (1st–15th c CE) (Asiatische Studien/Etudes asiatiques 62, 3), Bern *et al.*: Peter Lang, 677–737.

Lukonin, Vladimir G. (1983), "Political, Social, and Administrative Institutions, Taxes and Trade", in: Ehsan Yar-Shater, ed., *The Cambridge History of Iran 3 (2): The Seleucid, Parthian, and Sasanian Periods*, Cambridge: Cambridge University Press, 681–746.

Lurje, Pavel (2008), "*Khamir* and Other Arabic Words in Sogdian Texts", in: Étienne de la Vaissière, ed., *Islamisation de l'Asie Central: processus locaux d'islamisation du VIIe au XIe siècle* (Studia Iranica, Cahier 39), Paris: Association pour l'Avancement des Études Iraniennes, 29–57.

Luxenberg, Christof (2000), *Die syro-aramäische Lesart des Koran ein Beitrag zur Entschlüsselung der Koransprache*, Berlin: Das Arabische Buch.

Lynch, Ryan J. (2015), "Sons of the Muhājirūn: Some Comments on Ibn al-Zubayr and Legitimizing Power in Seventh-Century Islamic History", in: Alessandro Gnasso *et al.*, eds., *The Long Seventh Century : Continuity and Discontinuity in an Age of Transition* Oxford *et al.*: Peter Lang, 251–268.

Mabra, Joshua (2017), *Princely Authority in the Early Marwānid State: the Life of ʿAbd al-ʿAzīz ibn Marwān* (Islamic History and Thought 2), Piscataway: Gorgias Press.

MacAdam, Henry I. (1986), "Some Notes on the Umayyad Occupation of North-east Jordan", in: Philip Freemann and David Kennedy, eds., *The Defence of the Roman and Byzantine East. Proceedings of a Colloquium Held at the University of Sheffield in April 1986* (British Archaeological Reports 297), Oxford: B. A. R., 531–547.

Mac Coul, Leslie S. B. (1987), "Coptic Egypt during the Persian Occupation: the Papyrological Evidence", *Studi Classici e Orientali* 36, 307–313.

Mac Coul, Leslie S. B. (1988), "The Coptic Papyri from Apollonos Ano", in: Vasileios G. Mandilaras, ed., *Proceedings of the XVIII international Congress of Papyrology, Athens 25–30 Mai 1986*, II, Athens: Greek Papyrological Society, 141–160.

MacDonald, Michael C. A. (2000), "Reflections on the Linguistic Map of pre-Islamic Arabia", *Arabian Archaeology and Epigraphy* 11, 28–79.

MacDonald, Michael C. A. (2004), "Ancient North Arabian", in: Roger D. Woodard, ed., *The Cambridge Encyclopedia of the World's Ancient Languages*, Cambridge: Cambridge University Press, 488–533.

MacDonald, Michael C. A. (2008), "Old Arabic", *Encyclopedia of Arabic Language and Linguistics*, 3, 464–477.

MacDonald, Michael C. A. (2009a), *Literacy and Identity in pre-Islamic Arabia* (Collected Studies Series 906), Aldershot: Ashgate.

MacDonald, Michael C. A. (2009b), "ARNA Nab 17 and the Transition from the Nabataean to the Arabic Script", in: Werner Arnold, Michael Jursa, Walter W. Müller, and Stephan Procházka, eds., *Philologisches und Historisches zwischen Anatolien und Sokotra. Analecta Semitica in Memoriam Alexander Sima*, Wiesbaden: Harassowitz, 207–240.

MacDonald, Michael C. A. (2010), "Ancient Arabia and the Written Word", in: Michael MacDonald, ed., *The Development of Arabic as a Written Language. Papers from the Special Session of the Seminar for Arabian Studies held on 24 July, 2009* (Supplement to the Proceedings of the Seminar for Arabian Studies 40), Oxford: Archaeopress, 5–27.

MacDonald, Michael C. A. (2015), "Arabs and Empires before the Sixth Century", in: Greg Fisher, ed., *Arabs and Empires before Isalm*, Oxford: Oxford University Press, 11–79.

MacKenzie, David (1986), *A Concise Pahlavi Dictionary*, reprinted with corrections, London: Oxford University Press.

Macuch, Maria (2016), "The Legal Context of the Tabarestan Court Records (Tab.1–8,10)", in: Rika Gyselen, ed., *Words and Symbols: Sasanian Objects and the Tabarestān Archive* (Res Orientales 24), Bures-sur-Yvette: Groupe pour l'Etude de la Civilisation du Moyen-Orient, 145–170.

Macuch, Maria (2017), "Pahlavi Legal Documents from Tabarestan: On Lease, Loan and Compensation", in: Rika Gyselen, ed., *Sassanian Coins, Middle-Persian Etymology and the Tabarestān Archive* (Res Orientales 26), Bures-sur-Yvette: Groupe pour l'Etude de la Civilisation du Moyen-Orient, 165–195.

Malandra, William W. (1996), "Day", *Encyclopaedia Iranica*, 7, 163–164.

Mâle, Emile (1923), "Les influences arabes dans l'art roman", *Revue des Deux-Mondes* 18, 311–343

Malek, Hodge M. (2004), *The Dābūyid Ispahbads and Early 'Abbāsid Governors of Tabaristān: History and Numismatics* (Royal Numismatic Society, Special Publication 39), London: Royal Numismatic Society.

Maraqten, Mohammed (1998), "Writing Materials in Pre-Islamic Arabia", *Journal of Semitic Studies* 48, 287–310.

Marcone, Arnaldo (2008), "A Long Late Antiquity?: Considerations on a Controversial Periodization", *Journal of Late Antiquity* 1, 4–19.

Maresch, Klaus (1994), *Nomisma und Nomismatia: Beiträge zur Geldgeschichte Ägyptens im 6. Jahrhundert n. Chr* (Abhandlungen der Rheinisch-Westfälischen Akademie der Wissenschaften, Sonderreihe Papyrologica Coloniensia 21), Opladen: Westdeutscher Verlag.

Marsham, Andrew (2009a), *Rituals of Islamic Monarchy: Accession and Succession in the First Muslim Empire*, Edinburgh: Edinburgh University Press.

Marsham, Andrew (2009b), "The Early Caliphate and the Inheritance of Late Antiquity, *c.* 610–750", in: Philip Rousseau, ed., *A Companion to Late Antiquity* (Blackwell Companions to the Ancient World), Oxford: Wiley Blackwell, 479–492.

Marsham, Andrew (2011), "Public Executions in the Umayyad Period: Early Islamic Punitive Practice and its Late Antique Context", *Journal of Arabic and Islamic Studies* 101, 101–136.

Marsham, Andrew (2018), "God's Caliph' Revisited: Umayyad Political Thought in Its Late Antique Context", in: Alain George and Andrew Marsham, eds., *Power, Patronage and Memory in Early Islam: Perspectives from Umayyad History*, Oxford: Oxford University Press, 3–37.

Marthot-Santaniello, Isabelle (2013), *Un village égyptien et sa campagne: étude de la microtoponymie du territoire d'Aphroditê (VIe-VIIIe s.)*, 2 vols., Ph.D. thesis, Paris.

Marx, Michael Josef / Jocham, Tobias J. (2019), "Radiocarbon (^{14}C) Dating of Qurʾān Manuscripts", in: Andreas Kaplony and Michael Marx, eds., *Qurʾān Quotations Preserved on Papyrus Documents, 7th–10th Centuries and the Problem of Carbon Dating Early Qurʾāns* (Documenta Coranica 2), Leiden/Boston: Brill, 188–221.

Marzouk, Muḥammad A. A. (1954), "The Turban of Samuel Ibn Musa: The Earliest Dated Islamic Textile", *Bulletin of the Faculty of Arts (University Of Cairo)* 16, 143–151.

Mavroudi, Maria (2008), "Arabic Words in Greek Letters: The Violet Fragment and More", in: Jérôme Lentin and Jacques Grand'Henry, eds., *Proceedings of the First International Symposium on Middle Arabic and Mixed Arabic Throughout History (Louvain-la-Neuve, 11–14 May 2004)*, Louvain: Peeters, 321–354.

Mavroudi, Maria (2015), "Greek Language and Education under Early Islam", in: Behnam Sadeghi *et al.*, eds., *Islamic Cultures, Islamic Contexts. Essays in Honor of Professor Patricia Crone* (Islamic History and Civilization 114), Leiden/Boston: Brill, 295–342.

Mayer, Leo A. (1946), "Note on the Inscription from al-Muwaqqar", *Quarterly of the Department of Antiquities in Palestine* 12, 73.

Mayerson, Philip (1994), "'Pουζικον' and 'Ρογα' in the Post-conquest Papyri", *Zeitschrift für Papyrologie und Epigraphik* 100, 126–128.

Mayerson, Philip (1995), "An Additional Note on Pουζικον (ar. *rizq*)", *Zeitschrift für Papyrologie und Epigraphik* 107, 279–281.

Mayerson, Philip (2003), "The κάγκελλον Artab Measure Equals Five Modii Xysti?", *The Bulletin of the American Society of Papyrologists* 40, 179–185.

McCormick, Michael (2001), *Origins of the European Economy Communications and Commerce, A.D. 300–900*, Cambridge: Cambridge University Press.

McLean, Bradley H. (2002), *An Introduction to Greek Epigraphy of the Hellenistic and Roman Periods from Alexander the Great down to the Reign of Constantine (323 B.C.-A.D. 337)*, Ann Arbor: University of Michigan Press.

McMillan, M.E. (2011), *The Meaning of Mecca: The Politics of Pilgrimage in Early Islam*, London: Saqi.

Medjell, Gunvor (2008), "'Middle Arabic' across Time and Medium/Mode. Some Reflections and Suggestions", in: Jérôme Lentin and Jacques Grand'Henry, eds., *Moyen arabe et variétés mixtes de l'arabe à travers l'histoire: actes du premier colloque international (Louvain-la-Neuve, 10–14 mai 2004)* (Publications de l'Institut Orientaliste de Louvain 58), Louvain: Peeters, 355–372.

Meinecke, Katharina (2014), "The Encyclopaedic Illustration of a New Empire. Graeco-Roman-Byzantine and Sasanian Models on the Facade of Qasr al-Mshatta", in: Stine Birk, Troels Myrup Kistensen, and Birte Poulsen, eds., *Using Images in Late Antiquity*, Oxford/Philadelphia: Oxbow, 283–300.

Meinecke, Katharina (2016), "Antike Motive in der frühislamischen Kunst: Neue Beobachtungen zur Bauornamentik des Palastes Mschatta in Jordanien (8. Jh.)", in: Gerald Grabherr and Barbara Kainrath, eds., *Akten des 15. Österreichischen Archäologentages in Innsbruck 27. Februar–1.März 2014* (IKARUS 9), Innsbruck: Innsbruck University Press, 215–226.

Meinecke, Katharina (2020), "Umayyad Visual Culture and its Models 1", in: Andrew Marsham, ed., *The Umayyad World* (The Routledge Worlds 46), London: Routledge, 103–132.

Melchert, Christopher (2013), "Whether to keep Unbelievers out of Sacred Zones: a Survey of Medieval Islamic Law", *Jerusalem Studies in Arabic and Islam* 40, 177–194.

Metlich, Michael A. / Schindel, Nikolaus C. (2004), "Egyptian Copper Coinage from the 7th Century AD: Some Critical Remarks", *Oriental Numismatic Society Newsletter* 179, 111–115.

Mikhail, Maged S. (2014), *From Byzantine to Islamic Egypt. Religion, Identity and Politics after the Arab Conquest*, London/New York: I.B. Tauris.
Miles, George C. (1938), *The Numismatic History of Rayy* (Numismatic Studies 2), New York: The American Numismatic Society.
Miles, George C. (1939), "A Byzantine Weight Validated by al-Walid", *Numismatic Notes and Monographs* 87, 1–11.
Miles, George C. (1948), "Early Islamic Inscriptions near Tâ'if in the Hijâz", *Journal of Near Eastern Studies* 7, 236–242.
Miles, George C. (1950), *The Coinage of the Umayyads of Spain* (Hispanic Numismatic Series 1), New York: American Numismatic Society.
Miles, George C. (1957), "Mihrab and ʿAnaza – a Study in Early Islamic Iconography", in: George C. Miles, ed., *Archaeologica Orientalia in Memorian of E. Herzfeld*, Locust Valley: J.J. Augustin, 156–171.
Miles, George C. (1963), "On the Varieties and Accuracy of 8th Century Arab Coin Weights", *Eretz-Israel* 7, 78–87.
Miles, George C. (1967), "The Earliest Arab Gold Coinage", *Museum Notes (American Numismatic Society)* 13, 205–229.
Miles, George C. / Matson, Frederick R. (1948), *Early Arabic Glass Weights and Stamps: With a Study of the Manufacture of Eighth-Century Egyptian Glass Weights and Stamps* (Numismatic Notes and Monographs 111), New York: The American Numismatic Society.
Milik, Jozef T. (1953), "Une inscription et une lettre en araméen christo–palestinien", *Revue Biblique* 60, 526–530.
Milstein, Rachel (1988–1989), "A Hoard of Early Arab Figurative Coins", *Israel Numismatic Journal* 10, 3–26.
Milwright, Marcus (2016), *The Dome of the Rock and Its Umayyad Mosaic Inscriptions*, (Edinburgh Studies in Islamic Art) Edinburgh: Edinburgh University Press.
Mittwoch, Eugen (1935), "Eine arabische Bauinschrift aus dem Jahre 136H", *Orientalia* 4, 235–238.
Mochiri, Malek I. (1981), "A Pahlavi Forerunner of the Umayyad Reformed Coinage", *The Journal of the Royal Asiatic Society of Great Britain and Ireland* 2, 168–172.
Montevecchi, Orsolina (1956), "Pantokrator", in: Edoardo Arslan, ed., *Studi in onore di Aristide Calderini e Roberto Paribeni*, vol. 2, Milano: Ceschina, 401–432.
Montevecchi, Orsolina (1988), *La papirologia. Ristampa, riveduta e corretta con addenda*, (Trattati e manuali) Milano: Vita e pensiero.
Morelli, Federico (1996), *Olio e retribuzioni nell'Egitto tardo (V–VIII d.C.)*, Florence: Istituto papirologico "G. Vitelli".
Morelli, Federico (2001), *Documenti greci per la fiscalità e la amministrazione dell'Egitto arabo*, 2 vols. (Corpus Papyrorum Raineri 22), Vienna: Hollinek (= *CPR* XXII).
Morelli, Federico (2002), "*Gonachia* e *kaunakai* nei Papiri con due Documenti Inediti (P. Vindob. G 1620e P. Vindob. G 18884) e uno riedito (P. Brook. 25)", *The Journal of Juristic Papyrology* 32, 55–81
Morelli, Federico (2010a), *L'archivio di Senouthios* anystes *e testi connessi (I). Lettere e documenti per la costruzione di una capitale* (Corpus Papyrorum Raineri 30), Berlin/New York: De Gruyter (= *CPR* XXX).
Morelli, Federico (2010b), "Consiglieri e comandanti. I titoli del governatore arabo d'Egitto symboulos e amîr", *Zeitschrift für Papyrologie und Epigraphik* 173, 158–166.
Morelli, Federico (2013), "Egitto arabo, papiri e papirologia greci", *The Journal of Juristic Papyrology* 43 (2013), 163–186.

Morelli, Federico (2019), *I prezzi dei materiali e prodotti artigianali nei documenti tardoantichi e del primo periodo arabo (IV* ex. – *VIII d.C.)* (Mitteilungen aus der Papyrussammlung der Nationalbibliothek in Wien: Papyrus Erzherzog Rainer XXIII), Berlin: De Gruyter.

Morimoto, Kosei (1981), *The Fiscal Administration of Egypt in the Early Islamic Period* (Asian Historical Monographs 1), Kyoto: Dohosha.

Morony, Michael G. (2004), "Social Elites in Iraq and Iran: After the Conquest", in: John Haldon and Lawrence I. Conrad, eds., *The Byzantine and Early Islamic Near East VI: Elites Old and New* (Studies in late Antiquity and Early Islam 1), Princeton: Darwin Press, 275–284.

Morony, Michael G. (2005), *Iraq after the Muslim Conquest* (Perspectives on Society and Culture 3), 2nd edition, Piscataway: Georgias Press.

Morrisson, Cécile (1972), "Le tresor byzantin de Nikertai", *Revue Belge de Numismatique* 118, 29–91.

Morton, Alexander H. (1985), *A Catalogue of Early Islamic Glass Stamps in the British Museum*, London: British Museum Publications (= *EIGS*).

Morton, Alexander H. (1986), "A Glass Dīnār Weight in the Name of ʿAbd al-ʿAzīz b. Marwān", *Bulletin of the School of Oriental and African Studies* 49, 177–182.

Morton & Eden LTB (In Association with Sotheby's) (2012), *Important Coins from the Islamic World*, Morton & Eden Auctions, London, Auction 54 (23rd April 2012).

Motyl, Alexander J. (2001), *Imperial Ends: The Decay, Collapse, and Revival of Empires*. New York: Columbia University Press.

Moubarac, Youakim (1957), *Les études d'épigraphie sud-sémitique et la naissance de l'Islam: Eléments de bibliographie et lignes de recherches* Paris: Paul Geuthner.

al-Muaikel, Khaled I. (1994), *Study of the Archaeology of the Jawf Region*, Riyadh: King Fahd National Library.

Mugridge, Alan (2010), "Writing and Writers in Antiquity: Two "Spectra" in Greek Handwriting", in: Traianos Gaos, ed., *Proceedings of the 25th International Congress of Papyrology Ann Arbor, July 29–August 4, 2007*, Ann Arbor: The University of Michigan Library, Scholarly Publishing Office, 573–580.

Mullen, Alex / James, Patrick (eds) (2012), *Multilingualism in the Graeco-Roman World*, Cambridge: Cambridge University Press.

"Multilingual Archives and Documents in post-conquest Egypt", in: Arietta Papaconstantinou, ed., *The Multilingual Experience in Egypt, from the Ptolemies to the ʿAbbasids*, Burlington: Ashgate, 105–124.

Münkler, Herfried (2005), *Imperien. Die Logik der Weltherrschaft: Vom alten Rom bis zu den Vereinigten Staaten*, Berlin: Rowohlt.

Munt, Harry (2016), "Caliphal Imperialism and Ḥijāzī Elites in the Second/Eighth Century", *Al-Masāq* 28, 6–21.

Munt, Harry (2018), "Caliphal Estates and Properties around Medina in the Umayyad Period", in: Alain Delattre, Marie Legendre, and Petra Sijpesteijn, eds., *Authority and Control in the Countryside: From Antiquity to Islam in the Mediterranean and Near East (6th-10th Century)* (Leiden Studies in Islam and Society 9), Leiden/Boston: Brill, 432–463.

Nadler, Rajaa (1990), *Die Umayyadenkalifen im Spiegel ihrer zeitgenössischen Dichter*. Ph.D. thesis: Erlangen-Nürnberg.

Naldini, Mario (1968), *Il Cristianesimo in Egitto: lettere private nei papiri dei secoli II–IV*, (Biblioteca patristica 32), Florence: Le Monnier.

Naveh, Joseph / Shaked, Shaul (2012), *Aramaic Documents from Ancient Bactria (Fourth Century BCE.): From the Khalili Collections*, London: The Khalili Family Trust.

Naymark, Aleksandr / Treadwell, Luke (2011), "An Arab-Sogdian Coin of AH 160: an Ikhshid in Ishtihan?", *The Numismatic Chronicle* 171, 359–366.
Nebes, Norbert (2009), "The Martyrs of Najrān and the End of Ḥimyar: On the Political History of South Arabia in the Early Sixth Century", in: Angelika Neuwirth, Nicolai Sinai, and Michael Marx, eds., *The Qur'an in Context, Historical and Literary Investigations into the Qur'anic Milieu* (Texts and Studies on the Qur'ān 6), Leiden *et al.*: Brill, 27–59.
Nehmé, Laïla (2010), "A Glimpse of the Development of the Nabataean Script into Arabic based on Old and New Epigraphic Material", in: Michael MacDonald, ed., *The Development of Arabic as a Written Language. Papers from the Special Session of the Seminar for Arabian Studies held on 24 July, 2009* (Supplement to the Proceedings of the Seminar for Arabian Studies 40), Oxford: Archaeopress, 47–88.
Nehmé, Laïla (2016), "A 'Transitional' Inscription from Dûmat al-Jandal", in: Guillaume Charloux and Romolo Loreto, eds., *Dûma 2. The 2011 Report of the Saudi-Italian-French Archaeological Project at Dûmat al-Jandal, Saudi Arabia*, Riyadh: SCTH, 231–233.
Nehmé, Laïla (2017a), "New Dated Inscriptions (Nabataean and pre-Islamic Arabic) from a Site near al-Jawf, Ancient Dūmah, Saudi Arabia", *Arabian Epigraphic Notes* 3, 121–164.
Nehmé, Laïla (2017b), "Aramaic or Arabic? The Nabateo-Arabic Script and the Language of the Inscriptions Written in this Script", in: Ahmad al-Jallad, ed., *Arabic in Context. Celebrating 400 years of Arabic at Leiden University* (Studies in Semitic Languages and Linguistics 89), Leiden/Boston: Brill, 75–98.
Nelson, Robert S. (2005), "Letters and Language / Ornaments and Identity in Byzantium and Islam", in: Irene A. Bierman, ed., *The Experience of Islamic Art on the Margins of Islam*, Reading: Ithaca, 61–88.
Nevo, Yehuda (1994), "Towards a Prehistory of Islam", *Jerusalem Studies in Arabic and Islam* 17, 108–141.
Nevo, Yehuda / Heftman, Dalia / Cohen, Zemire (1993), *Ancient Arabic Inscriptions from the Negev I* (New Sources for the History of the Byzantine and Early Arab Periods 3), Midreshet Ben-Gurion: IPS Ltd.
Nevo, Yehuda / Koren, Judith (2003), *Crossroads to Islam: The Origins of the Arab Religion and the Arab State*, New York: Prometheus.
Niehoff-Panagiotidis, Jannis (1996), "Lat. *signum* > σίγνον > arab. *sign*", in: Jens Lüdtke, ed., *Romania Arabica: Festschrift Reinhold Kontzi zum 70. Geburtstag*, Tübingen: Narr, 1–19.
Nikitin, Alexander (1992), "Middle Persian Ostraca from South Turkmenistan", *East and West* 42, 103–129.
Nikitin, Alexander / Roth, Günther (1995), "The Earliest Arab-Sasanian Coins", *The Numismatic Chronicle* 155, 131–137.
Noeske, Hans-Christoph (2000), *Münzfunde aus Ägypten I: Die Münzfunde des ägyptischen Pilgerzentrums Abu Mina und die Vergleichsfunde aus den Dioecesen Aegyptus und Oriens vom 4.-8. Jh. n. Chr* (Studien zu Fundmünzen der Antike 22), Berlin: Mann.
Nöldeke, Theodor (1875), *Mandäische Grammatik*, Halle: Verlag der Buchhandlung des Waisenhausens.
Nöldeke, Theodor (1876), "Kalilag und Damnag. Alte syrische Uebersetzung des indischen Fürstenspiegels by Gustav Bickell and Theodor Benfey", Review of *Kalilag und Damnag* by G. Bickel and T. Benfey, eds., *Zeitschrift der Deutschen Morgenländischen Gesellschaft* 30, 752–772.
Nöldeke, Theodor (1879), *Geschichte der Perser und Araber zur Zeit der Sassaniden aus der Chronik des Tabaris*, Leiden: Brill.

Nöldeke, Theodor (1908), "Arabs (Ancient)", *Encyclopaedia of Religion and Ethics*, 1, 659–673.
Nöldeke, Theodor (1910), *Neue Beiträge zur semitischen Sprachwissenschaft*, Strassburg: Trübner.
Nyberg, Henrik S. (1964), *A Manual of Pahlavi, Part I: Texts*, Wiesbaden: Harrassowitz
Nyberg, Henrik S. (1974), *A Manual of Pahlavi, Part II: Glossary*, Wiesbaden: Harrassowitz.
O'Connor, Michael P. (1986), "The Arabic Loanwords in Nabatean Aramaic", *Journal of Near Eastern Studies* 45, 213–229.
Oddy, Andrew (1991), "Arab Imagery on Early Umayyad Coins in Syria and Palestine: Evidence for Falconry", *The Numismatic Chronicle* 151, 59–66.
Oddy, Andrew (2012), "Symbolism and Design on the Early Umayyad Coinage", in: Tony Goodwin, ed., *Arab-Byzantine Coins and History: Papers Presented at the 13th Seventh Century Syrian Numismatic Round Table Held at Corpus Christi College Oxford on 11th and 12th September 2011*, London: Archetype, 109–124.
Oddy, Andrew / Schulze, Wolfgang (2012), "Terminology for the Transitional Coinage Struck in 7th Century Syria after the Arab Conquest", in: Tony Goodwin, ed., *Arab–Byzantine Coins and History. Papers presented at the Seventh Century Syrian Numismatic Round Table held at Corpus Christi College, Oxford on 10th and 11th September 2011*, London: Archetype, 187–200.
Olister, David (2006), "Ideological Transformation and the Evolution of Imperial Representation in the Wake of Islam's victory", in: Emmanouela Grypeou, Mark N. Swanson, and David Thomas, eds., *The Encounter of Eastern Christianity with Early Islam* (The History of Christian-Muslim Relations 5), Leiden/Boston: Brill, 45–72.
Orbeli, Josef (1981), "Sasanian and Early Islamic Metalwork", in: Arthur Upham Pope and Phyllis Ackerman, eds., *A Survey of Persian Art from Prehistoric Times to the Present*, New York: Oxford University Press, 716–770.
Ory, Solange (1967), "Les graffiti umayyades de ʿAyn al-Ǧarr", *Bulletin du Musée de Beyrouth* 20, 97–148.
Ory, Solange (1969), *Monuments et inscriptions des époques Umayyade et Salǧukide à Buṣrā*, Ph.D. thesis, Paris (= *MI*).
Ory, Solange (1970), "Les monuments et inscriptions islamiques de la tille de Buṣrā aux époques umayyade et salǧūqide", *Annuaires de l'École pratique des hautes etudes. 4e section, Sciences historiques et philologique*, 769–772.
Ory, Solange (1990), "Aspects religieux des textes épigraphiques du début de l'Islam", *Revue des mondes musulmans et de la Méditerranée* 58, 30–39
Ory, Solange (1999), "L'inscription de fondation de la mosquée al-'Umarī à Buṣrā", *Damaszener Mitteilungen* 11, 371–378.
Ory, Solange (2005), "Inscriptions arabes du Musée de l'Emir Manǧak", in: Michael Meinecke and Flemming Aalund, eds., *Bosra – Islamische Architektur und Archäologie* (Orient-Archäologie 17), Rahden: Leidorf, 161–167.
Palma (de), Giovanna / Palumbo, Gaetano / Birrozzi, Carlo / Mano, Marie-Josée / Gaetani, Maria Carolina / Shhaltoug, Asma / Imbert, Frédéric (2012), "Quṣayr ʿAmra World Heritage Site: Preliminary Report on Documentation, Conservation and Site Management Activities in 2010–2012", *Annual of the Department of Antiquities of Jordan* 56, 309–340.
Palma (de), Giovanna / Palumbo, Gaetano / Shhaltoug, Asma / Arce, Ignacio / Arrighi, Chiara / Atzori, Angela / Birozzi, Carlo / De Vivi, Giulia Sara / Di Marcello, Stefania / Esaid, Wesam / Gaetani, Maria Carolina / Ghraib, Romel / Haron, Jehad / Hjazeen, Hossam / Khirfan, Hussein / Lash, Ahmed / Mano, Marie-José / Mariani, Francesca / Meschini, Alessandra / Sarra, Alex / Tomassett, Cristina (2013), "Quṣayr ʿAmra World Heritage Site: Preliminary

Report on Documentation, Conservation and Site Management Activities 2012–2013", *Annual of the Department of Antiquities of Jordan* 57, 425–439.
Palmer, Andrew (1993), *The Seventh Century in the West-Syrian Chronicles* (Translated Texts for Historians 15), Liverpool: Liverpool University Press.
Papaconstantinou, Arietta (2001), *Le Culte des saints en Égypte des Byzantins aux Abbassides: l'apport des inscriptions et des papyrus grecs et coptes* (Monde byzantin), Paris: CNRS.
Papaconstantinou, Arietta (2009), "'What Remains behind: Hellenism and *Romanitas* in Christian Egypt after the Arab Conquest", in: Hannah M. Cotton, Robert G. Hoyland, Jonathan J. Price, and David Wasserstein, eds., *From Hellenism to Islam: Cultural and Linguistic Change in the Roman Near East*, Cambridge/New York: Cambridge University Press, 447–466.
Papaconstantinou, Arietta (2015), "The Rhetoric of Power and the Voice of Reason", in: Stephan Procházka, Lucian Reinfandt, and Sven Tost, eds., *Official Epistolography and the Language(s) of Power. Proceedings of the First International Conference of the Research Network* imperium & officium*: Comparative Studies in Ancient Bureaucracy and Officialdom, University of Vienna, 10–12 November 2010* (Papyrologica Vindobonensia 8), Vienna: Österreichische Akademie der Wissenschaften, 267–281.
Paret, Rudi (1976–1977), "Die Entstehungszeit des islamischen Bilderverbots", *Kunst des Orients* 11, 158–181.
Payne Smith, Robert (1879–1901), *Thesaurus Syriacus*, 2 vols., Oxford: Clarendon Press.
Pedersen, Johs (1991), "Madjid (a.–g.)", *Encyclopaedia of Islam*, 2nd ed., 6, 644–677.
Penn, Michael Ph. (2011), *When Christians first Met Muslims: A Sourcebook of the Earliest Syriac Writings on Islam*, Oakland: University of California Press.
Perrot, Charles (1963), "Un *fragment christo-palestinien découvert à Khirbet Mird (Actes des Apôtres, X, 28–29; 32–41)*", *Revue Biblique* 70, 506–555.
Phillips, J. R., (1962), "The Byzantine Bronze Coins of Alexandria in the Seventh Century", *Numismatic Chronicle* 2, 225–241.
Phillips, Marcus / Goodwin, Tony (1997), "A Seventh-Century Syrian Hoard of Byzantine and Imitative Copper Coins", *The Numismatic Chronicle* 157, 61–87.
Pinder-Wilson, Ralph (1960), "An Islamic Ewer in Sassanian Style", *The British Museum Quarterly* 22, 89–94.
Popp, Volker (2010), "Die frühe Islamgeschichte nach inschriftlichen und numismatischen Zeugnissen", in: Karl-Heinz Ohlig and Gerd-Rüdiger Puin, eds., *Die dunklen Anfänge: Neue Forschungen zur Entstehung und frühen Geschichte des Islam* (Inârah 1), Berlin: Hans Schiler, 16–123.
Porten, Bezalel / Yardeni Adah (1986–1999), *Textbook of Aramaic Documents from Ancient Egypt, I: Letters, II: Contracts, III: Literature, Accounts, Lists, IV: Ostraca and Assorted Inscriptions*, Winona Lake: Eisenbrauns.
Potthast, Daniel (2019), "Qurʾān Quotations in Arabic Papyrus Letters from the 7th to the 10th Century", in: Andreas Kaplony and Michael Marx, eds., *Qurʾān Quotations Preserved on Papyrus Documents, 7th–10th Centuries and the Problem of Carbon Dating Early Qurʾāns* (Documenta Coranica 2), Leiden/Boston: Brill, 42–85.
Pottier, Henri / Schulze, Ingrid / Schulze, Wolfgang (2008), "Pseudo-Byzantine Coinage in Syria Under Arab Rule (638–c. 670), Classification and Dating", *Revue Belge de Numismatique* 154, 87–155.
Preisigke, Friedrich (1925–1931), *Wörterbuch der griechischen Papyrusurkunden*, 3 vols., Berlin: Selbstverlag der Erben.

Putten (van) Marijn / Stokes, Phillip W. (2018), "Case in the Qur'ānic Consonantal Text", *Wiener Zeitschrift für die Kunde des Morgenlandes* 108, 143–179.

al-Qāḍī, Wadād (2012) [repr. 1994], "The Religious Foundation of Late Umayyad Ideology and Practice", in: Fred M. Donner, ed., *The Articulation of Early Islamic State Structures* (The Formation of the Classical Islamic World 6), Ashgate: Franham, 37–79.

al-Qāḍī, Wadād (2016), "Non-Muslims in the Muslim Conquest Army in Early Islam", in: Antoine Borrut and Fred Donner, eds., *Christians and Others in the Umayyad State* (Late Antique and Medieval Islamic Near East 1), Chicago: The Oriental Institute of the University of Chicago, 83–127.

Rabbat, Nasser (1999), "Ṭirāz", *Encyclopaedia of Islam*, 2nd ed., 10, 534–538.

Raby, Julian (1999), "*In vitro veritas*: Glass Pilgrim Vessels in Seventh-Century Jerusalem", in: Jeremy Johns, ed., *Bayt al-Maqdis, Part 2: Jerusalem and Early Islam* (Oxford Studies in Islamic Art 9, 2), Oxford/New York: Oxford University Press, 113–183.

Rāġib, Yūsuf (1984), "Pour un renouveau de la papyrologie arabe: Comment rassembler les archives dispersés de l'Islam médiéval", *Comptes-rendus des séances de l'Académie des Inscriptions et Belles-Lettres* 128, 68–77.

Rāġib, Yūsuf (1991), "La plus ancienne lettre arabe de marchand", in: Yūsuf Rāġib, ed., *Documents de l'Islam médiéval. Nouvelles perspectives de recherche* (Textes arabes et études islamiques 29), Cairo: Publications de l'Institut Français d'Archéologie Orientale, 1–9 (= *P.RagibPlusAncienneLettre*).

Rāġib, Yūsuf (1996a), "Les esclaves publics aux premiers siècles de l'Islam", in: Henri Bresc, ed., *Figures de l'esclave au Moyen Âge et dans le monde moderne: Actes de la table ronde, organisée les 27 et 28 octobre 1992*, Paris: L'Harmattan, 7–30.

Rāġib, Yūsuf (1996b), "Les plus anciens papyrus arabes", *Annales islamologiques*30, 1–19.

Rāġib, Yūsuf (1997), "Sauf–conduits d'Egypte Omeyyade et Abbaside", *Annales islamologiques* 31, 143–168 (= *P.RagibSaif-conduits*).

Rāġib, Yūsuf (2013), "Les premiers documents arabes de l'ère musulmane", in: Constantin Zuckerman, ed., *Constructing the Seventh Century* (Travaux et mémoires 17), Paris: Association des Amis du Centre d'Histoire et Civilisation de Byzance, 679–729.

Randall, William M. (1933), "Three engraved stones from the Moritz Collection at the University of Chicago", in: William, G. Shellabear *et al.*, eds., *The Macdonald Presentation Volume: A Tribute to Duncan Black Macdonald*, Princeton: Princeton University Press, 325–330.

al-Rāshid, Sa'd b. 'Abdul'azīz (1992), "A new 'Abbāsīd milestone from al-Rabaḏa in Saudi Arabia", *Arabian Archaeology and Epigraphy* 3, 138–143.

al-Rāshid, Sa'd b. 'Abdul'azīz (1993), *Darb Zubayda, Ṭarīq al-ḥajj min al-Kūfa ilā Makka al-mukarrama*, Riyadh: Riyadh University Libraries.

Rathbone, Dominic (1983), "The Weight and Measurement of Egyptian Grains", *Zeitschrift für Papyrologie und Epigraphik* 53, 265–275.

Reenen (van), Daan (1990), "The 'Bilderverbot': a New Survey", *Der Islam* 67, 27–77.

Reinfandt, Lucian (2012), "Administrative Papyri from the Abbasid Court in Samarra (AD 836–892): a First Report", in: Paul Schubert, ed., *Actes du 26e Congrès international de papyrology*, Géneve: Droz, 639–645.

Reinfandt, Lucian (2015), "Empireness in Arabic Letter Formulae", in: Stephan Procházka, Lucian Reinfandt, and Sven Tost, eds., *Official Epistolography and the Language(s) of Power. Proceedings of the First International Conference of the Research Network* imperium & officium: *Comparative Studies in Ancient Bureaucracy and Officialdom, University of Vienna, 10–12*

November 2010 (Papyrologica Vindobonensia 8), Vienna: Österreichische Akademie der Wissenschaften, 281–292.

Reinfandt, Lucian (2020a), "Petosiris the Scribe" in: Sabine R. Huebner *et al.*, eds., *Living the End of Antiquity – Individual Histories from Byzantine to Islamic Egypt* (Millennium Studien/Millennium Studies 84), Berlin: De Gruyter, 141–152.

Reinfandt, Lucian (2020b), "Iranians in 9th Century Egypt", in: Johannes Preiser-Kapeller, Lucian Reinfandt, and Yannis Stouraitis, eds., *Migration Histories of the Medieval Afroeurasian Transition Zone: Aspects of Mobility between Africa, Asia and Europe, 300–1500 C.E.* (Studies in Global Social History 39), Leiden/Boston: Brill, 225–246.

Reinfandt, Lucian / Tost, Sven (2017), "Mehrsprachigkeit und ihre gesellschaftlichen Hintergründe im spätantiken Ägypten", https://www.onb.ac.at/forschung/forschungsblog/artikel/news/aller-anfang-ist-schwer/ (accessed Oct. 7, 2020).

Retso, Jan (2006), "Aramaic/Syrian Loanwords", *Encyclopedia of Arabic Language and Linguistics*, 1, 98–101.

Reynolds, Gabriel S. (2008), "Introduction: Qurʾānic Studies and its Controversies", in: Gabriel S. Reynolds, ed., *The Qurʾān in its Historical Context* (Routledge Studies in the Qur'an), *London*: Routledge, 1–26.

Rezakhani, Khodadad (2010), "Balkh and the Sasanians. The Economy and Society of Northern Afghanistan as Reflected in the Bactrian Economic Documents", in: Maria Macuch, Dieter Weber, and Desmond Durkin-Meisterernst, eds., *Ancient and Middle Iranian Studies: Proceedings of the 6th European Conference of Iranian Studies, Held in Vienna, 18–22 September 2007* (Iranica 19), Wiesbaden: Harrassowitz, 191–204.

Rezakhani, Khodadad (2017), *Reorienting the Sasanians: Eastern Iran in Late Antiquity*, (Edinburgh Studies in Ancient Persia) Edinburgh: Edinburgh University Press.

Richter, Tonio S. (2001), "Arabische Lehnworte und Formeln in koptischen Rechtsurkunden", *The Journal of Juristic Papyrology* 31, 75–89.

Richter, Tonio S. (2003), "Spätkoptische Rechtsurkunde neu bearbeitet (III): P.Lond.Copt. I 487 – arabische Pacht in koptischem Gewand", *The Journal of Juristic Papyrology* 33, 213–230.

Richter, Tonio S. (2004), "O.Crum Ad. 15 and the Emergence of Arabic Words in Coptic Legal Documents", in: Petra M. Sijpesteijn and Lennart Sundelin, eds., *Papyrology and the History of Early Islamic Egypt* (Islamic History and Civilization 55), Leiden/Boston: Brill, 97–114.

Richter, Tonio S. (2008a), *Rechtssemantik und forensische Rhetorik. Untersuchungen zu Wortschatz, Stil und Grammatik der Sprache koptischer Rechtsurkunden* (Philippika 20), 2nd edition, Wiesbaden: Harrassowitz.

Richter, Tonio S. (2008b), "Coptic Letters", in: Eva M. Grob and Andreas Kaplony, eds., *Documentary Letters from the Middle East: The Evidence in Greek, Coptic, South Arabian, Pehlevi, and Arabic (1st–15th c CE)* (Asiatische Studien/Études Asiatiques 62, 3), Bern *et al.*: Peter Lang, 739–770.

Richter, Tonio S. (2009), "Greek, Coptic and the 'Language of the Hijra'", in: Hannah M. Cotton, Robert G. Hoyland, Jonathan J. Price, and David Wasserstein, eds., *From Hellenism to Islam: Cultural and Linguistic Change in the Roman Near East*, Cambridge/New York: Cambridge University Press, 401–446.

Richter, Tonio S. (2010), "Language Choice in the Qurra–dossier", in: Arietta Papaconstantinou, ed., *The Multilingual Experience in Egypt, from the Ptolemies to the 'Abbasids*, Burlington: Ashgate, 189–220.

Richter, Tonio S. (2013), "An unseren Herrn, den allberühmten Korra, den herrlichsten Gouverneur, durch Dich, glorreichster Herr Basilios, Pagarch von Djkow mit seinen Gehöften. Verwaltung und Verwaltungssprachen Ägyptens im 8. Jh. nach den Qurra–Papyri", in: Frank Feder and Angelika Lohwasser, eds., *Ägypten und sein Umfeld in der Spätantike vom Regierungsantritt* Diokletians *284/285 bis zur arabischen Eroberung des Vorderen Orients um 635 – 646. Akten der Tagung vom 7. – 9. 7.2011 in Münster* (Philippika 61), Wiesbaden: Harrassowitz, 121–139.

Richter, Tonio S. / Schmelz, Georg (2010), "Der spätkoptische Arbeitsvertrag P.Heid. kopt. inv. 451", *The Journal of Juristic Papyrology* 40, 185–203.

Rippin, Andrew (2008), "Syriac in the Qur'ān", in: Gabriel S. Reynolds, ed., *The Qur'ān in Its Historical Context* (Routledge Studies in the Qur'an), London: Routledge, 249–261.

Ritter, Markus (2010), "Kunst mit Botschaft: Der Gold-Seide-Stoff für den Ilchan Abu Sa'īd von Iran (Grabgewand Rudolfs IV. in Wien) – Rekonstruktion, Typus, Repräsentationsmedium", in: Markus Ritter and Lorenz Korn, eds., *Beiträge zur islamischen Kunst und Archäologie*, vol. 2, Wiesbaden: Reichert, 105–135.

Ritter, Markus (2016a), "Umayyad Foundation Inscriptions and the Inscription of al-Walīd from Khirbat al-Minya: Text, Usage, Visual Form", in: Hans-Peter Kuhnen, ed., *Khirbat al-Minya: Der Umayyadenpalast am See Genezareth* (Orient Archäologie 36), Rahden: Marie-Leidorf, 58–83.

Ritter, Markus (2016b), "Cloth of Gold from West Asia in a Late Medieval European Context: The Abū Sa'īd Textile in Vienna – Princely Funeral and Cultural Transfer", in: Juliane von Fircks and Regula Schorta, eds., *Oriental Silks in Medieval Europe* (Riggisberger Berichte 21), Riggisberg: Abegg-Stiftung, 231–51.

Ritter, Markus (2017), *Der umayyadische Palast des 8. Jahrhunderts in Khirbat al-Minya am See von Tiberias: Bau und Baudekor* (Studien zur islamischen Kunst und Archäologie 1), Wiesbaden: Reichert.

Robin, Christian J. (2006), "La réforme de l'écriture arabe à l'époque du califat médinois", *Mélanges de l'Université Saint-Joseph* 59, 319–364.

Robin, Christian J. (2012), "Les rois de Kinda", in: Abdulaziz ak-Helabi, Dimitrios G. Letsios, Moshalleh al-Moraekhi, and Abdullah al-Abduljabbar, eds., *Arabia, Greece and Byzantium. Cultural Contacts in Ancient and Medieval Times. Proceedings of the International Symposium on the Historical Relations between Arabia, the Greek and Byzantine world (5th c. BC-10th c. AD)*, vol. 2, Riyadh: King Saud University, 59–130.

Robin, Christian J. (2014), "Inscriptions antiques de la région de Najrān (Arabie séoudite méridionale): nouveaux jalons pour l'histoire de l'écriture, de la langue et du calendrier arabes", *Comptes rendus de l'Académie des Inscriptions & Belles-Lettres* 2014/3, 1033–1128.

Robin, Christian J. (2015), "Ḥimyar, Aksūm, and *Arabia Deserta* in Late Antiquity", in: Greg Fischer, ed., *Arabs and Empires before Islam*, Oxford: Oxford University Press, 127–171.

Robin, Christian J. (2016), "Die Kalender der Araber vor dem Islam", in: Nora Schmidt, Nora K. Schmid, and Angelika Neuwirth, eds., *Denkraum Spätantike. Szenarien der Reflexion von Antiken im Umfeld des Koran* (Episteme in Bewegung 5), Wiesbaden: Harrassowitz, 299–386.

Robin, Christian J. (2020a), "*al-ʾIlāh* et *Allāh*: les deux noms de Dieu chez les Arabes chrétiens de Najrān au 6e siècle de l'ère chrétienne", *Hawliyāt* 19 (Special Issue), 55–109.
Robin, Christian J. (2020b), "*Allāh* avant Muḥammad", *Jerusalem Studies in Arabic and Islam* 49 (Studies in Honour of Ella Landau-Tasseron I), 1–146.
Robin, Christian J. / Gajda, Iwona (1994), "L'inscription du Wādī ʿAbadān", *Raydān* 6, 113–137.
Robinson, Chase F. (2000), *Empire and Elites after the Muslim Conquest: The Transformation of Northern Mesopotamia* (Cambridge Studies in Islamic Civilization), Cambridge: Cambridge University Press.
Robinson, Majied (2016), "From Traders to Caliphs: Prosopography, Geography and the Marriages of Muḥammad's Tribe", *Al-Masāq* 28, 22–35.
Rose, Jenny (2001), "Sasanian Splendor: The Appurtenances of Royalty", in: Stewart Gordon, ed., *Robes and Honor: The Medieval World of Investiture* (The New Middle Ages), New York: Palgrave Macmillan, 35–56.
Rosenthal, Franz (1962), "Nabatean and Related Inscriptions", in: Dunscombe H. Colt, ed., *Excavations at Nessana (Auja Hafir, Palestine) I*, Princeton: Princeton University Press, 198–210.
Rosenthal, Renate / Sivan, Renée (1978), *Ancient Lamps in the Schloessinger Collection*, (Qedem 8) Jerusalem: Institute of Archaeology.
Rosser-Owen, Mariam (2015), "Islamic Objects in Christian Contexts: Relic Translation and Modes of Transfer in Medieval Iberia" (*Art in Translation* 7, special issue: 'Translation and Hispanic Visual Culture'), 39–64.
Rossi, Adriano (2015), "Once again on Iranian **kund*", in: Uwe Bläsing, Victoria Arakelova and Matthias Weinreich, eds., *Studies on Iran and the Caucasus Presented to Prof. Garnik S. Asatrian in the Occasion of his 60th Birthday*, Leiden/Boston: Brill, 351–364.
Rousseau, Vanessa (2004), "The Emblem of an Empire: The Development of the Byzantine Empress' Crown", *Al-Masāq* 16, 5–15.
Rousseau, Vanessa / Northover, Peter (2015), "Style and Substance: A Bust of a Sasanian Royal Woman as a Symbol of Late Antique Legitimacy", *Journal of Late Antiquity* 8, 3–31.
Rückert, Friedrich (1856), "Bemerkungen zu Mohl's Ausgabe des Firdusi, Band I", *Zeitschrift der Deutschen Morgeländischen Gesellschafft* 10, 127–282.
Rustow, Marina (2020), *The Lost Archive: Traces of a Caliphate in a Cairo Synagogue* (Jews, Christians, and Muslims From the Ancient to the Modern World), Princeton/Oxford: Princeton University Press.
Sahner, Christian C. (2017), "The First Iconoclasm in Islam: A New History of the Edict of Yazīd II (AH 104/AD 723)", *Der Islam* 94, 5–56.
al-Salameen, Zeyad (2010), "Early Islamic Inscriptions from Danqūr al-Khaznah at Petra", *Arabian Archaeology and Epigraphy* 21, 71–79.
al-Ṣandūq, ʿIzz al-Dīn (1955), "Ḥajar Ḥafnat al-Abyaḍ", *Sumer* 11, 213–218.
Sauvaget, Jean (1944), "Notes de topographie omeyyade", *Syria* 24, 96–112.
Sauvaget, Jean (1947), *La Mosquée Omeyyade de Médine étude sur les origines architecturales de la mosquée et de la basilique*, Paris: Vanoest.
Schall, Anton (1960), *Studien über griechische Fremdwörter im Syrischen*, Darmstadt: Wissenschaftliche Buchgesellschaft.
Schall, Anton (1982), "Geschichte des Arabischen Wortschatzes – Lehn- und Fremdwörter im Klassischen Arabischen", in: Wolfdietrich Fischer, ed., *Grundriß der Arabischen Philologie*, vol. 1, Wiesbaden: Ludwig Reichert, 142–153.
Schindel, Nikolaos C. / Hahn, Wolfgang (2010a), "Imitations of Sicilian folles of Constantine IV from Bilad al-Sham", *Israel Numismatic Journal* 17, 213–233.

Schindel, Nikolaos C. / Hahn, Wolfgang (2010b), "Notes on Two Arab-Byzantine Coin Types from Seventh Century Syria", *The Numismatic Chronicle* 170, 321–330.

Schlumberger, Daniel (1939), "Les fouilles de Qasr el-Heir el-Gharbi (1936–1938), Rapport préliminaire", *Syria* 20, I: 195–238 and II: 324–372.

Schlumberger, Daniel (1986), *Qasr al-Heir el Gharbi relevés et dessins de Marl Le Berre contributions de Michel Ecochard et al.* (Bibliothèque archéologique et historique 120), Paris: Librairie orientaliste Paul Geuthner.

Schmidt, Rüdiger (1971), "'Méconnaissance' altiranischen Sprachgutes im Griechischen", *Glotta* 49, 95–110.

Schmidt, Stefanie (2020), "Economic Conditions for Merchants and Traders at the Border between Egypt and Nubia in Early Islamic Times", in: Sabine R. Huebner *et al.*, eds., *Living the End of Antiquity – Individual Histories from Byzantine to Islamic Egypt* (Millennium Studien/Millennium Studies 84), Berlin: De Gruyter, 207–222.

Schmidt, Stefanie (in press), "'The most ancient Islamic monument' reconsidered", in: Jelle Bruning, Janneke De Jong, and Petra M. Sijpesteijn, eds., *Egypt in the Eastern Mediterranean World: From Constantinople to Baghdad, 500–1000 CE*, Cambridge: Cambridge University Press.

Schoeler, Gregor (1992), "Schreiben und Veröffentlichen: Zu Verwendung und Funktion der Schrift in den ersten islamischen Jahrhunderten", *Der Islam* 69, 1–43.

Schoeler, Gregor (1997), "Writing and Publishing: on the Use and Function of Writing in the First Centuries of Islam", *Arabica* 44, 423–435.

Schoeler, Gregor (2009), *The Genesis of Literature in Islam from the Aural to the Read*, (New Edinburgh Islamic Surveys) Edinburgh: Edinburgh University Press.

Schopen, Armin (2006), *Tinten und Tuschen des arabisch-islamischen Mittelalters Dokumentation, Analyse, Rekonstruktion: ein Beitrag zur materiellen Kultur des Vorderen Orients*, (Abhandlungen der Akademie der Wissenschaften zu Göttingen. Philologischhistorische Klasse, 3: 269) Göttingen: Vandenhoeck & Ruprecht.

Schulze, Ingrid (2010), "The *al-wafā lillāh* Coinage: A Study of Style (Work in Progress)", in: Andrew Oddy, ed., *Coinage and History in the Seventh Century Near East 2: Proceedings of the 12th Seventh Century Syrian Numismatic Round Table held at Gonville and Caius College, Cambridge, on 4th and 5th April 2009*, London: Archetype, 111–121.

Schulze, Wolfgang (2007), "A Hoard of Seventh Century *Folles* Found Near Aleppo", *The Numismatic Chronicle* 167, 27–76.

Schulze, Wolfgang (2012), "The Syrian 'orans figure' Copper Coins", in: Tony Goodwin, ed., *Arab-Byzantine Coins and History: Papers presented at the 13th Seventh Century Syrian Numismatic Round Table held at Corpus Christi College Oxford on 11th and 12th September 2011*, London: Archetype, 131–144.

Schulze, Wolfgang / Goodwin, Tony (2005), "Countermarking in Seventh Century Syria", *Supplement to the ONS Newsletter* 183, 23–56.

Schwabe, Moshe (1946), "Khirbat Mafjar. Greek Inscribed Fragments", *Quarterly of the Department of Antiquities in Palestine* 12, 20–30.

Schwiderski, Dirk (2000), *Handbuch des nordwestsemitischen Briefformulars: Ein Beitrag zur Echtheitsfrage der aramäischen Briefe des Esrabuches* (Beihefte zur Zeitschrift für die alttestamentliche Wissenschaft 295), Berlin: De Gruyter.

Scribner, Sylvia / Cole, Michael (1981), *The Psychology of Literacy*, Cambridge, MA: Harvard University Press.

Sears, Stuart D. (1997), *A Monetary History of Iraq and Iran, ca. CE 500 to 750*, Ph.D. thesis, Ann Arbor.

Sears, Stuart D. (1999), “The Sasanian Style Drachms of Sistan”, *Yarmouk Numismatics* 11, 18–28.

Sears, Stuart D. (2003a), “The Legitimation of al-Hakam b. al-'As: Umayyad Government in Seventh-Century Kirman”, *Iranian Studies* 36, 5–25.

Sears, Stuart D. (2003b), “Before Caliphal Coins: Transitional Drahms from the Umayyad North”, *American Journal of Numismatics* 15, 77–110.

Segni (di), Leah (1997), “The Greek Inscriptions of Hammat Gader”, in: Yizhar Hirschfeld, ed., *The Roman Baths of Hammat Gader: Final Report*, Jerusalem: The Israel Exploration Society, 185–266.

Segni (di), Leah (2009), “Greek Inscriptions in Transition from the Byzantine to the Early Islamic Period”, in: Hannah M. Cotton, Robert G. Hoyland, Jonathan J. Price, and David Wasserstein, eds., *From Hellenism to Islam: Cultural and Linguistic Change in the Roman Near East*, Cambridge/New York: Cambridge University Press, 352–373.

Semenov, Gregory (2002), “MUGH, MOUNT”, *Encyclopaedia Iranica*, online edition, available at http://www.iranicaonline.org/articles/mugh-mount (accessed Nov. 21, 2020).

Serjeant, Robert B. (1983), “Early Arabic Prose”, in: Alfred F. L. Beeston *et al.*, eds, *The Cambridge History of Arabic Literature: Arabic Literature to the End of the Umayyad Period*, Cambridge *et al.*: Cambridge University Press, 114–153.

Shahbazi, Shapur A. (2004), “Hormozd IV”, *Encyclopaedia Iranica*, 12, 466–467.

Shahid, Irfan (1989), “Ghassān *post* Ghassān”, in: Clifford E. Bosworth, Charles Issawi, Roger Savory, and Abraham L. Udovitch, eds., *The Islamic World: From Classical to Modern Times, Essays in Honor of Bernard Lewis*, Princeton: Darwin Press, 321–328.

Shahid, Irfan (1992), “Ghassānid and Umayyad Structures: A Case of *Byzance après Byzance*”, in: Pierre Canivet and Jean-Paul Rey-Coquais, eds., *La Syrie de Byzance à l'Islam VIIe–VIIIe siècles: actes du colloque international: Lyon, Maison de l'Orient méditerranéen; Paris, Institut du monde arabe, 11–15 septembre 1990* (Publications de l'IFD 137), Damascus: Institut Français de Damas, 299–307.

Shahid, Irfan (2001), “Sigillography in the Service of History: New Light”, in: Claudia Sode and Sarolta Takács, eds., *Novum Millennium. Studies on Byzantine History and Culture Dedicated to Paul Speck, 19 December, 1999*, Aldershot: Ashgate, 369–378.

Shaked, Shaul (1986), “From Iran to Islam: on Some Symbols of Royality”, *Jerusalem Studies in Arabic and Islam* 7, 75–91.

Shaked, Shaul (1993), “Some Iranian Themes in Islamic Literature”, in: Philippe Gignoux, ed., *Recurrent Patterns in Iranian Religions from Mazdaism to Sufism: Proceedings of the Round Table held in Bamberg (30th September–4th October 1991)* (Studia Iranica, Cahier 11), Paris: Association pour l'Avancement des Études Iraniennes, 143–158.

Shalem, Avinoam (2006), “Manipulations of Seeing and Visual Strategies in the Audience Halls if the Early Islamic Period: Preliminary Notes”, in: Franz A. Bauer, ed., *Visualisierung von Herrschaft: Frühmittelalterliche Residenzen – Gestalt und Zerimoniell*, Internationales Kolloquium, 3./4. Juni 2004 in Istanbul (BYZAS 5), Istanbul: Ege Yayınları, 213–232.

Shalem, Avinoam (2007), “Islamische Objekte in Kirchenschätzen der lateinischen Christenheit: Ästhetische Stufen des Umgangs mit dem Anderen und dem Hybriden”, in: Christine van Eickels and Klaus van Eickels, eds., *Das Bistum Bamberg in der Welt des Mittelalters* (Bamberger interdisziplinäre Mittelalterstudien Vorträge und Vorlesungen 1), Bamberg: University of Bamberg Press, 163–175.

Shams Eshragh, Abdolrazagh (2004), "An Interesting Arab-Sasanian Dirhem", *Oriental Numismatic Society Newsletter* 178, 45–46.

Sharon, Moshe (1966), "An Arabic Inscription from the Time of the Caliph ʿAbd al-Malik", *Bulletin of the School of Oriental and African Studies* 29, 367–372.

Sharon, Moshe (2018), "Witnessed by Three Disciples of the Prophet: The Jerusalem 32 Inscription from 32 AH/652 CE", *Israel Exploration Journal* 68, 100–111.

Shatzmiller, Maya (2017), "Prices and Price Formation in the Islamic Middle East: The Role of Money Supply and State Policies", in: Giampiero Negri, ed., *Prezzi delle cose nell'età preindustriale: selezione di ricerche = The Prices of Things in Pre-industrial Times Selection of Essays* (Atti delle "Settimane di Studi" e altri Convegni 48), Florence: Firenze University Press, 15–35.

Shatzmiller, Maya / Pamuk, Şevetek (2014), "Plagues, Wages, and Economic Change in the Islamic Middle East, 700–1500", *The Journal of Economic History* 74, 196–229.

al-Shdaifat, Younis / al-Jallad, Ahmad / al-Salameen, Zeyad / Harahsheh, Rafe (2017), "An Early Christian Arabic Graffito Mentioning 'Yazīd the King'", *Arabian Archaeology and Epigraphy*, 315–324.

Shenkar, Michael (2014), *Intangible Spirits and Graven Images: The Iconography of Deities in the Pre-islamic Iranian World* (Magical and Religious Literature of Late Antiquity 4), Leiden/Boston: Brill.

Shenkar, Michael (2017), "The Religion and the Pantheon of the Sogdians (5th–8th centuries CE) in Light of Their Sociopolitical Structures", *Journal Asitique* 305, 191–209.

Siddiqi, Abdusattar (1919), *Studien über die Persischen Fremdwörter im klassischen Arabisch*, Göttingen: Vandenhoeck & Ruprecht.

Sijpesteijn, Petra M., (2007a), "The Arab Conquest of Egypt and the Beginning of Muslim Rule", in: Roger S. Bagnall, ed., *Egypt in the Byzantine World, 300–700*, Cambridge: Cambridge University Press, 437–459.

Sijpesteijn, Petra M., (2007b), "New Rule over Old Structures: Egypt after the Muslim Conquest", in: Harriet Crawford, ed., *Regime Change in the Ancient Near East and Egypt: From Sargon of Agade to Saddam Hussein* (Proceedings of the British Academy 136), Oxford: Oxford University Press for the British Academy, 183–202.

Sijpesteijn, Petra M. (2007c), "The Archival Mind in Early Islamic Egypt: Two Arabic Papyri", Petra M. Sijpesteijn, Lennart Sundelin, Sofia Torallas Tovar, Amalia Zomeno, eds., *From al-Andalus to Khurasan: Documents from the Medieval Muslim World* (Islamic History and Civilization 66), Leiden/Boston: Brill, 163–187.

Sijpesteijn, Petra M. (2008), "Palaeography", *Encyclopedia of Arabic Language and Linguistics*, 3, 513–524.

Sijpesteijn, Petra M. (2009), "Landholding Patterns in Early Islamic Egypt", *Journal of Agrarian Change* 9, 120–133.

Sijpesteijn, Petra M. (2010), "Multilingual Archives and Documents in post-conquest Egypt", in: Arietta Papaconstantinou, ed., *The Multilingual Experience in Egypt, from the Ptolemies to the ʿAbbasids*, Burlington: Ashgate, 105–124.

Sijpesteijn, Petra M. (2011), "Army Economics: An Early Papyrus Letter Related to ʿAṭāʾ Payments", in: Adam A. Sabra, Abraham L. Udovitch, Petra M. Sijpesteijn, and Roxani E. Margariti, eds., *Histories of the Middle East: Studies in Middle Eastern Society, Economy and Law in Honor of A.L. Udovitch* (Islamic History and Civilization 79), Leiden/Boston: Brill, 245–267.

Sijpesteijn, Petra M. (2012a), "Coptic and Arabic Papyri from Deir al–Balā'izah", in: Paul Schubert, ed., *Actes du 26e Congrès International de Papyrologie*, Geneva: Droz, 707–714.

Sijpesteijn, Petra M., (2012b), "Seals and Papyri from Early Islamic Egypt", in: Ilona Regulski *et al.*, eds., *Seals and Sealing Practices. Proceedings of the International Workshop on "Seals and Sealing Practices from Ancient Times till the Present Day: Developments in Administration and Magic through Cultures"* (Orientalia Lovaniensia Analecta 219), *Cairo, Netherlands–Flemish Institute in Cairo*, Louvain: Peeters, 163–174.
Sijpesteijn, Petra M. (2013), *Shaping a Muslim State: The World of a Mid–Eighth Century Egyptian Official* (Oxford Studies in Byzantium), Oxford: Oxford University Press.
Sijpesteijn, Petra M. (2014), "An Early Umayyad Papyrus Invitation for the Ḥajj", *Journal of Near Eastern Studies* 73, 179–190 (= *P.SijpesteijnInvitation*).
Sijpesteijn, Petra M. (2017), Delegation of Judicial Power in Abbasid Egypt", in: Maaike van Berkel, Léon Buskens, and Petra M. Sijpesteijn, eds., *Legal Documents as Sources for the History of Muslim Societies* (Studies in Islamic Law and Society 42), Leiden/Boston: Brill, 61–84.
Sijpesteijn, Petra M. (2018), "Expressing New Rule: Seals from Early Islamic Egypt and Syria, 600–800 CE", in: Brigitte Bedos-Rezak and Carol Symes, eds., *Seals – Making and Marking Connections across the Medieval World* (Medieval Globe 4), Leeds: ARC Humanities Press, 99–148.
Sijpesteijn, Petra M. (2020a), "Visible Identities: In Search of Egypt's Jews in Early Islamic Egypt", in: Alison Salvesen, Sarah Pearce, and Miriam Frenkel, eds., *Israel in Egypt: The Land of Egypt as Concept and Reality for Jews in Antiquity and the Early Medieval Period* (Ancient Judaism and Early Christianity, 110), Leiden/Boston: Brill, 424–440.
Sijpesteijn, Petra M. (2020b), "The Arabic Script and Language in the Earliest Papyri: Mirror of Change", *Jerusalem Studies in Arabic and Islam* 49 (Studies in Honour of Ella Landau-Tasseron I), 433–494.
Sijpesteijn, Pieter J. / Worp, Klaas A. (1983), *Griechische Texte V* (Corpus Papyrorum Ranieri 8), Vienna: Hollinek (= *CPR VIII*).
Silverman, Katja (2007), "The Fifth Mīl from Jerusalem: Another Umayyad Milestone from Southern Bilād Al-shām", *Bulletin of the School of Oriental and African Studies* 70, 603–610.
Silverstein, Adam (2001), "Etymologies and Origins: A Note of Caution", *British Journal of Middle Eastern Studies* 81, 92–94.
Silverstein, Adam (2007), *Postal Systems in the Pre-Modern Islamic World* (Cambridge Studies in Islamic Civilization), Cambridge: Cambridge University Press.
Sima, Alexander (2004), "Der Lautwandel s^3>s^1 im Sabäischen: Die Wiedergabe fremden Wortgutes", *Zeitschrift der Deutschen Morgeländischen Gesellschafft* 154, 17–34.
Sims–Williams, Nicholas (1999), "From the Kushan-Shahs to the Arabs: New Bactrian Documents Dated in the Era of the Tochi Inscriptions", in: Michael Alram *et al.*, eds., *Coins, Art, and Chronology* (Beiträge zur Kultur- und Geistesgeschichte Asiens 31; Denkschriften der Österreichischen Akademie der Wissenschaften, Philosophisch-historische Klasse 280; Veröffentlichungen der Numismatischen Kommission, 33), vol. 1, Vienna: Verlag der Österreichischen Akademie der Wissenschaften, 245–258.
Sims-Williams, Nicholas (2000), "Some Reflections on Zoroastrianism in Sogdiana and Bactria", in: David Cristian and Benjamin Craig, eds., *Realms of the Silk Roads: Ancient and Modern: Proceedings from the Third Conference of the Australasian Society for Inner Asian Studies (A.S.I.A.S.), Macquarie University, September 18–20, 1998* (Silk Road Studies 4), Turnhout: Brepols, 1–12.

Sims-Williams, Nicholas (2001), "Bactrian Legal Documents from 7th- and 8th-Century Guzgan", *Bulletin of the Asia Institute* 15, 9–29.

Sims-Williams, Nicholas (2002b), "Ancient Afghanistan and Its Invaders: Linguistic Evidence from the Bactrian Documents and Inscriptions", in: Nicholas Sims-Williams, ed., *Indo-Iranian Languages and Peoples* (Proceedings of the British Academy, 116), Oxford: Oxford University Press, 225–242.

Sims-Williams, Nicholas (2007), *Bactrian Documents from Northern Afghanistan II: Letters and Buddhist Texts* (Corpus Inscriptionum Iranicarum 2,6,2; Studies in the Khalili Collection 3,2), London: The Nour Foundation (= *BD* II).

Sims-Williams, Nicholas (2008), "The Arab-Sasanian and the Arab-Hephthalite Coinage: A View from the East", in: Étienne de la Vaissière, ed., *Islamisation de l'Asie Centrale: processus locaux d'islamisation du VIIe au XIe siècle* (Studia Iranica, Cahier 39), Paris: Association pour l'Avancement des Études Iraniennes, 115–130.

Sims-Williams, Nicholas (2010), *Bactrian Personal Names* (Iranisches Personennamenbuch II. Mitteliranische Personennamen 7), Vienna: Österreichische Akademie der Wissenschaften.

Sims-Williams, Nicholas / Blois (de), François (2018), *Studies in the Chronology of the Bactrian Documents from Northern Afghanistan with Contributions by Harry Falk and Dieter Weber* (Veröffentlichungen zur Iranistik 83; Denkschriften der Österreichischen Akademie der Wissenschaften, Philosophisch-historische Klasse 505), Vienna: Österreichische Akademie der Wissenschaften.

Sizgorich, Thomas (2004), "Narrative and Community in Islamic Late Antiquity", *Past & Present* 185, 9–42.

Smirnova, Ol'ga I. (1963), *Katalog monet s gorodishča Pendžikent: materialy 1949–1956 gg.*, Moskow: Izd-vo vostočnoĭ lit-ry.

Smirnova, Ol'ga I. (1981), *Svodnyĭ katalog sogdiĭskikh monet. Bronza*, Moskow: Izd-vo vostočnoĭ lit-ry.

Snijders, Tjamke (2015), *Manuscript Communication: Visual and Textual Mechanics of Communication in Hagiographical Texts from the Southern Low Countries, 900–1200* (Utrecht Studies in Medieval Literacy 32), Turnhout: Brepols.

Snyder, Janet E. (2011), *Early Gothic Column-Figure Sculpture in France: Appearance, Materials, and Significance*, Burlington: Ashgate

Sokoloff, Michael (1992), A Dictionary of Jewish Palestinian Aramaic of the Byzantine Period, (Dictionaries of Talmud, Midrash and Targum 2) Ramat-Gan: Bar Ilan University Press.

Sokoloff, Michael (2002), *A Dictionary of Jewish Babylonian Aramaic of the Talmudic and Geonic Periods* (Publications of the Comprehensive Aramaic Lexicon Project), Ramat-Gan: Bar Ilan University Press.

Sokoloff, Michael (2009), *A Syriac Lexicon: a Translation from the Latin, Correction, Expansion, and Update of C. Brockelmann's* Lexicon Syriacum, Winona Lake: Eisenbrauns.

Sokoloff, Michael (2014), *A Dictionary of Christian Palestinian Aramaic* (Orientalia Lovaniensia Analecta 234), Louvain/Paris/Walpole: Peeters.

Sonego, Leonora (2019), "Qurʾān Quotations in Papyrus Legal Documents", in: Andreas Kaplony and Michael Marx, eds., *Qurʾān Quotations Preserved on Papyrus Documents, 7th–10th Centuries and the Problem of Carbon Dating Early Qurʾāns* (Documenta Coranica 2), Leiden/Boston: Brill, 86–111.

Soulier, Gustave (1924), "Les caractères coufiques dans la peinture toscane", *Gazette des Beaux-Arts* 5, 347–258.

Spitaler, Anton (1955), "*Materialien* zur Erklärung von Fremdwörtern im Arabischen durch retrograde Ableitung", in: Hans Krahe, ed., *Corolla Linguistica. Festschrift Ferdinand Sommer zum 80. Geburtstag am 4. Mai 1955 dargebracht von Freunden, Schülern und Kollegen*, Wiesbaden: Harrassowitz, 211–220.
Spitaler, Anton (1960), "Die Schreibung des Typus صلوة im Koran. Ein Beitrag zur Erklärung der koranischen Orthographie", *Wiener Zeitschrift für die Kunde des Morgenlandes* 56 (1960), 212–226.
Spittle, S. Denys T. (1953), "Cufic Lettering in Christian Art", *The Archaeological Journal* 110, 138–152.
Sprengling, Martin (1939), "From Persian to Arabic", *The American Journal of Semitic Languages and Literatures* 56, 175–224.
Starcky, Jean (1954), "Un contrat nabatéen sur papyrus", Revue Biblique 61, 161–181.
Stein, Peter (2008), "Correspondence by Letter and Epistolary Formulae in Ancient South Arabia" in: Eva M. Grob and Andreas Kaplony, eds., *Documentary Letters from the Middle East: The Evidence in Greek, Coptic, South Arabian, Pehlevi, and Arabic (1st–15th c CE)* (Asiatische Studien/Etudes asiatiques 62, 3), Bern *et al.*: Peter Lang, 771–802.
Stein, Peter (2010a), *Die altsüdarabischen Minuskelinschriften auf Holzstäbchen aus der Bayerischen Staatsbibliothek in München* (Epigraphische Forschungen auf der Arabischen Halbinsel 5), 2 vols., Tübingen: Wasmuth (= X.BSB).
Stein, Peter (2010b), "The Monetary Terminology of Ancient South Arabia in Light of New Epigraphic Evidence", in: Martin Huth and Peter G. van Alfen, eds., *Coinage of the Caravan Kingdoms: Studies in Ancient Arabian Monetization* (Numismatic Studies 25), New York: The American Numismatic Society, 303–343.
Stein, Peter (2013), *Lehrbuch der sabäischen Sprache, 1. Teil: Grammatik, 2. Teil Chrestomatie* (Subsidia et Instrumenta Linguarum Orientis 4), Wiesbaden: Harrassowitz.
Stein, Peter (2017), "Schreiben, meißeln, Fehler machen. Zur Funktion von Schriftim öffentlichen Raum im antiken Südarabien", in: Laïla Nehmé and Ahmad Al-Jallad, eds., *To the Madbar and back again Studies in the Languages, Archaeology, and Cultures of Arabia Dedicated to Michael C.A. Macdonald* (Studies in Semitic Languages and Linguistics 92), Leiden/Boston: Brill, 154–201.
Stein, Peter / Jocham, Tobias J, / Marx, Michael (2016), "Ancient South Arabian Correspondence on Wooden Sticks: New Radiocarbon Data", *Proceedings of the Seminar for Arabian Studies* 46, 263–276.
Stempel, Reinhard (1998), *Abriß einer historischen Grammatik der semitischen Sprachen* (Nordostafrikanisch-westasiatische Studien 3), Frankfurt *et al.*: Peter Lang.
Stock, Brian (1983), *The Implications of Literacy: Written Languages and Models of Interpretation in Eleventh and Twelfth Centuries*, Princeton: Princeton University Press.
Stroumsa, Rachel (2008), *People and Identities at Nessana*. Ph.D. thesis: Durham, NC.
Stroumsa, Rachel (2014), "Greek and Arabic in Nessana", in: Alexander T. Schubert and Petra M. Sijpesteijn, eds., *Documents and the History of the Early Islamic World* (Islamic History and Civilization 111), Leiden/Boston: Brill, 143–157.
Sundermann, Werner (1993), "An Early Attestation of the Name of the Tajiks", in: Wojciech Skalmowski and Alois van Tongerloo, eds., *Medioiranica: Proceedings of the International Colloquium Organized by the Katholieke Universiteit Leuven from the 21st to the 23rd of May 1990* (Orientalia Lovaniensia Analecta 48), Louvain: Peeters, 163–173.
Szaz, Margarett C. (2001), *Between Indian and White Worlds: The Cultural Broker*. Norman: University of Oklahoma Press.

Tadmor, Uri (2009), "Loanwords in the World's Languages: Findings and Results", in: Martin Haspelmath and Uri Tadmor, eds., *Loanwords in the World's Languages: A Comparative Handbook*, Berlin: De Gruyter Mouton, 55–75.

Talgam, Rina (2004), *The Stylistic Origins of Umayyad Sculpture and Architectural Decoration*, 2 vols., Wiesbaden: Harrassowitz.

Tanaka, Hidemichi (1989), "Oriental Scripts in the Paintings of Giotto's Period, *Gazette des Beaux-Arts* 113, 214–226.

Tannous, Jack (2008), "Between Christology and Kalām? The Life and Letters of George, Bishop of the Arab Tribes", in: George Kiraz, ed., *Malphono w-Rabo d-Malphone: Studies in Honor of Sebastian P. Brock* (Georgias Eastern Christian Studies), Piscataway: Gorgias Press, 671–716.

el-Tayib, Abdulla (1983), "Pre-Islamic Poetry", in: A. F. L. Beeston *et al.*, eds., *The Cambridge History of Arabic Literature: Arabic Literature to the End of the Umayyad Period*, Cambridge *et al.*: Cambridge University Press, 27–113.

Teule, Herman G.B. (2009), "The Maronite Chronicle", in: David Thomas and Barbara Roggema, eds., *Christian-Muslim Relations: A Bibliographical History. Volume I (600–900)* (The History of Christian-Muslim Relations 11), Leiden/Boston: Brill, 145–147.

Thomas, David / Roggema, Barbara (eds), (2009), *Christian-Muslim Relations: A Bibliographical History. Volume I (600–900)* (The History of Christian-Muslim Relations 11), Leiden/ Boston: Brill.

Thomason, Sarah G. (2001), *Language Contact: An Introduction*, Washington: Georgetown University Press.

Thomason, Sarah G. / Kaufmann, Terrence (1988), *Language Contact, Creolization, and Genetic Linguistics*, Berkley: University of California Press.

Thompson, Deborah (1976), *Stucco from Chal Tarkhan-Eshqabad near Rayy Including Illustrations of the Excavated Ostraca from the Same Site* (Colt Archaeological Institute Publications), Warminster: Aris and Phillips.

Till, Walter C. (1958), *Die koptischen Rechtsurkunden der Papyrussammlung der Österreichischen Nationalbibliothek* (Corpus Papyrorum Raineri 4), Vienna: Adolf Holzhausen (= *CPR* IV).

Tillier, Mathieu (2009), "Le statut et la conservation des archives judiciaires dans l'Orient abbasside (IIe/VIIIe-IVe/Xe siècle): un réexamen", in: SHMESP, ed., *L' autorité de l'écrit au Moyen Âge (Orient – Occident): XXXIXe congrès de la SHMESP (Le Caire, 30 avril – 5 mai 2008)* (Histoire ancienne et médiévale), Paris: Publ. de la Sorbonne, 263–275.

Tillier, Mathieu (2013), "Du pagarque au cadi: ruptures et continuités dans l'administration judiciaire de la Haute–Égypte (Ier–IIIe/VIIe–IXe siècle)", *Médiévales* 64, 19–36.

Tillier, Mathieu (2015), "Dispensing Justice in a Minority Context: The Judicial Administration of Upper Egypt under Muslim Rule in the Early Eighth Century", in: Robert G. Hoyland, ed., *The Late Antique World of Early Islam. Muslims among Jews and Christians in the East Mediterranean* (Studies in Late Antiquity and Early Islam 25), Princeton: Darwin Press, 133–156.

Tillier, Mathieu / Vanthieghem, Naïm (2019), "Recording Debts in Sufyānid Fusṭāṭ: A re-examination of the Procedures and Calendar in Use in the First/Seventh Century", in: Victor Tolan, ed., *Geneses: A Comparative Study of the Historiographies of the Rise of Christianity, Rabbinic Judaism, and Islam*, London: Routledge, 148–188.

Tilly, Charles (1997), "How Empires End", in: Karen Barkey and Mark von Hagen, eds., *After Empire: Multiethnic Society and Nation Building*, Boulder: Westview Press, 1–11.

Tohme, Lara (2009), "Spaces of Convergence: Christian Monasteries and Umayyad Architecture in Greater Syria", in: Alicia Walker and Amdanda Luyster, eds., *Negotiating Secular and Sacred in Medieval Art: Christian, Islamic and Buddhist*, Farnham: Ashgate, 129–145.

Toll, Christopher (1990), "Die aramaischen Ideogramme im Mittelpersischen", in: Werner Diem and Abdoldjavad Falaturi, eds., *XXIV. Deutscher Orientalistentag, vom 26. bis 30. September 1988 in Köln: ausgewählte Vorträge* (Zeitschrift der Deutschen Morgenländischen Gesellschaft – Supplement 8), Stuttgart: Franz Steiner, 25–45.

Toral-Niehoff, Isabel (2014), *Al-Ḥīra: eine arabische Kulturmetropole im spätantiken Kontext* (Islamic History and Civilization 104), Leiden/Boston: Brill.

Travaini, Lucia (1995), *La monetazione nell'Italia normanna* (Nuovi Studi Storici 28), Roma: Istituto storico italiano per il medio evo.

Treadwell, Luke (1999), "The 'Orans' *drachms* of Bishr Ibn Marwān", in: Jeremy Johns, ed., *Bayt al-Maqdis. Jerusalem and Early Islam* (Oxford Studies in Islamic Art 9, 2), Oxford: Oxford University Press, 223–269.

Treadwell, Luke (2005), "'Mihrab and ʿAnaza' or 'Sacrum and Spear'? A Reconsideration of an Early Marwanid Silver Drachm", *Muqarnas* 22, 1–28.

Treadwell, Luke (2007), "The Monetary History of the Bukharkhuda Dirham ("Black Dirham") in Samanid Transoxania (204–395/819–1005)", in: *Coinage and History in the Seventh Century Near East: Papers from the Seventh Century Syrian Numismatic Round Table 2007* (Supplement to the ONS Journal 193), Croydon, Surrey: Oriental Numismatic Society, 25–40.

Treadwell, Luke (2008), "The Copper Coinage of Umayyad Iran", *The Numismatic Chronicle* 168, 331–381.

Treadwell, Luke (2012a), "Qur'anic Inscriptions on the Coins of the *ahl al-bayt* from the Second to Fourth Century AH", *Journal of Qur'anic Studies* 14, 47–71.

Treadwell, Luke (2012b), "Byzantium and Islam in the Late 7th Century AD, a 'Numismatic War of Images?'", in: Tony Goodwin, ed., *Arab-Byzantine Coins and History, Papers Presented at the Seventh Century Syrian Numismatic Round Table held at Corpus Christi College, Oxford on 10th and 11th September 2011*, London: Archetype, 145–155.

Treadwell, Luke (2015), "Symbolism and Meaning on the Early Islamic Copper Coinage of Greater Syria", in: Andrew Oddy, Wolfgang Schulze, and Ingrid Schulze, eds., *Coinage and History in the Seventh Century Near East 4. Proceedings of the 14th Seventh Century Syrian Numismatic Round Table held at The Hives, Worcester on 28th and 29th September 2013*, London: Archetype, 73–95.

Treadwell, Luke (2017) "The Formation of Religious and Caliphal Identity in the Umayyad Period", in: Finbarr B. Flood and Gülru Necipoğlu, eds., *A Companion to Islamic Art and Architecture* (Blackwell Companions to Art History 12), Oxford: Wiley-Blackwell, 89–108.

Trombley, Frank R. (2014), "From Kastron to Qaṣr: Nessana between Byzantiumand the Umayyad Caliphate ca. 602–689. Demographic and Microeconomic Aspects of Palaestina III in Interregional Perspective", in: Ellen Bradshaw Aitken, ed., *The Levant: Crossroads of Late Antiquity. History, Religion and Archaeology / Le Levant: carrefour de l'antiquité tardive. Histoire, religion et archéologie* (McGill University Monographs in Classical Archaeology and History 22), Leiden/Boston: Brill, 181–224.

Trombley, Frank R. (2015), "Fiscal Documents from the Muslim Conquest of Egypt: Military Supplies and Administrative Dislocation, ca 639–644", *Revue des Études Byzantines* 71, 5–38.

Turner, Eric G. (1978), *The Terms* recto *and* verso*: The Anatomy of the Papyrus Roll* (Papyrologica Bruxellensia 16), Bruxelles: Fondation Egyptologique Reine Elisabeth.

Tütüncü Mehmet (2013), *Cezayir'de Osmanlı izleri (1516–1830): 314 yıllık Osmanlı hâkimiyetinde Cezayir'den kitâbeler, eserler ve meşhurlar* (Çamlıca Basım Yayın 123), Istanbul/Haarlem: SOTA Türk ve Arap Dünyasi Araştırma Merkezi.

Ullmann, Manfred (1997), *Zur Geschichte des Wortes barīd "Post"* (Beiträge zur Lexikographie des Klassischen Arabisch 13), Munich: Bayerische Akademie der Wissenschaften.

al-Ushsh, Muḥammad A. F. (1963), "Inscriptions arabes inédites à Djabal ʿUsays", *Les Annales Archéologiques de Syrie* 13, 225–237.

Vaissière (de la), Étienne (2007), *Samarcande et Samarra: Elites d'Asie centrale dans l'empire abbasside* (Studia Iranica, Cahier 35), Paris: Association pour l'Avancement des Études Iraniennes.

Vaissière (de la), Étienne / Riboud, Pénélope / Grenet, Frantz (2003), "Les livres des Sogdiens (avec une note additionnelle par Frantz Grenet)", *Studia Iranica* 32, 127–136.

Vandorpe, Katelijn (2009), "Archives and Dossiers", in: Roger S. Bagnall, ed., *The Oxford Handbook of Papyrology* (Oxford Handbooks), New York: Oxford University Press, 216–255.

Vanthieghem, Naïm (2014a), "Le plus ancien sauf–conduit arabe", *Der Islam* 91, 266–271 (= *P.VanthiegemSauf-Conduit*).

Vanthieghem, Naïm (2014b), "Un exercice épistolaire arabe adressé au gouverneur Ǧābir ibn al-ʾAšʿaṯ", *Archiv für Papyrusforschung und verwandte Gebiete*, 402–405 (= *P.VanthieghemExercice*).

Vedeler, Marianne (2014), *Silk for the Vikings* (Ancient Textiles Series 15), Oxford: Oxbow.

Versteegh, Kees (2001), "Linguistic Contacts between Arabic and Other Languages", *Arabica* 48, 470–508.

Versteegh, Klees (2010), "Contact and the Development of Arabic", in: Raymond Hickey, ed., *The Handbook of Contact Languages* (Blackwell Handbooks in Linguistics), Chichester: Wiley Blackwood, 634–651.

Versteegh, Klees (2015), "An Empire of Learning: Arabic as a Global Language", in: Christel Stolz, ed., *Language Empires in Comparative Perspectives* (Koloniale und Postkoloniale Linguistik / Colonial and Postcolonial Linguistics 6), Berlin: De Gruyter, 41–54.

Versteegh, Klees (2018), "Language of Empire, Language of Power", in: Klees Versteegh, ed., *Language of Empire, Language of Power* (Special Issue of Language Ecology 2, 1/2), Amsterdam: John Benjamins Publishing Company, 1–17.

Vibert-Guigue, Claude / Bisheh, Ghazi (2007), *Les peintures de Qusayr ʿAmra un bain omeyyade dans la bâdiya jordanienne* (Bibliothèque archéologique et historique 179; Jordanian Archaeology 1), Beirut: Institut français du Proche-Orient.

Vierros, Maria (2018), "The Greek of the Petra Papyri", in: Antti Arjava, Jaakko Frösén, and Jorma Kaimio, eds., *The Petra Papyri V* (American Center of Oriental Research Publications 8), Amman: American Center of Oriental Research, 8–34.

Violet, Bruno (1901), "Ein zweisprachiges Psalmfragment aus Damascus", *Orientalische Literaturzeitung* 4, 384–403, 425–441, and 475–488.

Vollandt, Ronny (2015), *Arabic Versions of the Pentateuch: A Comparative Study of Jewish, Christian, and Muslim Sources* (Biblia Arabica 2), Leiden/Boston: Brill.

Vollers, Karl (1887–1897), "Beiträge zur Kenntniss der lebenden Arabischen Sprache in Aegypten", *Zeitschrift der Deutschen Morgenländischen Gesellschaft* 41, 365–402; 50, 607–657; and 51, 291–326 and 343–364.

Vondrovec, Klaus (2014), *Coinage of the Iranian Huns and Their Successors from Bactria to Gandhara (4th to 8th century CE)*, 2 vols. (Denkschriften der Österreichischen Akademie der Wissenschaften, Philosophisch-historische Klasse 471; Veröffentlichungen zur

Numismatik 59; Studies in the Aman ur Rahman Collection 4), Vienna: Österreichische Akademie der Wissenschaften (ed. Michael Alram and Judith A. Lerner).
Vorderstrasse, Tasha (2015), "Terms for Vessels in Arabic and Coptic Documentary Texts and Their Archaeological and Ethnographic Correlates", in: Alexander T. Schubert and Petra M. Sijpesteijn, eds., *Documents and the History of the Early Islamic World* (Islamic History and Civilization 111), Leiden/Boston: Brill, 195–234.
Walker, Alicia (2015), "Pseudo-Arabic 'Inscriptions' and the Pilgrim's Path at Hosios Loukas", in: Anthony Eastmond, ed., *Viewing Inscriptions in the Late Antique and Medieval World*, Cambridge: Cambridge University Press, 99–123.
Walker, John (1941), *Catalogue of the Muhammadan Coins in the British Museum Part 1: A Catalogue of the Arab-Sassanian Coins*, London: British Museum (= *BMC* I).
Walker, John (1952), "Some New Arab-Sassanian Coins", *The Numismatic Chronicle and Journal of The Royal Numismatic Society* 12, 106–110.
Walker, John (1956), *Catalogue of the Muhammadan Coins in the British Museum Part 2: a Catalogue of the Arab-Byzantine and Post-Reform Umayyad Coins*, London: British Museum Publications (= *BMC* II).
Walmsley, Alan (1999), "Coin Frequencies in Sixth and Seventh Century Palestine and Arabia: Social and Economic Implications", *Journal of the Economic and Social History of the Orient* 42, 326–350.
Walmsley, Alan / Blanke, Louise / Damgaard, Kristoffer / Mellah, Aicha / McPhillips, Stephen / Roenje, Lars /Simpson, Ian / Bessard, Fanny (2008), "A Mosque, Shops and Bath in Central Jarash: the 2007 Season of the Islamic Jarash Project", *Annual of the Department of Antiquities of Jordan* 52, 109–137.
Walmsley, Alan / Macumber, Phillip / Edwards, Phillip C. / Bourke, Stephen / Watson, Pamela M. (1993), "The Eleventh and Twelfth Seasons of Excavations at Pella (Ṭabaqat Faḥl): 1989–1990", *Annual of the Department of Antiquities of Jordan* 37, 165–240.
Wansbrough, John E. (1977), *Quranic Studies: Sources and Methods of Scriptural Interpretation*. Oxford: Oxford University Press.
Wansbrough, John E. (1978), *The Sectarian Milieu: Content and Composition of Islamic Salvation History*, Oxford: Oxford University Press.
Wärmländer, Sebastian K.T.S. / Wärmländer, Linda / Saage, Ragnar / Rezakhani, Khodadad / Hamid Hassan, Saied A. / Neiß, Michael (2015) "Analysis and Interpretation of a Unique Arabic Finger Ring from the Viking Age Town of Birka, Sweden", *Scanning* 37, 131–137.
Wasserstein, David J. (1998), "The Language Situation in *al-Andalus*", in: Manuela Marín and Maribel Fierro, eds., *The Formation of al-Andalus II: Language, Religion, Culture and Sciences* (The Formation of the Classical Islamic World), Aldershot: Ashgate, 3–18.
Webb, Peter (2016), *Imagining the Arabs: Arab Identity and the Rise of Islam*, Edinburgh: Edinburgh University Press.
Weber, Dieter (1992), Ostraca, Papyri und Pergamente (Corpus Inscriptionum Iranicarum /3, 4/5, 1: Pt. 3, Pahlavi inscriptions, vol. 4, Ostraca, and vol. 5, Papyri), London: Humphries.
Weber, Dieter (2003), "Die Pahlavi-Ostraca von Čāl Tarxān-Ešqābād", in: Ludwig Paul, ed., *Persian Origins: Early Judaeo-Persian and the Emergence of New Persian; Collected Papers of the Symposium, Göttingen 1999* (Iranica 6), Wiesbaden: Harrassowitz, 275–282.
Weber, Dieter (2005), "A Pahlavi Papyrus from Islamic Times", *Bulletin of the Asia Institute* 19, 225–231.

Weber, Dieter (2008a), *Berliner Pahlavi-Dokumente. Zeugnisse spätsassanidischer Brief- und Rechtskultur aus frühislamischer Zeit. Mit Beiträgen von Myriam Krutzsch und Maria Macuch* (Iranica 15), Wiesbaden: Harrassowitz.

Weber, Dieter (2008b), "New Arguments for Dating the Documents from the 'Pahlavi Archive'", *Bulletin of the Asia Institute* 19, 215–222.

Weber, Dieter (2008c), "Sassanidische Briefe aus Ägypten", in: Eva M. Grob and Andreas Kaplony, eds., *Documentary Letters from the Middle East: The Evidence in Greek*, Coptic, *South* Arabian, Pehlevi, and Arabic (1st–15th c CE)</i> (Asiatische Studien/Etudes asiatiques 62, 3), Bern *et al.*: Peter Lang, 803–826.

Weber, Dieter (2010), "Villages and Estates in the Documents from the Pahlavi Archive: The Geographical Background", *Bulletin of the Asia Institute* 24, 37–65.

Weber, Dieter (2011), "Testing Food and Garment for the "Ōstāndār": Two Unpublished Documents from the "Pahlavi Archive" in Berkeley, CA", *Bulletin of the Asia Institute* 25, 31–37.

Weber, Dieter (2012), "Studies in Some Documents from the "Pahlavi Archive"", *Bulletin of the Asia Institute* 26, 61–95.

Weber, Dieter (2013a), "Die persische Besetzung Ägyptens 619–629 n. Chr. – Fakten, Spekulationen", in: Frank Feder and Angelika Lohwasser, eds., *Ägypten und sein Umfeld in der Spätantike vom Regierungsantritt* Diokletians *284/285 bis zur arabischen Eroberung des Vorderen Orients um 635 – 646. Akten der Tagung vom 7. – 9. 7.2011in Münster* (Philippika 61), Wiesbaden: Harrassowitz, 221–246.

Weber, Dieter (2013b), "Taxation in Pahlavi Documents from Early Islamic times (late 7th century CE)", in: Sergej R. Tochtas'ev and Pavel Lurje, eds., *Commentationes Iranicae. Vladimiro f. Aaron Livschits nonagenariodonum natalicium*, St. Petersburg: Nestor-Historia, 171–181.

Weber, Dieter (2014), "Arabic Activities Reflected in the Documents of the 'Pahlavi Archive'", in: Ryka Gyselen, ed., *Documents, argenterie et monnaies de tradition sassanide* (Res Orientales 22), Bures–sur–Yvette: Groupe pour l'étude de la civilisation du Moyen–Orient, 179–189.

Weber, Dieter (2016a), "Court Records of Lawsuits in Tabarestan in the Year 86/7 PYE (737 CE): A Philological Examination", in: Rika Gyselen, ed., *Words and Symbols: Sasanian Objects and the Tabarestān Archive* (Res Orientales 24), Bures-sur-Yvette: Groupe pour l'Etude de la Civilisation du Moyen-Orient, 121–144.

Weber, Dieter (2016b), "Two Documents from Tabarestan Reconsidered (Tab. 12 and 26)", in: Rika Gyselen, ed., *Words and Symbols: Sasanian Objects and the Tabarestān Archive* (Res Orientales 24), Bures-sur-Yvette: Groupe pour l'Etude de la Civilisation du Moyen-Orient, 185–192.

Weber, Dieter (2017), "Pahlavi Legal Documents from Tabarestān on Lease, Loan and. Compensation: A Philological Study (Tab. 13, 14, 15, 17, 18 and 23)", in: Rika Gyselen, ed., *Sasanian Persia and the Tabarestan Archive* (Res Orientales 27), Bures–sur–Yvette: Groupe pour l'étude de la civilisation du Moyen–Orient, 131–163.

Wensinck, Arent J. (1927), *Handbook of Early Muhammadan Tradition Alphabetically Arranged*, Leiden: Brill.

Wensinck, Arent J. (1936–1988), *Concordance et indices de la tradition Musulmane*, 8 vols., Leiden: Brill.

Whitcomb, Donald W. (1989), "Evidence of the Umayyad Period from the Aqaba Excavations", in: Muḥammad A. Bakhit and Robert Schick, eds., *The Fourth International Conference on the*

History of Bilād al-Shām during the Umayyad Period: Proceedings of the Third Symposium, Amman: University of Jordan Press, Bilad al-Sham History Committee, 164–184.
Whitcomb, Donald W. (1995), "Two Glass Medallions: Sasanian influence in early Islamic Aqaba", *Iranica Antiqua* 30, 191–206.
Wolf, Eric R. (1956), "Aspects of Group Relations in a Complex Society: Mexico", *American Anthropologist, New Series* 58, 1065–1078.
Wright, George H. R. / Milik, Jozef T. (1961), "The Archaeological Remains at El Mird in the Wilderness of Judaea", *Biblica* 42, 1–20.
Wroth, Warwick W. (1908), *Catalogue of the Imperial Byzantine Coins in the British Museum*, 2 vols., London: Trustees of the British Museum.
Wurtzel, Carl (1978), "The Coinage of the Revolutionaries in the Late Umayyad Period", *Museum Notes (American Numismatic Society)* 23, 161–199.
Yakubovich, Ilya (2002), "Mugh 1.I. Revisited", *Studia Iranica* 31, 231–253.
Yarbrough, Luke (2012), "Upholding God's Rule: Early Muslim Juristic Opposition to the State Employment of non-Muslims", *Islamic Law and Society* 19, 11–85.
Yarbrough, Luke (2016), "Did ʿUmar b. ʿAbd al-ʿAzīz Issue an EdictConcerning Non-Muslim Officials?", in: Antoine Borrut and Fred Donner, eds., *Christians and Others in the Umayyad State* (Late Antique and Medieval Islamic Near East 1), Chicago: The Oriental Institute of the University of Chicago, 173–206.
Yardeni, Adah (2001), "The Decipherment and Restoration of Legal Texts from the Judaean Desert: A Reexamination of Papyrus Starcky (P.Yadin 36)", *Scripta Classica Israelica* 20, 121–137.
Yarshater, Ehsan (1998), "The Persian Presence in the Islamic World", in: Richard G. Hovannisian and Georges Sabagh, eds., *The Persian Presence in the Islamic World. Proceedings of the Giorgio Levi Della Vida Biennial Conference held at the University of California, Los Angeles, May 10–12, 1991*, Cambridge: Cambridge University Press, 4–125.
Younes, Khaled (2013), *Joy and Sorrow in Early Muslim Egypt: Arabic Papyrus Letters Text and Content*. Ph.D. thesis: Leiden (= *P.JoySorrow*).
Younes, Khaled (2018), "New Governors Identified in Arabic Papyri", in: Alain Delattre, Marie Legendre, and Petra Sijpesteijn, eds., *Authority and Control in the Countryside: From Antiquity to Islam in the Mediterranean and Near East (6th-10th Century)* (Leiden Studies in Islam and Society 9), Leiden/Boston: Brill, 13–43.
Zaborowski, Jason R. (2010), "Arab Christian Physicians as Interreligious Mediators: Abū Shākir as a Model Christian Expert", *Islam and Christian–Muslim Relations* 21, 185–196.
Zaehner, Robert Ch. (1937), "Nāmak-nipēsišnīh", *Bulletin of the School of Oriental and African Studies* 9, 93–109.
al-Zalaʿī, Aḥmad b. ʿUmar (2010), "Les inscriptions arabo-islamiques sur pierre", in: Ali Ibrahim al-Ghabban *et al.*, eds., *Routes d'Arabie: Archéologie et Histoire du Royaume d'Arabie Saoudite*, Paris: Somogy, 486–487.
Zammit, Martin R. (2002), *A Comparative Lexical Study of Qurʾānic Arabic* (Handbuch der Orientalistik 61), Leiden/Boston/Köln: Brill.
Zbiss, Slimane M. (1960), *Corpus des Inscriptions Arabes de Tunisie II: Inscriptions de Monastir*, Tunis: Direction des Antiquités et Arts.
Ziadeh, Joseph (1915–1917), "Apocalypse de Samuel, superieur de Deir-el-Qalamoun", *Revue de l'Orient Chretien* 20: 374–407.
Zimmern, Heinrich (1915), *Akkadische Fremdwörter als Beweis für Babylonischen Kultureinfluss*, Leipzig: Edelmann.

Indices

General Index

ʿAbbāsa bt. Jurayj 122, 208, 209, 212, 245
Abbasid(s) 10, 11, 34, 40, 89n323, 100, 110, 116, 124n61, 160, 163, 182, 199, 218, 259, 263, 264, 329
– art 98
– book production 125
– coinage *see* coinage/coins
– documentary scripts 128n88
– official documents 109, 171n2, 177–178n45, 180–181, 182, 188, 199–200, 332, technical vocabulary of 265, 271, 308, 318–321, 328, 331
– official inscriptions 50, 93–94, 117, 119, 193–194, 195, 196–198
ʿAbd Allāh b. ʿAbd al-Raḥmān (pagarch) 220
ʿAbd Allāh b. Abī Hāshim/ʿĀṣim (governor) 82–83
ʿAbd Allāh b. ʿĀmir (governor) 325n300
ʿAbd Allāh b. ʿAmr 57, 240
ʿAbd Allāh b. Asʿad 49, 73, 206, 240
ʿAbd Allāh b. Jābir (*amīr*) 56
ʿAbd Allāh b. Khāzim (governor), coinage of 257n192
ʿAbd Allāh b. Qays 74
ʿAbd Allāh b. al-Rabīʿ (governor) 126
ʿAbd Allāh b. Saʿd (governor), seal of 146
ʿAbd Allāh b. al-Zubayr *see* Ibn al-Zubayr
ʿAbd al-ʿAzīz b. ʿAbd Allāh (governor) 145
– coinage of 144, 244, 245
ʿAbd al-Azīz b. Marwān (governor) 61, 64, 66, 116, 180, 197
– coinage of 65–66, 149, 157. *See also* coinage, coins – *ABAZ* and – Arab-Byzantine (Greek)
– dossier of 61, 80, 129, 236
– glass weights of 66
– seal of 146
ʿAbd al-ʿAzīz b. Mundhir (*amīr*) 235
ʿAbd al-Ḥamīd (secretary) 22n88
Abdīn (*amīr*) 96
ʿAbd al-Malik b. Marwān (caliph) 40, 61, 153, 163, 197, 243
– coinage of 11, 20, 139, 143, 144, 151
– graffito by 90
– language reforms of 40, 145, 245
ʿAbd al-Malik b. Yazīd (pagarch) 73
ʿAbd al-Raḥmān b. Abī ʿAwf (pagarch) 70, 220
ʿAbd al-Raḥmān b.ʿAwf 82
ʿAbd al-Raḥmān b. Khayr (commander) 60n138
ʿAbd al-Raḥmān b. Muḥammad *see* Ibn al-Ashʿath
ʿAbd al-Raḥmān b. Ṣubḥ (*amīr*) 102, 103
Abraha (king) 290
Abū ʿAbd Allāh, archive of 53n85
Abū ʿAmr *al-qahramān* 320
Abū Ghālib b. al-Iṣbahbadh (*amīr*) 106
Abū Manṣūr Bukhtegin 165n290
Abū Mūsā al-Ashʿarī (commander) 95
Abū ʿUbayda b. al-Jarraḥ 82
Abū Yūsuf 319n281
Acre 93, 117, 192, 193
al-Afshīn (prince) 104n418
Aleppo 46, 153, 200
– Great Mosque 123
Alexandria 54, 60n136, 64n157
– Byzantine conquest of 9
– mint of 59, 66, 246
ʿAlī b. Sulaymān(governor) 298n193
Amman 44, 92, 135n136
– mint of 153n228
ʿAmr b. al-ʿĀṣ 57, 240
– mosque of 65n146
– seal of 146n188
ʿAmr b. ʿUbayd (pagarch) 220
Anbā Magnillē (preacher) 86, 212
Anbā Yusūf 86
Anbīr 160, 257n192
al-Andalus *see* Spain
Aninou (village) 64
Antonio de Nebrija 40
Apakyros (pagarch) 57
ʿAqūlā *see* Kūfa
Arabic language. *See also* Arabization
– as a *lingua franca* 52–54, 109
– as an imperial language Ch. I *passim*, 199–200, 211–212, 314–321, lexical features of Ch. V *passim*

https://doi.org/10.1515/9783110740820-041

– official formal varieties of 171–187, 194–198, difference from private formal varieties 201–213
– orthography 200, 332, 334
– pseudo-Arabic inscriptions 127, 163–164
– scribes *see* scribes – Arabic
Arabic script 22, 43, 46, 78, 104
– as a visual medium 3, 71, 116–121, 124–125, 166–167
– origins of 43–45
– pre-Islamic use of 45–46
– use of in Western Europe 162–165
"Arab-style" documents
– Bactrian 255–256
– Coptic 225–228, 231, 237, 239, 253, 327, 346–342
– Greek 219–225, 231, 236–237,253, 254–255, 327, 346–352
– Middle-Persian 232–233, 239, 253, 327, 346
– Sogdian 228–231, 236–237, 253, 327, 346–350
Arabization 33, 35. *See also* Arabic language and Arabic script
– among Christians 33, 40, 48, 239–240, 325
– and conversion to Islam 86, 106, 107, 110, 132, 239–240
– of coinage 51–52, 81–82, 94–95, 103, 136–143, 151–155, 162, 243–244, 251–252, 325–326
– of onomastics 16, in Egypt 108n440, in Greater Syria 86–87, in Bactria 106–108, 267, in Sogdiana 104, 321
– of scribal practices Ch. I *passim*, 324–325, 331–332. *See also* "Arab-style" documents
Aramaic
– Achaemenid Official Aramaic 88, 171, 284, letters 178, 180
– Christian Palestinian Aramaic 87, inscriptions 43, loanwords in Arabic 314, papyri 17, 78, 85
– Imperial Aramaic *see* Achaemenid Official Aramaic
– Jewish Babylonian Aramaic loanwords in Arabic 314
– Jewish Palestinian Aramaic loanwords in Arabic 314
– loanwords in Arabic Ch. V *passim*, 329
– logograms 44n33, 201, 243
– Nabatean Aramaic *see* Nabatean language
Arcadia 63
Ardashīr Khurra, mint of 144–145n181
Ascalon 193
ʿĀṣim b. ʿĀʾib 190
Aswān 30, 50, 60, 212, 245
– "Fatimid" cemetery 50, 53
Athanasios (pagarch) 58
Athanasios br. Gumōyē (secretary) 318
ʿAṭīya b. Juʿayd (duke) 63, 64, 65, 220, 235
– archive of 63–64
ʿAwf b. Nāfi (pagarch) 220

Bāb b. Bēk (II) 106, 107, 256
Bactria 178, 313, 329
– Aramaic documents from 178
– Bactrian pantheon 239n114
Bactrian language
– coinage 257n192. *See also* coinage/coins – Arab-Hephtalite
– documents 284, 286, 289, 292, 308n226, 311, 312n247, 315, 325, formal features of 174, 187, 255–256
– loanwords in Aramaic 281n113
– script 257n192, 311n239
Baghdad 314, 328
al-Bakrī 46
al-Balādhurī 93, 146n187
Balāʾizah, Apa Apollo monastery 49n56, 227n48
Balkh 101, 105, 311, 312n247
Banū ʿAbd al-Muʾmin, archive of 52n85
basmala 129, 138, 176–177, 184, 185, 188, 189, 190, 191, 195, 196, 197, 198, 202, 205, 207, 208, 223, 226, 233, 250, 253, 256, 257, 258
– Bactrian renditions of 255
– Coptic renditions of 225, 226, 257
– "Eastern" 150n220
– Greek renditions of 220, 222, 226, 257
– in letters by Christians 86, 184, 257
– Latin renditions of 250

- Middle Persian renditions of 97, 145, 232, 233, 256, 257
- pre-Islamic antecedents 177n42
- "short" 136, 150, 188, 195, 208, 250
- Sogdian renditions of 229
Baṣra 115, 127n82, 138n153, 139, 325n300
- mint of 157, 160
Bāwiṭ, Apa Apollo monastery 49n56, 72, 239
Baysān 92, 117, 123, 193
Bayyān b. Qays 79
Bēk (I), family of 49, 105, 106, 107, 108, 147, 187, 206, 255, 256
Bēk (II) b. Kamird-far (I) 107
al-Bīrūnī 121n44
Bīshāpūr, mint of 145n181, 157n157, 161
Bishr b. Marwān (governor) 157, 160
- coinage of 157, 161
Bohemond I (prince) 164
Bosra
- era of 45n40, 46
- Mibrak *madrasa* 50n64
- al-ʿUmarī Mosque 93, 117, 192, 193
Byzantine(s)
- art and architecture 133–134, 140–141
- *regalia* 135, 151

Cairo 126. *See also* al-Fusṭāṭ
- Genizah 16n58
calendar 183n86
- Egyptian 63, 68, 222
- Mulsim 31, 63, 68
- Roman 84, 222, 255n175
Carthage 9
- mint of 59, 146
Chalkis *see* Qinnasirīn
Chāl Tarkhān-ʿEshqābād 98–99, 134
- ostraca from 49n56, 99
Christian(s) 3, 29, 40, 45, 48, 85, 116, 117, 148, 227–228, 237, 333
- access to mosques 120
- Arabic letters addressed to 65–66, 71, 327, formal features of 183–184, 218–219, 223–224, 240–241. *See also* "Arab-style" documents
- as cultural brokers 217n4, 241, 317–318, 327
- literary sources 11, 13
- officials 57, 60, 74, 96, 110, 147, 218–219, 240–241, 317–318
- pre-Islamic Arabs 45–46, 84, 176, 182
- *spolia* 115–116
- symbols 45, 147, 150, 154, 237, 240, on documents by Muslims 237, on Islamic coinage 136, 137, 158–161, removal from Islamic coinage 144, 148–149, 151
- workshops 133–134
- writing in Arabic 14n45, 45–46, 48, 53–54, 86–87, 74, 87, 171n3, 176, 184, 200–201, 212–213, 231n66, 241, 257, 308, 325, 333–334
coinage, coins
- *ABAZ* 65–66, 149, 157
- Abbasid 21n84, 24n94, 52, 98, 298
- Arab-Byzantine, Greek 51, 65–66, 139, 142, 152, 242, Latin 20, 52, 129, 140, 158, 245–253
- Arab-Hephtalite 149, 160, 257n192, 286
- Arab-Sasanian, copper 129, 139, 154n231, 158, 235, 245n149, silver 51–52, 81–82, 94–95, 97, 137–140, 142, 143–145, 149–151, 157, 160, 232, 242–243, 244, 250n160, 257
- Byzantine, imitations of 9n17, 59–60, 137, 148–149, import of 137, 143
- *mancusi* 163–164
- *orans* 139n159, 149, 157, 160–162
- Pseudo-Damascus 157, 161
- reformed 24n94, 51–52, 66, 125, 142–150, 158, 162–163, 242–244, 246, 249, 252, 298, 300, 301, 311, 326
- Sasanian 94–95, 128, 138, 149–150, 244
- standing caliph 51, 149–150, 152–162, 242–243, 250n159, 298
- Umayyad Imperial Image 51, 81–82, 94, 137, 245
- *al-wafāʾ li-llāh* 161, 245
Constantine III (emperor) *see* Heraclius Constantine
Coptic language 14, 55, 70n189, 179, 186, 219, 259
- Arabic loanwords in 317n267
- inscriptions 235

– in the early Islamic administration 27, 57–58, 60, 63–64, 66–67, 69–77, 110, 220, 236–237, 240, 311, 329, 330. *See also* "Arab-style" documents – Coptic
– literary sources 12n41, 40
– loanwords in Arabic 271, 280n105, 317
– papyri 15–16, 47–48, 53, 54n96
Coptic revolts 9
Cook, Michael 11
Crone, Patricia 11

Dābūyids 100
al-Ḍaḥḥāk b. ʿAbd al-Raḥmān (secretary) 66
Damascus 49, 54, 61n140, 92, 116, 117, 126, 314, 328
– mint of 51, 110, 142, 149, 151, 153n228, 154, 155, 159, 160, 162, 253n168
– Pseudo-Damascus mint *see* coinage/coins – Pseudo-Damascus
– Umayyad Mosque 14n46, 53, 93, 115, 117, 120n26, 123, 133, 134, 148, 192, 193. *See also* Umayyad(s) – art and architecture
Darab-gird, mint of 138, 144–145n181
Darb Zubayda 51, 117, 194, 197. *See also* milestones
Decapolis 87
Dēwāshtīch (king) 102, 181, 207, 239
– archive of 49n56, 102–103, 186–187 104n418, 228–231
Diem, Werner 64
Dikaiou (village) 64
doxology
– disappearance of 318
– Greek renditions of 221, 223–224, 350
– in inscriptions 90–91, 193–194, 195, 196, 340
– in official letters 175, 179, 181, 185, 189, 204, 205, 206, 207, 219, 227, 337, 350
– omission of in private letters 203
– Sogdian renditions of 228–231, 350
– variants of for Christians 183, 241
– variants of in private letters 203–204

Egypt 9, 77, 109, 116, 127, 136, 174, 221, 234, 236, 240
– administrative idiolect of 268–307, 327–328, compared to Greater Syria 314–318, compared to Khurāsān 319–321
– Arabic-inscribed objects from 50, 53, 127
– Arabic inscriptions from 53, 60, 65, 193, 194, formal features of 207–209
– Arabization of scribal practices in 54–77, 180–183, 228, 325–326, compared to Greater Syria 77, 79–83, 85–87, 109–110, 128, 231, 240, 257, compared to Iran 96, 110, compared to Khurāsān 103, 110, 177n45, 231
– Aramaic documents from 178
– as a province of the Early Islamic Empire 24–26, 264–265, 328–330
– Delta 18, 116n9, 194
– Islamic coinage from 51, 59–60, 65–66, 137, 140, 149, 159
– Lower 64n157, 71
– Middle 72
– Muslim conquest of 3, 52, 54, 226
– Palmyrene conquest of 54
– Persian invasion of 31, 54
– Roman 235
– seals from 52, 146–147
– standard weights from 52, 66n166, 243n137, 300n194, 304n210
– survival of papyri in 15–18, 46–48, 53, 219
– Upper 54n94
Étienne de Blois (count) 165n290

Fasā, mint of 144n181
Faṭrīq 86n306
Fayyūm 52, 61, 62, 64, 73, 74, 75, 126, 188, 219
– pagarchs of 63, 65, 73, 74, 185, 206, 220
Flavius Atias *see* ʿAṭīya b. Juʿayd
al-Fusṭāṭ 50, 54, 58, 59, 64, 65, 66, 67, 68, 70, 93, 115, 193
– mint of 59

Gabriel 227
Gabriel (monk) 85
Gaza 78, 79
Georgios (*dioikētēs*), 121n40, 79–80
Georgios (*symmachos*) 74, 240
Georgios Pachymeres 166
Georgios s. of Patrikios (abbot) 78
Georgios s. of Victor (scribe) 84
Ghassānid(s) 8, 44, 46, 115, 201

Gōzgān 257
Greek language 8, 14, 42–43, 120n39, 121, 128, 129, 147n196, 177, 179, 186, 201n176, 207, 243, 257, 330
– graffiti 88, 133, 239–240
– inscriptions 18, 45, 82, 88, 92n338, 119, 133, 176, 242
– in the early Islamic administration 27, 33, 40n5, 139, 146, 152, 174, 188–189, 234–235, 236–237, 245, in Egypt 51, 55–77, 220, 240, 251n162, 329, in Syria 77–85, disappearance of 53, 75, 76–77, 87, 145, 151, 162, 218, 325. *See also* "Arab-style" documents – Greek
– literary sources 11, 12n41, 29
– loanwords in Arabic 54, 74, 152, 240, Ch. V *passim*, 329
– loanwords in Middle Persian 159n263
– orthography of Arabic terms 43, 248n157 291, 332n308
– papyri 15–18, 47–48
Grob, Eva 25–26
Gzella, Holger 171

Ḥabbān b. Yūsuf 86, 184
Ḥajj 172n7. *See also* Darb Zubayda
al-Ḥajjāj b. Yūsuf (governor) 11, 101, 149
– coinage of 149
ḥamdala 204, 318. *See also* doxology
– Greek renditions of 350
– Sogdian renditions of 350
– variants of in private letters 204
– verbalized 204
Hamdān 97
Ḥamra bt. Mīr 106, 107
al-Ḥārith b. Jabala (phylarch) 46n47, 201
Ḥarrān 266
– inscription 18n72, 46, 266
– mint of 153
Hārūn al-Rashīd (caliph) 319
Haspīn-raz (village) 100
Ḥassan al-Qommī 96, 98
Heidemann, Stefan 23
Heracleopolis/Heracleopolite *see* Ihnās
Heraclius (emperor) 59, 60, 148, 151
Heraclius Constantine (emperor) 151
Heraclonas (emperor) 151
Hermopolis/Hermopolite *see* al-Ushmūnayn
Ḥijāz 18, 50, 88, 110, 117, 123, 292, 294, 309
al-Ḥīma 45, 46
Ḥimṣ 152
– mint of 51, 151
Ḥimyar 8, 46, 174, 201
Hind bt. al-Ḥārith (queen) 46
al-Ḥīra 46, 115
Hishām b. ʿAbd al-Malik (caliph) 123, 124, 148, 189, 197
Honorifics
– Roman 8, 63, 234, 235, 259
– Sasanian 235, 259
Hosios Lukas 164
Ḥujrid(s) 8, 46, 201
Ḥumā al-Numūr 89
al-Ḥumayma (palace) 160
Hyrkania *see* Khirbat al-Mird

Ibn ʿAsākir 218
Ibn al-Ashʿath 10, 101
Ibn Hishām 314
Ibn Isḥāq 267, 314
Ibn al-Nuʿmān, Ḥassān (governor) 52
– coinage of 140, 247, 250n158
Ibn Rustah 93, 197
Ibn al-Zubayr (anti-caliph) 145n183
– Zubayrid(s) 90n325, 151, 161, coinage 140, 144, 145, 149, 150, 244–245, 250n160, 326
Ibrahīm b. Yaḥyā (pagarch) 73, 220
– seal of 73, 147
Idrīs (I) b. ʿAbd Allāh (emir) 193
Ihnās 56–58, 62n147, 70, 71, 73, 74, 188, 241
– pagarchs of 56, 57, 68, 72, 183, 220n15
Imruʾ al-Qays (b. ʿAmr?) 8, 201
Iran 3, 9, 39, 94, 242, 325, 326, 327
– Arabization of scribal practices in 94–100, 110, 217–218
– documents from 17, 98–99, 186, 329. *See also* Pahlavi Archive
– inscriptions from 50
– Iranian influences on Arabic scribal practices 33, 284, 318–321, 329. *See also* Pahlavi script – influence on Arabic documentary scripts

– Islamic coinage from 51, 137, 150, 158–161, 235, 245, 248, 312, 329. *See also* coinage – Arab-Sasanian
– seals from 136, 157
Iraq 3, 117, 150, 217
– inscriptions from 50, 207
– Islamic coinage from 51, 137, 139, 158n258. *See also* coinage – Arab-Sasanian
– Jewish revolts in 9
– pre-Islamic Arab presence in 3, 42, 201
– seals from 136
ʿĪsā (*ʿāmil*) 241n128.
Isḥāq b. Qabīsā (governor) 123
Ishtikhān 103
Islam
– and iconophobia 147–150
– appropriation of late antique symbols 131–141, 150–162, 330–331
– conversion to 86, 106–107, 239–240, 333
– *dhimma* 82
– early adherents of 29–30
– expressions of 89, 122, 140
– Islamization of landscape 115–116
– relation with Arabization 53, 259–260, 326
Iṣṭakhr 131
– mint of 144–145n181, 157n253, 161

Jabala b. Ayhām (phylarch) 8n15
Jabal Usays 45, 126, 201
al-Jahshiyārī 66, 93
Jaffa 92, 125
Jafnid(s) *see* Ghassanid(s)
Jarhom, mint of 144–145n181
Jarīr b. ʿAṭīya 131–132
al-Jarrāḥ b. ʿAbd Allāh (governor) 102, 103, 181, 239
al-Jawālīqī 266, 322n297
Jayy 97, 243
– mint of 144n181, 244n140
Jerusalem 54, 82, 85, 87, 92, 117, 125, 209
– al-Aqṣā Mosque 115, 123n52, 133, 155
– Dome of the Rock 115, 133–134, 148, 155, inscriptions of 27, 93, 117, 118, 119, 121n41, 123, 125, 192, 193, 196, 198
– mint of 51
Jīruft, mint of 144n181
John of Damascus 13
John of Nikiou 12n42
jund 282
– Damascus 152
– Filasṭīn 78, 152
– Ḥimṣ 152
– Qinnasirīn 156
– Urdunn 152, 161
Jurayj 86n306
Justinian I (emperor) 46, 201
Justinian II (emperor) 40, 163
– coinage of 156

Kairouan, Great Mosque 15n46
Kamird-far (II) b. Bēk (II) 106, 107
Kaplony, Andreas 23, 171, 173
Kēra Tonga Spara (*sēr*) 255, 258
Keshsh 103
Khālid b. Slkyān (witness) 106
Khālid b. Yazīd 70, 74
Khārijite(s) 145
– coinage 122, 149
Khaydar b. Kāwūs *see* al-Afshīn
Khirbat al-Mafjar (palace) 133, 134, 148, 156n246, 189
Khirbat al-Minya (palace) 92, 198
Khirbat al-Mird 17, 85, 86, 87, 212
– papyri 85, 86, 87, 184
Kos 49
Knidos 49
Kūfa 51, 115, 138n153
– mint of 157, 160
al-Kutubī 117n23

Lakhmid(s) 8, 44,
Latin language 5, 14, 163–164, 240n123
– in the early Islamic administration 20 27, 52, 129, 140, 245–253, 259, 327
– Latino-Arabic letter 53–54, 248n157
– literary sources 12n41, 42, 189
– loanwords in Arabic 152 and Ch. V *passim*
– orthography of Arabic terms 248n157
– papyri 53, 77–78
Ludd 92, 120, 125

Maʿagan Mikhael 87n309
Maʿarrat Miṣrīn, mint of 153
Madā'in Ṣāliḥ 88

Madr 105n421
al-Mahdī (caliph) 105
Manbij, mint of 153
al-Manṣūr (caliph) 163
Manṣūr family 13
al-Maqdisī 316n262
al-Maqrīzī 64, 93
Mardaites 9–10
Maria (princess) 132
Marthot-Santaniello, Isabelle 68
Marwān (courier) 103
Marwān (I) b. al-Ḥakam (caliph) 61, 117
Marwān (II) b. Muḥammad (caliph) 50, 197
Marwanid(s) *see* Umayyad(s)
Maskan (claimant) 106
Maslama b. Mukhallad (governor) 61, 65n164
al-Mas'ūdī 93
mawālī 86, 234, 239–240
al-Māwardī 146n187
Maymūn b. Ka'b (pagarch) 70, 74, 220n15
Maysara *mawlā* of Ghālib 105
Mecca 50, 51, 117
– Bay'a Mosque, inscriptions 197
– al-Ḥarām Mosque 123, 133, inscriptions 193, 194, 197
– pilgirmage to *see Hajj*
Medina 90, 91, 117, 126
– Constitution of 29
– Medinan Caliphate 54, 55, 70, 82, 87, 89n323, 94, 101
– Prophet's Mosque 123, 133, 134n123, inscriptions 50, 93, 192, 193, 197
Mēnas s. of Senouthios, archive of 49n56, 71
Merv 132n107
– mint of 145n181
Meshkinshahr inscription 232
Meyam s. of Bēk 105
Middle Persian language 14, 105, 120n39, 177, 184, 229. *See also* Pahlavi script
– documents 17, 54n96, 95n361, 236, 239, 257, 330
– inscriptions 201
– in the early Islamic administration 27, 33, 81–82, 94–100, 110, 129, 145, 242–243, disappearance of 97–98, 145, 160, 218, 243, 245, 325. *See also* "Arab-style" documents – Middle Persian
– loanwords in Arabic 265n12, 267, 271, 272, 282, 283, 289, 300, 308, 309, 318–321
milestones 51, 92, 116–117, 125, 194, 196–197, 308
Mīr b. Bēk (II) 106, 107, 256
Monastir 117
Mshatta (palace) 135
Mu'āwiya (I) b. Abī Sufyān (caliph) 10, 20, 82, 137–138, 196, 325n300
– coinage of 138, 139, 148
– inscriptions 83, 90–91, 237n112, 295n178
Mugh, Mount 49n54, 101, 102, 103, 187, 228, 229, 256. *See also* Dēwāshtīch
Muḥammad (prophet) 12, 31, 82, 129, 140, 142, 143, 145, 148, 149, 150, 151, 160, 166, 183, 195, 203, 208, 209, 224, 244, 251
– depicted on coins 149, 150, 153
Muḥammad b. Abī al-Qāsim (pagarch) 71n192, 220
Muḥammad b. Marwān (governor) 150
Muḥammad *mawlā* of Ṣayfī (witness) 106
Muḥammad b. Sa'ī d (governor) 321
Muḥammad b. 'Umar (or 'Amr) 190
al-Mundhir (III) b. al-Nu'mān (king) 46
Mūsā al-Ash'arī (governor) 95
Mūsā b. Ka'b (governor) 16n59, 24, 183, 223
Mūsā b. Nuṣayr (governor) 52, 247
– coinage of 140, 247–253, 250n159. *See also* coinage, coins – Arab-Byzantine (Latin)
Muṣ'ab b. al-Zubayr (governor)
– coinage of 145, 243
Muslim (scribe) 76n243

Nabatean language 44, 178, 263, 295n180, 315
– Arabic loanwords in 315n254
– inscriptions 39, 42, 43, 78, 88, 176
– Nabateo-Arabic graffiti 44–46, 178, 200, 201
– papyri 44
Nājid b. Muslim (pagarch) 73, 185, 206, 220, 237
– seal of 147
Najrān 45, 49
Namāra inscription 8, 201

Nanā (deity) 239
Narseh (prince) 9
Naṣr b. al-Qāsim 106
Naṣr b. Sayyār (governor) 188
Naṣrid(s) *see* Lakhmid(s)
Nessana 16n58, 17, 63n148, 77, 119, 180, 234n89, 235n92, 310n235
– inscriptions 78
– papyri 78–81, 83–85, 206, 207, 222, 236, 254–255, 311, 315–316
– St. Sergius Church 77, 78
– Theotokos Church 77

Offa (king), coinage of 163–164

Pahlavi Archive 49n56, 95–98, 232–234, 237, 329
Pahlavi script 120n39, 138. *See also* Middle Persian language
– influence on Arabic documentary scripts 174–175, 318
– on coins 9n17, 81–82, 94–95, 128–129, 138, 145, 150n217, 154n231, 159n263, 242–243, 244, 256–257
– on documents 97, 232, 284
Paikuli inscription 201, 232
Panjakent 102, 181, 239
Papaconstantinou, Arietta 217
Papas (pagarch) 58
– archive of 58
papyrus protocols 25, 47, 52, 85, 109, 113, 118, 119, 121, 173, 174, 196, 326
– Arabic 94, 127
– bilingual 61, 72, 75, 76, 83, 129, 205, 251n162
– Byzantine 56, 58, 60, 83
Pērōz III (King of Kings) 9
Petosiris (scribe) 241, 260
Petra papyri 84
Phiēou (monk) 227
Phocas (emperor) 148

Qārwāl b. Mīr, archive of 49n54, 104
al-Qāsim b. ʿUbayd Allāh (financial director) 70
– seal of 147n194
Qaṣr Burquʿ (palace) 92, 192, 195, 196, 200, 201
Qaṣr al-Ḥayr al-Gharbī (palace) 92, 124, 134, 135, 148, 155, 189, 192, 202
Qaṣr al-Ḥayr al-Sharqī (palace) 92, 134, 156, 160, 192
Qaṭarī b. al-Fujāʾa (anti-caliph), coinage of 145n181
Qinnasirīn 152, 156
Qom 95, 96, 97, 98, 110, 330. *See also* Pahlavi Archive
– mint of 97n373
Qurʾan 12, 29, 33
– loanwords in 265n12, 268, 269, 276, 278, 283, 285, 287, 289, 292, 295, 296, 297, 300, 303, 307, 312–313, 314n251, 319
– manuscripts 14–15, 124, 125, 126n76
– quotations 15, 122, 267n26, 327, in inscriptions and graffiti 19, 89, 117, 193, 210–211, in papyri 129, 175–180, 184, 204, 222 (*see also* "Arab-style" documents), in coins 162, 243–244, 251–253. *See also basmala*, *ḥamdala*, and *shahāda*
Quraysh (tribe) 266
Qurra b. Sharīk (governor) 47n50, 63n148, 65n164, 79, 113n2, 180, 183, 217
– dossier of 66–69, 75, 76, 80, 103, 118, 119, 146n193, 185, 236
– glass weights of 243n137
– seals of 146
Quṣayr ʿAmra (palace) 92, 119, 124, 132, 134, 135, 148, 192, 195
Qutayba b. Muslim (governor) 101, 132

(...) al-Raḥmān b. al-Dibīr 104, 321
Rāshid (*amīr*) 227
Rāshid b. Khālid (pagarch) 49, 72, 73, 147, 220
Rayy 97, 98
– mint of 98
al-Rayyān b. ʿAbd Allāh 89
Reinfandt, Lucian 23, 76, 118
Rōb 105, 315
rutbīl 10, 101, 256

Sabaic language 263, 292
– Arabic loanwords in 295n180
– documents 177, 178, 186, 237, 298

– inscriptions 176–177, 290
– loanwords in Arabic 267, 270
– theonyms 177
Sabas monastery 85
safe-conducts 70, 71, 182, 183, 241n128, 269
Sahl b. ʿAbd al-Azīz (prince) 172
Saʿīd (copist) 76n243
Saʿīd. *See* Kamird-far (II) b. Bēk (II)
Saʿīd b. ʿAbd al-ʿAzīz (governor) 102, 229, 230, 237
Saʿīd b. ʿAmr (governor) 102
Ṣāliḥ b. ʿAbd al-Raḥmān (secretary) 40n6, 218
Ṣāliḥ b. Abī Rāshid (pagarch) 220
al-Ṣalt (b. Masʿūd?) (copist) 76n243
salutation
– absence of from short prescript letters 181
– Coptic renditions of 225–228, 349
– Greek renditions of 221–222, 223, 224, 349
– in official letters 73n218, 175, 178–180, 185, 188n181, 188, 205, 207, 219, 230, 337, 349
– omission of in letters to Christians 183, 223
– omission of in private letters 203
– pre-Islamic antecedents of 179
– variant of for Christians 183–184, 223
– variants of in private letters 203, 327
Sām *mawlā* of Ghālib (witness) 105
Samangān 105n421, 315
Samarkand 102, 188, 228, 229, 230, 239
Sāmarrāʾ 188
Ṣanʿāʾ, Great Mosque 14n46, 115n7, 126n76, 193
Sanjar-Shah 106, 181
Saqqāra, Apa Jeremias monastery 49n56, 70, 241n128
Sarjūn b. Manṣūr (secretary) 13, 218. *See also* Manṣūr family
Sarmīn, mint of 153
Sasanian(s)
– art and architecture 133, 140–141, 147
– coinage. *See* coinage/coins – Sasanian
– honorifics 235
– *regalia* 133–135, 138, 139, 242, 258, 331
Scribes 172
– Arabic 65, 67, 74, 76, 84, 110, 182–183, 204, 207, 212, 236, 323
– bilingual 74, 77, 104, 188, 240–241
– Greek 76, 84, 218, 255, 291, 332n308
– Pahlavi 96, 104, 217–218, 321
– scribal exercises 74–75, 77, 99n394, 174, 188–190, 240, 326
– scribal politesse 103, 108, 183–184, 199–200, 218, 240–241, 260
– scribal signatures 63, 76, 84, 91, 175 182–183, 196
– Sogdian 102, 103–104, 207, 229
– training 74–75, 76, 188–191
Scythopolis *see* Baysān
Senuthios (*anystes*) 57
– archive of 58
Sergios s. of Georgios (witness) 84
shahāda 253, 318. *See also* doxology
– "Eastern" 150n220, 208n216
– "Egyptian" 209
– forming one semantic unit with the *basmala* 208
– in official documents 350
– in official inscriptions 209
– in private inscriptions 209–211
– "Jerusalem" 208n216
– Latin renditions of 247–248, 250–251
– Middle Persian renditions of 145, 245
– on coins 150–152, 153n228, 163
– short 150, 160, 208n216
– "Syrian" 208n216
Shāh-ī-Āfrīd (princess) 132
Sharaḥīl b. Ẓālim (phylarch) 46, 266. *See also* Ḥarrān – inscription
Shīrīn (queen) 132
Sidon 93, 117, 193
Sijistān 312
Sistān 10, 52, 144, 244
– "later Sistān" series 243n140
Sogdian(s) 16, 101
– bilingual coinage 82n278, 103–104
– documents 14, 17, 35, 98n381, 99n389, 101–104, 186–187, 188, 228–231, 237, 253, 259, 292, formal features of 187, 256, 327, 346–350
– pantheon 239
– scribes *see* scribes
Sogdiana 9–10, 101–104
Spain 39, 136, 312

– Islamic coinage from 20, 52, 140, 247–251, 298, 301, 311
– Muslim conquest of 3, 246
Spūr (*martān shāh*) 257, 258
– coinage of 256
Sufyanid(s) *see* Umayyad(s)
Sulaymān (craftsman) 126
Sulaymān b. Mūsā 126
Sunbādh 9
Susa 158
– mint of 129, 157n253, 158–159, 161, 243, 329
al-Suyūṭī 322n297
Sykomazon (village) 79
Syria (Greater) 3, 9, 17, 18, 19, 26, 33, 35, 39, 50, 51, 58, 65, 93, 103, 109–110, 128, 136, 180, 181, 183, 184, 199, 207, 222, 231, 234, 320, 321, 325, 326
– administrative idiolect of 282–312
– Arabization of scribal practices in 16n50, 77–87, 218
– as an imperial metropole 263–264, 314–318, 327–329, 331
– Islamic architecture in 50, 115, 120n36, 123, 133–134, 187, 331
– Islamic coinage from 51, 81–82, 94, 136–139, 144, 148, 151–153, 156–157, 160, 161, 245–246, 298. *See also* coinage/coins
– pre-Islamic Arabic inscriptions from 42, 45, 78, 201
Syriac language 12, 14, 29, 176, 297n186
– manuscripts 29
– inscriptions 45, 46, 176
– literary sources 11, 12n41, 148
– loanwords in Arabic 85, 176, 314
– papyri 78, 314n252

Ṭabaristān 52, 99, 100, 101
Ṭā'if 89, 90, 91
Tāq-i Bostān 134
Ṭāriq b. Ziyād (commander) 247
Tawwaj, mint of 144–145n181
Taxes
– collection of 74–75, 79, 96, 105–106, 181, 206n200, 227, 241, 268n33, 272, 319n278
– *dēmosion* 227n48,
– *gazīdag* 96. *See also jizya*
– *gazito* 285, 286. *See also jizya*
– *harg* 284, 320
– instalments 270
– *kharāj* 86, 96, 98, 188, 268, 283–284, 312–313, 320, 330
– *jāliya* 319
– *jizya* 285–286, 312, 314, 319, *j. al-ra's* 285, 319, *j. al-arḍ* 285, 320
– *nā'iba* 269, 313, 317
– requisition orders 61–63, 67–69, 79–80, 173, 181–183, 219, 236, formal difference from tax demands 80
– *rhouzikon* 289–290
– *rizq* 56, 289–290, 312–313
– *ṣadaqa* 269, 270, 314
– tax demands 68, 71–73, 75, 80, 109, 128, 173, 181–183, 219, 220n15, 236
– tax receipts 52, 56–57, 70–71, 74n229, 78n263, 105n421, 106, 147n196, 181, 183, 220n15, 318
– *zakāt* 270, 314
Tha'laba b. 'Amr (king) 201
Thebaid 58, 61, 63, 220n15
Theodorakios and Christophoros (pagarchs) 56, 57
– archive of 49n56
Theodore Abū Qurra (bishop) 33, 53
Theophanes (historian) 75, 163, 218
Tiberias 92
ṭirāz 50, 165
Tlemcen, Great Mosque 50, 193
Tost, Sven 76
Tustar 131
Tyssaphernēs (satrap) 150

'Ubayd Allāh b. al-Ḥabḥāb (financial director) 194
al-'Ulā 88
'Umar (II) b. 'Abd al-'Azīz (caliph) 120
'Umar (I) b. al-Khaṭṭāb (caliph) 3, 8, 89
– Pact of 3
Umayya b. 'Abd Allāh (governor)
– coinage of 257n192
Umayyad(s) 6n10, 9, 10, 22, 32, 34, 90n325, 97, 101, 102n404, 109, 110, 132–133

– administration 13, 33, 84n296, 109
– art and architecture 98, 115–116, 118–119, 123–127, 133–136, 140–141, 148, 156–157
– book production 15, 125
– coinage *see* coinage/coins
– official documents, formal features of 15, 62–64, 67–68, 79–81, 127–129, 174–191, 219–233, 236–238, 240–241, 337, 345–352, difference from private documents 202–207, 333, influence on Christian and Zoroastrian scribal practices 226–227, 228–229, 233, 237, 254–258, 329, 333–334, technical vocabulary of Ch. V *passim*
– official inscriptions 50, 116–125, 135–136, 193–194, formal features of 90–94, 195–198, 341–343, difference from private epigraphy 207–211
– poetry 131–132
Umm al-Ḥakam bt. al-Ḥakam 241
Umm Sulaymān bt. Marqōs 86
ʿUqba b. Muslim (governor) 172
al-Ushmūnayn 58, 61, 64, 70, 75, 182, 240
– pagarchs of 68, 70, 72, 220n15
– postmaster of, archive of 182
ʿUthmān b. ʿAffān (caliph) 10, 203

Vaheshtābādh Ardashīr 115
valediction
– absence of from short prescript letters 181
– Coptic renditions of 226, 227, 352
– Greek renditions of 221–222, 224, 228, 352
– in official letters 73n218, 146n193, 175, 180, 185, 207, 219, 231, 241, 333, 352
– omission of in letters by Christians 241n128
– pre-Islamic antecedents of 180
– variants of for Christians 146n193, 183–184, 224
– variants of in private letters 203, 204, 333
Visigoths/Visigothic 3, 136, 312

Wādī Sarga, Apa Thomas monastery 49n56, 69
Wahb b. al-Munabbih 14n45
Wahran b. Bēk (II) 106
Walker, John 246
Webb, Peter 30
Weber, Dieter 232

Yaqṭīn b. Mūsā 197
Yāqūt 45, 316n262
Yazd, mint of 144–145n181
Yazd (accountant) 233n78
Yazdānfādhār (landowner) 96
Yazdānpādār *see* Yazdānfādhār
Yazdgerd III (King of Kings) 94, 132, 137
– era of 138
– frozen name on coins 138
– post-Y. era 95, 100, 138
Yazīd b. Ḥātim (governor) 70
Yazīd b. al-Muhallab (governor) 160
– coinage of 149, 160, 257n192, 286

Zābulistān 10, 101, 256–257
Zacharias 227
Zādān Farrūkh (secretary) 40n6, 217–218
Ziyād b. Abī Sufyān (governor) 139
– coinage of 139
Zoroastrian(s) 95–96, 241, 257, 325, 329, 333
– officials 40n6, 96–97, 102, 229, 233
– symbols on Islamic coinage 94, 137, removal from Islamic coinage 143, 149, 154, 157, 161, 244
– theonyms 229, 232–233
Zubayr b. Ziyād (pagarch) 70n189, 71n192
Zuhayr *mawlā* of Bint Shayba 88, 89

Index Locorum I: Papyri

BD I
– al 289n153
– Q 284n131
– R 308n226
– T 105n423
– U 105n423
– V 105n423, 301
– W 105nn421 and 423, 106n429, 286, 292, 308n226, 301
– X 105n423, 106n429
– Y 105nn421 and 423, 106n429, 187n105, 255n178, 256 and n189, 257n191
Berk.
– 27 96, 284n129
– 67 96
– 187 97, 232 and n74, 233, 347
– 188 232 and n74, 233n78, 346
– 197 232 and n74, 233n78, 346
– 244 96 and n370

Chrest.Khoury I
– 19 254n173, 298
– 48 *see P.TillierDebts* 1
– 64 254n173, 298
– 66 274, 276, 284, 286, 292
– 72 *see CPR* XXI 1
– 90 67n171, 128n91, 281, 282, 285, 292
– 91 128n91, 146n190, 273, 276, 278, 282, 286, 288, 289, 292, 298
– 92 *see P.GascouQurra*
– 93 *see P.Mudun* 11
– 94 67n176, 285, 286, 292, 298
– 96 282, 283
– 98 241n127, 276, 300
Chrest.Khoury II
– 17 *see P.Vente 14*
– 22 254n173, 298
– 26 *see CPR* XXI 4b
CII
– *O.* 197 98
CPR II
– 7 220n15
– 225 225, 227n42, 349, 351
– 228 *see P.Gascou* 24
CPR III
– 1 292
– 2 61n145, 129n99
– 4 61n144, 129n99
– 8 61n142
– 9 61n143
– 10 61n145
– 35 121n42
– 37 121n42
– 65 128n91, 251n162
– 108 129n100
– 109 129n100
– 170 319n284
– 325 121n42
CPR IV
– 3 63n152, 220n15
– 4 63n152, 220n15
– 5 63n152
– 6 63n152
CPR VIII
– 72 63n152
– 73 63n152
– 74 63n152, 64 nn153, 154, and 158
– 75 63n152, 64 nn154 and 158
– 76 63n152
– 77 63n152
– 78 63n152, 237n107
– 79 63n152
– 80 63n152
– 81 63n152
– 82 63n152, 270n49
– 83 63n152
– 84 63n152
CPR XIV
– 33 291
CPR XVI
– 4 240, 292, 298
– 7 269
– 8 204n193
– 9 274, 288
– 11 220n15
– 12 220n15
– 14 53n88
– 17 293

https://doi.org/10.1515/9783110740820-042

– 18 203n187, 293
– 27 205n197, 293
– 33 293
CPR XIX
– 27 220n15, 237n111, 315n255
CPR XXI
– 1 269, 284
– 2a 274, 284, 298
– 2b 284, 286, 293
– 3 270, 274, 276, 284, 298
– 4b 270, 274, 284, 286, 293, 298
– 5 274, 284, 286, 293, 298
CPR XXII
– 7 220n15
– 8 73n211, 220n15
– 9 73nn211 and 213, 147n194, 220n15
– 10 220n15
– 13 73nn215–216, 220n15
– 17 276
– 18 74n224, 75n231, 220n15
– 20 75n231, 220n15
– 43 296
– 52 220, 221, 346, 348, 350, 351
– 53 296
– 55 307n220
CPR XXVI
– 16 298
– 17 276
– 36 254n173
– 37 271
CPR XXX
– 12 330n303
CPR XXXIV
– 22 188n115
CT
– 40 99n389
– 75 99n388
– 85/1 99n388
– 85/2 99n388
– 92/1 99n389
– 94 99n388
– 97 99n388
– 101 99n388
– 102 99n388
– 110 99n388
– 123 99nn389 and 392
– 133/1 99n388
– 133/2 99n388
– 133/3 99n388
– 133/4 99n388
– 134 99n388
– 135/2 99n388
– 135/4 99n388
– 135/5 99n388
– 139 99n388
– 140/1 99n388
– 162/2 99n389
– 195 99n389
– 205/1 99n388
– 205/3a 99n388
– 205/3b 99n388
– 205/ 99n388

KSB II
– 912 73n212

MPER XV
– 106 v 74n224
– 106a r 74n224
Mugh
– 1.I 228 and n52, 229, 230–231, 236, 239n117, 243, 347, 348, 350
– A-14 103n410, 187n104, 229n55
– B-15 187n104
– B-16 187n104
– B-18 187n104
– Nov. 2 187n104
– Б-15 292

Nilus IV
– 1 72n209, 147n194
– 17 146n188
– 18 146n190
– 21 147n194
– 23 147n194
– 25 147n194
– 30 147n194
– 32 147n194
– 33 146n188

O.Crum
– 356 235n95
O.CrumVC
– 116 225 and n35, 226, 346, 352

P.AbbottUbaydAllah 75n232, 288, 289
P.AnawatiPapyrusChretien 53n88, 87n308, 184n96
P.Apoll.
– 4 220, 346
– 5 221, 224n29, 352
– 7 220 and n16, 222, 224n30, 346, 348, 352
– 8 220 and n16, 221, 224n29, 346, 348, 352
– 27 291
– 33 291
– 49 290
– 64 291
– 82 58n125
– 94 290
– 95 290
– 97 58n125
– 105a 58n125
– 105b 58n125
– 105c 58n125
– 105d 58n125
P.Bal.
– 181 69nn184–185
– 182 69nn184–185
– 214 225, 227n48, 349
– 256 226, 352
– 262 225, 227n43, 349
– 277 226, 227, 352
P.BaranskiArabisation 220
P.Bas. I
– p. 6–7 146n193
P.Bawit Clackson
– 76 72n201
P.BeckerLateinisches 2
– 2 *see CPR* III 2
– 6 *see CPR* III 37
P.BeckerNPAF
– 1 *see P.Cair.Arab.* 146
– 2 *see P.Cair.Arab.* 148
– 3 *see P.Cair.Arab.* 149
– 4 *see P.Cair.Arab.* 147
– 5 *see P.Cair.Arab.* 151
– 6 *see P.Cair.Arab.* 153
– 7 *see P.Cair.Arab.* 150
– 8 *see P.Cair.Arab.* 154
– 9 *see P.Cair.Arab.* 155
– 10 *see P.Cair.Arab.* 152
– 11 *see P.Cair.Arab.* 156
– 12 *see P.DietrichTopkapi* 1
– 13 *see P.Cair.Arab.* 160
– 14 *see P.Cair.Arab.* 161
– 15 *see P.Cair.Arab.* 162
– 16 *see P.Cair.Arab.* 163
– 17 *see P.Cair.Arab.* 175
P.BeckerPAF
– 1 76n243, 286, 293, 298
– 2 288, 293, 295
– 3 *see P.VanthieghemCorrespondance* II
– 4 293
– 5 293, 307
– 7 *see P.Cair.Arab.* 147
– 8 67n174, 281, 282, 283
– 9 *see P.Mudun* 32
– 10 67n175, 182n77, 273, 274, 276, 298
– 11 293
– 12 *see P.Cair.Arab.* 150
– 13 *see P.Cair.Arab.* 153
– 14 *see P.Cair.Arab.* 151
– 16 *see P.Christ.Musl.* 1
P.BeckerPapyrusstudien 63n148, 67n174, 281, 282, 283, 298
P.BerkesCareers 73, 271
P.BerkesTrilingualScribe 288
P.Berl.Arab. I
– 2 271, 293
– 3 293
P.Berl.Arab. II
– 23 74n229, 203n187, 285, 288, 293
– 24 270, 293
– 25 204n192, 293
– 26 284, 286, 293
– 38 53n85
– 39 53n85
– 40 53n85
– 41 53n85
– 42 53n85
– 43 53n85
– 49 205n197, 293, 298
– 50 293, 305
– 72 293
– 73 203n187
– 75 203n187, 288, 293
– p. 20–21 284, 286, 288, 293
P.BruningDevelopments 274, 276, 279, 298

P.BruningSunna 55n99, 56n109, 174n13, 202, 205n196
P.Brux.Bawit
– 9 72n201
– 17 72n201
– 19 72n201
– 44 72n201
P.Cair.Arab.
– 77 *see CPR* XXI 3
– 146 146n190, 293
– 147 288
– 148 128n91, 282, 288, 293
– 149 272, 285, 286, 293, 295, 298
– 150 282, 286, 288, 293
– 151 146n190, 293
– 152 282, 298
– 153 76n243, 285, 288, 290, 293
– 154 76n243, 128nn91–92, 286, 288, 293, 298
– 155 76n243, 286, 293, 298
– 156 293
– 157 293
– 158 295
– 159 293
– 160 67n177, 128n91, 146n190, 276, 285, 286, 293, 298
– 161 67n176, 146n190, 285, 286, 293, 298
– 162 67n176, 285, 288, 293, 298
– 163 67n176, 285, 286, 293
– 167 286, 293
– 169 270, 285, 286, 288, 293
– 174 285, 293
– 175 285, 293
– 180 75n233, 285, 286, 293, 298, 304
– 197 269
– 231 267
– 260 293, 298
– 274 298
– 285 319n276
– 286 *see P.Christ.Musl.* 1
– 317 *see P.DiemCair.Arab.* V 317
– 342 279
– 343 279
– 371 276
– 420 320
P.Christ.Musl.
– 1 70n190, 273, 276
– 2 70n190
– 5 290
– 6 74n223
– 7 74n223, 269, 279
– 11 269, 287
– 15 220n15
– 17 220n15
– 19 74n229
– 20 74n229
– 21 74n229, 182n83
– 23 70n187, 74n229, 287
– 24 284, 287
P.Clackson
– 45 72n202, 75n235, 270, 285, 288, 293, 298, 303
– 46 73n216
P.David-WeilEdfou
– A 53n85
– B 53n85
P.David-WeillLouvre
– 11 332n307
– 12–13 205n197, 276, 298, 302
– 16 284, 286, 295, 298
– 24 298
– 26 289
– 27a *see P.DiemDienstschreiben* d
– 30 203n181, 286
P.DelatterEntagion 62n147, 276, 279, 281, 282, 286
P.DelattreSymbole 121n42
P.DiemAmtlicheSchreiben
– 1 *see P.BerkesCareers*
– 3 288
P.DiemAphrodito
– p. 261 272n69
– p. 261–264 293, 298
– p. 272 *see P.RagibAn22*
P.DiemCair.Arab. V
– 317 293, 298
P.DiemDienstschreiben
– b 293
– d 191, 283
P.DiemFrueheUrkunden
– 1 62n147, 267, 276, 281, 286, 305
– 2 62n147, 286
– 3 270, 284, 298
– 4 274, 284, 293, 298

– 5 281, 284, 293
– 6 *see P.Berl.Arab.* II p. 20–21
– 7 284, 285, 286, 293, 298, 319n280
– 8 285, 293
– 9 285, 293
– p. 150 *see P.DiemAmtlicheSchreiben* 3
P.DiemGouverneur 64n159, 128n91, 293
P.DiemMauleselin 298
P.DiemRemarkableDocuments
– 1 203nn182 and 184, 205n196, 298
– 2 271, 290
P.DiemStelle 294
P.DietrichTopkapi
– 1 146n190, 289, 298
P.DonnerFaagments
– 1 69nn183 and 185, 72n205
– 3 70n186, 72n205, 285
PERF
– 566 *see Nilus* IV 17
– 572 73n214
– 577 *see Nilus* IV 1
– 578 72n209
– 587 *see Nilus* IV 33
– 593 *see Nilus* IV 18
– 594 77n247
– 614 282, 283, 286
– 667 *see Nilus* IV 25
– 776 *see Nilus* IV 30
– 896 319n278
– 959 147n194
P.Fay.Copt.
– 12 227 n49
– 26 225, 227 n43, 346, 349, 351
P.Gascou
– 24 288
– 27a 61n144, 64, 83n286, 129n99, 146n188
– 27b 62n147, 64, 146n188, 220, 289
– 28 63n152, 64, 220n15
P.GascouQurra 281, 283, 289, 293
P.Giss.Arab.
– 6 285
– p. 33 a *see P.RagibSauf-conduits* 4
P.Grenf II
– 105 70n190
– 106 *see SPP* III 259
P.GrohmannApercu
– p. 41 *see SB* VI 9576
– p. 50 *see CPR* XXI 2b
– p. 55 *see P.Cair.Arab.* 175
– p. 85 *see CPR* XXI 2a
– p. 90 no. 2 *see P.DiemAmtlicheSchreiben* 3
P.GrohmannBeziehung
– p. 338 *see Chrest.Khoury* I 66
– p. 339 *see CPR* XXI 4b
P.GrohmannMuhadara II
– p. 12 *see SB* VI 9576
P.GrohmannPapyrusProtokoll
– 1 56nn105–106, 254n173
– 2 83n285, 129n99
P.GrohmannProbleme
– 5 270, 285, 298
– 6 285, 298
– 14 319n278
– 17 *see P.Berl.Arab.* II p. 20–21
– III p. 143 *see CPR* XXI 2a
– III p. 148 no. 3 *see P.DiemAmtlicheSchreiben* 3
P.GrohmannQorraBrief 68n180, 183, 272
P.GrohmannSteuerpapyrus 298
P.GrohmannUrkunden
– 9 318n276
P.GrohmannWirtsch.
– 2 *see P.World* p. 168
– 11 *see P.World* p. 153a
– 17 267
P.GuestPapyrus see P.Cair.Arab. 167
P.HaimPaper
– 1 102n407, 103n409, 174n14
– 2 102n407, 174n14
– 3 102n407, 174n14
P.Hamb.Arab. II
– 203nn181–183
P.HanafiBusinessLetter 298, 305
P.HanafiCairoCopenhagen
– 1 298–299, 300, 303, 304, 305
P.HanafiTwoPaperDocuments
– 3 48n54, 293, 299
P.HanafiWill 293
P.Heid. XI
– 490 225, 349
– 491 226, 349
P.Heid.Arab. I
– 1 *see Chrest.Khoury* I 90
– 2 288, 293
– 3 *see Chrest.Khoury* I 91

– 4 286, 288, 293
– 5 *see P.Mudun* 11
– 6 *see Chrest.Khoury* I 94
– 7 *see P.BeckerPAF* 8
– 8 *see P.Mudun* 32
– 9 *see P.BeckerPAF* 10
– 10 68n181, 76n243, 287, 299
– 11 76n243, 288, 299
– 12 *see P.Cair.Arab.* 151
– 13 273, 289
– 22 67n174, 283
– a 67n177, 146n190, 276, 285, 286, 293, 299
– b 67n176, 146n190, 285, 293, 299
– c 67n177, 146n190, 276, 285, 286, 293, 299
– d 67n176, 146n190, 285, 286, 293, 299
– e 146n190, 276, 285, 299
– f 67n176, 146n190, 236n104, 285, 286, 293, 299
– g 67n177, 146n190, 276, 285, 286, 293, 299
– h 67n176, 146n190, 236n104, 285, 286, 293, 299
– i 67n176, 146n190, 285, 286, 293, 299
– k 67n177, 146n190, 276, 285, 286, 299
– l 67n177, 146n190, 276, 285, 286, 293, 299
– p. 7 *see P.Jahn* 2
P.Heid.Arab. II
– 1 r *see Chrest.Khoury* I 96
– 1 v 282, 283, 293
– 5 299
– 24 293, 299
– 25 293
– 34 53n88
– 42 293
P.HerzfeldSamarra
– 1 98n381
– 2 98n381
– 3 98n381
– 4 98n381
– 5 98n381
– 6 98n381
P.HindsNubia 16n59, 24, 30n115, 75n232, 128n92, 183–184, 269, 299
P.Horak
– 85 293, 300
P.HoylandDhimma
– 1 180n68, 206n200, 207, 254, 294
– 2 180n68, 206n200, 254, 288
P.Jahn
– 1 *see ChrestKhoury* I 96
– 2 174n15
– 3 *see P.Christ.Musl.* 6
– 4 *see P.Christ.Musl.* 7
– 5 203n187, 205, 293
– 9 300
– 10 48n54, 201, 203 nn181–182, 204n192, 300
– 12 *see ChrestKhoury* I 98
P.JoySorrow
– 1 205n196
– 3 293
– 4 203n183, 293, 299
– 5 203n186, 293, 307
– 9 283, 293
– 10 293
– 11 293
– 12 293
– 13 293
– 14 293
– 15 293
– 16 288
– 17 300, 302
– 20 *see P.YounesCondolence* 5
– 21 189, 205n197
– 23 293
– 24 293
– 25 293
– 26 293
– 27 294
– 28 294
– 30 294
– 31 294, 299
– 33 300
– 34 294, 299, 300
– 35 294, 299
– 36 294
– 37 299
– 38 203
– 39 294
– 41 294
– 42 287
– 43 273, 284, 289, 294
P.KarabacekBemerkungenMerx 62n147, 287, 289, 304
P.KarabacekKuenstler
– p. 67 279

P.KarabacekPapiergeschichte
– p. 107 279
P.KarabacekPapyrusprotokolle
– p. 42 *see CPR* III 235
P.Khalili I
– 1 299, 300, 304
– 2 269n40, 274, 287, 288, 294
– 7 279, 281, 282, 283
– 9b 299
– 14 273, 288, 294, 299
– 15 203n185, 289, 294
– 21 203 and nn182 and 184, 205n197, 300
– 24 203nn181 and 183, 288, 294
P.Khalili II
– 5 *see P.BruningDevelopments*
P.KhanBerkeley
– 1 97n378
– 2 97n378
– 3 97n378
– 4 97n378
– 5 97n378, 320n289
P.KhanLegalDocument 299
P.KhanLegalPapyrus 254n173, 294, 299
P.Khurasan
– 1 105n422, 182n79, 284, 287, 295, 301
– 2 105n422, 182n79, 284, 295, 301
– 3 105n422, 128n92, 182n79, 295, 301, 303
– 4 105n422, 182n79, 284, 301
– 5 105n422, 182n79, 267, 284, 295, 301, 303
– 6 105n422, 182n79, 284, 292, 295, 301, 303
– 7 105n422, 182n79, 284, 295, 301
– 8 105n422, 182n79, 295, 301
– 9 105n422, 182n79, 284, 295, 301, 303
– 10 105n422, 182n79, 284, 295, 301, 303
– 11 105n422, 182n79, 284, 296, 301, 303
– 12 105n422, 182n79, 284, 295, 301, 303
– 13 105n422, 182n79, 284, 295, 301, 303
– 14 105n422, 182n79, 284, 295, 301, 303
– 15 105n422, 182n79, 284, 301
– 16 105n422, 182n79, 206n207, 284, 296, 301, 303
– 17 105n422, 182n79, 284, 296, 301, 303
– 18 105n422, 284, 296, 301, 303
– 19 105n422, 182n79, 284, 296, 301, 303
– 20 105n422, 182n79, 284, 296, 301, 303
– 21 105n422, 182n79, 284, 296, 303
– 22 105n422, 182n79, 296, 303
– 23 105n422, 284, 301
– 24 105n422, 106n426, 295, 296, 308, 309
– 25 105n422, 106, 295, 302n201, 308
– 26 105n422, 106n432, 107n437, 295, 301
– 27 105n422, 106n432, 295, 301
– 28 105n422, 106n432, 205n196, 206, 301
– 29 105n422, 107, 108n439, 255n173
– 30 105nn422 and 425, 107n433, 295
– 31 105n422, 107n433, 301
– 32 105n422, 107n433, 255n173, 301
P.KisterLetter see P.DiemStelle
P.Kratchkovski 17n66, 102, 128n91, 181n74, 230, 231, 239n117, 292
P.Laur. V
– 204 223n22
– 1892 224n30
P.L.Bat. XXXIII
– 65 267, 273n71
P.LiebrenzQuittung 296, 299
P.Lond. IV
– 1334 123n52, 296, 315n255
– 1335 290
– 1336 291
– 1341 123n52, 296
– 1342 123n52
– 1343 113n2
– 1345 67n171
– 1346 146n190
– 1349 67n171
– 1350 220, 221, 346, 348, 350, 351
– 1351 220, 221, 291, 346, 348, 350, 351
– 1352 221, 348, 350, 351
– 1353 220, 221, 291, 346, 348, 350, 351
– 1356 220, 221, 287, 291, 307n220, 346, 348, 350, 351
– 1359 67n171, 220, 221, 346, 350, 351
– 1360 220, 221, 346, 350, 351
– 1362 220, 221, 291, 346, 350, 351
– 1363 146n190
– 1368 123n52, 220, 221, 291, 296, 346, 350, 351
– 1369 220, 221, 346, 350, 351
– 1370 220, 221, 291, 346, 350, 351
– 1374 146n190, 220, 221, 346, 350, 351
– 1375 220, 221, 289, 346, 350, 351

– 1376 220, 221, 346, 350, 351
– 1378 220, 221, 346, 348, 350, 351
– 1379 220, 221, 346, 348, 350, 351
– 1380 220, 221, 291, 346, 348, 350, 351
– 1381 220, 221, 346, 348, 350, 351
– 1383 291
– 1385 146n190
– 1389 67n171
– 1394 220, 221, 346, 348, 350, 351
– 1397 123n52, 296
– 1399 221, 348, 350, 351
– 1401 220, 221, 291, 346, 348, 350, 351
– 1403 123n52, 291, 296
– 1404 290
– 1407 290
– 1411 123n52, 296
– 1412 129n99
– 1414 123n52, 296
– 1416 291
– 1419 291
– 1433 123n52, 291, 296
– 1434 67n172, 290, 291
– 1435 290, 296
– 1439 296
– 1440 291
– 1441 291, 296
– 1443 291
– 1447 67n172, 318n271
– 1451 296
– 1463 291
– 1464 291
– 1492 146nn190–192
P.Lond. V
– 1892 222, 352
P.Lond.Copt.
– 551 *see P.Fay.Copt.* 12
P.Loth
– 1 *see CPR* XXI 1
– 2 *P.Berl.Arab.* II 75
P.MalczyckiInstructions 209n222
P.MargoliouthSelectPapyri
– 2 *see P.RagibLettresdeService* 2
– 3 *see P.RagibLettresdeService* 4
– p. 413–414 *see CPR* XXI 5
P.MarrowExchanges
– 1 *see P.YounesDeuxLettres* 1
– 2 *see P.YounesDeuxLettres* 2
P.MerxDocuments
– p. 55 *see P.KarabacekBemerkungenMerx*
P.Mich.Copt.
– 12 225, 227nn45 and 47, 346, 349
P.Mil.Vogl. I
– 8 a-b 75n236, 299
P.Mird
– 8 86
– 10 294
– 18 86n302, 128n91
– 19 86n302, 287, 288
– 20 86n302
– 23 86n303, 294
– 24 86n303
– 25 86n302, 294
– 27 309
– 29 86n302
– 30 86n302
– 31 86n302
– 33 86n306
– 35 306
– 36 301, 303, 304
– 38 309
– 41 304
– 43 294
– 44 294
– 45 48n55, 86, 87, 184, 201
– 46 48n55, 86, 87, 184, 201
– 47 *see P.DiemStelle*
– 48 86
– 50 86
– 51 203n181
– 53 294
– 55 294
– 57 203n184
– 61 205n197
– 68 294
– 71 85n298
– 72 85n298
– 73 85n298
– 82 307
– 83 301
– 95 287
P.Mon.Apollo
– 28 72n203
– 29 72n203
– 30 72n203

P.Mudun
– 11 67n177, 276, 285, 286, 292, 298
– 32 67n174, 281, 283, 285, 295, 298, 305
P.MuslimState
– 1 206n202
– 2 206n202, 270, 287, 288, 315n255
– 3 206n202, 270, 307n220
– 4 206n202, 287, 288
– 5 206n202, 288, 294
– 6 206n202, 294
– 7 206n202, 267, 287
– 8 30n115, 128n91, 204n189, 206n202, 269, 274, 288, 294, 299
– 9 206n202
– 10 206n202, 288
– 11 206n202, 287, 288
– 12 206n202, 288, 294
– 13 203n187, 206n202, 270
– 14 74n220, 206n202, 272, 288, 294
– 15 206n202, 272, 294
– 16 206n202
– 17 206n202, 294
– 18 206n202, 288, 294
– 19 206n202, 273, 294
– 20 206n202, 270, 299
– 21 206n202, 288
– 22 206n202, 285
– 23 206n202, 270, 273, 274, 276, 279, 285, 288, 294, 299, 306
– 24 206nn203 and 206, 240n120, 272, 294, 299
– 25 203n187, 206nn203 and 206
– 26 206n203, 294, 299
– 27 206n203, 299
– 28 206nn203 and 206, 281, 299
– 29 206n203, 281, 294, 299
– 30 206n203, 299
– 31 206nn203 and 206, 294, 295
– 32 206nn203 and 206, 294
– 33 204n194, 206n203, 294
– 34 74n221, 206nn203 and 206, 294
– 35 206n202, 285, 294, 320n288
– 36 268n33, 269, 270
– 37 206n202
– 38 204n192, 206nn204 and 206, 294
– 39 206n204
P.Ness.
– 1 78n254
– 2 78n253
– 3 77n252
– 4 77n252
– 5 77n252
– 6 77n252
– 7 77n252
– 8 77n252
– 9 77n252
– 10 77n252
– 11 77n252
– 12 77n252
– 13 77n252
– 55 78n263, 79n267
– 56 83, 205, 206, 254, 255, 300
– 57 255
– 58 79n267
– 59 78n263, 79n267
– 60 83, 128n91, 236n102, 287, 289n151, 290, 307, 309, 316n261
– 60a *see P.GrohmannPapyrusProtokoll* 2
– 61 236n102, 287, 289n151, 290, 307, 309, 316n263
– 62 236n102, 287, 289n151, 290, 307, 309
– 63 220, 236n102, 309, 347
– 64 79, 128n92, 236n10, 302, 300, 309
– 65 236n102, 300, 309
– 66 236n102, 309
– 67 236n102, 307, 309
– 68 79n264, 222, 224n30, 352
– 69 79n266, 289n151, 290
– 70 78n263, 221, 224n29, 352
– 71 79n264, 220, 347
– 72 79n264, 120n34, 220, 221, 347, 348, 351
– 73 78n263, 79n265, 120n34, 220, 221, 311n238, 347, 348, 351
– 74 78n263, 79n264, 221, 224n29, 352
– 76 79, 83n288
– 77 79n266
– 89 83n292, 310n235
– 92 79n266
– 93 79n266, 289n151, 290
– 158 311n238
P.Oxy.
– LIV 3758 291n164
P.RagibAn22 55n99, 297n186, 299

P.RagibEdfou
– 1 53n85
P.RagibJuridiction
– 1 55n101, 56n109, 84n293, 205n196, 299
– 2 *see P.TillierDebts* 2
P.RagibLettreFamiliale 203n189, 204n192, 205n197, 287, 294
P.RagibLettres
– 2a 74n229, 285, 288, 294
– 2b 74n229
– 8 299
– 9a 294
– 9b 204n192, 205n197
– 10 203n185, 205nn196–197
– 11 205n197, 294
– 12 332n307
P.RagibLettresdeService
– 1 *see P.Ryl.Arab.* II 6
– 2 271, 290
– 3 272, 290
– 4 290
– 5 *see P.Ryl.Arab.* II 7
P.RagibPlusAncienneLettre 174n13, 294, 299
P.RagibQurra
– 1 *see P.GascouQurra*
– 2 299
– 3 287, 294
P.RagibSauf-conduits
– 1 71n195, 294
– 3 71n196, 287, 294, 296
– 4 285
– 5 71n195, 285, 287, 294
– 6 71n195, 285, 287, 294
– 7 71n195, 287, 294
– 8 71n195, 285, 287, 294
P.ReinfandtLeinenhaendler 205n197, 283, 299
P.RogersNotice
– p. 15 *see P.RagibLettres* 2 a
P.Ross.Georg. III
– 23 63n152
P.Ross.Georg. IV
– 2 146n190, 220, 221, 346, 348, 351
– 3 123n52, 296
– 4 146n190
– 10 283
– 11 146n190
– 13 220, 221, 291, 346, 348, 351
– 14 220, 221, 346, 348, 351
– 15 291
– 27 291
P.Ross.Georg. V
– 11 223n22, 347
P.Ryl.Arab. I
– I 5 *see P.YounesGovernors* 1
– IV 1 *see P.RagibLettresdeService* 3
– IV 2 *see P.RagibLettresdeService* 2
– IV 3 *see P.Ryl.Arab.* II 6
– IV 4 *see P.RagibLettresdeService* 4
– IV 5 *see P.RagibLettresdeService* 5
– VI 12 *see P.Ryl.Arab.* II 8
– IX 6 *see CPR* XXI 5
– XV 14 b 284, 299
– XV 56 a 299
– XV 59 *see P.DiemGouverneur*
P.Ryl.Arab. II
– 4 *see CPR* XXI 5
– 6 272, 287, 290
– 8 332n307
– 7 182n80, 291
– 9 299
P.Ryl.Copt.
– 214 77n248, 273
– 277 67
– 285 227n41
– 321 225, 226, 227n45, 346, 349, 351
P.ShahinScheltbrief 294
P.ShahinSchreibubung
– 1b 294
– 3 188, 284, 287
PSI XV
– 1570 220, 221, 223n28, 224n29, 347, 348, 349, 351, 352
P.SijpesteijnInvitation 128n91, 172n7
P.SijpesteijnQurra 285
P.SijpesteijnTravel 204n192, 274, 294, 299, 304
P.SilvestredeSacyPapyrus
– A *see P.RagibSauf-conduits* 7
– B *see P.RagibSauf-conduits* 8
P.SilvestrePaléographie p. 84 *see P.RagibSauf-conduits* 5
P.Sorb.
– 2346 76n243

P.Steuerquittungen
– 1 287
P.StoetzerSteuerquittung 57n111, 70n190, 237n107, 273n71, 299
P.StoetzerSteuerquittungen
– 2 57n110, 70n190, 220, 287, 299, 304
P.ThungWrittenObligations
– 1 *see CPR* XXVI 16
– 2 *see CPR* XXVI 17
P.TillierDebts
– 1 44n100, 254n173, 281, 287, 299
– 2 299
– 3 55n101
P.TillierFustat
– 2 205n196, 299
– *Annexe* 299, 300, 302
P.Tyl.Arab. I
– 10 175n28
P.VanthieghemAbuHurayra 52–53n85
P.VanthieghemCorrespondance II 67n171, 294
P.VanthieghemMiel
– 1 279
– 2 279
– 3 279
P.VanthieghemPlusAncienPapier 175n28
P.VanthieghemRecu 284, 287, 294
P.VanthieghemSaufConduit 71n194, 287
P.Vat.Aphrod.
– 135 72n203
P.Vente
– 14 254n173, 299
– 15 254n173, 299
– 16 53n85
– 17 53n85
– 18 53n85
– 19 53n85
– 20 53n85
– 21 53n85
– 22 53n85
– 23 53n85
P.World
– p. 113 *see SB* VI 9576
– p. 116 *see CPR* XXI 2b
– p. 124 *see Chrest.Khoury* I 90
– p. 126 *see P.Cair.Arab.* 148
– p. 129 *see P.Cair.Arab.* 154
– p. 130 *see P.DiemAphrodito* p. 261–264
– p. 132 287, 294
– p. 141 a 279
– p. 153a 304
– p. 160 299
– p. 162 202, 203 nn181–182, 270, 299
– p. 168 320n290
– p. 171 *see P.YounesGovernors* 1
– p. 186 203n187, 299, 302
P.YounesCondolence
– 1b 332n307
– 3 205n197, 294
– 4 205n197
– 5 205n197
P.YounesDeuxLettres
– 1 203n187
P.YounesGovernors
– 1 276, 284, 287, 294
– 2 272, 287, 288, 294
– 3 272, 321n293

SB I
– 4826 220, 221, 223n28, 346, 349
– 5130 73n211, 220n15
– 5644 *see P.Heid.Arab* I a
– 5645 *see P.Heid.Arab* I b
– 5646 *see P.Heid.Arab* I c
– 5647 *see P.Heid.Arab* I d
– 5648 *see P.Heid.Arab* I e
– 5649 *see P.Heid.Arab* I f
– 5650 *see P.Heid.Arab* I g
– 5651 *see P.Heid.Arab* I h
– 5652 *see P.Heid.Arab* I i
– 5653 *see P.Heid.Arab* I k
– 5654 *see P.Heid.Arab* I l
SB III
– 7240 63n152, 220n15
SB V
– 7520 221, 351
SB VI
– 9262 220n15
– 9460 *see CPR* VIII 82
– 9752 347
– 9576 56, 57, 254n173, 283
SB VIII
– 9748 220, 221, 222, 223n28, 224n30, 346, 348, 349, 351, 352
– 9752 220, 221, 223n28, 348, 349, 351

– 9755 57n116
– 9760 73n216, 220n15
SB X
– 10454 296
– 10459 220, 221, 351
SB XVI
– 12575 220, 221, 347, 348, 351
– 12857 73n211, 220n15
SB XVIII
– 13247 74n224, 220n15
– 13249 220n15
– 13268 71
– 13269 71
– 13771 *see P.StoetzerSteuerQuittungen* 2
– 13870 220n15
SB XX
– 14234 71, 220n15
– 14443 180n69, 237n107
– 15100 291
SB XXIV
– 16219 63n152, 220n15
SB XXVI
– 16754 220n15
SB XXVIII
– 17257 220n15
SB Kopt. I
– 280 225, 349
SB Kopt. IV
– 1783 63n152, 220n15
– 1785 63n152, 220n15
SPP III
– 259 70n190, 71
– 260 75n234, 220n15, 237n111
SPP VIII
– 1083 220n15
– 1184 73n211, 220n15
– 1194 220n15
– 1195 220n15
– 1198 *see P.BaranskiArabisation*
– 1199 220n15
– 1200 220n15
– 1333 74n224
– 1345 *see P.Christ.Musl.* 1
SPP X
– 64 220n15
– 169 75n230
– 197 220n15
Tab.
– 1 100n397
– 2 100n397
– 3 100n397
– 4 100n397
– 5 100n397
– 6 100n397
– 7 100n397
– 8 100n397
– 10 100n397
– 11 100n397
– 12 100n397
– 13 100n397
– 14 100n397
– 15 100n397
– 16 100n397
– 17 100n397
– 18 100n397
– 19 100n397
– 20 100n397
– 23 100n397
– 24 100n397
– 25 100n397
– 26 100n397
– 27 100n397

X.BSB
– 48 178n52
– 49 178n52
– 50 178n52
– 52 178n52
– 53 178n52
– 54 178n52
– 62 298n192
– 145 298n192

Documents Quoted by Inventory Number

Ms. BM
– add. 14,666 29n111
P.BL
– 3124 54, 248n157
– 65541(?) 232
P.Berl.inv.Arab.
– 15014⅔ 270n49
P.Berol.inv.
– 2791 219n12
P.Bodl.inv.

– MS. Copt. b 7 269n42
– MS. Copt. b e 35 269n42
P.Cair.EgLib.inv.Gen.
– 39825 174n16
P.Cambr. UL Inv. Michael.
– 893 *see P.TillierDebts* 3
P.CtYBR inv.
– 71 62n147
P.Gen.inv.
– 713 75n233, 285
P.Heid.inv.Arab.
– 28 269
– 856 220n15
P.Khalili inv.
– 129 105
P.Louvre inv.
– 6420
P.Michael.inv.
– Q 5 184n91
P. Paris BNF Inv. 7075(9)
– 55n101
P.Utah inv.
– 520 55n99
P.Vind.inv. A. Ch.
– 1207 147n194
P.Vind.inv. A. P.
– 849 48n54
– 8711 77n246, 83n290
– 11012 55n101
– 11074 55n101
– 11076 55n101
– 11086 55n101
– 11153 55n101
– 11163 205n196
– 13986
P.Vind.inv. G
– 39752 77n247
– 43234 62n147
– 44498 222, 224n30
P.Wash.Libr. of Congress inv. Ar.
– 1 + 40 61

Index Locorum II: Inscriptions

Abdeljauad 2001
– no. 2 50n68, 117, 339, 340, 341
AI
– Y 287 208n218
– Z 68 90–91, 192, 340, 342
– Z 69 91n327
– Z 72 312n242

Bartoccini 1964
– no. B-1630 209n225

CG I
– 1 60, 211n235, 292n169, 294
– 2 50n60, 209n220, 211n235
– 3 50n60, 209n220, 210n230
– 4 50n60, 209n220
– 7 50n60, 209n220
CG VII
– 2466 209n226
CG VIII
– 3187 209n220
CG IX
– 3201 30, 245
– 3203 209n220
CG X
– 3977 209n220
CIAP I
– p. 4, no. 1 92n336, 194, 198n156, 296, 309, 339, 340
– p. 30–31, no. 1 93n350, 192, 342
– p. 31, no. 2 93n351, 117n16, 193, 341, 342
– p. 103, no. 1 193, 198n156
– p. 144, no. 1 193, 198n156, 296, 339, 340, 341, 342
CIAP II
– p. 5, no. 1 92n336, 194, 198n156, 309, 339, 340–341
– p. 207, no. 1 92n332, 117n19, 123n54, 193, 198n156, 339, 340, 341, 342
– p. 215, no. 1 193, 339, 340, 341, 342
– p. 221, no. 3 193, 339, 340, 341, 342
– p. 286, no. 19-A 188n111
CIAP III
– p. 104, no. 1 92n337, 194, 309, 339, 340, 341
– p. 104–105, no. 2 92n337, 309, 339, 340, 341
– p. 162, no. 2, 182n85
– p. 179 267n26
– p. 220, no. 1 92n335, 309, 339, 340, 341
– p. 221, no. 2 92n335, 309, 339, 340, 341
– p. 230, no. 13 207n210
– p. 230, no. 14 207n210, 211n235
– p. 232, no. 15 207n210, 211n235
– p. 232–233, no. 16 207n210, 211n235
CIAP VI
– 58 187n109
– 59 187n109, 294
– 60 187n109
– 61 187n109
– 62 187n109
– 63 187n109
– 64 187n109
– 65 187n109
– 66 187n109
– 67 187n109
– 68 187n109
– 69 187n109, 189, 294
– 70 187n109
– 71 187n109
– 72 187n109
– 73 187n109
– 74 187n109
– 75 187n109
– 76 187n109
– 77 187n109
– 78 187n109
CMC
– 1 194

DZ I
– p. 229, no. 1 309
DZ II
– p. 430 292
– p. 487 309

EIA
– no. 67 294
– no. 82 294

https://doi.org/10.1515/9783110740820-043

EPI
- 14941 193, 296, 341
- 14944 193, 296, 341, 342
- 14993 296, 341
- 40352 297
- 43922 209n220

Flood 2001
- p. 252–253 30n115, 93n348, 192

Gadjev/Shikhsaidov 2002
- p. 4 50n70, 193, 198n156, 339, 341, 342

Hamilton 1946
- p. 70 92n333, 194, 198n156, 339
el-Hawary 1930 *see CG* I 1
el-Hawary 1932 *see CG* IX 3201
Hoyland 2006
- p. 413 90, 192, 339, 342

IM
- p. 28–29 50n68, 193, 198n156, 297, 339, 341
Imbert 2016
- p. 344–346 92n338

Jumʿa/al-Maʿānī 1999
- p. 247–248 294

al-Kilābī 1995
- no. 163 209n224

Litmann 1949
- no. 31 *see* Ory 1969 p. 137 no. 3

Mayer 1946
- p. 73 192, 193, 198n156, 297, 339, 341
MCIA I
- 546 65n164
MCIA IV, 1
- p. 40, no. 1 193, 296, 339
- p. 43, no. 2 193, 339, 341, 342
- p. 44, no. 3 193, 296, 341
- p. 44, no. 4 193,198n156, 339, 341, 342
- p. 46, no. 5 193, 194, 339
- p. 47, no. 6 193, 197, 198n156, 339, 341, 342
- p. 47, no. 7 193, 197, 296, 341
- p. 48, no. 8 193, 197, 296, 341, 342
Mittwoch 1935
- p. 235–236 50n69, 193, 339, 340, 341, 342

Ory 1967
- no. 55 209n227
Ory 1969
- no. 1 342
- no. 3 193, 198n156, 339, 340
- no. 15 342
- no. 21 208n212
- no. 22 207n210
- no. 23 207n210
- no. 24 208n212
- no. 27 208n212
- no. 28 207n210
- no. 55 211n235
- no. 56 211n235
- no. 79a 207n210
Ory 1999
- p. 376 192, 198n156, 341
Ory 2005
- no. 1 118n24, 193
- no. 2 93n344, 193, 339, 341

P.HerzfeldSamarra
- 8 188n111
PoI
- 1.22 294
- 1.25 209n225
- 1.26 210n228
P.SchlumbergerQasr 189

Randall 1933
- p. 328 209n220
al-Rāshid 1992
- p. 138 194, 292, 309
al-Rāshid 1993
- p. 335, no. 1 194
- p. 335–336 no. 2 194
- p. 336 no. 3 194, 197n150
- p. 337 194
RCEA I
- 1 39n1, 178n49, 201n172
- 2 176n31, 192n124, 200n166
- 5 31n120, 192n124

– 6 *see CG* I 1
– 8 65n162, 93n348, 182n85, 193, 197n152, 237n71, 341, 342
– 9a 93n342, 192, 193, 339, 340, 342
– 9b 93n342, 193, 339, 340, 342
– 10 93nn340 and 343, 192, 339, 340, 341
– 11 93n341, 192, 339, 340
– 12 92n331, 118n24, 192, 339, 341
– 14 *see CIAP* III p. 104–105 no. 2
– 15 *see CIAP* II p. 5 no. 1
– 16 *see CIAP* III p. 104, no. 1
– 17 *see CIAP* I p. 4, no. 1
– 18a–b *see* Flood 2001, 252–253, 296, 341
– 19 193
– 23 *see* Imbert 2016, 344–346
– 25 *see* Sauvaget 1944 no. 1
– 26 93n347, 339, 341
– 27 92n328, 118n24, 192, 339, 340, 341, 342
– 28 92n330, 192, 198n156, 339, 340, 341, 342
– 32 *see CIAP* I p. 30–31 no. 1
– 37 *see CIAP* I p. 31 no. 2
– 38 193, 294
– 40 *see MCIA* IV 1, p. 40, no. 1
– 46 *see* Sauvaget 1947 p. 58 D and E
– 47 *see* Sauvaget 1947 p. 56 B
– 48 *see MCIA* IV, 1 p. 44, no. 3
– 49 *see MCIA* IV, 1 p. 44, no. 4
– 50 *see MCIA* IV, 1 p. 47, no. 7
– 51 *see MCIA* IV, 1 p. 47, no. 6
– 52 *see MCIA* IV, 1 p. 48, no. 8
– 53 *see RCEA* V additions and corrections 53
– 54 193, 339
– 55 *see CG* I 2
– 56 *see CG* I 3
– 57 50n60, 209n220
– 58 *see CG* I 4
– 59 50n60
– 60 50n60
– 61 *see CG* I 7
– 62 50n60
– 63 50n60, 209n220
– 163 *see CMC* 1
RCEA V additions and corrections
– 53 193, 198n156, 339, 341, 342
RCEA XIV
– p. 275 93n346
Ritter 2016a
– p. 65 92n329, 118n24,192, 198n159, 339, 341, 342
Ritter 2017
– p. 49

Sauvaget 1944
– no. 1 92n334, 198n156, 340, 341, 342
Sauvaget 1947
– p. 52 no. 2 *see* Ory 2005 p. 161–162
– p. 56 A 197n154
– p. 56 B 197n154, 296
– p. 58 D 197n154, 296
– p. 58 E 93n346, 197n154, 296, 341
– p. 66 93n345, 192, 296, 341
– p. 79 193n130
Schick/Salameh 2004
– no. 1 209n221
Sharon 2018
– p. 101 198n156
Silverman 2007
– p. 605 92n336, 194, 198n156, 309, 339, 340

TKN
– p. 191–192 296
– p. 194 296

WS
– 001 296
– 003 296
– 004 208n212

www.ingramcontent.com/pod-product-compliance
Lightning Source LLC
Chambersburg PA
CBHW061924220426
43662CB00012B/1795
* 9 7 8 3 1 1 1 5 4 3 8 6 4 *